W9-ARX-815

WEB CATALOG COOKBOOK

Cliff Allen

Deborah Kania

WILEY COMPUTER PUBLISHING

JOHN WILEY & SONS, INC.
New York • Chichester • Brisbane • Toronto • Singapore • Weinheim

Executive Publisher: Katherine Schowalter
Editor: Tim Ryan
Assistant Editor: Pam Sobotka
Managing Editor: Erin Singletary
Associate Editor, Electronic Products: Mike Green
Text Design & Composition: Pronto Design & Production, Inc.

Designations used by companies to distinguish their products are often claimed as trademarks. In all instances where John Wiley & Sons, Inc., is aware of a claim, the product names appear in initial capital or ALL CAPITAL LETTERS. Readers, however, should contact the appropriate companies for more complete information regarding trademarks and registration.

This text is printed on acid-free paper.
Copyright © 1997 by John Wiley & Sons, Inc.

All rights reserved. Published simultaneously in Canada.

This publication is designed to provide accurate and authoritative information in regard to the subject matter covered. It is sold with the understanding that the publisher is not engaged in rendering legal, accounting, or other professional service. If legal advice or other expert assistance is required, the services of a competent professional person should be sought.

Reproduction or translation of any part of this work beyond that permitted by section 107 or 108 of the 1976 United States Copyright Act without the permission of the copyright owner is unlawful. Requests for permission or further information should be addressed to the Permissions Department, John Wiley & Sons, Inc.

Library of Congress Cataloging-in-Publication Data:
Allen, Cliff, 1948–
     Web catalog cookbook / Cliff Allen, Deborah Kania.
        p. cm.
     Includes index.
     ISBN 0-471-18331-8 (pbk./CD-ROM : alk. paper)
     1. Commercial catalogs. 2. Commercial catalogs—
Software. 3. Web sites—Design and construction—Software.
4. Internet advertising. 5. Internet marketing. 6. Electronic commerce. I. Kania, Deborah, 1963– . II. Title.
HF5862.A44 1997
380.1'029'4—dc21   97-9529
                                               CIP

Printed in the United States of America

10 9 8 7 6 5 4 3 2 1

Contents

Acknowledgments

We would like to thank the following people for their invaluable assistance in making this a book of quality:

- Our families, who did an exceptional job supporting our book obsession

- Chris Allen, creator of the GuestTrack software used in this book

- Carolyn Allen, the visionary who prompted this book

- Michael Kania, whose support allowed the fulfillment of this dream (and obsession!)

- Beth Yaeckel, outstanding Web expert in her own right, for her valuable contributions to this book

- David and Sherry Rogelberg, our first-class partners at Studio B and the Computer Book Cafe

- Assistant Editor Pam Sobotka, an asset to John Wiley & Sons and to us

- The wonderful people at Allen Marketing Group, Inc. and Indelible Blue Inc.

- All of the organizations that spent time answering our pestering e-mails, especially Jeanne Dietsch at ActivMedia, Jeff Bezos-president extraordinaire of Amazon.com, Tony Levitan-enthusiastic leader at Greet Street, Jason Olim-innovator at CDNow, Tony Ruggery-Webinator at New Pig, and the enterprising folks at Insight Direct, Levenger, Cyberian Outpost, Hot! Hot! Hot!, The Sharper Image, and Overton's

Introduction

Welcome to the Web Catalog Cookbook. You are now among the thousands of people who recognize the incredible opportunity of informing, marketing and selling to, or supporting customers using the Internet. According to a recent research report from International Data Corporation (IDC) in December 1995, $1.1 billion of sales were conducted on or initiated by the Web. This means that sales resulted from information a customer saw on a company's Web site or actually purchased products and services from the Web site. IDC estimates that commerce on or because of the Web will reach $116.8 billion by year's end in 2000. This kind of potential, coupled with the fact that creating a Web site is relatively easy, makes the argument for developing a Web catalog a strong one. The purpose of this book is to show you how to create an online catalog to sell products and services on the Web, help you find the business partners you need to get your catalog online and fulfill orders, and give you ways to market your new online catalog. The accompanying CD-ROM contains light versions of the GuestTrack personalization software and the GT/Catalog software. Both enable you to create your Web site and catalog.

Who will find this book useful

A Web catalog is very versatile. It can be used to simply contain a database of documents for viewing or downloading, or it can be robust enough to allow you sell, receive payment, and ship products. Here are some people that will find this book and software very helpful.

- Entrepreneurs setting up shop. There are many success stories such as Amazon.com, CDNow, Greet Street, and others that have created entire businesses only on the Web.

- Existing mail-order and catalog companies taking their catalogs to the Web. The Web makes a lot of sense for these companies. If products can be sold through mail-order, then more than likely they can be sold using a Web site.

- Existing businesses or organizations who want to communicate with the Web marketplace. A Web catalog can be used to inform, market, and support—though not necessarily sell—online. For example, a Web catalog can be a database of product data sheets, press releases, technical support release notes, and so forth.

- Companies and organizations that want to communicate within organizations using *Intranets*. A Web catalog can be created for an internal company network or Intranet. The catalog can contain documents and files that are to be accessed by employees, investors, trade association members, non-profit organization committee members, and so on.

- Anyone who wants to create a Web site that contains information, documents, or multimedia files, where a catalog format is the best way to organize and manage these items, as well as non-profit organizations, school classroom students, families, and support organizations.

Chapter overviews

The chapters of this Cookbook are arranged to take you from a starting point of wanting to establish a catalog on the Web, through the planning phases, creation, and implementation, and then to information about how upcoming technologies will affect your Web catalog business. In addition, the resources toward the back of the book will help you to explore the Web to see what others are doing and to locate businesses that can help your business succeed.

Since different people come to the Web with different experiences and different sets of skills, we've included three different types of Web catalogs from which to choose. The Basic Web Catalog is a very simple Web catalog that will be adequate for companies with a small number of products and for people creating their very first Web site. The Intermediate Web Catalog uses the GuestTrack personalization software and a shopping cart system to build upon the Basic Catalog to produce Web pages on-the-fly and based on the interests of the customers. The Advanced Web Catalog builds upon the Intermediate Catalog to use a database of product information instead of static Web pages.

The CD-ROM included with this book contains the Web server software and Web template files you will need to implement the catalogs described in the book, as well as a set of Web clip art designed especially for readers of this book.

Chapter 1—Benefits of an online Web catalog

This chapter provides you with an understanding of the current catalog activities on the Web by looking at several of the more famous online catalogs from such companies as The Sharper Image, as well as the demographic characteristics of the people who are buying products on the Web. It also provides you with a framework for planning your Web catalog.

Chapter 2—Basics of online sales and marketing

Selling your products over the Internet is similar to traditional selling situations—with some key exceptions. This chapter provides you with a view of one-to-one marketing where you immediately provide information to customers based on their requests on your Web site. Other key parts of online marketing covered in this chapter are how to determine a position for your Web catalog in the minds of your prospects. The interactivity described in this chapter is one of the key advantages of the Web as a marketing tool, and the examples are some of the best on the Web.

Chapter 3—Planning a Web catalog

As Web sites have become more complex, especially catalog Web sites, it has become more important to plan the marketing content, the technical requirements, and the operations aspect of fulfillment. This chapter helps you manage these diverse parts of implementing an online Web catalog.

Chapter 4—Designing a Web catalog

After you've developed a strategic Web plan in Chapter 3, this chapter takes you through the tactical planning of a Web site, from creating a site map that shows how pages are linked to one another, to explaining the different elements of your Web pages. As you work through the design process, you will learn more about not only your Web site, but also your business and how your customers view your business and your products. Be prepared to focus on planning how you are going to help your prospective customers learn about, evaluate, and purchase your products.

Chapter 5—The Basics of HTML

Learning to format Web pages with HTML tags is similar to learning how to format word processing documents—except you see the actual codes that most word processing programs hide from the user. This chapter takes you from the very basics of HTML through the process of creating well-organized tables of information. If you've never used HTML, then this chapter will help you understand the codes used for the templates on the CD-ROM provided with this book.

Chapter 6—Preparing your text and graphical content

There are a number of techniques for creating and managing the text and graphic files used on your Web site that can make the life of a Web developer much easier—and we've packed many of them into this chapter. Even if you've used a graphics program to produce your print catalog, you will find the tips and techniques described in this chapter very helpful. In addition to the more technical side of preparing graphic files, this chapter also includes some insights about the use of color so that the image of your Web catalog will match the image of your company and your products.

Chapter 7—Working with a Web Service Provider

The technical complexities of creating your first Web site normally require a programmer experienced in the ways of the Web. To make it easy for you to accomplish all of the technical tasks without needing an experienced Webmaster, this chapter contains the step-by-step process for using the automated software installation that we have created. Whether you use the automated programs available through leading Web service providers, or you use the manual installation steps outlined in the chapter, you will have the catalog software on the enclosed CD-ROM uploaded to your Web sight and installed very quickly.

Chapter 8—Building your basic Web catalog

This chapter shows you step-by-step how to turn a set of template files on the CD-ROM into a Web catalog that will capture orders for your products. Since different companies need different images, there are three sets of templates, each with a slightly different look and feel for the customer. Screen shots are included that show you how each page within a Web site looks so you'll have both a step-by-step guide and a pictorial reference to keep you on track.

Chapter 9—Building your Intermediate Web catalog

The chapter takes you through the steps of adding the GuestTrack personalization software and a shopping cart to the Web sites described in Chapter 8. All of the Web pages used in the Intermediate catalog are created on-the-fly by the Web server, so you will be able to add the customer's name to pages they see, as well as personalize the list of products based on their interests. Providing a personalized Web experience is one of the greatest advances in Web technology today, and your Intermediate Web Catalog will put you ahead of your competition that doesn't provide this level of attention to customer needs.

Chapter 10—Building your advanced Web catalog

As the number of products in a Web catalog grows into the hundreds, so does the development and maintenance time. The way to keep control over the catalog as it grows is to store product information in a database and to display product pages using the formats stored in template files. This chapter shows how to add the special version of GT/Catalog's product database software to create an Advanced Web Catalog.

Chapter 11—Web catalog operations and fulfillment

Creating an online Web catalog is the start of operating a business on the Web. This chapter answers questions about what is entailed in fulfilling online orders or inquiries, options for handling orders and inquiries, and resources. Whether you already operate a business using a print catalog, or if this will be your first catalog business, this chapter provides important business information about the operations and fulfillment aspects of a catalog business.

Chapter 12—Web site marketing and promotion

There are many important parts to having a successful online catalog business, and one is attracting prospective customers to your Web site. If you have wondered how to announce and promote your Web site online and in other media, this chapter is what you've been looking for.

Chapter 13—The next step

The Internet and the World Wide Web are growing very rapidly both in the number of companies using it for commerce and in the technologies available to attract prospects and communicate with customers. This chapter gives you overview information about emerging Web technologies and how to leverage GuestTrack personalization capabilities.

Appendix A—Resources

One of the most valuable aspects of the World Wide Web is that you can easily tap into information about products and services available to help your catalog business succeed. The list of resources in the Appendix will help you locate many of the tools, resources, and business partners you will need as you grow your Web catalog business.

And, in the spirit of the online worlds, the Web sites shown in the Appendix are also available in a Web file on the CD-ROM so you can use your Web browser to link directly to the sites listed.

Appendix B—Posting an announcement on a newsgroup

This Appendix contains a useful FAQ (Frequently Asked Questions) document of how to post announcements on a Usenet newsgroup. It covers what to do and what *not* to do to ensure your posting will be acceptable.

 # Summary

You've heard the growth rates. You've heard the predictions about the Web. You now hold in your hands the tools to help you establish an online Web catalog that can reach thousands more prospective customers than a print catalog—and at a fraction of the cost.

You also have the information needed to follow the latest technological developments in Web marketing so you will be able to keep out in front in this ever-changing, ever-growing electronic medium.

Welcome to the World Wide Web!

CHAPTER ONE

BENEFITS OF AN ONLINE WEB CATALOG

Electronic commerce is the future, and it is happening now. You must decide if you want to take advantage of the World Wide Web's promise. If you cut through the news hype about the Web's greatness, you will see that the Web is a viable way to do business now and, most definitley, in the future. Many of the technologies needed to perform sales transactions and maintain customer relations (like the GT/Catalog Light on this book's accompanying CD-ROM) are available now, and in the future even more sophisticated solutions will make marketing and selling as easy as traditional methods such as retail, face-to-face sales, telephone sales, fax, and voice. This chapter will spell out what Web commerce is and its benefits.

What is electronic commerce on the Internet and why is it important?

Electronic commerce is the computerized buying and selling of goods and services between individuals or companies. The computerization spans the entire purchase process including product information and specifications, sales transactions (electronic funds transfer, digital cash, credit card authorization, inventory allocation), confirmation of the delivery of goods or services, either digital goods (information, software, publication, video, audio) or physical goods (books, clothing, furniture, supplies, services), and customer service. For example, when you visit the World Wide Web site of The Sharper Image—a traditional mail-order and retail company that opened shop on the Internet in 1994—you can browse through an online catalog looking for the latest high-tech gadget, and order and pay for it using your credit card, all electronically. By the year 2000, The Sharper Image Web site is expected to yield 20-25 percent of the company's total revenues. Figure 1.1 shows The Sharper Image home page.

According to a September 1996 Computer Intelligence study, 2.7 million people have used the Internet for shopping or for commercial services such as banking or travel information. In 10 years it is predicted by Booz Allen & Hamilton (http://www.bah.com) that 20 percent of household spending will be funneled through the Internet. In 1996, many companies saw results from selling on the Web. For example, CDnow (Figure 1.2), a popular Web site for purchasing music and videos, expects to reach $6 million in revenues for 1996 and expects signficant growth in the future. Jason and Matthew Olim, the founders, attribute this success to selection and an intimate understand of what the Internet is technologically and how it makes their business better.

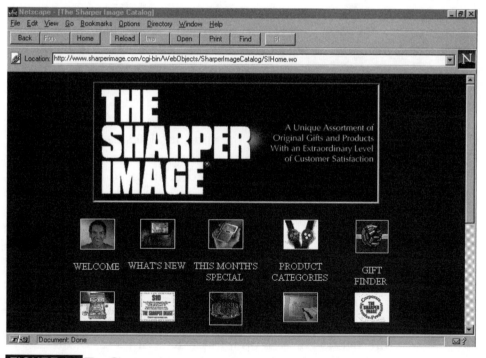

 **FIGURE 1.1** The Sharper Image home page.

Netscape - [CDnow : Main : Homepage]

File Edit View Go Bookmarks Options Directory Window Help

| Back | For | Home | Reload | Ima | Open | Print | Find | Stop |

Location: http://www.cdnow.com/

**ALL THE HOTTEST NEW RELEASES
AVAILABLE FOR ADVANCE ORDER**
click here

CDNOW FIND MUSIC FIND CLASSICAL [Find Video] SHOPPING ACCOUNT [Other Stuff] HELP

Homepage

Information

Sales
Album Charts
New Releases
Advance Orders

To find an artist, album, song or record label, fill out the form below and click the Find It button. Additional searches for classical music and movies are available by using the blue Find Classical and Find Movies buttons above.

Artist ▼ Alphabetically ▼

Find It

ADVANCE ORDERS
AVAILABLE NOW

CDNOW'S TOP 50 MOVIES NOW ON SALE!
CLICK HERE CLICK HERE CLICK HERE CLICK HERE CLICK HERE

[Bjork]   [Dave

3% of 3K

FIGURE 1.2 The CDnow home page.

History of Web commerce

The history of commerce on the Internet is quite brief, but much has been accomplished within a short amount of time. The inception of the Internet dates back to the 1960s during the Cold War when it was created for national security reasons. The Internet is a decentralized network of computers and its purpose was to ensure that in case one portion of the network was destroyed the rest of the network continued to operate. The design was based on a network that was not organized *point-to-point*—which requires each computer to be dependent on the computer link before it. The network design is much like a fishnet of connected computers that allows information to find its own path. For example, when you send an e-mail across the Internet it is broken up into packets, or pieces of message. Each packet finds its own way to the person you are sending the e-mail. The e-mail message arrives in pieces and is reconstructed when it arrives at its destination.

Many uses for the Internet have emerged: research, education, newsgroups, public information, and now, a place for anyone to get information, communicate with others, and buy products and services.

Surprisingly, the Internet wasn't suitable for commercial use until 1991 when the World Wide Web—a tool that allows people to view and navigate the Web graphically—was developed by Tim Berners-Lee, a consultant working at CERN, a particle physics laboratory in Switzerland. The initial purpose for developing the Web was to allow scientists to share data in a graphical form. It wasn't until mid-1993 when the first commercial Web sites set up shop on the Internet. It was estimated that there were 130 Web sites, two of which were commercial. According to Network Wizard's (http://www.nw.com) Internet Domain Survey, January 1997, there are more than one-half million commercial (.com) Web sites worldwide in 1996. Of these, about 90,000 are selling or initiating sales of products online, according to Activmedia (http://www.activmedia.com). An interesting statistic about new Web site growth from the The NPD Group (http://www.npd.com) is that 20 percent of their "PC Meter Top 500 Web sites" are new to the list each month.

↳ The potential of Web commerce

There are a lot of statistics soothsaying the prosperity of the Web. The growth of the Web is tied to the emergence and adoption of computer and Internet technology. According to The NPD Group in a July 1996 address to the ARF Interactive Media Research Summit II, the Web has nearly 11 percent penetration among consumers at home. The following statistics give you an idea of the Web's potential.

- Number of Web users in 1996: 35 million. (International Data Corporation, Internet Commerce Market Model, 10/96)

- Number of Web users in 2000: 163 million. (International Data Corporation, Internet Commerce Market Model 10/96)

- 84 million persons 12 or older indicate they or someone in their household have a computer. (Nielsen Media Research, Home Technology Report, 7/96)

- 23.4 million households were online in 1996, and it is estimated that online households will reach over 66 million by 2000. (Jupiter Communications, World Online Markets Report, 11/96)

- 15 percent of households with online services have made an online purchase. (Nielsen Media Research, Home Technology Report, 7/96)

- $6.6 billion in Web sales transactions in the year 2000. (Forrester Research, Retail's Online Advances, 7/96)

- 31 percent of Web-based businesses are profitable and 28 percent expect to be in 12-18 months. (ActivMedia, Web Commerce 1996-2001 Report, 9/96)

- Average Web sales transaction is currently $200 or less. (Forrester Research, Retail's Online Advances, 7/96)

- In 1996, 55 percent of online households made purchases via their PCs and 58 percent plan to do more online shopping in 1997. (NFO Research Survey, 2/97)

Cyber-demographics and other information about Web users

Beyond the statistics, you will need to know even more specifically who visits or buys from your Web site and why. This type of information is key to initial and continued success with a Web-based business. For example, if you are selling women's apparel you need to know if there are enough women who are online, purchase products on the Web, and are within the target age group and economic status. You do not want to commit a large amount of resources to building a Web catalog if there is no sign of a market for you on the Web. However, there are businesses that have set up shop knowing that their Web site will emerge as the customers get to know they are there. It is somewhat of a "which came first, the chicken or the egg?" situation. The following demographics of Web users show how they use the technology, and more information about home technology.

- Average age of a World Wide Web user is 34.9. (Georgia Tech Graphic, Visualization & Usability Center, 6th WWW User Survey, 10/96)

- 55 percent of longtime Internet users (online before 9/95) have at least a college degree and 27 percent have annual household income of over $80,000. (CommerceNet and Nielsen Media Research, Internet Demographics Survey, 10/96)

- 42 percent of Web users are women. (CommerceNet and Nielsen Media Research, Internet Demographics Survey, 3/97)

- Average annual household income of a Web user is $59,000. (Georgia Tech Graphic, Visualization & Usability Center (GVU), 5th WWW User Survey, 5/96)

- Nearly 51 percent of Internet users live in households with children under 17 years of age. (Neilsen Media Research, Home Technology Report, 7/96)

- 47.5 percent of Web users are married and 36.7 percent are single. (GVU's 6th Study, 10/96)

- 16 percent of home Web users are children ages 12 to 17. (Neilsen Media Research, Home Technology Report, 7/96)

- Occupations of Web users: 29.6 percent are in Education, 27.8 percent are in computer-related jobs, and 18.9 percent are in Professional/Managerial occupations. (GVU's 5th Study, 5/96)

- 63.6 percent of Web users access the Web from home. (GVU's 6th Study, 10/96)

- Almost 37 percent of Web users claim they use the Web instead of watching TV on a daily basis. (GVU's 6th Study, 10/96)

- 51.4 percent use a 28.8 Kb/ps modem; 19.69 percent use a 14.4 Kb/ps modem. (GVU's 6th Study, 10/96)

Since the Web is still an emerging place to buy and sell we should see these demographics change over time. The following statistics about Web usage can be very useful in deciding to build a Web site, selecting products for your Web site, and promoting your Web site.

- 2.7 million Web users purchased products or services online in 1996. (Computer Intelligence, 9/96)

- Online households are spending an average of 9.4 hours a week on line. (Odyssey, Homefront Study, 3/97)

- During a Web site visit a Web user spends 28 minutes on the site and views about 21 pages. (PC Meter, "Getting A True Picture of What Consumers Are Doing Online," 5/96)

- Internet access by computing platform: Windows (59 percent), Macintosh (28 percent) and Unix (5 percent). (GVU's 5th Study, 5/96)

- Primary uses of the Web: entertainment (51 percent), news (49 percent), computer products (41 percent), travel (30 percent) and financial (26 percent). (Nielsen Media Research, Home Technology Report, 7/96)

- How Web users find out about a Web site: word-of-mouth referrals (44 percent), traditional media such as magazine advertising and TV (39 percent), Web browsing (32 percent) and "hot links" from one Web site to another Web site (10 percent). (Coopers & Lybrand, Electronic Access '96 Study, 6/96)

Interesting facts about personal computer use

The adoption of personal computers and the online services are key to making the Web a viable marketplace, along with enhancements to technologies that speed up communications, and improve graphics, video and audio applications on the Web. The Nielsen Home Technology Report (1996) sheds some light on the adoption of computer technology in the home.

- Approximately 40 percent (84 million) persons 12 years of age or older have, or someone in their household has, a personal computer.

- More than half of persons with children ages 12 to 17 in their household have a computer in their home.

- Almost half of persons in households with computers reported using the computer during the past two days and used it for two hours, while 64 percent reported using their computer during the past week, and 32 percent of home computer users used their computer at least once a day.

- Business/Work was the most frequent use of home computers (22 percent), entertainment/games (21 percent), and school (19 percent) followed closely.

Most of the information presented about the potential of the Web shows a very promising future. At the same time, you should do some of your own research in order to make decisions about building a Web-based business or what goods and services you'll provide on your Web site. Many owners of successful Web stores advise you how to plan and implement your Web site; however, you should be prepared to evolve the site to meet the changes of Web technologies and the changing demands of your Web customers.

Benefits of the Web to retail, direct, and mail-order companies

Considering the prediction that in 10 years people will be spending 20 percent of their household expenditure on the Web, it is easy to see many benefits of setting up an online store. For companies that are used to taking orders via mail order or an 800 number, the transition to the Internet should be a natural one. A company can market, prospect, sell, provide customer service, provide information, establish a sense of community, and personalize relationships with customers. For companies that want to open a Web store, the cost of building it is not out of reach relative to creating a new mail-order catalog. Estimates of initial set-up range from a few thousand dollars to millions, based on the complexity of the site. By establishing an online presence, a company can reach additional markets, move with its market if its customers seem to be adopting the Web as a primary information tool, and support retail stores, resellers, and other selling outlets.

Reaching additional markets

Patronage on Web sites that have historically sold through traditional vehicles such as mail order is a mix of existing and new customers on the Web. This means that you can reach additional markets on the Web that you cannot reach through your existing methods of selling. This also means that you will need to move some of your marketing and selling costs to promote your Web site on the Information Superhighway. Existing customers who go online will do so if they promote their Web site on any and all of their traditional marketing communications (i.e., magazine advertising, TV, radio, direct mail, telephone messages, press releases, brochures, business cards, etc.).

FIGURE 1.3 Adobe Publishing.

The Home Depot (http://www.homedepot.com) is well known for its in-store customer service and its Web site also reflects the company's customer-oriented business practices (Figure 1.4). Along with company information such as history and stock reports, it contains a map and database of store locations so you can easily find a store near you by street address and phone number. Other nice features include company news, community service activities, and environmental tips.

Increased productivity

A Web site can streamline communications as well as automate the buying process, which can translate into

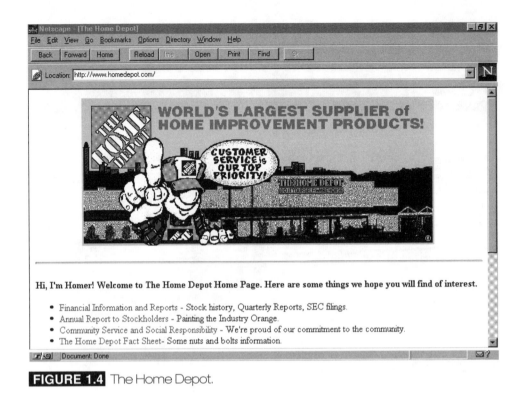

FIGURE 1.4 The Home Depot.

higher productivity and reduced costs. By automating the sales, order, and fulfillment process for the Web, you can reserve valuable customer sales, service, and human resources for more complex tasks such as resolving customer service issues, handling highly customized or large orders, handling complex requests for information, and so forth. Overall sales should increase because Web orders will be automated and you can handle more orders (Web and telephone/retail) without adding more staff.

✔ Make the Web better than the 'real-world" buying experience.

If Web customers are not satisfied, they will call you for sales and service. This defeats the purpose of having the

Web site. We will discuss the concept of interactivity and the integration of backend operations that should allow you to accomplish this objective in Chapter 11.

Why now?

You may be asking, "If my customers aren't online yet, why should I be?" This is a valid question to ask yourself and you should do some analysis to determine the best time for you create a Web site. One argument for "Why now?" is that you will be there first, before your competition. And if you create a great Web experience for online customers, they will keep coming back to your site, not your competition's site. Yes, the Web is still very young and companies that make the commitment now will have to evolve with the rapidly changing technology, but the Web customer base is growing just as rapidly.

↳ Applications of the Web catalog

The Web allows all types of entities to do a variety of things to build relationships with customers and members including providing information, marketing and selling products, providing customer service, and getting feedback. Just look at the following list:

- Businesses—Lotus Corporation (http://www.lotus.com), Spiegel (http://www.spiegel.com)

- Organizations—trade organizations like the World Wide Web Consortium (http://www.w3c.org), nonprofit organizations like the Habitat for Humanity (http://www.habitat.org)

- Government—the White House (http://www.whitehouse.gov), the Internal Revenue Service (http://www.irs.ustreas.gov)

- Education—SciEd: Science and Mathematics Education Resources (http://www-hpcc.astro.washington.edu/scied/science.html)

A Web catalog can help organizations accomplish all of these things. It also allows a company to serve itself through an Intranet, an internal network that uses Internet technology and protocols to distribute information within an organization and typically uses a Web browser interface. For example, a company can create an Intranet to store internal product information and price lists, or to manage employee communications.

The Web catalog advantage

The advantage of building a Web catalog versus individual HTML-based pages is productivity, flexibility, and smaller resource requirements. A Web catalog works with a database and allows you to build page templates that are populated with information from a database when a user selects a subject. If you need to modify or add product information, you simply update the database instead of modifying the Web page or creating a new one. Below is an in-depth discussion of applications of a Web catalog for the Internet and an Intranet.

Web catalog for the Internet

A primary reason for creating a Web catalog is to store product information in order to sell the products online. A Web catalog can store a product's name, description, part number, price, shipping weight, graphics, Web site URLs, video clip, ratings/testimonials by customers or industry, manufacturer or reseller, and so forth, and you can store the information in a way that the online patron can locate a product by category (i.e., price, size, new, bestseller, genre, age group, you name it). Here's summary of reasons for businesses to put information in the form of a Web catalog.

- Product information—to inform and/or sell using as much product or service data as needed: part number, description, price, how to buy, graphic or picture, video, award/rating, category, example applications, customer testimonials, warranty/guarantee, shipping information, news articles, specials, new releases, requirements

- Corporate information—brochures, press releases, news stories about your company, information about divisions, newsletters, employees, awards, industry affiliations

- Customer service—reduce service costs by putting up databases of frequently asked questions (FAQs), service notes, warranty information, special announcements, service availability and contact information

- "Where to buy"—local store or office contact information, sales/account representative contact information, resellers, stores, Web sites that carry your products

- Web "hot links"—store all Web links such as links to manufacturers, organizations, resellers, favorite sites

- E-mail list mailings—store e-mail addresses and information about users that sign up to receive periodic e-mail notifications from you

American Airlines Interactive Travel Network (American Airlines' AAccess) is one of the first Web sites to link up several databases to allow customers a one-stop place for air travel (Figure 1.5). It is several Web catalogs in one place.

Here is a list of information and services customers can see on the site:

- AAccess Overview
  - Travel planning—ticket reservation and purchase, and AAdvantage sign up

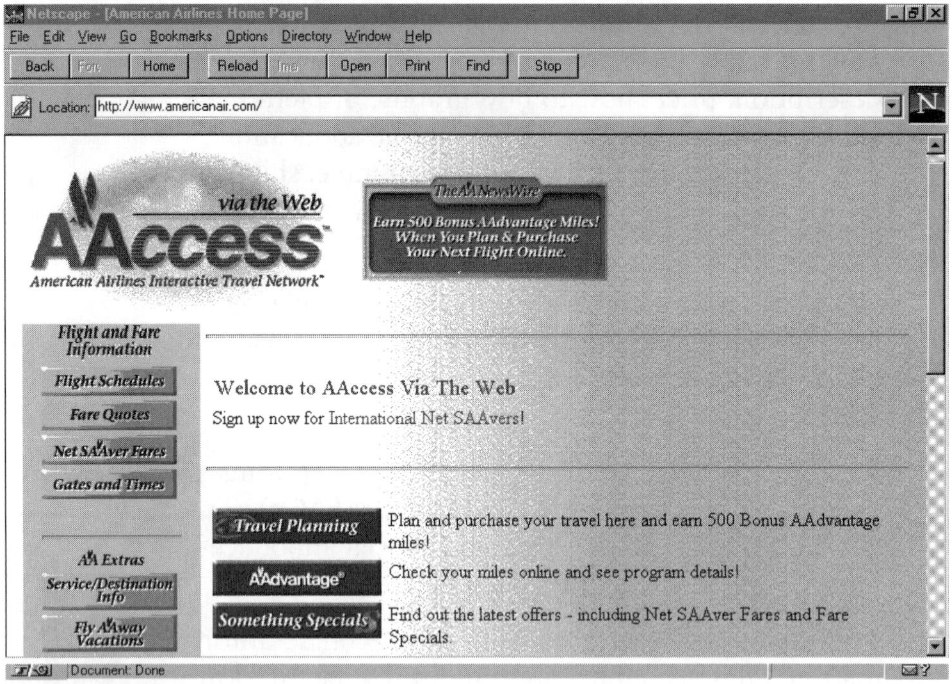

Netscape - [American Airlines Home Page]

File Edit View Go Bookmarks Options Directory Window Help

| Back | For. | Home | | Reload | Ima | | Open | Print | Find | | Stop |

Location: http://www.americanair.com/

via the Web
AAccess™
American Airlines Interactive Travel Network™

The AA NewsWire
Earn 500 Bonus AAdvantage Miles!
When You Plan & Purchase
Your Next Flight Online.

Flight and Fare
Information

Flight Schedules

Fare Quotes

Net SAAver Fares

Gates and Times

AA Extras

Service/Destination
Info

Fly AAway
Vacations

Welcome to AAccess Via The Web

Sign up now for International Net SAAvers!

Travel Planning — Plan and purchase your travel here and earn 500 Bonus AAdvantage miles!

AAdvantage® — Check your miles online and see program details!

Something Specials — Find out the latest offers - including Net SAAver Fares and Fare Specials.

Document: Done

FIGURE 1.5 American Airlines.

- Something Specials—latest fare specials
- AAdvantage—frequent flier account status
- Flight and Fare Info
  - Flight schedules—displays flight schedules, aircraft information, movies, and so on
  - Fare quote—quotes air fares
  - Net SAAvers—specially discounted air travel, hotel, car rental with e-mail notification
  - Gates and times—up-to-date flight arrival and departure information
- Service/Destination Info—route maps, reservations information, seat maps, and so on
- Fly AAway Vacations—vacation package planning
- AA Products—information on Admiral Clubs, duty-free shopping, and so on

- American Way Online—online version of inflight magazine

Oft hailed as a great Web site, Amazon.com Books (http://www.amazon.com), "The Earth's Biggest Bookstore," was never a retail or mail-order business. Amazon.com designed its business exclusively for the Web (see Figure 1.6). The company has experienced over annual 3,000 percent growth since opening in July 1995. More importantly, 44 percent of daily orders are from existing customers. Ninety percent of its customer service is handled via e-mail. The Web site contains a database of more than one million book titles. Locating a book is lightning-fast using its search engine. It also provides personalized e-mail notification services called *Eyes* which will let you know when a book is available from a favorite author or subject, and *Editors* which tracks new releases, in your favorite categories. Several databases are at the heart of this Web site's operation.

CDnow is another example of a business started solely on the Web. The music, movie, and game Web store was founded by two brothers who were frustrated by the lack of selection of jazz titles in music shops. The Web site debuted in August 1994 and is expected to generate more than $6 million in sales in 1996. The site contains several searchable databases and even allows you to buy or redeem CDnow gift certificates.

Web catalog for an Intranet—applications of internal Web catalogs

As quickly as the potential was realized for the Internet, companies began implementing Intranets. Internal use of the Internet has become very popular because it allows companies to give employees easy and secure access to information on a network that is not computing-platform specific. An Intranet can integrate data, fax, video conference, and other technologies to pull a decentralized organization together. It is estimated by Zona Research (http://zonaresearch.com) that purchase of Web servers for

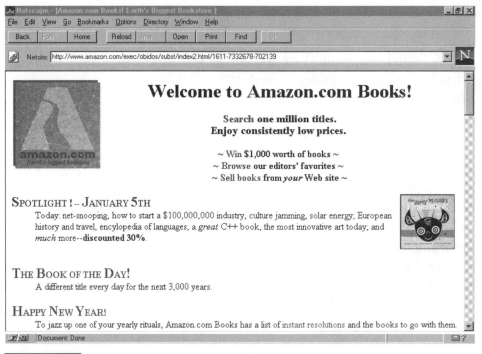

FIGURE 1.6 Amazon.com Books.

Intranets will considerably exceed Web servers purchased for the Internet. A Web catalog can be created for many internal communications including product information, internal price lists, and availability; vendor and manufacturer databases; personnel and benefit documents; competitive intelligence; company credit union; customer sales or service databases; account activity; and so forth. Private Intranets outside the company can also be useful to communicate to investors, distributors, manufacturers, strategic partners, and other constituents. For example, Digital Equipment Corporation has an Intranet in place to serve field offices, product development groups, business units, and marketing organizations throughout its worldwide organizations. DEC's Intranet consists of an internal Web page and over 375 internal Web servers, and allows over 20,000 employees access to up-to-date information. Any size company—from just a few employees to tens of thousands—can be more productive with an Intranet based on a Web catalog that allows easy access and the ability to quickly update the information.

> Explore the outer limits of the usefulness of a Web catalog. A Web catalog can be created for any information and databases you want to make available to any type of Web surfer: customer, employee, business partner, associate member, or personal/family Web page. Web catalogs are useful for Internet and Intranet applications and can contain many types of files including text, graphic, video, animation, spreadsheet, and photographs—basically any type of file that can be stored in a database.

↳ Summary

Whether you want to create a Web-based business or an internal Web for your company, using a Web catalog will make the site more flexible and manageable. Web site design and content is critical to the success of a Web site, and a database is a key component. We will discuss Web page and catalog design in greater detail in later chapters. Another critical success factor for a Web site is promotion—within the Web site, on the Web, and in traditional marketing media.

The next chapter discusses the basics of online marketing. It explains how the Web is different from traditional sales and marketing vehicles because of its one-to-one marketing capabilities. You will learn what online customers value in a Web site, how to communicate your Web site's unique nature, and how to design a satisfying Web experience.

BASICS OF
ONLINE SALES
AND MARKETING

The World Wide Web has opened up opportunities and challenges to how business is conducted. The Web IS different from traditional ways of doing business. On the Web, most business is initiated by the Web user, which is the exact opposite of traditional marketing and sales. So forming customers relationships, marketing, and selling will need a new process, a *one-to-one* process.

One-to-one future

In their 1993 ground-breaking book, *The One-to-One Future* (Doubleday, 1993), Don Peppers and Martha Rogers, Ph.D., predicted the emergence of new technology that would change the way we market our products and maintain customer relationships. In their book they foresaw a future characterized by the customized production of goods and services, the availability of "individually addressable media" (i.e., the Internet and World Wide Web), and a one-to-one method to marketing. An outcome from these new ways of doing business will be a highly competitive marketplace. It will require companies to give priority to differentiating themselves through customized products, giving superior specialized service, and establishing a unique relationship with every customer. The guiding principles of Peppers and Rogers' one-to-one marketing can be summarized in the following excerpt from their Web site (http://www.marketing1to1.com):

- The basic principles that govern dialogue marketing come directly from the practice of one-to-one marketing and relationship management

- Differentiating distributors, customers, and prospects individually, according to their value to, and needs from, an organization

- Maximizing share of customer with each end-user customer or distributor, measured individually, increasing the scope of the company's relationship with each one individually, over time; creating Learning Relationships with each customer or distributor, so that as interactions with the company occur, the relationship continues to improve, constantly reflecting the benefit of previous learning and transactions

• Generating collaborative opportunities with individual customers or distributors, which result in stronger relationships and gradually increasing "share of customer" for the firm

To succeed in the one-to-one future, you will need to grow a very loyal base of customers who buy only your goods or services instead of your competition's. Instead of focusing solely on attracting new customers to obtain more share of the market, you will need to concentrate on obtaining what Peppers and Rogers call "share of customer." This means that you will sell many products and multiple product lines to a single customer over a long period of time versus trying to sell single products to as many customers as possible. The economics of the share of customer approach are very attractive since it costs as much as five times more to obtain revenue from new customers as it does from existing customers. Peppers and Rogers advise that you take all the steps necessary to get your customers to choose your products more often. The following examples illustrate how companies effectively do one-to-one marketing:

• Levi's Personal Pair—Levi Strauss & Company has a program called the Personal Pair Service that allows customers to buy jeans that fit them better. Customers go into participating Levi's retail stores, and a salesperson takes the customer's measurements. A custom pair of Levi's jeans is created for that customer. The jeans are priced a little higher than off-the-rack jeans, but customer satisfaction with the way the jeans fit is higher than the off-the-rack alternative.

• Hallmark Card Kiosks—Hallmark card stores contain kiosks that allow customers to personalize cards. The customer browses the card database for occasion and message style (i.e., humorous or sentimental) that shows the card graphics and text, selects a card, and then types in a personalized message that is printed on the card.

In the past, it was too expensive to communicate with individual customers. During the first half of the 20th century mass advertising was the prevalent method of communicating with customers. Advertisers would broadcast single messages to a mass audience using magazines, newspapers, and television. Direct marketing has been a popular way to reach customers since the 1960s because it allowed companies to customize communications to different customer segments at less expense than mass advertising. Companies had many methods of reaching customer segments such as direct mail, mail order, and special interest media (i.e., cable television, magazines, radio). Now there is electronic marketing using the Internet, the World Wide Web, and commercial online services. The Web is the definitive one-to-one marketing medium. With powerful Internet search engines, e-mail, Web advertising banners that can be displayed based on special key words, electronic news services, news discussion groups and online chat forums, Web databases, Web tracking, and so on, you now have the ability to individually market and sell to customers at relatively low cost. The Internet allows any size of company from a one-person shop to a large corporation to set up an online business and conduct one-to-one relationships with its customers. With the highly competitive nature of the Web marketplace, companies will need to differentiate themselves based on one-to-one principles.

From the start, you can set up your Web catalog with information and activities that will enable you to build a loyal customer base. In addition to having a catalog of goods or services, you can provide customers with useful information that they cannot find easily elsewhere. While a customer is on your Web site, you can track their *click-stream*, or which additional Web pages they selected or clicked on. You can also track the purchase history of each customer and target information and communications based on this information. For example, if a customer always buys from one product category, the next time they visit your site you can alert them to some new information or specials for that specific product category. Additionally, there are other tools that allow you to profile customers based on their answers to questions. This allows you to know more about what your customers are interested in as well as customize communications and product offerings to each customer. All of the techniques and technologies mentioned previously will be covered later in this and other chapters.

Since the nature of the Web makes it the ultimate one-to-one marketing tool, here are some examples of Web

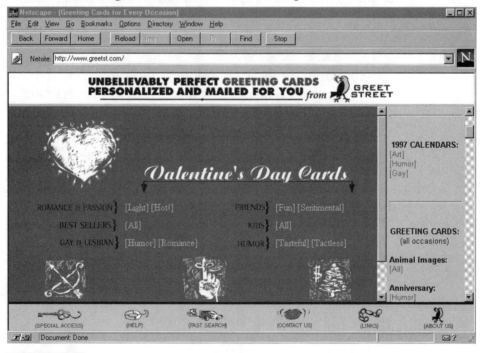

FIGURE 2.1 Greet Street (delivering physical product).

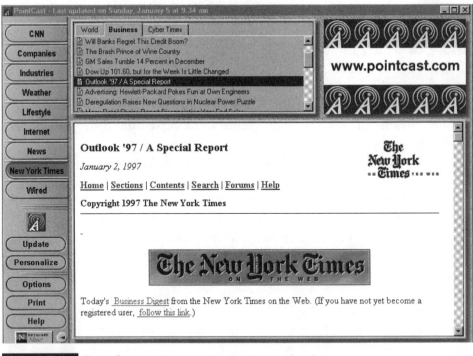

FIGURE 2.2 PointCast (delivering electronic product).

sites that practice these techniques. You can expect most all commercial Web sites to adopt a one-to-one marketing and service strategy. Figures 2.1 and 2.2 contain examples of one-to-one marketing on the Web.

Founders of the Greet Street Web site (http://www .greetst.com) opened their electronic card shop because of a need they had at a personal level: always missing birthdays, holidays, and anniversaries. The business idea for "The Coolest and Largest Selection of Personalized Paper Greeting Cards" was only for the electronic marketplace. Not only do they allow customers to select, inscribe, and instruct Greet Street where to send the card, they can sign up for an advanced card booking service called Perfect Memory. This service allows you to plan your cards in advance and receive an e-mail notification of the impending occasion so you won't miss it ever again.

PointCast is a free personalized Internet news service. It allows viewers to customize the news and information they choose to receive. PointCast broadcasts up-to-the-minute information such as national and international news, weather, stock information, industry updates, and sports according to a viewer's preference, throughout the day. The PointCast network broadcasts information from several sources, including Reuters, *Time Magazine*, *People Magazine*, *Money Magazine*, Accuweather, CNN, *The New York Times*, and several other newspapers.

The Sharper Image (http://www.sharperimage.com) is a good example of a retail and catalog company that has successfully opened a Web catalog (Figure 2.3). In addition to the regular Sharper Image fare of high-tech gifts, it has an online gift finder that allows customers to match gifts by categories like who you are buying for (male, female, kids),

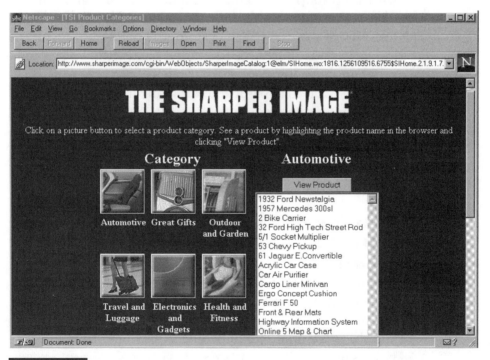

FIGURE 2.3 The Sharper Image (delivering physical product; also paper catalog and retail store).

gift category (automotive, entertainment, outdoor), and even career type. They also have specials specifically for Internet customers.

New Web catalogs selling a growing list of goods and services go online almost daily. What will separate successful catalogs from the others will be organizing the Web site in ways that treat customers as individuals through the entire process from product offerings, from marketing to sales to customer service and support.

↳ Which products will sell online

Products and services that are sold through mail-order can be sold using a Web catalog. Initially there were limitations that made only certain types of products popular with Web shoppers such as computers, books, and gifts. The limitations were both technical and due to the characterisitics of the early Web customer. The biggest technical limitation was speed due to limited bandwith. This posed a problem for many catalogs that rely on pictures to sell products such as apparel and home furnishings. The early Web patron was predominately male and had a interest in computing products. With the rapid improvements in Web communications and graphics technology and the broadening of the Web market, we will see every imaginable product marketed and/or sold on the Internet.

Products that have sold successfully to date

As stated in Chapter 1, online merchants can expect to generate more than $1 billion in sales today, and it should grow to more than $6.6 billion by the year 2000. However, with the rapid emergence of technology online and the incredible rate of people subscribing to online services, sales numbers may exceed everyone's current expectations. More specifically, low-risk, no trial, and digital products have sold very well on the Web. Another

Forrester Research report showed that computer products dominate online purchases at 27 percent. The rest of the online purchases are travel (24 percent), entertainment-books, music, videos (16 percent), apparel (9 percent), gifts and flowers (9 percent), food and drink (8 percent) and other (7 percent).

Currently, most of the products that sell successfully online are those that have sold successfully via mail order, 800 services, and catalogs. Table 2.1 lists of categories and products that have sold well during this very short period of electronic commerce on the Web.

TABLE 2.1 Products That Have Sold Successfully on the Web

Category	Products/Example Web Sites
Business-to-business	
1. Traditional	Parts/Supplies, manufacturing, distribution
	Hello Direct, http://www.hello-direct.com
	Lamp Technology, http://www.webscope.com/lamp tech/
	3M Innovation, http://www.mmm.com
	John Wiley & Sons publishing, http://www.wiley.com
2. High technology	Computers, telecommunications, biotechnology, pharmaceutical
	Hewlett Packard, http://www.hp.com
	Sun Microsystems, http://www.sun.com
	IBM, http://www.ibm.com

TABLE 2.1 Continued

Category	Products/Example Web Sites
	Microsoft, http://www.microsoft.com
	Cybercash, http://www.cybercash.com
	Netscape, http://home.netscape.com
	AT&T, http://www.att.com
	MCI, http://www.mci.com
	HOTLinx, http://www.hotlinx.com
	Motorola, http://www.mot.com
3. Services	Financial, information, magazines, business
	Morgan Stanley, http://www.ms.com
	Dun & Bradstreet, http://www.dnb.com
	Mastercard, http://www.master-card.com
	Visa, http://www.visa.com
	Wall Street Journal, http://www.wsj.com
	ZD Net (Ziff-Davis), http://www.zdnet.com
	FedEx, http://www.fedex.com
	UPS, http://www.ups.com
Consumer	
1. Mass merchant	Apparel, computers, home, hobbies, kids, gifts, food/drink
	Disney, http://www.disney.com

Category	Products/Example Web Sites
	800-Flowers, http://www.1800flowers.com
	Gateway Computer, http://www.gw2k.com
	Dell Computer, http://www.dell.com
	Elek-Tek, http://www.elektek.com
	Software.net, http://www.software.net
	Insight, http://www.insight.com
	Hot! Hot! Hot!, http://www.hot.presence.com
	Crutchfield, http://www.crutchfield.com
	Joe Boxer, http://www.joeboxer.com
	L.L. Bean, http://www.llbean.com
	Land's End, http://www.landsend.com
	Eddie Bauer, http://www.ebauer.com
	Sony, http://www.sony.com
	Wizzywygs, http://www.wizzywygs.com
	CyberShop, http//www.cybershop.com
	Internet Shopping Network, http://www.isn.com
	All-Internet Shopping Directory, http://www.webcom.com/~tbrown
2. Upscale merchant	Apparel, computers, home, hobbies, kids, gifts, food/drink

TABLE 2.1 Continued

Category	Products/Example Web Sites
	Sharper Image, http://www.sharperimage.com
	Levenger, http://www.levenger.com
	Godiva, http://www.godiva.com
	J. Peterman, http://www.jpeterman.com
3. Entertainment	Music, video, books, TV, radio, magazines, film
	CDnow, http://www.cdnow.com
	Amazon.com, http://www.amazon.com
	The Discovery Channel, http://www.discovery.com
	NPR, http://www.npr.org/index.html
	PBS, http://www.pbs.org
	Wired, http://www.hotwired.com
4. Services	Travel, investment/banking, real estate, information, shopping
	American Airlines, http://www.americanair.com
	PC Travel, http://www.pctravel.com
	Fidelity Investments, http://www.fid-inv.com
	PC Quote, http://www.pcquote.com
	Peapod, http://www.peapod.com

Category	Products/Example Web Sites
5. Automobiles	Manufacturers, dealerships
	Toyota, http://www.toyota.com
	Volvo, http://www.volvo.se/
	BMW, http://www.bmw.com
	Ford, http://www.ford.com
	Auto-By-Tel, http://www.autobytel.com

As you can see, there is quite a variety of companies with online stores. There are many examples of companies that are online but are focusing on information instead of sales. These organizations benefit from having a Web catalog just to manage and present information in an easy-to-use and easy-to-find way.

What will sell online in the future?

Everything! Need we say more? Many companies that do not fit in the categories initally predicted as the ones that will sell successfully on the Web have proven that just about any business can sell products online. Fine wine, fruit, burritos, boomerangs, art, beef Wellington, and just about anything you can imagine is being sold on the Web today. For example, Overton's (http://www.overtonsonline.com), a mail-order company catering to water sport enthusiasts, sells everything for boating from propellers and skis to wet suits and sunglasses. Figure 2.4 shows Overton's product selection.

The Web and Web catalog can be a successful tool for you whether you want to sell your goods or services, provide a useful place for customers to get information, or simply store human resource documents on an internal network (or Intranet) for employees to access, fill out, and submit to the personnel manager.

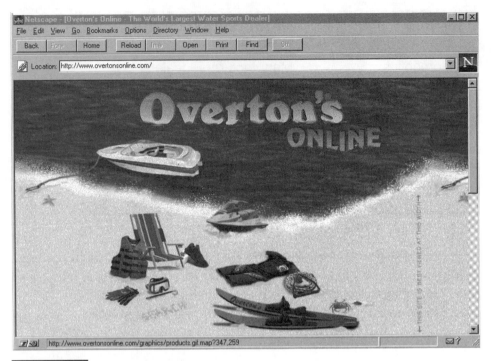

FIGURE 2.4 Overton's Web catalog.

🔙 How the Web is unlike other marketing vehicles

A common philosophy held by companies with experience in marketing and selling on the Web is to make sure you treat it as it is own entity. They advise that the Web is its own medium and marketers should not force traditional marketing methods and business processes onto this unique communication tool. Some Web site owners feel that Web experience should be better than traditional media. The Web's capability for interactivity and personalization, along with a higher level of competition due to users' ability to access competing Web sites, makes marketing and selling a whole new game.

One-to-one marketing

As mentioned at the beginning of this chapter, the Web is the ultimate one-to-one marketing, sales, and service tool. It requires a person to think of customers not as a whole, but as a set of individual customers. Your Web catalog should incorporate personalization and customization techniques to make the experience tailored to each customer. This will require you to leverage customer and product databases, as well as Web technology, to accomplish this personalization.

Customizing products and services allows you to better compete against other companies offering something similar, to create programs that allow you to encourage your customers to focus on the value you provide rather than just price, and to create a loyal customer following. Think of your Web site as being like the Levi's Personal Pair program mentioned earlier. Customers are willing to pay a little more for their custom-fitted jeans than off-the-rack jeans, and their satisfaction with the product is significantly higher, and that means that they will be back to take advantage of this personalized program every time they need a pair of jeans. With ever-increasing price competion, you will need to provide valuable and personal service to succeed on the Web. The search capabilities of the Web make it extremely easy to shop price, so differentiating yourself in other ways is important.

Customers are willing to continue to invest their precious time and hard-earned income if they are getting consistent value in exchange. If they have already made the comittment to your Web catalog, make it difficult to enable them to switch by providing an excellent value from their perspective.

Allow customers to provide feedback so you can gauge whether or not they continue to value your unique Web catalog.

According to Peppers and Rogers, "The Law of Repeat Purchases" means the more you sell to any single customer the easier it is the sell to him or her again. It can allow you to get higher return from selling an increasing volume of products to customers who repeatedly buy from you. The one-to-one approach can increase volume while giving you a greater return (i.e., higher profit margins) on sales over time. This goes back to the rule that it is five time more expensive to acquire a new customer than to sell to an existing customer. Figure 2.5 shows how Peapod gives one-to-one service.

Peapod (http://www.peapod.com) is an innovative personalized shopping service that allows you to e-mail a grocery list to a participating store. Peapod serves a few U.S. areas such as Chicago, San Francisco, Boston, and Columbus, Ohio, and has plans to continue adding areas to its service. Customers use special software to go on a "virtual trip" to the grocery or drug store, select items, and

FIGURE 2.5 Peapod online grocery service.

e-mail the order along with credit card information or Peapod Electronic Payment. Customers can display a picture of the item along with specifications like nutritional facts. The groceries are then sent to the customer in crush-proof bins. A customer can also create a personal list of items that can be stored and re-used as necessary.

Competition and positioning

Increasing competition, the global marketplace, and information overload have presented many challenges to all companies—in all industries. The Web itself embodies all three of these characteristics. This makes it more important to build a Web catalog that is designed to stave off competition, sell and compete in a global marketplace, and give customers easy access to very useful information. Currently, Web-based businesses are fighting for a relatively small share of the dollars that Web customers are willing to spend online. For example, there were an estimated 50,000 Web-based businesses in 1996 vying for $500 million online shopping dollars, spent by 2.7 million Web shoppers, which indicates a highly competitive marketplace. Even with the very attractive growth of the Web market, it will continue to be a competitve one. This means that you will want to differentiate, or *position*, your Web catalog relative to other Web catalogs that may offer similar services and/or products.

Positioning enables you to differentiate your Web site from another similar or competitive Web site. The information explosion on the Internet makes it easy for a customer to access nearly real-time information, leading to a more competitive environment for products and services. Therefore, there is a need to make product positioning an important part of your Web marketing strategy. To position your Web catalog effectively, you must know everything about your competition and your own company's strengths and weaknesses, as well as how customers perceive your products, in order to make sure they are getting the messages you are relaying.

With the accelerating availability of information and global competition, the positioning of a Web catalog should be simple, strong, and memorable-enough to leave an impression in the mind of the customer. A Web site needs a name, image/design, and statement that leaves no question why the customer should buy from your Web site instead of your competitor's Web site. The following list illustrates some classic examples of positioning statements you may recognize:

- FedEx—When it absolutely positively has to be there overnight
- Budweiser—This Bud's for you
- Timex—It takes a licking, and keeps on ticking
- Coca-Cola—The Real Thing
- Sara Lee—Nobody doesn't like Sara Lee

Here are a few you will see on the Web:

- Amazon.com—Earth's Biggest Bookstore
- Cyberian Outpost—The cool place to shop for computer stuff
- Excite Search—Twice the power of the competition
- PC Quote—The world's leading provider of online stock quotes
- Hot! Hot! Hot!—The Net's coolest hot sauce shop
- Peapod—Smart shopping for busy people

When you leave the appropriate impression in the customer's mind they will think of your Web site first when feverishly surfing the Internet and wading through the overwhelming amount of information. Of course, the content and services of the Web site must be implemented in a way that directly supports the positioning statement. Here are the steps to take to arrive at a positioning of your Web site.

1. Determine the degree of differentiation of your product from the competition by first classifying your Web catalog as innovative or imitative.

   - Innovative: strong consumer franchises, greater market exclusivity, higher/more rapid customer awareness, broad distribution, lower marketing expenditures per unit

     - Technical innovations—unique technical features and firsts (innovative use of the latest technology such as Java applications, sophisticated databases, live chat)

     - Superior performance—clearly superior benefits (specialized information, large selection, exclusive offerings, custom solutions)

     - Category innovation—whole new category of Web use (Web soap operas)

     - Market segmentation innovation—new segment within a category (kids-only news service)

   - Imitative: extensive competitive duplication, lower market share, potential customer confusion, frequent price fluctuations

     - Similar with major new feature—additional characteristic that appeals to customer

     - Similar with minor new feature—minor cosmetic feature

     - Identical—only differentiated based on lowest price

     - Commodities—no competitive differentiation

2. Select the specific selling message. Positioning concepts are selling ideas that explain a unique benefit or attribute.

   - Actual product attributes and benefits—success depends on importance of attribute to the customer

- Price and value differences—equal product quality at a lower price

- Unique applications—uses for the product not a part of customer's normal use

- Unique innovations—offers significant advantage to the customer

By going through this two-step process to create or evaluate the product or service your Web catalog will provide, you will come up with a few descriptive words or phrases that can be manipulated into a single statement that embodies the position. You will then apply this to how you design the Web site and its services and offerings. For example, Amazon.com's positioning as "Earth's Biggest Bookstore" explains that it has access to more than one million book titles. Customers can search Amazon.com's huge database of book titles and order a book while they are online.

Pull versus push

An interesting and challenging aspect of the Web is that it requires a *pull* method of generating demand, which requires a company to attract, or pull, people to its Web site. A feature of mass marketing at the beginning of this century was the *push* method of marketing that manufacturers used to promote products. Direct marketing uses a push method also, but to a targeted set of consumers. When a manufacturer uses a distribution channel to sell its products it uses a combination of push marketing at resellers and pull demand creation among customers. You will have several options to pull people to your Web catalog using a combination of marketing via traditional methods and online methods. Once you have pulled the customer to your site for the first time, it will be important to publish Web content that will pull the customer back to your site on their next excursion on the Web.

The challenge for a Web-based business is to get customers to want to come back on a regular basis.

> Design the Web site so that it has daily, weekly, monthly, and/or quarterly updates to information. Communicate the update timeframes to your Web audience so they make it a habit to visit periodically and consistently.

Your Web site should offer more than just information about your product and services; it must also give customers a whole view of your company. There are many things that you can do to pull your customers and prospects to your Web site:

- Useful and engaging content will be the key to regular visits to your Web catalog. Designing a schedule for periodic updates and communicating this to the customer will promote habitual visits.

- Post regular announcements about new products, special offers, company news, changes to the Web site, and so forth. Most Web sites have menu bars such as What's New, Weekly Specials, Daily Tip, or Monthly News to communicate to the customer of how often to visit.

- You can also build a mail list server that your Web customers can sign up on to receive regular e-mail notifications of happenings on your Web site. This will encourage customers to come to your site.

Web sites have begun to make the transition from simply relaying company and product information to developing a personality and sense of community. It will be important to build relationships through your Web site. Figures 2.6 and 2.7 show examples of how some Web sites have been designed to form relationships with their customers.

FIGURE 2.6 Gateway Computer.

Gateway 2000 Computer (http://www.gw2k.com) is a computer mail-order company that sells computers on its Web site. This site is a great example of a well-organized Web site and of leveraging the Gateway 2000 brand image.

Yahoo! (http://www.yahoo.com) is the most popular Web search engine, and has a special Web site just for kids called Yahooligans! (http://www.yahooligans.com). Kids can become members of Club Yahooligans! and receive e-mail that gives them advance notice of contests, special offers, and sneak previews of new Web sites. Yahooligans! also has New, Cool, Random, and Add Site buttons that keep kids coming back and gives them the feeling that this is a Web site just for them.

iVillage (http://www.ivillage.com) is a Web community (Figure 2.8). Currently, it is a Web environment for three Web sites: Parent Soup, About Work, and Vices and Virtues. It is a place for shopping, sharing though live

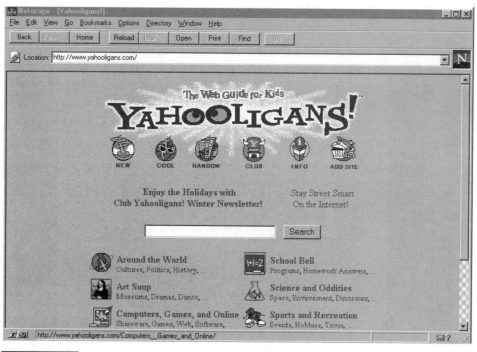

FIGURE 2.7 Yahooligans club.

online discussion groups, humor, advice, and accessing related resources.

What does an online customer value?

Shopping on the Internet is fast becoming a major reason why people use the Web. Studies have shown that the percentage of people using their Web browser to shop is increasing, though browsing, entertainment, and work still rank higher than shopping.

Web users are replacing some of their time spent watching television with browsing on the Web. They have four needs they are looking to fulfill when shopping the Web.

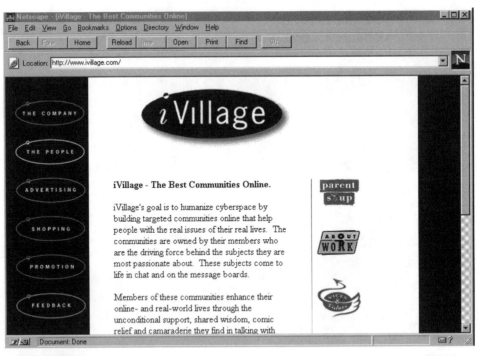

FIGURE 2.8 iVillage.

1. They want information that is easy to find and meaningful.

2. They want to find what they are looking for as quickly as possible, especially since modem speeds are relatively slow.

3. They want selection of products and services that is either large or specialized.

4. They want information, products, and/or services that address their personal needs.

Information

A Web catalog will need to incorporate essential elements found in traditional catalogs. These include product and service information, supporting graphics, and a level of information normally given by a telephone service representative. You will not want to so overload the Web user with information that they get frustrated while trying to find the product, but you will need to give a higher level of detail than what is normally found in a paper catalog. Catalog telephone sales representatives typically have much more supportive information that they actually communicate to a customer. For example, apparel catalogs have short descriptions and photographs, but only the telesales rep can tell you if the item tends to run large in size.

In addition to designing a home page that is informative and forms a perception of your Web catalog that communicates your positioning, product information should be presented in a friendly and informative way. Web catalog pages should give two levels of information whereby the user first locates a summary of product information and then clicks on a button or scrolls down a page to bring them more detailed information. The more detailed information can include specifications such as sizes and compatibility, benefits, applications for the product, customer testimonials, awards, complementary products, or competitive differentiation. For example, Amazon.com presents book information with the a summary of specifics such as title, author, price, description, publisher, ISBN number, and availability. A user can click on the author's name to find a short biography and can also scroll down for customer comments and a list of similar books by subject. Figure 2.9 shows Amazon.com's book page organization and information.

Time savings

Web users want instant gratification from a Web site. One of the most frequest complaints heard by Web shop owners is that information is difficult to find. If it is hard to locate information in your Web catalog, users will become frustrated and may not visit your site again. Web catalogs will need to give users a few options for finding information: a search engine, a menu grouped by category, and a navigational button at the bottom of every page. Your Web catalog home page should be simple and should present

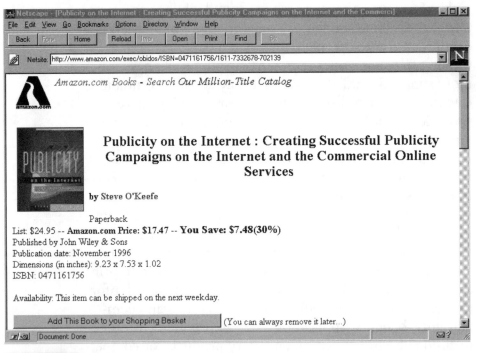

FIGURE 2.9 Amazon.com book pages.

subjects and ways for the user to get to desired information. You can think of the home page much like a book's table of contents. The search engine will act much like a book's index. The more information your Web catalog contains, the more critical it is to design a navigational structure. For example, Insight Direct (http://www.insight .com) has grouped product information, company, administrative, and entertainment into categories. There is also a sophisticated product search page and tool bar on subsequent pages to navigate to the most used Web pages. Figure 2.10 shows Insight Direct's easy-to-navigate Web site.

Selection and convenience

Selection and convenience are the primary reasons why people choose to shop the Internet. The early Web sites like Amazon.com, CDnow, and Insight Direct are successful because they provide a wide selection of goods. These

FIGURE 2.10 Insight Direct Web site navigation.

Web sites provide a broad selection that is organized in a very convenient way. This combination, no matter how many products your Web catalog contains, is a powerful tool for a successful Web site. If you are putting together your Web catalog from scratch, then your selection of products or services can be based on the market to which you are selling. If you already have a traditional catalog, you may want to tailor your offering so it closely matches the wants and needs of your Web customers. Most traditional mail-order catalog companies have put a large portion of or all their products online and some have created exclusive offers to Web customers, to encourage existing customers to try out their Web site.

Personalized service

Currently, a popular topic among Web marketing folks is the idea of customizing and personalizing the Web experience. This is the heart of the one-to-one marketing mantra given to you earlier. Few Web catalogs have exploited this idea to any great extent, but it will become a "must have" on the Web marketer's checklist in the future, just like a search engine and shopping cart are now absolute necessities. Many Web sites allow people to select products based on categories in which they are interested. This is one step toward personalizing the Web experience. The key to being able to provide a personal system is developing a Web catalog based on product and customer databases. Customer data will have to go beyond the basics like address and purchasing history to include demographics (age, gender, occupation) and psychographics (recreational interests, values, attitudes, preferences or tastes). (See Chapter 13 for more information about personalizing the Web experience). Figure 2.11 shows Firefly's personal approach.

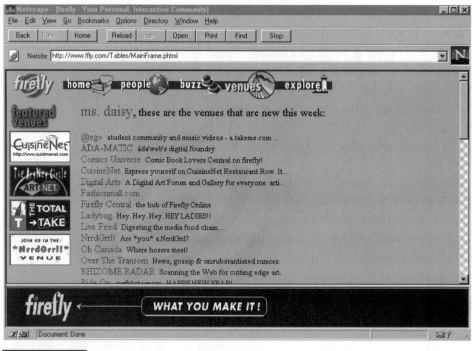

FIGURE 2.11 Firefly's personal Web experience.

Firefly (http://www.firefly.com) is a service Web site *community* where users can receive movie and music recommendations based on information users give to Firefly. It also uses this information to connect users to other Firefly customers. Users can get involved in online discussions about movies, music, and so on. Customers can listen to samples of music they are interested in and then order the music while they are online.

↳ Keys to a successful Web catalog: organization, content, interactivity, and feedback

According to Jim Sterne, in his book *World Wide Web Marketing* (John Wiley & Sons, 1995), a Web site is a combination of a magazine ad, brochure, trade show exhibit, demo diskette, and CD-ROM. Also, it must be easy to access, interesting, and valuable, or the Web surfer will not be back a second time. The site must be intuitive to the Web user and contain visual and textual cues. Be sure to take a look at the many example Web sites listed in this book for ideas. There are four basic requirements for building a Web site that customers will value: organization, content, interactivity, and feedback.

Organization

A well-organized and easy to navigate site is one that is clear and simple and gives Web users instant success. You can organize your Web site using a "table of contents" approach. The home page should be the major sections, and chapters would link from the home page sections. What follows is the basic content list of "usual suspects" on a home page Jim Sterne presented in his book *World Wide Web Marketing* (Wiley, 1995):

- What's New
  - What's been added since (date)
  - Press releases
  - Company and industry events
- About the company
  - History
  - Current accomplishments
  - Financials (for public companies)
  - Upper management "Who's Who"
- About the Industry
  - White papers
  - Special acknowledgement—we have what you want
- About our products
  - The line card
  - Product line A
  - Product line B
  - Product line C
  - How to order
- Customer Service
  - Frequently asked questions (FAQs)
  - Order processing support
  - Product support
  - How to contact us
- Employment Opportunities

You will want to eliminate any potential confusion of where a customer needs to go to get the information they need. You will want to spend as much time communicating as much as you can about the products and services you provide. Figure 2.12. shows C|Net's good Web home page organization.

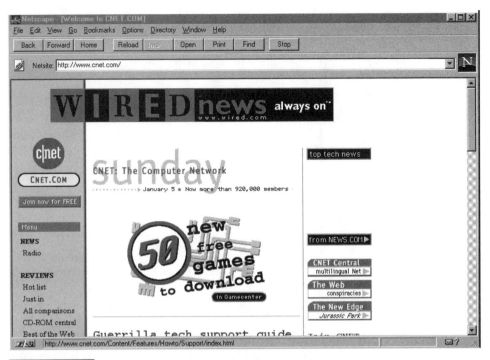

FIGURE 2.12 C|Net: good Web home page organization.

C|Net (http://www.cnet.com) is a computer news Web site (C|Net also has television shows called CNET Central, The Web, TV.COM, and The New Edge) filled with news, reviews, and much more.

> Being well organized is not enough. Your site must be easy to navigate.

No matter where Web users travel, the main menu follows them in the left margin. Since the Web site is chock-full of information, this is an extremely helpful way to navigate.

No matter where a user travels in your Web site, they should be able to get back to the basic book sections

FIGURE 2.13A Portion of CNet left vertical menu.

discussed earlier. A tool bar at the bottom of each page that contains the home page contents will allow users to find their way home or back to the major category in which they are interested. You can make your Web site as deep as possible by having users access more details of particular subjects, but allow them to easily get back to the shallow area (home page or major section page) at any time. You can give users the choice to surf deeper rather than plunging them into the deep. You will want to establish a hierarchical structure that starts with the home page and a tool bar that enables customers to flow to other areas easily. Remember to keep it simple and intuitive. You can even sit a few folks who have never seen your Web catalog site and observe them using it. This will give you

FIGURE 2.13B Gateway Computer bottom of page horizontal.

the information you need to make modifications before introducing your Web site to the rest of the world. Figures 2.13A and 2.13B show examples of menu and tool bars that aid users in navigating the Web.

Useful content

Even if you strictly want to sell products, you will need to give people an idea of what your company is all about. Otherwise, they will go to other companies on the Web or to a local retail store for the product. Unless you have an exclusive product line, marketing and service will be keys to a successful Web-based business. Also, if you are selling your own manufactured products or specialized services, you will still need to convince people to buy them instead of a competitor's products. This is why additional non-product or non-service content is important. You can add marketing and editorial information to your catalog of products and services that will do the job of not only selling products, but *selling a relationship* with the company. Beyond product descriptions, specifications, pricing, and ordering information, you can include the following types of marketing and editorial information:

- Information based
  - What's new
  - Special offers
  - Featured product of the day, week, month
  - Multilingual versions—if you serve the global marketplace
  - Company news—press releases and company newsletter
  - Company or products "in the news"
  - Industry news that is of interest to your customers
  - Related articles written by guest columnists
  - Employee profiles or Web pages

- Application stories, customer testimonials, product demos
- Awards and recognition
- Annual report
- Company brochure
- Community service activities
- In-depth information about products that is downloadable
- Favorite and related links to other Web pages
- Frequently Asked Questions (FAQ)
- Online periodical newsletter (it could be the container for a few items on this list)

- Activity based
  - E-mail notification service—send periodic e-mails with a summary of updates on your Web site and other news
  - Personalization—special offers or personal Web pages customized for Web user based on preferences
  - Games—online scavenger hunts, simple multimedia games
  - Surveys—surveys that allow customers to give feedback or "just-for-fun" surveys where results can be displayed to your Web customers
  - Contests—name a new product, most interesting product use, weekly or monthly random drawings for free gifts
  - Animation and Java applets—animated messages or graphics or a small Java application that gives the user a tool to enhance (product trivia game, quick quote calculator) their experience on your Web site. Most of this technology is new; therefore, real-world applications have been limited to special

effects and simple games. However, this technology is emerging so fast that applications will be turned out quickly. So suggest visiting the Web often to see what will come next.

As stated earlier, the Web is not a passive medium. Web users seek and deserve good information. Of course, you will want to make the information meaningful and even a bit fun. Figures 2.14 and 2.15 show examples of Web sites that serve as good informational resources.

Scholastic Place (http://www.scholastic.com) is the Web site of a large children's book publisher. The site contains many subjects, activities, and clubs for children in grades K-8. There is also an art gallery where children can submit hand-drawn and computer-generated art. There is a fun and games area with riddles, pictures to print and color, puzzles, games, and more. Scholastic now offers

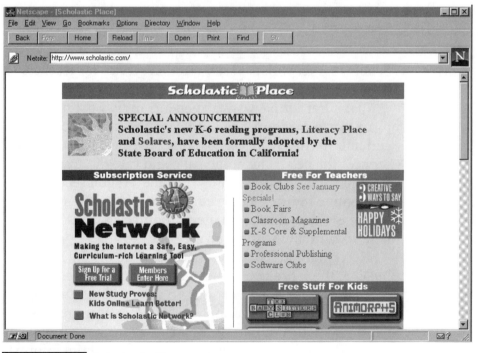

FIGURE 2.14 Scholastic Place.

FIGURE 2.15 Acme Pet.

Scholastic Network paid subscription service for teachers to help them integrate the Internet with the classroom.

Acme Pet (http://www.acmepet.com) is a pet marketplace that provides pet care information, resource links, and links to the Web sites of companies with products and services for pets. The home page and category pages have been nicely organized. The Welcome Wagon section even has a guide to using the Web site and Web terminology. There is also a chat room, news room, classifieds, what's new, favorite links, and club sections.

Keep in mind, however, that the more information you include, the more you will need to organize the site to make it easy for your customer to view and read. Also, make sure the information is useful. Web users get easily frustrated with Web sites that waste their time with lots of marketing and advertising content. You can write informative editorial that doesn't contain marketing speak. Guest columnists who are experts in a particular subject or a customer who writes articles are very effective additions.

Interactivity—a more satisfiying Web site experience

Interactivity and one-to-one marketing are related concepts for Web-based businesses. Interactivity is a way to implement one-to-one marketing methods. But interactivity is simply allowing customers to interact in a non-passive way with the content in your Web catalog. In his book (Wiley, 1995), Sterne advises that "A Web site is not something people read, it's something people do." The Web is not a passive activity; otherwise, there would be no reason to use it. You get passive communications in everyday life from the newspaper, product brochures, and television. Sterne defines interaction as making Web customers feel like they are getting the information themselves, rather than having it handed to them. Of course, interactivity only begins with the action of clicking and surfing through your Web catalog site. Interactivity for information as well as ordering and customer service can be incorporated in a variety of ways.

Interactive information

Interactivity for the informative portion of your Web catalog can be implemented in useful and fun ways. A simple source of interactivity is to allow Web users to obtain desired information using a search engine. Customers can give the search engine key words or criteria for a search of your Web site. The search engine will display a list of search results to the customer who will then make a selection to view the information. Other ideas for making information more interactive include making personalized Web pages for each customer based on criteria they select. This is becoming a popular idea for Web marketers. Currently, Web news services like PointCast, My Yahoo!, Excite Live!, and NewsPage build custom Web pages that contain the news you want to receive. This concept can be a powerful service to your Web catalog customers.

You can also provide pre-sales support such as an interactive quoting system, build your own product bundle (i.e, software bundle, gift basket), build a customize computer system, and much more if you let your imagination go.

Interactive ordering and customer service

Interactivity during ordering will be key to getting consumers more comfortable with this new way to shop. Pre-sales and post-sales interaction with customer service systems and people is the other half of the equation. Interactive ordering is based on the flow of a Web catalog, a shopping cart, and additional product, data that will allow cross-selling of complementary special offers, products, and/or services.

1. A customer will browse through your Web catalog and interactively add the items they want to an electronic shopping cart.

2. Then, they will prepare to purchase the items in their shopping cart. At this time, a message is displayed informing them that there is a special offer on a product that compliments an item they are planning to purchase.

3. The customer can decide to take advantage of this offer before finishing their purchase.

4. The customer completes the purchase and receives an order number.

This represents typical order interactivity on a site that sells products online. What if there is trouble with the order, or the customer wants to check on the status of an order? Another interactive process will need to assist the

Web customer. In this case, servicing these situations may require a human touch in addition to Web site or e-mail interactivity. Both of these subjects (order processing and customer service) will be discussed in nuts-and-bolts detail in Chapter 11.

Interacting just for fun

Making a Web site engaging can also mean making it fun. There are lighthearted and humorous technologies that allow you to include some activities related to what your Web catalog provides.

> Audio, video, chat, animation, Java, and VRML (Virtual Reality Modeling Language) can be used to add life to a Web catalog site.

You can begin with a simple activity such as animating your Web site logo banner so it comes to life. Contests and games can be a fun way to build stronger relationships with customers. The following list gives you some places to start getting familiar with the technologies and applications that make Web sites fun:

- Audio—RealAudio, http:www.realaudio.com
- Video—CU-SeeMe, http://www.goliath.wpine.com/cu-seeme.html
- Chat—WebChat, http://www.wbs.net
- Java—Gamelan, http://www.gamelan.com
- VRML—Moving Worlds at SGI, http://www.webspace.sgi.com
- Contests—WWW Contests Guide, http://www.4cyte.com/ThreadTreader/
- Games—Happy Puppy, http://www.happypuppy.com

Feedback—immediate and consistent

Some Web-based businesses had a test period before introducing their Web site to the rest of the world. You may want to choose a set of customers or others to use the feature of your Web catalog for a short period of time. This is a good way to get opinions as well as test the functionality of the Web site. This will minimize the possibility of a bad first impression, which on the Web means a lot.

After your initial introduction of your Web catalog, you'll want to receive additional feedback in general, and whenever you introduce a new feature or function. You solicit free-form feedback using a Comment or Suggestion button, and display formal online customer surveys for insight into their satisfaction and ideas for your Web site. Remember, results from these various feedback mechanisms are limited to the opinions of customers who use the Web site. It doesn't reflect the opinion of your entire customer base (if you have other types of customers such as retail or mail-order catalogs). You'll want to survey them as well when you want the opinions of all of your customers.

Summary

The basics of online sales and marketing are:

1. Treat the Web medium and Web customers differently from traditional media—both have their own idiosyncracies.

2. Web marketing and sales inherently embody one-to-one marketing and sales philosophies.

3. Design a Web catalog site that is useful, interactive, engaging, friendly, and differentiates itself from similar ones.

4. Give customers the whole company story in order to build relationships.

5. Open a dialog with customers using feedback mechanisms.

6. Change and enhance the Web catalog site often.

Chapter 3 explains how to plan your Web catalog. It outlines a step-by-step approach to planning, including the coordination of people and resources. Budgeting and outsourcing options are also explained to help you build a Web catalog that meets your objectives.

PLANNING A WEB CATALOG

By selecting this book your interest in creating a Web catalog is clear. By reading the first two chapters, you are likely convinced that the Web provides an opportunity for your organization. Before proceeding any further you will want to make a plan. Planning a Web catalog site is as important as actually building one. Going through the planning process will help you establish an objective and focus for your Web site, build a roadmap for creating the site, determine a budget, create goals and performance measurements, as well as reveal any issues you may not have anticipated. The plan will serve as a guide to all departments involved in building the Web site. Since there are so many pieces, parts, and people involved in the process it is good to have a plan everyone can follow. Before we discuss the planning process we will outline the technologies involved in conducting business on the Web as well as what you need to get yourself connected to the Internet—if you haven't done so already. It will be important for you to immerse yourself in the Web to gain a perspective of the true nature of the technology and market.

↳ What you need to know about Web commerce technology

Before tackling the Web planning process you will need to learn about the technology involved in the Web part of electronic commerce. By knowing more about the bits and bytes of the Internet you will be better prepared to outline the objectives, resources, and steps you need to take to build a successful Web site. Figure 3.1 depicts a typical set up for a Web-based business and how a customer accesses and uses a Web site.

How advanced are your customers?

The makers of the two most popular Web browsers, Netscape and Microsoft, have created what can be called

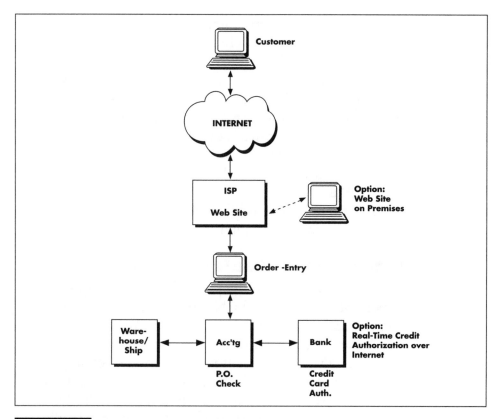

FIGURE 3.1 Typical set-up of a Web-based business.

an *open systems environment*, consisting of small software modules that automatically *plug into* the main browser software. These plug-ins offer the user a wide range of additional material and interactivity, such as animation, music, video, and other enhancements.

As great as these latest technologies are in terms of offering additional experience for the audience, there is one problem—the plug-in software modules must be downloaded and installed by the user, who is more accustomed to turning on and off their computer, television, and other appliances. We've all heard jokes about the number of people who cannot set the time on their VCR, and cannot program it to record their favorite television show. And yet, it's these members of the audience that third-party software developers expect to download software, run set-up programs, and configure for use with their Web browser software.

The end result is that merchants looking to sell products via the Web should keep these people in mind when planning to use advanced multimedia technologies. If your product lends itself to using video or animation to show off its features, and your market is likely to be sophisticated enough to handle plug-in software, then you should consider using an advanced technology. On the other hand, if your market is less sophisticated or the product can be displayed with photographs or illustrations, then you should put off planning to add multimedia to your site.

Know how You're connected

It's not enough to know you want a Web catalog. It's important to understand a bit about the technical side so you can make good decisions about where your Web site should be stored and how to help your customers access the site easily. The Internet is a collection of computer systems connected to a *backbone* of high-speed connection. When a customer decides to come to your Web site, many pieces of equipment must function together to complete the request for information. Since any one of the pieces of equipment—owned or operated by any one of several companies in the path—can malfunction, it's important for you to have a basic knowledge of Internet technology.

Here is the path that requests information from a Web site, and covers some of the potential problems that can occur. Keep in mind that this discussion is not a highly technical tutorial for a communications engineer. It simplifies the communications aspect of the Internet in order to help you understand the basic flow of data.

In step one, the user types a URL and presses Enter, or the user clicks on a hypertext link on the Web.

In step two, the browser sends a request to the user's *domain name service* (DNS) server to convert a Web address into a numerical address of the desired Web server. The numerical address is called an *IP address* (IP stands for Internet Protocol). Here are some examples of domains and IP addresses.

Web Address	IP Address
www.allen.com	207.59.6.98
www.mindspring.com	207.69.188.185

As you can see, the IP address is represented as four sets of numbers, each set having from one to three digits. It is these IP addresses that are used by the data communications equipment of the Internet to move data from one computer to another. Basically, an IP address represents a hierarchy of computers at a particular location or within a particular company. Using the example of www.allen.com, starting from the left, a router sending a request for a Web page would send it toward the 207 group of IP addresses, where it will be passed along to other routers as they move the packet to the machine with the IP address.

It's not uncommon for a customer in your city who uses a different Internet provider to have their packets go through 20 or more routers, in 3 to 5 states, before the packets of data reach your Web server. In addition, the 20 or so routers in the path are probably owned by 3 or 4 different companies, and the communications lines between the routers may be operated by several different telephone companies.

Figure 3.2 shows a *traceroute* report that traces the route of signals between a dial-up customer and a Web site three miles away. Notice how many routers are in the path and the different names of telephone companies that provide the service.

In step three, the browser software sends a GET request to the Web server located at the IP address that was supplied by the user's DNS server.

In step four, the Web server software looks up the page specified in the URL and sends it to the user's computer.

As you can imagine, the user needs an IP address for the Internet to know how to forward data to their com-

```
Server-3> traceroute www.mit.edu
traceroute to ANXIETY-CLOSET.MIT.EDU (18.181.0.21),
30 hops max, 40 byte packets
 1 router.domain.com (206.58.5.94) 3.574 ms 3.538 ms
   3.574 ms
 2 raleigh5.isdn.interpath.net (199.72.1.234) 35.239
   ms 31.365 ms 30.606 ms
 3 chain01.rtr.interpath.net (199.72.1.101) 34.662
   ms 34.043 ms 32.64 ms
 4 tysons.rtr.interpath.net (199.72.250.26) 117.767
   ms 43.915 ms 243.094 ms
 5 mae-east-plusplus.washington.mci.net
   (192.41.177.181) 82.878 ms 129.891 ms 227.725 ms
 6 core2-hssi2-0.Washington.mci.net (204.70.1.213)
   46.133 ms 45.002 ms 42.726 ms
 7 core2-hssi-2.Boston.mci.net (204.70.1.2) 53.44 ms
   core2-hssi-3.Boston.mci.net (204.70.1.10) 57.042
   ms 61.741 ms
 8 core2-hssi-3.Boston.mci.net (204.70.1.10) 55.552
   ms 55.889 ms 55.55 ms
 9 borderx2-fddi-1.Boston.mci.net (204.70.179.68)
   58.512 ms 56.139 ms 57.503 ms
10 nearnet.Boston.mci.net (204.70.179.122) 62.686 ms
   179.265 ms 58.363 ms
11 ihtfp.mit.edu (192.233.33.3) 236.184 ms 59.718 ms
   61.363 ms
12 W20-RTR-FDDI.MIT.EDU (18.168.0.8) 8 1.469 ms
   59.788 ms 57.678 ms
13 ANXIETY-CLOSET.MIT.EDU (18.181.0.21) 71.814 ms
   61.219 ms 57.878 ms
```

FIGURE 3.2 Traceroute report.

puter. You may be wondering how the Web server handles
requests for pages when no file with an HTML extension
is supplied. In this case, the Web server software tries to
find a file by the name of *index.html* to send to the user. If
the index.html file is not found, then it creates an index of
the files that are available at that URL and sends that to
the user. When the file index.html is sent to the user, the
user cannot see a list of other files available in that directory. However, when the index.html file is not available to
send, the user can link to all of the files—text and

graphic—that you are storing in that directory. From a security standpoint, we recommend that you always put a file named index.html in every directory on your Web site.

You have probably noticed that many Web sites are arranged into multiple levels of subdirectories, with each subdirectory used to store files about a different topic. For example, here is a fictitious URL for a baseball glove page within an online catalog: http://www.yourcompany.com /products/sports/baseball/gloves/glv001.html

You now know that by taking off the file name at the end (e.g., glv001.html), the Web server would try to send the file to http://www.yourcompany.com/products/sports /baseball/gloves/index.html.

Since you may be storing old product information—or upcoming product pages—in that directory and not want the public to see an index of those files, be sure to include an index.html—even a blank file—in that subdirectory.

In step five, as the Web browser program starts arranging text on the page, it probably finds inline images— product photos and other graphic images—that need to be included on the page. As it finds HTML tags that call for image files it sends requests to the Web server for them to be retrieved and sent to the browser.

Internet connection

The actual connection to the Internet from your Web server computer can be wide and varied. For instance, if you are using a commercial Web hosting service, their hardware will have one or more special pieces of data communications equipment connecting it to a phone line that carries their signal to their Internet access provider. Commercial Web hosting services will probably have a *T1* line connecting their computer to the communications network at their Internet access provider. All of these Internet connections funnel data into a special high-speed network, called the *backbone* of the Internet, that acts as a central *clearinghouse* for data, much like airlines use large airports called *hubs* to help passengers more easily connect with a large number of potential flights. Even though each passenger follows only one path into a hub airport and out to the final destination, the airline doesn't know where everyone wants to go, so they make provision for them to go anywhere in the airline system.

There are generally less than a dozen companies whose networks make up the backbone of the Internet, and who sell access to other companies such as Internet Access Providers and Web hosting services. Most of the companies providing Internet access and Web hosting buy their access from other companies that are *upstream* from them—and have more capacity (called *bandwidth*) than they do. Of course, Internet companies with substantial bandwidth are in position to provide a number of other valuable services, such as being able to serve more and larger files, have faster Web servers that can respond to users quicker, and perhaps have better technical support. In addition, larger Internet companies generally provide better backup services so you can retrieve accidentally lost files.

The bottom line for choosing a Web hosting service is, in fact, more than the bottom line. It's also service, reliability, capacity, and a variety of other factors. These criteria will be covered in more depth later so you'll know how to choose an Internet company that meets your needs and budget.

Secure Web server

In order to provide a secure environment for electronic commerce, it is necessary to have some way to encrypt data so that snoopers cannot monitor commerce data and use it. It's hard to call it stealing when the data does actually arrive at its intended destination, but the money snoopers take with that valuable data is indeed an act of stealing.

There are several encryption methods being used on the Web today, but it's more important to understand the relationship of a secure Web server program and a browser that can communicate with a secure Web server. Netscape popularized the idea of needing to use a secure Web server by freely distributing its Netscape Navigator browser which displays a blue line and the symbol of a solid blue key on the screen while communicating with its secure server. By having its Web browser display a warning box to users when form data is being transmitted to the Web server, Netscape is able to increase the public's awareness of the potential for data snooping. Because of this, many merchants on the Web use a secure Web server to receive form data containing especially sensitive information, such as credit card data. While many other pieces of data are transmitted between users and Web sites that are not encrypted, it appears that merchants selling to the public will need to use an encrypted Web server in order to reach their sales potential.

Web site

This is probably a good time to define just what a "Web site" and "home page" are because those two terms are tossed around quite a bit. Basically, a *Web site* is a collection of Web pages (files) that use hypertext links to allow the user to move from page to page. A *home page* is a specific page, the first page, that is generally seen by users. Since you can actually display practically any page within a Web site without going through the home page, we need to remember that every page could be a home page for someone. This means you need to keep these users in mind when you design Web documents, because some people will follow the link you carefully lay out, but others will enter at practically any page, so you must provide them with sufficient graphical and textual information to help them understand where they are and what they have found. There will be more about this topic later, but just keep in mind the need to treat every page as a home page for someone.

Forms

The interactive nature of the Web requires a way to send data to the Web server from the user. This is done through a form that can have fill-in-the-blank fields, checkboxes, radio buttons, and other input devices that accept information from the user.

When the user clicks the Submit button on the form, the Web browser tells the Web server to start a particular program that has been designed to handle the data from that form. The way the browser and the program at the server know where each piece of data goes is by giving the item a name, called a *variable* that stores data by programmers, and called a *field* of information by people who design databases. Either way, the item of data is passed to the program at the server, which processes the data and stores or displays the results.

Since you will not be doing any programming in the creation of your Web catalog, you may be wondering why this is being covered in such depth. The reason is that while using the procedures in this book for creating a Web catalog you will be installing one or more of these programs that are initiated by a Web form.

As you select a Web hosting service you will need to be conversant with the terminology used to describe the process of running programs from forms. One term you will hear is *cgi-bin*, which is the name of the directory where form-initiated programs are normally stored. This is why you see a cgi-bin directory in the URLs of many sophisticated Web sites, especially those with database programs, inquiry programs, or other similar programs.

In case you're wondering what the letters in "cgi" refer to, it's *Common Gateway Interface*, and "bin" stands for *binary* program—a program that has been converted from programming language into computer, or machine, language. The Common Gateway Interface refers to the ability of the Web server software to receive commands to start another program—in other words, to be a common gateway for many Web forms and many different programs stored in the cgi-bin directory. Later, you will copy binary programs from the CD-ROM included with this book into the cgi-bin directory using directions provided by your Web hosting service.

↳ Web planning steps

There are several steps to go through to come up with a plan for your Web catalog. Because things change so quickly with the Web, be open to revising any plan that you come up with. The planning process is important to enabling you to build a successful Web site. This section will detail the steps you will need to follow to design a plan.

1. Be a smart surfer

Immerse yourself in the Web. By using the Web yourself, you will be able to identify with the Web user community. This will allow you to be sensitive to the demands, likes, dislikes, and habits of a Web consumer. Do some online shopping of your own, so you can identify the traits of a good online catalog. If you like books, you should give the online book megastore Amazon.com (http://www.amazon .com) a browse. Amazon.com is one of the best Web catalog shopping sites available. A great online store for software is Software.Net (http://www.software.net). When you shop with a particular Web store, study the flow of the browsing and ordering process. Planning an order process that is smooth and increases the confidence of your customers is key to successfully selling on the Web.

2. Conduct your own Web research

Before creating a new Web site, you will want to see what is already on the Web. You need to find any competition for your Web idea and then design yours to be better or different. You also want to see what the more popular sites offer their Web users. You can surf to find out how good your Web site should be and what it should contain beyond Web standards for information, creativity, interactivity, shopping, and service. You will want to do some research on who is on the Web and what they are buying online to ensure that your customers will be there when you open up your e-shop, as well as finding out why certain Web sites have been successful. Good places to start your Web research include:

Point Communications Top 5%	http://www.pointcom.com
PC Magazine's Top 100	http://www.pcmag.com
Entrepreneurs on the Web	http://www.eotw.com
BizWeb	http://www.bizweb.com
CyberAtlas	http://www.cyberatlas.com
Internet Business Bureau	http://www.ibb.com

3. Develop an objective

Why do you want a commercial Web site, and what is its purpose? Is it an informational or awareness vehicle, an exceptional place for online shopping, or a company Intranet that improves employee communications? Defining an objective or a short list of objectives should be done before any work is done on your Web site. Once you have objective(s), you will have a benchmark to know if your Web site is performing as desired. Here are some sample objectives for building a Web catalog:

- Give existing and new customers another way to communicate with your company.

- Develop a company Intranet that gives employees a sense of pride and ownership through easy access of company news and employee documents.

- Create the best service-oriented Web catalog for home electronics buyers.

- Develop the premier online store that locates and sells rare books to collectors and enthusiasts.

- Build a not-for-profit organizational Web site, funded by sponsors, that heightens the awareness of our cause among parents of young children.

- Reduce order processing costs by creating a private manufacturer-supplier Web site where suppliers can create their own price quotes and place orders.

- Establish a Web community among older adults to exchange ideas and promote comradeship.

These are some common examples of why and how companies can embrace the Web. When you write your objective(s) for your Web site you want to have a clear vision of what you are accomplishing. The simple act of setting up a Web site just to have one is not enough reason to go online, unless the purpose of going online is to build a personal, family, or just-for-fun site. If your goal is to create a full-fledged Web-based business, you will need to go through all processes needed to set up a business, including the special activities associated with doing business electronically. Here are a few questions that will help you start developing an objective for your Web business.

1. What is nature of my business?

   - Selling and delivering physical products (mail-order).

   - Selling and delivering electronic products (software, information).

   - Creating awareness and demand for products and/or services (generate sales inquiries, support retail stores, support channel of suppliers).

   - Creating an online community for non-profit organizations (trade association, service organization, government, entertainment and dicussion, family).

2. Who are the customers/buyers?

- Consumer: age, income, lifestyle, how and why do they use the Web, and other demographic and psychographic information.

- Business-to-business: industry, how they buy (credit card, PO, mail order, direct sales), what type of products and services are they going to the Web to locate and purchase, title or function of most likely customer.

3. Why is my company and Web site different/better?

- Your company: if you are an existing business, your company's product and/or service reputation will be an important factor. If you are a new company, you will need to establish this reputation on your Web site.

- Your Web site: most complete product offerings, valuable information, best service, highly engaging, great interactivity, fastest order turnaround, highly secure, best prices or value, best selection of hard-to-find products, most personalized information/service, customized solutions. (Note: focus on one or two of these types of reasons to ensure that your customers have a unique reason to do business on your Web site.)

4. How and when will I know my site is a success?

- Determine a timeframe to evaluate the success of your Web catalog site. Develop a plan of reaction to enhance success or improve less than desirable results.

- Determine how you will measure success: daily/weekly/monthly hits or unique/new visitors, number of inquiries and the rate of conversion to sales, revenue, awards, media exposure.

See Step 6 for additional information and a handy Web planning worksheet.

4. Determine a budget

Setting up and maintaining a Web site can cost as little or as much as you want. A Web-based business can cost a few thousand dollars or millions to set up. It all depends on your objective and your available funds. Figure 3.3 is reprinted from *The New Internet Business Book*, by Jill and Matthew Ellsworth (John Wiley & Sons, 1996), where they outline a sample of high- and low-end set-up and maintenance costs of a Web site.

This is a very general cost example. Of course, you will need to make your own estimates based on your objective and how much money you have available. You may want to allocate more marketing dollars to include some Internet advertising.

5. Set up relationships with your outside Web partners

There are a few companies that you will need to partner with to set up your Web site. You will want to research each company carefully to examine its expertise as well as the satisfaction of its clients.

If you are a new Web-based catalog business, here is a list of services you'll need and the companies with whom you'll likely partner:

- Internet service provider account.

- Merchant account with bank or with credit card company such as MasterCard (http://www.mastercard .com), Visa (http://www.visa.com), American Express (http://www.americanexpress.com), Discover (http: //www.discover.com), Charge.com (http://www .charge.com).

- Payment processing with your bank or companies such as First USA Paymentech (http://www.fusa.com), First Virtual (http://www.fv.com), Open Market (http://www.openmarket.com), CyberCash (http: //www.cybercash.com).

Initial costs		
Set-up:	**High-end**	**Low-end**
Server hardware and software	$15,000 ($6000-$30,000)	$0
Leased line installation	$2500 (varies by locale)	$0
Personnel time and set-up	$13,200	$0
Account set-up	$10-$40	
Personnel to implement:		
Web site designers	$10,000-$40,000	$0
Content preparation	$5000-$10,000	$0
Image preparation	$3000-$8000	$0
Initial site support:		
Training	$500	$0
Ongoing costs (per year)		
Personnel to maintain and run	$30,000	your time
Leased line	$20,400 (varies widely)	$0
Cost of an account	$0	$20-$40
Marketing:		
Non-Internet	$9000 (paper-based)	$20
Hardware/software upgrades and maintenance:		
Upgrades	$2000	$0
Service contract	$3100	$0
TOTAL first year	$96,200-154,200	$50-$100

FIGURE 3.3 The costs of getting up and running on the Web.

- Purchase order-entry and fulfillment system(s). Some Web commerce server solutions will provide some or all of these functions.

- Shipping services from FedEx (http://www.fedex .com), UPS (http://www.ups.com), and other ship-pers. If your product is delivered electronically, you will want to set up relationships with companies such as Litle.Net (http://www.litle.net) that specialize in conducting and managing the delivery of digital prod-ucts such as software and information. An option would be to build this system internally.

Of course, you've got some options available to you that may save time or that you may need because of a lack of in-house resources:

- Option 1: Find an outside Web site development ser-vice company if you do not have the internal resources such as marketing, graphics, Webmaster.

- Option 2: Set up an account with an electronic payment merchant such as Digicash (http:///www.digicash.com) or CyberCash (http://www.cybercash.com).

- Option 3: Outsource order processing and fulfillment.

If you are an existing business with a new Web catalog shopping site, you'll need to do the following:

- Set up an Internet service provider account.

- Work with your payment processor to integrate Web order credit processing.

- Work with fulfillment and shipping services or sys-tems providers to make sure their services or systems can integrate with a Web commerce server. They will need to meet the data and communication challenges presented by the new electronic medium.

Again, the following options apply:

- Option 1: Find an outside Web site development ser-vice company if you do not have the internal resources such as marketing, graphics, Webmaster.

- Option 2: Set up an account with an electronic payment merchant such as Digicash (http://www.digicash.com) or CyberCash (http://www.cybercash.com)

- If you are an existing catalog or mail-order company, the previous Option 3 would not apply since you may already have an in-house fulfillment operation or have a relationship with a fulfillment service company

6. The Web planning session

It is important to get all personnel or outsourcing partners together for a planning session. This team approach allows all parties to set appropriate timelines and budget. You will want to choose a Web champion (even if it is you) to coordinate and communicate among all participants—this could be the Webmaster. If you are creating a Web catalog using internal personnel, then you want to invite a representative from marketing, graphics, information services, customer service, and find or choose a Webmaster. You will want to make sure there are active communications between the Webmaster and your ISP, and between your information systems manager and outside order processing, fulfillment, and payment processing services/systems companies. If you are outsourcing the development of your Web site, then you may want to work with a Web development firm. These firms are experts in Web development and manage relationships with ISPs, copywriters, graphic artists, and the like, and they can save you time. To help you with the planning process, it is helpful to have a Web planning worksheet similar to the one in Figure 3.4.

7. Building Web site infrastructure: equipment and software

You are almost done with your plan. You have become an official Web surfer, developed objectives, created a budget, and assembled the people and resources both in-house and outside. Now it is time to get the hardware and software you need to develop your Web catalog. If you are going to build your system in-house, then you will need:

• A secure Web commerce server

Web Planning Worksheet

Competitors:

URL   Strengths   Weaknesses   *(Learn from competition)*

Goal:

_____   *(Why do we want*
_____   *to be on the Web?)*

Objectives:

_____   *(How do we know*
_____   *we've met our goals?)*

Budget:

Web connection (hardware, software,   *(How much will*
Web account): _____   *each phase cost?)*
Design/Writing/Graphics: _____
Personnel: _____

Resources:

_____   *(Who will do what?)*
_____

Timeline:

_____   *(When should the*
_____   *Web site be opera-*
_____   *tional and how long*
_____   *will each phase take?)*

FIGURE 3.4 Sample Web planning worksheet.

- A phone connection to an ISP
- E-mail
- Databases
- Link to payment processor
- Hooking into your order processing, fulfillment, and shipping systems (if separate from commerce server)

If you are going to outsource all of your equipment needs such as the ISP Web commerce server, order processing, and fulfillment, then you will still need to maintain a connection with an ISP that transmits data to the order and fulfillment system. You will also want your own connection to the ISP for Web access and e-mail, and you will create and maintain product and customer databases using GT/Catalog Light.

Figure 3.5 summarizes the tools, resources, outside partners, and outsourcing options needed to set up a Web catalog site that conducts sales transactions. If you are not going to sell products, then you will not need order-entry, fulfillment, and shipping systems.

Web commerce server systems

If you plan to set up and maintain your own Web commerce server, you will want to research the several options available. Here is a list of the current commerce server solutions:

- IBM Net.Commerce—part of IBM's CommercePoint electronic commerce software and services solution. Net.Commerce allows businesses to open a retail store on the Web. Also offered, Net.Payment enables online stores to handle credit card transactions. http://www .internet.ibm.com/commercepoint/

- The Internet Factory Merchant Builder—a turn-key server solution for building an online store that includes administration, order processing, and credit

STARTING FROM SCRATCH	INTEGRATING WEB WITH MY EXISTING BUSINESS
Do it yourself	**Do it yourself**
Tools and equipment for you:	**Tools and equipment for you:**
GuestTrack Catalog - build and input data	GuestTrack Catalog - build and import data
PhotoShop or other graphics program	PhotoShop or other graphics program
Secure Web server	Secure Web server
Connection: dedicated phone line, ISDN or T-1	Connection: dedicated phone line, ISDN or T-1
Order-entry and fulfillment system	Software to link Web with existing systems*
Shipping system	
Services:	**Services:**
Internet access w/ Internet Service Provider (ISP)	Internet access w/ Internet Service Provider (ISP)
Payment: credit card merchant account, PO or e-cash	
Option: link Web catalog to online mall for transactions	Option: link Web catalog to online mall for transactions
	*Assumes you have order-entry, fulfillment and shipping systems; customer and product databases; and payment processing
Outsource everything	**Outsource Web graphics and transactions**
Tools and equipment for you:	Tools and equipment for you:
GuestTrack Catalog - build and input data	GuestTrack Catalog - build and import data
Phone connection to ISP for Web access and e-mail	Phone connection to ISP for Web access and e-mail
Outsource/Services:	**Outsource/Services:**
Graphic designer and copywriter	Graphic designer and copywriter
Account with Internet Service Provider (ISP)	Account with Internet Service Provider (ISP)
Payment: credit card merchant account or e-cash	Payment: credit card merchant account or e-cash
Fulfillment services	
Shipping services	
Option: link Web catalog to online mall for transactions	Option: link Web catalog to online mall for transactions

FIGURE 3.5 Summary of Web tools, resources, partners, and outsourcing options.

card processing. It includes the Commerce Builder secure Web server product. http://www.ifact.com

- Lotus Domino.Merchant—application that works with the Lotus Notes Domino Server. It enables companies to sell and process payment for products. http://www.lotus.com

- Microsoft Corporation Merchant Server—a Web server with order processing, tracking, payment processing, and fulfillment. http://www.microsoft.com /merchant/

- Netscape Netscape Commerce Solutions—a whole set of solutions for setting up shop on the Internet including SuiteSpot and extensions such as LivePayment, and the Netscape Merchant System http://www.netscape.com/comprod/products/iapps/in dex.html

- Open Market—full set of commerce-building products including OM-Transact, OM-Axcess, OM-SecureLink, and ActiveCommerce DB. http://www .openmarket.com

- Stronghold—secure Web server based on Apache server technology (http://www.apache.org). http: //stronghold.c2.net/

↳ Summary

You are now familiar with all that is needed to set up a Web site and build a Web catalog. It isn't as overwhelming as it may appear. Some companies have set up an initial Web site in a few weeks. As long as you have a solid plan of action and all of the right people and companies are involved, the process of building the Web site should not be difficult. You will want to keep an open mind to all of the new things you are learning as well as the issues that arise from tinkering with such a youthful technology and business medium.

In the next chapter, you will learn how to design your Web site. The chapter will help you map out how the Web site will be organized, how to write Web-oriented copy, what you need to know to use graphics, and how to *beta test* your new Web site.

DESIGNING A WEB CATALOG

Now that you have a plan for your Web site, you should plan the layout of your Web site. Since time is precious for Web users, you will need to make a visit to your Web site worth users' time. When designing your Web site you want to keep these principles in mind:

- Make it easy
- Make it fast
- Make it engaging
- Make it visually rewarding

A Web site that is easy is one that is very intuitive in its structure. A Web site that is fast is one that loads graphics and information quickly as well as one that allows users to find the information they need within a few minutes of arriving at your site. An engaging Web site is one that is both informational and graphically interesting. A visually rewarding Web site is one that contains attractive, fast-loading graphics that support the information on the site.

In order to balance all of these factors, it is best to start by assembling all of the text and graphics together. Then, sketch out how the Web site will be laid out. This chapter will give you a few approaches to laying out your Web site based on what you are trying to accomplish with the site, (whether shopping, informational, or something else.)

↳ Web site architecture

As we've discussed earlier in this book, the Web is different from traditional media such as TV, magazines, radio, newspapers, and face-to-face. Each medium has its own communication rules. For example, traditional media is generally passive: the person is being communicated to with minimal or no interaction. Whereas the Web requires interaction on the part of the viewer. If the Web user wants information, they have to actively click on textual or visual cues to access the information. One thing

90

Chapter 4

most of the media have in common is that all recipients are looking for immediate messages that tell them why they should bother listening, viewing, reading, or responding to the call-to-action (call 1-800-BUY-THIS, go to the nearest retail outlet, and so on). Web users want the Web business to show that they value their customers' time by rewarding them with a well-organized, well-written, and well-designed Web site.

Think about the Web sites that appeal to you. Most likely, they are the ones that make it easy for you to find what you need. So before you begin putting the Web site together, grab a sheet of paper and a pencil to lay out the site. This method works well, but remember to have an eraser because you will make many changes in the design process. It is easier (and cheaper) to make as many changes as you need on paper than while programming your Web site.

Establishing hierarchy and relationships

Visually mapping out your Web site will help you establish the hierarchy of information and relationships between certain information groups. Once you establish the hierarchical structure of the Web site, you will use visual cues using type or graphics to remind the user where they are located. After the layout of the site hierarchy is complete, you will select the most important areas and build a menu tool bar that helps users navigate to those areas. Nothing is more frustrating to a Web user than getting lost on your Web site. While the Web browser contains a backward and forward button, you should give users their own set of navigational tools within your Web site. Figure 4.1 is a diagram of the most common Web site content and its hierarchical and relational layout. Of course, the more complex or in-depth your Web site is, the more you need to carefully design the layout of the site.

You will then want to establish textual or visual cues that let Web users know where they are at all times. Each

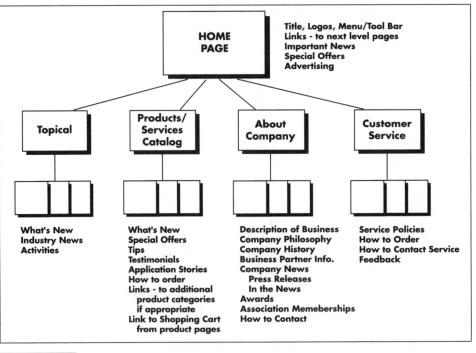

The figure shows a hierarchical web site layout diagram:

HOME PAGE

Title, Logos, Menu/Tool Bar
Links - to next level pages
Important News
Special Offers
Advertising

Four second-level categories branching from the home page:

Topical

What's New
Industry News
Activities

Products/ Services Catalog

What's New
Special Offers
Tips
Testimonials
Application Stories
How to order
Links - to additional
    product categories
    if appropriate
Link to Shopping Cart
    from product pages

About Company

Description of Business
Company Philosophy
Company History
Business Partner Info.
Company News
    Press Releases
    In the News
Awards
Association Memeberships
How to Contact

Customer Service

Service Policies
How to Order
How to Contact Service
Feedback

FIGURE 4.1 Simple Web site layout.

page should have a banner at the top that indicates on which category page they are located or which page they are on within a category. Figure 4.2 shows how the C|Net Web site (http://www.cnet.com) communicates to the Web user his or her location. In the Features section there are four topics: Digital Life, Techno, How To, and Events. Each title bar indicates that you are in Features section and are located on the topic Web page. If you substitute graphics for text, make sure that the graphic is very easy to understand. Another way to approach cues is to partner a graphic with text on more important pages.

Web page organization

Many of the difficulties of creating a successful Web site go beyond the technical challenges of working in this new medium. Probably the most challenging aspect of creating a Web site is understanding how your potential customers

features	digital life

features	techno

features	how to

features	events

FIGURE 4.2 ClNet's section-topic banners help users know where they are located within the Web site.

want to gather information and evaluate products such as yours. It's important to understand how your customers think and feel because that tells you what information to present and how to arrange that information in such a way to always have answers to their questions and lead them through the process of evaluating your products—and buying them.

Many times the principles and techniques marketing-communication people learned in the print world apply to online marketing as well. For example, a home page can be thought of as serving the same purpose as a full-page magazine advertisement in a key publication. Some of these are as follows:

- Gain attention
- Explain the overall benefit of using your product(s)
- Provide a limited amount of additional information
- Invite the reader to explore your products further

The pages linked from the home page serve the purpose of helping the reader find the information they are searching for. Pages of links to detailed content material are generally called *index* pages, *section* pages, *guide* pages, and other similar names.

The pages of detailed information, whether they are product description pages, general company information, or news of the day, are often heavily text-oriented with minimal graphics. The general thought is that when someone has linked down the hierarchy that far, they probably don't need extensive graphics to keep their attention.

In addition to the challenge of understanding your customer and their product information needs, there is also the challenge of what to say. Should the text from a print brochure be used? Should the text be modified? Should we hire a copywriter to create new material?

These are the questions that need to be answered as you move closer to creating a Web site. When the Web was new, people tried to determine which media was similar to the Web. It was found that long articles that worked well in the print world were hard to read online, and that the writing style that was most comfortable to readers was similar to the short, light style used in writing for radio. The Web is more personal, friendly, requires shorter attention spans and, of course, is interactive. The Web can be thought of as the best of television with its video; newspapers with its quick, in-depth reporting; and magazines with their complex, colorful layout page design.

Home page

Now that you know the marketing purpose for the home page—attention and interest—you can step through the concept stage of the planning process. Once you understand the underlying method, then you can apply it to your situation.

First, take an inventory of the marketing tools you have to work with that have attention-getting value, tell part of your overall story, or promise a big benefit. Here is a list of things you might have available:

- Product photo or graphic—good if a single photo can tell the story of your company or whole product line

- Money saving offer—good if yours is a price-sensitive market

- News about innovation—good if you are in a high-technology market

- Strong headline—good if your main benefit can be clearly stated in a few words

As you can see, not everyone can use the same marketing tool on their home page because products are different, and companies selling the same product lines are different. As you apply this method of conceiving a home page, keep two questions in mind.

1. Why do people really buy from us?—main benefit.

2. Why do they buy from us instead of our competition?—differentiation.

When you apply the answers to these questions to your design concepts, customers will be able to tell instantly if they should continue reviewing your Web site. For example, a well crafted headline on your home page can serve many purposes, from gaining attention to describing your specialty and promise overall benefits.

Make every square inch of the home page screen work for you!

Section or category pages

The *content* pages of your Web site are, of course, where the readers are really trying to get to, so we suggest limiting the number of section pages to a minimum, allowing section pages to be somewhat long if necessary in order to keep the *depth* of a Web site to a minimum. Even on a section page, it is possible to have links to content pages organized in such as way that material within the section can be found without using sub-section pages. For example, you could use an outline format on a section page to show a hierarchy of information. Here is how you could show links to products and educational information about outdoor clothing:

- How to buy gloves
  - Wool gloves for winter wear
  - Leather gloves for dress occasions
- How to buy hats
  - Sporty hats for special occasions
  - Hats that keep you warm

As you can see, we've included two types of links: educational information about how to buy our products and detailed product information. You can imagine that the how to pages also have links to the specific products in their sub-category, but we didn't force the customer to go through another layer of pages when they already know they want to look at—say, leather gloves.

You may have also noticed that the copy used on this section page includes words that conjure up emotional reactions to such things as special occasions where we want to look good, cold weather where we want to stay warm, and so on. The relationship you are building with your customer is built on a number of factors, one of which is how you help them feel better about themselves and their lives. By showing that you understand their emotional needs—even if you don't come right out and talk about their emotions—will help them feel better about doing business with you.

Product or individual pages

The product description pages in your Web site are the real focus of your customers. It's the object of their search. So, it's important to provide information on the detailed features they are looking for while showing how the emotional side of their lives will be improved with your products. As with other parts of your Web site, you will want to provide benefits for using your products and a description or list of features that substantiates these benefits.

Of course, you will want to include at least one product photo, illustration, or graphic so customers can see what they will be buying. The Web offers the unique opportunity to show prospects more than a simple product photo—you can show different views of the product, the product in use by a customer, and cutaway illustrations. If packaging is important to your customers (for example, if you are selling to retailers) you can also include photographs of the packaging, point-of-purchase displays, as well as other promotional support materials.

Navigation design—be kind to users

The wide variety of navigation techniques found on Web sites today ranges from simple text links to complex graphics, from intuitive to bizarre, and from helpful to confusing. This means that you have an opportunity to increase your customers' attraction to your Web site by making sure the navigation techniques you use help the customer find what they are looking for. It is good to use a combination of navigational techniques to make your site exceptionally easy to use and informative (Table 4.1).

Inquiries and Orders

The placement of inquiry forms is relatively easy: Place links everywhere. Seriously, links to inquiry forms should be available on practically every page so customers can have easy access to a response form. The easy way to allow customers to send e-mail to you is with the mailto: function that brings up the browser's general e-mail screen. If you would like to have specific information from the person inquiring, you will need to create an HTML page with the form tag and a program to run on the Web server to process data from the form. Since many Web service roviders use different programming techniques to facilitate

TABLE 4.1 Today's Standard List of Navigation Techniques and the Pros and Cons of Using Them

Description	Pros	Cons
Text links	Easy to implement Easy for customers to understand	Simple looking May not convey depth of linked page
Graphic icon	Adds to graphic impact of page Easy for customers to find	Difficult to design meaningful graphics Interferes with other graphics
Menu	Always available	Takes up screen area
Tool Bar	Always available, unobtrusive	Only contains a few links
Site Map	Good guide to site contents	Serves as overview, not navigation
Search engine	Very powerful	Very specific purpose; not to be used as the sole navigation technique

creating e-mail from forms, check with the technical support group of your provider on how to generate e-mail.

Order forms are, of course, a key ingredient to generating revenue from a Web catalog. Once a customer is ready to order, it should be easy for them place their order and have it fulfilled. The shopping cart software included with this book uses data that you've stored in the product page. It includes several items of data:

- Product number
- Quantity
- Description
- Price
- Shipping charge

There are a variety of techniques that can be used in a shopping cart system, from allowing the customer to enter or change quantities on the order form to providing buttons for adding or deleting entries and linking to other product pages. Just remember to make it clear, obvious, and simple for customers to place orders; because if they become frustrated, you have not only lost a sale, but have likely lost a customer.

After the order form is completed and submitted for processing, be sure to provide some sort of response to the customer, such as e-mail confirmation, letting them know the computer did receive their order and that you appreciate them shopping with you.

Web site checklist

The content on sites has changed a lot since the first graphical sites began appearing in 1993. Web sites have gone from single-page format, where users scrolled down through the entire Web site to the multidimensional sites of today. Early Web sites were simpler because their purpose was to display information and a few graphics. Now users can search, shop, view animation, play an online game, talk on a Web telephone, see 3-D product views, and chat with others online in real time. More sophisticated features such as video conferencing are just around the corner. The following section is a checklist of the "Must Haves" and "Nice to Haves" for Web sites today.

"Must haves"

☑ Useful, interactive content

Web users are looking for interesting information in addition to marketing and sales messages. You want Web customers to spend time on your site. The more time they invest using your site as a favorite place for getting good information, the more likely they will become a long-time customer. Building a Web site that is an electronic version of company brochures will not please Web users. The same information can be used, but it must be organized differently. Additional content that can be found only on the Web will help you draw existing customers to your Web site. Designing a Web site that allows users to be interactive is important to making a visit to your Web site worthwhile. The ultimate test is if they bookmark your site in their Web browser and return frequently.

CNN Interactive (http://www.cnn.com) is a good name for its Web site (Figure 4.3). This Web site is an online edition of the Cable News Network (CNN) television channel. In addition to reporting the news, the site has many interactive features that keep Web users interested such as a daily Almanac, News Quiz, and Video Vault,

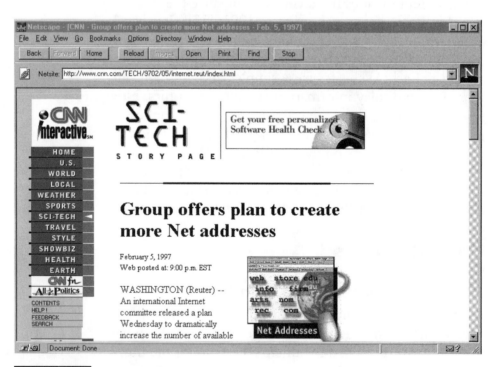

FIGURE 4.3 CNN Interactive.

which has video clips from the day and also an archive of news videos. The CNN Networks section provides a television program schedule, a studio tour, the news in its Headline News format, and an Anchors and Reporters page. A fun feature is a simulated pager that uploads the latest news to the computer; you can even have CNN broadcast the news to your own pager.

✔ Attractive but fast-loading graphics

The purpose of using graphics on your Web site is to form a visual perception of your company. You will want to make the graphics attractive, but you do not want them to take a long time to load. If your site has too many graphics that take too much time to load, then Web users will elect not to load your graphics. This will defeat the purpose of using graphics to give the Web user a perception of your company, and it can be a problem if you are promoting a brand image in a competitive market. Chapter 6 will address how to prepare graphics for use on your Web site. Figure 4.4 shows how cool Web graphics can be on the Hot! Hot! Hot! (http://www.hothothot.com) Web site.

✔ Navigational menu or tool bar

Remember that navigation is an important tool to make browsing and using your Web site satisfying—instead of frustrating. You can use a horizontal navigational tool bar that appears near the top and/or bottom of your Web pages, or a vertical menu in a column on the left-hand side of your Web site. You will want to put the most important Web sections on the menu or tool bar, either text-based or graphical. If you have a graphical menu or tool bar, you will want to always have a text-based alternative for people who may have slower computers and prefer to browse your Web site using text links. The menu or tool bar should appear on every Web page, no matter where the user is located within your Web site. Figures 4.5 A, B and C show samples of navigational menus and tool bars.

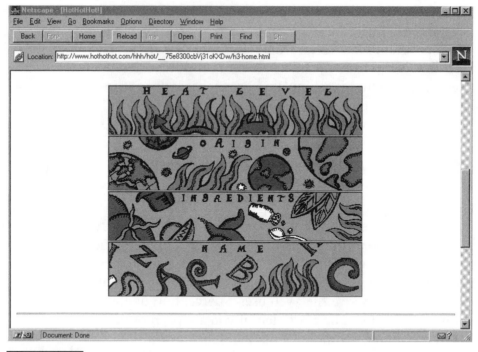

FIGURE 4.4 Cool graphics on Hot! Hot! Hot!

✓ Feedback mechanism

Give your Web customers an easy way to communicate with your organization. Having a Talk to Us button on your navigational menu or tool bar will make sure it is easy to find this important Web page. The Web user seems to have no problem saying what is on his or her mind. Make it easy for even the silent majority (neither extremely happy nor extremely upset) to let you know how they feel. The silent majority make up the part of your customer base who could move to your competitors if they are not satisfied and not even tell you. Encourage all customers to communicate with you by making it easy to get their ideas and issues. Chapter 11 discusses how to design a feedback mechanism for your Web site.

FIGURE 4.5A Godiva's menu.

FIGURE 4.5B Cyberian Outpost tool bar that appears on every section.

FIGURE 4.5C Hammecher Schlemmer's menu.

✔ Service policies

Without a doubt, if you sell products and/or services on the Web, make sure customers see and understand your service policies *before* they buy. Don't hide your service Web page; make it a necessary item for customers to view while they are shopping. Locate several links to it from various pages including: home page, catalog section, shopping cart, and of course, the navigational menu or tool bar. Write your service policies with the utmost clarity so customers cannot misinterpret your policies. Have a few people unrelated to your company review the policies and check them for clarity.

☑ Site map

A site map is a table of contents for your Web site. Some Web sites use their home page as a site map and some have a link to a special Web page that details the structure of the Web site as well as where to find information by section or category. A site map is different from a navigational menu or tool bar in that it outlines the entire site in detail versus listing a few or several important sections.

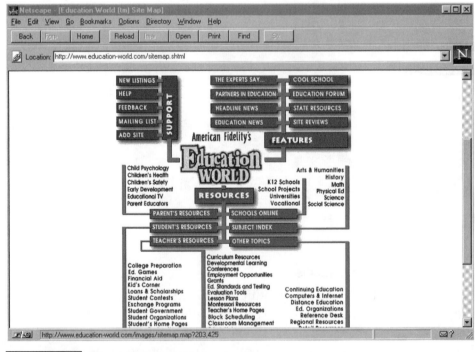

FIGURE 4.6 Education World Web site map.

Figure 4.6 shows the site map of Education World's (http://www.education-world.com) Web site.

☑ Shopping cart and inquiry forms

If you are taking orders for products on the Web you will need a shopping cart to allow customer to submit an order to you. The shopping cart will also need an area for customers to fill in their address information, payment method, shipping method if applicable, and so on. Inquiry forms can be used for Web sites whose its purpose is to generate sales leads. Customers can fill out these forms to request desired information to be sent or e-mailed to them, or for a representative to call them. Forms can also be used for subscription requests or to generate quotes.

☑ About the company and contact information

This is another absolutely necessary item for a Web site. This can be located in a few places. Many companies have an About Our Company link from a home page or navigational menu/tool bar. This Web page can include information and news about the company as well as instructions on how to contact particular departments in the company. Company contact information can also be located on, or linked from, the service policy and feedback areas.

"Nice to Haves"

With the "Must Haves" being taken care of, you will want to begin exploring some pretty neat technology that can help you solidify your relationship with your customer. Some "Nice to Haves" are very useful and some are just plain fun, which can be just as important as the useful ones. Many of the "Must Haves" were once "Nice to Haves," so you can expect some of the following Web functions to move to the "Must Have" list in the near future.

☑ Search engine

This is a "Must Have" for very large sites. It is another way for users to navigate your Web site. This is another Web page function that can be linked from a navigational menu or tool bar so that it is available to the customer no matter where they are located within your Web site.

Web sites built with GT/Catalog Light will not need a special search engine that works with databases. Since GT/Catalog Light Web sites tend to be small- to medium-sized Web sites, a Site Map and navigational menu/tool bar will be sufficient to allow users to find information easily.

☑ Mailing listserver

A listserver is a software program that administers a database of e-mail addresses and e-mail content for use in e-mail notifications or e-mail newsletters. Customers choose to sign up to receive periodic or occasional e-mails from your Web site. The e-mails should contain useful and timely information. They should be short and encourage the user to visit your site for more information. Refrain from using e-mail to do advertising or make sales pitches because users will get off the list. Appendix A includes a resource for listservers.

Some of the newest e-mail programs automatically turn URLs into live links that launch the reader's browser and go to the desired Web site. By including properly formatted URLs in your e-mails, you are improving your chances of having readers come to your Web site.

☑ Cross-selling

Imagine ordering a pair of pants on a Web site and receiving a message and a picture describing a special offer on a coordinating sweater. This is a technique used by traditional mail-order call centers and is effective in increasing average order size. You want to make sure that the cross-selling messages are informational in nature rather than aggressive sales pitches. Cross-selling on the Web can be accomplished as simply as using a standard message reminding customers to check out the special and new Web pages before completing their order. A more sophisticated approach involves using databases and programming logic that will allow you to display information on additional products based on the initial product(s) selected by the customer, past purchase history, or customer profile information.

☑ Chat

Providing an area for your Web customers to participate in a scheduled chat session with experts, celebrities, or other customers can build a sense of community among your Web customers. You will want to assign people within your company to host the chat sessions. Figure 4.7 shows a partial list of the many chat sessions happening on the Parent Soup (http://www.parentsoup.com) Web site.

☑ Personalization

Personalizing Web information and offers is powerful, but it is early in its implementation. Personalized news services such as PointCast (http://www.pointcast.com) allows customers to customize which news is delivered to them by selecting preferred categories. Product, information, and sophisticated customer databases are required to implement this function. The GuestTrack software that is contained on the companion CD-ROM has been configured to use personalization to display a page of products based on the interests of the customer. (Chapter 9 shows you how to use this feature, and Chapter 13 explains the personalizations concept further.) A few Web sites providing personalization today are Firefly (http://www.firefly.com), NetRadio Network (http:

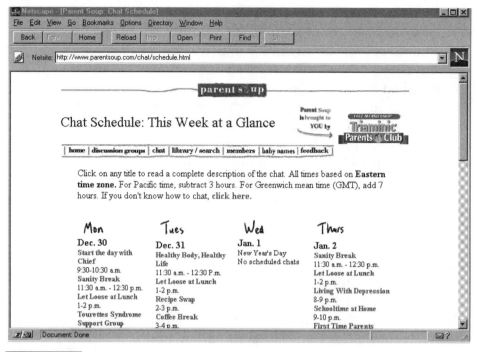

FIGURE 4.7 Chatting opportunities on the Parent Soup Web site.

//www.netradio.com), IntelliSource's Family Success
(http://www.intelli-source.com), and GuestTrack
(http://www.guesttrack.com). Figure 4.8 shows the
Casebook on IntelliSource's Family Success Web site that
allows users to build their own profile. This profile will be
used to provide personalized Web page content.

✔ Leading-edge technology

Animation, Java applets, virtual reality, video, sound, Web
phone, and video conferencing are emerging technologies
that have appeared on some Web sites. Because of current
technical limitations these technologies have been used in
a limited way. With technological improvements occurring
every day for the Internet, these "Nice to Haves" will be
used more prevalently in the future. These technologies
are explained in further detail in Chapter 13.

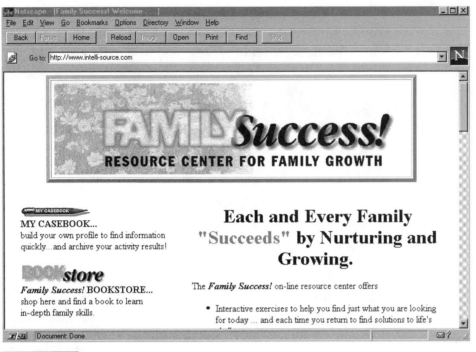

FIGURE 4.8 Personalization on IntelliSource's Family Success Web site.

↳ Web graphics guidelines

The part of a Web site that people see immediately and generates positive word of mouth is the graphical look of the site. At the same time, the part of a Web site that people criticize most is, of course, the graphics.

With a dilemma like this, how does a Web merchant have a chance of attracting customers and encouraging people to browse the catalog? The answer is relatively simple and somewhat easy to implement—make your graphics appropriate for the purpose.

This means applying good design techniques instead of using large graphics. It also involves applying some techniques that reduce download time without significantly affecting the quality of the graphics.

Many times using a small logo means leaving *white space* around the graphic, which increases the contrast between it and the background.

> A small logo can convey the company's image just as much as a large one—if it is placed in a graphical environment where it can do its job.

When you are designing your navigation scheme, keep in mind that browsers store graphic images in memory during the session, which means that when you reuse graphics, they don't have to be downloaded from the server, which not only reduces download time, it eliminates it. You've probably seen navigation bars with several sections of the Web site and links to each one. Sometimes these are really one piece of art with sections users can click on. Traditionally these large graphics used a technique called *image maps* to send the *x* and *y* coordinates of a mouse click to the server, where it would be turned into a URL, which is then treated as a link.

The safest approach to creating a *navigation bar* is to place individual icons next to one another so they form a visual bar or continuous graphic. In addition to reducing traffic over the Internet (which will speed things up), you have a graphical environment that will let you easily alter the page they are seeing, thereby helping the user know where they are within the Web site. On some Web sites you'll see the graphic or button for the displayed page turned a different color, grayed out, as an arrow or other additional graphic pointing at the current icon, and a host of other ways to differentiate one button from another. As you can imagine, because the browser stores each separate graphic in memory, all of the graphic buttons will pop onto the page while it downloads only the new button for the current page.

Animated graphics

As new versions of browsers support new features, Web sites spring up using or experimenting with these new features. As mentioned earlier, it is best to concentrate on using the features built in to the browser, instead of relying on plug-ins and *helper* applications (ones that run outside of the browser).

One of the recent additions to the browser feature lists is called *animated GIFs*. This is a technique where multiple GIF images are stored in one GIF file, then displayed in sequence by the browser. If the sequence of images is of the same item, say, moving across the piece of art, it will be seen as an animation. If the sequence is of completely different images, then it will be seen as *slide show*. Either way, animated GIFs open the door to a wide variety of graphic attractions.

During the concept stage of creating your Web site, keep in mind that it's easy to have too much of a good thing. If you've seen a home page with several different animations going on and didn't know what to look at, then you've experienced "animation overload." The thing to keep in mind is that graphics should be used to help, not distract your user, and guide them toward key parts of your Web site. An appropriate use of animation would be to highlight a new information section you've added to your home page. Another effective use of animation is in displaying headline text word-by-word using a large font. Not only do you attract attention with this technique, you also control the speed and flow of delivering the message. For example, here is a complete headline:

Save Time and Energy With an Electronic Memory

Since the headline is slightly long, the size of type would have to be considered in order to fit the entire line into a space on its page. If we convert this headline into a series of images in an animated GIF, it could be displayed as follows:

Save Time and Energy
With an
Electronic Memory

Just imagine the effect of having each line of text flash on the screen in large, bold type. Of course, it's possible to accidentally arrange words into short phrases where the meaning is less effective than the line as a whole, but that's the challenge of this medium—it requires seeing everything through the eyes of the audience and anticipating how they will react to the message, its presentation, and the interaction possible at that moment.

⤵ Web copy guidelines

The Web IS a communication tool. As much emphasis placed on designing must also be placed on writing. Both text and graphics play critical roles. The Web is its own medium, and writing copy for your Web catalog will require a different style than those used in writing brochures, TV and print advertisements, books, direct mail, paper catalogs, and other traditional media. Putting an electronic replica of existing product and company literature on the Web will not work. You will need to rework existing text and graphics to conform to the way Web users view and read information. When you write for the Web you will want to ensure that your Web copy is organized, concise, compelling, and informative.

> The Web is a very different communications medium. It will require a new way of writing that gets to the point quickly, conversationally, personally, interactively and exhibits the personality of your organization.

Organized Web copy

Writing for Web readers requires you to organize the material for them. Your task is to guide the reader through product and editorial information, anticipating their information needs at each step, then presenting them with information and links when they are receptive to that information. For example, a product information Web page should present information in a structured *template*, and each product page should be consistent with the template design so readers can locate a particular piece of data. A product page could be organized in the following manner:

Product Name

Description (100 words)

Attributes: Feature/Function/Benefit, size, weight, requirements for use, category, manufacturer, warranty, price, export information.

More detailed information: Specifications, application stories, customer testimonials, competitive benefits, complementary products, link to manufacturer Web site.

Add to shopping cart button

Navigational buttons

Headlines and subheads give the customer clues about where to look for particular information. Web users steer away from reading long streams of text. If you have a longer article, then you will want to break the article up with subheads to give the reader visual breaks, as well as visual cues to find information. Hyperlinks are cues to direct readers to other Web pages or Web sites.

Because hypertext links can be put within the body of text—and many Web developers do this—the question is whether or not you should sprinkle links throughout a document. Relevant links should be placed at the end of the actual text if you do not want the reader to go to another page within a story or block of information.

Concise Web copy

With so many sites to visit and so little time, Web surfers prefer that information gets to the point quickly. Long-winded, fluffy copy that might be found in a corporate brochure is not appropriate on the Web. Shorter sentences and paragraphs work well. One technique is to have a page of informational summaries with links to in-depth versions. Figures 4.9 A and B show the Godiva Web site and its use of this technique. No chocolate connoisseur can resist the desire for more information!

Compelling Web copy

Webster's New Universal Unabridged Dictionary gives this definition for "Compelling": requiring acute admiration, attention, or respect. Writing Web copy requires the creativity of an advertising copywriter and the nose-for-news of a journalist. This combination of good information that is presented in a interesting way can get customers to spend time on your Web site, and they will feel rewarded for the valuable time they gave to your site. Capturing and keeping their interest is key to a successful Web site. Figure 4.10 shows the compelling nature of the writing done on Virtual Vineyard's Web site (http://www.virtualvin.com). What makes the copy compelling is that it converses with the user. You feel like your are browsing in a gourmet shop and you meet up with a friend who tells you about a new recipe or wine they tried, or the owner of the shop who makes suggestions for a dinner party menu.

Informational Web copy

Web surfers can get marketing from many places—their mailbox, TV, radio, magazines, or newspapers. The original purpose of the Internet was for research and exchanging information. These purposes still hold true. Advertising has been added to the information, but has not replaced the informational nature of the Internet. Web marketing copy

INDULGE

The kids are in bed. The phone's ringer is turned off. The only light is the flickering glow of the nearby candle. This is your time. To be alone. Put on a fresh pot of coffee. Bake something sweet and really bad for you. Tonight it's just you, your favorite 45's and that dust-covered book you've kept under your nightstand. Go ahead. Indulge. You deserve it.

ROMANCE

Each of our lives could use a little spice, a dash of panache, a jolt of, shall we say, *je ne sais quoi*. And no, we're not talking about some dime-store novel with a pectorial prince on the cover. What you require is real romance. We understand your need to sing in the rain, to dance in the streets, to take long moonlit walks along a shimmering sea. Feel free to revel in romance, and be glad that those silly novels sometimes reflect real life. Perhaps even yours. That is why we created this little hideaway in cyberspace. Come in, light a fire, put on soothing sounds. You may just learn a thing or two from our own lessons of love. Or if it's something more you're longing for, we've crafted a fable for your fancy which we call "Love is a Mysterious Chocolate." Oh, how true.

FIGURES 4.9A AND 4.9B Use of summaries on the Godiva Chocolate Web site.

should not be presented as mere information, but as marketing. Web users don't mind advertising and marketing as long as it is identified as such and is placed in the correct formats, such as banner advertising. Information conveys

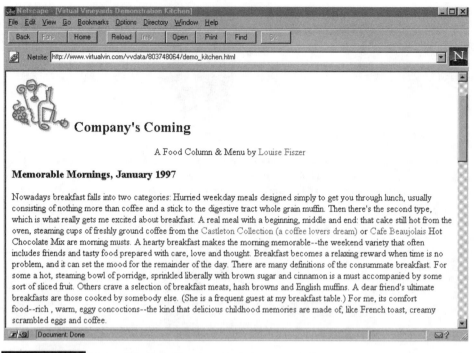

Netscape - [Virtual Vineyards Demonstration Kitchen]

File Edit View Go Bookmarks Options Directory Window Help

Back | Fory. | Home | Reload | Imes | Open | Print | Find | Str

Netsite: http://www.virtualvin.com/vvdata/803748064/demo_kitchen.html

Company's Coming

A Food Column & Menu by Louise Fiszer

Memorable Mornings, January 1997

Nowadays breakfast falls into two categories: Hurried weekday meals designed simply to get you through lunch, usually consisting of nothing more than coffee and a stick to the digestive tract whole grain muffin. Then there's the second type, which is what really gets me excited about breakfast. A real meal with a beginning, middle and end: that cake still hot from the oven, steaming cups of freshly ground coffee from the Castleton Collection (a coffee lovers dream) or Cafe Beaujolais Hot Chocolate Mix are morning musts. A hearty breakfast makes the morning memorable--the weekend variety that often includes friends and tasty food prepared with care, love and thought. Breakfast becomes a relaxing reward when time is no problem, and it can set the mood for the remainder of the day. There are many definitions of the consummate breakfast. For some a hot, steaming bowl of porridge, sprinkled liberally with brown sugar and cinnamon is a must accompanied by some sort of sliced fruit. Others crave a selection of breakfast meats, hash browns and English muffins. A dear friend's ultimate breakfasts are those cooked by somebody else. (She is a frequent guest at my breakfast table.) For me, its comfort food--rich , warm, eggy concoctions--the kind that delicious childhood memories are made of, like French toast, creamy scrambled eggs and coffee.

Document: Done

FIGURE 4.10 Virtual Vineyard's approach to compelling copy.

ideas, facts, figures, first-hand accounts, features, functions, and opinions in a straight-forward manner. There's a difference between the following two statements:

- Advertising copy: These are the best Widgets on earth.

- Informational copy: Our Widgets have been tested to withstand temperatures in excess of 400 degrees Fahrenheit, which makes them a superior solution for your equipment needs.

Marketing messages are acceptable as long as they are backed by some substantiated evidence that corroborates the messages. Figures 4.11A and B show how Dell successfully blends marketing and information. If you have ever seen a Dell direct mail piece, print advertisement, or Web banner, you will notice that the company's Web site is consistent but doesn't contain the same marketing volume as the advertising. Dell has succeeded in using each medium for what it is designed to accomplish.

Each Web site will have its own personality conveyed through graphics and text. Here are some places to start for more insight into writing for your Web site.

- The Electric Pages—http://www.electric-pages.com, http://www.electric-pages.com/articles/wftw1.htm, and http://www.electric-pages.com/articles/wftw2.htm

- Webmaster Magazine—http://www.cio.com /WebMaster/style.html

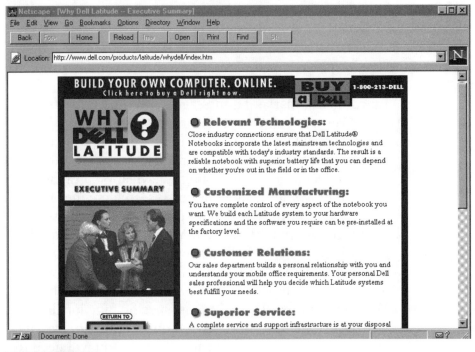 "Beta testing" your Web site

Testing your Web site is much like presenting an advertising ad campaign to a focus group or letting users test a

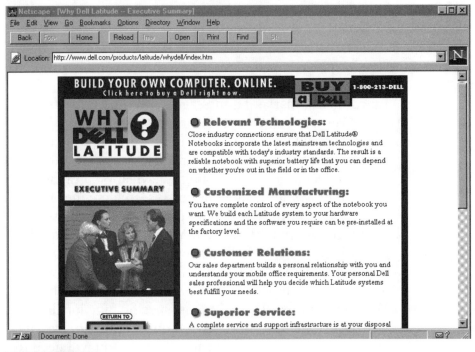

FIGURE 4.11A Screen of Dell's Executive Summary.

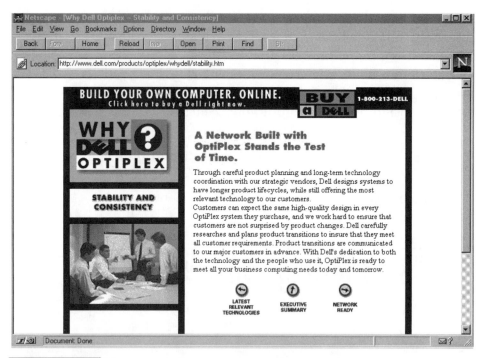

FIGURE 4.11B Screen of Dell's OptipLex's Stability and Consistency.

Beta, or pre-released version, of a software application. This process allows you to test the usability, information, functionality, marketing messages, and other aspects of your Web site before introducing it to millions of Web users. You will want to select a limited number of customers to use your Web site for a few weeks, or more, and give you feedback on the content, navigation, graphics, general impressions, shopping cart, search engine, and links. You want to select a group of people that closely represents your target market. You should select experienced Web users, as well as people new to the Web. To make sure that you are getting a good team of testers, include questions that will give you a profile of each tester. You will want to ask them to test specific functionality as well as give them an open-ended opportunity to give their opinions, likes, dislikes, and suggestions. You will need to

THE NATURE OF CYBERWRITING

Joe Vitale's new book, *Cyberwriting* (AMACOM, 1997) guides readers on how to write effective e-mail, FAQs, cyber-advertising, and copywriting. He starts the book by stating that cyberspace will change the way we do business, and is a powerful new medium where the old rules of writing, marketing, and etiquette no longer apply. He also offers these Twelve CyberCopywriting Tips.

1. Activate your writing—write using the active voice versus the passive voice
2. Be specific—use concrete phrases
3. Add excitement—give your Web site personality
4. Involve readers—bring readers into a relationship with the text
5. Focus on benefits—features are facts; benefits tell people why they should do business with you
6. Be human—write conversationally
7. Forget graphics—graphics ARE important, but don't rely on them
8. Remember how you look—make copy visually inviting
9. Deliver one message—give one main idea per screen
10. Remember that emotion sells—tell a story, use testimonials, paint a picture with words, and so on
11. Avoid sexist language—this one is clear
12. Remember the globe—it is the *World Wide* Web

be objective about the feedback provided by the users because they have an impartial and fresh perspective.

The next step will be to aggregate user feedback and make modifications. You will then ask the same set of people and some new users to test again. These two iterations will help you present your Web site in the best possible way. You can also use this approach whenever you add a new function, feature, or activity to the Web site or change the Web site significantly.

From a technical aspect, the testing of a Web site involves having people use different browsers on different computer platforms go through your site in as many ways as possible. Here are a few of the potential combinations that need to be tested:

- PC, Mac—Netscape Navigator 1.1 (introduced tables, color backgrounds, etc.)
- PC, Mac—Netscape Navigator 2.0 (introduced frames, Java, JavaScript, etc.)
- PC, Mac—Netscape Navigator 2.1 (it reacts differently on some Web sites than Netscape 2.0)
- PC, Mac—Netscape 3.x (introduced proper frame handling, advanced multimedia)
- PC, Mac—MS Internet Explorer 2.0
- PC, Mac—MS Internet Explorer 3.0

In addition, you should test using as many UNIX browsers as possible. Because the UNIX environment is really multiple environments, it is difficult to test on all UNIX systems. The more popular UNIX platforms are from Sun Microsystems, SGI, and Digital Equipment. In addition, the Linux and BSDI operating systems run on PCs.

Unfortunately, the early version of the same browser did not operate exactly the same on all platforms, which is why testing, and perhaps some adjusting of your HTML, is needed. Fortunately, the newer browsers are much more consistent across computing platforms. If you want to keep up on the latest browser news visit the Browser Watch Web site at http://www.browserwatch.com.

⤷ Summary

Taking the time to design your Web site before actually constructing it is crucial. By taking this important step you will minimize changes and headaches. The design process allows you to build a site that entices your customers to spend a lot of time with your site and your company. Now that we've given you the foundation for planning and designing a Web site, we are ready to roll up the sleeves and create a great Web catalog. The next chapter will show you the basics of HTML (Hypertext Markup Language).

Are you ready to create a Web site? Yes. You're in for an exciting time sharing your products with prospective customers in places you have never been. As we go through the following chapters, be sure to allow yourself enough time to learn the techniques of HTML and become accustomed to working in this new electronic medium.

THE BASICS OF HTML

As you search the Web you may have wondered just how those HTML pages were created, and just what makes the text and graphics appear where they do. Now that you are creating a catalog on the Web, you'll be very interested in just how the HTML tags are used—and how you can use HTML to create your Web catalog.

If you have never created an HTML page, then this chapter will help you through the sometimes confusing effort of getting into HTML. If you are experienced at using HTML tags, then you may want to review this chapter and proceed to selecting catalog templates and creating your catalog. This chapter covers the origin of HTML, its general use, and the basic *tags* that will get you going. If you become interested in using some of the advanced features of HTML that you see used on the Web, then you'll want to explore some of the resources in our Online Marketing Library (http://www.allen.com/online-marketing).

Just what is HTML?

HTML stands for *Hypertext Markup Language*, a technique of adding descriptions to text that causes the program on the reader's computer to display a formatted document. If you want certain text displayed in **bold**, *italic*, or ***bold-italic***, there are HTML tags that will cause this to happen on each graphical browser program for PCs, Macintosh, and UNIX.

Of course, there are more formatting tags than just these, just as there are many options for formatting a document with your word processor—and it's almost as easy to do. In order to be compatible with each computer platform, HTML uses text-based tags to describe the layout desired. This means that you could use a standard text editor program to key in the HTML tags—and some people tag documents this way. Most people, however, use a program that was specifically designed to apply HTML tags to text files because it's easier to click a mouse button than type long HTML tags. In addition, many HTML editors have screens that pop up and prompt you for information needed for that tag. After you've read this chapter, take a look at the section of resources in Appendix A or use your Web browser to go to our Online Marketing Library (http://www.allen.com/cookbook), where you'll find links to several currently popular HTML editor programs. In addition to their ability to format a page, HTML tags are used to link pages to one another and gather information from users, which is how you will create interactivity for your users.

Page layout

Displaying formatted text and graphics on a page is generally called *page layout*, a term taken from the graphics industry where columns of text were physically laid on cardboard sheets and glued down. Since the early page layout software started being used in 1985 to do desktop publishing, the idea is that pages be laid out to resemble typeset pages.

Hypertext links

Onscreen presentation of material is different from presentation of printed material in many ways. For example, there is the general difficulty of getting online users to move from one page to another page based on their interests. Hypertext linking allows the user to provide *jumps* or *links* to other parts of your material so your readers can navigate easily.

It's up to you, the HTML author, to provide appropriate links that are useful to your audience. This means you need to know your audience—what they're looking for and how they like to gather information—so you can include links that provide the additional material your audience wants when they're reading a particular Web page.

How hyperlinks work

Hyperlinking Web pages is accomplished by taking the reader from the *source* document to the *destination* document. By providing a visual *hot link*, the reader can easily move from one *page* to another.

↳ General features and capabilities of HTML

The formatting capabilities of HTML are similar to the features found in today's advanced word processing programs. For example, HTML can now place text in multiple columns on a page, wrap text around graphics, and link documents together. Like the newer word processors, HTML documents can now include multimedia components such as animation, audio, and can (through special programming) enter data into fields on a form.

While there is much that can be done with HTML, there are still limitations that HTML authors must be aware of:

- Text and graphics cannot touch
- Limited control over size of HTML text and font style

Why are there so many limitations in HTML? One of the original goals of HTML was to allow people with a wide range of equipment to view documents, so the end user's software—the browser—was charged with interpreting the HTML codes and displaying the page. This means the viewer—not the Web designer—has final control over how the Web pages look.

Limitations of HTML—we're not doing layout anymore

By placing control over the appearance of Web pages in the user's browser, the Web author must learn to live with the limitations of this environment and design Web pages

126

that will look good when viewed with a number of browsers, computers, and user preference settings. It's important to understand the range of variations that exist—and ways to design for (or around) those limitations. Table 5.1 describes many of the common variations.

TABLE 5.1 Typical Computer Configuration

Type of Environment	Typical Examples Found
Computer hardware and operating system	Windows 95
	Windows 3.1
	Macintosh
	UNIX
Monitor size	640 x 480 pixels
	800 x 600 pixels
	1200 x 1024 pixels
Number of colors displayed	16
	256
	Thousands
Window width	Full-size
	Less than full-size

In addition to the features of the computing environments, browsers have added various features along the way. Table 5.2 summarizes the major developments in browsers from Netscape and Microsoft:

TABLE 5.2 Major Features in Popular Browsers

	GIF	JPEG	Background	Image Alignment	Tables	Frames
Netscape 1.0	Y	N	N	N	N	N
Netscape 1.1	Y	Y	Y	Y	Y	N
Netscape 2.0	Y	Y	Y	Y	Y	Limited
Netscape 3.0	Y	Y	Y	Y	Y	Y
Explorer						
Explorer						

As you can see, designing Web pages for each combination of browser, computer, monitor, and user preference can be challenging. Fortunately, Web pages designed using the concepts included in these chapters will display well on most of the browsers in use today. If you are interested in using advanced features, and perhaps including multimedia or audio, you should obtain one of the books on advanced HTML and related programming.

Structure of HTML documents

Specially formatted tags are used in HTML to differentiate the formatting description from the actual test itself. HTML tags are enclosed in angle brackets (the characters "<" and ">") which are normally not found in documents. Most HTML tags have a *starting tag* and an *ending tag*. For example, the title of an HTML document is enclosed in a TITLE tag:

```
<TITLE>This is the Title of the Document</TITLE>
```

HTML pages are made up of two sections:

• HEAD element

• BODY element

This chapter will cover all of the HTML tags you will need to create your Web catalogs, including those required for the following:

• Page setup

• Text formatting

• Text links

• Graphic links, such as graphic icons and photos

• Tables of information in rows and columns

• Forms to gather information from the reader

Page setup tags

The HTML specifications that define precisely how HTML should be coded call for a number of tags to define the page itself, the heading area that contains information used by various computers in displaying and indexing the page, and the body area that contains the material displayed to the user.

Here is a very basic HTML version of a page (Figure 5.1) that we'll use to discuss setup tags.

```
<HTML>
<HEAD>
<TITLE>
Document Title Goes Here
</TITLE>
</HEAD>

<BODY>
```

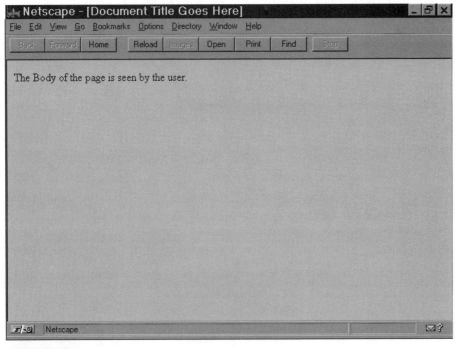

FIGURE 5.1 Basic HTML Web page.

The Basics of HTML

```
The Body of the page is seen by the user.
</BODY>

</HTML>
```

We've used extra blank lines to separate sections so they are easier to see, but Web browsers ignore blank lines and spaces (unless they are in special formatting tags covered later).

HTML tag

The HTML tag defines the beginning and end of the HTML document. Practically all Web browsers today recognize an HTML document and don't require the HTML tag, but some HTML editor programs automatically insert the HTML tag when you start a new document.

HEAD tag

The HEAD element includes the TITLE element as well as non-displaying tags, such as the META tag.

TITLE tag

The TITLE element contains a short piece of text that describes the contents of the page. Many Web browsers display the title in a bar at the top of the window. Since the title is usually a concise description of the topic, many search engines give extra weight to the words in the title when indexing a Web page.

BODY tag

The BODY tag alone is not required by many Web browsers, but practically all Web pages today apply either a background color or pattern to pages, which is specified in the BODY tag. In addition, some HTML authors like to override the default colors for text links, which is done in the BODY tag.

Background color

The easiest way to use the BODY tag to enhance your Web pages is to specify a background color. This is done with the bgcolor attribute by specifying the amount of red, green, and blue needed to create the desired background color.

For example, the format of the BODY tag with the background color attribute set to the color white is:

```
<BODY BGCOLOR="#FFFFFF">
```

The range of each of the three primary colors is from 0 to 255 using a two-character *hexadecimal* color code. (If you have been programming for some time, you'll be familiar with *hex* codes. For the rest of you, hang in there—it'll get easier in a minute.) Probably the easiest way to grasp the hexadecimal system is with an example.

```
Dec=Hex
01 = 01
02 = 02
03 = 03
09 = 09
10 = 0A
11 = 0B
12 = 0C
12 = 0D
14 = 0E
15 = 0F
16 = 10
```

As you can see, counting with hex up to 9 is easy—it's the same as we humans use. When you go past 9, it gets strange since six additional characters (the letters A through F) are added to the number system. This means that A equals 10, E equals 14, F equals 15, and so forth. But how do you represent 16? Well, like in the decimal number system, you put a 1 in the 16s column and set the 1s column back to zero.

To make it easy for you, the Online Marketing Library includes links to hex color calculators, color pallets, and examples so you can see a variety of colors and their background codes.

Background texture

Sometimes a single, flat background color doesn't convey the feeling or mood you want in your Web site. What you need is a background *texture*. You can have browsers use a repeating pattern by using the *background* attribute in the BODY tag, such as:

```
<BODY background="my_texture.gif">
```

or

```
<BODY background="my_texture.jpg">
```

The difference between these two examples is the file format—one is a GIF while the other is a JPEG. Browsers that can display background textures can use either a GIF or JPEG file. Since JPEGs are generally smaller files and take less time to download, most Web authors use JPEG format for backgrounds.

We'll discuss the techniques of creating backgrounds later when we cover graphics techniques, but for now keep in mind that the background *tiles*, or repeats from left-to-right and down the page, so it needs to be designed so the edges look good when aligned with each other.

META

The META element has several uses; the most common one is allowing HTML authors to specify to search engines which keywords and what description to use in indexing and describing the Web site. Since the META tag is in the HEAD element, the user does not see any of the text in the META tag—just the search engines programmed to use it. To use the META tag for keywords and descriptions, the format is as follows:

132

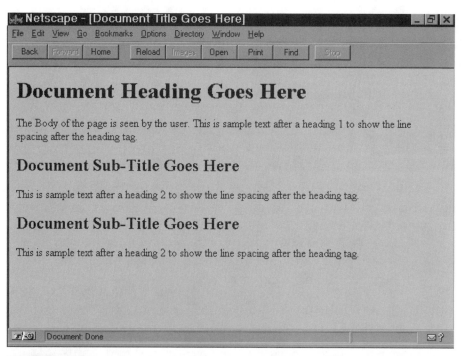

FIGURE 5.2 Basic HTML Web page with headings.

the page is displayed (Figure 5.2). We'll cover that tag shortly.

Paragraph and line breaks

As you saw in the HTML code for the basic document, text inside a Heading tag started on a new line, as did text starting after the Heading tag. However, the two sentences just after the <H1> tag were displayed together even though there is a blank line between them in the HTML. The reason is that the Line Break tag is needed to tell the browser to actually start on the next line, or the Paragraph tag is used to insert a blank line and start a new paragraph. Here is an example using the Paragraph tag (Figure 5.3), then an example using the Line Break tag (Figure 5.4):

```
<HTML>
<HEAD>
<TITLE>
```

```
Document Title Goes Here
</TITLE>
</HEAD>

<BODY>
<H1>Document Heading Goes Here</H1>

The Body of the page is seen by the user.
<P>
This is sample text after a heading 1 to show the
line spacing after the heading tag.
</BODY>
</HTML>
```

When you compare the HTML code to the actual
screen shot, you'll see that there is now a blank line
between the paragraphs of text.

```
<HTML>
<HEAD>
```

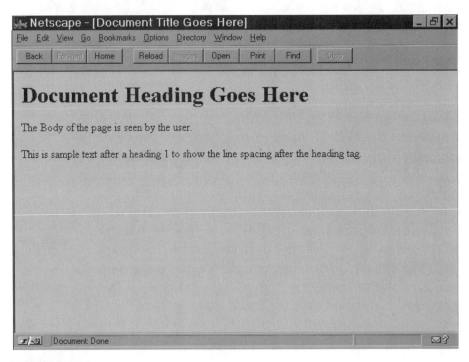

FIGURE 5.3 Illustration of the Paragraph tag.

```
<TITLE>
Document Title Goes Here
</TITLE>

</HEAD>

<BODY>
<H1>Document Heading Goes Here</H1>
The Body of the page is seen by the user. <BR>

This is sample text after a heading 1 to show the
line spacing after the heading tag.
</BODY>
</HTML>
```

In the screen shot for this example (Figure 5.4) you'll see that there is no blank line between the paragraphs—they just start on the next line.

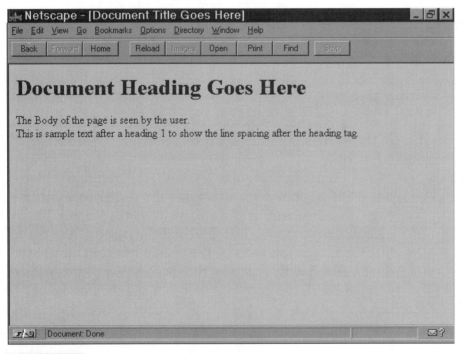

FIGURE 5.4 Illustration of the Line Break tag.

This is a good place to point out a difference between word processors and HTML when it comes to these tags. The HTML specification calls for recognizing only one paragraph tag between paragraphs—no matter how many <P> tags are used together. On the other hand, each <BR> tag actually moves to a new line. Try some experiments with different numbers of <P> and <BR> tags together to get the feel of how your browser interprets them. Just remember that different browsers may act differently, so obtain browsers from different companies to see how each acts. This will give you a feeling of how your audience will be seeing these formatting effects.

Horizontal rule

One HTML technique for breaking material into visual groupings is to use the *horizontal rule* tag to place a thin line across the page. Here is a standard tag.

```
Last line of a paragraph
<HR>
First line of next paragraph
```

Links

Linking to other documents is a key part of the attraction of the Web, so it's important to know how to use links effectively.

Let's start with a simple text link, the traditional blue underlined piece of text that takes the reader to another page. The first part of the link includes the anchor (denoted with the <A HREF=) and the name of the file to link to. This is followed by the visible text (blue underlined), which is followed by the closing part of the anchor (denoted with the </A>). When creating the link you should do the following:

1. Start the anchor with <A

2. Point to document with HREF="filename.html"

3. Follow with closing bracket: >

4. Enter text for link

5. Enter the ending anchor tag: </A>

For example, a link to the file nc-data.html using the link text of "Visit North Carolina," would be as follows:

```
<A HREF="nc-data.html">Visit North Carolina</A>
```

If the file nc-data.html is in the same directory on your Web site as the file with the link, all's well. If, on the other hand, you want to organize your Web site so all files in a topic are in their own directory, then you will need to include information about the path to those files. Before we cover how to link to files in various sub-directories, let's create a directory structure that will hold our files. In this example we are building a set of documents about tourism in various states.

/states

    /north-carolina

        /news

        /attractions

    /texas

        /news

        /attractions

    /california

        /news

        /attractions

As you can see, we have reserved sub-directories for News and Attractions for each of these states. If you use a PC and are familiar with the MS-DOS operating system, you may wonder why the slashes are *forward slashes* instead of the traditional *back slash* used in directory structures in

DOS. Since most Web servers are running on UNIX platforms, we're using the UNIX nomenclature, which uses a forward slash. Most Web browsers understand that PCs use back slashes, Macintoshes use colons, and UNIX platforms use forward slashes.

Links within documents

While links normally take a reader from one document to another, there are times when you just want to jump to a different place in the same document. The HTML technique to use in this case is to link to a *target* location, which is identified by the number character (#). For example, here is a link in one part of a Web page that links to another part:

```
<A HREF="#jump-to">For the rest of the story</a>
<A NAME="jump-to">Continued story</a>
```

Add anchor in target document

If you need to jump to a paragraph inside another document, then use the target with a standard link.

```
For the definition of <A
HREF="glossary.html#router">routers</A> see the
glossary document.
```

Inside the document glossary.html include the target:

```
<A NAME="router">Routers</a> are an important part
of the Net.
```

Lists, lists, and more lists

Many things in life—from grocery lists to product feature lists and software documentation—use lists to present information in an easy to understand way. With HTML it's easy to create indented lists with bullets or numbers.

Bullet lists in HTML are called *unordered* lists, while numbered lists are called *ordered* lists. The choice of which to use should be based on whether the list should be acted on in a certain order, or if there is no particular order to the items. These two types of lists, along with a special *definition* list, are illustrated in Figure 5.5.

The basic structure of these lists is to have enclosed the list items (denoted with <LI>) with tags defining the type of list. For example, a bullet list (unordered list) would be as follows:

```
<UL>
<LI> Feature A
<LI> Feature B
<LI> Feature C
</UL>
```

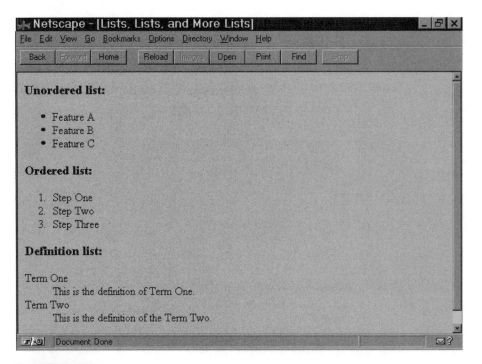

FIGURE 5.5 Three types of HTML lists.

An ordered list would appear as follows:

```
<OL>
<LI> Step One
<LI> Step Two
<LI> Step Three
</OL>
```

You've probably noticed that the <LI> tag is one of the few examples that does not have a closing </LI> tag.

Another type of list that comes in handy is the *definition* list that has both a word or phrase and an indented piece of text (usually a definition of the word or phrase).

```
<DL>
<DT>Term One<DD>This is the definition of Term One.
<DT>Term Two<DD>This is the definition of the Term Two.
</DL>
```

Character formatting

Let's apply some basic character formatting to our HTML documents using <B> to make text bold and <I> to display text in italic (Figure 5.6). Here's an example.

```
<HTML>
<HEAD>
<TITLE>
Document Using Bold and Italic
</TITLE>

</HEAD>

<BODY>

<H1>Document Using Bold and Italic</H1>

This is sample text to show the <B>bold charac-
ters</B>, <I>italic characters</I>, and <B><I>bold-
italic</I></B> characters.

</BODY>
</HTML>
```

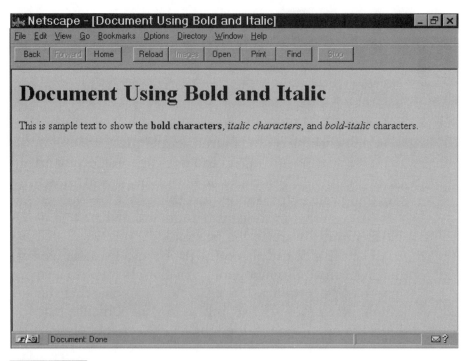

FIGURE 5.6 Illustration of Bold and Italic tags.

Images

One of the key advantages of the Web in marketing is its ability to show off your products in an attractive graphical environment. There are a number of options for including graphics in your Web catalog, just as in print catalogs. There are also things you can do with graphics on the Web that can never be done in print materials—such as animation, mixing sound with pictures, and allowing the shopper to interact with your products.

In addition, there are several types of graphics you can include in your Web pages:

- Product photos
- Logo art
- Banner art indicating the section of the catalog
- Lines and rules separating products on a page

- Icons for buttons

- Image art and photos

It's important to understand how each of these types of graphics are perceived and the actions they evoke. A piece of art that looks like a button will cause the audience to feel that clicking on the button should make something happen, such as moving to another page. A piece of art that also looks like a clickable button but doesn't link to anything causes frustration. Just think back to Web pages you've seen that included three-dimensional art that didn't do anything—weren't you frustrated?

The flip side can also cause problems. Take the idea of having a small product photo as a clickable link to a larger photo of the product. If there is no visual clue that the thumbnail photo is a live link, then your audience may miss the opportunity to see the product in its full glory.

Including images

The first Web browsers could only display graphics stored in the GIF file format. Netscape and others quickly added the ability to display graphics stored in the JPEG format as well. Since many people still use browsers that display only GIF files, it is best to use the GIF format for product photos and use JPEGs on optional pages seen by people who want larger photos.

The HTML tag used to include a graphic image is the IMG SRC tag. Here is an example that uses the file logo.gif.

```
<IMG SRC="logo.gif">
```

When you want to use a graphic as a hotlink, just include the IMG SRC within an anchor link.

```
<A HREF="company-info.html"> <IMG SRC="logo.gif">
</A>
```

In this example, the logo becomes a link with a blue border that indicates it is a live hyperlink (just as underlined blue text indicates a live hyperlink). Since most art looks better without the border, you can turn off the border with border=0 in the IMG tag:

```
<A HREF="company-info.html"> <IMG SRC="logo.gif bor-
der=0"> </A>
```

Aligning graphics

When graphics are included in Web documents, the default is to align the bottom of the graphic with the line of text around the graphic, which is not very attractive. HTML includes optional commands that cause graphics to be aligned on the right or left edge of the window, with text wrapping around the graphic. In addition, alignment options allow you to specify that the top or bottom of a graphic is to align with the text surrounding them.

By default the bottom of an image is aligned with the text as shown in this paragraph.

```
<IMG SRC=megalogo.gif>
```

Add the ALIGN=TOP option if you want the browser to align adjacent text with the top of the image.

```
<IMG SRC=megalogo.gif ALIGN=TOP>
```

Add the ALIGN=MIDDLE option if you want the browser to align adjacent text with the middle of the image.

```
<IMG SRC=megalogo.gif ALIGN=MIDDLE>
```

Add the ALIGN=LEFT option if you want the browser to wrap adjacent text around the image on the left side of the page.

```
<IMG SRC=megalogo.gif ALIGN=left>
```

Add the ALIGN=RIGHT option if you want the browser to wrap adjacent text around the image on the right side of the page.

```
<IMG SRC=megalogo.gif ALIGN=right>
```

Tables

HTML tables provide a wide range of capabilities for you to use in your Web pages, so let's first cover the ways to use tables, then how to build tables to meet your needs.

As you've seen, standard HTML creates lines of text that are as wide as the window. Change the width of the window and the browser *word wraps* the text to fill the width of the window. What do you do if you want columns of text? The answer is use tables.

It has been known for a long time that readability of text is maximized when there about 40 characters across in a line. When the line is wide, the size of type must be increased to reduce the number of characters. With a Web window wide enough to display 80-100 characters, increasing the size of type would be unworkable. Therefore, creating columns of text—each about 40 characters wide—solves this problem.

Let's start with a simple table using the default settings, then use options to enhance the look of the table. Here is the HTML used to create a two-column, three-row table.

```
<HTML><HEAD><TITLE>Table #1</TITLE></HEAD>
<BODY><H2>Table Example 1</H2>
<TABLE>
<TR>
<TD>SKU-001</TD>
<TD>$49.95</TD>
</TR>

<TR>
<TD>SKU-999</TD>
```

```
<TD>$9.95</TD>
</TR>

<TR>
<TD>SKU-555</TD>
<TD>$55.55</TD>
</TR>

</TABLE>
</BODY>
</HTML>
```

Figure 5.7 shows what this particular table looks like when displayed by a browser.

Let's review each of the tags used to create a basic table.

<TABLE>   Defines start of a table

<TR>   Defines the start of a new row

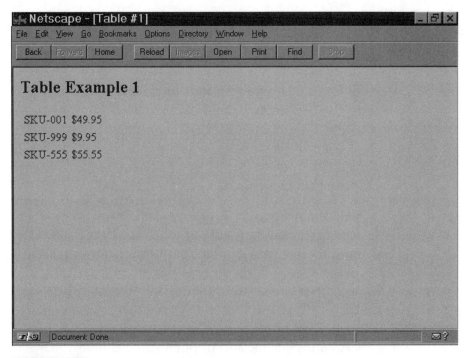

FIGURE 5.7 HTML table.

FIGURE 5.8 HTML table with border.

<TD>	Defines the start of an individual cell across a row
</TD>	Defines the end of a cell on a row
</TR>	Defines the end of a row
</TABLE>	Defines the end of a table

As you see in Figure 5.7, a basic table is just that—basic. Let's enhance that table to make the data easier to read and understand. First, let's put borders around each cell so we can see where the cells are.

Figure 5.8 is the same as Figure 5.7 except for one tag: <TABLE BORDER=10>.

The optional border and size tells the browser to put lines between the cells, and to put a three-dimensional border around the outside edge. We've used a border size of 10 to illustrate how the border option works. Normally you would use a border size of only 1-3.

Now, let's use the width and height options to control how much more of the window the table will take. In Figure 5.9 we've reduced the border to a more normal value of 2. We've set the overall width of the table as 80 percent of the window and the overall height as 50 percent of the window. The HTML for this is as follows:

```
<TABLE BORDER=2 WIDTH=80% HEIGHT=50%>
```

This means that as the user resizes the window, the overall size of the table will change to keep these percentages. The width and height options allow you, not the browser, to control the overall look of a table.

Since we have prices in the table, we can improve their look by making that particular cell right-justified while the

![Netscape - [Table Example 3] browser window showing Table Example 3 with a two-column, three-row table: SKU-001 $49.95; SKU-999 $9.95; SKU-555 $55.55]

FIGURE 5.9 HTML table with reduced width and height.

descriptive text remains left-justified (Figure 5.10). In addition, let's add a product description to the two items we now have for each product. The option to cause a cell to align its contents on the right is as follows.

```
<TD ALIGN=right>$49.95</TD>
```

To complete our table, let's add headers above each field (Figure 5.11). The <TH> tag is an easy way to add column headers that are centered and bolded. The new row looks as follows:

```
<TR>

<TH>Product</TH> <TH>Description</TH> <TH>Price</TH>

</TR>
```

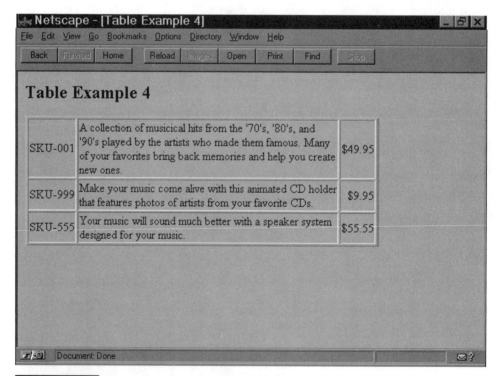

FIGURE 5.10 HTML table with justified text.

Table Example 5

Product	Description	Price
SKU-001	A collection of musicical hits from the '70's, '80's, and '90's played by the artists who made them famous. Many of your favorites bring back memories and help you create new ones.	$49.95
SKU-999	Make your music come alive with this animated CD holder that features photos of artists from your favorite CDs.	$9.95
SKU-555	Your music will sound much better with a speaker system designed for your music.	$55.55

Document: Done

FIGURE 5.11 HTML table with headings.

As you can see, tables have a great deal of flexibility—so much that we've not covered it all. Now that you've seen the basic HTML tables, look for ways to organize information on your pages with tables. Then, review more in-depth guides to using tables in one of our online references in our Online Marketing Library (http://www.allen.com/online-marketing) under "HTML Tools and References."

↳ Forms

The Web is an interactive marketing medium, so we need ways to receive information and responses from the people who visit our Web site. Forms provide an easy way for people to respond, either with text keyed into blanks on the form, by clicking on radio buttons and check boxes, or through drop-down menus.

One of the difficulties of using forms is that certain software is required to receive the data and process it. Typically, these programs are written in a language called *Perl*. Occasionally, Webmasters write these programs in the C language; however, most form handling programs can be written much more quickly with Perl. While Perl is sometimes called a *scripting* language, it is as complex to use as any other programming language. For this reason, many Web sites use existing Perl scripts to generate e-mails containing form data.

The GuestTrack system included with this book includes a special program that can handle a large number of items from forms without needing any special programming. It uses standard HTML form tags to tell what information is coming and how to handle that data.

For now, let's cover the basics of HTML forms, then we'll cover how to use these tags to tell form.pl how to handle your form data.

Here is an example (Figure 5.12) of the most basic of all forms: a simple, one-field form that asks the user for their name.

```
<HTML>
<HEAD><TITLE>Form #1</TITLE></HEAD>
<BODY>
<H2>Form Example #1</H2>
<FORM ACTION="form.pl" METHOD="Post">
<INPUT NAME="name" TYPE="text" SIZE=30><BR>
<INPUT TYPE=SUBMIT> <INPUT TYPE=RESET>
</FORM>
</BODY>
</HTML>
```

This example has a single field that is 30 characters wide plus a button to submit the data to the Web server and a button for the user to reset (or *blank out*) each field on the form if they want to start over.

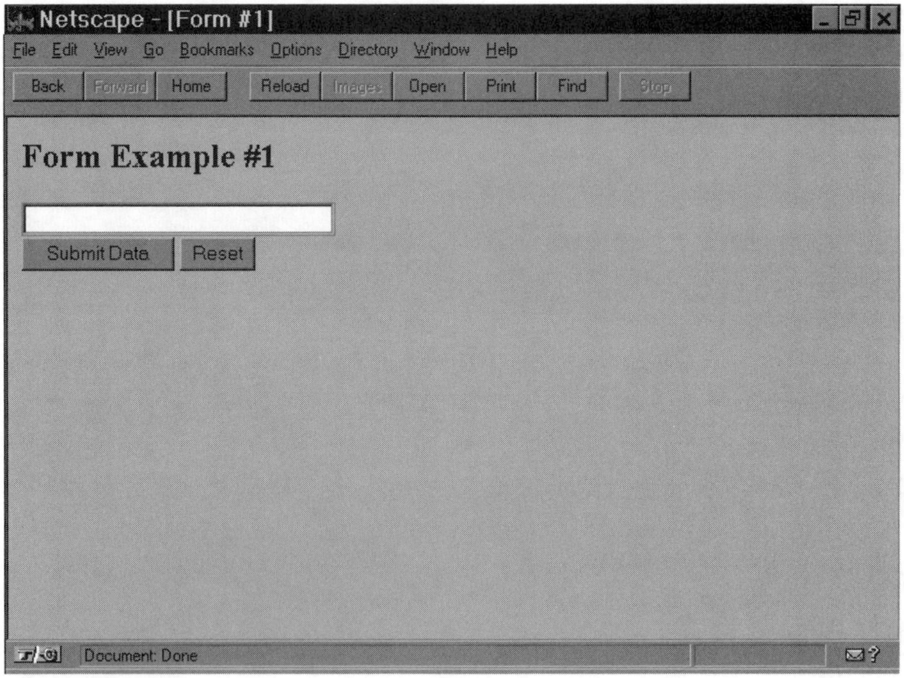

FIGURE 5.12 HTML basic form example.

There are several more ways for the user to provide information. Some of these include the following:

- Radio button—a group of buttons that allow only one of the group to be selected
- Check box—an individual selection box
- Drop-down menus—list of possible selections

Let's add these to our example (Figure 5.13), in order to add guidance for the user.

```
<HTML>
<HEAD><TITLE>Form #2</TITLE></HEAD>
<BODY>
<H2>Form Example #2</H2>
<FORM ACTION="form.pl" METHOD="Post">

Name:  <INPUT NAME="name" TYPE="text" SIZE=30><BR>
Sex:  <INPUT NAME="Male" TYPE="radio"> Male — <INPUT
```

Netscape - [Form #2]

File Edit View Go Bookmarks Options Directory Window Help

| Back | Forward | Home | | Reload | Images | Open | Print | Find | | Stop |

Form Example #2

Name: [   ]
Sex: ○ Male -- ○
Main Hobby: [Gardening ▼]
[Submit Data] [Reset]

Document: Done

FIGURE 5.13 Illustration of form elements.

```
NAME="female" TYPE="radio"> Female<BR>
Send Catalog:  <INPUT NAME="Cat"
TYPE="checkbox"><BR>
Main Hobby:  <SELECT NAME="hobby">
<OPTION>Golf
<OPTION SELECTED>Gardening
<OPTION>Hiking
</SELECT>
<BR>
<INPUT TYPE=SUBMIT> <INPUT TYPE=RESET>

</FORM>

</BODY>
</HTML>
```

In this example, we've added labels in front of each
input item to tell the user what information we want
entered or selected. Unfortunately, it's not graphically

pleasing because input items are unaligned. There are two ways to align form items:

1. Use monospaced type with the <PRE> tag and add enough spaces to make each input item align.

2. Put each label and each input item into cells of a table.

We're going to use the <PRE> tag because it's easier to see the form tags while we establish alignment (Figure 5.14).

```
<HTML>
<HEAD><TITLE>Form #3</TITLE></HEAD>
<BODY>
<H2>Form Example #3</H2>

<FORM ACTION="form.pl" METHOD="Post">
<PRE>
Name:             <INPUT NAME="name" TYPE="text"
                  SIZE=30><BR>

Sex:              <INPUT NAME="Male" TYPE="radio">
Male — <INPUT NAME="female" TYPE="radio"> Female<BR>

Send Catalog:  <INPUT NAME="Cat"
TYPE="checkbox"><BR>

Main Hobby:    <SELECT NAME="hobby">
<OPTION>Golf
<OPTION SELECTED>Gardening
<OPTION>Hiking
</SELECT>
<BR>
<INPUT TYPE=SUBMIT> <INPUT TYPE=RESET>
</FORM>
<PRE>
</BODY>
</HTML>
```

If you're wondering why the form suddenly became double-spaced, it's because the <PRE> tag acts on every piece of non-tagged text, and that includes the carriage

Form Example #3

Name:

Sex: ◯ Male -- ◯

Main Hobby: Gardening ▾

[Submit Data] [Reset]

FIGURE 5.14 Form.

returns (or paragraph marks in a word processor) in addition to the line break tags, (<BR>), that are also in the form. In most cases you will find that single spacing is best for most of a form, such as contact information, but you might want to set off payment information with either carriage returns or <BR> tags.

This covers the basics of creating forms that gather information and product orders. We'll use all of these techniques—and a couple of additional ones—when we cover using forms with the GuestTrack guest book and catalog order forms.

CHAPTER SIX

PREPARING YOUR TEXT AND GRAPHICAL CONTENT

Now that you have the basics of HTML down, you're ready to start creating your own Web catalog—well, almost. You may be ready to "jump right in" and start preparing HTML and graphic files, but we encourage you to stop and plan your approach. Why? Because you'll save time and frustration if you use a few planning techniques.

In addition to covering the general techniques of preparing your text and graphic files, this chapter covers the selection of a Web hosting company that will store your Web site files and make them available to your customers. Since the selection of a Web hosting company is one you will probably live with for some time—in contrast to the changing nature of Web files—you will want to pay particular attention to selecting a Web hosting vendor.

Getting started

There are many things to take into consideration when preparing the text and graphic files for your Web catalog. When possible, it's best to divide the work among a team of people, each responsible for certain types of tasks best suited to their skills, interests, and knowledge.

Web development firms normally have a team of people creating Web sites that include the following:

- Creative Director—directs the graphic designers, writers, and HTML developers

- Graphic Designer—creates original art elements and converts product photos

- Writer—edits existing copy and writes original copy for use on the Web

- HTML Developer—converts text files into HTML files, adding tags to include graphics and other elements according to the overall design provided by the Creative Director

- Technical Director—directs the programmers in creating and maintaining software needed to receive and process orders
- Programmer—creates and configures software to process data from forms, databases, as well as the interface between the Web server and the in-house data processing system

With the GuestTrack Light software on the accompanying CD, you will be able to build a Web catalog without having to hire a team of people. If you have a small business with only a few employees, you will be able to build the Web catalog yourself. You may want to employ the assistance of a writer or artist as needed, and you will be able to leave the technical details to the Internet service provider. Alternatively, if your company is larger, you can build your Web catalog using an internal team and the GuestTrack Light software. The other option for Web catalog development will be a combination of internal people and outside experts. How the Web catalog is developed and who is involved will depend on your business model.

For the past few years we've helped companies of all sizes establish their first Web presence, and we've seen that there are basically two approaches for companies of any size:

1. Jump into the creation of a Web site, experience the inevitable confusion that occurs when learning a new technical skill, then modify Web pages based on what has been learned.

2. Study the process of creating a Web site, carefully plan the look of the home page and additional pages, develop and refine pages as the Web site is created.

Both processes work—and work well—so how you proceed is a matter of your personal preference or the preference of your company. Based on our experience in helping companies develop a wide range of Web sites, we recommend that if you want to jump in and create a Web site to experience the creation process, then start with the chapter on creating a Basic Web site so you can master the basics of creating Web art and converting text files to HTML, and quickly experience the thrill of retrieving your first Web pages from the Internet. Then, if you feel you need the more advanced capabilities described in later chapters, such as displaying product pages from a database of information, you will be prepared to move to the next level of Web creation. On the other hand, if you are interested in using a methodical process for creating art, files, and are interested in using Web database technology, then consider using the procedures described in Chapter 9 on using the GuestTrack profile system and Chapter 10 on adding the GT/Catalog product display system to a Web catalog.

No matter which approach you take, you'll find step-by-step instructions based on the techniques and technologies we've used for several years in developing Web sites. In addition, remember to visit the Online Marketing Resource Center so you can keep up on developments especially for readers of the *Web Catalog Cookbook*.

Using the banners and icons on the *Web Catalog Cookbook* CD-ROM

The art files included on the accompanying CD-ROM were designed specifically for this book so you can review the look of these items and choose art that best projects your image.

Review groups of art

The art that has been created for this book is arranged into compatible groups. The groups have all been given names to make it easier for you and others working with you to refer to them. Then, the groups are arranged into three sections: conservative, moderate, and dramatic. In addition to the raw art for your use is a set of sample home pages using art from the collection.

The easiest way to review the various sets of art and sample home pages on the CD-ROM is to point your browser to the master index page located in the directory "web-art" on the CD-ROM. The page "index.htm" (Figure 6.1) in the directory contains links to each of the HTML pages that display the component pieces of art in that group.

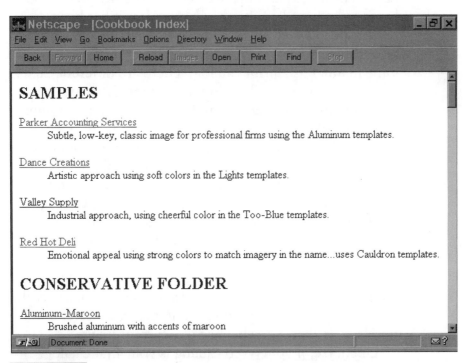

FIGURE 6.1 Index to clip art library and sample home pages.

If you know the type of look you want for your Web catalog, then start browsing through the groups until you find what you are looking for. On the other hand, if you are unsure of exactly which colors and styles are best for your Web catalog, following are a few suggestions.

Selecting the right image for your catalog

The first step in determining a look for your Web catalog is to decide what your customers are expecting from your catalog. If you already have a print catalog, then you probably have a feel for how customers react to the colors, graphics, and organization of the catalog. Sometimes, though, print catalog merchants hear negative reactions from their customers but don't feel they can make the needed changes and improvements in the design without loosing the brand equity they have. Also, it has been proven that simply putting your print catalog online is a mistake. Web users do not browse the Web catalog in the same manner as a print catalog. There are different expectations for online catalogs in terms of interactivity, depth of information, navigation, and experience. These important principles are covered in Chapters 2, 4, and 13.

If you have a print catalog that needs to be upgraded, now is a good time to break away from an old image because your Web catalog customers will be new to your company and have not seen the print catalog. As you promote the Web catalog in your print catalog, you will migrate prospects and customers to the Web, where they will see your new look and image—and hopefully appreciate your updated look. If you have invested time and money in an image that works well for you, then select the art that complements your existing image. Be careful not to select art that overwhelms your current image.

Of course, if your Web catalog is your first catalog, then you are probably still searching for the right look for your business. In both cases, the following tips and suggestions should prove helpful.

Selecting colors

If you have worked with a graphic designer in creating a new look for a company, then you have probably experienced being overwhelmed by the endless possibilities available when starting from scratch. In addition, you may have worked with an artist who had personal favorites in both design techniques and colors. It's natural for all of us to have our personal favorites (e.g., our college colors or the color of our first car), but in marketing to consumers and to businesses, it's important to blend our personal preferences with the preferences of the customers so that your catalog appeals to your target market.

Selecting colors based on how your audience will perceive them requires you to consider what you already know about how you react to colors and add input from what has been demonstrated by behavior research. Think of color in terms of a clothing outfit that a person wears. Just imagine the reaction if a new employee wears a red outfit into the office their first day, while another new employee wears a black outfit. The person in red would be thought of as having more energy, while the person in black would be seen as quiet and withdrawn. The same type of reaction would occur if one had worn a wild paisley outfit and the other wore a pastel and solid white outfit. The same color comparison reasoning can be applied to a catalog.

Let's take a few examples. If you sell stainless steel pipes, chances are that gray with blue or burgundy accents will work better than a combination of fire red and sunny yellow. So, to get an idea of the right colors for your Web page, here are some typical color associations:

> Industrial products suggest navy blue or gray with small accents of one bright color.

Human-related services suggest soft flesh and hair colors, beige, pink, brown, blue (for eyes), with accents of black, white, or a bright color.

Children's toys suggest that children enjoy bright, primary colors, so it's good to use a white background with a wide variety of accent colors.

Vacations suggest relaxation, so they could center around soft blues and greens. But an adventure vacation could be earth tones with heavy accents of vibrant colors. Vacations in sunny areas would call for liberal dashes of sunshine yellow.

Also, products can be categorized in other ways, too, such as commodities versus innovative, unique, or high-tech products. If you are selling commodity products, your customers want reliability and safety. Colors that reflect that feeling would include human tones, and traditional conservative business colors such as navy blue, mid-range blue, burgundy, gold, or gray.

Innovative products are selling excitement and energy, so a base of reliable colors allows you to add interesting dashes of bright, energized colors such as red, orange, green, purple, or the latest "trend" colors.

As you can see, there is some logic behind picking the colors used with different products, but there is also a big dash of imagination, observation, and innovation that you must draw upon, too.

After you have an idea about the basic colors and general look you would like to convey, you are ready to start gathering together art for banners and buttons, as well as other accent places on your Web catalog.

Copying art to the Images directory

Many HTML authors start developing Web sites by putting the image files (GIF and JPG) in one directory along with all of their HTML files. For small Web sites it is easier if all files are in the same place, but when the Web site gets larger—and they all do—the management of these files becomes unwieldy.

Just imagine starting an FTP session to your Web server directory and seeing hundreds and hundreds of files. The best approach is to have a plan for directory names, and a consistent way of naming files, too.

If you have looked at the HTML source for some of your favorite Web sites, you have probably seen that the HTML files are stored in different directories by topic. A tradition has also been established among HTML authors to place graphics in a directory structure with the title images so the graphics are separated from the HTML files.

Let's create a directory structure for images as we did in Chapter 5 for HTML files. First, let's review some of the directory structure for HTML files with additional sections called *transportation* and *accommodations*:

```
/states
        /north-carolina
                /news
                /attractions
/transportation
/accommodations
```

We don't want to create an images directory exactly like this because so many of the graphics are used on multiple pages in multiple HTML directories. With our sample tourism Web site, it's likely that graphics will be used throughout the /states section of the Web site, while the graphics used in /transportation and /accommodations will probably be used just in those sections.

Knowing how graphics will be used in a Web site gives us a sense of how the directory structure should be set up to make it easy to reference in Web pages and easy for designers to manage the files. As a general rule, logos and other art common to many pages should be stored in the images directory, while graphics that are used only in one particular section can be stored in a sub-directory within the images directory.

Managing text and art files

While we're on the topic of file names and directory names, let's cover the guidelines for naming files. With Microsoft Windows 3.1, the length of filenames is limited to eight characters with a three-character extension (sometimes referred to as an "8.3" format), so we need a way to make each of those eight characters meaningful so everyone on the Web development team can easily identify files they need to create and update.

Since the length of file names in Windows 95, Macintosh, and UNIX environments is not limited to the 8.3 convention, they can use words that are meaningful to everyone on the team.

Win 3.1 example	d3logo2b.gif
Win 95/Mac example	Division 3-Product 2-option b.gif
UNIX example	division_3-product_2-option_b.gif

Determining file names and directory paths

In creating HTML files and testing their links, you will need to store these files in a directory structure on your local computer that is similar to the directory structure on the Web server so that the links with absolute paths can locate the target files. If you are creating a Basic Web Catalog, you will be able to use relative links and store all of your HTML files in a single directory on the Web server. This will allow you to easily test links in your HTML documents as long as they are all stored in the same directory on your local computer.

If you are creating an Intermediate or Advanced Web Catalog using the GuestTrack software, you can use relative links during the initial development on your local hard drive, but since the GuestTrack software uses links that include things such as the user's ID, you will want to have a good connection to your Web site so you can upload files and test online.

If you are creating HTML files in Windows 3.1, you will need to enter a filename that conforms to the standard 8.3 format. The three letter extension for HTML files should be .htm, while other computers can create files with the four letter extension of .html.

If you are using Windows 95 or Macintosh, the filename can be long and have spaces or special characters. However, the restrictions of the UNIX environment (where your Web files are likely to be stored) make it advisable to avoid spaces or unusual characters in filenames. It is best to use only hyphens (-) or underscore characters (_) in filenames with letters and numbers. Note the following examples:

Win 3.1 example	prodlist.htm
Win 95/Mac example	Product List - Complete.html
UNIX example	product_list-complete.html

Another difference between the filenames in UNIX and those in PC and Macintosh computers is that UNIX recognizes upper case letters as different from lower case letters, while Macintosh and Windows 95 computers see upper case and lower case letters as the same. This means that on your computer the filename My-logo.GIF is the same as my-logo.gif, but your UNIX Web server sees them as two separate filenames. The potential problems you can encounter include:

- Filenames in HTML files use a different case for graphic files

- Filenames using upper case letters become lower case letters in the FTP program

- Filenames with spaces (and referenced correctly in HTML files) have the spaces replaced with underscore characters in the UNIX file system

- Filenames with slashes are not accessible by the UNIX system (since slashes designate sub-directories)

As you can see from this sample of the problems caused by using uppercase letters and special characters, you will save yourself many headaches by using only lowercase letters, hyphens, and underscore characters.

Backup, backup, backup...and then backup again!

It should be clear to everyone who uses computers that problems develop that make files inaccessible—from disk drive failures to accidental erasure of important files. In addition, changes made to HTML or art files frequently need to be *reverted*, or use a previous version of the file.

While a commercial backup software program should be used on a regular basis to restore files after a catastrophic disk problem, good file management techniques can help eliminate problems during the creation of files. During creation and initial testing of HTML files, a good technique is to make a copy of a file prior to editing it. This ensures that you have a copy handy without the current set of changes. The steps of creating this copy are as follows:

1. Rename the file to include a letter or phrase at the end indicating that it is a backup copy.

2. Open the backup version of the document.

3. Save the document using the Save As command, removing the backup letter or code.

4. Edit the HTML file and save frequently.

This procedure is easy to use and will save many hours trying to recreate the exact HTML technique that was lost during a set of changes.

Once your Web site goes live and several people on your team are updating Web files, you may find yourself editing what you thought was the latest version of a Web page, only to discover that someone else had updated the file on the Web server. Since it can be difficult to know whether the version of a Web document on your local computer is the latest version, here is a procedure to ensure that you always edit the latest version and have a set of previous versions to draw upon when necessary. The following steps have you downloading fresh copies of HTML files from your Web server each time you start on a set of updates so that you will know you have the latest version of each document.

1. Create a folder on your local computer that includes the type of files you will be editing and the date you created the folder. Examples would be prod1025, prod1109, or prod1112.

2. Start your FTP program and download the files to be edited into the new folder.

3. Edit the HTML files and view them locally.

4. Use your FTP program to upload the files back to the production Web server.

5. Test each of the newly uploaded files to ensure that the links work properly.

You probably noticed that the date included in the example used two digits for the month and two digits for the day of the month. This ensures that directory listings keep these folders sorted by date so you'll know which is the last one you used.

↳ Creating original banners and icons

You can create new or use existing graphics or photographs with the GuestTrack software. If you prefer to use imagery that you've created for other catalogs or brochures, or if the art contained on the accompanying CD-ROM doesn't quite fit the image you are looking for, then you can create or add your own art to the Web catalog templates. Typically, banners are thin strips of art with the name of the section that go at the top of all pages within a section. For instance, you might have several pages about your company, each having the same banner (e.g., Company Information) at the top. Each page in the section would have an identifying piece of text in HTML that explains the specific material on that page (e.g., History, Officers, Plants and Warehouses, etc.)

Determining final sizes for art and photos

One of the biggest differences between creating photos and other graphics for use in print versus Web catalogs is how to measure the size of graphics. In the print world, the width and height of graphics are normally measured in inches or in picas (a *pica* is $\frac{1}{72}$nd of an inch). Art for the Web is measured in *pixels*—the individual dots of color on a computer monitor. The challenge in creating Web graphics is that there are several standards for the number of pixels displayed by computer monitors. The following lists shows most of the current monitor dimensions in use by Web users today:

- 640 pixels wide by 480 high
- 800 pixels wide by 600 high
- 1,024 pixels wide by 768 high

Since practically everyone's monitor can display approximately 600 pixels wide, you can assume that users with browser windows open to the maximum size will see the art that wide.

Does this mean we recommend making art that is 600 pixels wide? No, we're not encouraging large art for several reasons. In the first place, large art is slower to download, but more importantly, your customers may not have their browser window set to full size. What's more, there are more efficient ways to create art than to use the full screen width.

Options for adding product photographs and logos

Now there are more options to create illustrations of your products and application photos for your Web catalog. Here are a few of the techniques available, in the generally preferred order:

- Convert photo files used in a previous print catalog created on computer

- Scan slide prints or negatives on a drum scanner at a traditional prepress service bureau

- Scan slide prints or negatives at a Kodak Photo-CD service bureau

- Scan prints on a flatbed desktop scanner

- Scan slides on a desktop slide scanner

- Scan slides on a flatbed desktop scanner with slide attachment

- Shoot original product photos using an electronic camera, creating disk files

Scanned art is typically saved in a file format that preserves the quality of the image, such as TIFF, BMP, and so on. The GIF file format used on the Web does not maintain all of the color, so art files need to be converted to GIF after all modifications have been made.

Are you ready to create some art? Well, let's get cooking.

Adding text to banner art

Once you have picked art for your banners and buttons, you're ready to open the base art in your graphics program, add text, and save—that's all there is to it. Well, almost.

While it is easy to use a program that automatically saves art in GIF format, one of the more popular programs, Adobe PhotoShop, is a little more difficult to use, so we have included steps for using PhotoShop once you've chosen a graphic to use as background for your banners. The following are the general steps in using PhotoShop to add a word or short phrase describing the section text to a piece of banner art.

1. Open the raw art file.

2. Under Mode, set the mode to RGB. If you find that the raw art needs to be resized, make sure the mode is in RGB instead of Indexed Color.

3. Set the foreground color to white if the background is mostly dark, or to black if the background art is mostly white.

4. Select the Text Tool and click the middle of the graphic.

5. In the dialog box, select the following:

   Middle

   Anti-aliases

   Pixels

   Font of Arial (PC), Helvetica (Macintosh), or other sans serif font.

6. Select the number of pixels high for the text. Start with 75-100 pixels, adjusting to a larger or smaller size as needed.

7. Enter the text for the banner. Text for banners will normally look best in all uppercase letters because uppercase letters maximize the number of pixels used for the letters. In addition, the consistent, thick strokes of sans serif letters increase the number of pixels used. If you find the standard sans serif font to be too wide for the text, try using a condensed version of the font, or select another condensed font.

8. Under Mode, change to Indexed Color.

9. In the Indexed Color dialog box, check Adaptive, 8 bit, and No Diffusion.

10. Under File, select Save As in order to change the file name to one representing the text of the banner.

11. Set the file format to GIF, enter a filename, and save the file.

In addition to creating long banner art used at the top of section pages, you will want to create small navigation buttons for use at the bottom of pages. In some cases you will want to place the name of a section over a piece of art that can serve as a background (Figure 6.2). In cases where your button art may actually illustrate the information in the section (e.g., a telephone for a section of contact information), you should put the name of the section below the art.

Converting an existing print catalog

There are a number of advantages to starting the Web catalog creation process from an existing print catalog, such as having existing product photographs and descriptive copy. At the same time, there are potential drawbacks. Perhaps the greatest problem is the temptation to use the existing material without adjusting it for the Web environment. Not adapting current data, information, or

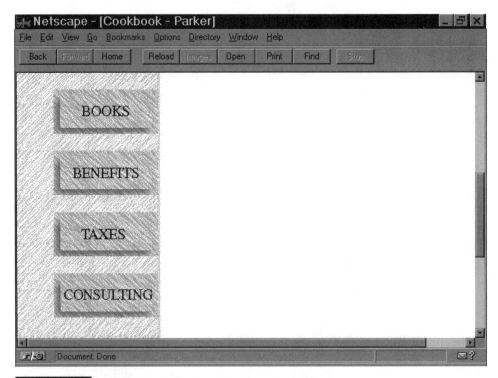

FIGURE 6.2 Navigation buttons using text over art.

graphics for the unique Web medium will impede a Web site's success.

Most Web catalogs are designed to display one product per Web page, instead of the approach used in print catalogs of having many products on a page or spread. Since you can focus your audience's attention on a particular product, take advantage of the medium by listing more product features and benefits than you would ordinarily do in a print catalog. In addition, you can add more photographs and show more features.

For example, if you are selling equipment with dials, knobs, switches, and jacks, then take advantage of the strong interest your customers have in seeing these features by using close-up photographs. Customers are interested if those dials have grooves on the edge, a pointer to see where the dial is set, and how much room is available between dials. These are things that cannot normally be seen in a small product photo of a whole piece of equipment. Don't forget that just as customers are interested in close-ups of the front, many people want to see the back of equipment to understand how it connects to other equipment.

If you sell products with cloth or other texture (e.g., clothing, seat covers, or wallpaper) then include close-up photographs of the material. While the colors displayed on the screen will not match the actual cloth, you can give your customers an idea of the weave and texture by using photographs that highlight the depth of the weave.

If you have observed how your customers evaluate and decide to buy products like yours, then you know how to display them on your Web catalog to show off their best features. Here are a few examples of catalog companies that have done a good job bringing their traditional paper-based catalogs to the Web. Pay particular attention to how photographs and graphics are displayed on their sites.

- Spiegel   http://www.spiegel.com
- Eddie Bauer   http://www.ebauer.com
- Levenger   http://www.levenger.com
- The Sharper Image   http://www.sharperimage.com
- Overtons   http://www.overtonsonline.com
- Crutchfield   http://www.crutchfield.com
- Insight Direct   http://www.insight.com
- Elek-Tek   http://www.elektek.com
- DECDirect   http://www.systems.digital.com/DIcatalog
- New England Business Supply   http://www.nebs.com
- Lab Safety Supply   http://www.labsafety.com

Using a QuarkXPress-to-HTML converter

Many print catalogs have been created using the QuarkXPress page layout software. QuarkXPress gives the designer and layout artist control over every aspect of how pages look, from font size and other attributes to various spacing and wrapping. As we've mentioned, HTML provides the author with only a few of these controls.

One of the difficulties of using QuarkXPress files in creating Web pages is that most artists place each piece of text in separate Quark *stories*. The standard export capability of QuarkXPress can only export one story at a time—not an entire page or entire document.

Fortunately, there are now software programs that can export text in a QuarkXPress file and convert graphics to GIF format. One of the first converter programs was BeyondPress from AstroByte. This software is an XTension that runs inside the QuarkXPress program on Macintosh computers. While some HTML authors use BeyondPress to arrange blocks of text and graphics into complete Web pages, many people use BeyondPress as a utility program to export all of the text into one HTML file, where it can be edited using traditional HTML editing software and techniques.

For a list of QuarkXPress-to-HTML converters, see the Online Marketing Library for a page of links to software you can use.

Summary

The purpose of this book is to help you get started creating your Web catalog without requiring an experienced team. Whether you are starting a Web catalog business as an individual or if you are converting your first print catalog to the Web, the following chapters will build on the topics we've covered so far and give you detailed steps in moving from the planning processes (covered in Chapter 3) and the preparation of files in this chapter to pulling these elements together into a live Web catalog.

CHAPTER SEVEN

WORKING WITH A WEB SERVICE PROVIDER

Creating great graphics and compelling copy for a Web catalog is only one challenge that faces an online merchant today. In addition, the technical challenges of working with computer software and hardware will keep you working hard. The first technical question that must be answered is which Web service provider should be used to host your Web site. Once that decision has been made, the next steps are to upload the software used to display Web pages and handle orders, followed by uploading the HTML graphic files that customers will see, then testing the system to ensure that it is working properly.

The focus of this chapter is on the Web service company and preparing your Web site for the text and graphic files that you will develop in the next chapter.

Selecting a Web service provider

The process of selecting a company to host your Web catalog can be quite complex since there are a number of factors that need to be considered—but we've made it easy for you. We researched the national Web service providers and evaluated their capabilities using the criteria listed, then we made special arrangements with two leading companies for readers of the *Web Catalog Cookbook* to automate the software installation process.

Selection criteria

The criteria we used in evaluating Web hosting services include the following:

- Bandwidth of connection from Web server datacenter to the backbone of the Internet

- Number of connections from the datacenter to the backbone

- Number of servers in the datacenter

- Brand, speed, and operating system of servers
- Number of Web sites on a server
- Brand and version of Web server software
- Easy access to an encrypted commerce Web server
- Quality and accessibility of technical support
- Support for scripts in the cgi-bin directory
- Number of years providing Internet/Web services
- Setup and monthly charge

Bandwidth and connections to the backbone of the Internet

The growth in number of Internet access providers and Web hosting companies has resulted in many small companies buying access to the Internet from other Internet access providers and Web hosting companies. This has resulted in a network that resembles a tree with a large trunk (the backbone of the Internet) with large limbs (major Internet providers), which are connected to smaller and smaller companies.

Smaller Internet providers often boast that they use a *T1* line (the equivalent of about 50 28.8 Kbps modems)—which would be very good if only 50 people were using the line. Unfortunately, when several providers each have a T1 connection to a provider that is itself using a T1 line to connect to another provider, then the effective bandwidth of the last provider in the chain is much lower than its connection can provide.

This means that you need to find out how many connections and providers are between your provider and the backbone and try to select a vendor that is close to the backbone.

Brand, speed, and operating system of servers

Another set of factors affecting performance of your Web site is the brand, speed, and operating system of the Web servers your provider uses. Sun Microsystems was an early-pioneer of developing high performance servers for the Internet, which is why its hardware has been used by leading Web service providers for several years. In addition to providing exceptional speed for a modest cost, the UNIX operating system used on Sun servers has proven to be a stable, reliable operating system that supports a large number of simultaneous users with very good security.

A version of the UNIX operating system called Linux has been popular with some Web providers because it runs on Intel-based computers that are less expensive than Sun computers. Their low cost has allowed Web providers to acquire more computers in order to spread the load. This doesn't necessarily provide greater throughput than a Sun server, but it does tend to reduce the number of Web sites sharing the same computer. This reduces the chances of traffic for another Web site causing your Web site to be difficult to contact.

Number of Web sites on a server

Even when a Web hosting service uses high-speed UNIX computers it can still have poor performance if it tries to place too many Web sites on each server. There is no magic number of Web sites that can be supported on a server. A high-speed server with a large amount of memory can support hundreds of Web sites with relatively low traffic. Ask prospective Web hosting companies how many Web sites they host on each server to get an idea of the load you will be sharing with other Web sites.

Easy access to an encrypted commerce Web server

Many consumers hesitate to provide their credit card number to Web sites that do not use an encryption technique because they are afraid that a thief will be able to steal their card number. For this reason, many Web merchants use a secure server for forms that ask for credit card data. Since not every Web hosting service has a secure server, be sure to ask potential vendors if they have one available.

Quality and accessibility of technical support

Technical problems can occur at any time of the day or night, so find out how your Web hosting company handles not only the first-line technical support group, but also the experience of the senior technical people and whether those experts are on call evenings and weekends.

Support for scripts in the cgi-bin directory

The Web is growing toward using more programs and scripts to control the presentation of material, so find out if your Web service provider allows you to use programs and scripts to process forms, display pages, and access databases. The GuestTrack Light software provided on the CD-ROM runs in the cgi-bin directory, so if you are going to take full advantage of this software you will need to select a Web hosting company that allows you to run programs on your Web site.

Number of years providing Internet/Web services

The World Wide Web has been a graphical marketing tool for only a few years, but the Internet has been in existence for many years. Web hosting companies that have been serving the Internet market for several years are generally better at solving the technical challenges of the Internet, so it's best to use a company with a history of providing Internet service.

Recommended Web hosting companies

While evaluating Web hosting companies we found some name brand companies that we expected to be at the top of the list actually have less capability than we expected, while other companies with long histories of providing Internet services actually have datacenters and Internet connections that meet the most demanding Web hosting needs.

Two companies we found to be among the best Web hosting companies are Interpath and MindSpring.

Interpath

Interpath, a division of Capitol Broadcasting Company, Inc., began commercial Internet access service in 1994 by acquiring the Internet operation of a government-funded organization that had been providing Internet access services for years (Figure 7.1). Interpath is one of the few Internet providers with a connection directly to one of the backbone hubs of the Internet (instead of buying access through another Internet provider).

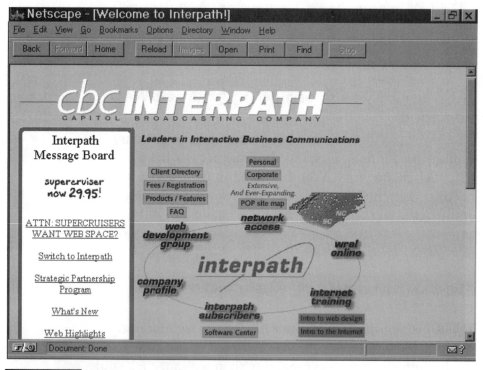

FIGURE 7.1 Interpath home page.

Interpath

711 Hillsborough Street

Raleigh, NC 27605

800-849-6305

fax (919) 890-6319

sales-mktg@interpath.net

http://www.interpath.net

MindSpring

MindSpring has become a national Internet provider with the acquisition of a number of regional providers (Figure 7.2). MindSpring consistently ranks high in lists of national Internet providers because of its service and pricing.

MindSpring Enterprises, Inc.

1430 West Peachtree St. NW, Suite 400

FIGURE 7.2 MindSpring home page.

Atlanta, GA 30309

404-815-9845 or 888-932-1997

websales@mindspring.com

http://web.mindspring.com

Establishing a Web hosting account

The steps for obtaining a domain and establishing an account with either of these Web service providers is as follows.

1. Determine what domain name you want to use for your Web catalog. Be sure to check if your preferred domain is available by using MindSpring's database query at http://web.mindspring.com/whois.html. If your preferred domain has another company associated with it, then select another domain.

2. Call the sales department at either Interpath or MindSpring and tell the representative you want to establish a Web hosting account for a site described in the *Web Catalog Cookbook* and that you want them to register the available domain you identified in the previous step.

   You will need to enter your official domain into the configuration program for the software provided with this book, so start the domain registration process early so it will be approved when you are ready to load the catalog software.

3. When you receive your account information from your Web service provider, look for the following information:

- Host computer name (used in your FTP program to identify the server)

- Login ID (used in your FTP program to identify you)

- Password (used in your FTP program to authenticate your ID)

- Location of Web pages (some providers require special directories for Web pages)

- Location of cgi-bin programs (the directory that stores the programs used with your Web catalog) such as: /usr/local/etc/httpd/htdocs/domain/cgi-bin

- Operating system of your Web server. The catalog software provided on CD-ROM has been developed for the popular versions of the UNIX operating system, which is used by practically all of the major Web hosting companies

4. After you receive information from your Web service provider, then follow the steps in the next section and use your Web browser to go to the GuestTrack Registration Server to enter your official domain, the directory information you received from your Web hosting company, and your e-mail address.

5. If you select one of the two companies previously described, you will automatically be linked to a special Web page on its server and the GuestTrack software will automatically be installed using the information it provides to you. If you select a Web service provider other than Interpath or MindSpring, then you will need to install the GuestTrack software using the procedure described later in this chapter.

Installing the GuestTrack Light Software

If you are going to use either MindSpring or Interpath for your Web hosting, then use the simplified software installation procedure. If you will be using a Web hosting service other than these two companies, then use the standard installation procedure described later in this chapter.

Simplified software installation (MindSpring and Interpath)

Special arrangements have been made with two Web hosting companies (MindSpring and Interpath) to allow us to pre-install a copy of the software from the CD-ROM on their Web server so you can use a simplified installation process. (If you are using a Web hosting company other than these two companies, please skip to the next section where the manual installation process is described.)

Once you have your Web server account with one of these two companies, use your Web browser to run the special GuestTrack Light configuration program located at http://www.allen.com/cookbook (Figure 7.3). Then follow the steps shown here.

1. Enter your name, company, address, telephone number, and e-mail address into the form fields and click the Submit button.

2. The page following the initial registration page will display your contact information. It is recommended that you bookmark this page so you can quickly return to it in the future if you need to change any configuration information.

3. Review your name, address, e-mail, and other information that is displayed in the fields. Change the data that may have been entered incorrectly. After you bookmark this page, click the Submit button.

4. Enter the domain name that you have registered through your Web service company.

5. Click on the Radio button that describes which Web service option you will be using (Figure 7.4):

   • I have established a Web hosting account with Interpath.

   • I have established a Web hosting account with MindSpring.

   • I have established a Web hosting account with another company.

6. Click the Submit button to continue the automated configuration process.

It is important to enter a correct e-mail address because this is the address to which the system will send your GuestTrack configuration file.

If you selected Interpath or MindSpring for your Web hosting service, you will see a Web page with blank fields requesting information that you received from these companies about your account (Figure 7.5). Be sure to enter information into every field. The installation software will use this information to access your account area and copy into your Web server area all of the GuestTrack Light files stored in a master directory on that Web hosting service.

If you didn't receive certain information, stop the configuration process and call your sales representative to obtain the information. (When you are ready to resume the configuration process, use your bookmark to return to the information page and resume with step #3.)

Once you complete all of the information, click the button to continue the automatic installation of the GuestTrack Light software that will occur by copying software into your cgi-bin directory. In addition, it will set all appropriate file permissions so the GuestTrack software

GuestTrack/Light Registration

Your Name:

Title:

Company:

Address:

City:

State: Zip:

Country:

Telephone:

Fax:

Email:

Register

FIGURE 7.3 Initial GuestTrack Light registration form.

will run properly. Since it may take several minutes for the process to be completed, be sure to wait until you see the page that says the installation process has been completed.

Once the installation has been completed there is only one more step before you can proceed to upload your HTML and graphic files that you will create in the following chapters.

While the software was being copied from a special library into your area of the Web server, the configuration software was preparing an e-mail to you that contains a special GuestTrack configuration file that must be present in your cgi-bin directory for the software to know how to access your programs and files. Once you receive the e-mail, copy the text between the lines of text marked *cut here* and paste the material into a completely blank file in your HTML editor program or your word processing

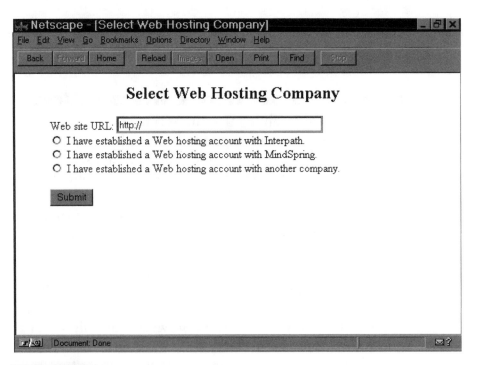

FIGURE 7.4 Web hosting selection screen.

program (that can save a text file). Save the file on your hard drive into the Web directory under the name config.txt.

The next step is to FTP the config.txt file you received during the registration process into the cgi-bin directory.

Here are the steps needed to copy the config.txt file into your Web server directory.

1. Start your FTP program and connect to your Web server account.

2. Change to the cgi-bin directory on the Web server.

3. Locate on your hard drive the Web directory and the config.txt file you saved earlier.

4. Set your FTP program to Text mode (instead of Binary mode) so the file will be transferred without changing the end-of-line character.

5. Upload the file config.txt into your cgi-bin directory.

Once you have completed these steps you are ready to upload your HTML and graphic files to the server and start testing your Web site.

Standard software installation

The process of installing the GuestTrack Light software in your Web server area is very similar to uploading traditional HTML files—with a few additional steps. The following steps will take you through the process of creating the sub-directories needed for the system and applying standard commands used to allow the software to run. Since we're expecting that you will be using an outside Web hosting service (instead of operating your own Web server computer at your office), and since most of the commercial quality Web hosting services use one of the UNIX operating systems, we're providing commands that are found on most Web hosting services. You will need to check with your hosting service to make sure it uses UNIX and that these commands are appropriate for its system.

Uploading software files from the CD-ROM enclosed with this book requires that you use your FTP program. There are a number of FTP programs available for Windows and Macintosh environments, such as WS_FTP (Windows) and Fetch (Macintosh). You probably received an FTP program from your Internet provider as part of a *dial-up kit*. If you are unfamiliar with your FTP program, check with the Internet Service Provider that you use to access the Internet, or check with your Web hosting service to see what it recommends and can provide.

If you would like to review a short tutorial on the program WS_FTP, use your Web browser to access the on-line tutorial at http://www.wiley.com/gilster.

In general, the process of installing software on a Web server is as follows.

1. Ensure that the cgi-bin directory has the proper permissions.

2. Upload files to the cgi-bin directory.

3. Ensure that the files are named properly.

4. Change the mode of the programs to EXE-CUTABLE so they will run properly.

Before you begin uploading software from the CD-ROM to your Web server account, make sure you know the type of UNIX operating system used by your Web service hosting, then use the version of software that matches its operating system.

Once you have your server account with your hosting service, use your browser to run the special GuestTrack Light configuration program located at http://www.allen.com/cookbook and follow these steps.

1. Enter your name, company, address, telephone number, and e-mail address into the form fields and click the Submit button.

2. The page following the initial registration page will display your contact information and blank fields and buttons for other configuration information. It is recommended that you bookmark this page so you can quickly return to it in the future if you need to change any configuration information.

3. Review your name, address, e-mail, and other information that is displayed in the fields. Change the data that may have been entered incorrectly. After you bookmark this page, click the Submit button.

4. Enter the available domain name that you have registered through your Web service company.

5. Click on the Radio button (Figure 7.6) that describes which Web service option you will be using: "I have established a Web hosting account with another company."

6. Click the Submit button to continue the automated configuration process.

7. Enter into the fields the information about your account.

It is important to enter a correct e-mail address because this is the address to which the system will send your GuestTrack configuration file.

Since you will be using a company other than Interpath or MindSpring for your Web hosting service, you will see blank fields requesting information that you should have received from these companies about your account. (Figure 7.7) Be sure to enter information into every field.

Netscape - [GuestTrack/Light Registration]

File   Edit   View   Go   Bookmarks   Options   Directory   Window   Help

| Back | Forward | Home | Reload | Images | Open | Print | Find | Stop |

GuestTrack/Light Registration

Your Name:

Title:

Company:

Address:

City:

State: Zip:

Country:

Telephone:

Fax:

Email:

Register

Document: Done

FIGURE 7.5 Initial GuestTrack Light registration form.

194   Chapter 7

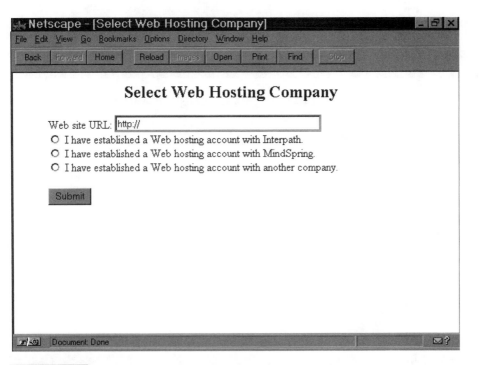

FIGURE 7.6 Web hosting selection screen.

Once you complete all of the information click the button to continue the automatic configuration process of sending an e-mail to you that contains a special GuestTrack configuration file that must be present in your cgi-bin directory for the software to know how to access your programs and files. Once you receive the e-mail, copy the text between the lines of text named "cut here" and paste the material into a completely blank file in your HTML editor program or your word processing program. Save the file on your hard drive into the Web directory under the name config.txt.

During the software installation process described in this list, you will also FTP the config.txt file you received into the cgi-bin directory.

Here are the steps needed to copy the GuestTrack software into your Web directory.

1. Start your FTP program and connect to your Web server account.

GuestTrack/Light Configuration

Base CGI directory (part of URL): `/cgi-bin`

Full path to the CGI directory:

`/usr/local/etc/httpd/cgi-bin`

Page directory (containing GuestTrack-parsed HTML:

`/usr/local/etc/httpd/htdocs/pages`

Obtain server prefix from your web service provider:

`http://`

Configure

FIGURE 7.7 Guest Track/Light Installation.

2. Change to the cgi-bin directory on the Web server.

3. Locate the directory on the CD-ROM appropriate for the set of software for your Web server's operating system.

4. Open the directory for the operating system you will be using and check that the following files (and the db directory, which will store your GuestTrack database) are included:

- gt
- gt-cat
- adduser
- idx
- cart
- gt-cart

- gt-final
- editprod

5. Set your FTP program to Binary mode (instead of Text mode) so the files will be transferred without being corrupting.

6. Copy each of the files listed in step 4 into your cgi-bin directory.

7. Rename the following files to their proper UNIX names:

   - gt to guesttrack
   - idx to indexbuilder

8. Create a sub-directory inside the cgi-bin directory called db.

9. Change into the db directory on the Web server.

10. On your local computer change into the db directory located with the program files you just uploaded.

11. You will see four files on the CD-ROM: users.def, products.def, products.db, and products.idx.

12. Copy users.def and products.def into the db directory on the Web server in ASCII mode.

13. Copy products.db and products.idx into the db directory in Binary mode.

Here are the steps needed to copy the config.txt file into your Web server directory.

1. Use your FTP program to connect to your Web server account.

2. Change to the cgi-bin directory on the Web server.

3. Locate on your hard drive the Web directory and the config.txt file you saved earlier.

4. Set your FTP program to Text mode (instead of Binary mode) so the file will be transferred without changing the end-of-line character.

5. Copy the file config.txt file into your cgi-bin directory.

Now that the GuestTrack program files have been copied to the Web server, it's necessary to change the mode of the programs so the Web server will know to treat them as programs instead of files of data.

First, let's cover the UNIX command used to change the mode of files, then we'll cover how to run the command. If your Web service provider has issued you what is typically called a *shell account* that allows you to issue UNIX commands from a command-line prompt (instead of using an FTP program), then you can just change to the cgi-bin directory and enter the chmod command. The change directory and change mode commands look like this:

```
cd cgi-bin
chmod a+x *
chmod a+w db
cd db
chmod a+w *.db *.idx
```

The chmod command changes the mode of the files specified in the command. The letter *a* says you want to change the mode for all of the users who run the programs, the plus sign says you want to add a mode to the list, and the letter *x* says you want the specified files set to *executable* as programs. The asterisk character is a *wildcard* that says you want all files in that directory changed.

Now that we know what the command does, here is how to run this command using the WS_FTP program to set the mode for files in the cgi-bin directory and for the db directory itself.

1. Run the WS_FTP program.

2. Log onto your Web server account.

3. Open the cgi-bin directory.

4. Right-click in the program to display the list of auxiliary functions.

5. Select the SITE command to enter a remote site-specific command.

6. Enter the change mode command:

```
chmod a+x *
```

7. Select the SITE command again to enter another chmod command.

8. Enter the chmod command to set the db directory world writable as follows:

```
chmod a+w db
```

9. Change into the db directory (that is inside the cgi-bin directory).

10. Select the SITE command and enter:

```
chmode a+w products.db
```

11. Select the SITE command and enter:

```
Chmod a+w products.idx
```

Some versions of WS_FTP have slightly different command menu options. Also, some versions of WS_FTP may not allow the wildcard option, so you will need to issue this command once for every file. If you experience problems with this step, contact the technical support group at your Web hosting service.

By following these steps to upload the GuestTrack software and set the mode, you are ready to upload HTML and graphic files to your Web site.

Keep in mind that if you have questions about this process, review the FAQ list at the Online Marketing Resource Library.

↳ Summary

In completing this phase of creating your online Web catalog, you have achieved one of the most difficult and challenging parts of any Web project—installing programs in the cgi-bin directory. As you move into creating the HTML files and templates that display catalog pages that appeal to your customers, you will experience one of the most rewarding accomplishments in today's technically challenging Internet environment—combining marketing and programming in a commerce-based Web site.

CHAPTER EIGHT

BUILDING YOUR BASIC WEB CATALOG

The Basic Web Catalog covered in this chapter allows you to create an online presence to promote a small number of products. We describe a general format that displays several products on a single Web page, along with an order form.

By keeping the product information, quantities being purchased, and the ordering information on the same Web page we make it very easy to transmit ordering information to your order-processing department.

Let's start by drawing the *site plan* for the Web site that shows the basic flow from the home page to the section pages. In Figure 8.1 the home page is linked to pages dealing with a description of the company, a general description of the products carried, and two *section* pages with details about the two product lines. In addition, the chart shows the page that appears after ordering—sometimes called the *Thank You* page.

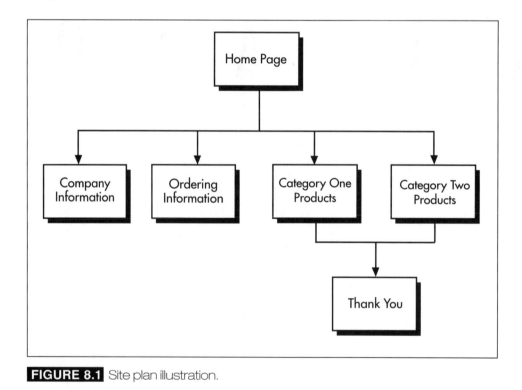

FIGURE 8.1 Site plan illustration.

The Web site in the diagram has two product lines, each with several products on those section pages. The home pages of the three example Basic Web Sites included on the CD-ROM are shown in Figures 8.2, 8.3, and 8.4.

The home page, of course, is the Web page where most visitors enter your Web site. The example home page has a company logo, a short description of the products available from the company, the general terms and conditions of buying from your company, and descriptive links that take the Web customer to the various section pages in the Web site.

The *Company Information* page is where customers turn to answer their questions about the credibility of the company and qualifications to provide quality products, so this is where you will want to express your corporate mission, biographies of officers, and other information that can help the customer understand your company's goals.

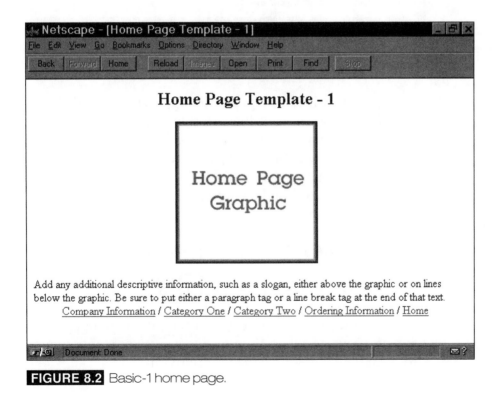

FIGURE 8.2 Basic-1 home page.

Netscape - [Home Page Template - 2]

File Edit View Go Bookmarks Options Directory Window Help

Back | Forward | Home | | Reload | Images | Open | Print | Find | Stop

Basic Home Page Template - 2

Home Page
Graphic

Category One

Category Two

Category One - The descriptive copy on the home page
for each category of products helps customers understand
the types of products you cary and idenfity which category
of products they might be interested in.

Document: Done

FIGURE 8.3 Basic-2 home page.

If you already have a print catalog, then you probably
already provide some of this information about your company and what makes your products distinctive.

The *Ordering Information* page should have the same
type of information that is included in print catalogs where
the objective is to build a relationship with the customer.

➥ Copying HTML templates and graphics from CD-ROM

As you've seen when we reviewed the sample templates
and art, you can select from a wide variety of components
to form your catalog's image on the Web.

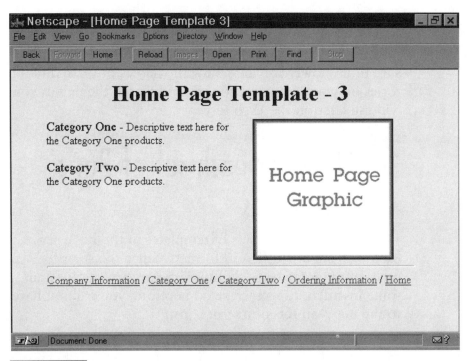

FIGURE 8.4 Basic-3 home page.

The first step in creating your own catalog is to set up a directory on your computer's hard drive where you will build your HTML files and a directory for your images. We recommend keeping your graphic images in a directory separate from your HTML files so it will be easier to manage the two separate types of files. In addition, as your catalog grows from a Basic to an Intermediate or Advanced Catalog, you'll find that the shopping cart software is easier to use when graphic images are separated from the HTML files.

While you can name the directory whatever you'd like, we suggest using the following names:

- raw-art—for original word processing files and original scans of art
- web—for the actual Web HTML files

• images—for the actual Web graphic files

Since you will be using a UNIX-based Web server, be sure to use lowercase letters for the names of these directories on your computer so they will match the names you will use later on the Web server.

↳ Steps for each set of Basic templates

We've included three sets of templates in the Basic series, each with slightly different formats. Since the steps for each set of templates is slightly different, we've repeated some instructions in each set. Therefore, you will not have to flip between sets of instructions.

↳ Using templates from Basic #1

The templates in the Basic #1 set are designed to allow you to provide a short summary of your products either in the heading or in the graphic, then direct the prospect to the links for company, product, and ordering information.

1. Open the basic-1 directory on the CD-ROM where you will see the following files and directories:

   • index.htm—home page

   • company.htm—information about the company

   • prod1.htm—product descriptions for category #1

   • prod2.htm—product descriptions for category #2

   • ordering.htm—terms and conditions of ordering products

   • thanks.htm—Thank You page following an order

- images—the directory of graphic images

2. Copy these files and the images directory to the web directory on your hard drive.

3. Open the file index.htm with your Web browser. Under the File Menu, select Open File, then select the file.

4. Test the links to ensure that all files are present and the links are set up correctly.

Home page

Now, let's edit the home page to include your catalog name, home page graphic, and any additional descriptive information you'd like to provide (Figure 8.5).

1. Open the index.htm template in your HTML editor.

```
Netscape - [Home Page Template - 1]                       _ 🗗 ×
File  Edit  View  Go  Bookmarks  Options  Directory  Window  Help
  Back   Forward   Home      Reload   Images   Open    Print    Find    Stop

                    Home Page Template - 1

                    ┌───────────────────────┐
                    │                       │
                    │                       │
                    │      Home Page        │
                    │       Graphic         │
                    │                       │
                    │                       │
                    └───────────────────────┘

  Add any additional descriptive information, such as a slogan, either above the graphic or on lines
  below the graphic. Be sure to put either a paragraph tag or a line break tag at the end of that text.
        Company Information / Category One / Category Two / Ordering Information / Home

  Document: Done                                              ⊠?
```

FIGURE 8.5 Basic-1 Home page.

2. Change the text "Home Page Template - 1" to the name of the catalog. For example, "Golf Accessories for the Avid Adventurer."

3. Add any additional descriptive information, such as a slogan, either above the graphic or on lines below the graphic. Be sure to put either a paragraph tag or a line break tag at the end of that text.

4. If you have prepared a home page graphic using a file name other than the one used in the template (e.g., homepage.gif), change that file name to the one you created. Be sure to maintain the reference to the images directory (e.g., images/filename.gif).

5. Change the text "Category One" to the name of your products (e.g., Gloves & Shoes).

6. If you will have only one category of products, then delete the text "Category Two /" and its link. If you have multiple categories of products, then create as many additional category links as you will need. You will notice that the links display well at any window width because they are inside a center tag.

7. Save the home page file in your web directory and view it in your browser to make sure it looks right.

Company Information page

1. Open the company.htm template in your HTML editor. (Figure 8.6).

2. Change the text "Company Information Template - 1" to be either the name of your catalog or just the words "Company Information."

3. Replace the paragraphs in the template with descriptive information about your company and the products you carry. Again, be sure to put either a paragraph tag or a line break tag at the end of each paragraph.

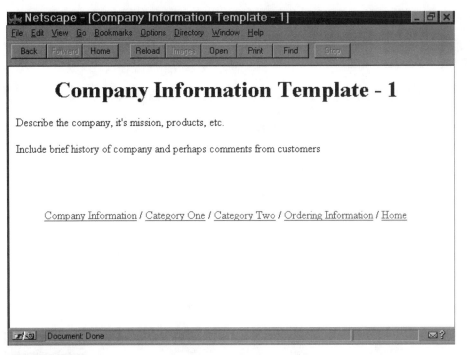

Company Information Template - 1

Describe the company, it's mission, products, etc.

Include brief history of company and perhaps comments from customers

Company Information / Category One / Category Two / Ordering Information / Home

Document: Done

FIGURE 8.6 Basic-1 Company Information page.

4. Since the text links at the bottom of the file index.htm are the same as you'll need for this page, if you have made any changes to the links in index.htm open the home page document, copy the section of links, then paste them over the links at the bottom of this template.

5. Save the Company Information page file in your web directory and view it in your browser to make sure it looks right.

Ordering Information

1. Open the ordering.htm template in your HTML editor. (Figure 8.7)

2. Change the text "Ordering Information Template - 1" to a descriptive word or phrase about your terms and conditions. For example, "Terms and Conditions," "Ordering Information," or "How to Order from Us."

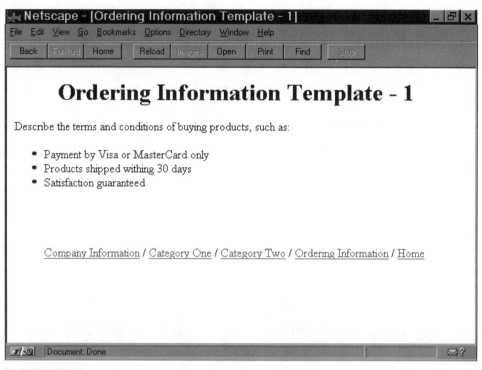

Ordering Information Template - 1

Describe the terms and conditions of buying products, such as:

- Payment by Visa or MasterCard only
- Products shipped withing 30 days
- Satisfaction guaranteed

Company Information / Category One / Category Two / Ordering Information / Home

Document: Done

FIGURE 8.7 Basic-1 Ordering Information page.

3. Replace the paragraphs in the template with descriptive information about your payment and shipping information. Again, be sure to put either a paragraph tag or a line break tag at the end of each paragraph.

4. If you have made changes to the links at the bottom of the page, then paste the text links at the bottom of the page as you did for the company.htm.

5. Save the Ordering Information page file in your web directory and view it in your browser to make sure it looks right.

Products page

Preparing the actual products HTML page will be easy if you have gathered electronic versions of the product descriptions and product photos, as well as the price for

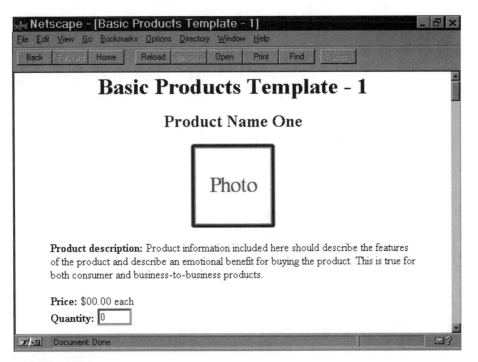

Basic Products Template - 1

Product Name One

Photo

Product description: Product information included here should describe the features of the product and describe an emotional benefit for buying the product. This is true for both consumer and business-to-business products.

Price: $00.00 each

Quantity: 0

FIGURE 8.8 Basic-1 Product Information page.

each product. There are two types of changes needed for these product pages:

- Changes to the material above the product descriptions and changes at the very bottom of the page
- Changes to each product description and price, as well as the hidden variables for the shopping cart

For this reason, changes to product pages are divided into these two sections. We suggest creating the material at the top and bottom of the page first so you will have the overall look established and have links that work (Figure 8.8).

Modifying the heading and navigation links

Here's how to do it.

1. Open the prod1.htm template in your HTML editor.
2. Change the text "Basic Products Template - 1" to be either the name of your product line that you used in

the link from the other Web pages or a banner graphic. If you have prepared banner art for the top of this page, replace the text at the top of the page (<H1>Basic Products Template - 1</H1>) with an IMG SRC tag such as <IMG SRC="images/banner1.gif">.

3. Since the text links at the bottom of the file index.htm are the same as you'll need for this page, if you have made any changes to the navigation links in the home page open the home page document, copy that section of links, then paste them over the links at the bottom of this template.

4. Save the prod1.htm file in your web directory and view it in your browser to make sure it looks right, then move on to modifying the specific product information.

Modifying the product information

For each product on the page use the following steps to replace the template material with actual material about the product.

1. Change the product name (e.g., Product Name One) to the actual name of the product being shown.

2. Look for the following tag for the product photograph: <IMG SRC="images/photo.gif">. Replace the graphic file name photo.gif with the actual graphic file name for this product. Be sure to keep the reference to the images directory and the slash (/) between them.

3. Replace the text in the template describing the product with descriptive information about the actual product. Be sure to put either a paragraph tag or a line break tag at the end of each paragraph.

4. Look for the following tags and text: <B>Price:</B> $00.00 each
. Change the price that is displayed to the actual price.

5. Several pieces of information stored in *hidden* form variables need to be changed, including the price, for the shopping cart to know about this product. The following three lines of tags and information set the part number, description, and price for the product: <INPUT NAME="part01" TYPE="hidden" VALUE="SKU-001">, <INPUT NAME="desc01" TYPE="hidden" VALUE="Product Name 01">, and <INPUT NAME="price01" TYPE="hidden" VALUE="$00.00">.

Notice that there are three elements used here in the input tag: name, type, and value. The variable names of part01, desc01, and price01 are the names of the variables and identify the data being supplied in the tag. The actual value of the data is inside the double quotes at the end of the tag.

First, change "SKU-001" to the part number you use in your order-processing system, keeping the double quotes around the text.

Second, replace the text in the desc01 tag with a short description that will appear in the order file.

Next, change the price of the product in the price01 tag. Make sure it is the same price you used for this product just above these hidden variables.

Repeat this for each product on the page. We've included placeholders for ten products in this form and designed the accompanying shopping cart system to handle up to ten products. The form variables are numbered from "01" to "10", so be sure that text, photo file names, and the shopping cart data all correspond.

If you have fewer than ten products, just delete the unused placeholders. If you need to display more than ten products, then you will need to use additional Category Template Forms.

Modifying the Thank You page

After an order is processed, the shopping cart program displays the page thanks.htm that contains a brief message thanking the customer for placing an order (Figure 8.9).

You may find that the text included in the template will suit your needs, but you might want to add text telling customers about specials available only to them or other information that should be given to customers after they have placed an order.

Many Web marketers like to provide links to Web sites that their customers would be interested in visiting, perhaps selling compatible products. It's best to display links to other Web sites after they have placed an order, so the Thank You page is the most appropriate page to display those links.

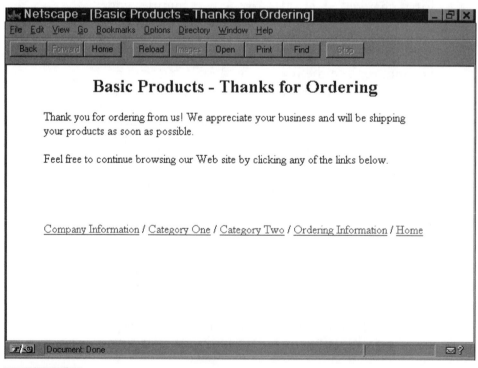

FIGURE 8.9 Basic-1 Thank You page.

↳ Using templates from Basic #2

The templates in Basic #2 set are designed to have a slightly more complex look than the templates in the Basic #1 set.

The home page in this set provides more information about your company and about the categories of products than in Basic #1, and the product category pages are designed to highlight the product photos at the top of the page. These photos are links to the full product information and larger photos lower on the page. This technique reduces the need for your customer to scroll through the page to find products of interest.

As with the other sets of templates, there are links to Company Information and Ordering Information in addition to the pages of product information.

The following steps will take you through the process of using the templates in Basic #2 to create a complete Web catalog.

1. Open the basic-2 directory on the CD-ROM where you will see the following files and directories:

   - index.htm—home page
   - company.htm—information about the company
   - prod1.htm—product descriptions for category #1
   - prod2.htm—product descriptions for category #2
   - ordering.htm—terms and conditions of ordering products
   - thanks.htm—Thank You page following an order
   - images—the directory of graphic images

2. Copy these files and the images directory to the web directory on your hard drive.

3. Open the file index.htm with your Web browser. Under the File menu, select Open File, then select the file.

4. Test the links to ensure that all files are present and the links are set up correctly.

Home page

The home page for this set of templates is designed to take advantage of the current design technique that uses a strip of color down the left side of the page, with text on a white background. In addition to displaying a small accent of color on the page, this layout reduces the width of the column of text, which research shows improves readability.

Multiple <blockquote> tags are used to indent the text enough so that it is to the right of the color bar. If you create your own color bar to replace the one in the template, you may need to add or delete <blockquote> tags to make the text indent the proper amount (Figure 8.10).

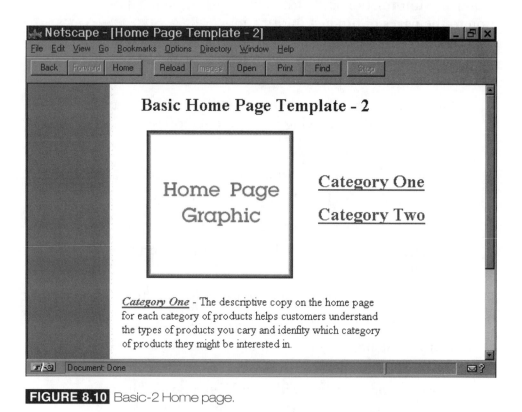

FIGURE 8.10 Basic-2 Home page.

This template also uses a table to align the home page graphic next to the category names, so you may want to familiarize yourself with the table tags described in Chapter 5.

Let's edit the home page to include your catalog name, home page graphic, and the description of your product categories.

1. Open the index.htm template in your HTML editor.

2. Change the text "Home Page Template - 2" to the name of your catalog.

3. If you have prepared a home page graphic using a file name other than the one used in the template (e.g., homepage.gif), change that file name to the one you created. Be sure to keep the reference to the images directory. Notice that the graphic is in the left cell of a two-cell table, so be sure to keep it within the <TD> and </TD> tags.

4. Change the text "Category One" to the name of your products (e.g., Gloves & Shoes). Be sure to keep these category names inside the <TD> and </TD> tags that make up the second cell of the table.

5. Change the text "Category Two" to the name of a second category, if you have one. If you are going to have only the one category of products, then delete the text "Category Two" and its link, as well as the descriptive paragraph.

6. Below the table are two paragraphs describing the two categories. Edit the phrase "Category One" (inside the bold and italic tags) to the name of your first category of products, then replace the descriptive text with a paragraph that describes the types of products in Category One.

7. If you have only one category of products, then delete the paragraph dealing with Category Two. If

you have a second category, edit the phrase "Category Two" (inside the bold and italic tags) and the descriptive text as you did for Category One.

8. Save the home page file in your web directory and view it in your browser to make sure it looks right.

Company Information page

1. Open the company.htm template in your HTML editor (Figure 8.11).

2. Change the text "Company Information Template - 2" to be either the name of your catalog or just the words "Company Information," or replace it with a graphic banner (using an IMG SRC tag) with similar words.

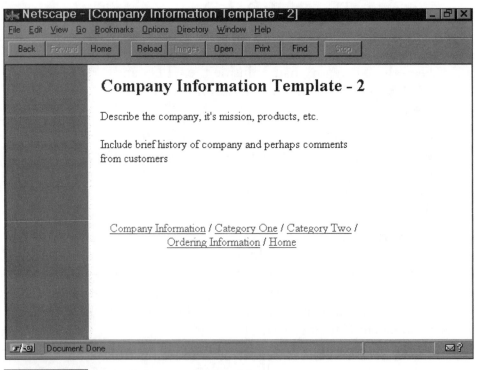

FIGURE 8.11 Basic-2 Company Information page.

3. Replace the paragraphs in the template with descriptive information about your company and the products you carry.

4. Since the text links at the bottom of the file index.htm are the same as you'll need for this page, if you have made any changes to these links on the home page open the home page document, copy the section of links, then paste them over the links at the bottom of this template.

5. Save the Company Information page file in your web directory and view it in your browser to make sure it looks right.

Ordering Information

1. Open the ordering.htm template in your HTML editor (Figure 8.12).

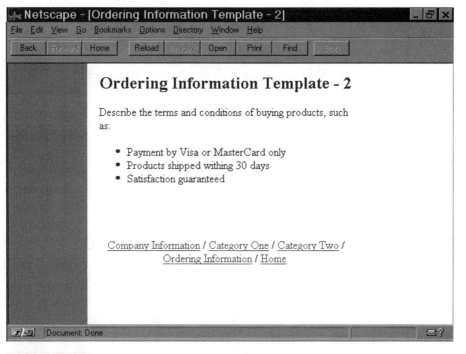

FIGURE 8.12 Basic-2 Ordering Information page.

2. Change the text "Ordering Information Template - 2" to a descriptive word or phrase about your terms and conditions, or use a graphic banner (using an IMG SRC tag) For example, "Terms and Conditions," "Ordering Information," "How to Order from Us," and so forth.

3. Replace the paragraphs in the template with descriptive information about your payment and shipping information. Again, be sure to put either a paragraph tag or a line break tag at the end of each paragraph.

4. If you have made changes to the links at the bottom of the page, then paste those text links at the bottom of the page as you did for the company.htm.

5. Save the Ordering Information page file in your web directory and view it in your browser to make sure it looks right.

Products page

Preparing the actual products HTML page will be easy if you have gathered electronic versions of the product descriptions and product photos, as well as the price for each product. There are two types of changes needed for these product pages:

- Changes to the material above the product descriptions and changes at the very bottom

- Changes to each product description and price, as well as the hidden variables used in the shopping cart

For this reason, the changes to product pages are divided into these two sections. We suggest making the changes to the material at the top and bottom of the page first so you will have the overall look prepared and have links that work (Figure 8.13).

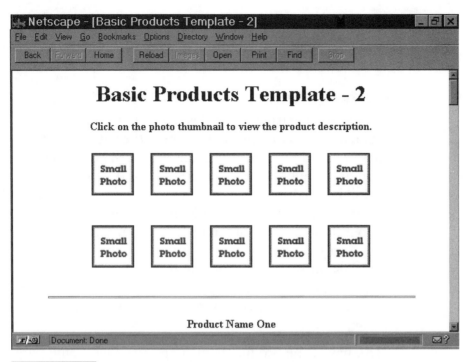

FIGURE 8.13 Basic-2 Product Information page.

Modifying the heading and navigation links

Here's how to do it.

1. Open the prod1.htm template in your HTML editor.

2. Change the text "Basic Products Template - 2" to be the name of your product line that you used in the link from the other Web pages. If you have prepared banner art for the top of this page, replace the text at the top of the page (<H1>Basic Products Template - 2</H1>) with an IMG SRC tag such as <IMG SRC="images/banner1.gif">.

3. The text links at the bottom of the file index.htm are the same as you'll need for this page. If you have made any changes to them just open the home page document, copy the section of links, then paste them over the links at the bottom of this template.

4. Save the prod1.htm file in your web directory and view it in your browser to make sure it is correct, then move on to modifying the specific product information.

Modifying the product information

The first step in customizing this template is to replace the thumbnail product photos at the top of the page with the names of actual thumbnail product photos. These thumbnail photos should be approximately 150-200 pixels wide so they will be small and load quickly. You'll notice that the name of the thumbnail photo file in the template ends in "tn" to indicate thumbnail. In order to keep the photo file names consistent, you might want to name the thumbnail photo files with a letter at the end to signify it's a thumbnail.

For each product on the page use the following steps to replace the template material with actual text about the product.

1. Change the product name (e.g., Product Name One) to the actual name of the product being shown.

2. Look for the following tag for the product photograph: <IMG SRC="images/photo.gif">. Replace the graphic file name photo.gif with the actual graphic file name for this product. Be sure to keep the reference to the images directory and the slash (/) between them.

3. Replace the text in the template describing the product with descriptive information about the actual product. Be sure to put either a paragraph tag or a line break tag at the end of each paragraph.

4. Look for the following tags and text: <B>Price:</B> $00.00 each
. Change the price that is displayed to the actual price.

5. Several pieces of information stored in *hidden* form variables need to be changed. The following lines of tags and information set the part number, description, price, and shipping charge for the product:

```
<INPUT NAME="part01" TYPE="hidden"
VALUE="SKU-001">, <INPUT NAME="desc01"
TYPE="hidden" VALUE="Product Name 01">,
<INPUT NAME="price01" TYPE="hidden"
VALUE="$00.00">.
```

Notice that there are three elements used here in the input tag: name, type, and value. The variable names of part01, desc01, and price01 are the names of the variables and identify the type of data being supplied in the tag, while the actual value of the data is inside the double quotes at the end of the tag.

First, change "SKU-001" to the part number you use in your order-processing system, keeping the double quotes around the text.

Second, replace the text in the desc01 tag with a short description that will be on the order form.

Next, change the price of the product in the price01 tag. Make sure it is the same price you used for this product just above these hidden variables.

Repeat this for each product in the product line. We've included placeholders for ten products in this form and designed the accompanying shopping cart system to handle up to ten products. The form variables are numbered from "01" to "10," so be sure that text, photo file names, and the shopping cart data all correspond.

If you have fewer than ten products, then just delete the unused placeholders. If you want to display more than ten products, then you will need to use additional Category Template Forms.

Modifying the Thank You page

After an order is processed, the shopping cart program displays the page thanks.htm that contains a brief message thanking the customer for placing an order (Figure 8.14).

You may find the text included in the template will suit your needs but you might want to add extra text telling customers about specials available only to them or other information that should be given to customers after they have placed an order.

Many Web marketers like to provide links to Web sites that their customers would be interested in visiting, perhaps selling compatible products. It's best to display links to other Web sites after customers have placed an order, so the Thank you page is the most appropriate page to display those links. Be sure the text and links are within the set of <blockquote> tags used to indent the text.

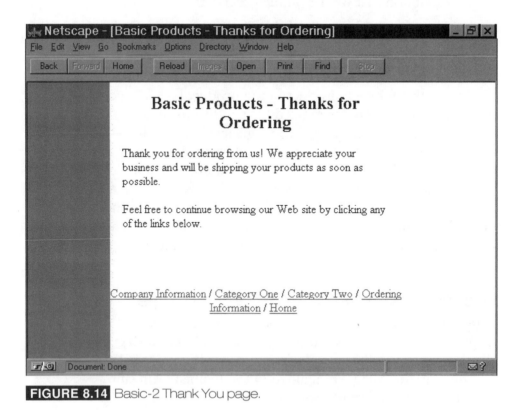 Using templates from Basic #3

The home page in this set provides more information about your company and about the categories of products

FIGURE 8.14 Basic-2 Thank You page.

than in Basic #1, while the product pages are designed to take advantage of the *grouping* effect of HTML tables.

As with the other sets of templates, there are links to company information and ordering information in addition to the pages of product information.

The following steps will take you through the process of using the templates in Basic #3 to create a complete Web catalog.

1. Open the basic-3 directory on the CD-ROM where you will see the following files and directories:

   • index.htm—home page

   • company.htm—information about the company

   • prod1.htm—product descriptions for category #1

   • prod2.htm—product descriptions for category #2

   • ordering.htm—terms and conditions of ordering products

   • thanks.htm—thank you page following an order

   • images—the directory of graphic images

2. Copy these files and the images directory to the web directory on your hard drive.

3. Open the file index.htm with your Web browser. Under the File menu, select Open File, then select the file.

4. Test the links to ensure that all files are present and the links are set up correctly.

Home page

This home page uses a colored background file instead of a plain white background to illustrate how this is done. The HTML tag that uses art from a file for this page is: <body background="images/green-bg.jpg">.

The use of colored backgrounds can be effective if the background doesn't overwhelm the text and other pieces of art on the page. While we used a solid color, you can use any type of pattern, such as watercolor paper, cloth, or other pattern that will look good when tiled across and down the page. If you scan a patterned texture, be sure to reduce the contrast and lighten the overall color.

Editing the home page to include your catalog name, home page graphic, and the description of your product categories will be similar to the two other Basic Sets with a couple of exceptions. This template has the home page graphic aligned to the right of the window and descriptive text wrapping to the left of the graphic (Figure 8.15).

Although you normally want an eye-catching graphic on the left so it pulls the reader's eyes into the text, there may be times when your catalog name and category names are stronger than the graphic.

1. Open the index.htm template in your HTML editor.

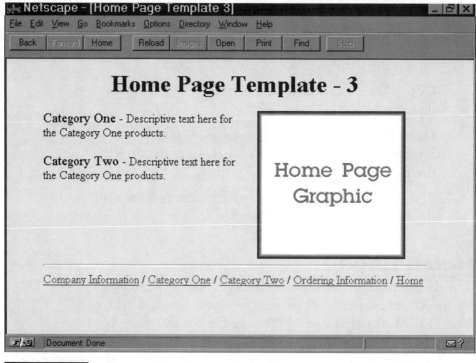

FIGURE 8.15 Basic-3 home page.

2. Change the text "Home Page Template - 3" to the name of your catalog.

3. If you have prepared a home page graphic using a file name other than the one used in the template (e.g., homepage.gif), change that file name to the one you created. Be sure to keep the reference to the images directory. Notice that the tag uses the align=right attribute that causes text to wrap around the left side of the graphic. The tag <BR clear=all> is used to stop the wrapping of text around the graphic.

4. Change the text "Category One" inside the font tag to the name of your products (e.g., Gloves & Shoes). Add any additional description of the category after the font tag.

5. Change the text "Category Two" to the name of a second category, if you have one. If you are going to have only one category of products, then delete the text "Category Two."

6. Save the home page file in your web directory and view it in your browser to make sure it looks right.

Company Information page

1. Open the company.htm template in your HTML editor (Figure 8.16).

2. Change the text "Company Information Template - 3" to be either the name of your catalog or the words "Company Information," or replace it with a graphic banner (using an IMG SRC tag) with similar words.

3. Replace the paragraphs in the template with descriptive information about your company and the products you carry.

4. Since the text links at the bottom of the file index.htm are the same as you'll need for this page,

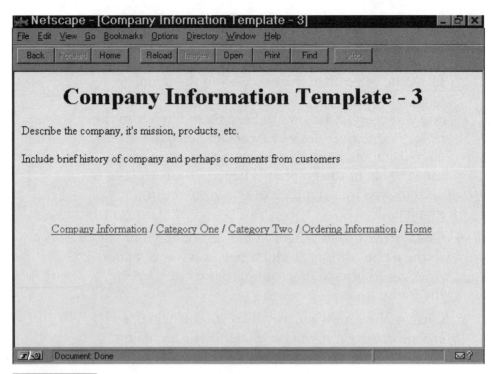

FIGURE 8.16 Basic-3 Company Information page.

copy that section of links, then paste them over the links at the bottom of this template.

5. Save the Company Information page file in your web directory and view it in your browser to make sure it looks right.

Ordering Information

1. Open the ordering.htm template in your HTML editor (Figure 8.17).

2. Change the text "Ordering Information Template - 3" to a descriptive word or phrase about your terms and conditions, or use a graphic banner (using an IMG SRC tag).

   For example, "Terms and Conditions," "Ordering Information," "How to Order from Us," and so on.

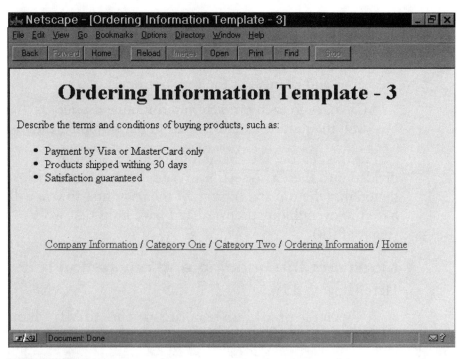

Ordering Information Template - 3

Describe the terms and conditions of buying products, such as:

- Payment by Visa or MasterCard only
- Products shipped withing 30 days
- Satisfaction guaranteed

Company Information / Category One / Category Two / Ordering Information / Home

FIGURE 8.17 Basic-3 Ordering Information page.

3. Replace the paragraphs in the template with descriptive information about your payment and shipping information. Again, be sure to put either a paragraph tag or a line break tag at the end of each paragraph.

4. Since the text links at the bottom of the file index.htm are the same as you'll need for this page, paste them over the links at the bottom of this template as you did for the company.htm.

5. Save the Ordering Information page file in your web directory and view it in your browser to make sure it looks right.

Products page

Preparing the actual products HTML page will be easy if you have gathered electronic versions of the product descriptions and product photos, as well as the price for each product. There are two types of changes needed for these product pages:

- Changes to the material above the product descriptions and changes at the very bottom
- Changes to each product description and price, as well the hidden variables used in the shopping cart

For this reason, the changes to product pages are divided into these two sections. We suggest making the material at the top and bottom of the page first so you will have the overall look prepared and have links that work (Figure 8.18).

Modifying the heading and navigation links

Here's how to do it.

1. Open the prod1.htm template in your HTML editor.

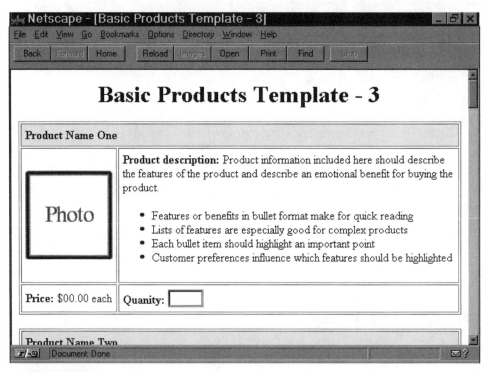

FIGURE 8.18 Basic-3 Product Information page.

2. Change the text "Basic Products Template - 3" to be the name of your product line that you used in the link from the other Web pages. If you have prepared banner art for the top of this page, replace the text at the top of the page (<H1>Basic Products Template - 3</H1>) with an IMG SRC tag.

3. Since the text links at the bottom of the file index.htm are the same as you'll need for this page, paste them over the links at the bottom of this template.

4. Save the prod1.htm file in your web directory and view it in your browser to make sure it looks right, then move on to modifying the specific product information.

Modifying the product information

The product pages used in the Basic #3 set of templates have a similar look to those used in the Basic #2 set except the data is arranged in cells of a table.

For each product on the page use the following steps to replace the template material with actual material about the product.

1. Change the product name (e.g., Product Name One) to the actual name of the product being shown.

2. Look for the following tag for the product photograph: <IMG SRC="images/photo.gif">. Replace the graphic file name photo.gif with the actual graphic file name for this product. Be sure to keep the reference to the images directory and the slash (/) between them.

3. Replace the text in the template describing the product with descriptive information about the actual product.

4. Look for the following tags and text: <B>Price:</B> $00.00 each
 Change the price that is displayed to the actual price.

5. Several pieces of information stored in hidden form variables need to be changed, including the price, for the shopping cart to know about this product. The following tags and information set the part number, description, price, and shipping charge for the product: <INPUT NAME="part01" TYPE="hidden" VALUE="SKU-001">, <INPUT NAME="desc01" TYPE="hidden" VALUE="Product Name 01">, and <INPUT NAME="price01" TYPE="hidden" VALUE="$00.00">.

Notice that there are three elements used here in the input tag: name, type, and value. The variable names of part01, desc01, and price01 are the names of the variables and identify the type of data being supplied in the tag, while the actual value of the data is inside the double quotes at the end of the tag.

First, change "SKU-001" to the part number you use in your order processing system, keeping the double quotes around the text.

Second, replace the text in the desc01 tag with a short description that will be on the order form.

Next, change the price of the product in the price01 tag. Make sure it is the same price you used for this product just above these hidden variables.

Repeat this for each product in the product line. We've included placeholders for ten products in this form and designed the accompanying shopping cart system to handle up to ten products. The form variables are numbered from "01" to "10," so be sure that text, photo file names, and the shopping cart data all correspond.

If you have fewer than ten products, then just delete the unused placeholders. If you need to display more than ten products, then you will need to use additional Category Template Forms.

Modifying the Thank You page

After an order is processed, the shopping cart program displays the page thanks.htm which contains a brief message thanking the customer for placing an order (Figure 8.19).

You may find the text included in the template will suit your needs but you might want to add extra text telling customers about specials available only to them or other information that should be given to customers after they have placed an order.

Many Web marketers like to provide links to Web sites that their customers would be interested in visiting, perhaps selling compatible products. It's best to display links to other Web sites after customers have placed an order, so the Thank You page is the most appropriate page to display those links.

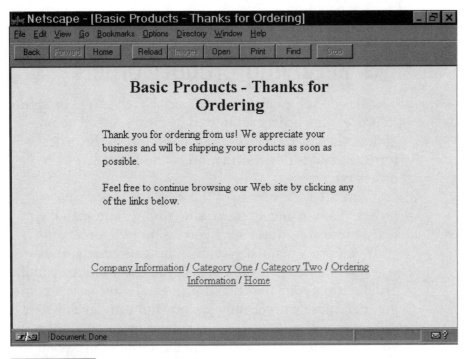

FIGURE 8.19 Basic-3 Thank You page.

Uploading your Web pages to the Web server

Once you have developed your Basic Web Catalog and tested the static pages on your local computer, upload the files from your web directory, along with the images directory, to your Web server account.

Once you have uploaded your files, test the links to each page and test the shopping cart program. If you find things that don't work properly or don't look the way you would like them to look, modify the affected files on your computer and upload the changed files. After you have tested each file, you're ready to promote your Web catalog and start receiving orders.

Receiving product orders

The Basic Web catalogs use a special Web server program to process the orders submitted by customers. The program, called *cart*, receives information from the order forms and adds the information to the file called orders.txt.

With the wide variety of methods for processing orders, from manually processing to fully automated systems, there are several ways you can use the orders file.

If you use a manual system to process orders, then you will want to print the orders file and use it to handle orders using your traditional process. If you have a computerized order processing system and can develop software that will import data to create a new order, then you will want to explore having a program developed to import the orders.txt file. In either case, you will probably want to send your customers an acknowledgment of their order via e-mail or fax, including their order number and final total charge.

The process for downloading the orders file is as follows.

1. Start your FTP program and log on to your account at the Web server. This should place you at the *root* (or top) level of your account on the Web server computer.

2. Change to the cgi-bin directory, then change to the db directory inside the cgi-bin directory.

3. Download to your local computer the file orders.txt.

4. Once you confirm that the orders file has been transferred to your local computer, then use the FTP program's *rename* function to change the name of the file to one that includes the date you downloaded the file. This creates a *backup* of the orders while allowing the shopping cart system to start a new orders file. While you can use any file-naming convention you like, a good one is to name the file oYYMMDD.txt, where the lowercase letter "o" stands for orders, "YY" is the year, "MM" is the month, and "DD" is the date. For example, if you make the backup file on February 1, 1998, the file would be called o980201.txt. By using a date in year-month-day format the directory listings of your files will show them in date order. Periodically, you should delete the old backup order files from your Web server to conserve disk space.

In order for the cart program to be able to create a new orders file each time, the directory storing the file must be set to be WORLD WRITABLE. If you suspect there is a problem writing to the orders file, review the steps in Chapter 7 on creating the db directory that stores orders.

↳ Summary

The Web site you created using the Basic templates will be the foundation for adding personalization using the techniques in Chapter 9 on Intermediate Web Catalogs and the database catalog in Chapter 10 on Advanced Web Catalog. After you have experience in creating HTML files in this chapter, consider enhancing your Web catalog with the techniques in the next chapter on adding personalization to a Web catalog.

CHAPTER NINE

BUILDING YOUR INTERMEDIATE WEB CATALOG

This chapter covers how to implement what we call an *Intermediate Web Catalog*—a catalog that uses Web personalization software called GuestTrack and introduces a more advanced approach to taking orders for products, sometimes called a *shopping cart*. The benefit of using an ordering system is that your customer can review the products you offer in detail, focusing attention on each product of interest. In addition, the Intermediate Web Catalog features an *index* page that helps customers choose which products to look at.

Once you decide you are ready to have a Web site that uses database technology, you must also be ready to pay closer attention to a wide variety of details because the increased complexity creates more opportunity for errors in creating the HTML code. Since mastering HTML while you are learning to use a database can be very challenging, we recommend that you start with the Basic Web Catalog described in Chapter 8, then enhance it with the techniques described in this chapter. If you already have a Web site and are looking to add the personalization and shopping cart features described in this chapter, then you're invited to read on and create a site with features you probably won't find on your competition's.

While the Basic Web Catalog had only two levels of Web pages (the Home Page and all other pages) the Intermediate Web Catalog features three levels of pages:

- Home page
- Index pages
- Content/Product pages

The addition of index pages is designed to help you present a rather large number of products in summary form so customers can review the names and short descriptions, then select a hypertext link to see the complete details and a photo.

A large number of levels in the Web site and an even larger number of product pages makes it difficult for the customer to find the right products while browsing through your Web site. One way around the problem of having many index pages is to use the customer's profile to prepare a customized page of links appropriate for that person—which is one of the main features you will add to your Web site in this chapter.

The general flow that occurs with the Intermediate Web Catalog is for the customer to come to your Home Page, decide they like the type of products you offer, then complete your Guest Book and select which areas they would like on their Personalized Product List. This chapter will walk you through the process of adding capability to the Web site you created in Chapter 8.

If you have just read Chapter 8 and did not create the Web site described, but now want to create the Intermediate Web Catalog described in this chapter, the templates on the CD-ROM in the intermed directory have the modifications described in this chapter. However, be sure to read this chapter to understand why these modifications were made so you can easily update your Web site using these techniques.

The first step is to create a *flow diagram* that shows how customers move from the Home Page through the intermediate pages to the product and other descriptive pages. Figure 9.1 shows each of the pages that we will develop for this Web site.

Since the Intermediate Web Catalog is more complex than the Basic Web Catalog, this is a good time to think through the information-gathering process of your prospects and customers.

There are basically two types of markets to which you may be selling: business or consumer. The business-to-business market is typically interested in facts about your products—the features, functions, and benefits—and secondarily interested in the emotional aspects, such as how it

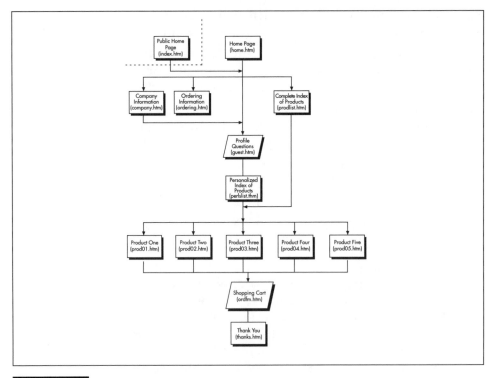

FIGURE 9.1 Intermediate Web Catalog site plan.

will help employee morale, how it will help them look good to their boss, or how their customers will benefit from the product.

Consumer markets, on the other hand, are typically interested in the more emotional aspects of buying products. Since consumers are typically more emotional, you will need to write copy with a different tone or style. In addition, the emotional nature of consumer products makes it important for the product photographs, illustrations, and graphics to be of high quality so the shopping experience will be pleasant and encourage prospects to order your products.

With these considerations in mind, it's time to gather the ingredients and follow the steps in creating your

Intermediate Web Catalog using the GuestTrack profile database system.

↳ Using GuestTrack to personalize Your Web site

One of the innovations that is taking place on the World Wide Web is the use of database technology to control the display of information to your prospects and customers. The difference between traditional static Web pages and the dynamic Web pages served by a database is that an additional level of software is added to the Web server software.

The main software programs that are part of the GuestTrack Light software system that are used in the Intermediate Web Catalog are:

- guesttrack—uses HTML template files to retrieve information from the GuestTrack profile database and insert those pieces of information into the HTML page displayed to the user on the fly (i.e., as the pages are created in real-time)

- adduser—creates a new entry in the GuestTrack profile database, stores information about the user in fields in the database, and creates a new GuestTrack ID

- gt-cart—displays an order form using product purchase information

- gt-final—creates a text file in a protected area of your Web site with new orders to process and ship

The use of this additional software requires several additional procedures that were not used in creating the Basic Web Catalog; none of these procedures require special programming.

Planning to use the GuestTrack personalization system

The use of a database in conjunction with a Web site is new, but the underlying concept of the GuestTrack Light system is similar to using the mail merge capability of your word processing software.

GuestTrack allows you not only to insert text into a Web page but it can include blocks of text and links based on the interest areas of the customer. For instance, the *Guest Book* form has space in the database reserved for up to five *interest* areas that you can use to display five groups of product descriptions and links.

You may group products by how the products are used, lifestyle interests (e.g., reading, shopping, outdoor activities), demographic characteristics (e.g., age, gender, income), or however your customers segment your products as they gather information to make buying decisions. By helping your customers to see only those products of interest to them, you help build the relationship based on how well you meet their needs.

The version of GuestTrack included with this book allows you to store information in a database on the Web server that is collected in the Guest Book form shown in Figure 9.2. In addition to the typical contact information, you can store answers to questions about their interests.

The five interest areas are coded in the database and the Guest Book as int1 through int5. You can label these interest areas on the Guest Book with whatever HTML text you like. For example, if you sell men's clothing items you might label the interest areas on the Guest Book check boxes as follows:

- int1 = Hats for All Seasons
- int2 = Shirts for the Distinguished Man
- int3 = Pants for Casual and Formal Settings

```
Netscape - [Guest Book]                                          _ ᵺ ×
File  Edit  View  Go  Bookmarks  Options  Directory  Window  Help

  Back   Forward  Home      Reload  Images   Open    Print   Find    Stop

        Personalized Product List - Interest Survey

   We would like to provide you with information about just the products that you are interested in, so
   you are invited to answer the following questions about your interests. The following page will
   present links to products in your interest areas.

   Which of the following categories are you interested in? Just check the boxes and we'll give you a
   personalized list of products that meet your criteria:
   ☑  Interest Number One
   ☑  Interest Number Two
   ☑  Interest Number Three
   ☑  Interest Number Four
   ☑  Interest Number Five


   Name:    [                                    ]

   Title:   [                                    ]

   Company: [                                    ]

   Document: Done
```

FIGURE 9.2 GuestTrack Guest Book.

- int4 = Shoes to Step Out In
- int5 = Accessories that Make the Man

Then, on a Personalized Shopping List page, use the special GuestTrack tags to show text and links for an interest area they checked on the Guest Book. For instance, if a customer had checked just "Accessories" on the guest book page, then the Personalized Shopping List page would just have text describing the accessories—and nothing displayed for the other four interest areas.

Of course, it's important to include a link to a page of all the products so customers can browse your entire product line, but Web customers appreciate the personalization that uses their interests to customize the Web experience because it saves them time and reduces the anxiety of information overload that shoppers sometimes feel when on the Web.

As previously mentioned, it's sometimes desirable to include information the customer has provided in Web pages. For instance, on the Personalized Shopping List template we've included the customer's name at the top of the page. When planning to use information from the customer's profile it's important to design the page to look good if the customer has not already provided information. In other words, if the customer doesn't provide a complete address and leaves out the city, you won't want to include their city in such a way that it would look awkward if it is missing.

Tracking a user on a Web site

The GuestTrack personalization software used in this chapter provides a number of features used to identify a user and display Web pages appropriate for them. One of the difficulties of developing Web sites that act like traditional software products used on a local computer is that the Web is *session-less*—there are no continuous sessions of data moving from the user's computer to the host computer.

This is different from traditional computing where some mechanism is used to continuously identify a user. Early computers used individual cables running from each desktop terminal to the host computer. That made it easy for the host to know whom to send answers back. Later, when Local Area Networks (LANs) became popular, each desktop computer had a unique identifier it sent on a shared cable. Having a unique ID was almost as easy to manage as unique cables, but it works well.

The network methodology of the World Wide Web causes a session of transmission to the host and a response from the host to be continuous only for the few seconds whenever a user requests a Web page from a Web server and when the Web server delivers that page to the user. While the user is reading the Web page or linking to another Web site and returning to the original Web site, there is no session going on, so there has been no easy way for the host Web server to tell when the user requests a second Web page, or a third page, and so on.

One way to overcome the problem of a session-less Web environment is to create a unique identifier for a user, then include their ID in each link and form request sent to the Web server. Since Web servers are not programmed to add IDs for users to hypertext links on the fly, special software is needed to handle this function.

Once a Web server database has a way to identify exactly which registered user is requesting a particular Web page, the database software is in a position to adjust what is displayed to that user as the Web page is being sent over the Internet. This is the function that GuestTrack provides a tag is given to each registered user in such a way as to allow Web pages to contain data retrieved from a profile database and make decisions about which information should be displayed to the user.

GuestTrack links

Now that we've covered the general approach to using a database in a Web environment, we need to cover the differences between static hypertext links and the links used with the GuestTrack software. Compare the following static link to a GuestTrack link that a user would see in a Web page link:

- Static: <A HREF="info.htm">

- GuestTrack: <A HREF="/cgi-bin/guesttrack?1234567 890ab&info.htm">

Here is a description of each component of the GuestTrack link:

- /cgi-bin/—This tells the Web server to look for a program stored in the cgi-bin directory.

- guesttrack—This is the name of the cgi-bin program to run.

- ?—The question mark is the standard separator used to identify input for a cgi-bin program.
- 1234567890ab—This is a typical GuestTrack user ID.
- &—The ampersand separates a GuestTrack ID from the file to be displayed.
- info.htm—The last item in the GuestTrack link is the name of the displayed HTML template file.

Why is the HTML file called a *template* file? We can't have an individual's GuestTrack ID stored in links stored in the HTML file because it would be used by all users. Instead, we need a *placeholder* that shows the GuestTrack software where to insert each user's ID. Compare the GuestTrack link stored in the template file to the GuestTrack link seen by our typical user 1234567890ab:

- Template: <A HREF="/cgi-bin/guesttrack#user _id#&info.htm">
- Displayed: <A HREF="/cgi-bin/guesttrack?1234567 890ab&info.htm">

Notice that the template's placeholder #user_id# is replaced with the question mark separator and the user's actual GuestTrack ID. As you can imagine, the HTML template file must have all links created using this format. If any links use the format of the static link, the user's ID will not be included in the link and, therefore, the session will be broken and the database will not be able to identify the user.

While we just said that every page in a Web site using GuestTrack much have the #user_id# placeholder in every link, there is one exception—the initial home page. The default home page needs to have a special ID, the guest ID of all f characters, in order for non-registered visitors to have an ID before they register in the guest book. This means the default home page needs to have all of its links look like the following:

- Displayed: <A HREF="/cgi-bin/guesttrack?ffffff ffffff&information.htm">

Keep in mind that the directories and program names need to be in lowercase letters. If you decide to use any uppercase letters for file names, then make sure the HREF links use uppercase letters in exactly the same way.

Directory usage for a GuestTrack Web site

The HTML template files need to be stored in a directory called *pages* so that the GuestTrack software can find them. In addition, the graphic image files should be stored in a directory called *images*.

If your Web service provider tells you to put all files at the *top level* within your directory, then a directory listing for your Intermediate Web site will have four items:

1. index.htm—Default home page

2. images—Directory for graphics

3. pages—Directory for HTML template files

4. cgi-bin—Directory for the GuestTrack software

Since pages are actually served to the user by software, references to graphic files (using the <IMG SRC> tag) must be fully specified from your root level (i.e., top level). This is necessary because when the GuestTrack software runs, the relative directory is within the cgi-bin directory, not the document tree of directories (i.e., pages). Compare the tag for the image logo.gif that would normally be used on a static Web site and the tag needed on a GuestTrack site:

• Static: <IMG SRC="logo.gif">

• GuestTrack: <IMG SRC="/images/logo.gif">

One of the differences you'll notice between the static link and the link used in a GuestTrack site is that there is a slash (/) in front of the directory name which tells the Web server to start looking for the image at your root level. The other difference, of course, is that the directory name images is included, as well as another slash (/) to separate the directory and the filename.

Now that we've touched on the differences in directory structure and links between a static Web site and a Web site that uses software to generate Web pages, we are almost ready to start developing the Intermediate Web Catalog. But first, let's take a shopping tour of the Web catalog we'll be building so we'll know what the audience member will experience.

Starting with the Home Page

The first page the typical Web shopper will see is the Home Page with its graphical image and descriptive headline (Figure 9.3). Then, come the links to the various sections of the Web site:

- Company Information
- Ordering Information
- Personalized Shopping List
- Complete Product Index

Since this is our first visit to this Web catalog, we click first on Company Information to learn about the company and general information about the products (Figure 9.4). While we see the links to the Personalized Shopping List and Complete Product List, we decide to learn more about the company's ordering policies so we click on Ordering Information. This page describes which credit cards are accepted, return policies, and other general information (Figure 9.5).

Now that we know about the company, it's time to return to the Home Page and see what else we can find on the Web site.

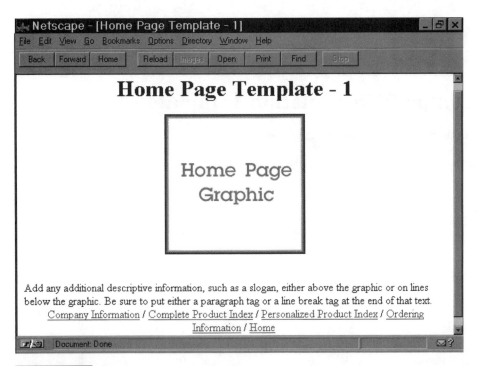

FIGURE 9.3 Intermediate Home Page.

By this time, we've probably become intrigued that a Web site claims to be able to give us a personalized list of products that meet our interest, so we click on the link to the Personalized Shopping List. We see a Web page with form fields asking for name, address, and other information—common on many Web sites (Figure 9.6). But we also see five checkboxes next to five descriptions of product categories carried by the merchant. Since we are interested in two of those categories—the first and third—we click on those checkboxes and click the Submit button.

After a few seconds, the Personalized Product List appears with the customer's name at the top and links to products in the two areas we checked on the guest book, but no links to the products in the other three categories that we didn't check (Figure 9.7).

As we look through the product links we spot one that catches our eye, so we click on that link. Next, the product

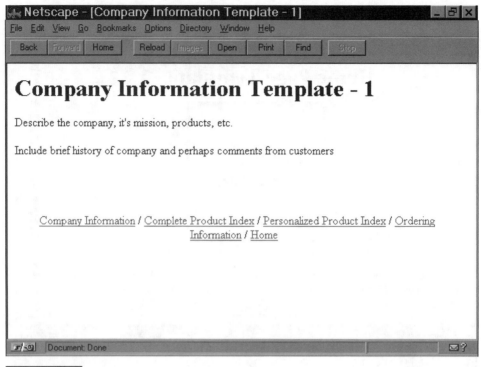

FIGURE 9.4 Company Information template.

page appears with a photograph of the product, description, and a bullet list of features (Figure 9.8). In addition, there is a checkbox offering to add this product to our shopping cart. Since we want to buy that product, we click on the checkbox, then back up to the index of products on our Personalized Shopping List where we see another product we want to purchase, so we go to that product's page, review the description, and click on the shopping cart checkbox.

At this point we're ready to finalize our order and continue our Web surfing, so we click on the Submit Order button to see both of the products we want to buy listed in an order form (Figure 9.9). Since we entered our name and address earlier in the guest book, that information is automatically entered in the form for us. All we need to do is review the quantities of each product (we

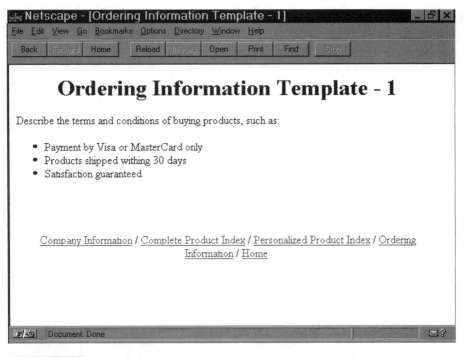

Netscape - [Ordering Information Template - 1]

File Edit View Go Bookmarks Options Directory Window Help

Back | Forward | Home | Reload | Images | Open | Print | Find | Stop

Ordering Information Template - 1

Describe the terms and conditions of buying products, such as:

- Payment by Visa or MasterCard only
- Products shipped withing 30 days
- Satisfaction guaranteed

Company Information / Complete Product Index / Personalized Product Index / Ordering
Information / Home

Document: Done

FIGURE 9.5 Ordering Information template.

change the second product since we need three of them),
enter our credit card information, and click the Submit
button.

After a few moments we see a page thanking us for our
order (Figure 9.10). We could click on the links leading
back to the home page, the complete index of all products,
or other pages in the Web site, but it's time to explore
another Web site.

Personalized shopping on the Web

While our shopping spree was very quick, it nonetheless
illustrates how a potential customer can interact with your
Web site. The Web site flow diagram shown earlier in
Figure 9.1 shows other potential paths your customers can
take through this site—such as first going to the complete

Personalized Product List - Interest Survey

We would like to provide you with information about just the products that you are interested in, so you are invited to answer the following questions about your interests. The following page will present links to products in your interest areas.

Which of the following categories are you interested in? Just check the boxes and we'll give you a personalized list of products that meet your criteria:

☑ Interest Number One
☐ Interest Number Two
☑ Interest Number Three
☐ Interest Number Four
☐ Interest Number Five

Name: Bob Roberts

Title: Automotive Engineer

Company: Accurate Bearing Co.

FIGURE 9.6 Personalized place holder text.

product list, or going through the Guest Book to register and then see the Personalized Shopping List.

Whether your customers go through the Guest Book and receive a personalized view of your products or go around the personalization, they can use the shopping cart system to select products to purchase, and then enter their credit card data to finalize the transaction.

↳ Creating the personalized Web site

The use of a database product such as GuestTrack can be difficult to implement as part of the very first Web site someone creates, so if you are new to the process of

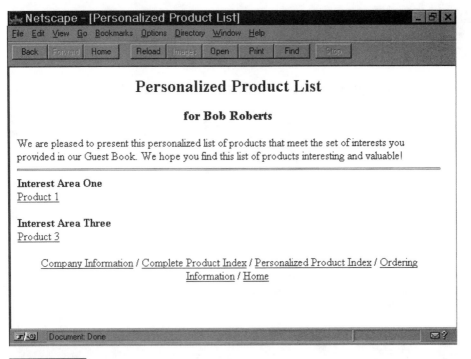

FIGURE 9.7 Personalized Product List page.

developing a Web site, you are encouraged to use the step-by-step instructions in Chapter 8 to create a Basic Web Catalog and gain experience with that before adding the personalization covered in this chapter.

If you have experience creating HTML files and want to start with the Intermediate Web Catalog templates, then we suggest you review Chapter 8 to see how we edit the template files to add descriptive copy and graphic illustration. Then you'll be ready to use the Intermediate Web Catalog templates, which already have the links that use the GuestTrack tags and the special codes for the shopping cart.

If you have experience with the Basic Web Catalog, or you have an existing Web site that uses static Web pages, then you are ready to add personalization to your Web site using the techniques described in this chapter. Basically, the

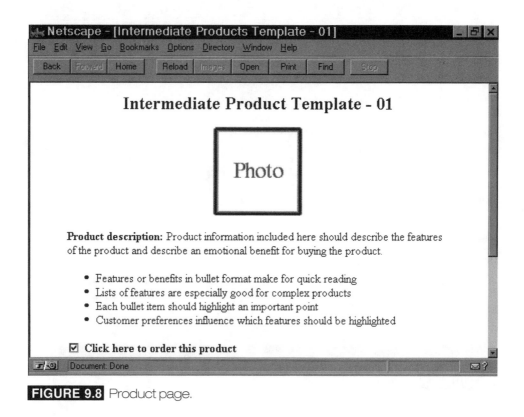

FIGURE 9.8 Product page.

steps to adding personalization to a Basic Web Catalog are as follows.

1. Make a copy of the Home Page file index.htm and name it home.htm.

2. Modify the navigation links in the file index.htm to use the guest ID of fffffffffff.

3. Modify the navigation links in the files home.htm, company.htm, ordering.htm, and any other static pages to use the GuestTrack *placeholder* format for links.

4. Create individual pages for each product (instead of having multiple products on a page, as in the file prod1.htm in the Basic set of templates). Name each

Intermediate Products Order Form

Part	Description	Quantity	Price	Total
SKU-001	Product Name 01	1	25	25
SKU-003	Product Name 03	1	25	25
Total Cost				50

Ordered by:

Name: Bob Roberts

Title: Automotive Engineer

Company: Accurate Bearing Co.

Address: 8514 S. 95 St.

FIGURE 9.9 Shopping cart order form page.

of the product pages prod01.htm through prod99.htm.

5. Create an index page called prodlist.htm that has links to all of your product pages.

6. Create a copy of prodlist.htm called perslist.htm that uses special GuestTrack tags to display the Personalized Shopping List page.

7. Add any desired copy and graphics to these new pages, as well as to the shopping cart pages.

Now that we have a Web flow chart and a general plan of action, let's create a personalized Web site using the software you loaded onto your Web server space in Chapter 7.

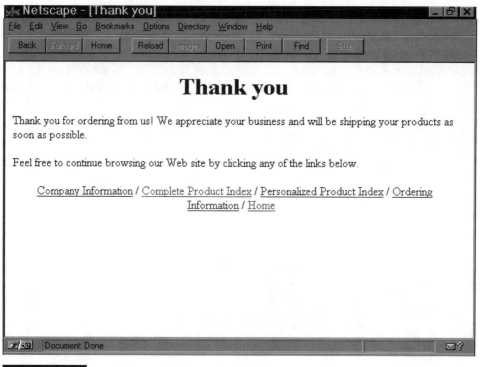

Thank you

Thank you for ordering from us! We appreciate your business and will be shipping your products as soon as possible.

Feel free to continue browsing our Web site by clicking any of the links below.

Company Information / Complete Product Index / Personalized Product Index / Ordering Information / Home

FIGURE 9.10 Thank You page.

Public Home Page

The process to convert your home page index.htm from being a static Web page to being a GuestTrack public home page is one of the easiest parts of this whole process. Before we cover the actual editing of the hypertext links, let's review where this file will be stored on your Web site and why it has links different from all other pages.

In earlier chapters we defined the root (or top) level on the Web server as the location that is the highest level in your directory structure. When a Web user accesses your domain, the Web server automatically looks in your root directory for a file called index.htm (or index.html if you can create long filenames) to use as your Home Page. This is what we call the *Public Home Page*—which is a different file from the identical-looking page named home.htm stored with other GuestTrack templates in the pages directory.

After you create the directories to store images, pages, and programs, and you upload your home page, the directory on your Web server will look something like the following:

```
drwxrwxr-x   3 cliff    users    cgi-bin
drwxrwxr-x   2 cliff    users    images
-rw-rw-r—    1 cliff    users    index.htm
drwxrwxr-x   2 cliff    users    pages
```

Once a user leaves the Public Home Page, the GuestTrack program handles displaying all of the pages seen by the user, which means that when the user wants to go back to your Home Page the program must have special GuestTrack tags and be stored inside the pages directory. This is why there are really two copies of your Home Page: the Public Home Page in the root level and another Home page inside the pages directory.

Before we begin modifying the files you created in your web directory for the Basic Web Catalog, be sure to make a backup copy of the files stored there because the files created in this chapter use a different hypertext link method.

1. Make a copy of the file index.htm called home.htm and save it in your web directory with all of the other files you used in making your Basic Web Catalog site.

2. Open the index.htm template in your HTML editor.

3. Open the file index.htm in the intermed directory on the CD-ROM, then copy the navigation links at the bottom of the file.

4. Change back to your index.htm file and paste the navigation links in place of the links that were there. If you have additional links on the page, add the text "/cgi-bin/guesttrack?ffffffffffff&" in front of the file-

names in all of the links. There are a few things to remember about doing this:

- There are 12 "f" characters that are the guest ID.
- The question mark (?) and ampersand (&) are required to be just before and just after the guest ID.
- The text "/cgi-bin" will be right for practically all Web sites that have been configured properly in Chapter 7, but your Web hosting service may tell you to use a slightly different path to the cgi-bin directory. Examples:
  - Static: <A HREF="company.htm">
  - GuestTrack: <A HREF="/cgi-bin/guesttrack?fff ffffffffff&company.htm">

5. Add the text "This site enhanced for Netscape 2.0" in order to let people with old Web browser software know you are using advanced features. The tags to add to your Public Home Page are:

```
<CENTER>
This site enhanced for Netscape 2.0<P>
</CENTER>
```

As you will see in the description of the product pages, these templates use JavaScript to temporarily store information about the products being purchased in the browser's cookie file.

6. Save the home page file in your web directory as index.htm. Keep in mind that since these links require the Web server to run the GuestTrack software in order to display the file in the HREF link, you will not be able to test these links on your local computer, but will need to upload the file to your Web server for testing.

7. Copy the following files from the intermed directory on the CD-ROM to your web directory on your

hard drive so you will have them to upload to the
Web server:

- guest.htm
- ordfm.htm
- prodlist.htm
- prodpers.htm

The files that should now be in your web directory are:

- company.htm
- guest.htm
- home.htm
- index.htm
- ordering.htm
- ordfm.htm
- prod01.htm
- prod02.htm
- prodlist.htm
- prodpers.htm
- thanks.htm

↳ Static Web pages

For each of the general information static Web pages
you created for the Basic site use the steps below to convert the links to GuestTrack links with the placeholder
#user_id#.

As mentioned above, the template's placeholder
#user_id# is used to tell the GuestTrack software where to
place the user's actual ID in each link as the page is generated on the fly and served to the user. As the template is
processed, GuestTrack replaces the placeholder with a question mark separator and the user's actual GuestTrack ID.

Since we will be creating new product description pages, you do not need to modify the Basic files prod1.htm and prod2.htm—they will be replaced with individual product files. For the files home.htm, company.htm, and ordering.htm, use the following steps to add the GuestTrack placeholder to each link in the file.

1. Open the template file in your HTML editor.

2. Open the file home.htm in the intermed directory on the CD-ROM and copy the navigation links at the bottom of the page.

3. Change back to the file you are editing and paste the navigation links in place of the ones previously in your file. If you have added links to other files, add the text "/cgi-bin/guesttrack#user_id#&" in front of the filenames in all of the links. Again, there are things to be aware of when doing this:

   - The question mark (?) is not used to separate the program name from the placeholder

   - The ampersand (&) is required to be just after the placeholder. Examples:

     Static: <A HREF="company.htm">

     GuestTrack: <A HREF="/cgi-bin/guesttrack #user_id#&company.htm">

⤶ Creating product pages

The next step in creating the Web catalog is to create individual Web pages for each of your products. As you edit the product template file prod01.htm you will see that most of the file is composed of a JavaScript routine that stores information about the product being purchased in the browser's cookie file. This information is used by the shopping cart to display the products in the order form prior to submitting the order to the Web server.

For each product you will be promoting on your Web site, use the template prod01.htm to create a product page. This is done as follows.

1. Open the template file prod01.htm and save it in your web directory with a unique product number.

2. Change the text "Intermediate Product Template" to the actual name of the product being shown.

3. Look for the following tag for the product photograph: <IMG SRC="/images/photo.gif">.

   Replace the graphic file name photo.gif with the actual graphic file name for this product. Be sure to keep the reference to the images directory and the slash (/) characters.

4. Replace the text in the template describing the product with descriptive information about the actual product.

5. Look for the text "SKU-001:Product Name 01:25:5" inside an INPUT form tag that has the product number ("SKU-001") and the product name ("Product Name 01"). Change the product number to the product number you use in your system (or the filename e.g., "prod33"). Change the product name to descriptive text to use in the order form. Change the number "25" to the actual price of the product (e.g., "12.95").

6. Look for the following tags and text: <B>Price:</B> $00.00 each
. Change the price that is displayed to the actual price.

7. Save the file in your web directory.

This file has several lines of hidden form fields that retrieve the user's name, address, and other information needed to fulfill the product order. These lines need to remain intact so the shopping cart software will receive this information.

Complete Product Index Page

This page has a bulleted list of product names and short descriptions that link to the individual product pages. After you have prepared the product pages, use a list of filenames and associated product names and short descriptions to modify the HREF tags so this page looks like the one shown in Figure 9.11. Here's how to do it:

1. Open the template file prodlist.htm.

2. Change the text "Intermediate Product Template" to the actual name of the product being shown.

3. Look for the following tag:

```
<LI><A HREF="/cgi-
bin/guesttrack#user_id#&prod01.htm"> Product 1 -
Short Description</A>
```

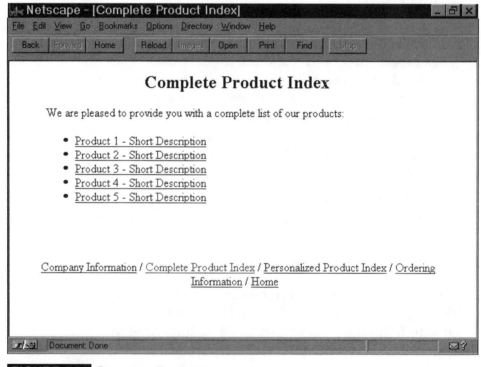

FIGURE 9.11 Complete Product Index page.

Replace the product filename with the actual product filename for this product.

4. Replace the text "Product 1 - Short Description" with the product name and a short description of the product that highlights the benefits of using the product. Add as many links as you need to include all products in the list.

5. Save the file in your web directory.

How to create the Personalized Product List

As we've mentioned earlier, the ability to provide your customers with a page of personalized product information is an exciting advance in Web marketing because it gives you an opportunity to interact with your customer. The Personalized Product List in Figure 9.12 shows how this page looks when the customer does not check the first two interest areas but does check the last three interests.

This page uses a GuestTrack block tag to determine whether to display a block of text based on the value of one of the interest area variables in the profile database. One of the sets of five block tags in the template looks like the following:

```
#user[int1|block|ifchecked]#
<B>Interest Area One</B><BR>
<A HREF="/cgi-bin/guesttrack#user_id#&prod01.htm">
Product 1</A><BR>
#end_block#
```

Let's step through each of the five lines that make up this set of tags and text. The first line can be read as follows: "Display the following block of text if Interest Area #1 was checked." The second line has the name of the interest area in bold type. The third line has an HREF link to a product in this interest area, and the fourth line

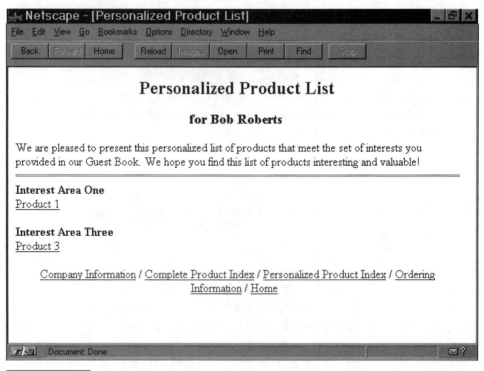

Personalized Product List

for Bob Roberts

We are pleased to present this personalized list of products that meet the set of interests you provided in our Guest Book. We hope you find this list of products interesting and valuable!

Interest Area One
Product 1

Interest Area Three
Product 3

Company Information / Complete Product Index / Personalized Product Index / Ordering Information / Home

FIGURE 9.12 Personalized Product List page.

has the text displayed to the user as part of the link. Any number of lines of text and links can be included in a GuestTrack block. The fifth line has a special GuestTrack tag that ends the current block.

The steps to editing each of the blocks for the interest areas are as follows.

1. Open the file prodpers.htm.

2. Edit the name of the Interest Area to be the actual name of the product category used.

3. Add as many HREF links and product names (and short descriptions) as needed.

4. Make sure the end of block tag #end_block# appears at the end of each block and before the beginning of the next block.

5. Save the file in your web directory.

 Guest Book

The Guest Book file guest.htm will operate without any modification. However, you may want to customize the text that describes the personalization so it better fits your target market. For instance, you may want a more detailed description of the interest areas used to create the Personalized Product List, or you way want to delete the credit card field (allowing the customer to enter that information after selecting products).

Customizing the Order Form

The file ordfm.htm is a template file used by the shopping cart software to create an order form that lists the products in the shopping cart. The template includes two spe-

Netscape - [Intermediate Products Order Form]

File Edit View Go Bookmarks Options Directory Window Help

| Back | Forward | Home | | Reload | Images | Open | Print | Find | Stop |

Intermediate Products Order Form

Part	Description	Quantity	Price	Total
SKU-003	Product Name 03	1	25	25
SKU-001	Product Name 01	1	25	25
Total Cost				50

Ordered by:

Name: Bob Roberts

Title: Automotive Engineer

Company: Accurate Bearing Co.

Document: Done

FIGURE 9.13 Order Form page.

cial GuestTrack tags that must be placed correctly for the shopping cart system to work. These are the #insert _javascript# tag (which is placed in the HEAD section of the document) and the #insert_order_table# tag (which is placed inside the form tags).

You can change the general format of the page, but these two special tags must not be moved outside their own areas on the page. When in use, the order form looks like the one in Figure 9.13.

After your customer clicks on the Submit button to approve their order, the information is appended to the orders file stored in the db directory.

Testing the Intermediate Web Catalog

After you have edited these HTML files to work with the GuestTrack software, you will need to upload the files to your Web server account in order to test your files.

Use your FTP program to connect to your server, then create a directory called pages in your root level and upload all HTML files (except index.htm) into the pages directory. You will recall that the Public Home Page file index.htm is stored in the root level. After you have uploaded your files, be sure to test each page to ensure that they display properly that each link works properly and that the catalog prices and descriptions are displayed accurately. And, of course, check that the orders file has stored all of the information entered by your customers.

Summary

The Intermediate Web Catalog uses a number of features that can help you personalize the presentation of your catalog and take advantage of technical features not found on most other Web sites.

The personalization you provide will be appreciated by your customers as you add products and categories of products. As you increase the scope of your Web site to include news and other general information in which your customers will be interested, you can use these personalization features to help customers sort through that information as well—and continue to build your online relationship.

Once the size of your catalog approaches a few hundred products, maintaining that size Web site will start to seem like an overwhelming task. That's when you need to upgrade your online catalog by using a database to store product information. That's the topic of the next chapter in your quest for success on the World Wide Web.

CHAPTER TEN

BUILDING YOUR ADVANCED WEB CATALOG

Marketing products on the World Wide Web presents merchants with many challenges, including the challenge of creating and maintaining product pages that describe and show products accurately and effectively.

As your catalog grows, so does the task of adding and updating products. When there are several hundred products in the catalog, the regular maintenance of several hundred Web pages becomes a chore. A better approach must be found, such as using database software to manage the data and automatically format the HTML pages.

The software included with this book is designed to store product information and create Web pages on the fly using a template to format the data into an HTML page.

The Advanced Web Catalog that you will create in this chapter uses the GT/Catalog Light software that builds on the catalog in Chapter 8 that uses GuestTrack Light. GT/Catalog uses a database file called products.db to store and serve data about your products according to a template file. The customization of GuestTrack tags in Chapter 8 was limited to formatting the personalized product list, so we didn't go into detail about how to customize GuestTrack templates. However, customization of the product template pages used in the Advanced Web Catalog will require that you understand how to retrieve data from the GT/Catalog database.

If you have never worked with database software, then you should understand two terms used to refer to the two key parts of a database: *records* and *fields*.

A database is made up rows of data called *records*, each of which is composed of several types of data, called *fields*. In Figure 10.1 you can see how a spreadsheet's rows and columns resemble a database's records and fields.

Each row in Figure 10.1 is a database record with fields of information typically found in a personnel database. The fields included are actually a few of the fields used in the GuestTrack user profile database in Chapter 9. Each field across the record has a name used to refer to the particular item of data for that person. The field names

Record #	Name	Address	Phone	Interest #1
001	Bob Smith	1234 E. 56 St.	555-333-4444	y
002	Sam Spade	84 E. Main St.	555-321-4567	n
003	Peggy Kernahan	123 N. Evergreen	555-876-5432	y
004	Mary Main	4341 S. 129 E. Ave.	555-859-5619	y

FIGURE 10.1 Records and fields in a database.

included in the figure are record, name, address, phone, and int1.

Every database system has a specific format for retrieving data from the database and a specific format for storing data in the database. Since the GuestTrack system always knows the ID of the current user, the only information needed in a GuestTrack database tag is the name of the database and the field name:

```
#DATABASE[FIELD]#
```

For instance, to retrieve the name and phone number from the user database and insert those fields of data into an HTML page that thanks them for their order, you would use the following tags:

```
<HTML>
<HEAD>
<TITLE>
Thank You
</TITLE>
</HEAD>

<BODY>
<H1>Thank You</H1>

We appreciate your order. We have the following
information on file for you:<P>

Name: #user[name]#<P>
Phone number: #user[phone]#<P>

</BODY>
</HTML>
```

↳ The GT/Catalog Light system

Now that you have an orientation to databases and how the GuestTrack database system is used to retrieve fields of data from the user database, it will be easier to work with the GT/Catalog Light system and its product database.

The GT/Catalog Light software system consists of several programs that run on the Web server to help you build a product database and create product pages on the fly as the user selects pages to view. As we've said earlier in this chapter, the Web pages displayed to the user are not actually stored on the server as individual HTML files, but are created using templates that specify where fields of data from the database are to be inserted in the format.

Let's cover the basic functions of each program so you'll have an overview of the components of GT/Catalog before we get into the specific uses of these programs:

- gt-cat—displays product information from the product database using an HTML template

- editprod—edits product information in the product database

- indexbuilder—creates an HTML file with links to each product so you can make index files for the Web site

- delprod—marks a product as *deleted* so it will not display

- makeadm—authorizes a GuestTrack ID to run administrative programs

The following sections of this chapter show you how to use each of these programs to create your Advanced Web Catalog.

Becoming the administrator of your product database

The GT/Catalog system is designed to allow only administrative users to edit and delete data in the products database, so it is very important that you use the following steps to authorize your GuestTrack ID. In addition, you should follow the security steps recommended to keep others from becoming administrative users and altering your products database.

The general process of becoming a GuestTrack administrative user, and restricting others from gaining administrative access, is to run the makeadm program with your GuestTrack ID, then remove the makeadm program from your Web server.

Since GuestTrack IDs are generated individually, we cannot show your exact ID in the examples below, so we will use a demonstration ID of "1234567890ab." Just remember to use your own ID in place of this demonstration ID.

In the following example, we assume that your Web provider uses a path to the cgi-bin directory, as we've shown throughout the book, and that the installation of the GuestTrack software that you did in Chapter 7 was successful. For the purpose of these examples, we'll assume the address for your Web site is www.domain.com. Therefore, you would use the following URL to run the makeadm program to become an administrative user: http://www.domain.com/cgi-bin/makeadm? 1234567890ab.

After you have run the makeadm program, be sure to delete this program from your Web server account so other people cannot run it.

↳ Entering product information

The general process of entering product information into the GT/Catalog database is as follows:

- Run the program editprod.
- Select a blank entry.
- Enter product information, product photograph file name, and so on.

As the administrator for your GuestTrack system, your GuestTrack ID is permitted to run the editprod program (as well as the delprod and indexbuilder programs). As part of the security for the system, there is no HTML page on the Web server with links that include your ID. This prevents unauthorized people from attempting to use it to alter your product database.

It also means you will need to manually create bookmarks (or *favorites* if you use a Microsoft browser) to have quick access to these administrative programs.

Creating a bookmark for editprod

You saw the general format of the GuestTrack administrative URL when you authorized your ID to run these programs. Since you will be running the editprod program often, you will find it convenient to make a bookmark with your administrative ID. Therefore, you should open the bookmarks window, select INSERT BOOKMARK, and manually enter the following URL to run the editprod program: http://www.domain.com/cgi-bin/editprod? 1234567890ab.

Entering product information

The next step is to enter a few products and then display the product pages. The catalog software used in this chapter has been configured to use the following fields:

![Edit Product Information form screenshot]

Netscape - [Edit Product Information]

File Edit View Go Bookmarks Options Directory Window Help

Back | Forward | Home | Reload | Images | Open | Print | Find | Stop

Edit Product Information

SKU:

Product name:

Short Desc:

Price (ex: 9.99):

Photo file path:

Description:

Document: Done

FIGURE 10.2 Product editing page displayed by editprod.

- sku—product number (also called "Stock Keeping Unit")

- product—name of product (e.g., "Award Clock")

- short-desc—short description of product (e.g., "Award plaque with clock and stand")

- price—price to Web customers of the product (e.g., "9.95")

- photo—path and filename of product photo (e.g., "/images/clock999.gif")

- description—lengthy description of the product (up to 300 characters)

When you run editprod you will see the Web form shown in Figure 10.2 that has blank fields for each of these database fields.

The steps to entering data with editprod are as follows:

1. Run editprod. An index page will be displayed with links to each of the 400 product records in the database.

2. Click a link to select a product record to edit.

3. Enter product information into the fields on the screen.

4. Click the Edit Product button to store the product information in the product database.

After you edit a product record, editprod displays the updated product index so you can select another product record to update.

After you have updated the product database, you will want to run the indexbuilder program to generate a page of links to product pages. The output of indexbuilder is an index page for your Web catalog, which is described in the next section.

↳ Creating a Product Index

Just as you need to create a bookmark to run the editprod program, you will need to create a bookmark to run the indexbuilder program.

Creating a bookmark for indexbuilder

Once you have a bookmark that includes your GuestTrack ID, it's easy to copy a bookmark, paste a copy into your bookmarks list, and change the program from editprod to indexbuilder so that you have a bookmark that looks like the following: http://www.domain.com/cgi-bin /indexbuilder?1234567890ab.

Creating an index file

One of the key elements to a successful Web site is making it easy for customers to find the products in your catalog that interest them. As you saw in Chapter 9, index pages with links to products grouped by category or interest area provide customers with an easy way to quickly locate specific products.

When you are dealing with product pages that are actually records in a database, it becomes more complex to identify just which products are associated with which database records. This is where the indexbuilder program can help because it creates an HTML file that is sorted on SKU or product name. Once you have an HTML file with links to all of your products, it is easy to add category labels to create one or more Web pages that help customers navigate through your catalog.

The indexbuilder program uses the Web form in Figure 10.3 to display the sort options available.

Netscape - [Build Product Index Page]

File Edit View Go Bookmarks Options Directory Window Help

Back | Forward | Home | Reload | Images | Open | Print | Find | Stop

Build a Product Index Page

Please specify the field to sort on: sku

Please specify the path to the template page to use in generating the product index page:

indxtmpl.htm

Please specify the path of the file to create, in the page directory:

prodindx.htm

Generate Index | Reset Options

Document: Done

FIGURE 10.3 Index creation page displayed by indexbuilder.

The steps to creating an index file are as follows:

1. Use your bookmark to run the indexbuilder program.

2. A Web page will appear asking you to select a sort field, either SKU or Product Name.

3. Enter a filename for the index. You will see that the field automatically recommends the filename prodindx.htm.

4. Enter a filename to use as a template in generating the index file. It automatically recommends the filename indxtmpl.htm.

5. After the index file has been created, use your FTP program to copy it to your personal computer for any additional editing.

When you view the HTML source for the file created by indexbuilder you will see that it has created HREF tags around text that includes the product name and short description. The HREF tags use the GT/Catalog format, which is slightly different from the GuestTrack format of tags:

GT/Catalog   <A HREF="/cgi-bin/gt-cat?12345 67890ab0001111">

Here is a description of each component of the GT/Catalog link:

- /cgi-bin/—This tells the Web server to look for a program stored in the cgi-bin directory.

- gt-cat—This is the name of the cgi-bin program to run.

- ?—The question mark is the standard separator used to identify input for a cgi-bin program.

- 1234567890ab—This is a typical GuestTrack user ID.

- 0001111—The last item in the GT/Catalog link is the record number in the products database.

In keeping with the Web site flow diagram used to create the Intermediate Web Catalog in Chapter 9, two index files are needed: one that lists all products and one that is personalized by interests used in the catalog you developed in Chapter 9.

Using the page of links created by indexbuilder, you can create an index page called prodlist.htm that has links to all of your products. Then, create a copy of prodlist.htm called perslist.htm and paste into it the tags that control the display of categories based on the user's interest areas.

Formatting the Product template page

Now that we've entered product information into the products database and created index pages that link to individual products, we turn our attention to the product template page.

The general steps to creating the template file used by GT/Catalog to format product pages (product.htm) are as follows:

1. Copy one of the product pages used to create the Intermediate Web Catalog (such as prod01.htm) into a new file called product.htm.

2. Replace the actual product information in the file with special GT/Catalog tags that retrieve information from the product database.

You'll notice that throughout this process of creating each of these three types of Web catalogs, we have used different filenames for the product pages. We have done this to reduce the potential problem of upgrading a catalog that may be live on the Web. In other words, your product.htm template file can be tested while your static product pages (e.g., prod01.htm, etc.) are still being viewed by customers.

Modifying the product page template

As you edit the template file product.htm, remember that most of the file is composed of a JavaScript routine that stores information about the product being purchased in the browser's cookie file. This information is used by the shopping cart to display the products in the order form prior to submitting the order to the Web server.

After creating the file product.htm in the next steps, you will have an HTML file that resembles Figure 10.4 which includes all of the GT/Catalog tags to retrieve product data and display a product page on the fly.

The steps in modifying the product.htm file are as follows:

1. Open a product file in your HTML editor (e.g., prod01.htm) and save it in your web directory using the filename product.htm.

2. Change the actual name of the product being shown to the GT/Catalog tag #product[product]#. When a customer clicks on a product page link, GT/Catalog will retrieve the database record for the product number specified in the link and replace the tag with the actual product name.

3. Change the tag for the product photograph that looks like <IMG SRC="/images/photo.gif">, and replace the path and filename with the GT/Catalog tag #product[photo]#. This tells GT/Catalog to retrieve the path to the product photo and insert it into the IMG SRC tag.

4. Replace the actual text describing the product with the tag #product[description]#.

5. Look for the text used in the shopping cart system that looks like SKU-001:Product Name 01:25:5, and

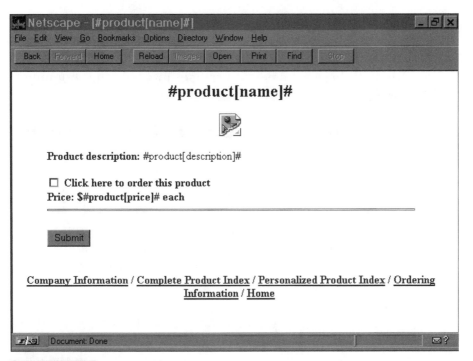

FIGURE 10.4 Product template file product.htm with GT/Catalog tags.

replace it with the following combination of tags that retrieve the product number, name, and price: #product[sku]#:#product[product]#:#product[price]#:0.

Be sure to keep each GT/Catalog tag—from beginning pound character (#) through the ending pound character—on the same line, and do not allow your HTML editor to word wrap any part of it to a second line. In addition, this entire line of shopping cart code needs to be on a single line with no word wrapping.

6. Look for the text and tags used to display the price to the customer that looks like <B>Price:</B> $00.00 each
, and replace the actual price with the tag #product[price]#.

7. Save the file in your web directory.

This file has several lines of hidden form fields that retrieve the user's name, address, and other information from the profile database needed to fulfill their product order. These lines need to remain intact so the shopping cart software will receive this information.

Creating a bookmark for gt-cat

You will find it helpful for testing purposes to create a bookmark that runs the gt-cat program to create a complete index list of active products in the database. As with the other administrative bookmarks you've made, copy one of the bookmarks with your GuestTrack administrative ID, paste a copy into your bookmarks list, and edit the program name to be gt-cat so that you have a bookmark that looks like http://www.domain.com/cgi-bin/gt-cat?1234567890ab.

When you run gt-cat using this bookmark (i.e., without a product number after your ID) it will generate a complete index of all active (non-deleted) products in the database. You can display any product by clicking on its link. This is a helpful testing technique when you have just updated product information but are not yet ready to create a new master index page.

Deleting a product

The GT/Catalog Light system has been configured to reserve database records for up to 400 products, but you may need fewer than this maximum, and you do not want your index pages to have links to blank records.

The process of deleting product records (actually marking them as inactive) is to use the delprod program to specify which active product record should be marked as inactive.

As with other administrative functions, we will create a bookmark so you can easily access the program using your administrative ID, then we will run the delprod program.

Creating a bookmark for delprod

Create one more bookmark by copying one of the existing GuestTrack bookmarks that has your GuestTrack administrative ID, paste a copy into your bookmarks list, and edit the program name to be delprod so that you have a bookmark that looks like http://www.domain.com/cgi-bin /delprod?1234567890ab.

Deleting a product with delprod

When you run delprod using this bookmark it will generate a complete index of all active (non-deleted) products in the database. You can delete any product by clicking on its link. The program will display a page asking for confirmation that you want to delete the product. After you confirm the deletion, that product record will be marked as inactive and the product information stored in the database will be deleted. This blank product record is then

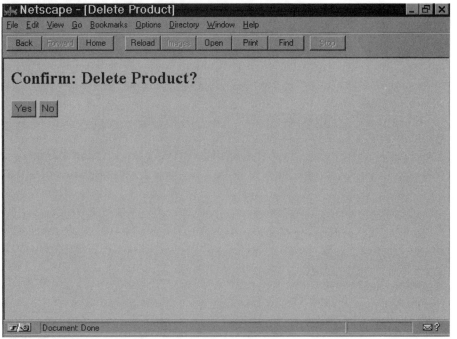

FIGURE 10.5 Product deletion page displayed by delprod.

available for you to add new product information with the editprod program.

When you run delprod you will see the Web form shown in Figure 10.5 that asks for confirmation that you want to delete this product record.

Summary

The process of creating a product information database is relatively simple—but very powerful. As you become accustomed to editing product information in a database and you experience the joy of updating only one HTML template file—instead of hundreds of static Web pages— you will have a more accurate catalog and more time for the other aspects of managing a Web catalog operation.

**EXPERIENCING PROBLEMS?
WE HAVE HELP FOR YOU!**

If you experience problems using the GuestTrack software, or just feel you need a specific question answered, you are encouraged to read the online Frequently Asked Questions (FAQ) at the Online Marketing Resource Library (http://www.allen.com/cookbook).

We realize that the world of Web servers can be confusing, so this list will have as many answers as possible.

CHAPTER ELEVEN

WEB CATALOG OPERATIONS AND FULFILLMENT

So far you have learned how to create an attractive and useful Web catalog. Now you will need to make your Web catalog actually conduct business. In addition to having a Web site, a database for your products, and services and/or information, you will need to allow customers to conduct transactions on your Web catalog. GT/Catalog Light will allow you to display product information and take online orders. If you are generating inquiries, you will want to automate the collection and tracking of these leads. If you are selling products and services, you will want to take orders, process payments, allocate inventory, ship orders, and confirm orders with customers. Also, you may want to conduct all or a portion of customer service online. You may need to still use an 800 number for service because some customer issues deserve the human touch.

Web shopping confidence

If you are building a Web catalog business from scratch, you will need to decide if you want to stock products and ship them yourself or outsource the order processing and fulfillment. If you already have a catalog and want to put a Web face on it, you may want to integrate the Web catalog with your existing order and fulfillment system. In either case, you will need to pay special attention to implementing a secure Web order-processing system that gives customers immediate feedback. This will build customer confidence in this new sales transaction medium.

Customers need to feel at least as confident ordering online as they do when they order from a traditional catalog using an 800 number or shopping at a retail store. How Web orders are processed and fulfilled is an important factor in enabling customers to order products online. The way you process orders, provide customers with information about their orders, and handle any customer services issues is extremely critical to the success of your Web catalog.

It is already difficult gaining the confidence of an online consumer of because on their concern over privacy and security, so having a well-implemented order-entry, processing, and fulfillment system will help you make customers feel comfortable in the ordering process. If customers have a satisfying buying experience, then they will come back often. In fact, an easy-to-use and stable order-processing system can be a competitive advantage. Insight Direct is a well-known computer mail-order company that is a leader in conducting online catalog sales. Figure 11.1 shows Insight's online order system.

Insight Direct (http://www.insight.com), a traditional mail-order company that sells computer hardware and software, created its Web catalog in March of 1995. Since it is a technology company, it built its own Web site and then integrated it with their catalog fulfillment system. It focused on keeping the order processing very streamlined

FIGURE 11.1 Insight Direct's online order system.

for the customer. From the time an order is placed to when it ships is approximately 15 minutes. Order entry, inventory allocation, and payment processing and shipping all happen during this time. You can expect to see the order-processing time shorten to real-time, where the customer enters the order and receives confirmation that it has shipped instantaneously.

Build your Web customers' confidence in shopping online. Many Web users are concerned over the security of their credit information and the privacy of their personal information. Educate customers about the security of your system by communicating how your system is secure, how the system meets industry standards for security, how you handle credit card fraud, and how their information is kept secure and private. Some Web sites such as Software.net (http://www.software.net) go to great lengths to make customers comfortable through a very well-designed order-entry process. Other Web sites have encouraged customers to purchase online by using special online promotions.

Overview of Web catalog transaction and fulfillment

There are several steps and systems involved in processing a Web catalog order. When an order is received in the shopping cart, order processing, wherein the order and customer information is sent to the order-processing system, occurs. The Web catalog should be an order-entry system or integrated with one that holds customer, product, inventory, shipping, tax, and other databases so that customers receive immediate information on product availability, pricing, tax amount, and the cost for shipping. This allows customers to receive the same level of feedback as they would receive if they called an 800 number to place an order with a customer service representative. The next step is payment processing (e.g., credit card authorization, e-cash, or PO), and inventory is allocated for soft goods (e.g., information, software code, etc.) or hard goods (e.g., books, apparel, food, flowers). Currently, the availability of real-time credit authorization is limited, but this will be the standard in the future. Until then, processing an order will involve a few extra steps and confirmation. Finally, the order-entry system releases the order to a warehouse to be fulfilled and shipped. An e-mail confirmation is sent to the Web customer. If all goes well, this should be the end of the process. If there are problems with the order, a customer service process will deal with exceptions such as declined credit or some other problem that occurred regarding the availability of an item. The following list outlines the steps and options involved with processing a Web catalog order:

- Web catalog shopping cart

  - The order-entry system—secure Web commerce servers that provide order-entry and inventory management capabilities

  - Integrating with existing order-entry system—solutions to allow the Web catalog to send order data to an existing system

- Processing and fulfilling the Web order

  - Processing options

    - Manual processing—orders can be processed either by actual persons, which does provide a way to handle a low volume of orders, or by testing a system before it is introduced to the Web public

    - Building the order processing system—secure Web commerce solutions that are Web servers capable of handling inventory management, payment authorization, and integration with a shipping system

- Integrating existing order-processing system—middleware software solutions or development of solutions to transmit data between each system and the Web

- Customer service loop

  - Automation of exception processing—system builds report of orders that cannot be processed because of problems such as declined payment authorization and product availability. The system automates the e-mail message.

  - E-mail notifications—can be automated or handled by dedicated customer service personnel.

  - When a human touch is needed—an 800 service number should be available to the customer when service issues are more complex.

  - Handling information inquiries and feedback—handle sales leads like Web orders by putting information into a database or by contacting a manager. You can automate the fulfillment of information or quotes. Inquiries that contain specific product questions should be handled by customer service representatives.

Design your Web site to direct customers to the appropriate area for particular information or feedback. Make specific e-mail addresses for each activity instead of one e-mail for all inquiries or comments. For example, have a Feedback button for customer suggestions; have a For More Information About button for inquiries and give buttons for each product or category of products; have an Ask an Expert button for specific questions; and have a Have a Sales Representative Contact Me button for inquiries. Each button will have its own database and routing process if there are dedicated areas for each need, or even if it is just a one-person operation. This will be discussed further in the customer service section of this chapter.

Typical flow of a Web catalog order

Most of the current Web catalogs allow customers to place orders, but are only beginning to provide the interactivity or order-processing capabilities of traditional catalog systems. Much of the technology and know-how needed is still very new. However, solutions are rapidly being developed and implemented. Web catalogs should provide the same or better customer interaction as when a customer calls an 800 number to order products. Following is the flow of a typical call into a traditional catalog call center.

1. Customer service representative (CSR) greets customer.

2. CSR enters customer and payment information, including the source of the call (key code).

3. CSR enters items being ordered.

4. CSR informs customer of availability of items in/out of inventory.

   • CSR asks customer if they would like to back order

      • Customer back orders, partial ship option

      • Customer chooses not to back order, order modified

5. CSR cross-sells specials, complemetary products, services, etc.

6. CSR gives customer an order number.

7. Several order-processing and fulfillment steps occur including processing credit card or PO, inventory allocation, and processed order forwarding to fulfillment and shipping systems using a catalog order-processing system.

Web catalogs should provide the ability to exchange information with the customer and the order-processing system. This interaction builds a relationship with a customer and minimizes the problems that can occur without the interaction such as accurate product, pricing, and availability information. Informing customers about the availability of an item, special offers, complementary products, or an item substitution for a discontinued product in a single Web transaction is provided by a small percentage of Web catalogs today. What is possible is allowing a customer to enter an order and receive later notification by e-mail whether or not their order was completely fulfilled, including the authorization of payment, and whether or not the item was shipped. The following list shows the flow of a Web catalog order and the interactivity needed using GT/Catalog Light.

1. Customer places Web order into a shopping cart on a secure Web server, which is a holding place for part numbers, pricing, shipping weights, etc. Customer receives immediate message telling him or her that there is a special offer on a popular product or using purchase history, alert them of a new product that fits their interest.

2. Customer enters payment information and submits order. Web displays order and payment information (e.g., credit card, P.O. number, special online account number, digital cash) to customer. Customer reviews and re-submits or has the option to modify the order and re-submit.

3. A Thank You Web page is displayed to customer.

4. Catalog order/entry system processes the order: inventory is allocated and payment processing occurs.

   • If credit is declined or there are any problems with product availability, an e-mail can be sent to the customer. The e-mail notification can aprise the customer of back-order situations, discontinued products with alternative offerings, etc. The customer can send a reply e-mail with changes, or they can call a customer service representative.

5. Fulfillment and shipping system processes order and confirmation of order is e-mailed to the customer, with order number and instructions to contact customer service by e-mail or phone number if there is a problem. The e-mail process can be handled manually or with an automated process. If a problem occurs, a separate service process will occur using e-mail. This may require the human touch.

6. Package is shipped (or electronic media/information is delivered via e-mail or other electronic method), and another confirmation is e-mailed to the customer.

Currently, the interaction points between the order system and the customer vary among Web sites because of the availability of technology. When designing the order-processing and fulfillment process, draw a diagram that shows the points of interaction with all people and systems. If you are starting from scratch, you will need to work with all external companies and/or internal personnel involved to design the back-end order system, which includes your Internet service provider, payment processor, fulfillment, and shipping information.

The Web order system can be set up to notify customer segments or individual customers with personalized e-mail notifications of new product offerings, special offers, news, and more. All of this can be automated by using databases and building logic that handles each segment or customer in a personalized way. Plus, it will be a critical process for getting people back to your Web site to visit and place orders often, much the same way you frequently mail catalogs or direct mail pieces to your customer base. The personalization concept will be discussed further in Chapter 13.

↳ Web order processing and fulfillment options

Once you have built your Web catalog using the GT/Catalog Light software on this CD and your Internet service, now you need to set up order processing and fulfillment. Whether you are starting from scratch or have an exisiting catalog that you want to make available online, you have many options to process, fulfill, ship, and manage orders. You can do it all yourself within your organization, or you can outsource everything except the development and maintenance of the product/service catalog and customer information. This section outlines your options for setting up catalog operations depending on how you want to run your Web catalog business. No matter which option you take, you will need to do the following first.

1. Learn about the Internet and the Web. Research other Web sites and your competition.

2. Establish objectives and outline a Web business plan.

3. Buy hardware and software for Internet access and e-mail (at minimum).

4. Purchase a phone connection.

5. Set up an account with an Internet Service Provider (ISP). The service you need will vary according to what option you implement.

6. Set up a merchant account with a credit card provider and a payment processor.

7. Take care of the legal requirements for doing business, copyrights, and trademarks.

8. Plan and design your Web site.

9. Build your GT/Catalog templates and databases.

These are the basic steps to begin setting up shop on the Web. Do not hesistate to ask questions of your Internet partners to better understand how to run your Web catalog smoothly. Other steps vary for each Web catalog operations option.

Starting from scratch, but doing it yourself

Monica Bosserman Lopez, co-founder of the Web site Hot! Hot! Hot! (http://www.hothothot.com), is ecstatic about the results from setting up the Web catalog known as "the Net's coolest hot sauce shop!" A retail store was set up at the same time as the Web store, and while they enjoy the retail shop, they would like to dedicate themselves even more to the Web site. Ms. Lopez likes that the store is open 24 hours a day, but you do not have to physically be there like you do with a retail store. Currently, they process Web orders by hand but have made automating order processing and fulfillment a top priority. Figure 11.2 shows the Web site of Hot! Hot! Hot!.

Steps and resources for "do it yourselfers"

In addition to the necessary steps outlined at the beginning of this section, you will need to do the following.

1. Assemble a team consisting of representatives from information systems (who handles networking and databases), marketing, sales, and customer service. Find or assign a person to be your Webmaster. A Webmaster creates, manages, and updates the Web site. The Webmaster can coordinate the efforts of each area and manage the relationship with your Internet service provider.

2. Buy the hardware and software to set up your own secure Web commerce server, Web authoring tools, and graphics application. You will want to choose Web commerce server solutions that provide

FIGURE 11.2 Hot! Hot! Hot! Web site.

security and databases for inventory, tax, and shipping as well as the ability to communicate with outside systems such as payment processing.

3. Call your telephone service company to set up a dedicated ISDN or T-1 connection between you and your ISP. Get your ISP to talk with you and your telephone company in order to set it up according to the ISP's specifications.

4. Hook up a router to connect the phone line, Web server, and firewall on your external network. The firewall protects your internal network from unauthorized access. The router basically allows different networks, which have different communication protocols, to communicate. This is also called internetworking. You will then set up an internal server protected by the firewall to conduct transactions and house customer, product, and other databases.

5. Develop Web site graphics, templates, and content, and build your GT/Catalog Light template and databases.

6. Upload Web content to your in-house commerce server and test the site for usability and functionality. Have a limited set of customers use the Web site to give you feedback on any problems or impressions about the Web site—what they liked or did not like. Make modifications and have another more limited re-testing of the Web site including the changes.

7. Announce and promote your Web catalog.

8. Update as often as needed or planned.

Have an existing catalog, but want to put it on the Web yourself

If you have an existing paper-based mail-order catalog and want to create your Web catalog yourself, then you will follow the steps above with some modifications. Since you already have graphics, product databases, customer databases, an order processing, and fulfillment and shipping systems, you will integrate them with the Web commerce server. Here are the steps you take to leverage existing systems and resources.

1. Assemble a team consisting of representatives from information systems (handles networking and databases), marketing, sales, and customer service. Find or assign a person to be your Webmaster. A Webmaster creates, manages, and updates the Web site. The Webmaster can coordinate the efforts of each area and manage the relationship with your Internet service provider.

2. Buy the hardware and software to set up your own secure Web commerce server, Web authoring tools, and graphics application. You will want to choose

Web commerce server solutions that provide security, databases for inventory, tax, and shipping as well as the ability to communicate with outside systems such as payment processing.

3. Call your telephone service company to set up a dedicated ISDN or T-1 connection between you and your ISP. Get your ISP to talk with you and your telephone company in order to set it up according to the ISP's specifications.

4. Hook up a router to connect the phone line, Web server, and firewall on your external network. The firewall protects your internal network from unauthorized access. The router basically allows different networks, which have different communication protocols, to communicate. This is also called internetworking. You will then set up an internal server protected by the firewall to conduct transactions and house customer, product, and other databases.

5. Have your information systems group develop programs to integrate various databases and systems. Basically, your existing catalog systems must be able to export and import data so that it can be brought into GT/Catalog Light databases and Web orders can be brought into your order-entry system. GT/Catalog can be configured so that order data can be sent via e-mail and imported into your order-entry system. Your systems team can also write a program that can e-mail the Web buyer a confirmation of their order including items ordered, order total including tax, shipping method, order number, and other messages for customer service or even marketing. These systems should allow the movement of data between different systems.

6. Modify current graphics and photographs for use on the Web, configure GT/Catalog Light database and template, and enter/paste/import product data.

7. Upload Web content to your in-house commerce server and test the site for usability and functionality. Have a limited set of customers use the Web site to give you feedback on any problems or impressions about the Web site—what they liked or did not like. Make modifications and have another more limited re-testing of the Web site including the changes.

8. Announce and promote your Web catalog.

9. Update as often as needed or planned.

Even though there are many costs associated with building a Web site and catalog yourself, there are many benefits as well. You control the process and the systems, you find additional uses for the Web server such as an Intranet, you have a better understanding of the potential of Web technology, you can add additional Web sites with incremental investments, and you change the Web content instantaneously versus getting on the Web provider's queue with other client's requests. If the cost of setting up and maintaining a Web site is prohibitive, then there are many options to outsource some or all of the activities associated with building a site, managing customer transactions, order fulfillment, shipping, and maintaining the site.

New Pig (http://www.newpig.com) is a company with an interesting name, to say the least. The company is the leader in leak and spill solutions for manufacturing, government, corporations, utility companies, the military, and other institutions. New Pig has sold its products using mail-order catalogs. In 1996, they opened their Web catalog (Figure 11.3). They view it as another way to keep in touch with customers as well as another avenue to sell products. Customers can view the online catalog in two ways.

1. Log in (once only!) and see catalog with prices and can perform online purchases.

2. Do not log in and view catalog without prices for browsing only.

FIGURE 11.3 How traditional mail-order company New Pig processes Web orders.

Once they choose a route, customers can browse the entire catalog or use a search engine to find product information.

If they browse the catalog, customers flip through pages of the online catalog and select products or families of products in which they would like more information. If they use the search engine, customers can type in product names, keywords, applications, product family names, and so forth, to find specific information.

To order products customers click on an icon that adds products to their shopping cart. When they are finished customers click on an icon to view the shopping cart. The shopping cart will show item number, description, price, and so on.

If the shopping cart is ready for order, customers give their name and company name along with order-specific information such as how they wish to be billed or purchase order number. Then they click an icon to submit the order.

Once they submit the order, their name and company name will be matched against a customer information database. If a match is found (if they have logged in to the site at least once before), all the demographic information will come up and the cusotmer will be asked to verify their information (e.g., shipping address, billing address, etc). If no match is found, the customer will be asked to log in and provide information that is needed to place an order.

In the first phase, Web orders went to New Pig as a secure transaction. A dedicated customer service representative checked for online orders. Orders were manually entered into the operational system to be processed, fulfilled, and shipped. The representative who entered orders immediately sent an e-mail acknowledgment of products shipped to the customer. It included ship method, price verification, and estimated arrival time of the order.

The second phase involved tying the Web site into operational systems so that customers could access inventory levels, shipping options, and estimated lead times. The customer then placed the order directly into the New Pig order system themselves.

Want to outsource some or all the functions of Web development, order processing, and fulfillment?

You may be able to do some of the things required to develop and maintain a Web catalog. You can get the assistance of a variety of specialists to help you. Some benefits of outsourcing include: lower cost and time to get online or reliance on the experts rather than trying to learn and understand their business. This way you can focus on your expertise, and it's a good way to test the new Web medium. Eventually you may want to bring the Web in-house.

Outsourcing Web server, design, development, and maintenance

You will want to plan and build your GT/Catalog templates and databases even if you want to use your ISP's secure Web server, and/or have a Web development company design, build, and maintain your Web catalog site. If the Web development company does not create graphics or write copy, you will want to locate computer graphic artists and copywriters that understand the Web medium. There are some companies that have all the staff, resources, and relationships to provide one-stop Web solutions. Here is a short list of resources to begin locating ISP and Web services:

The List	http://thelist.iworld.com
Dan Kegel's List of ISDN ISPs	http://alumni.caltech.edu /~dank/isdn/isdn_ip.html
Providers of Commercial Internet Access	http://www.celestin.com/pocia
Internet Source Book	http://www.internet sourcebook.com
Online Connection	http://www.barkers.org/online

Outsourcing Web order processing and fulfillment

You can set up a Web catalog without carrying any physical inventory. Order processing (call center) and fulfillment services have been available to traditional catalogers. That same business model can be applied to doing business on the Web. It allows you to focus on building an image, forming relationships with customers, selecting products, and providing information via your Web site. It allows you to open shop on the Web without incurring the initial costs of warehouse, order processing, and fulfillment-systems and personnel. It also allows you to offer competitive prices since you can immediately receive the volume advantage for costs such as shipping rates and the average cost of fulfilling the order from the fulfillment service company. Here are a couple of resources and fulfillment service companies with Web specialties:

- Yahoo! search

  http://www.yahoo.com/Business_and_Economy
  /Companies/Marketing/Fulfillment_Services/

- The Electronic Marketplace Fulfillment

  http://www.emrkt.com/fulfill.html

- Interactive Marketing Services (min. 2000
  orders/mo.)

  http://www.fulfillment.com

- AB&C Group

  http://www.abcgroup.com

- Neodata Services

  http://www.neodata.com

Hosting services and Web malls

Hosting services and Web malls are also great ways to
enter the Web marketplace without a large initial investment. They present an alternative savings model—instead
of investing in lots of Web development, you focus on
order processing and fulfillment. This is a good option for
traditional mail-order catalogs that want to establish a
Web presence. You can build your Web catalog using
GT/Catalog and then enlist a hosting service. Another
option is to join an Internet mall. A popular, well-publicized Web mall site can give you an online presence for no
or low cost. Malls will generally charge a percentage of
sales generated by the mall or a fee for a link. Here are a
couple of resources for hosting services and online malls:

- Yahoo! search

  http://www.yahoo.com/Business_and_Economy
  /Companies/Computers/Networking/Online_Services/

- Providers of Commercial Internet Access

  http://www.celestin.com/pocia

ParentsPlace.com | Reading Rooms | Dialog/Chat Rooms

THE MALL @ ParentsPlace.com

Welcome to the ParentsPlace.com™ Mall

The only on-line shopping center designed exclusively to meet the needs of the parenting market.

FIGURE 11.4 ParentsPlace home page.

• Internet Shopping Directory

http://www.shoppingdirect.com/supersites.html

Do some research to locate the hosting service and online mall that best serves you and your customers. Figures 11.4 and 11.5 show two examples of how you can take advantage of the presence of an online mall. One is a Web link, and the other carries products within their mall.

If you have a Web catalog that is related to the family, kids, or parenting, then ParentsPlace (http://www .parentsplace.com) would be a good place to link to your Web catalog site.

Internet Shopping Network (http://www.isn.com) is an online shopping mall for computer products. ISN carries over 35,000 products from 1100 manufacturers—IBM, Microsoft, Texas Instruments, Compaq, and Apple are just

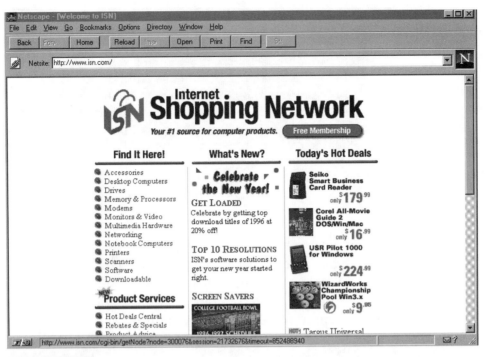

FIGURE 11.5 Internet Shopping Network (ISN) home page.

a few of the manufacturers represented. This would be a good place if you wanted them to sell your products.

There are a couple of Web sites that specifically cater to promoting mail-order/Web catalogs: The Catalog Site (http://www.catalogsite.com) and the Catalog Mart (http://catalog.savvy.com). Both provide the ability for Web surfers to subscribe to paper-based catalogs, but The Catalog Site also provides links to online catalogs, as shown in Figure 11.6.

⮡ Handling Web customer service

Customer service is a standard among all businesses whether they are on the Web or not. Things will and do go wrong when selling on the Web. Your objective will be to make sure you have enough good, accurate information

Your primary objective and budget will help you determine which order-processing and fulfillment option you need. Remember to assemble an in-house team or use your out-sourcing partners to outline a plan to build an order and fulfillment process that gives your Web customers the highest confidence in keeping their payment data private and ensuring that the process is as good or better than what the customer is used to when they purchase from mail-order or retail. Count on the experts to implement the system, but make yourself very familiar with the process and technology.

about your products and your company. You will also want to make customer service policies crystal clear and customer service contact information easy to find. Anticipating the needs of your customers up-front will be key to keeping problems to a minimum.

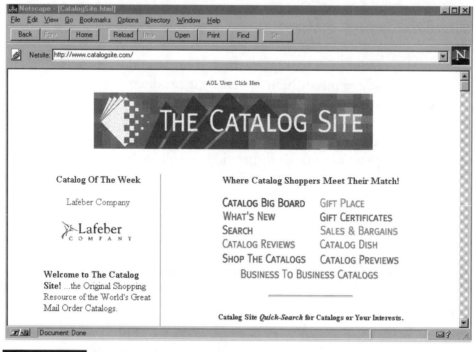

FIGURE 11.6 The Catalog Site.

What to do to make sure things go right

"What is your return policy?" "Will this product work with that product?" "How can this product help me do this?" "Why haven't I received my shipment yet?" "How much does the product cost?" These are all questions received by customer service representatives answering the 800 number. The Web site needs to answer the most frequent questions asked by customers. You can to give them enough information to let them find the answers they need and then reserve customer service and sales personnel for the more complex and unique questions. Figure 11.7 shows Greet Street's easy access Help Center.

> Communicate service policies clearly and link to the policy Web page from as many appropriate sections of your Web site as possible. Since customers cannot exchange dialog with customer service representatives about policies, then it will be important to write them so that they can be easily understood.

Reading your customers' minds: good, accurate, up-to-date, and easy-to-find information

You can never give too much information—if it is extremely well organized and easy to find. Company, product, and service information needs to be accessible and clearly communicated. As discussed in Chapter 2, an easy-to-navigate Web site will give users the instant gratification they are seeking. A good, fast search engine is a mainstay that helps customers find information quickly. One method that has become commonplace on the Internet is use of the FAQ, or Frequently Asked Questions, page. You can create a FAQ for products, company information, how to use your Web catalog, service

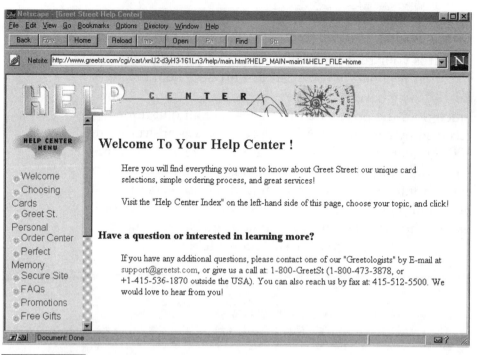

Here you will find everything you want to know about Greet Street: our unique card selections, simple ordering process, and great services!

Visit the "Help Center Index" on the left-hand side of this page, choose your topic, and click!

Have a question or interested in learning more?

If you have any additional questions, please contact one of our "Greetologists" by E-mail at support@greetst.com, or give us a call at: 1-800-GreetSt (1-800-473-3878, or +1-415-536-1870 outside the USA). You can also reach us by fax at: 415-512-5500. We would love to hear from you!

FIGURE 11.7 Greet Street's Help Center.

policies, and so forth. Figures 11.8 and 11.9 illustrate sample FAQs.

If you already have sales/service representatives, ask each of them for the top ten questions customers ask about products, services, the company, and the like. This is a good place to start in designing a useful FAQ.

Answering your customers' questions via e-mail

Even with the best available information, customers will have questions. You will want to structure your Web site to handle different types of questions differently. You can direct all questions to dedicated customer service representatives and they can answer or route them to specific departments or people. Alternatively, you can assign different people or departments to handle particular questions (Table 11.1).

Netscape - [Compaq Online - Frequently Asked Questions]

File Edit View Go Bookmarks Options Directory Window Help

Back Forward Home | Reload Imag Open Print Find Stc

Netsite: http://www.compaq.com/support/faqs/

FREQUENTLY ASKED QUESTIONS   **COMPAQ** Online

Notebooks
    Concerto, Contura, Contura Aero, LTE Elite

Desktops
    Deskpro, Presario, ProLinea

Systems
    ProLiant, ProSignia

HOME   SEARCH   CONTENTS   HELP   COMMENTS

© Copyright 1994, 1995, 1996 Compaq Computer Corporation.
Revised: 31 January 1996

COMPAQ
Online

Document: Done

FIGURE 11.8 Compaq Computers FAQ Web page.

> The Webmaster is not the right person to handle customer issues. The Webmaster should handle problems related to the Web site only.

If you are a few-person company, then you will want to have one or two e-mail addresses for customer service and feedback. If your company is large, it will be more efficient to point customers in the right direction from the start. The most important thing about e-mails is that they be monitored and responded to in a timely manner. The customer should receive an automated response from your e-mail program that thanks them for their feedback or inquiry. Some Web companies include a service FAQ and

FIGURE 11.9 World Wide Web FAQ.

a reminder of where information can be found on the Web site. This e-mail should contain information on how to contact someone or another e-mail address for urgent requests. It should also contain the phrase "Someone will respond to your e-mail within 24 hours. If someone does not respond within this time frame, contact [name] at the following e-mail address or phone number." This will give customers a way to contact someone if they are not responded to within a reasonable time. This is also a service standard that should be maintained. Your customers will hold you to it.

What to do when things go wrong

Things will go wrong. If you already have a customer service department, then you will want to train some or all of the representatives to handle Web service using and writing e-mail. If you are starting from scratch and do not have customer service representatives, then hire one. Your alternative is to do the service yourself, but be prepared to dedicate a fair amount of time to handling inquiries and issues.

TABLE 11.1 You Can Dedicate People and E-mail Addresses By Area or Subject

Question Type	E-mail/Department	Monitored By
General/Company	public_relations@ mycompany.com	Corporate communications
Service Policies/ Issues	service@ mycompany.com	Customer service/ support
Suggestions	feedback@ mycompany.com	Marketing
Product/Service Inquiries	sales@ mycompany.com	Sales
	product_specialist@ mycompany.com	"Technical" sales
Employment	human_resources@ mycompany.com	

E-mail dialog with customer

E-mail communication is different from face-to-face and telephone communications. It is missing the facial expressions or voice intonations that help ensure positive communications with customers. The written word can be misunderstood since it is void of the emotion that occurs on someone's face or tone of voice. You will want to make sure people are trained in written communications, especially on how to write e-mails in a professional, concise, and clear manner. Take care to not communicate with customers too informally using e-mail. Remember, e-mail is equivalent to writing a letter. Also, set appropriate expectations of response time because customers now have your promise in writing. One online resource for writing e-mail communications is the Beginner's Guide to Effective E-mail (http://www.webfoot.com/advice/email.top.html).

Toll-free customer service telephone number

Even though you may only want a Web-based business, you should have a toll-free service phone number to handle escalated customer service issues that need the human touch. Until e-mail customer service becomes a comfortable service medium for the customer, telephone service will be an important option when e-mail conversations have met their limit, or when the customer issue is at a highly critical state from which you may lose their business. If you already have a customer service department a portion or all of the staff could be trained to handle e-mail service.

Other important customer dialog

Web customers are more willing to give feedback on the Web because it is easy and a less intimidating medium. Giving customers ways to communicate with your company online will help build loyal, lasting relationships. Asking customers to rate satisfaction or give their opinions and suggestions can engage customer dialog. A feedback e-mail address, online customer satisfaction surveys, market surveys, and e-mail newsletters are a few dialog methods. Allowing customers to sign up to receive a monthly e-mail that contains newsletter-like information is a way to remind them that your Web site is still out there and encourage them to visit. Appendix A contains resources for how to use an e-mail list server to build, maintain, and send information to an e-mail database.

↳ Summary

How you process Web orders will vary based on how your organization and systems are set up. The key to processing and fulfilling Web orders is to make it easy and satisfying for customers. Otherwise, they will stick with the tried-and-true mail-order method of calling an 800 number and talking with a person. If you are commited to the online market, then you will want make the shopping experience instantly rewarding so customers have confidence in your Web catalog. If you already have order processing and fulfillment systems, you will want to make sure the companies who develop and support these systems understand Web technology and how to integrated the systems. If you do not have an order system, you can build one or you can outsource to a fulfillment services company, hosting service, or an online mall that is equipped to process and fulfill Web orders. Appendix A lists a few resources and organizations that specialize in fulfilling Web orders.

The next chapter outlines how to promote your new Web catalog site. It will allow you to develop an integrated Web marketing plan that incorporates traditional and online promotions and publicity. Since the introduction of a new Web site no longer heralds a lot of attention, you will want to emphasize your Web site's uniqueness.

CHAPTER TWELVE

WEB SITE MARKETING AND PROMOTION

You have done all of your research and created a useful, interactive, and unique Web catalog. You have tested the site and have worked out all of the kinks. Now is the time to introduce your Web site to the world and start selling. You will need to prepare a plan to attract customers—both existing and new. The marketing plan will contain a mixture of traditional and online communication activities. The Web marketing job is not complete without customer satisfaction and retention programs, as well as measuring the impact and performance of Web marketing plans and the Web site itself.

Getting the word out— integrated marketing communications plan

The best way to approach marketing your Web site is to create a marketing communications plan that includes your objectives, a list of all activities and, when they will happen, how much they cost, and how you will measure the success of the overall effort as well as individual activities. Because the Web is still new to marketing and sales, you will want to dedicate a portion of your time and budget to traditional marketing activities such as print or broadcast advertising, direct mail, corporate and employee communications (especially those employees who work directly with customers), and public relations for print and broadcast media. The following is a sample list of marketing activities you can do to announce and promote your Web catalog:

1. Traditional media—print and broadcast

- Marketing communications

   - Announce Web site in letter to existing customers and other company partners. Make sure you communicate the value of the Web since it may be new to them, too.

- Promote site to existing customers with direct mail that outlines special Web-only offers and contests, which will encourage them to give it a try.

- Put Web address (URL) on every communications piece: company letterhead, brochure, newsletter, catalog, promotional items (e.g., T-shirts, pens, memo pads), business cards, customer satisfaction cards, directories, or packaging, annual report. Basically, put Web information on all appropriate customer communications.

- Put Web address in and on any of your advertising and direct marketing: whether print advertising, direct mailers, television, radio, signage, or what-have-you.

- Provide a special announcement on the Web home page introducing the Web site with a feed-back button at the bottom of category pages or on every page. You can replace this introductory message with a general welcome message in a few months.

- Public relations

  - Announce your new Web site to selected print and broadcast media. For example, if your Web catalog sells tools for car repair, then you will want to send your press release to *Car and Driver*, *Automobile*, *Road & Track*, *AutoWeek*, *Popular Mechanics*, and other car magazines. Send and/or e-mail announce-ment information and call editors to explain the significance of your Web site news to him/her and the publication's readers.

  - Send press releases to all constituencies including investors, manufacturers, resellers, industry insiders and analysts, strategic partners, and so on.

- Sponsor events related to your Web catalog business. For example, if your Web site markets and sells wine, then sponsor wine tastings. Make sure this is well publicized (before and after) to the press, customers, and prospects, and on your Web site (including pictures and a story about the event).

- Employee relations

  - Internet—Announce the site to employees, especially those who maintain relationships with customers. Your Web catalog can be a good tool for your employees as well as your customers. Teach employees how to use the Internet, e-mail, and your Web site so they can effectively direct customers to the site. Communicate the value of the Web site as it relates to the customer.

  - Intranet—You may want to create an Intranet to enhance employee communications, provide a two-way communications mechanism, and cost-effectively manage personnel documents.

2. Online media—advertising and PR

- Advertising options and costs

  - Search engines: Home page, category pages, or key word searches are ways to place Web banner advertising. Advertising rates on the Yahoo! search engine range from a few hundred dollars per month for a key word to $20,000/month for its main page.

  - Online publications and other Web sites: There are lots of print and broadcast media with Web sites on which you can buy advertising.

  - Your partners' Web sites: Try to get free links from manufacturers, resellers and other business partners. Advertising on a partner's Web site can be less expensive and yield a higher rate of response.

- Paid sponsorship of contests on other Web sites: This is a good way to launch a new Web site or generate awareness for your Web catalog.

- Public relations

  - Web site registration and announcements and link campaigns

  - Online publications—announce new business and new Web sites

  - Newsgroups announcements and discussion groups.

  - Web site sponsorship—industry and community service

  - E-mail signature

- Online Launch: contest, free stuff, and introductory offers

This list is a summary of activities. The next section shows examples of Web site marketing as well as an in-depth explanation of the new Web advertising and public relations methods.

Design a marketing plan that contains both traditional and electronic media. The Web marketplace and its marketing technology, such as banner advertising and e-mail lists, are still young and should not be your only means of communication. Paper-based marketing and public relations activities will still be key ingredients to getting customers to visit your Web site.

INCREASED WEB SITE PROMOTION IN TRADITIONAL MEDIA

It has become a common occurrence to see companies promote their Web site in television advertising, print ads, radio, brochures, and so forth. Web site promotion in other marketing communications can be as simple as a Web address in small type at the close of Ford Motor Company's magazine ads and is the central theme to all communications by a Web-based business such as Auto-by-Tel.

A *Business Week* survey suggested that more and more companies are building Web sites and promoting them in their advertising (TV, radio, magazines, etc.) and other communications. In Jim Sterne's book, *World Wide Web Marketing* (Wiley, 1995), he discussed a quick, unscientific study by Sunil Gupta of the University of Michigan where Mr. Gupta analyzed ads in the April 17, 1995 issue of *Business Week*. He discovered that 9 out of the 54 display advertisements (17 percent) had the company's e-mail or Web site address. We discovered in the November 18, 1996 issue of *Business Week*, 50 out of the 95 display advertisements (53 percent) had a Web site address. There were some companies that did have Web sites but did not include their URLS in their advertisement. So, although not all companies have caught on to this new marketing strategy, there has been a considerable increase in the number of Web sites listed in print advertisements (Table 12.1).

TABLE 12.1 Ads of Web Information in Business Week

Company	Web Address Placement
Canon	in copy
3M	below logo how to contact information with 800 number
Unisys - 3 ads	below logo how to contact information with 800 number
Acquion	below logo how to contact information with 800 number

Company	Web Address Placement
AMP	with contact information in very small type
Cadence	in copy
Lotus - 2 Ads	in copy
AMD	below logo, relatively prominent, no 800 number
Bell South - 2 ads	in copy
Sun Microsystems	above logo how to contact information with 800 number
Comsat	below logo how to contact information with 800 number
Banco de Brasil	by itself, small
Toshiba	in copy
Ford	below logo how to contact information, no 800 number
Compaq	in copy
Oldsmobile	below logo how to contact information with 800 number
Digital	in copy
Transamerica	below logo, relatively prominent, no 800 number
Ericsson	below picture with other contact info, small type
Auto-by-Tel	prominent (Web-only business)
Acer	below logo how to contact information with 800 number
Sprint - 2 Ads	below logo how to contact information with 800 number
Cadillac	with how to contact information with 800 number
Arthur Andersen	in copy
Fujitsu PC Co.	with how to contact information with 800 number

TABLE 12.1 Continued

Company	Web Address Placement
Imation	in copy
Blue Cross Blue Shield	in copy
NCR	in copy
Buick	in copy
Westin Hotels	below logo how to contact information with 800 number
Motorola	in copy
Vanstar	below logo how to contact information with 800 number
Pagenet	below logo how to contact information with 800 number
Chrysler	in copy
Liberty Mutual	in copy
SAS Institute	below logo how to contact information with 800 number
US Robotics	in copy
UPS	in copy
Lincoln Cars	below picture with other contact info, small type
NEC	in copy
Roadway Express	below logo how to contact information with 800 number
Air Liquide	in copy
Chromatic Research	in copy
JP Morgan	in copy
Chevrolet	below logo how to contact information with 800 number

Auto-by-Tel (http://www.autobytel.com) is a Web-based electronic automobile marketplace that enables customers to find a car to buy or lease (Figure 12.1).

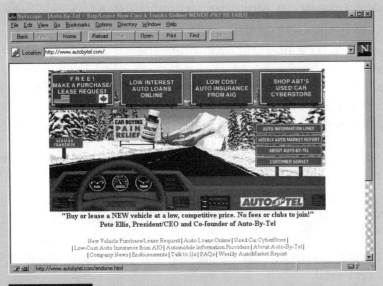

FIGURE 12.1 Auto-By-Tel jingle.

Auto-By-Tel links customers with dealerships as well as with automobile insurance companies. It has based broadcast advertising on its Web site URL address. The advertisment is a jingle that centers around "www.autoby-tel.com." This is an innovative way to promote a Web site address if you are serious about getting users to your site.

More about online advertising and public relations

Since the Web is so different from traditional media, a detailed discussion about the various ways to market and promote your Web catalog on the Web is necessary. You will want to be cognizant of the distinct characteristics of this new marketing medium.

Marketing on the Web is different from traditional marketing methods such as print and broadcast advertising and direct mail. You will want to gain an understanding of how marketing on the Web is different from other marketing vehicles.

Web search engine advertising

Search engines can be a cost-effective way of launching your Web catalog and promoting special Web catalog activities. It can become a regular part of your advertising plan. As stated earlier, advertising rates in general are around $100 per 1000 impressions. An impression occurs when the Web banner ad is displayed. When a user selects the Web banner ad, this is called *click-through*. This click-through is translated into a conversion rate percentage that identifies your response rate, or the percentage of people who viewed the banner ad and actually selected it. In general, the conversion rate of Web banner ads is about 2 percent. This response rate is much like the average response rates achieved in traditional print advertising or direct mail.

Search engines have the capability to display your advertisments to target audiences or segments of the entire Web user base. For example, if your Web catalog sells women's clothing you can select to advertise to only users who search on keywords such as "women," "clothing," "apparel," and other related words. When a user searches on the word, the search results are displayed along with a Web banner advertisement for your Web catalog. This can be an inexpensive way to find your market. Figures 12.2A and 12.2B show some well-designed Web banner ads.

FIGURE 12.2A Amazon.com's banner.

FIGURE 12.2B Cyberian Outpost's banner.

Web publication advertising

As far as online publications and other Web sites are concerned, there are lots of print and broadcast media with Web sites on which you can buy advertising. For example, if you want to place a banner ad on *Time Magazine*'s Web site, it will cost $10,000 per month. *Popular Mechanics*' Web advertising costs $5000-$10,000 per month. ParentsPlace.com is a Web-only publication whose ad rates range from $175 per month to $4000 per month. Most ad rates are about $100 per 1000 impressions (the number of times the ad is displayed). Visit Net Creation's Web site for a list of some advertising rates (http://www.NetCreations.com/ipa/adindex/index.html).

Free links and advertising on other Web sites

As for other Web sites, try to get free links from manufacturers, resellers, and other business partners. Advertising on a partner's Web site can be less expensive than advertising with a search engine or online publication and can yield a higher rate of response. Getting links to your Web site can be a relatively inexpensive or even free way to gain awareness. A link (or Hyperlink) is a graphic or text that a user selects and automatically brings the user to another Web site or section of the Web site they are within. Links from many Web sites can increase traffic to your Web site.

Links from other Web sites fill in the gaps that registering with search engines and directories leave, and these links are the very ones targeted to your audience. Some sites have registration forms you can use to add your site. If not, you can e-mail the Webmaster with information about the Web site and state why it would be a useful link for their Web users and provide exact wording for the description along with the HTML for the link and/or a graphic. Of course, since they are doing you a favor be professional and kind in your request e-mail. It also helps to approach a person at the organization to request such a link. This will help you establish a relationship, and this person may be able to influence the decision to link to your Web site. Many sites will ask you to link to their Web site in exchange, so make sure you are willing to do this before getting the other site to commit. The following is a list of types of links:

- Links from complementary Web sites and business partners
- *SuperSites* are Web sites, according to Steve O'Keefe in his book *Publicity on the Internet* (Wiley, 1996), that are special-interest Web sites that contain a huge list of related Web links. Generally, these sites are very popular resources for a specific group of people that are representative of your market. You will need to spend time locating these resource sites. For example, BizWeb is a popular business link resource directory

FIGURE 12.3 BizWeb—A SuperSite of business links.

Netscape - [Insight/Manufactures Listings]

File Edit View Go Bookmarks Options Directory Window Help

Back For Home Reload Ima Open Print Find Stop

Location: http://www.insight.com/web/1maufact.html

Special Offers
Accessories
Computer Systems
CD-ROM Drives
Controllers
Hard Drives
Input Devices
Internet
Memory
Modems
Monitors
Multimedia
Networking
Notebooks
PC Cards
Printers
Processors
Power Protection
Removable Storage
Scanners
Software
Tape Backups
Video Cards
Manufacturer Index

Insight's Manufacturer Index

Manufacturers	Categories	
3COM	Networking	
Acer	CD–ROM Drives	
Adaptec	Controllers	
ADI	Monitors	
Adobe	Software	
Andover	Internet	Software
APC	Power Protection	
Arcada	Software	
AST	Computer Systems	Notebook Computers
ATI	Video Cards	

Document: Done

FIGURE 12.4 Insight Direct links its manufacturers.

for companies to provide information about their products and/or services (Figure 12.3).

- Internet Link Exchange (http://www.linkexchange.com) is an Internet advertising network where you can get free links and advertising on other sites that belong to the Internet Link Exchange.

Links and advertising on compatible Web sites is much like advertising in a specialized magazine, which allows you to narrow your marketing focus to those people who are most likely to buy your type of products and services. Figures 12.4 and 12.5 show examples of Web links and advertising.

Insight Direct (http://www.insight.com) is a reseller of software and hardware products that provides an index of manufacturers to allow users to locate the Web site or contact information on the products from the manufacturer.

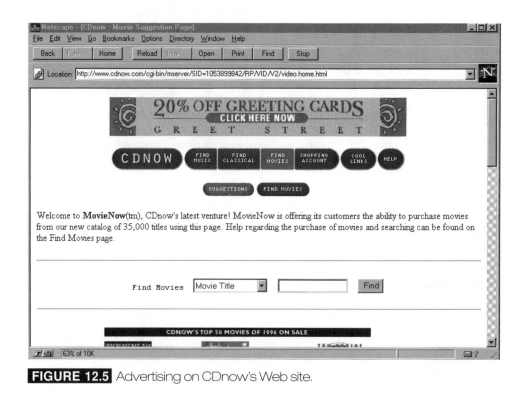

FIGURE 12.5 Advertising on CDnow's Web site.

This is beneficial to both Insight and the manufacturers: Insight can direct users to the manufacturer's site for more detailed information than they want to maintain on their site. The manufacturers benefit from the link because it acts like an advertisement if there is a linked Web site.

CDnow (http://www.cdnow.com) is an online music and video catalog that sells Web banner advertising on its site (Figure 12.5). The advertisers have products and services that would also be attractive to CDnow shoppers. Magazines, music news, and related Web sites are advertised on the CDnow Web site. This is a beneficial relationship to advertisers and CDnow because CDnow can generate revenue selling advertising and the advertiser gets to reach targeted Web users that would also typically buy their products.

Graphical link buttons and banner ads

If you are able to give a Web site a graphical link or banner ads, keep in mind that they should be small and simple. Since you are getting a free service from a site, then you should provide a graphic that does not take up to many computing resources (about 10K). Figures 12.6 and 12.7 are examples of good graphical links.

Web sponsorships and promotions

Paid sponsorship of contests on other commerical Web sites is a good way to launch a new Web site or generate awareness for your Web catalog. In general, these promotions are sponsored by more than one company so it can be a good value. Online contests and promotions get a lot of attention from Web users and online media, which helps increase awareness of the promotion to more people that just Web banner advertising. The purpose of these promotions is to make people aware of your Web site, so make sure that your Web site is ready for a high level of exposure. You can introduce a new Web site or new content and functionality of an existing Web site at the time of the promotion.

Web site registration and announcement services

There are free and paid services to register and announce your new Web site. You will want to take advantage of this low-cost way to get Web users to find your site. At minimum, you want to register your Web site with the search

FIGURE 12.6 Sample graphical links from CDNow's Web site.

Microsoft Internet Explorer N NETSCAPE Now!

FIGURE 12.7 Sample banner links: the ever-prevalent Netscape and Microsoft banners.

engines. If you go to the Yahoo! search engine and enter these words "Web announcement services" and select the category "Computers and Internet: Internet: World Wide Web: Announcement Services" you will get a long list of announcement services. According to Steve O'Keefe in his book *Publicity on the Internet* (Wiley, 1996), you should individually register your Web site with the most important directories and then use a free or fee-based registration service to reach the rest.

Free Services

Submit It! (http://www.submit-it.com) is a free service that allows you to fill out one registration form for your Web site. The service automatically submits the information to about 16 search engines and directories including Yahoo!, Whatsnew on the Internet, Infoseek, WebCrawler, Apollo, Starting Point, ComFind, InfoSpace, Yellow Pages Online, What's New Too!, Metroscope, LinkStar, BizWiz, WebDirect!, New Rider's WWW YP, Nerd World Media, Alta Vista, and Mallpark. Figure 12.8 shows the Submit It! Web site's services.

Other notable freebies include the following:

- Add It! (http://www.liquidimaging.com/liqimg/submit)

- Add Me! (http://www.addme.com)

- AutoSubmit (http://www.autosubmit.com)

- FreeLinks (http://www.freelinks.com)

- Expose Free Web Site Promotion Center (http://www.dev-com.com/~cmg/expose1.html)

- Go Net-Wide (http://www.GoNetWide.com /gopublic.html)

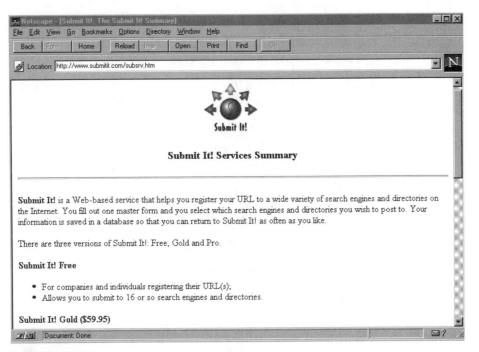

FIGURE 12.8 Submit It! announcement services.

- Multi-Submit (http://users.boone.net/yinon /multisub/default.html)

- SubmitAll (http://www.hometeam.com/addurl)

- NCSA What's New (http://www.ncsa.uiuc.edu/SDG Software/Mosaic/Docs/whats-new-form.html)

- Promote It! (http://www.iTools.com/promote-it/pro-mote-it.com)

As with anything that is free, there is no guarantee and it may take more time that you desire.

So here are some fee-based registration and announcement services that could save you a lot of time:

- Submit It! Gold (http://www.submit-it.com) is a fee-based version of its free service. The current price of $59.95 allows you to submit your Web site to over 300

Web Site Marketing and Promotion

331

search engines and directories. The service is good for one year and allows you to update information, register with new sites, and receive Web support.

- !Register-It! (http://www.register-it.com) will register your Web site to 100 directories for $39.00.

- PostMaster2 (http://www.netcreations.com /postmaster), allows you to submit information about your new Web site to over 400 sites including search engines, directories, what's new, what's cool, media outlets, and over 4,000 interested individuals. It currently costs $500 per Web site submitted.

- WebPromote (http://www.webpromote.com) is a full-service organization that will promote your Web site with directory listing, press release, and targeted promotion packages.

Depending on your time or budget, you may want to do it yourself or outsource some of the announcement work. Figure 12.9 shows a typical registration form reprinted from Mr. O'Keefe's book that will guide you into the information you should prepare before beginning the submission process.

Online media announcements

You can announce a new business and the associated Web site online and announce a significant enhancement or special newsworthly functionality/service you have added to your existing Web site. There are a couple of ways to announce your new Web site to online media and publications:

- Make a list of key Web sites and Web publications. Many print publications radio and television media now have companion Web sites. There are also Web-based sites that provide the same type of information and service as the traditional media's companion sites. You will need to locate Web sites covering news about your type of products and/or services. Make a

Company Name and Address
    Company Name
    Mailing Address
    City, State, Zip Code
    Country
Contact Name, e-mail Address, Toll-Free, Phone, Fax Numbers
    Web site administrator
    E-mail: Webmaster@mysite.com
    Toll-free: 1-800-555-1212
    Voice: (212) 555-1212
    Fax: (212) 555-1212
URL to be used in postings
    http://www.mysite.com
The Title of the Site
    My Site
Categories/Headings
    1. Widget Manufacturers
    2. Widget Industry
    3. Fictitious Products
    4. Businesses
    5. Awesome Web Sites
Keywords for Automatic Search Engines (Limit 10)
    Widget Tools Fake Web Business
Description of Service (10 words or less)
    What's long, smooth, rigid and reliable? Come see our
    Widgets!
Description of Service (25 words or less)
    Widgets are the most versatile of tools. They're long and
    strong, smooth and sleek.
    We make 'em and sell 'em. Come see for yourself.

FIGURE 12.9 Sample Web site registration form.

Your registration program should include monitoring Web index sites, search engines, and key Web sites. Ensuring that your Web site is registered, appears on key sites, and has accurate descriptions of your Web site is up to you. Here is a newsgroup FAQ that is a good summary of how to announce your site on the Web: http://ep.com/faq/webannounce.html.

list of the most important sites to tackle first and then make a secondary list to send or e-mail information. Your first step will be to find the right person to e-mail an announcement by perusing the Web sites or calling the organization. Then, e-mail a news release (see Figure 12.10) with a succinct message in the subject line of the e-mail that will give the editor a quick summary of the news. Editors, especially those on the Web, have very little time and appreciate your making their job easier by getting to the point and supplying all of the information they need. If you search on Yahoo! for magazines, you'll find numerous general-and special-interest publications as well as some of these recognized broadcast media: CNN, National Public Radio (NPR), Public Broadcasting System (PBS), FOX, CBS, or NBC.

• There are several news services that will put your announcement on the newswires. These services may cost a bit more than registration services, but they save you time and reach more media, and can provide full-service public relations programs. Check out these online news wire services: BusinessWire (http://www.businesswire.com), a full-service news wire service that has many examples; PR Newswire (http://www.prnewswire.com); and Global Internet News Agency (http://www.gina.com).

Newsgroup postings and announcements

The Usenet is a place to post messages and exchange information with people who have the same interests. If you post an announcement you are sure to get *flamed*, which occurs when many newsgroup participants publicly criticize and spread bad tidings about you. Just one phrase: "tread lightly." Historically, the Internet was used solely for the exchange of information, and the Web is the commercial side of the Internet. So, when you go to the Internet's tra-

SUBJECT: NEWS RELEASE
Web Site Profile and Tracking Software Tracks Hits
and Customizes Pages
RALEIGH, NC — April 15, 1996 — Allen Marketing
Group has developed a software application designed
to make the World Wide Web (WWW) an interactive,
informative marketing tool for both Web site owners
and members of their audience.
GuestTrack is the first of a series of products
used to monitor, track, and customize a Web site to
meet the needs of today's marketers and Web site
users. The product builds a profile of each individual who registers in a guest book and it tracks
user activity on a set of WWW pages. In addition,
scripts can be developed for a variety of purposes,
such as to create WWW pages "on the fly" based on
a visitor's preferences and to analyze demographic
information given by visitors.
"Since we've worked in the electronic media as well
as in the software industry, it was natural to combine this experience with our years of experience
with the Internet to create a line of products that
Web marketers have been looking for," said Cliff
Allen, president of Allen Marketing Group. "We
developed the GuestTrack series of programs based on
technology we developed a few years ago for the online game market. When the Web came along, we found
that the technology was perfect for developing a
profile of each member of a Web site's audience."
The visitor-tracking process begins when new users
are asked to register, either upon choosing a designated Guest Book link or as a requirement to
access certain parts of a site. New users can be
asked as many or as few questions as desired when

FIGURE 12.10 News release—GuestTrack announcement.

they register in the GuestTrack database.

As the user progresses through the Web pages, GuestTrack logs every Web page displayed to every user so that a marketer can determine exactly which pages are being viewed, for how long, and what pages motivate the user to take action.

Another way GuestTrack can be used is to script Web pages using its database of information about visitors in order to control the material provided to visitors. Scripts can be created that generate Web pages "on the fly" depending on the information given in the profile database. In addition, questions can be displayed throughout the Web site with answers added to the user's profile. Demographic preferences can be as detailed as one wishes by gathering information from several Web pages.

The information in the database includes the click-stream log file of user activity as well as the GuestTrack ID for each site visitor. This gives the marketer complete flexibility to sort, select, tabulate, and report the information that can help make the Web site more productive for the company and more valuable to members of the audience.

The license fee for GuestTrack is $1,000. It runs on all popular UNIX platforms. For more information, contact: Cliff Allen, Allen Marketing Group, Inc., 5540 Centerview Drive, Suite 411, Raleigh, NC 27606; 919-859-5619 phone ; 919-851-2969 fax; http://www.guesttrack.com; cliff@allen.com

FIGURE 12.10 Continued.

ditional sources for exchanging information, you will need to abide by special rules or *netiquette*. The best way to approach newsgroups, which can be a great word-of-mouth

> News releases should contain informative, not marketing-style, copy. The release should be straightforward and state the news clearly. Since many editors receive hundreds of news releases each day, you will need to make it fast and easy for an editor to get the gist of your news. A news release is typically designed to start with a news statement in the first paragraph and become more detailed. It also helps to have quotes from the CEO or business unit manager, customers, business partners, or well-known industry analysts or celebrities.

campaign, is to monitor the newgroups that are related to your business and answer questions for those folks needing information. For example, if your Web site specializes in educational products, you will want to monitor the k12 and misc.education newsgroups. One good newsgroup to post an announcement for your new Web site is comp .infosystems.www.announce. More information about posting an announcement on this particular newsgroup is located at http://boutell.com/info.html.

In order to post to a newgroup you will need to get newsreader software, build a list of relevant news, monitor the newsgroups, and post. When you post, you want to make sure you identify yourself, your Web site, and other ways for newsgroup users to get in touch with your organization. You can also create a signature for yourself to use in e-mails and postings. Finally, there some newsgroups that accept announcements. These newsgroups usually have the ".announce" suffix. Appendix B contains some information on how to announce your Web site on newsgroups.

Some newsgroups give users exact directions on how to post to a newsgroup, which is helpful to the newsgroup moderator and to you when you post an announcement. By following instructions you have a greater chance of getting your announcement posted. Appendix B gives you specific instructions from the news.announce.newusers Usenet newsgroup, but they are good guidelines to refer to when posting to any .announce newsgroup.

Community relations over the Web

Web site sponsorships of industry or community service Web sites help others and help you develop a whole company relationship with your customers. There are many Web sites that need industry and socially responsible partners to help fund them. This is a good way to match the interests of your company with good causes that need funding. Figure 12.11 highlights the American Fidelity's Education World (http://www.educationworld.com) Web site that calls itself "The World's Educational Resource on the Web." This Web site is sponsored by American Fidelity Assurance Company (http://www.af-group.com).

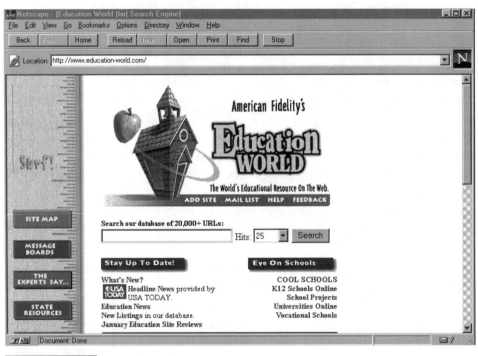

FIGURE 12.11 Education World.

Sponsors are usually the only advertisers and have top billing and links to their Web sites.

E-mail signature

Whether you are posting to a newsgroup, participating in online discussions, or sending e-mails, you'll want to create a special signature that lets everyone know who you are and what your Web site is all about. Figure 12.12 shows the e-mail signature of one of the authors of this book.

↳ Web launch!

Announcing your Web site to world can have greater impact when you tie in promotional acitivities such as contests (e.g., treasure hunts, trivia, quiz, or survey), free stuff, introductory offers, auctions, or special offers for Web users. They can also be lots of fun. These types of events always attract attention. If you have a Web catalog that offers products and/or services for anyone on the Web, then you may want to select a search engine like Yahoo! or other general-interest Web site to promote it. Since the goal is to find customers and capture names for a mailing list (regular or e-mail), then choose Web sites that have Web users who match the profile of your customers. For example, if you sell gourmet food gift baskets, you want to promote your Web event on sites that would reach people who buy these types of gifts such as *Gourmet* (http://www.epicurious.com/g_gourmet/g00_home /gourmet.html), and *Bon Appetite* (http://www.epicurious.com /b_ba/b00_home/ba.html). The Yahoo! search engine can

```
Cliff Allen            cliff@allen.com              GuestTrack —
Allen Marketing Group  919-859-5619                 Web Site Profile
Raleigh, NC            http://www.guesttrack.com    and Tracking
                                                     Software
```

FIGURE 12.12 Co-author's e-mail signature.

allow you to pick certain categories such as food, gifts, shopping, and catalogs.

You want to pick prizes that will appeal to participants and make the contest instructions and regulations very clear. According to Steve O'Keefe in his book *Publicity on the Internet* (Wiley, 1996) there are shared attributes of a great promotion:

- Integrity: A promotion grows out of the product being promoted.

- Appeal: The promotion is irresistible to the target market.

- Scope: The scale is perfectly suited to the product and the audience.

- Timing: The right gimmick at the right time.

- Novelty: The concept has a unique twist to it.

- Preparation: You must be ready to capture the lightning.

The promotion's success will be determined by your measuring the traffic on your Web site. Sales, inquiries, and the size of your customer and prospect database (e-mail or direct mail) are also ways to measure success. Also, monitor any negative or positive feedback to give you an idea of how the promotion is being received.

Absolutely, positively, and right away: satisfaction and retention programs

The Web's benefits of relative ease for locating information and businesses where users do not need to jump in their car and go from store to store or wade through stacks of store circulars to find what they need at a good price also makes it more competitive for Web-based businesses.

Also, it has been stated numerous times that the cost of acquiring a new customer is about five to seven times more than the cost of selling to a happy, loyal customer. Therefore, a Web catalog needs to build a loyal customer base from the day of its grand opening. Knowing what a Web user wants and the particular needs of your customers will assist you in building a customer retention program. A customer's satisfaction and your ability to retain it go hand in hand. Before you create a formal rewards or loyalty program, you will need to make sure that your customers are satisfied with your service and support. Even the best formal customer retention program will not make up for poor service.

Highest customer service standards

One of main purposes of a Web site is to provide service. With the highly competitive nature of the Web, marketing and customer service must be of high quality. There are organizations such as Point Communications (http://www.pointcom.com) and many Internet and computing magazines that review Web sites in order to let people know which Web sites to visit with their limited browsing time. There are even Web sites that publicize a list of bad Web sites. For example, Web Watchdog (http://www.webwatchdog.com) provides lists of Web sites that rate high (Web Watchdog certified) in customer satisfaction. Plus, it is easy for a user to communicate with others through e-mail or newsgroups about a good or bad experience with your company. Instead of conversations with a few people, users can potentially tell thousands of people about a bad experience. People tend not to rush out and tell others about a good experience because this is to be expected. People tend to make it a point to share bad stories. When you are communicating your service policies, make sure you live up to them. It is also important for you to allow a two-way communication with your customers so they will come to you first when they have a problem—rather than broadcasting their dissatisfaction with your company. Finally, the purpose is not to create a large customer service operation to handle all of the problems. It is to make sure customer service is handled up-front with a well-designed Web catalog and service process. Remember, good customer service does not make promises that cannot be kept and then clean up the mess. Refer back to Chapter 11 for information on conducting customer service on the Web.

Why loyal customers are your most profitable customers

As mentioned earlier, it is more expensive to find and convince new customers to do business with you. Of course, you will be incurring the expense to acquire new customers when you first launch your Web catalog. However, at the same time you are bringing new customers aboard, you will need to convince customers to buy from you as much as possible. With each additional purchase and increased time a customer continues his or her relationship with your company, they become less costly to serve. Not only is it not necessary to continue to spend marketing dollars to convince these customers to buy from you, good service will keep *make-good* customer service costs down. A make-good cost is anything you use to repair damage caused by poor service, such as waiving shipping costs, free products, money-off coupons, and the cost of people and telephone charges. This can be accomplished through exceptional service (both customer and marketing) and loyalty programs.

Amazon.com is considered an exceptional Web catalog for its huge book selection, ease of ordering, interactivity, and most importantly its service. Jeff Bezos, president of Amazon.com, is proud of its current rate of repeat purchases. "Every day 44 percent of the orders we receive are from customers who have ordered from us before," Mr. Bezos stated. It handles 90 percent of its customer service via e-mail and the other 10 percent by telephone. Amazon.com has a few e-mail confirmation steps with their ordering process that helps it deal with potential problems on the front end rather than during the frustration stage when an order is discovered to be incorrect. Figure 12.13 shows Amazon.com's customer service Web page and its adulation page for customers to view positive feedback, which helps people reduce their feelings of risk with an initial purchase.

Ideas for building a loyal Web customer following

First and foremost, the Web site must be effectively designed to give customers a feeling that the time they spend on your site is valued. As you recall, we discussed

FIGURE 12.13 Amazon.com's customer service and customer comments pages.

the importance of useful content, easy-to-navigate site organization, selection, convenience, and interactivity in earlier chapters. Personalized content and service are becoming very important functions for an exceptional Web site, which can be accomplished with the effective use of catalog and customer databases. Customer dialog and formal loyalty programs can help establish a loyal customer base. Of course, all of these efforts will yield terrible results if they are not backed up by high-quality customer service.

The Web merchant: personalized content and service

The idea of personalized content and service was introduced in Chapter 2. Having a one-to-one relationship with customers is a lot like the traditional local merchant model. Customers enjoyed walking in an being greeted by name and receiving special attention. The customer felt like they were more than a patron and they felt the merchant truly appreciated their patronage. This is the type of relationship a Web-based business needs to achieve with customers to retain customers and remain competitive. The key to personalizing Web information and service is to build a database of customer information. Many Web sites are giving users the ability to view their account information, track packages, receive special notifications based on their individual interests, display certain products that may be of interest to users based on prior purchasing patterns, or even better, based on their stated preferences that you have captured in a database. There are a couple of pioneers in the area of personalizing the Web experience: Firefly (discussed in Chapter 2) and NetRadio. Figure 12.14 outlines NetRadio's features for a personalized Web content.

NetRadio Network (http://www.netradio.net) is a 24-hour Internet radio network that provides users with custom Web pages that contain music, news, and entertainment geared to customer preferences. Users register their preferences with NetRadio and download the free NetCompanion and StreamWorks software. Web users can hear the latest news and weather and listen to music while they are surfing the Internet.

Customized offerings can also be a way to build long-term and loyal customers. Dell Computer (http://www.dell.com) allows customers to build their own computer with a feature on the company's Web site. American Airlines (http://www.americanair.com) has a service called FareQuote that allows users to receive quotes based on the flight information they enter. The Gist (http://www.gist.com) allows users to customize based on their preferences for time, category, channels, and geographic viewing area. Users receive listings meeting this criteria six days in advance and can receive e-mail reminders. Figure 12.15 shows a sample of what users will get with the The Gist personal TV listing service.

FIGURE 12.14 NetRadio fine tunes its service to customers.

FIGURE 12.15 The Gist: Personalized TV listings.

Chapter 13 will explain how to use the customer information in the GuestTrack Catalog program to provide some personalized services.

Customer dialog

In Terry Vavra's book, *Aftermarketing: How to Keep Customers for Life Through Relationship Marketing*, (Richard D. Irwin Inc., 1992) there is one statement that exemplifies the importance of two-way communications with customers: "Engaging in dialog with customers tells them that they are important." He states that direct contact with customers is key to building lasting customer relationships. Additionally, he outlines the primary benefits of this type of dialog:

- Customers will tell you what you are doing wrong and how to do it better.

- Give you new product/service ideas.

- Make the customer more loyal and committed to your company.

- Add value to your product or service.

- Provide testimonials or references.

It has been said that when customers are satisfied with your company they will tell a few people, but when they are dissastisfied they will tell many. You will need to make it easy on your Web for customers to establish an ongoing dialog with you. Places for feedback, suggestions, market surveys, satisfaction surveys, and other feedback mechansims should be a standard element on your Web site and easy to locate. Also, you'll want real human beings monitoring the feedback and responding...yes, responding. This should be part of the job for those folks who provide customer service. Customer service representatives can manage the feedback process where they will respond to the suggestion or issue within a reasonable time frame. An initial response within 24 hours with a quick answer or message that tells the customer that research needs to be done and a response will be sent within 48-72 hours is appropriate. Response times on the Web should be the same or faster than the response times normally found in traditional customer support operations. It is unfortunate that many Web sites have treated this as a secondary element. There have been instances of well-known companies with Web sites that take weeks to respond, and in some cases, never respond. To be sure, many of those customers were left feeling a bit insignificant.

Dialog is a two-way medium, so if a customer takes the time to provide feedback, you should take the time to respond. Since this can be resource-intensive, you can formulate answers for the most often asked questions into a FAQ (Frequently Asked Questions) Web page. The FAQ should take care of the majority of questions that occur and should be updated regularly. Some methods for customer dialog include the following:

- Feedback button on the general menu bar that appears on all Web pages

- Online satistfaction survey with closed- and open-ended questions

- E-mail with satisfaction survey sent immediately after online purchase

- Periodic customer surveys

- Chat sessions with management and/or employees

- Private discussion group

You can also provide a special service like the folks at Virtual Vineyards (http://www.virtualvin.com) do to answer questions about wine and food. Figure 12.16 shows where users can submit questions to the Cork Dork and the Food Dude.

Structured loyalty programs—no cost, low cost

The goal of loyalty programs is to generate as much repeat business from customers over the long term. Loyalty programs will not work it they are thought of as quick promotions to increase sales. Those type of promotions are like light switches—they work great until they are turned-off. Loyalty programs are building best customers and reward-

> All aspects of a Web-based business have an impact on the loyalty of your customers. Formal customer retention promotions will not work if the basics, such as marketing and customer service, are shaky. Content, how orders are taken, how customer service is handled, and how you market your Web site all have influence on building a loyal customer following.

┌───┐
│ Netscape - [Ask The Cork Dork]   _ □ ✕   │
│ File Edit View Go Bookmarks Options Directory Window Help │
│ ┌──────┬──────┬──────┬──────┬──────┬──────┬──────┬──────┬──────┐ │
│ │ Back │ For. │ Home │Reload│ Imag │ Open │ Print│ Find │ Sto │ │
│ └──────┴──────┴──────┴──────┴──────┴──────┴──────┴──────┴──────┘ │
│ Netsite: http://www.virtualvin.com/vvdata/81601662/askdork.html ▼ │ N │
│   │
│ Virtual Vineyards | Food & Wine Pairing-- Order form   │
│ ───   │
│   │
│   Ask The Cork Dork   │
│   │
│   I am the Cork Dork (are you the walrus?), and this is a forum for your questions, comments, and │
│   critiques. Virtual Vineyards provides this avenue for entertainment and learning, both yours and ours! │
│   You can browse through previously asked questions, or ask one of your own! If I do not know the │
│   answer to a question or have an immediate response to a comment, I will do the necessary research. If │
│   the reply is not posted to *Ask the Cork Dork*, I will respond to you personally. │
│   │
│   ──   │
│   │
│   ●**Read** the 20 most recently asked questions in the ***Questions*** section below. │
│   ●**Browse** questions by topic with The Cork Dork's Table of Contents. │
│   ●**Send mail** to: corkdork@virtualvin.com.   │
│   │
│   ──   │
│   │
│   *Questions*   │
│   │
│ Document: Done   ✉?   │
└───┘

FIGURE 12.16 Virtual Vineyards' Cork Dork.

ing them for their continued relationship with you. Airline frequent flier programs, word-of-mouth referrals, membership clubs, and "buy ten and get the next one for free" programs are typical loyalty programs.

↳ Measuring Web site success

There are a few quick ways to measure the success of a Web site: Web site hits, leads or orders generated, initial feedback from customers, and media coverage. These are sufficient early on, but more sophisticated tools are available or soon will be available that create, analyze, and generate log reports for your Web site. Since the Web medium is so new, hard and fast numbers for relative success are not available. It will take time to see if thousands of visits by your customers and your conversion rate of shoppers to buying customers is considered successful.

Web site hits

A Web *hit* is when someone clicks on a Web home page or pages within your site. These logs are accessible through a password-protected account at your Internet Service Provider (ISP). You can view these logs to see how many people visited your site, which pages are most popular, what country they are located in, and so forth. In general, you want to see your hits skyrocket up when you open your Web catalog for business and increase over time. Figure 12.17 shows a sample log report for a Web site.

Inquiries and orders

This is why you are on the Web in the first place. Keeping an eye on the number of inquiries and sales or the percentage of inquiries turned into sales (conversion rate) will give you an indication that you are going to meet your goals. You can calculate the average number of hits per day (after a few months of operation) and the average dollar amount of a sale then project future revenues to see if you are progressing to your goal. Make sure that if the Web is just another marketing and sales vehicle you are tracking sales that are specifically generated on the Web. This tracking is important in measuring the success of the site relative to other vehicles.

Customer feedback

It is important to monitor initial customer feedback closely when you introduce your new Web site or introduce a major change. People are more apt to tell you what they think on the Internet so it is important to listen. Also, if customers communicate in other ways with your organization (such as with sales respresentatives or an 800 number) make sure feedback is captured.

```
Web Server Statistics
HTTP Server General Statistics
Server: http://www.domain.com
Requests last 7 days: 27182
HTML requests last 7 days: 15311
Total unique hosts: 872
 Go to: [Monthly report] [Weekly report] [Daily summary] [Daily
 report] [Hourly summary] [Hourly report] [Full (host) report]
 [Request report] [Domain report] [Directory tree report]
# of requests : Request
5077 : /index.html
2397 : /admin/index.html
1586 : /admin/index2.html
 982 : /health.html
 741 : /casebook.html
 676 : /admin/newsservice.html
 592 : /admin/
```

FIGURE 12.17 Sample Web log report from a typical Web site.

Media coverage

Take time to scan publications or Web sites to see if your
new Web catalog made news. This should be an ongoing
effort to ensure that what is written about your Web site is
positive and accurate. The introduction of a new Web site
does not make the news like it did earlier. What makes
news is a unique approach, impressive use of the latest
technology, a promotional event, a "first" in something, an
engaging function, or great content.

Web tracking tools

There are several tools that allow you to track your customers' usage of your site. The tools allow you to create
reports to analyze site traffic by page views, length of visit,

most popular pages, or which site they came from to visit your site. These more sophisticated log analysis tools will be important for you if you have a larger site with many content areas and product categories. Available tools include I/Audit (www.ipro.com), Interse (www.interse .com), NetCount (www.netcount.com), WWWStat and Gwstat (http://www.ics.uci.edu/pub/websoft/wwwstat/), and free tools suchs as AccessWatch (http://netpressence .com/accesswatch/) and NetStore (http://www.netstore .de/Supply/). There is also a tracking tool that incorporates demographic and psychographic information in addition to accessing log information that provides Web user tracking, profiling, and content personalization called GuestTrack (http://www.guesttrack.com).

Sideline: Selling ads on your Web site

Selling ads on your Web site can be a nice way to generate revenue at a low cost. However, you must first determine if selling ads matches your Web site's purpose. If you are a reseller of other companies' products, then it may make sense to give manufacturers a chance to promote their products. If your site is solely an informational resource, then you will need to sell ads or Web site sponsorships to cover costs. Once you have decided to sell Web ads, make sure they do not inundate the user or slow them down during their quest for information. Also, reserve certain Web pages or sections for ads such as the home page, category introduction pages, or products section. You want your Web customers to focus on your information and products first, not the advertisements of others. One problem with Web ads is when a user clicks on them, they go to the advertiser's Web site. A technique to keep them on your Web site is to create an informational ad page on your Web site for the advertiser. In this case, the user will click on the banner ad and be linked to a page on your Web site for further information. Then you can have a link at the bottom of this page that will allow them to go to the advertiser's Web site or another link back to the page they were viewing on your site. Refer to Chapter 2 for Web banner ad information such as advertising rates and graphic specifications.

NEW PIG: A PEEK AT HOW ONE TRADITIONAL CATALOGER IS TACKLING WEB SITE MARKETING

New Pig (http://www.newpig.com) is a traditional business-to-business catalog company specializing in industrial products (Figure 12.18).

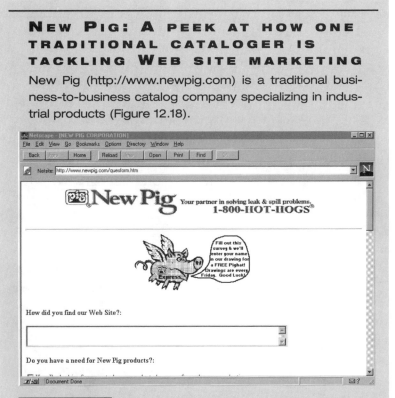

FIGURE 12.18 New pig site featuring pig hat promotion

New Pig is among the frontier organizations that saw the potential in doing business on the Internet. This is how they tackle the marketing of their Web site.

1. Objectives for promoting the Web site.

   • Promote/encourage current customers to visit the Web site

- Recruit new customers via the Web site

- Use Web site to expand awareness of New Pig to new markets

- Support our leadership position in the leak and spill industry

2. Marketing activities to support objectives.

- Heavily promote the Web site in all printed catalogs and media ads

- Using postcard mailings to customers and prospects—the postcard is used to promote aware-ness. The postcard also includes a brief survey to get an idea of the customers' impression of their Web site and how customers use the site.

- Encourage customers to place orders on the Web site using incentive and merchandise programs offered exclusively for Web orders

- Prepare special press releases for announcing the Web site

- Promote the Web site at all trade shows. The trade show booth will have a computer with Internet access to educate customers about the benefits of the infor-mation on the Web as well as how to do business with New Pig using the Internet.

- Continuous Web updates and testing key words used in 25 Web search engines to make sure they are effective

- Advertise on the Industry.net Web site (http://www.industry.net) which is an online sourcing and informational Web site that is very popular in New Pig's industry

- Investigation of opportunities for allowing other com-panies to have a link to their Web site, but New Pig is very selective about which companies can have a link

- Telephone service reps are promoting the Web site. The customer service staff is letting customers know about the Web site. The sales team uses the Web site to help sell product and direct customers to use the site as a place to find good industry information. The technical service staff are using the site to educate customers (e.g., technical articles and online newsletter) and they respond to technical questions that come to them via e-mail and Web.

3. Web site public relations.

- All New Pig press releases that are sent to traditional media are also put online. The company puts the announcements in a section on the Web site that is titled "More About New Pig." Every company announcement includes Web information including the Web site and e-mail addresses.

4. Marketing and promotions featured on the Web site itself.

- The New Pig Web site contains the same information that is found in the printed catalog. Currently, an online promotion features a drawing for a free pig hat to customers who respond to an online survey. New Pig plans to create a frequent buyers club and other online-only promotions and offers.

5. Measurement of Web site and online promotions.

- Success of the Web site itself has been measured according to the amount of site traffic and customer requests received via the site. New Pig keeps track of the number of viewers, how frequently they visit, what sections of the site they visit, and how long they spend at each section. The company uses customer communications as a key measure. New Pig plans to use Internet technology and an internal database of customers to measure even more directly the viewing preferences of individual customers and to customize the site to each viewer's preferences.

- Each promotional activity has specific measures attached to it. In typical direct marketing fashion, New Pig uses keycodes that identify where the customer heard about New Pig, one of its products, or a promotion. Customers who respond to the marketing activity are asked to reference a number or code to get an offer. This has proven to be very successful for New Pig in the past and continues to work well. New Pig keeps track of the customer communications received via the Web site. They track the number of orders, the number of catalog requests, and the number and type of questions asked. Changes in these communications help determine the success of a particular promotion.

6. Web marketing differences

- In principle, online marketing and traditional direct marketing are similar. The Web is another vehicle to deliver a message or offer. Great marketers know their customers intimately. They know what their customers want, need, and enjoy, and they deliver it. That priniciple holds true on the Web. There are differences at more intricate levels, however.

- The biggest and most important difference to remember is that on the Web, customers must come looking for the Web site versus how direct marketers mail a catalog to the customer. New Pig customers need not do anything special to receive a catalog. Media ads show up in magazines people read. Billboards pop up as we drive down the road. But in all cases, the customer has no choice but to see your message. Conversely, on the Web, customers must type the Web site address or look for a Web site via a search engine. Customers need a reason to come looking for your message. Therefore, promotion of the New Pig Web site is an important part of the company's Internet strategy.

- Another difference is the frequency of site visits. Direct marketers know the shelf-life of their catalog. When it expires, they mail again with new and fresh information. Media ads get changed. Billboards are changed. Again, customers have no choices to make; they just see the updated information. Web sites must offer something that brings customers back on their own. Information that is updated regularly, interactive services, fun and games, and so forth. Whatever the promotion, it must be something customers want and/or need on a regular basis so they visit the Web site often.

- Finally, there is a difference in how information is laid out physically on a Web site. Printed marketing pieces have very structured and well-proven rules of layout, design, and color. Television ads have their own sets of rules that are totally different than those for print. Likewise, the Web is developing its own set of standards or rules for marketing. For example, online catalogs typically use one product per page versus printed catalogs which often have four to ten products on a page.

Summary

"Build it and they will come" is a concept that does not apply to the Web—or much else anymore. You will need to take an active role in announcing and marketing your Web site to ensure the success of your Web-based business. There are many Web sites competing for a relatively small share of online revenue, so it is important to spend time getting people to your site. It is important that your Web site be well-designed, full of great information, is interactive, easy and painless to use, and even a little bit fun (or a lot, if that is your business). As many marketers have said, good advertising cannot make a bad product successful. In fact, the saying goes "nothing kills a bad product faster than good advertising." This chapter outlined the activities you can undertake to promote your Web site. See Appendix A for a list of resources on any of the concepts presented here.

The next chapter outlines advanced Web catalog techniques including ways to keep in touch with customers, enhancing your Web site experience using multimedia, animation, video, audio and new Web technologies such as Java and VRML (virual reality), and using your GT/Catalog Light profiling database to personalize the Web for customers. Once you have your Web site up-and-running you will want to plan the implementation of new features and functionality to keep customers coming back and bind your relationship with your customer base.

THE NEXT STEP

Now that you have a Web catalog site open for business, you will want consider enhancements to ensure that your Web site keeps up with what Web users are expecting. This chapter outlines the technologies and methods available to make the most of your Web-based business into the future. You will want to devise a plan to add some additional content and functionality in an acceptable time frame for you and for your customers. Customers will also help you determine new functionality that they prefer by sending comments to you or by filling out your periodic online survey.

Some nifty technologies, such as a search engine, an e-mail newsletter and chat, can be applied in a very meaningful way to build solid relationships with your customers. You can even use "old-fashioned" communications such as a telephone call, a paper newsletter, catalog, direct mailers announcing specials, and so on, to continue dialog with your customers.

There are also some Web technologies available to enhance your Web users' experience such as animation, Java, virtual reality, sound, and video. These technologies are new and exciting, but still have some limitations for most Web surfers such as the time it takes to download the pieces required to make these technologies work.

You should consider adding these technologies in a meaningful, fun, and non-obtrusive way because the real purpose is to help you build a relationship with your prospect—and help them become a customer. While it is neat to deliver a video clip to a prospect, the use of these technologies needs to be considered in a manner that improves communication, thereby improving your relationship with your customers.

Another way Web sites are being enhanced is through personalization. By customizing the material presented to Web visitors you can build a relationship by providing just the information your prospect is looking for. The GuestTrack Light software used in Chapter 9 to display the Personalized Product List is just one way to use personalization.

The more you know about someone, the more likely you are to be able to tailor your presentation to their background, education, and interests—which increases the likelihood that the prospect understands what you're trying to communicate. For instance, if you sell golf equipment you could use different copy promoting different benefits if you knew whether a Web visitor was just learning to play the game or if they had been playing for 20 years!

Keeping in touch with your customers

We touched on the subject of customer relations and support in a few previous chapters. It is important to encourage dialog with your customers, using both electronic and traditional communications tools. In addition to providing contact information and feedback mechanisms on your Web site (see Chapters 11 and 12 for discussions on customer service and dialog), there are three methods for keeping in touch with your customers: mail list server, chat, and real-world communications.

Mail list server

Electronic mailings of messages and brief newsletters using a mail list server are popular ways to remind customers to visit your Web site. You will achieve the best results if you use both electronic and physical mailings to your customers, and use each according to their benefits. The benefit of an electronic mailing is to give users some brief, useful information that will encourage them to visit your Web site for additional information. This method will also allow you to provide a consistent and periodic reminder to customers that you are still out in the vast World Wide Web. The most important factor to the success of a mail list server is that the e-mail messages be useful because users have the choice of signing up to receive the message, which also means that they can choose to take their name off the e-list if they don't find the mailings meaningful to them. The nice thing about a list server is that you can measure their success very easily by monitoring the number of users who sign on as well as monitoring attrition.

How a mail list server works

A mail list server allows customers to sign up to receive e-mail from you. The user submits their e-mail address to you, which is put into a database. A mail list server program allows you to build an e-mail database, send e-mail messages and administer the list. When you write an e-mail message or newsletter, the list server program will broadcast that message to all customers on the e-mail list. Majordomo and Listserv are the most widely used mail list server programs. Here are some resources for learning about and acquiring mail list server software:

• Listserver FAQ	ftp://ftp.uu.net/usenet /news.answers/mail/list -admin/software-faq
• Yahoo!	http://www.yahoo.com /Computers_and _Internet/Software /Internet/Electronic _Mail/Mailing_Lists/
• Majordomo (free)	http://www.greatcircle .com/majordomo
• Listserv	http://www.lsoft.com /listserv.stm
• Mailserv (free user interface program that makes administering a list server easy)	http://iquest.com /~fitz/www/mailserv/

Ideas for electronic mailings

You can have one or more mail list servers on a Web site. The most popular use of a mailing list is to periodically broadcast a *What's New* e-mail. This e-mail could contain a list of new products, services, Web site changes and additions, etc. Here is a list of what you could include in electronic mailings:

- What's new: products, services, Web site changes

- News: company, product, Web, and industry news that affects customers

- Special offers: current specials with description and offer expiration date

- Product technology/applications: technology briefs, articles about how customers are using products, services

- Customer/Technical support: include changes in service policies, technical notes

- Electronic newsletter: can include condensed versions of some or all of the items above, and include a link to a special Newsletter page with the full-text and graphical edition

- Multiple lists: can provide a list for a product or service category, technical support, news

Chat

Online chat has been a very popular recreational activity on the Web. Chat allows people to talk to each other online. Users converse with each other by typing messages during a chat session. Chat has the ability to establish a community of customers that can share ideas with each other and with your organization. Many companies are beginning to use it for customer support and public relations. Traditionally, customers have needed to have chat client software, also known as Internet relay chat (IRC), most of which is free to download.

Recently, other types of chat software have become available that allows people to chat in real time by typing into a Web page. You will need to obtain chat server software from companies such as Quarterdeck (http://www.qdeck .com), iChat (http://www.ichat.com), and others. You will want to do some research on the chat server software that meets your requirements. Web sites have regularly scheduled chat sessions, or special sessions, that are promoted on the Web. There is usually a dedicated person who moderates a chat session. 3-D Virtual chat sessions are the newest applications of the technology. Here are a few places to see chat in action:

- World Village Chat Central   http://www .worldvillage.com /wv/chat/html /chat.htm
- WebChat Broadcasting System   http://wbs.net/
- Parent Soup   http://www.par- entsoup.com/chat /indexnew.html

Real-world communications

Since the Web is still new, it will take time for people to make the Web a primary source for obtaining information and buying products. Even if you eventually have a majority of your customers using the Web, you will still need to give them physical reminders to visit your Web site. Letters, postcards, newsletters, direct mail pieces, catalogs, telephone calls, personal visits, and other physical communications are equally important to a successful Web-based business. Depending on the type of business you are in, you will want to select specific communication activities that make sense. The Web should not take the place of any real-world communications that are critical to your company's overall success. For example, if your business traditionally made sales calls to key customers, the Web is not a good substitute for important face-to-face communications. Alternatively, if you are a small online catalog, you may want to do some periodic postcard mailings—direct mail can be expensive, so evaluate each mailing based on its cost and what response you expect from it. Build a communications program that uses electronic and traditional communications methods to their distinct advantages.

Enhancing the Web experience

The Web site you have built using the GT/Catalog Light software is a fantastic start! On the otherhand, Web technology is changing so quickly as soon as you set up your Web catalog site, you will want to begin developing additional features and functions to meet the likes and demands of the Web community. You will want to consider researching and implementing some of these technologies that will enhance your site: search engine, sound, audio conferencing, video, videoconferencing, animation, Java applets, and 3-D/Virtual reality.

Search engine

As your site grows in size, you will want to consider including a search capability. In addition to other navigation tools, such as a menu, tool bar, or site map, a search engine considerably enhances a Web site. Here are a few resources to help you learn more about search engine technology and software:

- Boutell.com Search FAQ   http://www.boutell
                                .com/faq/search.htm

- Wais and WWW Pointers   http://www.cs.vu.nl
                                /~anne007/waissearch
                                /pointers.html

Sound

Sound can enhance a Web site's appeal. It can be used as part of brief multimedia presentations on your Web site. Some companies have used it in banner advertising and short advertisements within their site. Media sites have used sound to broadcast stories. Typical formats for sound include: u-law (UNIX), AIFF (Mac and Silicon Graphics), WAV (Windows) and MPEG. RealAudio (http://www .realaudio.com) has developed streaming audio technology for sound files that allows users to listen to the sound file while it is being downloaded. The technology is still new and limited in its use since it takes time to download a sound file. For more information on sound technology visit *WebMaster Magazine* at http://www.cio.com /WebMaster/wm_sound.html.

Video and videoconferencing

Video is much like sound in that you can enhance your Web site to provide a multimedia experience, the technology is new, and there are some speed hurdles that need to be gotten past in order for widespread use of video or video conferencing. Video allows you to enhance marketing messages and to showcase products or events and other applications that will allow a more personal approach. For example, some sites have used sound and video to broadcast messages from their CEO. Media sites are applying video technology to broadcast news stories. Videoconferencing is a very new idea to be added to Web communications. As picture and sound quality improves, you will see this medium gain more acceptance. To enable videoconferencing, users' computers need to outfitted with software, camera, and special hardware that allows the computer to capture and process video. Here are some sites to visit to learn more about video and videoconferencing:

- Digital Video Primer   http://www.raley .com/video.htm

- *WebMaster Magazine*   http://www.cio.com /WebMaster/resources _confe.html

- *WebMaster Magazine*   http://www.cio.com /WebMaster/resources _videocon.html

- Videoconference Resource Center   http://www.video conference.com/

- CU-SeeMe   http://cu-seeme .cornell.edu

Animation

Animation can add life to your Web site and Web advertising. The easiest animation to create on your Web site is an animated .GIF (bit-mapped color graphics format), which is a series of illustrations or text that is in .GIF format that are brought together to build a moving image. It is much like traditional cartoon animation or like those flip books most of us had during childhood. For more information, see an online animation tutorial at http://www .bendnet.com/users/brianhovis/tutorial/. Animation is very popular and will be very prevalent on the Web. There are tools available that make creating an animated .GIF very easy.

Java applets

Java was developed by Sun Microsystems as a programming language that allows developers to create programs that can run on PC, Macintosh, and UNIX computing platforms. Until now, programs written in the Java language were more for fun than for business. However, Java is now considered one of the most important Web technologies available. If you have cruised the Web and seen a site that contained scrolling text or animation, then you've probably seen a Java applet (small application) at work.

Check out Gamelan (http://www.gamelan.com), one of the most popular Java sites, to learn more.

3-D and virtual reality

The use of 3-D graphics and virtual reality is growing and becoming another leading-edge technology that is capturing everyone's attention. These technologies can and will make Web sites very engaging. Some sites such as Insight Direct (http://www.insight.com/#cybertai) have used 3-D and virtual reality technology to showcase products. Visit http://www.3d-web.com/3dfaq.htm to learn more about 3-D images on the Web. Virtual Reality Modeling Language (VRML) is the programming language that allows more than one person to participate in interactive 3-D simulations. To find out more about VRML, check out the VRML FAQ at http://vag.vrml.org/VRML_FAQ.html.

Here are a few resources for multimedia on the Web, which gives detailed information about many of the technologies discussed here:

- *WebMaster Magazine*   http://www.cio.com /WebMaster/resources _multi.html

- Cambridge Digital Media   http://www.cdmi.com /Lunch/multimedia .html

Improving communications builds relationships

All of the technologies we've covered in this chapter are interesting and novel ways to gain attention and provide more information to your prospects and customers. But just pumping out information is not enough—the information needs to be right.

As marketers, we need to be very aware of the wants, needs, and desires of our customers so we can help them evaluate our products and make good purchasing choices. For many years marketers have tried to use mass media to target specific groups of customers. Media buyers select television shows based on the demographic characteristics of the audience. The problem has been that the surveys of age and sex of a TV program's audience are based on a few hundred interviews, which leads to a wide error in actual measurement of the audience.

Direct-mail marketers have done a better job of targeting their audience through the use of list selection techniques based on data collected annually through magazine subscription forms and other sources of data about people. Of course, the problem with this technique has been that the questions asked a year ago probably don't pertain to the products a particular merchant is selling today. One of the key concepts in successful direct-marketing techniques is "test, test, test," which means to try different lists and see which ones work, and to try different brochures, letters, and inserts to see which ones provide a better return. The problem with this approach, of course, is that all measurement is after the fact instead of as you are interacting with the prospect.

↳ Personalizing the Web experience

The Web now affords marketers the ability to adjust the presentation based on actual answers while the prospect is in the market for your type of product. In addition, a Web site can be programmed to use the same observational techniques that an experienced salesperson uses when they make a sales call on a prospect or customer.

Why is this important? People appreciate being recognized as special. By providing information targeted to their specific questions about your products, you are reducing the anxiety of purchase decisions and showing how your products meet their unique needs, wants, and desires.

The version of GuestTrack Light included with this book allows much of the personalization that is possible with the full version of the product. This means that you could use the interest profile fields to customize pages of industry news, new product announcements, targeted specials, and other information that a salesperson or telemarketer would provide to the individual based on knowing a little about their interests.

The future of commerce on the Web is moving toward becoming as personalized as the customer will allow. For instance, the full version of GuestTrack allows a merchant to store hundreds of pieces of information about a customer and have very complex personalization rules that could result in no two customers seeing exactly the same information! In addition, continually updated monitoring and tracking allow the profile database to be updated throughout the customer's visit to the site using not only answers to questions, but through observation of which pages the customer viewed.

One way to personalize your customers' online buying experience is through cross-selling. Cross-selling is a way to inform customers about special offers, new products and complementary products. Let's say a customer decides to purchase a book in the History product category. When the customer adds the book to the shopping cart, you can display a Web page that informs the customer of related History books, or a more general Web page that contains information about current book specials. From there, the customer can review the book descriptions and make additional book purchases. The Web catalog you built using this book can have links on product pages to related products. You can also use the GuestTrack personalization software to add cross-selling links based on their interest.

As you can see, the opportunities for personalizing a Web site are as open as your imagine will allow. By combining the profile of a customer with actual viewing of Web pages you can learn a great deal about the effectiveness of your Web site, who it appeals to, and learn ways to increase your success.

 Summary

As you look to the future of online marketing and commerce, you will find that new technologies will lead to new ways of doing business—and that will lead to new opportunities to build relationships with your customers.

APPENDIX A

RESOURCES

⮑ Special Web site for Web Catalog Cookbook readers

A special Web site has been built for readers of this book (http://www.allen.com/online-marketing). It contains additional information to help you build and promote your Web site. Tips, Frequently Asked Questions, additional Web site links, and other useful content will help keep your Web site on the cutting edge.

⮑ General computing and the Internet

These Web sites contain great information about computer hardware and software, Internet/World Wide Web technology, the business side of Web computing, research, and statistics, and so on. These are great sites to begin your travels on the Web:

C⏐net	http://www.cnet.com/
PC Magazine Online	http://www.pcmag.com
Communications Week Interactive	http://techweb.cmp .com/cw/cwi/
ZDNet	http://www5.zdnet.com/
Boutell.com	http://www.boutell.com
CyberAtlas	http://www.cyberatlas .com/
World Wide Web Consortium W3C	http://www.w3c .org/pub/WWW/
Internet News Database	http://www.conceptone .com/netnews/netnews .html
Newspage	http://www.newspage.com
News.com	http://www.news.com

 Web commerce

These electronic and Web commerce resources will help you keep up with the happenings in this quickly emerging industry. These sites will help you understand how the Web fits into the larger electronic commerce community and how you can tie your business electronically to your customers, suppliers, manufacturers, financial, and other commerce relationships.

CommerceNet	http://www.commerce.net
iWorld's Guide to Electronic Commerce	http://e-comm.iworld.com/
Internet Survey on Electronic Commerce	http://www.earthweb.com/coopers/strategy/

The following book should prove helpful: *Frontiers of Electronic Commerce* by Ravi Kalakota and Andrew Whinston, published by Addison-Wesley Publishing, 1996.

Web development and Internet Service Providers

Building your catalog with the GT/Catalog Light software is one part of conducting business on the Web. You will want to locate partners that will help you get your business on the Web. Here are some good resources to assist you.

General

Internet Source Book	http://www.internetsourcebook.com Gateway Publishing 1-800-774-4410 or 1-413-664-6185 P.O. Box 786 North Adams, MA 01247

| Online Connection | http://www.barkers.org/online |

Web development and design

Domain Lookup	http://www.harold .com/whois.html
	http://web.mindspring .com/whois.html
WebReference.com	http://www .webreference.com/

Web graphics

| The Pixel Foundry | http://the-tech.mit.edu /KPT/KPT.html |

The following book should prove helpful: *Designing Web Graphics* by Lynda Wienman, published by New Riders Publishing (1996).

Internet service providers

The List	http://thelist.iworld.com
Dan Kegel's List of ISDN ISPs	http://alumni.caltech.edu /~dank/isdn/isdn_ip.html
Providers of Commercial Internet Access	http://www.celestin .com/pocia

↳ Web fulfillment resources and companies

If you are creating a Web catalog to sell products online, then you will need some assistance in finding order processing and fulfillment solutions. If you already have order processing, fulfillment, and shipping systems, you will want to talk with those partners to help you integrate your

Web catalog with existing systems. If you are starting from scratch and are anticipating a volume of orders that cannot be handled by existing personnel or systems, then refer to these resources for help.

Resources

Yahoo!	http://www.yahoo.com /Business_and_Economy /Companies/Marketing/ Fulfillment_Services/

Companies specializing in Internet fulfillment

The Electronic Marketplace (low volume)	http://www.emrkt .com/fulfill.html
	1860 East 28th Street Minneapolis, MN 55407 1-800-535-8470
Interactive Marketing Services (high volume)	http://www.fulfillment .com
	410-634-2060; Fax 410-634-1908 2 North Maple Ave. Ridgely, MD 21660
LitleNet Direct Commerce	http://www.litle.net
	508-551-5000; Fax: 508-551-5050 900 Chelmsford Street, Lowell, MA 01851
ABC Group Neodata Service	http://www.abcgroup .com http://www.neodata.com

↳ Hosting services and Web malls

If you prefer to have someone else worry about operating your Web catalog, then you may want to check out these resources for Web site hosting and online malls. If you plan to manage your Web site yourself, being a part of an online mall may be a way to get additional exposure and sales.

Yahoo!	http://www.yahoo.com /Business_and_Economy /Companies/Computers/ Networking/Online _Services/
Providers of Commercial Internet Access	http://www.celestin .com/pocia
Internet Shopping Directory	http://www.shopping direct.com/supersites .html

↳ Credit card merchant accounts, payment processors, and electronic cash

A very important issue for Web catalog merchants is how to receive payment for your goods and services securely. The following sites are worth investigating to ensure that you offer secure Web transactions, and to minimize potential credit fraud:

First USA Paymentech	http://www.fusa.com
Mastercard	http://www.mastercard .com

Visa	http://www.visa.com
American Express	http://www.americanexpress.com
Discover	http://www.discover.com
Charge.com	http://www.charge.com

Payment processing with your bank or companies

First USA Paymentech	http://www.fusa.com
First Virtual	http://www.fv.com
Open Market	http://www.openmarket.com
Yahoo!	http://www.yahoo.com/Business_and_Economy/Companies/Financial_Services/Credit/Credit_Cards/Merchant_Services/
	http://www.yahoo.com/Business_and_Economy/Companies/Financial_Services/Transaction_Clearing/e-cash
Digicash	http://www.digicash.com
CyberCash	http://www.cybercash.com

↳ Web marketing and promotion

The adage "build it and they will come" does not work on the World Wide Web. You will need to take control of your success through active marketing and public relations. The following Web sites offer good information and additional Web site links.

General

Marketing Resources	http://www.lib.lsu.edu/bus/marketin.html
Internet Advertising Resource Guide	http://www.voyager.net/adv/internet-advertising-guide.html
/Mousetracks/	http://www.nsns.com/MouseTracks/
Direct Marketing Asociation	http://www.the-dma.org
Marketing 1:1	http://www.marketing1:1.com
Web site announcement FAQ	http://ep.com/faq/webannounce.html

Web writing

Good Web content that is interesting, informative, and keeps customers coming back relies on great editorial and product/service copy. You'll find additional information with these resources:

Webmaster Magazine	http://www.cio.com/WebMaster/style.html
Electric Pages	http://www.electric-pages.com/articles/wftw1.htm
Elements of Style Online	http://www.columbia.edu/acis/bartleby/strunk/

The following book should prove helpful: *Cyberwriting* by Joe Vitale, published by AMACOM (American Management Association, 1997).

List server resource

An e-mail mailing list is fast becoming a requirement on all good Web sites. The following Web sites have free or low-cost software and information on how to create a mail list server:

Listserver FAQ	ftp://ftp.uu.net/usenet /news.answers/mail /list-admin/software-faq
Majordomo (free)	http://www.greatcircle .com/majordomo/
Listserv	http://www.lsoft .com/listserv.stm
Mailserv (free user interface program that makes administering a list server easy)	http://iquest.com/~fitz /www/mailserv/

Advertising and publicity

In addition to what was discussed in this book, these resources will help you build a good advertising and public relations plan to increase the awareness of your site.

Digital Direct Marketing	http://www.netcreations .com/ddm

The following book should prove helpful: *World Wide Web Marketing* by Jim Sterne, published by John Wiley & Sons Publishing, 1996

The following book should prove helpful: *Publicity on the Internet* by Steve O'Keefe, published by John Wiley & Sons Publishing, 1996.

↳ Customer service

Most great Web sites are not just attractive and fun to read. How customer service is handled is key to the success of a good Web site. There are few resources online at this moment, but we expect more to be written on the Web about this subject. All of the golden rules of customer service apply to doing business on the Web. Here is one book that specifically addresses customer service on the Internet:

Jim Sterne's Eight Ways — http://www.targeting .com/eightways.html

The following book should prove helpful: *Customer Service on the Internet* by Jim Sterne, published by John Wiley & Sons Publishing, 1996.

Search engine resources

Visit the following Web sites to learn more about how to add a search engine to your Web site:

Boutell.com Search FAQ — http://www.boutell .com/faq/search.htm

Wais and WWW Pointers — http://www.cs.vu.nl /~anne007/waissearch /pointers.html

General business and catalog resources

There is a wealth of business information on the Web. Here are just a few sites to visit for more information about general business and conducting business on the Web:

Better Business Bureau — http://www.bbb.org/

FinanceHub (venture capital) — http://www.FinanceHub .com/vc/vctab.html

Entrepreneurs on the Web — http://www.eotw.com

Small Business Administration Online — http://www.sbaonline .sba.gov/index.html

Catalog Age   http://www.mediacentral
.com/index/CatalogAge

 Legal resources

Legal Web sites should be on the top of your list of sites to visit. There are numerous legal issues surrounding copyright, trademark, international trade, and taxation for Web-based businesses.

American Intellectual Property Law Assoc.	http://www.aipla.com/
Copywright Web Site	http://www.benedict .com/index.html
U.S Patent and Trademark Office	http://www.uspto.gov/
Advertising Law Internet Site	http:www.webcom.com /~lewrose/home.html

POSTING AN ANNOUNCEMENT ON A NEWSGROUP

Subject: Advertising on Usenet: How To Do It, How Not To Do It
Date: Sat, 28 Dec 1996 09:00:12 GMT
From: jfurr@acpub.duke.edu (Joel K. Furr)
Newsgroups: news.announce.newusers, news.admin.misc, misc.entrepreneurs, news.admin.net-abuse.misc, news.misc, misc.answers, news.answers
Followup-To: news.newusers.questions

Original-author: jfurr@acpub.duke.edu (Joel K. Furr)
Archive-name: usenet/advertising/how-to/part1
Last-change: 23 Jul 1996 by jfurr@acpub.duke.edu (Joel Furr)
Changes-posted-to: news.misc

Introduction

Advertising on Usenet is a frequently misunderstood subject. The purposeof this message is to explain some Usenet conventions regarding advertising to new users and, hopefully, spare everyone involved a lot ofneedless worry.

To start with, let's define the term. "Usenet" is *not* synonymous with "Internet." Usenet is the system of online discussion groups, called "newsgroups," e.g. rec.humor, comp.misc, news.announce.newusers, talk.origins, misc.rural, alt.sex, and so forth.

This FAQ does not attempt to describe in detail all the various ways in which one can conduct commercial activity over the Internet and attempts simply to explain the issues involved in advertising in Usenet newsgroups.

The philosophy of Usenet

Usenet started out in 1980 as a UNIX network linking sites which needed to talk about and receive prompt updates on UNIX system configuration and other UNIX questions. Message traffic started out at a few messages per week, but the system was so useful that traffic quickly boomed and Usenet almost immediately expanded to include forums on science fiction, humans and computers, and other subjects.
In the beginning, Usenet was largely confined to

educational institutions such as universities and
colleges, and to research companies and other commercial enterprises with UNIX machines on-site. It
has now grown to include millions of users at commercial sites such as America Online and at companies around the world involved in every sort of
business imaginable. Nevertheless, many of the customs found on Usenet today have their origins in the
days when Usenet was very small and most Usenet
sites were universities.

That these customs and traditions began when Usenet
was much smaller and quite different in nature in no
way lessens the anger many users feel when these
customs and traditions are violated.

One such custom is the tradition and belief that it
is rude to advertise for profit in Usenet newsgroups.

Advertising is widely seen as an 'off-topic' intrusion into the discussions of any particular newsgroup (newsgroup is the Usenet word for discussion
group or bulletin board). Each newsgroup has a specific set of subjects it is intended to cover, and
in order for newsgroups to function as effective
discussion forums, it is important that people stay
'on-topic'. If everyone disregarded the particular
topics each newsgroup is intended to cover and simply posted whatever they wanted wherever they want,
the entire system would break down.

Due to the decentralized nature of Usenet, there is
no one person or body which can "enforce" the custom
of staying on-topic. It falls on each user to help
preserve the culture of open discussion and free
speech that Usenet has come to embody by not posting
off-topic material.

This, of course, includes advertising. Advertising
is by far the most

pervasive form of off-topic posting, and therefore,
gets most of the heat.

An analogy

If an analogy will help you to visualize the situation, imagine a meeting at your workplace or school.

At this meeting, people are discussing a certain
issue -- for example, getting new sidewalks
installed downtown or getting new schoolbooks for
the elementary school, or what to do about the new
product your company is planning on introducing.

In the midst of the discussions on the new sidewalks
or textbooks or product, someone walks into the
room, interrupts everyone, then reads an advertisement for a local restaurant. He or she then leaves
without waiting for comment.

Now imagine if this happened over and over again each
time your group tried to hold a meeting. Every time
someone tried to make a point, in walks some other
stranger who reads an ad for some business that has
nothing to do with the subject of the meeting.

It would soon become rather difficult to hold effective meetings, wouldn't it?

Similarly, it's very difficult to keep Usenet newsgroups interesting and useful when people deluge
newsgroups with advertisements.

The hidden cost

One of the things that attracts some people to the
idea of advertising via Usenet is that it costs so
little to do it. You pay $20 or $30 per month for
an Internet account, and you can post literally
millions of advertisements at no additional cost.

But there *is* a cost. Each message you post takes
up disk space on each site around the world where it
lands. People don't much mind paying for disk space
to hold Usenet discussions since they know that people like taking part in those discussions and since
they know that it's sort of like mutual backscratch-
ing: "I let your messages reside on my site for
free, and you let the messages I post reside on your
site for free." Everyone benefits from interesting,
informative, or amusing discussions, so no one
really minds paying for the space.

But there's only one person who benefits from advertising: the advertiser. Sure, you can say that the

people who see the ad benefit from the product or service advertised, but when you balance that against what they lose when their favorite discussion group is taken over by non-stop advertising, it's a poor trade.

No one wants to give their disk space for free to someone who selfishly posts a copy of an advertisement to every newsgroup on Usenet.

How to advertise on Usenet

There *are* acceptable ways to advertise in Usenet newsgroups.

1. The on-topic notice

If you have a product or a message that is specifically related to a particular Usenet newsgroup, and you want to let people know about it, it's *usually* all right to post *one* notice about it.

Note the word "notice." A notice is a brief mention of the product with information about how interested persons can find out more. It's not a sales pitch. It's not an advertisement. It's not a "BUY BUY BUY" sort of message. It's a notice.

You are encouraged to make such postings one-time-only. When your polite informational notice starts getting posted every week, people are going to start getting irked at you.

You are also *strongly* encouraged to keep such postings hype-free. What often works very well is to post information about your services or product and include a contact address, World Wide Web site, or phone number for people to use to get more information.

For example, if you want to post a notice about your immigration law services, you could post a message to alt.visa.us or the various misc.immigration.* newsgroups, where you'd find a large population of people interested in that or related subjects. Posting the same ad to rec.sport.football.college would *not* be appropriate because rec.sport.football.college has nothing to do with immigration law, visas, or becoming a citizen of another country.

One way to tell if a post is appropriate is to look at a newsgroup's charter. The charter is the formal declaration of what is on topic and what is not, and was generated at the time the group was created if the group was created in the so-called Big 7 hierarchies of comp.*, soc.*, rec.*, talk.*, misc.*, news.*, sci.*, and humanities.*. Some other groups have charters as well, but not all -- and if they do, they're often one or two lines in length. Where can you find a charter? Well, in some cases the charter is regularly posted to the newsgroup or is contained in the newsgroup's Frequently Asked Questions files. In other cases, the charter has been all but forgotten. Charters can occasionally be difficult to locate, so you may have to use your best judgment and/or ask someone who's been reading the group for a while if a particular message would be appropriate.

This is not to say that on-topic notices will always be welcome; the proliferation of inappropriate advertisements (ads posted in the wrong way to the wrong place) has resulted in *all* ads, even informational notices posted to appropriate newsgroups, tending to get a cold shoulder. You can help by limiting your ads to *informational* postings posted *only* *where* *appropriate*, and abiding by any local restrictions a given newsgroup's readers have placed on advertising.

2. *.forsale and *.marketplace newsgroups

There are many newsgroups directly involved in selling. You can generally spot them by the word "forsale" or "marketplace" in their names.

For example, rec.games.board.marketplace is a newsgroup where people post for-sale and want-to-buy notices about board games they want to buy or sell.

Similarly, the misc.forsale.* hierarchy is full of newsgroups for buying and selling various computers, monitors, printers, devices, and so forth, as well as misc.forsale.non-computer.*, for selling stuff that's not computer-related. However, the misc.forsale.* policy is rather resistant to *commercial* ads -- the hierarchy is intended as a place to post classified-style ads.

Many parts of the Net have local hierarchies as well where you can post for-sale and want-to-buy ads.

For example, in central North Carolina, the triangle.* hierarchy has triangle.forsale and triangle.wanted, where classified-style advertisements are the rule of the day.

It's generally considered rude, though, to crosspost a notice about your product to every forsale newsgroup, even ones on the opposite side of the country or world. Post your notice only to your *local* for-sale newsgroup, if one exists.

3. comp.newprod

If and only if you are with a computer company which is releasing a new product and you want to make word of this new product known to the computing community, you can post a notice to the moderated newsgroup comp.newprod. The moderator of comp.newprod requires submissions to be informative and hype-free so people will use comp.newprod as a reliable way of gaining information.

4. biz.*

There is a hierarchy of newsgroups called "biz.*" which exists mainly for announcement from companies of new products, fixes and enhancements, postings of demo software, and so forth. If your site carries biz.*, and you feel that a biz.* hierarchy group would suit your purposes, go to biz.config and ask for it.

Be warned, though, that if your goal is to create a biz.* newsgroup for posting hype-filled advertisements, no one would read such a newsgroup. People only want to read newsgroups that are of benefit to them; they're not about to subscribe to a newsgroup that's nothing but ads for Bob's Bait and Tackle.

There are a few dozen biz.* newsgroups, some of which get used regularly and some of which are essentially defunct. If your site carries biz.*, you can find out more about the hierarchy by asking in biz.config, biz.general, and biz.misc.

5. .signature advertisements.

A .signature is a mini-file that is automatically appended (stuck at the end of) to any Usenet messages that you post -- regardless of what the content is. Whether or not you can create and use a .signature depends on what sort of system you're using to access Usenet news. Many UNIX systems simply equire you to create a file called ".signature" in your root directory within your shell account and put whatever you want your .signature to say within that file. Other systems, like America Online, allow you to do something similar, but the implementation varies from system to system. If you can't figure out if your system supports a .signature, ask the people in charge for help.

Typically, it is considered bad manners to put more than four lines of information in your .signature, regardless of what those four lines might say or contain. Gigantic ASCII pictures of dragons, for example, are annoying when you have to see them every time a certain person posts.

Similarly, it's considered bad manners to put an advertisement in your .signature and then post a lot of empty or nearly-empty articles simply to get your .signature into various newsgroups.

On the other hand, if you post meaningful, responsible messages in groups you're actually interested in, and those messages happen to have the address of your Web page tacked on at the end, few people will complain.

Just keep .signature advertisements extremely short and sweet. Let your Web page contain the sales pitch -- the .signature should usually be little more than a listing of your URL and perhaps a mention of what sort of business you're in.

Restraint and responsibility are everything -- if you've got those, people will sit up and listen to you.

How *not* to advertise on Usenet

Unfortunately, there are just about as many *inappropriate* ways to advertise on Usenet as there are appropriate ways.

1. Posting off-topic messages in unrelated newsgroups

Each message you post to Usenet, regardless of its content, should only be posted to related news-groups.

For example, you run a rug company. You want to sell lots of rugs. So, you post an advertisement about your rugs in sci.physics. Not surprisingly, a lot of people send you email telling you what a jerk you are.

Why'd they do this, you ask? It's simple: sci.physics has nothing to do with selling rugs. Your ad was as off-topic as if someone had tried to get a discussion going there about the upcoming football season or started posting a lot of messages about their recent vacation.

Suppose you own that rug company, and you regularly read rec.crafts.textiles.weaving. Would you like it if someone started coming in and posting a lot of ads to the newsgroup about ginseng tablets, and then someone else came in and started trying to sell mag-azine subscriptions, and before you knew it, it became hard to find any actual discussion of weaving going on?

Try to look at it from the other person's point of view. If you'd resent someone posting an ad for *their* product to *your* favorite newsgroup, why would you post an ad for *your* product to thousands of other people's favorite newsgroups?

Remember the Golden Rule: "Do unto others as you would have them do unto you."

2. Spamming

Spamming is defined as posting identical or nearly-identical messages (not just ads, although ads are usually what spammers post) to a lot of newsgroups, one right after the other. Since it's really not that difficult to write a program that will post the same advertisement to dozens, if not hundreds or thousands of newsgroups, a lot of people have taken to doing this.

What's happened to people who've spammed?

They've lost their accounts, been mail-bombed (had thousands of pieces of junk email sent to them), had people call up and yell at them in the middle of the night, had people forward their mail (by this I

mean paper mail, not email) to someplace strange,
had people sign them up for thousands of unwanted
magazine subscriptions, had people send them thousands of pages of condemnatory faxes, and so forth.

Nothing is as hated on Usenet as spamming. It's
extremely, unbelievably rude and if you do it, you
will come to regret it.

This is not a threat -- it's an observation. Any benefits spamming might have brought you will be more
than counteracted by the intense public outcry
against you in every newsgroup you posted your ad to.

Some members of the media have gotten the mistaken
impression that spamming is hated because it's
advertising. While it's true that Usenet users
don't have much fondness for advertising, the real
reason spamming is hated so much is because it's
unbelievably *rude*.

If you don't regularly read a newsgroup, why would
you post an ad to it? In so doing, you're basically
saying that you don't care what the people in that
newsgroup think or whether your ad might inconvenience them; you're out to benefit yourself. When
you spam by posting the same advertisement to hundreds or thousands of newsgroups, you're saying that
your personal profit is more important than the discussions of millions ofpeople.

Would *you* like it if someone came by your house
day after day and shoveled several thousand copies
of an advertising circular through your windows?

Each copy of the ad takes up disk space on thousands
of machines around the world -- and if you post the
ad 1,000 times, that's millions of copies of your
message that *you* are making other people pay to
store copies of. When you spam, you're hogging hundreds of thousands of dollars worth of other people's storage space.

So please, don't do it. I've already explained that
one copy of an off-topic ad is rude because it has
nothing to do with the group it was posted to.
Multiply that by a thousand times to get an idea of
how rude it is to spam.

A quick note about what happens to spam:

Another consideration against spamming is that
Usenet readers developed defenses against it, so
it's not very effective. There are quite a few spam
detectors running on Usenet, and if one of them
detects that the same message has been posted
repeatedly to multiple newsgroups, the humans who
run those spam detectors will step in and actually
erase the spamming messages with 'cancel' messages
which are honored at most sites around the world.

A common misconception shared by many members of the
media is that spam is bad because it's *advertising*
and that people who cancel spam are doing so to get
rid of *advertising*. In actual point of fact, most
Usenet users consider cancellation to be extremely
bad manners and something to be done only as a last
resort. When spam-cancellers cancel spam, it's done
because of the *volume* (posting hundreds of times),
not because of the content.

The analogy that's often used is that yes, you have
the right to walk down the street and say whatever
you like -- but you do NOT have the right to stick
your head in someone's house at 3 am and shout
through a bullhorn.

So if you *do* spam, you're likely to lose your
account, have your personal life made a living hell,
possibly get sued by people whose storage space
you're taking up, and in the end, not very many people are even going to see your advertisement. It's
just not worth the grief you'll get.

Sorry to be unpleasant about it, but spam's a really
bad idea.

Finally, if you're wondering where the term "spamming" came from, it came from a Monty Python sketch
in which the characters were in a restaurant which
mainly sold Spam. Items on the menu included things
like "Spam, Spam, Spam, eggs, ham, and Spam."
Whenever the waitress recited the menu, a group of
Vikings in the corner would chime in with her,
chanting the word "Spam" over and over, drowning out
everything else.

Some members of the media have spread the explanation that the word "spamming" derives from throwing chunks of Spam into a fan. This is not where the term comes from.

3. Unsolicited junk email

Another often-practiced and often-punished scheme is to send email to thousands of strangers whose addresses you found in various Usenet newsgroups. In the last year, dozens of people have lost their Internet access after sending thousands of strangers ads for timeshare condos in Cancun or dubious credit schemes, and yet, the junk email continues to flood in.

Suffice it to say that junk email, using Usenet posters' addresses, is a really bad idea. Most sites will yank your account if you do that kind of thing.

4) 'Mail-Merged' ads

Some advertisers noticed that it was only *identical* postings that were getting cancelled by the spam cancellers, and cleverly came up with a way to post their ad to dozens of newsgroups while varying a line or two to make it look sufficiently different to avoid being cancelled.

For example, one book editor posted ads to dozens of newsgroups about his book, essentially giving a sales pitch for said book, while adding a paragraph to each article that purported to contain the text that had been printed about each newsgroup in said book.

It was rather obvious that the editor wasn't interested in getting feedback on the text since the book had already been published; eventually an employee at the company admitted that the technique had been used to try to avoid triggering the spam cancellers -- and that the point had indeed been to broadcast the ad widely without getting cancelled.

Don't do postings that say things like "Congratulations,

REC.FOOD.DRINK.BEER reader, you are among the lucky few to be included in this amazing offer." Spam that makes a token effort to relate to each newsgroup it's posted to is still spam, and will still be erased on sight.

Conclusion

To make a long story short, off-topic advertising and advertising that equates to a bullhorn stuck into someone's window in the middle of the night are bad ideas.

Please exercise restraint and don't make the mistake many have of thinking that just because there's no central authority that can punish you for spamming newsgroups, that there will be no consequences if you do.

There will be consequences if you spam -- and you might be surprised by the lengths that vengeful Usenet users can go to when someone spams their favorite group with yet another off-topic advertisement.

If you want to advertise on Usenet, you can, but please follow the tips contained in this document's "How to" section and don't make the mistakes listed in "How not to do it."

Stay on topic; keep your notices hype-free; only post your notices to newsgroups where they are appropriate.

Do unto others as you would have them do unto you.

Afterword: Advertising on the Internet

It should be noted that there are many ways to advertise on the Internet that don't involve Usenet at all.

Usenet, you see, is NOT the same thing as the Internet. Usenet is transmitted via the Internet, but is also transmitted via other means (see "What is Usenet" in news.announce.newusers for more information). The Internet also includes services like ftp, telnet, gopher, and the World Wide Web.

A World Wide Web page allows you to put up graphics, text, and sound in an interactive hypertext format that's remarkably easy to set up and use. Many thousands of companies and individuals and organizations have put up World Wide Web pages that can be viewed by anyone around the world with a Web browser such as Mosaic or Netscape.

Since the only people who see a Web page are people who *choose* to see it, and since the person who pays for the storage space necessary to hold the Web page is the person or business or organization who put it up and designed it, a Web page is a *much* better way than advertising on Usenet to put your company's information up on the Internet.

If you need help getting going, ask the people who run your site for help on getting started; usually, all you really need to do is go buy a book on basic HTML (Hyper-Text Markup Language) design and/or scout out the newsgroup comp.infosystems.www.author-ing.html. It's really not that hard to set up a Web page, and it's much, much, much more neighborly to put your advertising message on a Web page than to barrage the readers of Usenet.

IF YOU HAVE FURTHER QUESTIONS:

A board of experienced Usenet users stands ready to help suggest non-destructive ways to use Usenet for your commercial purposes. Send mail to commerce@acpub.duke.edu if you have questions or would like help.

This FAQ can also be found online at http://www.danger.com/advo.html.

WHAT'S ON THE CD-ROM

The CD-ROM that accompanies the *Web Catalog Cookbook* contains HTML template files, special Web server software, and a clip-art library that you can use to create an online catalog to display products and take orders. In addition, a special Resource Library of links to valuable Web sites is included on the CD-ROM.

HTML Templates that are ready to use

The Basic Web Catalog described in Chapter 8 uses the HTML templates on the CD-ROM to quickly create a catalog to display a small product line. Chapter 8 takes you step-by-step through the process of adding your product descriptions and photos to the product pages, as well as customizing the company and ordering information pages.

Chapter 9 tells how to add personalization to the catalog created in Chapter 8 to create an Intermediate Web Catalog through the use of a special version of the GuestTrack profile and personalization software. Adding GuestTrack Light to your Web site allows you to create Web pages on the fly based on each customer's personal profile, and a *shopping cart* system that lets customers add products to their order as they browse. The HTML templates on the CD-ROM have the special GuestTrack tags so you're ready to go.

Chapter 10 shows how to upgrade the Web site created in Chapter 9 into one that uses a database to store and retrieve product and photo information. The Advanced Web Catalog uses a special version of the GT/Catalog software on your Web site to create product pages using an HTML template file. The GT/Catalog Web database allows you to store information on hundreds of products, yet Web site maintenance is easy since the system uses a single template file to format product pages quickly and efficiently.

GuestTrack and GT/Catalog to create a personalized Web catalog

The Web provides catalog merchants with the ability to build relationships based on the interests and demographic profile of each of their customers.

While most Web personalization techniques require a staff of programmers to accomplish it, the GuestTrack Light and GT/Catalog Light software included on the CD-ROM puts the power of personalization within reach of HTML developers.

The versions of GuestTrack Light and GT/Catalog Light included on the CD-ROM are special versions of the full commercial versions of these software products. This version of GuestTrack includes many of the personalization capabilities of the full commercial version. GT/Catalog Light has the same functions as the full commercial version, but the number of products it will store is limited to 400.

Clip art designed for the Web

Web catalogs are more than just descriptive copy and product photographs—they are also about image. If you are just starting to create your first Web site, then you will want to create buttons and banners that help position your products in your customer's mind. The clip-art library on the CD-ROM has many complete sets of art you can use to enhance your Web site. Each of the over 50 sets are grouped into three sections so you can select a set that reflects the image of your company and your products.

↳ Resource library

The text refers to many companies and products that can help a Web merchant enhance their Web site and other aspects of their company. Links to these Web sites are included in a special HTML file on the CD-ROM, as well as on the special Web site that provides support for readers of the book.

Hardware requirements

The Internet has traditionally used UNIX computers to serve the Internet community, so most commercial Web hosting companies use UNIX computers for Web servers. The GuestTrack software on the CD-ROM requires a UNIX operating system and a Web server that uses the traditional *Common Gateway Interface*, or CGI, for running external programs.

Installing the software

Installation of the GuestTrack software on UNIX servers is described in Chapter 7, including the process of using the CHMOD command to set the mode of programs.

In addition to the manual process of installing software on the Web server, special arrangements have been made with leading Web hosting companies to allow readers of the *Web Catalog Cookbook* to use an automated installation process that copies all of the software, configuration files, and database files into the Web server directories. This automated installation process is also described in Chapter 7.

User assistance and information

Creating Web catalogs that accept orders is a complex process, so an online resource center has been created on the Web to assist readers. A Frequently Asked Questions

(FAQ) section is updated with new material to help answer unusual or unique questions. In addition, a resource Library of links to valuable Web sites is included on the CD-ROM and a frequently updated version of the Online Marketing Resource Library is available on the Web at http://www.allen.com/cookbook.

The software accompanying this book is being provided as is without warranty or support of any kind. Should you require basic installation assistance, or if your media is defective, please call our product support number at (212) 850-6194 weekdays between 9 AM and 4 PM Eastern Standard Time. Or, we can be reached via e-mail at: wprtusw@wiley.com.

To place additional orders or to request information about other Wiley products, please call (800) 879-4539.

INDEX

Receive 20% off the full versions
of
GuestTrack™
and
GT/Catalog Web Software

As a special "thank you" for purchasing the Web Catalog Cookbook, you will receive a 20% discount when upgrading to the full versions of the software contained on the book's accompanying CD-ROM. The Web Catalog Cookbook contains "light" versions of GuestTrack and GT/Catalog software that will help you create your own catalog of up to 400 products. Here is the additional functionality:

GuestTrack   Retail Price $1,000   **Your Price $800**

- ❖ Expand personalization capability
- ❖ Gather profile data throughout the Web site
- ❖ Track Web page displays by users

GT/Catalog   Retail Price $2,000   **Your Price $1,600**

- ❖ Includes complete GuestTrack functionality
- ❖ Increased number of products in database
- ❖ Expand the descriptive text and graphics
- ❖ Add selection capability to display personal catalogs

Here's how to obtain the full versions of GuestTrack and GT/Catalog:

Call: **919/859-3073**

Fax: **919/851-2969**

Web: **http://www.guesttrack.com/cookbook**

Address: **GuestTrack, Inc.**
5540 Centerview Drive, Suite 411
Raleigh, NC 27606

WHAT'S ON THE CD-ROM

The CD-ROM that accompanies the Web Catalog Cookbook contains the following items to help you create your own online catalog:

HTML templates for beginner, intermediate, and advanced Web catalogs

GuestTrack Light and GT/Catalog Light software to help you personalize your Web catalog

A clip-art library of over 50 sets of buttons and banners to enhance your catalog

A resource library of links to valuable Web sites

USING THE SOFTWARE

This software contains files to help you utilize the models described in the accompanying book. By opening the package, you are agreeing to be bound by the following agreement:

This software product is protected by copyright and all rights are reserved by the author, John Wiley & Sons, Inc., or their licensors. You are licensed to use this software on a single computer. Copying the software to another medium or format to use on a single computer does not violate the U.S. Copyright Law. Copying the software for any other purpose is a violation of the U.S. Copyright Law.

This software product is sold as is without warranty of any kind, either express or implied, including but not limited to the implied warranty of merchantability and fitness for a particular purpose. Neither Wiley nor its dealers or distributors assumes any liability for any alleged or actual damages arising from the use of or the inability to use this software. (Some states do not allow the exclusion of implied warranties, so the exclusion may not apply to you.)

GOVERNANCE AND POLICY IN **sport** ORGANIZATIONS

SECOND EDITION

Mary A. Hums
UNIVERSITY OF LOUISVILLE

Joanne C. MacLean
BROCK UNIVERSITY

Packianathan Chelladurai
CONSULTING EDITOR, SPORT MANAGEMENT SERIES

Holcomb Hathaway, Publishers
Scottsdale, Arizona

Library of Congress Cataloging-in-Publication Data

Hums, Mary A.
   Governance and policy in sport organizations / Mary A. Hums, Joanne C. MacLean. — 2nd ed.
     p. cm. — (Sport management series)
   ISBN 978-1-890871-89-5
1. Sports administration.   2. Sports--Management.   I. MacLean, Joanne,
II. Title.
   GV713.H86 2009
   796.06'9—dc22

                                    2008022644

Photo on p. 245 © Diademimages, p. 281 © Shariffc, p. 303 © Serega, downloaded from Dreamstime Photos, www.dreamstime.com.

Copyright © 2004, 2009 by Holcomb Hathaway, Publishers, Inc.

Holcomb Hathaway, Publishers, Inc.
6207 North Cattletrack Road
Scottsdale, Arizona 85250
(480) 991-7881
www.hh-pub.com

10 9 8 7 6 5 4 3

ISBN 978-1-890871-89-5

All rights reserved. No part of this publication may be reproduced, stored in a retrieval system, or transmitted in any form or by any means, electronic, photocopy, recording, or otherwise, without the prior written permission of Holcomb Hathaway, Inc.

Printed in the United States of America.

CONTENTS

Managerial Activities Related to Governance 19

Strategic Management and Policy Development 41

Ethics in Sport Organizations   59

Scholastic Sport   77

Amateur Sport in the Community   105

Campus Recreation   137

Intercollegiate Athletics   169

The Major Games in Amateur Sport   215

Olympic Sport   245

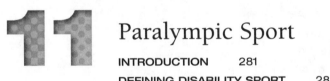

Paralympic Sport   281

North American Professional Sport   303

International Professional Sport   327

The Future of Sport Governance   343

FOREWORD

by Packianathan Chelladurai

In the past decade scholars have published books on many of the topics suggested in the guidelines of the National Association for Sport and Physical Education and the North American Society for Sport Management. Yet there was a deficiency in the list, with few texts on the important topic of governance. Mary Hums and Joanne MacLean filled that gap with this text.

While the research on and the teaching of management topics at the organizational level are legitimate and needed, they tend to overlook the significance and influence of governance organizations, which are at the apex of the organizational network in a given industry segment. In general, these governance organizations serve to achieve the individual and collective goals of the member organizations. They may be authorized to control and regulate the activities of the member organizations. Such organizations also serve the member organizations by generating valued resources and facilitating the interactions and exchange of information among members.

Given the significant role of these governance organizations and the extent and manner of how they govern their respective segments of the sport industry, one would expect that discourse regarding them would have been more extensive than it is now. Notable exceptions are the work of Trevor Slack and his associates, who have studied extensively the national sport governing bodies in Canada, and James Thoma and Laurence Chalip, who have studied governing bodies at the international level. Similarly, the National Collegiate Athletic Association has been the focus of much research and discussion. But such works have been largely confined to governing bodies representing elite sport, just one segment of the sport industry. Hums and MacLean identify and describe this as well as other segments. This book includes chapters on scholastic sport, amateur sport in the community, campus recreation, intercollegiate athletics, major games in amateur sport, Olympic sport, Paralympic sport, North American professional sport, and international professional sport. The conception and selection of these segments is obviously justified by the existence of governing bodies for each of the selected segments. It is also noteworthy that Hums and MacLean cover segments of the industry that encompass participant sport, elite sport, professional/commercial sport, and sport for individuals with disabilities.

The chapters on each of these segments are unique in their inclusion of history of the segment, the governance structures and programming within the segment, and the policy issues faced in each segment. Readers will appreciate and enjoy the presentation in each chapter of the mission statements and financial and membership aspects of the respective governance organizations.

While the chapters on the governance of the segments are the substance of the text, the authors have prefaced these chapters with four introductory chapters. The first chapter is a lucid introduction to the sport industry, its segments, and the concept of governance. The authors argue rightfully that students should gain insight into the "Big Picture" of sport governance in addition to understanding individual organizations within a segment. The second chapter is devoted to a treatise on managerial activities including planning, organizing, and decision making. The critical concepts of strategic management and policy development are dealt with separately in the third chapter. The fourth chapter is devoted to ethics in sport organizations. This is an important chapter because a major responsibility of governance organizations is to foster ethical conduct by member organizations and the individuals therein. These four introductory chapters lead nicely into the substance of the book. The book's final chapter is fittingly devoted to raising issues that will confront sport governing organizations in the future.

It is a matter of great pleasure and pride to present the credentials of the authors. The pleasure is professional in the sense that I am referring to two outstanding professionals in the field. The pride is personal and stems from the fact that my association with these scholars began as they were developing as academics. Mary Hums and Joanne MacLean are not new to the science and art of writing scholarly papers and texts. Each has published in leading journals and each has published texts and/or chapters in texts. And each has been associated with the governance organizations about which they write. These practical experiences have provided them with the insights that they admirably bring to bear on the discussion of the governance of sport industry organizations and segments.

The authors suggest in their preface that the book is written for upper-level undergraduate or graduate students. I am inclined to believe that the substance of the text would be equally appealing to students at all levels. An instructor may adopt the strategy of introducing the industry segments and their governance mechanisms, and then follow it up with classes on management of the governance and member organizations. By the same token, classes on marketing activities of the governance and member organizations may also follow the introduction to industry segments and their governance.

In sum, Hums and MacLean have written an excellent text on the governance of segments of the sport industry and I am pleased and proud to offer this foreword. I thank the authors and the publisher for granting me this honor.

G*overnance and Policy in Sport Organizations* is designed for use in governance or policy development courses with upper-level undergraduate students, and can also be used with some graduate-level courses that introduce students to business aspects of the sport industry.

Sport management students enter the workforce and are employed in various segments of the sport industry. An important part of their training is learning the structure and function of the various sport organizations they will work within or interact with. Successful sport managers understand the big picture of how their sport organizations are structured. They also know what issues their organizations—and they as managers—will have to confront. This book challenges students to integrate management theory with governance and policy development practices. It discusses where the power lies in an organization or industry segment and how individual sport organizations fit into the greater industry.

This second edition of the book provides up-to-date numbers, figures, and examples. Numerous websites for sport organizations are featured throughout the text, to prompt in-class discussions and facilitate further research. These websites are displayed in the margins of the text and thus are easily referred to. In this edition, we have also increased the number of case studies and have addressed policy areas currently of interest in the various sport segments, such as MLB's Mitchell Report, sport and human rights, and the impact of technology in disability sport. Issues such as these will continue to emerge and evolve, and this text will provide a springboard for class discussions and projects.

Although the focus of this book is primarily on North American sport organizations, it presents sufficient information on international sport organizations to provide students with working models and an understanding of these organizations. For example, this edition highlights how North American scholastic, intercollegiate, and professional sports differ from those in other regions of the world. This expanded knowledge is necessary to succeed and be a well-informed manager in the increasingly global sport industry. Our backgrounds as authors—one American and the other Canadian—contribute to the international scope of this book.

Both of us have had hands-on experience in international sport settings as researchers and practitioners. This combination brings a unique skill set and knowledge base to the text.

This book also features a chapter on the Paralympic Games, a growing international operation. As an internationally recognized researcher in the area of management issues affecting disability sport, Mary Hums contributes her expertise to this chapter.

Governance and Policy in Sport Organizations is written and organized with the goal of being teacher- and student-friendly so that instructors will be comfortable with the topic and can present the material to students in a clear, organized fashion. To this end, we now include useful information on this book's application to the NASPE/NASSM sport management curricular guidelines, the organization of the book's chapters, and the teaching tools in the chapters.

NASPE/NASSM Curricular Application

Sport governance is one of the content areas required for Sport Management programs to achieve NASPE/NASSM program approval. Even though the movement to program accreditation (rather than approval) is currently underway, these topics remain relevant. For undergraduate programs, the NASPE/NASSM Standard 12 content area is Governance in Sport. According to this standard, the following content is required:

- Identification of governing bodies in professional and amateur sport
- Organizational structure of a variety of governing bodies
- Authority and functions of various governing bodies
- Requirements for membership in governing bodies
- Sanctions and appeals processes utilized by governing bodies
- Influence of governmental bodies and sports commissions on sport governing bodies

Governance and Policy in Sport Organizations weaves these content areas throughout the chapters. The information is presented for the various industry segments, and students will use relevant concepts to work through the case studies in each chapter. Reading this text will enable your students to meet NASPE/NASSM Standard 12 for content knowledge in sport governance.

Organization of the Chapters

The book is divided into two main sections. The purpose of this division is to first establish the theoretical knowledge bases related to governance and policy development that sport managers need to operate their sport organizations, and then to present ways the theoretical bases play out in practical sport governance environments.

The first section, Chapters 1 through 4, presents the basics of specific managerial activities necessary for governance and policy development in sport organizations. This section includes material that is more theoretical in nature, covering an introduction to sport governance, planning, organizing, decision making, strategic management, and ethics. Because sport managers face ethical dilemmas on a regular basis, the book devotes a chapter to ethical decision making and the importance of corporate social responsibility.

The second section of the book, Chapters 5 through 13, details the governance structures of various sport industry segments, including

- scholastic sport
- amateur sport in the community
- campus recreation
- intercollegiate athletics
- major games in amateur sport
- Olympic sport
- Paralympic sport
- North American professional sport
- international professional sport

The content of this section is much more applied in nature. These chapters on the specific industry segments include sections on history, governance structures, and current policy issues. Organizational policies often develop as a reaction to current issues faced by sport organizations and sport managers. These issues change and evolve over time. For each industry segment, the text presents a selection of current policy issues and strategies that sport organizations are implementing to deal with these issues. As mentioned earlier, topics that have come to the forefront since the initial edition are now included. Often, such organizational policy decisions have ethical underpinnings as well. Throughout the sections on current policy issues, the book addresses the ethical questions sport managers must confront when developing policies. These ethical issues are integrated into many of the case studies as well.

Finally, in Chapter 14, with the goal of stimulating student thought and class discussion, we consider issues with which sport governing bodies may have to grapple in the future.

Instructional Tools

Each chapter includes Chapter Questions, for use either as homework assignments or for class discussion. In addition, all chapters in this edition contain Case Studies, many of which have been used successfully in governance classes and have proven useful for students. The first edition of this text included case studies only in the industry segment chapters.

The ancillary materials for this text include an Instructor's Manual and PowerPoint presentation. The Instructor's Manual contains student learning objectives, exam questions (multiple choice, short answer, and true/false), and suggestions for additional assignments. The PowerPoint presentation focuses on key points from the chapters to help instructors deliver the material as effectively as possible. New to this edition, to help readers easily access the many websites cited throughout the book, the ancillary materials also include an electronic document containing links to the sites. You may distribute this file to your students or post it on your website. These ancillary materials are available to instructors with adoption of the text.

It is our hope that instructors and students will find this book to be an interesting and useful tool for learning the fundamentals of sport governance and its relationship to current policy and ethical issues facing today's sport managers. It is a book designed to help readers understand the big picture of the sport industry, and their place in it as future sport management professionals.

Note: We have made every effort to verify the website addresses that appear in this book. Such information changes frequently, however, so readers are likely to encounter some URLs that are no longer active. We regret any inconvenience this may cause.

ACKNOWLEDGMENTS

A book project, truly a labor of love, cannot be undertaken and successfully completed "flying solo," so many thanks are in order. I would like to specifically acknowledge my Sport Administration colleagues at the University of Louisville: Chris Greenwell, Dan Mahony, Anita Moorman, and Simon Pack. Without their ongoing and daily support and encouragement, as academics but more importantly as friends, this project would never have reached completion. I am especially thankful for all they have done for me during the past ten years. I would also like to thank the student research assistants who helped me with this book in one or both of its editions: Yung Chou (Enzo) Chen, Morgan Fishman, Robert Sexton, and Mark Perry. They put in numerous hours at the computer and in the library searching for information.

My thanks to Dr. Chelladurai for contributing his foreword to the book, but even more for his valuable guidance and mentorship in my academic life. Thanks to Colette Kelly and all the good people at Holcomb Hathaway, and to the following reviewers, who did a thoughtful and thorough job: Gala Bank, Northwood University; Carol A. Barr, University of Massachusetts; Dennis Bechtol, Northwood University, Florida Campus; Richard C. Bell, Mesa State College; Mel Brennan, Towson University; Susan Brown Foster, Saint Leo University; Karen Danylchuk, University of Western Ontario; Stephen W. Dittmore, University of Arkansas; John Harris, Kent State University; Timothy Henrich, University of the Incarnate Word; Sue Inglis, McMaster University; E. Newton Jackson, Florida State University; Darlene Kluka, Kennesaw State University; John D. McMillan, Bowling Green State University; Steven Ross Murray, Mesa State College; Barry J. Nicholson, Southeast Missouri State University; Jeff Noble, Wichita State University; Cecile Reynaud, Florida State University; James T. Reese, Ohio University; B. David Ridpath, Mississippi State University; Raymond G. Schneider, Bowling Green State University; Robert Taylor, California University of Pennsylvania; Bernadette M. Twardy, Flagler College; Susan Vail, York University; and Michael Wynn, Northwood University.

Thanks to David Grevemberg from the International Paralympic Committee in Bonn, Germany, for his assistance with the chapter on Paralympic sport.

I would also like to thank all of our professional colleagues who adopted the book and made it as successful as it is. I sincerely appreciate that support. And to all the students who read it—a big thank you! Without the students, we wouldn't have had the opportunity to write this book.

Finally, I would like to thank my family and friends here and around the world for their support and encouragement. Once again I cannot say enough about the good work of my coauthor, Joanne MacLean. One of the main reasons I asked Joanne if she wanted to team with me on this project was because I knew she was a "do-er." I was not disappointed, as she motivated me and kept me going on more occasions than she will ever know! I enjoy working with people like her—people who make me better.

Thanks to all of you!

—*Mary Hums*

I have been challenged by the magnitude of writing the second edition of this book and want to thank the many individuals who have assisted and encouraged me. I am fortunate for the support and inquisitiveness of my students and colleagues at Brock University. I wish to thank and applaud the efforts of one undergraduate student in particular: Josh Kruger worked scrupulously as a research assistant in the updating of this book. His attention to detail in researching a myriad of questions and suggestions for examples has summarily improved the text, and I am indebted to Josh for his thoroughness and hard work.

I appreciate and wish to acknowledge the reviewers of the manuscript, listed above, who brought both relevance and depth of thought through their comments, making a significant contribution to the usefulness of this edition. I also wish to thank Colette Kelly and Gay Pauley of Holcomb Hathaway for their support and insightful comments throughout the second edition process. I continue to be grateful for my family and friends who have always encouraged and shown interest in my academic pursuits.

Finally, I am thankful for my coauthor, Mary Hums, who has simply been terrific to work with chapter by chapter, displaying a wonderful work ethic, breadth of knowledge of governance in sport organizations, and a sense of humor that helps me keep perspective on the important things in life. My thanks to you all!

—*Joanne MacLean*

ACRONYMS DEFINED

Here is a reference list defining the many organizational acronyms you will encounter in this book.

AAU	Amateur Athletic Union
ACLU	American Civil Liberties Union
ACT	American College Test
AD	Athletic Director
ADA	Americans with Disabilities Act
AFC	American Football Conference
AFC	Asian Football Confederation
AFL	American Football League
AFL-CIO	American Federation of Labor–Congress of Industrial Organizations
AGM	Annual General Meeting
AIA	Arizona Interscholastic Association
AIAA	Atlantic Intercollegiate Athletic Association
AIAW	Association for Intercollegiate Athletics for Women
APR	Academic Progress Rate
ASAA	Alberta Schools' Athletic Association
ASC	Australian Sports Commission
ASCOD	African Sports Confederation for the Disabled
BAA	Basketball Association of America
B.A.S.S.	Bass Anglers Sportsman Society
BUSA	British Universities Sporting Association
CAAWS	Canadian Association for the Advancement of Women in Sport and Physical Activity
CAF	Confédération Africaine de Football
CAHPERD	Canadian Association for Health Physical Education Recreation and Dance
CBA	collective bargaining agreement
CCAA	Canadian Collegiate Athletic Association
CCES	Canadian Centre for Ethics in Sport
CEO	Chief Executive Officer
CGF	Commonwealth Games Federation
CIAU	Canadian Interuniversity Athletic Union
CIRA	Canadian Intramural Recreation Association
CIS	Canadian Interuniversity Sport
CISS	International Committee of Sports of the Deaf
COC	Canadian Olympic Committee
CONCACAF	Confederation of North Central American and Caribbean Association Football
CONMEBOL	Confederaciön Sudamericana de Fútbol
COO	Chief Operating Officer
CP-ISRA	Cerebral Palsy International Sport and Recreation Association
CPR	cardiopulmonary resuscitation
CSR	corporate social responsibility
CU	Cornell University
DI	Division I
DI-FBS	Division I Football Bowl Series
DI-FCS	Division I Football Championship Series
DII	Division II
DIII	Division III
DU	Drew University
ED	Executive Director
EPC	European Paralympic Committee
EPL	England's Premier League
FA	Football Association of England
FAR	Faculty Athletics Representative
FARA	Faculty Athletics Representatives Association
FARE	Football Against Racism in Europe
FIA	Fédération Internationale de l'Automobile
FIBA	Fédération Internationale de Basketball Association
FIFA	Fédération Internationale de Football Association

FISU	Fédération Internationale du Sport Universitaire
FIVB	International Volleyball Federation
GOC	Games Organizing Committee
GPA	grade-point average
HBCUs	Historically Black Colleges and Universities
HHSAA	Hawaii High School Athletic Association
IAAUS	Intercollegiate Athletic Association of the United States
IBSA	International Blind Sports Association
ID	identification
IF	international federation
I–FBS	Football Bowl Subdivision
IFC	International Sports Federation
I–FCS	Football Championship Division
IHF	International Handball Federation
IHSAA	Iowa High School Athletic Association
IIS	Institute for International Sport
INAS-FID	International Association of Sport for People with an Intellectual Disability
IOC	International Olympic Committee
IOSDs	International Organizations of Sport for the Disabled
IPC	International Paralympic Committee
IPSFs	International Paralympic Sport Federations
ISFs	International Sport Federations
ISHSAA	Indiana State High School Athletic Association
ISOD	International Sport Organization for the Disabled
ITTF	International Table Tennis Federation
JCC	Jewish Community Centers
JFA	Japan Football Association
JrNBA	Junior National Basketball Association
JrWNBA	Junior Women's National Basketball Association
JSL	Japan Soccer League

KHSAA	Kentucky High School Athletic Association
LLB	Little League Baseball
LOCOG	London Organizing Committee for the Olympic Games
LPGA	Ladies Professional Golf Association
MCAHA	Muskegon (Michigan) County Amateur Hockey Association
MIA	Motorsports Industry Association
MIAA	Massachusetts Interscholastic Athletic Association
MLB	Major League Baseball
MLBPA	Major League Baseball Players Association
MLS	Major League Soccer
MMA	Mixed Martial Arts
MVP	most valuable player
NAIA	National Association of Intercollegiate Athletics
NAIB	National Association of Intercollegiate Basketball
NASCAR	National Association of Stock Car Auto Racing
NASPE	National Association for Sport and Physical Education
NASSM	North American Society for Sport Management
NBA	National Basketball Association
NBL	National Basketball League
NBPA	National Basketball Players Association
NCAA	National Collegiate Athletic Association
NCCAA	National Christian College Athletic Association
NCHSAA	North Carolina High School Athletic Association
NEA	National Education Association
NFC	National Football Conference
NFHS	National Federation of State High School Associations
NFL	National Football League
NFLPA	National Football League Players Association
NGBs	national governing bodies
NHL	National Hockey League

NHLPA	National Hockey League Players Association		PIAA	Pennsylvania Interscholastic Athletic Association
NIA	National Intramural Association		QU	Queen's University
NIAAA	National Interscholastic Athletic Administrators Association		RBI	Reviving Baseball in the Inner Cities
NIRSA	National Intramural-Recreational Sports Association		SAT	Scholastic Aptitude Test
			SBHCS	Saint Barnabas Health Care System
NJCAA	National Junior College Athletic Association		TSSAA	Tennessee Secondary School Athletic Association
NMAA	New Mexico Activities Association			
NOC	National Olympic Committee		UCLA	University of California Los Angeles
NPC	National Paralympic Committee		UEFA	Union of European Football Associations
NSAA	Nebraska School Activities Association		UM	University of Michigan
NSCAA	National Small College Athletic Association		UN	United Nations
NSF	National Sport Federation		USADA	United States Anti-Doping Association
NSOs	Canadian National Sport Organizations		USFL	United States Football League
NYSPHSAA	New York State Public High School Athletic Association		USNZ	University Sport New Zealand
			USOC	United States Olympic Committee
OCOG	Organizing Committee for the Olympic Games		VANOC	Vancouver–Whistler Canada Organizing Committee
OFC	Oceania Football Confederation		VHSL	Virginia High School League
OFSAA	Ontario Federation of School Athletic Associations		WADA	World Anti-Doping Agency
OQWIA	Ontario–Quebec Women's Intercollegiate Athletics		WFL	World Football League
			WHA	World Hockey Association
OSAA	Oregon School Activities Association		WIAU	Women's Intercollegiate Athletic Union
OSU	Ohio State University		WMSC	World Motor Sports Council
OUA	Ontario University Athletics		WNBA	Women's National Basketball Association
OUAA	Ontario University Athletics Association		WSF	Women's Sports Foundation
OWIAA	Ontario Women's Intercollegiate Athletic Association		WTA	Women's Tennis Association
			WWE	World Wrestling Entertainment
PAs	Players Associations		XFL	Xtreme Football League
PAR-Q	Physical Activity Readiness Questionnaire		YMCA	Young Men's Christian Association
PASO	Pan American Sports Organization		YMHA	Young Men's Hebrew Association
PBA	Professional Bowlers Association		YWCA	Young Women's Christian Association
PBRA	Professional Bull Riders Association		YWHA	Young Women's Hebrew Association
PGA	Professional Golfers' Association			

1

INTRODUCTION TO SPORT GOVERNANCE

INTRODUCTION

The National Collegiate Athletic Association (NCAA) passes a new rule about eligibility. A Major League Baseball (MLB) player gets suspended for using performance-enhancing drugs. A city's Parks and Recreation Department creates a new program for people with disabilities. A campus recreation center requires an identification card to enter the facility. The International Olympic Committee changes the sports on the official program of the Olympic Games. These are regular

1

occurrences in the sport industry, each of which deals with issues of membership, regulation, programming, or organizational structure. All are related to governance and policy development in sport organizations. Many organizations in the sport industry act as governing bodies and make decisions about the everyday operation of the industry. This chapter will set the groundwork for you to see governance and policy development in action in the sport industry.

What Is the Sport Industry?

Today's sport industry is continually expanding and evolving on a global scale. Sport is distinctive and remarkable in magnitude and influence, reaching billions of participants and followers. The mass media devote special coverage to the sporting world, recounting competitive, recreational, and leisure-time activities for a variety of age groups and participant levels. Scholars study sport from each angle as well, including sport history, sport psychology, and sport management.

In your sport management academic career, you are by now well aware of the industry segments of this global industry, including professional sport, intercollegiate athletics, the Olympic and Paralympic Movements, recreational sport, facility management, event management, sport for people with disabilities, health and fitness, sport club management, interscholastic sport, sport marketing, and legal aspects of sport. Considering the numerous segments comprising the sport industry, what is the size and monetary value of this business we call sport?

Scope of the Industry

According to an annual survey (Street & Smith's Sport Group, 2007), in the year 2006 the value of the United States sport industry was estimated at approximately $213 billion; higher than twice the size of the U. S. auto industry and seven times the size of the movie industry. Among the components that make up this value are advertising (14.1%), spectator spending (13.4%), sporting goods (13.2%), operating expenses (11.8%), gambling (9.7%), travel (8.3%), personal services (7.8%), medical spending (6.5%), licensed goods (5.4%), media broadcast rights (3.6%), sponsorship (3.3%), facility construction (1.3%), multimedia (1.1%), endorsements (0.5%), and Internet (0.1%) (Street & Smith's Sport Group, 2007).

Despite its size, the sport industry is a people-oriented, service-oriented industry. The importance of treating one's customers and employees in a positive manner has been widely discussed throughout all of your coursework. Most Sport Management courses deal with a micro approach to the industry, focusing on various specific areas such as marketing, facility management, event management, or financial issues. Governance courses, on the other hand, take a macro view of sport organizations and will help you understand the big picture of how the various sport industry segments work together. Successful sport managers need the conceptual skills (Chelladurai, 2005) to see the big picture, an important element in governance. Governance is more closely related to courses dealing with management, organizational behavior, or most especially, legal aspects of sport, which deals specifically with governance-related and policy-oriented issues. What, then, is the definition of *governance?*

Definition of Governance

A common dictionary definition of *governance* is "the exercise of authority." Often, we associate governance with power, authority, control, and high-level policy making in organizations. People involved in governance make decisions that set the tone for the entire organization.

Sport governance occurs mainly on three different levels—local, national, and international. Examples of a local governance organization are the Kentucky High School Athletic Association (KHSAA) at the state level and the Ontario Federation of School Athletic Associations (OFSAA) at the provincial level. On the national level, examples include the National Football League (NFL), the National Intramural-Recreational Sports Association (NIRSA), USA Hockey, Hockey Canada, and the Hellenic Basketball Federation in Greece. International organizations include the International Olympic Committee (IOC), the International Paralympic Committee (IPC), FIFA (Fédération Internationale de Football Association), which is the international governing body for soccer, and FIBA (Fédération Internationale de Basketball Association), the international governing body for basketball.

Governance structures within such organizations, while often similar, are not universally the same. Governance structures in North American sport differ from governance structures in European sport. For example, professional leagues in Europe use the promotion and relegation system in which basketball teams that finish at the bottom of a Division I league are relegated to Division II while the top teams in Division II are promoted to Division I. This system is not used in the professional sport leagues in North America. Even within North America, differences exist between governance structures in Canada and the United States. NCAA rules and regulations governing collegiate sport in the United States are different from the Canadian Interuniversity Sport (CIS) rules and regulations governing college sport in Canada. The role of a country's government in sport also differs. Some countries may have a separate Ministry of Sport while others may have a sport governing body within a Ministry of Education or Culture. Again, this differs from the United States, where no federal government office exists to oversee all sport in the country.

In the professional sport industry segment, Sharp, Moorman, and Claussen (2007, p. 60) describe *governance* as being "roughly divided into governance of team sports by professional sport leagues and governance of individual sports by players associations operating professional tours." For international sport managers, according to Thoma and Chalip (1996), governance involves making effective choices among policy alternatives. They suggest three techniques sport managers can use in the international setting: ideology analysis, political risk analysis, and stakeholder analysis.

Sport governance is often easy to identify but difficult to define. For purposes of this textbook, the authors define *sport governance* as follows:

> Sport governance is the exercise of power and authority in sport organizations, including policy making, to determine organizational mission, membership, eligibility, and regulatory power, within the organization's appropriate local, national, or international scope.

We will study each element of this definition in this book.

What Is an Organization?

In order for sport governance to take shape, we must first have an organization that needs governing. Certainly plenty of groups are involved with sport, but what truly identifies a group as an organization, rather than just a group of people?

Chelladurai (2005) lists several attributes of an organization, including the following:

1. identity
2. program of activity
3. membership
4. clear boundaries
5. permanency
6. division of labor
7. hierarchy of authority
8. formal rules and procedures

To illustrate how an organization is different from just a group a people, let's attempt to apply these attributes to (1) a professional basketball team and (2) the group of people you met in college and regularly go out with on weekends.

1. Identity. Teams establish an identity to the public by their name, whether that name is the Lakers, the Monarchs, Real Madrid, or Olympiakos. Teams also have an established corporate identity separate from the players or the fans. In contrast, your group of friends usually does not have a name and is not an established business entity.

2. Program of activity. A program of activity implies that an organization has a certain set of goals it wishes to achieve and that these goals are tied to its mission statement and its successful business operation. A basketball team wants to win a championship, and the people who work in its front office want to maximize revenues. A group of friends may have goals (for example, to go to an event), but it does not have a written set of goals it wishes to accomplish or a written mission statement.

3. Membership. Organizations have set rules about membership. In order to play professional basketball, one would need a certain amount of experience at a certain level of play to be considered for membership in the league. In a group of friends the rules for membership may depend on who is mad at someone this week or whom you met at a party last week.

4. Clear boundaries. We know who plays on the Lakers or the Monarchs because they have published, league-approved rosters. Any claim that "I play for the Lakers" can be easily verified. Groups of friends change from year to year, often from week to week or day to day, depending on who is now dating whom.

5. Permanency. True organizations are permanent, although the organizational members come and go. For example, the Lakers' current players are not the same people as when the franchise was new, but the Lakers' organization still exists. A group of friends also changes over time and eventually may simply disappear as a group.

6. Division of labor. Within organizations labor is divided among members. Tasks are determined, and then people are assigned to the tasks. Organizations clearly illustrate division of labor with organizational charts. The front office of a basketball team has specialization areas such as Marketing, Media Relations, Community Relations, and Ticket Sales. On the other hand, a group of friends has no organizational chart with assigned duties, except perhaps for the designated driver.

7. Hierarchy of authority. An organizational chart also reflects an organization's hierarchy of authority. Who reports to whom is clear from the lines and levels within the chart. At the top of the chart a basketball team has a General Manager in charge of the day-to-day operations of the club; all others answer to her. In a hierarchy, people higher up are responsible for the actions of the people below them. In a group of friends, one seldom has any personal responsibility for the actions of others in the group.

8. Formal rules and procedures. Organizations have formal rules and procedures, such as constitutions, bylaws, and operational manuals. Friends don't have policy manuals outlining how the group will operate, where they will go, and who can come along on Saturday night.

As you see from these very simplified examples, organizations are formalized entities with rules about mission, membership, structure, operation, and authority. You will read about these fundamental concerns of governance in the chapters focusing on the different segments of the sport industry.

Regulatory Power

Another significant aspect of governance is that organizations have regulatory power over members, an ability to enforce rules and impose punishments (sanctions) if necessary. Different governing bodies possess this sanctioning power to different degrees. For example, the National Federation of State High School Associations, referred to as NFSH, establishes set competition rules for individual sports. Failing to follow these rules may prevent a particular school from participating in a certain event. The IOC has the power to ban athletes from participating in future Olympic Games if they test positive for performance-enhancing drugs, and MLB can impose a luxury tax on teams whose payrolls exceed a certain amount.

External and Internal Influences on Sport Organizations

Sport organizations do not exist in a vacuum. As part of the greater society in which they exist, they must anticipate changes in both their external and their internal environments, preferably before they *must* react. Chelladurai (2005) subdivides the organization's external environment into two categories: (1) the task or operating environment, sometimes referred to as the *proximal* (close) environment, and (2) the general environment, also called the *distal* (further removed) environment. Sport organizations must be cognizant of what is happening in their external environments and adapt accordingly. Their internal environments are created through each organization's specific policies and procedures (Chelladurai, 2005).

As open systems with inputs, throughputs, and outputs, sport organizations are in a constant state of interaction with their various environments (Minter, 1998). Governance structures, therefore, must be adaptable to changes in an organization's internal and external environments. For example, as society increasingly disapproves of the use of performance-enhancing drugs by athletes, more and more sport organizations are toughening their policies and procedures regarding the use of banned substances, and as a result, we see the formation of organizations such as the World Anti-Doping Agency (WADA). As more professional athletes receive negative publicity for breaking the laws of their nations, leagues and teams adapt by codifying policies and procedures to deal with athletes in trouble with the law. These *internal* reactions to trends in the sport organization's *external* environment are made to stay current with the times.

The Five R's of Good Governance

For a governing body to operate successfully, it must be structured in such a way that important information can flow throughout the organization and be disseminated externally to others needing this information. But what types of information are most important? According to Grevemberg (1999, p. 10), sport organizations need to be mindful of what he calls the "Five R's":

1. *Regulations*—systems that report organizational governance structures, constitutions, legal control mechanisms, event selection criteria, and codes of eligibility, conduct and ethics
2. *Rules*—systems that report technical rules for the officiating and management of the respective sport's competitive events
3. *Rankings*—systems that report and place athlete/team performances based on results and competitive criteria in to numerical order from first to last place
4. *Records*—systems that report the best performances ever accomplished by athletes/teams within competitions, time periods, or overall
5. *Results*—systems that report the final standings and performance statistics from competitions

If sport organizations can consistently apply the Five R's across all their operations, they will find that governance can be consistent and efficient.

Organizational Units and Documents in Sport Governance

Governance has a certain language, with terms and concepts we must know to understand governance and the inner workings of sport organizations. In terms of sport governance, organizations are made up of distinct organizational units with varying degrees of authority and responsibility. In addition, sport organizations usually maintain a set of documents dealing with governance structures. This section briefly introduces some of these organizational units and documents.

General Assemblies

Many sport organizations (for example, the IOC, IPC, NCAA, and NIRSA) are voluntary in nature. Nevertheless, these organizations employ paid staff members. The size of the headquarters staff can vary widely. NIRSA, for example, has approximately 20 employees, while the NCAA headquarters has approximately 350. However, the paid staff members are not the ones who govern the organizations.

The primary governing body is usually called a General Assembly; it may also be called a Congress or a General Business Meeting. In many sport organizations, the members of this governing body are often volunteers. According to Chelladurai and Madella (2006, p. 84), "Voluntary organizations are truly political systems; power is continuously exerted by professionals and volunteers to influence decisions and actions in order to satisfy personal or group needs."

A General Assembly for a sport organization usually convenes on a regular basis (often yearly). The members of the General Assembly, selected in accordance with an organization's constitution and bylaws, vote as a group on legislation, rules, policies, and procedures. This type of governing body generally elects officers such as the President, Vice Presidents, and Secretary. It also has several standing committees assigned specific tasks, as will be discussed later. Its meetings, or sessions, are generally conducted using a common set of rules of operation. One of the most commonly used set of guidelines for running a meeting is called "Robert's Rules of Order." Those of you who are in a fraternity or sorority may recognize these from house meetings you have attended. These rules are often referred to as Parliamentary Procedure, and most organizations designate a person who is familiar with Robert's Rules as the organizational Parliamentarian. It is the Parliamentarian's job to make sure the group members properly follow Robert's Rules of Order so that discussions can proceed in an orderly manner. Meetings organized using Robert's Rules usually follow this order of events:

Robert's Rules of Order
www.robertsrules.org

1. call to order
2. approval of the minutes of the previous meeting
3. committee reports
4. old business
5. new business
6. announcements
7. a call to adjourn the meeting

During the meeting, when someone wants to make a suggestion for action by the group, he makes what is called a motion to take the action. Another person from the group must then second the motion. Then, the meeting chair allows debate on the action to begin. During this time the motion can be amended and if so, the members must then vote on the amended motion. When the debate is complete, the chair calls for a vote. Votes are taken by a count of hands, by voice, or sometimes by a paper ballot, depending on the topic. If no decision can be reached because, for example, the members need more information, a motion can be tabled—that is, set aside for action at the next meeting. When all the business of the group is complete, someone makes a motion to adjourn the meeting, and after another member seconds that motion, the meeting ends. Using these rules for the standard operation of a business meeting helps ensure fairness and enables all members to voice their opinions in an orderly manner (Introduction to Robert's Rules of Order, n.d.).

Often the agendas for General Assembly meetings and the issues on which they vote come from a body known as an Executive Committee or Management Council.

Executive Committees, Governing Boards, and Management Councils

Executive Committees, sometimes called Governing Boards or Management Councils, are small subsets of an organization's General Assembly. Members of the General Assembly select a group, usually from 5 to 20 members, to serve on the organization's Executive Committee. Many believe that the Executive Committee is where the "real power" in a sport organization lies. This group usually generates the agenda action items on which the General Assembly votes. If the Executive Committee does not endorse an idea, it will almost never be brought to the General Assembly for a vote. In addition, this group meets formally more frequently, often two or three times a year, in order to deal with issues that may come up between General Assembly meetings. It may also deal with special issues via scheduled video conferences and conference calls, or through e-mail.

Standing Committees

Sport organizations also designate standing committees with specific responsibilities within their governance structures. The type and number of standing committees vary by organization. The International Table Tennis Federation (ITTF) has committees for the following areas:

- Media
- Nominations

- Ranking
- Rules
- Sports Science
- Technical
- Umpires and Referees
- Veterans
- Commissions and Working Groups (Juniors, Women's Working Group, Calendar Working Group)
- New Technologies & Research Advisory Board (ITTF, 2007)

FIFA, the international governing body for football (soccer), has the following standing committees (FIFA, 2007, p. 30):

- Finance Committee
- Internal Audit Committee
- Organising Committee for the FIFA World Cup
- Organising Committee for the FIFA Confederations Cup
- Organising Committee for the Olympic Football Tournaments
- Organising Committee for the FIFA World Youth Championships
- Committee for Women's Football and FIFA Women's Competitions
- Futsal Committee
- Organising Committee for the FIFA Club World Championship
- Referees Committee
- Technical and Development Committee
- Sports Medical Committee
- Players' Status Committee
- Legal Committee
- Committee for Fair Play and Social Responsibility
- Media Committee
- Associations Committee
- Football Committee
- Strategic Committee
- Marketing and Television Advisory Board

Ad Hoc Committees

At times, sport organizations face issues that need to be dealt with on a short-term basis. For example, perhaps the organization is planning to host a special fundraising event. Because the event may just occur one time, the organization will assemble an *ad hoc,* or temporary, committee that is in charge of the event. Unlike standing committees that deal with ongoing concerns, once the event is over, the ad hoc committee ceases to exist.

Executive Staff

The people who serve on a General Assembly or Executive Council are almost always volunteers. Their business expenses may be paid, but they are not employees of the sport organization. The people who are employed by the sport organization to run the daily operations are called Executive or Professional Staff. People in these positions have titles such as Executive Director, Marketing Director, Sport Administrator, Technical Director, or Event Coordinator. These individuals are paid sport management professionals, employed by the governing body. They work in the organization's headquarters, as opposed to volunteers who may be located anywhere in the world. For example, the Executive Staff of the NCAA works daily in offices in Indianapolis, Indiana. The Athletic Directors on the NCAA Management Councils are located at their home institutions across the nation and come together only at designated times during the year. The staff members for the IPC work in the office in Bonn, Germany. The volunteers who work with a specific sport such as Ice Sledge Hockey, may be located in Canada, Norway, and the United States. They may meet together at a Sport Technical Committee meeting, for example, at a designated time and place each year or may hold a session during the Paralympic Games. The Executive Staff runs the organization on a daily basis, planning events, handling financial matters, and marketing upcoming events.

Constitutions and Bylaws

Almost all sport organizations have documents outlining the basic functions of the organization, usually called the constitution and bylaws. An organization's constitution acts as a governing document that includes statements about the organization's core principles and values. Bylaws, also governing documents, are more operational in nature, outlining how an organization should conduct its business in terms of elections, meetings, and so on. For examples of what these types of documents include, see Figure 1.1, a Table of Contents from the Constitution of the International Volleyball Federation (FIVB), and Figure 1.2, a Table of Contents from the Bylaws of the International Handball Federation (IHF).

These different organizational units and documents will be discussed throughout each of the industry segment chapters in this text.

FIGURE **1.1** Table of contents of the FIVB constitution.

CHAPTER I

Preamble

1.1 Definitions

1.2 Foundation

1.3 Headquarters

1.4 Objectives

1.5 Fundraising Principles

CHAPTER II

Composition of the FIVB

2.1 National Federations

2.2 Affiliation

CHAPTER III

Institutions of the FIVB

3.1 General Provisions

3.2 Congress

3.3 Board of Administration

3.4 Executive Committee

3.5 Presidency

3.6 International Volleyball Tribunal (IVT), Judiciary Institution

3.7 Councils

3.8 Commissions

3.9 Confederations

3.10 Secretariat

CHAPTER IV

Financial Provisions

4.1 Fiscal Year

4.2 Financial Resources

4.3 Budget

4.4 Annual Accounts and Balance Sheets

4.5 Auditors

4.6 Regulations

CHAPTER V

General Provisions

5.1 Sports Events

5.2 Disciplinary Matters

CHAPTER VI

Special Provisions

6.1 Official and Working Languages

6.2 Dissolution

CHAPTER VII

Entering Into Force and Amendments

7.1 Effective Date

7.2 Supersedes Previous Constitution

7.3 Modifications

Source: Condensed from Siekman, R.C.R. & Soek, J. (1998). *Basic documents of international sports organizations.* The Hague, The Netherlands: Kluwer Law International.

Table of contents of the IHF bylaws.	**FIGURE**	**1.2**

I   **Name, Composition, Domicile**

II   **Purpose**

III   **Membership**

IV   **IHF Bodies**

V   **Finances**

VI   **Official Languages, Correspondence, Announcements, and Publications**

VII   **International Events**

VIII   **Rules of the Game**

IX   **Representatives, Officials, Technical Delegates, Referees**

X   **IHF Adjudicating Bodies**

XI   **Dissolution of the IHF**

Source: Condensed from Siekman, R.C.R. & Soek, J. (1998). *Basic documents of international sports organizations.* The Hague, The Netherlands: Kluwer Law International.

Why Study Governance?

With all the areas there are to study within the academic discipline of Sport Management, why do students need to study governance?

Understanding the Big Picture

Governance is one class where you will be truly challenged to put together all the pieces of the sport industry. As mentioned earlier in this chapter, studying sport governance requires the ability to see the big picture, to understand how individual sport organizations fit into the greater industry, and to see the similarities and differences among the various industry segments. With an understanding of sport governance, you will see how the governing structures of seemingly dissimilar organizations such as Campus Recreation and the Olympic Movement have much in common.

Meeting NASSM/NASPE Program Guidelines

As the number of sport management academic programs has increased greatly in the past few decades, so have issues of program quality. In response, in 1987 two academic organizations, the North American Society for Sport Management (NASSM) and the National Association for Sport and Physical Education (NASPE), joined to form a task force to develop curricular standards (Parkhouse, 2001). Recognizing the importance of learning governance, the task force included sport governance as one of the content areas required for Sport Management programs to attain NASSM/NASPE approval. The premise is that students must be familiar with governance agencies, their authority, organizational structure, and functions. According to this standard, the following content knowledge is required:

www

Sport Management Program Standards

www.aahperd.org/naspe/
template.cfm?template=
ns_smps.html

- identification of governing bodies in professional and amateur sport
- organizational structure of a variety of governing bodies
- authority and functions of various governing bodies
- requirements for membership in governing bodies
- sanctions and appeals processes utilized by governing bodies
- influence of governmental bodies and sports commissions on sport governing bodies (NASSM/NASPE, 2000)

Throughout this book information on these content areas will be presented for the various industry segments, and you will apply these concepts from the content areas to work through the case studies in each chapter.

As of this writing, discussion is on-going concerning whether the NASSM/NASPE approval process will evolve to an accreditation process. If the change occurs, accreditation will involve a different type of assessment system for Sport Management academic programs.

How You Will Use Knowledge of Governance in Your Career

Understanding governance structures is important for any sport manager. If you work at a bank, you need to know the rules for your workplace, and probably some basic federal and state laws. But for the most part, especially at an entry-level position, you will not be interacting with the people who make the policies for your bank or for the broader banking industry. In sport, however, especially because of the ramifications of enforcement, you will need to be keenly aware of governance structures and issues. You will need to know where the power lies in your organization, and studying governance can help you understand that. You will need to know which governing body you will be dealing with in your industry segment. If you work in a college athletic department, you must understand how you relate to governance structures of your university, your conference, and the NCAA or CIS. In professional sport, if you deal with players associations or players unions, you will need to know how they relate to the decisions you make. In high school sport, the power rests at the state or provincial level in organizations such as the Indiana State High School Athletic Association (ISHSAA) and the OFSAA. A recreation director in a City Parks and Recreation Department may answer to the mayor or the City Council. If you work for a sport federation such as the Fédération Internationale de l'Automobile, you will have to be knowledgeable about the federation's rules and regulations dealing with athlete eligibility.

Studying sport governance gives you a perspective of where you fit into your sport organization and of where your sport organization fits into your industry segment. For example, if you work in the front office of an MLB team, you will need to understand various levels of governance in your job, from the club's front office to the League Office to the Commissioner's Office. In Olympic and Paralympic Sport, you may be involved in interactions among International Federations, National Governing Bodies, National Olympic Committees, and Organizing Committees of the Olympic Games. In intercollegiate athletics, you will need to know basic NCAA compliance rules to avoid placing your school in danger of NCAA sanctions. If you work for the Commonwealth Games Federation (CGF), you will need to understand eligibility rules for athletes, so that any athletes you are responsible for do not jeopardize their eligibility. In sport, you are likely to have more direct interactions with governing bodies and policy makers than you might in many other industries. In any sport organization you work for or interact with, you need to understand who has the power and where the power lies.

Finally, the importance of sport managers acting in an ethical manner in any sport governance situation cannot be overstated. Sport managers face ethical dilemmas on a daily basis. How they decide to deal with them is a measure of their and their organizations' ethical nature. For this reason this textbook devotes a chapter to ethical decision making and the importance of corporate social responsibility and discusses various ethical issues sport managers may face in different industry segments.

The sport industry continues to grow and develop on a global scale. Studying sport governance allows you to take a big-picture approach to this global industry. Learning about the governing structures and documents for sport organizations illustrates where power and authority exist within the industry. This area of study is important enough to have warranted its own content area within the NASSM/NASPE program approval guidelines, reemphasizing the importance of understanding this complex, fascinating aspect of the sport industry.

In your previous Sport Management classes, you learned about basic managerial activities and functions. For purposes of this textbook, we will focus on four of these important areas—planning, decision making, strategic management and policy development, and ethical decision making. These activities are the heart and soul of the governance process and have separate chapters devoted to them, further explaining their roles in the governance of sport organizations.

The next chapter addresses basic managerial activities vital to effective sport governance. The remainder of the text then guides you through selected industry segments and explains how sport governance is implemented in those segments, using numerous examples to illustrate governance in action. It is our hope that you will enjoy these challenging and interesting areas of study within sport management.

CASE STUDY | *Introduction to Governance*

You are the Sport Director for the State Summer Games in your home state. The Games take place every year, and the program for which sports and events should be included has to be agreed upon by the Games' General Assembly two years in advance of the next Games. A group of people is proposing to add a new sport to the program—Judo. How would the organization proceed with making the decision on whether or not to add Judo to the program?

1. What type of committee should be appointed to study this proposal, and what type of information should it gather to help in making this decision?

2. When the proposal comes to the General Assembly, describe how Robert's Rules of Order would work at that meeting in order to make the decision about Judo being added the program.

CHAPTER QUESTIONS

1. Choose a sport organization and then use Chelladurai's model from this chapter to define the different elements of that organization.
2. Find two sample sport organization constitutions or bylaws. Compare the two for content. Explain why you think they are different or similar.
3. Using the definition of *sport governance* from this chapter, choose a sport organization and identify the different parts of the definition in that sport organization.

REFERENCES

Chelladurai, P. (2005). *Managing organizations for sport and physical activity: A systems perspective* (2d ed.). Scottsdale, AZ: Holcomb Hathaway.

Chelladurai, P., & Madella, A. (2006). *Human resource management in Olympic sport organizations.* Champaign, IL: Human Kinetics.

FIFA. (2007). FIFA statutes. Retrieved October 8, 2007, from www.fifa.com/mm/document/affederation/federation/fifa%5fstatutes%5f0719%5fen%5f14479.pdf.

Grevemberg, D. (1999, May). Information technology: A solution for effective Paralympic Sport administration. Paper presented at the VISTA 1999 Paralympic Sport Conference, Cologne, Germany.

Introduction to Robert's Rules of Order. (n.d.). Retrieved August 20, 2007, from www.robertsrules.org/rulesintro.htm.

ITTF. (2007). Committee nominations 2007. Retrieved October 8, 2007, from www.ittf.com/main/menus/menu_directory.html.

Minter, M. K. (1998). Organizational behavior. In J. B. Parks, B. R. K. Zanger, & J. Quarterman (Eds.), *Contemporary sport management* (pp. 79–89). Champaign, IL: Human Kinetics.

NASSM/NASPE. (2000). *Sport management program standards and approval protocol.* Reston, VA: Author.

Parkhouse, B. L. (2001). *The management of sport: Its foundation and application* (3d ed.). Boston, MA: McGraw-Hill.

Sharp, L. A., Moorman, A. M., & Claussen, C. L. (2007). *Sport law: A managerial approach.* Scottsdale, AZ: Holcomb Hathaway.

Street & Smith's Sport Group. (2007). *About us—The sports industry.* Retrieved April 30, 2007, from www.sportsbusinessjournal.com/index.cfm?fuseaction=page.feature&featureId=43.

Thoma, J. E., & Chalip, L. (1996). *Sport governance in the global community.* Morgantown, WV: Fitness Information Technology.

2

MANAGERIAL ACTIVITIES RELATED TO GOVERNANCE

INTRODUCTION

Sport managers carry out a myriad of managerial activities and functions on a daily basis. The four functions of management have been defined as planning, organizing, leading, and evaluating (Chelladurai, 2005). Sport managers dealing with governance issues must be able to carry out all these functions, but two functions, planning and organizing, are more critical than others and will be discussed in this chapter. Decision making, a subset of leading, is also essential to sport managers dealing with governance issues, and it will also be discussed. Sport managers perform these functions daily. This chapter provides a brief overview of these important managerial activities and their relationship to sport governance.

Planning

The Importance of Planning for Sport Organizations

Sport organizations need to plan because the sport industry is a complex entity. Whether it is the Olympic Games bringing together nations or a high school softball tournament featuring local teams, the sport industry requires interaction and cooperation in order for teams, leagues, tours, and events to be successful. What are the specific purposes of planning? According to Bridges and Roquemore (1996), planning serves to (1) formalize objectives, (2) determine time standards and efficiency, (3) minimize problems, and (4) achieve effective end results. These authors state the benefits are that sound planning (1) gives direction to the efforts of employees, (2) helps an organization determine its own destiny, (3) is key to effective control, and (4) is essential for managerial success. Why, then, do some people insist on resisting efforts to plan?

Resistance to Planning

Some people develop comfort zones. They do things a certain way because "We've always done it that way." To these individuals, trying to implement a plan to do something different or new is a challenge they do not wish to undertake. Sometimes people who have been with an organization for many years respond to planning initiatives with "Why should we do this? We've done this a million times before, and we know no one really looks at these things. Then five years later they ask us to do it again, and they ignore us again." Finally, there are those who simply lack the ability to plan and are intimidated by the process. Good sport managers make planning a priority and learn how to deal effectively with those employees who resist the importance of planning.

Types of Plans

Sport managers must be able to develop both short-term and long-term plans. They must develop timetables so projects and events will take place as smoothly as possible. *Short-term planning* refers to planning projects and events that will occur within the next one to three years. For example, with the Olympic Games, test events in all venues are run within a year or two of the start of the Games. At a new stadium, contracts with concessionaires and security are finalized in the year before the stadium opens.

In contrast, *long-term planning* involves planning that extends three or more years. For example, an Olympic Games is awarded to a host city seven years before the flame is lit to open the Games in that city. Teams deciding to build new stadiums must begin working with architects and contractors at least five years before the first beverage is poured at a game. Within these long-term plans, short-term plans must be implemented. Returning to our stadium example, the people who work in Presentation (coordinating the music, announcements, etc., during an event) need to be able to work with the sound system (short-term planning). However, before a sound system in a venue can be checked, all the proper infrastructure for the power must be in place (long-term planning). All these plans must be carefully sequenced for the sport organization to be successful.

Long-term and short-term plans are not the only types of plans sport managers need to develop. For example, there are standing plans and single-use plans (Chelladurai, 2005). *Standing plans* refer to plans that are put in place and then referred to continuously as certain events repeat. For example, a facility manager who develops a plan for a security check of a venue before a home event would implement the plan repeatedly for each home event. *Single-use plans* refer to plans developed for events that may occur just once. For example, executives at a local Sport Commission may develop a parking plan for an event such as a Ryder Cup or Special Olympics World Games, which may be awarded to their city only one time.

The Planning Process

Sport organizations need to follow a set process to establish effective short-term and long-term plans. For some sport organizations, this process may begin with a vision statement. Other organizations will start with a mission statement and then take the following steps (adapted from VanderZwaag, 1998):

1. vision/mission statement
2. goals
3. objectives
4. tactics
5. roles
6. evaluation

The next sections examine each step in the planning process and use examples to illustrate the different steps. The focus is on the sport organization's front-office planning, rather than on-the-field plans such as the Cincinnati Reds' objective to win the World Series and the University of

Tennessee Lady Vols basketball team's objective to win the NCAA women's basketball tournament. Since you most likely will be working in off-the-field careers, the focus of this chapter is on goals and objectives dealing with front-office matters such as increasing ticket sales or securing sponsorship packages. For sport organizations to effectively move into the future, they must establish both long- and short-range plans. Because sport governance issues are generally broad in nature and affect the entire sport organization, any course of action dealing with governance issues must be carefully planned.

Vision Statements

A number of sport organizations are beginning their planning process by developing what is known as a vision statement. According to Heathfield (2007, Vision Statement section), a *vision statement* is

> a statement about what your organization wants to become. It should resonate with all members of the organization and help them feel proud, excited, and part of something much bigger than themselves. A vision should stretch the organization's capabilities and image of itself. It gives shape and direction to the organization's future.

Vision statements are different from mission statements in that vision statements focus on the organization's future aspirations and values while mission statements focus on an organization's purpose.

The vision statement for the Amateur Athletic Union (AAU) is as follows:

> To offer amateur athletes and volunteers opportunities to develop to their highest level through a national and local network of sporting events. Through participation in AAU, we achieve our dreams as athletes and as valued citizens of our communities. (AAU, 2007)

The vision statement of the Northern British Columbia Winter Games Society is as follows:

> To gain province-wide recognition as a respected, dynamic leader and partner in community and sport development because of our achievement in fostering successful Games. (Northern British Columbia Winter Games Society, 2006)

Another good example of a sport organization's vision statement is that of the International Paralympic Committee, which is presented in Chapter 11.

Mission Statements

Sport organizations are a lot like sailboats. Without a rudder to steer, it does not matter how much or how little wind one has; the boat will not go in its intended direction. It will still float, but it will not get where the crew wants it to go. What gives a sport organization its direction?

Its direction is established early in the planning process with the organization's mission statement. As previously stated, a *mission statement* focuses on an organization's purpose. More specifically, it

1. describes who we are
2. describes what we do
3. uses concise terms
4. uses language that is understandable to people inside and outside the sport organization
5. communicates the organization's purpose, philosophy, and values

A well-written mission statement does not need to be a lengthy document; it may be only 30 to 40 words, or two or three sentences long. All organizational planning documents should flow from the mission statement. As you read the mission statements in this book, keep in mind that they are living documents that are subject to change.

In this section we will use a minor league baseball team as an example, starting with the mission statements of existing franchises. The mission statement for the Everett AquaSox reads:

> The Everett AquaSox Baseball Club upholds a tradition of family owned and operated minor league baseball in the Puget Sound region. Our goal in maintaining the public trust has always been to provide our community with a fun and affordable form of family entertainment in a safe, clean and positive environment. (Everett AquaSox, 2007)

The mission statement for the Lexington Legends states:

> It is the philosophy of this company to serve Central Kentucky and the region by providing affordable, accessible, family-oriented entertainment in an environment that is clean, safe, and fun for all ages. We strive to promote and support our communities in a professional manner through service, leadership and employment opportunities that are available to everyone while earning a responsible profit for our shareholders. The hope of our company is to always dream of what can be; to determine how goals can be accomplished; and to work together in a collaborative style that maintains a family, team-driven effort that continues to seek the perfect vision. (Lexington Legends, 2007)

These mission statements are relatively similar; both clearly state that minor league baseball is about fun and affordable family entertainment. Anyone who has attended a minor league baseball game recently would agree that these statements describe what it is all about—mascots, inexpensive food, and between-inning promotional contests for fans of all ages.

Goals

Different textbooks use differing definitions for *goals* and *objectives*. Sometimes the terms are even used interchangeably. In this textbook, however, *goals* are defined as broad, qualitative statements that provide general direction for a sport organization. They are statements of purpose that are achievable (Mulrooney & Farmer, 2001). For example, a minor league baseball team may have the following goals:

Goal #1 Increase attendance

Goal #2 Increase sponsorship revenues

Objectives

As opposed to goals, which are qualitative in nature, *objectives* are defined as quantitative statements that help a sport organization determine if it is fulfilling its goals. Because objectives are quantitative and can be measured (Mulrooney & Farmer, 2001), they are useful tools in evaluating employee and organizational performance. To be measurable, objectives always contain quantifiable measures such as numbers, percentages, or monetary values. Objectives are tied directly to achieving specific goals. For example:

Goal #1 Increase attendance

Objective #1 Increase game-day walk-up sales by 5 percent

Objective #2 Increase group ticket sales by 10 percent

Goal #2 Increase sponsorship revenues

Objective #1 Secure five new corporate sponsors

Objective #2 Increase the value of existing sponsorships by 5 percent

Measurable objectives are important in two ways: First, they can be used in employee and organizational evaluation and, second, they are necessary because it is difficult to manage something you cannot measure!

Tactics

Once a sport organization has established its goals and objectives, it must determine specifically how it is going to achieve them. These specific how-to steps are called tactics. (Some textbooks use the term *strategies;* to avoid confusion with strategic planning principles, *tactics* is the term used here.) *Tactics* are the specific actions the organization takes to achieve its objectives. For example:

Goal #1 Increase attendance

Objective #1 Increase game-day walk-up sales by 5 percent

Tactic #1 Add two new promotional nights (bobble-head doll giveaway and autographed baseball card giveaway)

Tactic #2 Purchase ten 30-second advertising slots on the new local country radio station

Goal #2 Increase sponsorship revenues

Objective #1 Secure five new corporate sponsors

Tactic #1 Have each sales rep contact ten new local corporations

Tactic #2 Offer special first-year benefits to new sponsors (extra tickets)

Roles

After the tactics have been determined, the responsibilities for carrying out those tactics must be assigned. Roles refer to the organizational units specifically responsible for carrying out the sport organization's tactics and the behaviors that will be necessary to achieve success (VanderZwaag, 1998). For example:

Goal #1 Increase attendance

Objective #1 Increase game-day walk-up sales by 5 percent

Tactic #1 Add two new promotional nights (bobble-head doll giveaway and autographed baseball card giveaway)

Role Ticket Office

Goal #2 Increase sponsorship revenues

Objective #1 Secure five new corporate sponsors

Tactic #1 Have each sales rep contact ten new local corporations

Role Marketing, Sales

Evaluation

In the final step in the planning process, the sport organization must evaluate itself to see if it is fulfilling its mission statement by successfully completing its stated goals, objectives, tactics, and roles. For example:

Goal #1 Increase attendance

Objective #1 Increase game-day walk-up sales by 5 percent

Tactic #1 Add two new promotional nights (bobble-head doll giveaway and autographed baseball card giveaway)

Role Ticket Office

Evaluation Determine the actual percentage increase and compare to 5 percent target. Reward responsible employees appropriately.

Goal #2 Increase sponsorship revenues

Objective #1 Secure five new corporate sponsors

> *Tactic #1* Have each sales rep contact ten new local corporations
>
> *Role* Marketing, Sales
>
> Evaluation Determine the actual number of new sponsors and compare to target (five new sponsors). Reward responsible employees appropriately.

This brief example shows how the planning process flows from one step to the next. This example also shows that the planning process does not consist of a number of separate, fragmented steps but rather is a seamless garment, and it illustrates how the process is part of the big picture of the entire organization. Note, too, that all the steps in the process can be traced directly back to, and should be consistent with, the organization's mission statement.

The Role of Planning in Governance

Sport governance is complex and ever-changing. Sport organizations can be as small as a city soccer league or as massive as the Olympic and Paralympic Movements. Whatever the size of the sport organization, those in charge of the governance structures must plan accordingly. An organization without a well-thought-out and organized plan complete with a mission statement, goals, objectives, tactics, roles, and an evaluation system is destined to fail. Remember: If you fail to plan, you plan to fail.

Organizing

The traditional view of organizing revolves around staffing. We usually think of establishing tasks, determining who will be responsible for those tasks, and then placing those people into a hierarchy, commonly illustrated by an organizational chart. *Organizing* can be defined as "dividing the organization into work units and subunits so their efforts will mesh and fulfill the overall objectives" (Quarterman & Li, 2001, p. 109).

An organizational chart is a diagram showing all positions and reporting relationships within the organization. Sport organizations vary from small units with only a few employees to large, complex organizations with numerous employees. Many of the larger ones are departmentalized into subunits according to the division of labor within the organization and the responsibility of members within each subunit of the organization. Figure 2.1, an example of an organizational chart for a departmentalized sport organization, depicts the division of labor and coordination of divided tasks among members of the organization. The organization might have been subdivided differently, by business function (Figure 2.2) or strategic business unit structure (Figure 2.3). Other organizational charts may reflect departmentalization by geographic region (Figure 2.4), or some mixture of elements (Figure 2.5).

FIGURE **2.1**

Organizational chart for college athletic department organized by internal department.

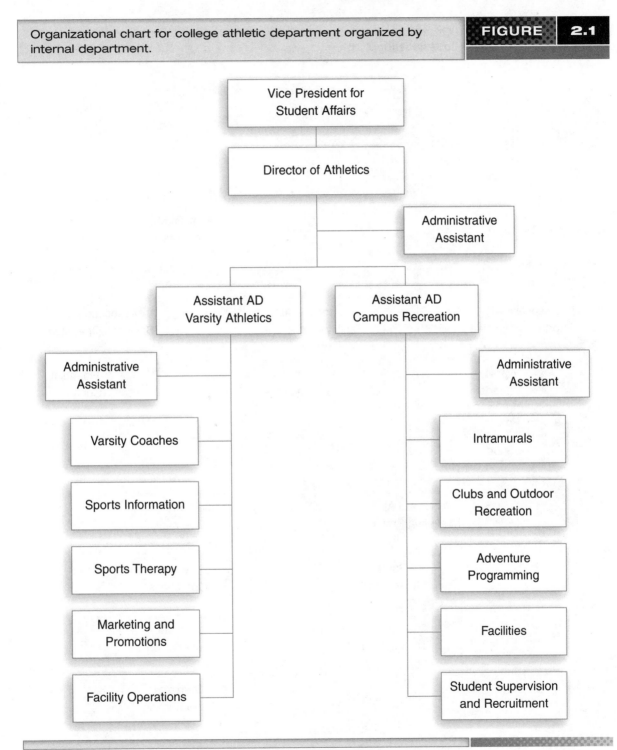

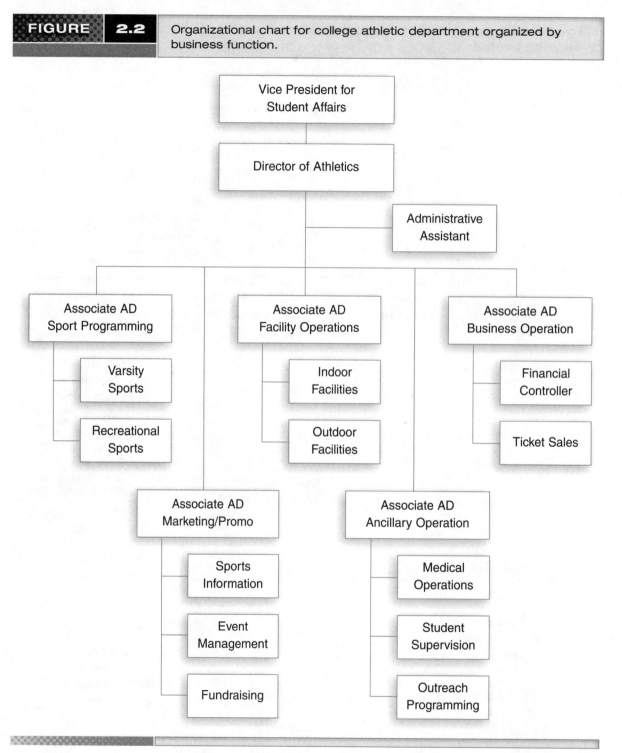

Organizational chart for sporting goods company organized by strategic business unit.

FIGURE   2.3

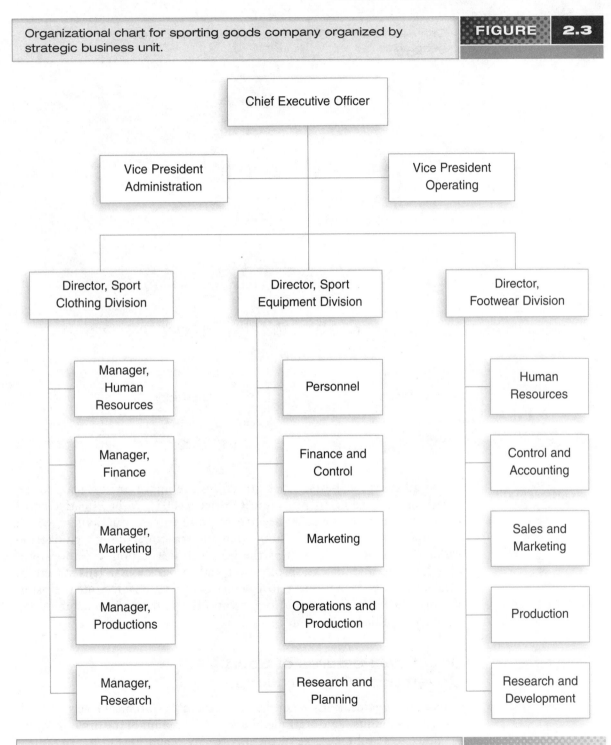

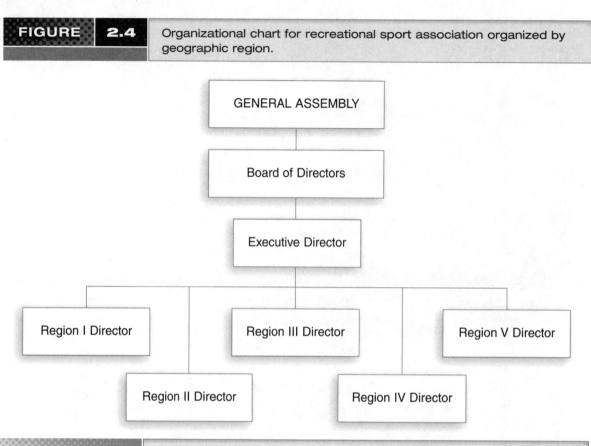

FIGURE 2.4 Organizational chart for recreational sport association organized by geographic region.

In all cases, well-established structures are important for sport organizations. According to Amis and O'Brien (2001), to be effective sport organizations must be structured to respond to the situations in which they operate. Miller (1987) states that the structure of an organization influences many areas, such as the flow of information, collaboration, coordination, and allocation of power and responsibility. This structural influence can be seen in sport governance organizations. Despite their similarities, the structures of sport organizations also have elements unique to their sport industry segment.

Structural Features of Sport Governance Organizations

Governing organizations generally have several hierarchical levels of work units and subunits. Paid staff members usually maintain the organization's headquarters and take care of the day-to-day operations of the organiza-

| Organizational chart for athletic department using a mixture of elements. | **FIGURE** | **2.5** |

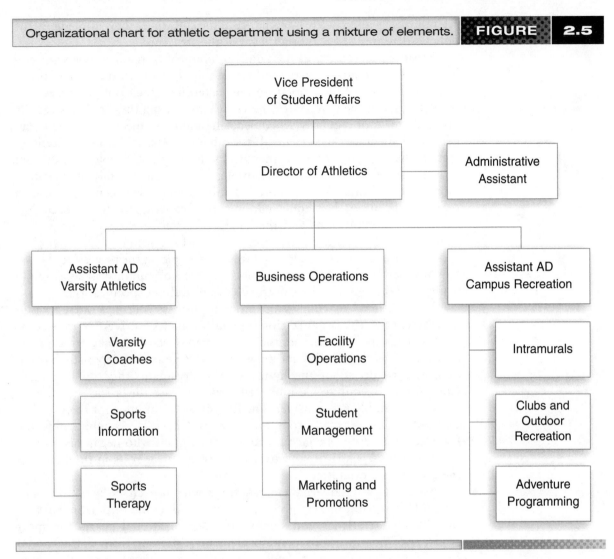

tion. As stated previously, for high school sport, this is the state or provincial athletic association, such as IHSAA. Major professional sport leagues operate league offices such as the National Basketball Association (NBA) League Office in New York City. The headquarters for the IOC resides in Lausaunne, Switzerland, while the IPC is housed in Bonn, Germany. The sport managers employed in these offices have titles such as Executive Director, League Vice President, and Marketing Director. These employees keep the organization moving along, and their responsibilities include budgeting, staffing, scheduling tournaments and events, marketing, and media relations. However, this level of the organization does not typically set policies dealing with governance issues. Rather, they implement the policies determined by another level of the structure.

Most major sport organizations are nonprofit organizations with voluntary membership—not individual people, but institutions or nations. The membership of these organizations determines their policies, rules, and regulations, not the paid staff. The vehicle for setting these policies usually takes the form of regularly scheduled, often annual, meetings of the membership. Sometimes called General Assemblies or Annual Business Meetings, these gatherings are where the members vote to establish policies and rules or to modify existing ones. For example, at the Winter Paralympic Games, Nordic Skiing holds its own Sport Assembly, and the voting members, each representing his or her home nation, vote on issues such as acceptable equipment modifications and the length of different races. While professional sports leagues are for profit, they still have meetings at which they make governance decisions. Every year, for example, at the professional baseball Annual Winter Meetings, representatives of minor league baseball teams vote on issues such as draft rules and stadium specifications.

These General Assemblies and Annual Business Meetings often appoint a President for the organization as well as an Executive Committee or Executive Council. Sometimes the organization needs to make adjustments between General Assembly meetings, and so it vests the responsibility and authority to do so in the hands of the President and the Executive Committee. Executive Committees also generate ideas for the Annual General Assemblies to consider. The Executive Committee for the IOC has eight members selected from the Annual General Assembly, plus the President, currently Mr. Jacques Rogge of Belgium who began his term in 2002. For most sport organizations, the true power rests in the hands of the Executive Committee.

Naturally, the governance structures within each industry segment differ. This section merely gives an overview of some important organizational characteristics and shows how organizational charts for sport governance organizations contain elements different from a traditional sport front-office organizational chart. In each industry segment chapter, the organizational structures for that industry segment are explained in more detail.

The Role of Organizing in Governance

The organizational structures in any sport governing body dictate the flow of information, the setting of policies and rules, and the philosophical statements about the organization. Power is distributed differently within these structures. Sometimes power rests with the membership, and other times it rests with the Executive Committee or the President. It is important to note that the organizational charts for sport-governing structures parallel traditional organizational charts with one difference: In traditional organizational charts we see people or titles in certain places; in governance structures we see governance units. This difference shows us how governing bodies transcend individual responsibility and also shows us the big picture.

Decision Making

The decision-making process is essential in sport governance. We all make decisions every day. Some decisions are very simple. You chose what to wear to class on Monday. What did you consider when deciding what clothes to wear? You probably considered the weather, what was clean, what matched, whom you might sit next to in class, or if you had to give a presentation. Even this simplistic example shows the two basic parts of decision making—gathering and analyzing information. Sport managers must also make decisions on an everyday basis (after they decide what to wear to work).

Routine and Complex Decisions

Sport managers face a variety of decisions in the workplace, some are and some are not routine. *Routine decisions,* sometimes referred to as *programmed decisions,* are repetitive and are based on policies and procedures (Amis & O'Brien, 2001). During a New Jersey Nets basketball game, if a toilet overflows, the decision to call Maintenance to fix it is easy. When the University of Nebraska Sports Information Office is running short of copy paper (a recurring situation), the decision to order more paper is routine.

All decisions are not so easy. Many problems are unique. *Complex, nonroutine decisions* involving unique situations are referred to as *nonprogrammed decisions* (Amis & O'Brien, 2001). For example, baseball stadiums often shoot fireworks after the home team hits a home run. But suppose Stadium Operations personnel discover that some fireworks have been stolen. What types of decisions do they have to make about public safety? Which public safety departments need to be informed? What does the public need to know? Or suppose a violent thunderstorm is quickly approaching a crowded high school football stadium. Again, what types of decisions must be made to ensure safety? How much advance notice is needed to safely clear the stadium? Where will the players and officials go for safety? Or suppose you are a college athletic director facing budget cuts. How do you decide which teams' budgets will be decreased and which won't, and how will you implement those decisions? These examples illustrate the complexities sport managers face in decision making.

The Rational Model

One thing is of great importance to sport managers when they make decisions: They must have an organized, thoughtful decision process to follow. Decisions of great magnitude cannot be left to chance. Rather, the sport manager's thought process must be detailed and organized. One such process, the Rational Model based on Robbins (1990), is outlined here:

1. Identify the REAL problem.
2. Identify the decision objective.
3. Gather all pertinent information.
4. Identify any hurdles.
5. Brainstorm for alternatives.
6. Narrow down the options.
7. Examine the pros and cons of each option.
8. Make the decision.
9. Evaluate the decision.

To illustrate this decision-making process, assume that you are the Athletic Director at Big State University (BSU), home of the Fightin' Saugers. Recently, a group of female athletes came to you asking to add rowing and golf to your roster of women's sports. You are aware of the Title IX regulations pertaining to providing appropriate opportunities for female athletes, particularly the "proportionality" interpretation, whereby the percentage of male–female athletes must reflect the percentage of male–female students in the greater university population. Currently the university has a student-body enrollment of 53 percent women and 47 percent men, while the Athletic Department's athlete breakdown is 35 percent female athletes and 65 percent male athletes. You know the financial implications of adding sports, but the group is also threatening legal action if the university does not do as they are asking.

Let's apply the Rational Model:

1. *Identify the REAL problem.* The real problem is that the university is not in compliance with Title IX, which guarantees athletic opportunities for men and women athletes.

2. *Identify the decision objective.* The decision objective is to bring the department into compliance.

3. *Gather all pertinent information.* Look at the different program areas Title IX covers, such as facilities, coaches, equipment, travel and per diem, scholarships, and so forth.

4. *Identify any hurdles.* You are aware not only of tangible hurdles, such as budgetary constraints, but also of intangible hurdles, such as people's attitudes toward women's sports.

5. *Brainstorm for alternatives.* When brainstorming for ideas, it is important to note that any and all ideas are OK, no matter how far-fetched they may seem at face value (Chalip, 2001). The idea is to list all possible ideas now and sort through them later. In this case, the options could include adding sports without increasing the budget, asking the university for additional funding, cutting some men's nonrevenue sports to free up money, dropping football, and finding additional funding sources such as sponsorship dollars or new donors, or increasing ticket prices for the major revenue sports. Not all the ideas may be reasonable, but when brainstorming, remember to put all ideas on the table.

6. *Narrow down the options.* Then narrow down your list of options to three or four. Let's say that the best options appear to be finding additional funding sources and dropping some men's nonrevenue sports.

7. *Examine the pros and cons of each option.* Carefully weigh the pros and cons of these options. Dropping men's sports is a quick fix in terms of budgets, but in terms of public relations, it may be a nightmare. Finding additional sponsorship dollars is a possibility as the university is located in a major metropolitan area, but you may be limited in how much can you ask for. Increasing ticket prices will help, but the increase will be limited to how much fans will pay, and the increase will not finance the entire venture.

8. *Make the decision.* You decide on a combination approach, using the tactics of finding additional sponsorship dollars and increasing ticket prices.

9. *Evaluate the decision.* These tactics will have to be evaluated over the coming years. Once the teams are in place, BSU's Athletic Department will need to continually account for sponsorship dollars and fans' responses to increased ticket prices by measuring the impact on tickets sold.

This simplified version of a very complex decision-making process illustrates how an organized approach to decision making can help a sport manager decide on a course of action.

The SLEEPE Principle

Another decision-making method, which takes a more global view of the organization and the implications of sport managers' decisions, is called the SLEEPE Principle. The decisions sport managers make are often very public, subject to scrutiny by the media, fans, and people in general. Therefore, when sport managers make decisions, they must be able to use their conceptual skills to see the big picture. By using the SLEEPE method, decision makers can analyze decisions, especially decisions affecting policy development or interpretation. Originally set up as the SLEEP model (W. Moore, class lecture, Ohio State University, 1990), this decision-making model has been modified (Hums, 2006; Hums, Moorman, & Wolff, 2002) and applied in the sport industry to help sport managers see the big picture by analyzing the many different ramifications of their decisions. The components of the SLEEPE Principle are as follows:

S—Social

L—Legal

E—Economic

E—Ethical

P—Political

E—Educational

Using this model helps sport managers understand how their decisions will be viewed in different ways by various constituencies in society. The following example will illustrate this variety:

You are the Athletic Director at Big State University. Your potential NFL first-round draft pick, star running back Clinton Blanford, has been arrested and is in jail on charges of domestic violence. Your team is headed for a bowl game to determine the national championship. Of course, this story has received extensive national coverage in the press and is the talk of the bowl season. The decision you have to make, in conjunction with your head coach, is whether to allow Blanford to play in the upcoming bowl game. Let's use the SLEEPE Principle to analyze this situation:

S—Social. Look at the social ramifications of the decision: Allowing Blanford to play makes the statement to society in general that domestic violence is not serious enough to warrant his not playing in the game. This decision could lead to protests by both on- and off-campus groups, including faculty, students, and alumni groups, opposing domestic violence. It also suggests winning the bowl game is more important to the Athletic Department than standing up against domestic violence by athletes. On the other hand, if you do not allow Blanford to play, many fans and university supporters will be angry, especially if your team loses the game. However, you will have made a statement that BSU will not tolerate this sort of player misconduct.

L—Legal. From the legal standpoint, one may argue that Blanford should be allowed to play because he has not actually been convicted of anything yet. However, extending the definition of legal beyond just the traditional legal system, one can ask, has he violated team or university rules related to such conduct? How would a student who is not an athlete be treated by the university? If he does not play and the team loses, is it possible to hold him in some way legally responsible for the loss of revenue resulting from losing the game (Moorman & Hums, 1999)?

E—Economic. The economic ramifications for both the university and Blanford himself are as follows: Allowing him to play maximizes the opportunity to win the game, meaning increased revenue for the university, especially in terms of sales of licensed products and perhaps ticket sales for the upcoming year. Keeping the team highly ranked will help with recruiting and potential future earnings. On the personal level, if Blanford plays well, he could increase his potential professional earnings. On the other hand, if he does not play, there is greater potential that BSU would lose the game and the national championship and all the revenue streams associated with these events. Blanford's draft status could suffer, costing him money in his contract and potential endorsement deals.

E—Ethical. Next are the ethical considerations. Saying Blanford cannot play takes the ethical stance that domestic violence is wrong and will not be tolerated. It also says athletes are not above the law and must be held accountable for their actions, as they often are not (Benedict & Yaeger, 1998). On the other hand, allowing him to play may make the ethical statement that a person is innocent until proven guilty. He has not yet been tried by a court of law, so he should not be convicted in the court of public opinion. Of all the parts of the SLEEPE Principle, this is the most complex and challenging to sport managers.

P—Political. Politically there are a number of constituencies to consider. In this context, the term *political* is not limited to elected officials only; it is broader, including any groups or stakeholders who may exert some type of political power or influence in a given situation. In our example, if Blanford is allowed to play, the university's faculty, staff, and administration will most likely make public statements about the decision. They may place public pressure on the school's Athletic Department. The school's conference or even the NCAA may also make statements about the decision. Since BSU is a state university, the state legislature may also voice its opinions. If he is not allowed to play, some of these same groups may make supportive comments, publicly supporting and strengthening the Athletic Department's stance.

E—Educational. Finally there is the educational component to consider. This aspect of the SLEEPE Principle is used only when the decision situation is in an educational setting. If Blanford is allowed to play, it certainly makes the statement that athletics, rather than education, is the primary concern of the Athletic Department and, correspondingly, the university itself. However, not allowing him to play says that athletics is not above the law at the university and that education is the primary focus, not winning football games.

This example illustrates the complexity and public nature of many decisions sport managers face on a daily basis. Athlete misconduct, substance abuse, equity and diversity, violence, and other pressing social issues are present in the sport industry just as they are in general society. Because of the far-reaching ramifications of their decisions, forward-thinking sport managers must learn to examine all potential results of and reactions to their decisions before they make them.

This section outlined various decision-making models sport managers can incorporate when solving problems. Often, sport managers' decisions will be ethical in nature. Do the same decision-making models apply? To address the importance of dealing with ethical issues, Chapter 4 discusses ethical decision making.

The Role of Decision Making in Sport Governance

Sport managers dealing with governance issues are faced with decisions that have far-reaching implications. Their decisions, from simple to complex, shape the direction of the organization. The decisions sport managers make are open to public scrutiny and media discussion. As such, sport managers must make sure they have a concrete method for analyzing any decisions they need to make.

SUMMARY

Sport managers need to be able to perform the major management functions of planning, organizing, leading, and evaluating. This chapter focused on planning, organizing, and one subset of leading, decision making. It is important to have a solid foundation in these areas before further examining specific industry segments.

Planning is the basis for everything a sport organization does. Sport organizations must make both short- and long-term plans. The planning process is sequential: organizational goals, objectives, tactics, roles, and evaluation all flow from the mission statement. Sport organizations are organized with different levels of responsibility. Determining the tasks an organization needs to accomplish and the people needed to accomplish those tasks is essential for organizational success. Sport managers must make decisions every day. Some of their decisions are routine; others are unique. Two structured methods to help sport managers make solid decisions are the Rational Model of Decision Making and the SLEEPE Principle. By mastering these important skills, sport managers can successfully conduct the business of governance and policy development in their sport organizations.

Managerial Functions

You are the General Manager for the Elkhart Komets, a struggling AA baseball franchise. Playing in an old, poorly maintained Riverfront Stadium and stuck with a dull logo (a gold star with a silver tail), you need to make some decisions on how to increase revenues. Keep in mind that it is a minor league team, and you have no control over which players you can acquire.

1. Use the rational decision-making model to determine your course of action.

CHAPTER QUESTIONS

1. Locate organizational charts for three different sport organizations. Compare and contrast the titles and structures of each. Why are some aspects similar and others different?

2. Choose one of the following:
   - minor league baseball team
   - public assembly facility
   - college or university athletic department
   - high school athletic department
   - charity golf tournament
   - campus recreation department
   - sporting goods store

   After you choose one of these sport organizations, develop the following:
   a. mission statement
   b. one goal
   c. two objectives for that goal
   d. two tactics for each objective
   e. the roles for each tactic

3. For a sport organization of your choosing, identify two situations that would involve routine decision making and two situations that would involve complex decision making.

REFERENCES

AAU. (2007). About AAU. Retrieved December 31, 2007, from www.aausports.org/default.asp?a=pg_about_aau.htm.

Amis, J., & O'Brien, D. (2001). Organizational theory and the study of sport. In B. L. Parkhouse (Ed.), *The management of sport: Its foundation and application* (3d ed.) (pp. 72–92). Boston: McGraw-Hill.

Benedict, J., & Yaeger, D. (1998). *Pros and cons: The criminals who play in the NFL.* New York: Warner Books.

Bridges, F. J., & Roquemore, L. L. (1996). *Management for athletic/sport administration* (2d ed.). Decatur, GA: ESM Books.

Chalip, L. (2001). Group decision making and problem solving. In B. L. Parkhouse (Ed.), *The management of sport: Its foundation and application* (3d ed.) (pp. 93–110). Boston: McGraw-Hill.

Chelladurai, P. (2005). *Managing organizations for sport and physical activity: A systems perspective* (2d ed.). Scottsdale, AZ: Holcomb Hathaway.

Everett AquaSox. (2007). Mission statement. Retrieved September 20, 2007, from www.aquasox.com.

Heathfield, S. M. (2007). Build a strategic framework: Mission statement, vision, values. . . . Retrieved December 31, 2007, from http://humanresources.about.com/cs/strategicplanning1/a/strategicplan.htm.

Hums, M. A. (2006, May). Analyzing the impact of changes in classification systems: A sport management analysis model. Paper presented at the VISTA 2006 International Paralympic Committee Congress, Bonn, Germany.

Hums, M. A., Moorman, A. M., & Wolff, E. (2002). Examining disability sport from a sport management perspective. *Proceedings of the VISTA 2001 Conference,* Vienna, Austria.

Lexington Legends. (2007). Mission statement of the Lexington Legends Baseball Club. Retrieved August 25, 2007, from www.minorleaguebaseball.com/fans/page.jsp?ymd=20061221&content_id=149629&vkey=fans_t495&fext=.jsp&sid=t495.

Miller, D. (1987). Strategy making and structure: Analysis and implications for performance. *Academy of Management Journal, 30,* 7–32.

Moorman, A. M., & Hums, M. A. (1999). Student athlete liability for NCAA violations and breach of contract. *Journal of Legal Aspects of Sport, 9*(3), 163–174.

Mulrooney, A., & Farmer, P. (2001). Managing the facility. In B. L. Parkhouse (Ed.), *The management of sport: Its foundation and application* (3d ed.) (pp. 272–297). Boston: McGraw-Hill.

Northern British Columbia Winter Games Society. (2006). Mission, vision and values. Retrieved December 31, 2007, from www.bcgames.org/nbcwgs/gs_mission.html.

Quarterman, J., & Li, M. (2001). Managing sport organizations. In B.–L. Parkhouse (Ed.), *The management of sport: Its foundation and application* (3d ed.) (pp. 103–118). Boston: McGraw-Hill.

Robbins, S. P. (1990). *Organizational theory: Structure, design and applications* (3d ed.). Englewood Cliffs, NJ: Prentice Hall.

VanderZwaag, H. J. (1998). *Policy development in sport management.* Westport, CT: Praeger.

STRATEGIC MANAGEMENT AND POLICY DEVELOPMENT

INTRODUCTION

As discussed in Chapter 1, sport is an industry with considerable reach and impact on consumer-spending indices and the economy in general. Sport is acknowledged as big business, given the sheer numbers of participants, its exponential growth over the past 30 years, and the healthy percentage of the economic marketplace attributed to sport worldwide (DeSchriver & Mahony, 2007). Ozanian's (1995) earlier comment still applies: "What's all the excitement about?

41

Sports is not simply another big business. It is one of the fastest-growing industries in the U. S., and it is intertwined with virtually every aspect of the economy . . . sports is everywhere, accompanied by the sound of a cash register ringing incessantly" (p. 30).

The magnitude and reach of the sport industry is important in terms of economic impact, employment opportunities, and consumer interest. The extent of the business of sport is understandable, considering the vast numbers of both participants and activities involved. The popularity of different sporting activities, for participants and spectators, provides a rationale for the proliferation of organizations delivering the business of sport. Such organizations are involved in providing entertainment (amateur and professional spectator sport) or facilities (gyms and clubs for participation); offering structures within which competitive sport is delivered (minor, scholastic, or college, and club sport leagues and championships); designing and manufacturing equipment used by all levels of participants (clothing, sporting equipment, and other apparel); and promoting and delivering sporting competitions and festivals (World Championships and Paralympic Games). These organizations can be public or private, for-profit or not-for-profit. Regardless of the specifics of the business, sport as a consumer product is massive, technological advances occur daily, and focused marketing and promotion efforts are resulting in the further globalization of the sport industry (Pitts & Stotlar, 2002).

Without a doubt, the competition is fierce and the stakes high. For students interested in a career in the sport industry, learning the breadth and depth of the businesses and understanding how these organizations are strategically managed and governed is an important, early step in defining your career. According to Mahony and Howard (2001), the need for effective and strategic management practices and the development of meaningful policy has never been more important for sport organizations. Therefore, the focus of this chapter is the development of business strategy, the implementation of the principles of strategic management, and the development of policy in sport organizations. Even though the 1990s represented a period of great expansion in the sport industry, continued growth will only result from the implementation of creative business strategy (Mahony & Howard, 2001). It follows, then, that strategic management is an important concept to the sport manager. Future sport managers need to ask themselves:

- Is there a link between the macro approach (assessing the organization as a whole) to strategic management and what a manager does as an individual?
- Will strategic management enable managerial activities to be more successful in defining and setting policy for the organization?
- Is it important to understand strategic management and policy development in order to understand the governance of a sport organization and its pursuit of effectiveness?

The answer to each question is a resounding "Yes." This chapter provides further insight into the importance of strategic management and policy development for sport organizations.

Strategic Management

Strategy refers to the plans and actions implemented to achieve a goal. Strategy is a common tool used by organizations as a whole or in part to achieve a goal or gain some advantage. Chapter 2 described *tactics* as the specific steps that need to be followed to implement the strategy. You might consider strategy an organization's game plan. Sport is the perfect example to illustrate the concept because strategy is a normal part of competitive sports. A coach develops a game plan or strategy based on her team's strengths and weaknesses in comparison to the competition. The plan, of course, is to negate the opposition's strengths and find ways to capitalize on the strengths of one's own team. Managers of organizations seek to achieve these same results. They set goals and strive to realize them through a series of tactics or steps that will help the organization realize a goal. Strategy, then, is an important component in the management of an organization because it helps paint a picture of where the organization is headed. Again, tactics relate to the specific steps used to carry out the broader game plan. Let's focus our attention on the development of overall organizational strategy by first defining *strategic management*.

Defining Strategic Management

The terms *strategic management, business strategy,* and *organizational strategy* are often used synonymously to refer to both a purpose and a plan of action enabling an organization to reach its goals (Belcourt & McBey, 2000). For the purpose of this text, we will use the term *strategic management*. According to Pearce and Robinson (2007), strategic management

- involves decisions and action plans evolving from the organization's mission
- takes into account both the internal and the external environment
- involves both short- and long-term objectives (tactics) and plans
- requires strategic choices in budget resource allocation with respect to tasks, people, structures, technologies, and reward systems

To summarize, strategic management involves the planning, organizing, leading, and evaluating of an organization's strategy-related decisions and actions (Pearce & Robinson, 2007). On a larger scale, the term *corporate strategy* refers to global strategy for the larger *corporation*, an entity that may include several smaller businesses. Thus a strategy can be developed in a global organizational sense to deal with corporate-wide plans (corporate-level strategy), it can deal with factors impacting the main organizational mission (business- or management-level strategy), or it can be implemented to enable specific managerial functions such

TABLE	3.1	Defining levels of strategy.

Type of Strategy	Definition
Corporate-Level Strategy	General, overall strategic planning for the entire organization and all its business
Business-Level Strategy	Specific, individualized strategic planning for individual products or services
Functional-Level Strategy	Specific, individualized strategic planning concepts implemented by personnel

as planning or decision making (functional-level strategy) (Pearce & Robinson, 2007). See Table 3.1.

For example, Maple Leaf Sports & Entertainment Ltd. is the parent company managing the Toronto Raptors basketball and the Toronto Maple Leafs hockey franchises. The organization's corporate strategy might involve a focus on growing the games of basketball and hockey by encouraging grassroots development and opportunities for participation and strengthening the national fan base for these teams. The business-level strategy of the Raptors and Maple Leafs might include a commitment of a certain budget to hire staff and run programming, thereby encouraging the accomplishment of the corporate goals. Partnerships with other sport delivery groups and contributions to both facilities and program development might result. The outcome of these investments will strengthen the functional-level strategies, such as delivering a 3-on-3 mini hoops program for kids prior to an NBA game, by helping to develop a following in a particular sport, widening the fan base, and enabling marketing activities that promote ticket sales. Each level of strategy is critically important and contributes to the overall success of the organization. Then tactics such as advertising, acquiring facilities, and developing rules and regulations are employed to enact the overall strategy.

Strategic management often occurs as a result of some environmental factor impacting the operation of the organization and its ability to achieve defined goals. Specifically, strategy involves creating mission, goals, and objectives statements, along with action plans (tactics) accounting for both the organization's environment and its competition (Anthony, Perrewe, & Kacmar, 1993). With an ultimate goal or several goals in mind, the organization's decision makers will maneuver activities and decisions based upon factors in the organization's environment to achieve them. Strategic management is dynamic, both short and long term in nature, and sometimes results in structural changes to organizational arrangement.

Mintzberg (1988) offered the five Ps of strategy as a way to understand the meaning of strategic management. He suggested that strategic management involved the following:

1. *Planning:* setting a course of action to deal with a situation
2. *Purpose:* actions that are sometimes deliberate and other times emergent that deal with change and opportunity
3. *Ploy:* some specific maneuver to deal with an issue
4. *Position:* the location of the organization relative to its business and competitors
5. *Perspective:* the culture or perspective of the organization

It is important to remember that organizational strategy involves not only goals and objectives but also the tactics by which goals are achieved (Mintzberg, Lampel, Quinn, & Ghoshal, 2002). The chief executives of the organization commonly develop business strategy.

Although defining specific business strategy is important, it is not more important than executing the strategic management plan. According to Belcourt & McBey (2000), this is accomplished by

1. defining the vision or clear purpose
2. converting the vision to measurable objectives
3. defining a plan to achieve the end goal
4. implementing the plan
5. measuring the results and revising the plan based upon actual versus planned events

The flow of information leading to strategic action involves looking backward and forward prior to assessing the current organizational environment. Managers will evaluate historical, current, and forecasted data in light of the values and priorities of the organization's stakeholders (Pearce & Robinson, 2007). Stakeholders are usually subdivided groups of professionals, volunteers, and customers that have an interest in the product or service being developed.

To be effective, an organization must create a good fit between its strategy, organizational structure, and governance plan (Slack & Parent, 2006). This means the managerial activities related to governance discussed in Chapter 2 are critical to success. If those sport managers responsible for planning, organizing, and decision making are not cognizant of their environment and in tune with the mission and action plans of the organization, then ineffective outcomes are bound to result. Consider the negative results likely to occur if the United States Olympic Committee (USOC) were to work at cross-purposes with the National Governing Bodies. The result of divergent policy or unacknowledged shifts in the environment could lead to chaotic, illogical management illustrated by inconsistent decision making, poor planning, and inadequate organization. For instance, suppose the USOC were to establish a common policy dictating how athletes were selected to Olympic Teams but not effectively accounting for the differences between selecting an individual athlete in track and field versus a team sport athlete in volleyball. The end result might involve selecting the wrong athletes and might well be illustrated by decreased medal performances at the Olympic Games.

Planning and organizing are critical components of the process because determining goals and the means to achieve them (tactics) are core items of strategic management. After all, it's hard to achieve "success" if you cannot define "success" and the steps needed to achieve it. Developing policies that empower action are equally vital. However, perhaps even more important to the concept of strategic management is strategic decision making. Knowing what to do at the right time is a critical component of strategic management.

Strategic Decision Making

As discussed in Chapter 2, decision making is the act of deciding a course of action based on the available alternatives related to a particular issue. Strategic decision making attaches a global organizational perspective to individual decisions. Strategic decision making usually involves top management decisions related to substantial resources. The long-term prosperity of the organization may even be affected, as strategic decisions sometimes have enduring effects. Strategic decision making involves forecasting both the environment and the effects of a particular decision in the acquisition of long-term goals. Normally several alternatives and "if–then" scenarios are played out to gain perspective on the results of the decision. Strategic decision making is employed in an attempt to ensure the most profitable decision is made. Follow-up evaluations are used to promptly correct negative outcomes that might accrue once a decision is made. Examples of common strategic decisions in sport organizations include developing partnerships with sponsors or other organizations, long-term planning, establishing the organizational brand, and dramatic shifts in programming.

Decision making in sport organizations is among the manager's most important functions (Chelladurai, 2005). Although some decisions will be routine and repetitive with precedent and policy defining the decision choices, others will involve unique situations with little in the way of established guidelines to assist the decision maker (Amis & O'Brien, 2005). Given the magnitude and importance of the outcome to the entire organization, some decisions require business strategy. In each case, a procedure for framing and solving the problem is critical to ensure a well-thought-out decision. In line with the Rational Model of Decision

Making presented in Chapter 2, Chelladurai (2001) summarizes strategic decision making in the following steps:

1. defining the problem
2. listing all possible alternatives, taking into consideration the internal and external organizational environments
3. assessing the pros and cons of the alternatives
4. considering the global and the long-term impact of the alternatives
5. selecting the best course of action

Step 4 is included in order that the best and most strategic decision for the overall organization is considered, emphasizing the importance of strategy in sport management.

The Importance of Strategy in Sport Management

Sport organizations must embrace strategic management practices to maximize their potential for several reasons:

1. To plan effectively. Strategy is extremely important because sport organizations have historically had reputations for ineffective planning. Many amateur sport groups developed from informal beginnings and were dominated by volunteer, nonprofessional staff. Today, the stakes are high, and poor management can mean not getting to the medal podium or losing a billion-dollar product line. It is accepted that planning is the foundation of effective strategic management.

2. To capitalize on opportunities. Capitalizing on opportunity is enhanced by the tenets of strategic management. Today's turbulent environment can result in a warp-speed, frenetic business climate. Only those organizations with a strategy and an understanding of alternatives will truly capitalize on the opportunities. Suppose that you manage a privately owned fitness club and that you, the owner, and the three investors who provided the original capital to start the club have engaged in regular meetings, charting strategy for the current and future activities of the club. Now suppose that you receive an inside tip that your main competitor who runs three local clubs is about to sell the business. Having a strategic management plan that includes designs for acting relative to both future acquisitions and outselling the competition might well enable you to merge your business with your main competitor. In the absence of such strategic management and planning, you may be ill equipped to make such a decision or to make it in a timely manner. Capitalizing on this opportunity is critical, given the competition among sport organizations for customers, fans, athletes, and consumers.

3. To make effective decisions. An organization charting a specific course of action is most likely to make effective decisions. Strategic management will enable strategic decision making by keeping the organization in tune with environmental realities and reducing internal resistance to change.

4. To enhance the manager's entrepreneurial role. Many years ago Mintzberg (1975) described four decisional roles of a manager: entrepreneur, disturbance handler, resource allocator, and negotiator. The sport organization with a clear business strategy has the greatest potential of enhancing the manager's entrepreneurial role, encouraging the development or acquisition of innovative goods and services, and effectively managing organizational change.

In addition to strategic management, effective sport organizations will be administered through effective policy. Strategic management involves specific action or patterns of action. The ultimate goal of this action is to achieve objectives defined by the organization while respecting the guiding principles and policies of the organization. Let's turn our attention now to the definition of policy, the importance of policy in the governance of sport organizations, and the concept of policy development.

Policy

All organizations deal with different types of difficult situations, often issues related to human resources, service delivery, risk management, or finance. The issue could result from deviating from the strategic business plan, straying from past practice, or confronting some new, uncharted ground. It may be difficult or tricky, the answer may not be immediately clear, and the potential consequences could be far-reaching within the organization. Sport organizations require policy in the areas of finance, human resources, facility use and control, equipment, travel, public relations, promotion, and other items related to managing risk. For example, travel is a pressure point in college athletics. How will the college Athletic Director react when an athlete asks to travel to a particular road game on his own? Should this concern the administrator? Are there larger issues to consider? Will granting the request set a precedent? Would it matter if the athlete were to travel with his parents as opposed to his girlfriend? Who would be responsible in the event of an accident? How will the athlete's coach view the situation? Each of these questions, and possibly others defined by the college risk manager and insurance carrier, provide the framework for developing policy to deal with this issue. Let's take a further look at defining policy and answer the questions posed above.

What Is a Policy?

Policies are broad guidelines or procedures an organization follows as it moves toward its objectives. Policies are normally general, written statements providing a framework for enabling decisions while allowing employees some flexibility and discretion in problem solving. These guiding statements are meant to provide common direction for all facets of the organization. It is important to understand that policies are different from objectives, strategies, procedures, or philosophy (VanderZwaag, 1998). Policies have wide ramifications and are formal expressions of an organization's standing decisions on important, often recurring, issues. They are different from procedures, which are established to guide the work of an individual or a division within the organization. Policies are also different from goals, objectives, and tactics. They emerge from the organization's philosophy by creating a framework for resolving issues directly and consistently. Effective policies evolve over time in reaction to the environment within which the organization exists. For example, an amateur sport organization often has a fiscal responsibility policy that prevents its departments from spending beyond their budgets. The policy does not dictate how or on what items to spend, but rather creates a bottom line principle specific to the importance of only spending within the means of the organization. As significant savings occur, the policy might be amended to allow quarterly reports on budget savings to reallocate funds to a list of items not funded in the original budget. Over time, this practice might be changed slightly so that the savings remain within the original department budget to further encourage fiscal responsibility to managers concerned with losing part of their original resources.

Organizations rely upon policy and precedent (or past practice) to solve problems fairly and consistently. In the example of the athlete who wishes to travel by his own means to the college game, the Athletic Director will likely rely on a college policy or a departmental policy for an answer to help ensure consistency when another athlete asks. Further, the administrator will be concerned with the following:

- the college's responsibility for the safety and the behavior of athletes when traveling
- the coach's wishes about team cohesion and togetherness
- the athlete's understanding of his responsibilities and expectations
- the circumstances and rationale surrounding the request

In such a case, the Department of Athletics may approve the policy shown in Figure 3.1 regarding athletes traveling to competitions. In its policy, the department defines an expectation that athletes will travel with their team, but it acknowledges that there are circumstances in which this may not be

| FIGURE | 3.1 | Sample policy for athletes traveling to competitions. |

It is expected that athletes will travel to and from athletic contests with their teammates on carriers provided by the College. In the event an athlete wishes to make alternate travel plans, he or she must obtain the form "Permission for Alternate Travel Plans—Varsity Athletes" from the Athletic Office. This form requests information regarding the intended mode of transportation and a rationale for the request. Permission may be granted on a case-by-case basis only when the form is signed off by both the head coach and the Athletic Director. Permission requests must be made 48 hours prior to travel.

possible and that such cases will be dealt with on an individual basis. The definition of those circumstances will then be left to the discretion of those involved. Perhaps the athlete has an exam that will not permit him to leave with the team but is able and willing to drive on his own and arrive in time for the game. A parent might be at the game and want to take her son home for the weekend after the game. Together, the case-by-case decisions begin to establish a precedent. An example of the Athlete Permission Form is presented in Figure 3.2.

The Importance of Policy in Sport Organizations

Developing policies permitting effective decision making has never been more important for sport organizations, especially given their current size and complexity. Rapid growth over the past decade coupled with an increase in the complexity and business orientation of sport organizations has made it necessary to expand managers' breadth of decision-making responsibility. This trend toward decentralized decision making means effective policy development is crucial. A policy manual can be an invaluable tool that helps personnel to deal quickly and effectively with issues. Policies also promote fair, equitable decisions supported by rationales that are both reasonable and easy to understand. Policies encourage consistency, ensuring the same answer to a problem is applied between organizational units and over time. Perhaps even more important, policy development enables the organization to link its mission statement and management strategy to operation, ensuring the business strategy is implemented through overall policies and tactics. Let's consider this point in more detail.

Department of Athletics
**Statement of Personal Responsibility for Alternative
Travel Arrangements Chosen by Student–Athletes**

REQUEST   Date: _____

I (_____) request permission to _____

_____

_____

and will not **travel with / return with** the _____ **prior to / following**
        (circle one)   (team)   (circle one)

the contest played at _____
                             (location/opponent)

on _____.
          (date)

If my request is approved, I will assume all the responsibilities for my travel, conduct, and well-being while traveling to and/or from the contest. I will not hold the college liable in any way for any harm or injury I may suffer, or for any loss or damage to my property that may occur during this journey.

_____   Date: _____
(Signature of student making request)

Address: _____

_____

_____

Telephone: _____   Birth Date: _____

Permission Granted by Department of Athletics

_____   _____
(Athletic Director)   (Coach)

Date: _____   Date: _____

Suppose you become the Athletic Director for a college competing in Division I of the NCAA. You are in the leadership role for directing the department. The mission statement of the department might be "to provide student-athletes opportunities for the pursuit of excellence in a broad range of competitive athletics." You need to ensure that department policies are developed that link to the pursuit of the mission relative to how you operate (management strategy) on a day-to-day basis. The mission clearly reflects the need to offer as many sports as possible and to operate them at the highest possible competitive level in order to win. Policies about funding, recruiting, program breadth, competitive schedules, excellent facilities, and so on will help to link the management and business strategies. This organization wants to offer lots of sport opportunities and to operate them at the highest competitive level. The steps necessary to achieve these goals involve specific tactics to follow. For instance, your tactic might include having a balance of sports that use both indoor and outdoor facilities, with no more than four sports sharing any one facility. This tactic ensures that each team's competitive schedules and necessary practice times can be accommodated.

Remember, too, that sport organizations are held to standards of fairness and principle as defined by law. Policies provide for a systematic framework that aids in decision making. For example, a gender-equity policy may call for an equal number of competitive sport opportunities for females as there are for males within the athletic program. When decisions are being made relative to adding or dropping sports, this policy helps to guide the discussion. Of course, this does not ensure the policy is legally defensible, but it does promote actions based upon reasoned statements of organizational intent, developed for a purpose.

Developing Policy

Armed with an understanding of what a policy is and why it is important, let's now turn our attention to developing policy. *Policy development* is an ongoing process through which a framework for decision making is developed relative to issues broadly encountered throughout the organization. Policy is developed on recurring issues or problems and is usually directed to guiding decision making around critical organizational resources such as finances and personnel (VanderZwaag, 1998). Policy areas are those parts of an organization's operation where important decisions have surfaced and several alternative actions are possible. The stakes connected to the issues are high; thus the organization forms policy to solve a problem or take a stand on an issue that is likely to recur. Issues or problems that arise, especially those issues that are recurring or that impact a large proportion of organization members or activities, frequently result in the development of policy. Thus policies are active, living documents that can change in response to changes in the environment of the organization. Since policies are meant to clarify actions, embed fairness within operations of what and how things are done, and to help manage risk, it is understandable that policies result from issues that arise. Ultimately, a policy guides the actions of all members of the organization facing a particular issue or dilemma, speeding decision making and unifying the thinking of managers and subordinates.

An effective way to develop policy and to be strategic about the development of policy is through the case method analysis for understanding the problem and properly framing the issue (VanderZwaag, 1998). Essentially, the case method analysis is a procedure for looking at a problem, collecting information to assess the available options for solving the problem, and then choosing the alternative most closely aligned with the strategy and philosophy of the organization. This method involves four main steps, as outlined in Figure 3.3. As an example for using the case method analysis outlined, let's consider Major League Soccer (MLS) in the United States and Canada:

1. *Define the problem.* MLS executives have been aware that soccer, or football as the sport is known around the world, is highly popular worldwide, but does not draw the same fan or media following as other professional leagues in North America such as the NFL, NHL (National Hockey League), NBA, PGA (Professional Golfers' Association), and LPGA (Ladies Professional Golf Association). In a strategic move, MLS executives decided that increasing the league market share was an issue for the league to strategically manage and that its impact on MLS was a major problem for realizing potential levels of profit.

Case method analysis steps for developing policy.　　　　**FIGURE　3.3**

1. Define in detail the issue and the facts describing the scope of the problem and its impact on the organization.

2. Collect and assess information on both sides of the issue. What are the options for action?

3. Evaluate how and to what extent each of these options will ultimately affect the organization.

4. Choose the favored option for solution and specifically define the action. This, then, becomes the written policy statement.

2. *Collect information and formulate options.* Those same executives spent considerable time studying the other leagues including England's Premier League (EPL), identifying ways and means for increasing MLS North American profits through team expansion, player acquisitions, promotion and publicity, television, merchandizing, and stadium capacity.

3. *Evaluate the options.* Evaluate the pros and cons, as well as the potential impact of each of the options identified above.

4. *Choose the favored option and define the action.* MLS executives identified and pursued player acquisition as a means for increasing the exposure for soccer within the North American professional sport market (Step 4) and thus as a strategic move to increase profit. As an example, David Beckham was enticed to join the MLS's Los Angeles Galaxy. The impact for virtually all MLS teams in ticket sales, merchandizing, and television revenues was immediate.

At the end of each industry segment chapter in this book, a case study gives you an opportunity to deal with real-life policy issues confronting sport managers working in that industry segment. After reading the cases, you may wish to refer to Figure 3.3 and follow the steps presented to frame your response to the case.

Once policy is defined, it must be communicated within the organization and properly enforced. This is possible only by developing clearly delineated, written policy (see Figure 3.3) and a procedure for communicating the policy throughout all levels of the organization. Such a procedure includes the specific communication method (face-to-face meetings, e-mail, or written memo) and the timing for announcing and clarifying the policy, and it identifies exactly who announces what. Commitment and understanding from every level of the organization are necessary for organizational policy to serve its intended purpose. In addition, the developed policy needs to be affiliated with the mission, business pursuits, strategy, and environment of the sport organization. Policies need to remain current and closely aligned with the strategic management activities of the overall management process. In fact, policies play an important role in strategy implementation.

Strategic Management Activities and Policy Development

█ n Chapters 1 and 2 you were introduced to managerial activities related to governance. Planning, organizing, and decision making are actions carried out by sport managers at the *micro,* or departmental, level of analysis. These actions are considered everyday activities performed as the functions of management. The alternative to the micro level of analysis is the *macro* approach to managing the organization. A macro orientation looks at those issues impacting the organization as a whole, assessing things from the perspective of the larger, more complex structure. The content presented earlier in this chapter takes on a macro perspective by investigating the concepts of strategic management and policy development, two concepts that embrace the organization as a whole.

It is important to understand the link between the macro and micro levels of managerial activities guiding an organization. In essence, the managerial activities carried out at the micro level of analysis (planning, organizing, decision making) provide information for the construction of the business strategy and policy development occurring at the macro level of organizational activity. Departmental activities such as planning, organizing, and decision making provide fundamental information for defining organizational strategies. The business strategies then contribute a foundation from which organizational policy is derived. This process should be viewed as a dynamic operation in which information flows both ways in response to the changes that occur in the organizational environment (Figure 3.4). Policies empower the action of strategic management.

The interaction of three factors—managerial activities; strategy; and the size, technology, and environment of the organization's structure—is the primary determinant of organizational design (Moorhead, Griffin, Irving, & Coleman, 2000). The structure of an organization reflects the division of labor and the hierarchy of authority and power that exists to maximize the use of available resources (Chelladurai, 2005). The actual structural configuration of the organization can be analyzed from several different perspectives, including (1) its size and shape as depicted on the organizational chart, (2) how it operates via decision making, specialized tasks, and procedures, and (3) the responsibility and authority accorded

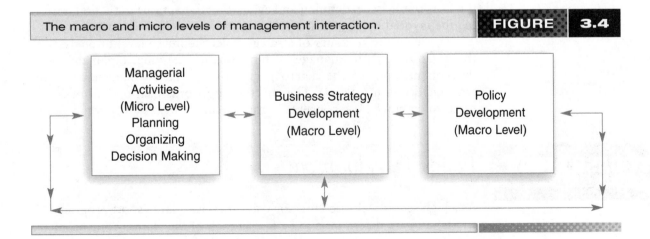

The macro and micro levels of management interaction.   FIGURE 3.4

its members (Moorhead et al., 2000). The chapters that follow describe the governance structures present in several different sport industry segments from these perspectives.

SUMMARY

Sport pervades society, and sports is big business. Organizations delivering the business of sport have grown in response to the interest and economic impact of the sport industry. Accordingly, the importance of effective management has emerged, and the concept of strategic management for sport organizations has evolved. Business strategy involves the development of purposeful plans, actions, and decisions that enable an organization to reach its goals. The strategic level of management involves global, organization-wide strategy dealing with issues that have important financial or human resource consequences for the organization as a whole. Such factors are related to the mission of the organization and are affected by the organizational environment. Strategy involves the creation of mission, goals, and objective statements, along with tactics. Strategy should enable action and is a factor in decision making as well. Strategic decision making involves making the right decision at the right time. Strategic management and decision making are critically important for sport organizations in the pursuit of their organizational goals. Strategy encourages planning, capitalizing on opportunities, and overall competitiveness.

Strategic management is enabled through policy development. A policy is a written statement providing guidelines to solve recurring problems fairly and consistently. Policy is written for issues broadly impacting the organization and its constituent groups. They provide for equitable decision making that can be enacted throughout the organization on a consistent basis. Policy is developed using case method analysis: collecting the facts of the issue, defining and evaluating the options for action, selecting the favored option, and developing the written policy statement.

The inclusion of issues of strategy links the micro level of analysis of the organization (the managerial functions of planning, organizing, and decision making) to the macro perspective (strategic management and strategic decision making). The effective sport organization will be structured to embrace both concepts in the pursuit of its organizational goals.

CASE STUDY | *Policy Development*

As a high school Athletic Director you supervise a large sport program (19 sports) and are determined to be fair to each of the teams. Your problem:

8 sports (girls field hockey, boys football, and boys and girls soccer, lacrosse, and archery) require practice and game time on the one outdoor field you have to schedule.

1. Follow the steps in Figure 3.3 to culminate in writing a policy that (a) covers the use of the field by your teams (you are not in a position to drop any sports) and (b) describes the boundaries for using fields off school property.

CHAPTER QUESTIONS

1. Suppose you are sitting in an interview for a management position with your favorite professional sport organization. One member of the interview panel says: "The business of sports is fiercely competitive. We have to be very strategic in our management decisions. Tell us what strategic management means to you." List five answers you would provide, given your understanding of this chapter.

2. Consider the following statement: *Timing is everything in strategic decision making.* Is this statement true? Why, or why not? How do you know the best time to make a decision?

REFERENCES

Anthony, W. P., Perrewe, P. L., & Kacmar, K. M. (1993). *Strategic human resource management.* Fort Worth, TX: Harcourt Brace Jovanovich.

Amis, J., & O'Brien, D. (2005). Organizational theory and the study of sport. In B. L. Parkhouse (Ed.), *The management of sport* (4th ed., pp. 76–95). New York: McGraw-Hill.

Belcourt, M., & McBey, K. J. (2000). *Strategic human resources planning.* Scarborough, Canada: Nelson Thomson Learning.

Chelladurai, P. (2001). *Managing organizations for sport and physical activity: A systems perspective.* Scottsdale, AZ: Holcomb Hathaway.

Chelladurai, P. (2005). *Managing organizations for sport and physical activity: A systems perspective* (2d ed.). Scottsdale, AZ: Holcomb Hathaway.

DeSchriver, T. D., & Mahony, D. F. (2007). Finance, economics, and budgeting in the sport industry. In J. B. Parks, J. Quarterman, and L. Thibault Eds.), *Contemporary sport management* (3d ed.). Champaign, IL: Human Kinetics.

Mahony, D. F., & Howard, D. R. (2001). Sport business in the next decade: A general overview of expected trends. *Journal of Sport Management, 15*(4), 275–296.

Mintzberg, H. (1975). The manager's job: Folklore and fact. *Harvard Business Review, 53,* 49–61.

Mintzberg, H. (1988). *In the strategy process.* Englewood Cliffs, NJ: Prentice Hall.

Mintzberg, H., Lampel, J., Quinn, J., & Ghoshal, S. (2002). *The strategy process: Concepts, context, and cases* (4th ed.). Englewood Cliffs, NJ: Prentice Hall.

Moorhead, G., Griffin, R. W., Irving, P. G., & Coleman, D. F. (2000). *Organizational behavior: Managing people and organizations.* Scarborough, Canada: Nelson Thomson Learning.

Ozanian, M. K. (1995, February 14). Following the money: FW's first annual report on the economics of sports. *Financial World, 164,* 26–27, 30–31.

Pearce, J. A., & Robinson, R. B. (2007). *Strategic management: Formulation, implementation, and control.* Toronto, Canada: Irwin/McGraw-Hill.

Pitts, B. G., & Stotlar, D. K. (2002). *Fundamentals of sport marketing* (2d ed.). Morgantown, WV: Fitness Information Technology.

Slack, T., & Parent, M. M. (2006). *Understanding sport organizations: The application of organization theory* (2d ed.). Champaign, IL: Human Kinetics.

VanderZwaag, H. J. (1998). *Policy development in sport management.* Westport, CT: Praeger.

4

ETHICS IN SPORT ORGANIZATIONS

INTRODUCTION

Sales representatives alter receipts to get more money than they are entitled to. Managers lie to their bosses about using company-owned cars. Bosses lie to their employees about company policies. Accountants alter the books to cover up questionable spending practices. Major corporations are forced to close down because of income mismanagement. Large manufacturers violate the human rights of their workers. Companies use production processes that are

59

not friendly to the environment. Such negative news from the corporate world calls into question the ethics we see practiced in business and industry on a daily basis.

All of you hope to work in the sport industry some day. The world of sport is a place where we want to believe in fair play and good sporting conduct. But is the world of sport somehow immune to the ethical issues confronting managers and businesspeople in general society? Unfortunately, the answer to this question is "No," as can be illustrated by the following examples:

- The father of a youth hockey player sues his son's league because his son was not awarded the most valuable player (MVP) trophy.
- A college basketball player accepts thousands of dollars in cash from a booster.
- MLB players and Tour de France riders use banned substances to improve performance.
- A coach fabricates information on her resume when pursuing a new job.
- An agent promises a young player more than he can deliver.
- International officials accept bribes to swing the votes for the selection of a host city for the Olympic Games.
- The PGA remains silent on courses that exclude women as members where the PGA holds its events.
- An NBA official is accused of gambling on NBA games.

Unfortunately, these types of incidents appear with regularity in the sports pages and are often the lead stories on the evening sports broadcasts. According to Ridinger and Greenwell (2005, p. 156), "This is problematic as the sport industry prides itself on providing wholesome entertainment, promoting positive values, building character, and creating good role models. Unethical behavior threatens all of the positive benefits." All the above scenarios involve behavior that is considered unethical. As sport managers, you will confront situations that will present you with ethical dilemmas. How, then, should you respond to these situations?

Sport as a Mirror of Society

Every society faces its own unique issues, including violence, substance abuse, domestic abuse, racism, sexism, homophobia, ableism, economic downturns, and corporate cheating. These issues also appear in all levels and facets of industry, including the sport industry. It has been said that sport is a mirror or reflection of society, not just in the United States, but other nations as well (Asser, 2000; Coakley, 2006; Maguire & Nakayama, 2006; Oprisan, 1999). It should come as no surprise, therefore, that sport managers face the very same issues.

ASC Ethics in Sports
www.ausport.gov.au/
supporting/ethics

The Australian Sports Commission provides a comprehensive list of key sport ethics issues. A partial list is shown in Figure 4.1 (Australian Sports Commission [ASC], n.d.a).

Partial list of key sport ethics issues (ASC, n.d.a).	FIGURE 4.1

- Corruption, gambling, cheating, bribery, match fixing
- Corporate governance—cronyism, paternalism, nepotism, favouritism, discrimination and/or bias in organisational and board governance and in the appointment of people to paid or voluntary positions
- Verbal and physical abuse (including death threats) of officials/referees/umpires
- Victimisation of those who speak out or make a complaint about something they consider to be inappropriate
- Sportsmanship/fair play/sporting values
- Expectation for athletes to be role models/ambassadors at all times (both on and off the field)
- Performance enhancing drugs
- Excessive alcohol consumption and use of recreational drugs
- Racial harassment and vilification

- Spectator violence
- Abusive/aggressive parental behaviour
- Sexuality discrimination and homophobia
- Transgenders (questions regarding participation at the elite level by male to female transgender athletes)
- Genetic doping/therapy/manipulation
- Science and technology (at what point does the technology surpass the influence of the athlete's performance and in the process devalue the performance; are some technological innovations [other than drugs] dangerous?)
- Eating disorders (are some sports contributing to the prevalence of eating disorders?)
- Sponsorship demands
- Sexualisation and/or exploitation of athletes
- Violence on the sporting field
- Questionable game tactics
- Media's role

Note that the second point in Figure 4.1 particularly mentions ethical issues related to governance, many of which have obvious parallels as societal issues. So how do these societal issues manifest themselves in sport?

The simple diagram in Figure 4.2 illustrates how societal issues are reflected in sport. As an example, violence is a daily issue in society, and fighting and killing are often depicted by the media on television or in films. Violence, the societal issue, appears on the left-hand side of the model. As the issue is filtered through sport, we see, for example, the Detroit Pistons and the Indiana Pacers in a court fight at an NBA game. Another example is the recent altercation at a college football game in which two teams started an all-out brawl. Fights have broken out at Little League Baseball games, high school football games, and youth soccer matches. Officials are accosted at an alarming rate, prompting more states to make it a felony offense to strike an official (Robinson, Hums, Crow, & Phillips, 2001).

FIGURE 4.2   Societal issues reflected in sport.

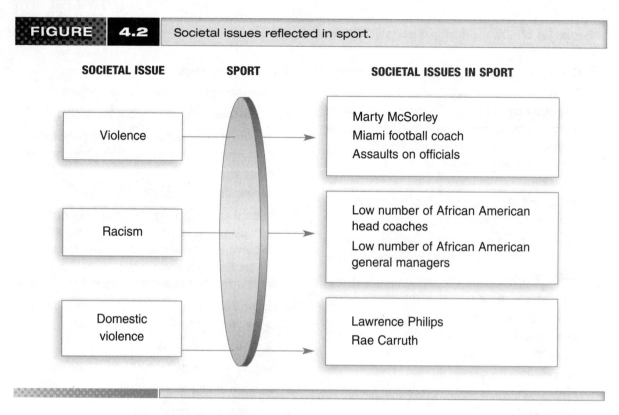

SOCIETAL ISSUE   SPORT   SOCIETAL ISSUES IN SPORT

Violence → Marty McSorley / Miami football coach / Assaults on officials

Racism → Low number of African American head coaches / Low number of African American general managers

Domestic violence → Lawrence Philips / Rae Carruth

The second example shown in Figure 4.2, racism, still exists in society, as evidenced by the disproportionate number of African American males on death row in the United States and by incidents of racial profiling. In sport, the number of African American head coaches in the NCAA Division I football is extremely small. The overwhelming majority of positions with any decision-making power in professional sport are held by white people (Lapchick, 2005).

The third example illustrated in Figure 4.2 is domestic violence. Every nine seconds in the United States, a woman is beaten (University of Nebraska Medical Center, 2007). In sport, we have read all too many times about a star athlete allegedly abusing a wife, girlfriend, or female companion. The coach or general manager must decide whether the player should be allowed to play or should be punished in some way, such as a suspension or fine.

This diagram could include other examples, but its purpose is not to provide a comprehensive list of examples. Rather, its purpose is to ask, "As sport managers, when we are confronted by these issues, how will we react?" Responding to these incidents is never easy, for sport managers feel pressure from many constituencies to "do the right thing." But what is "the right thing," and more important, how should a sport manager decide on "the right thing"? Remember, too, as mentioned in Chapter 2, the decisions sport managers make will be publicly analyzed and scrutinized by the media, fans, and casual readers of the news. As a sport manager, you will be faced with ethical dilemmas on a regular basis. But will you know how to recognize an ethical dilemma?

Ethics Defined

What do we mean when we talk about ethics in sport? *Sport ethics* is a field of practical or applied ethics that aims at a critical understanding and evaluation of

- the moral values and norms that inhere in and that condition the practice of sport, as well as
- the contribution sports render to the realization of general societal and moral ends and values. (Etheik Instituut, 2005, para. 1)

More specifically, according to the Canadian Centre for Ethics in Sport (CCES) (2007, What Is Ethics in Sport? section), sport ethics should address the following considerations:

- respect for persons
- protection from harm
- development of ethical conduct toward others
- notions of justice, fairness, equity
- ethics of care (meaning the ethics of relationships, not just ethics of individual conduct)
- freedom to enjoy, to flourish
- respect for the institution of sport

The CCES (2007, By Fair and Ethical Means section) goes on to elaborate that sport should be practiced through fair and ethical means. It defines *fair and ethical means* as follows:

- the presence and acceptance of codes of ethics for athletes, coaches, and officials
- basic human rights, like the absence of exploitation, respect for the dignity and worth of human beings, self-determination, and privacy
- principles of due process, including such things as informed consent, rights of appeal, and absence of bias and conflicts of interest
- responsibility of care for self and others
- business practices

www

Canadian Centre for Ethics in Sport
www.cces.ca

- quality control systems
- other policies and practices on such things as gender equity, disabled integration, harassment, multiculturalism, access, safety, discrimination, racism, drug-free sport, violence, privacy, and consent

Often, when people think of sport ethics they think only of good sporting conduct and fair play *on* the field. From the information above, it is obvious that ethics and ethical concerns spill over into the business aspects of sport as well. As stated by Council of Europe Committee of Ministers (2001, Aims section), "ethical considerations leading to fair play are integral, and not optional elements, of all sports activity, sports policy and management, and apply to all levels of ability and commitment, including recreational as well as competitive sport." Fair play extends to the management of sport as well. It is in the business venue of sport where sport managers will find a myriad of ethical issues and dilemmas.

Ethical Dilemmas

What is an ethical dilemma? An *ethical dilemma* occurs in situations where the course of action is unclear, or where reasonable people cannot agree on what should or should not happen (CCES, 2007). According to McNamara (2007, Definitions section), a manager faces a significant ethical conflict when the following exist: "(1) significant value conflicts among differing interests, (2) real alternatives that are equally justifiable, and (3) significant consequences to stakeholders in the situation." For example, a star athlete is arrested for driving while intoxicated one week before the final game for the league championship. Should the player be allowed to play?

- Are value conflicts present? Some people would say the athlete should not play because of the arrest; others would say she has been arrested but not convicted, so let her play.
- Do real alternatives exist that are equally justifiable? Real alternatives may include playing the athlete, not playing the athlete at all, or limiting playing time.
- Are there significant consequences to stakeholders, including owners, sponsors, or investors? If the athlete does not play and the team loses the championship, there could be a significant loss of revenue; if the athlete does play, there will be significant negative publicity.

When faced with an ethical dilemma, what is a sport manager to do? What should guide the sport manager when making a decision about an ethical dilemma like this?

Ethical Decision-Making Models

As discussed in Chapter 2, a sport manager must have an organized and sequential method for making decisions. It is no different when the problem is ethical in nature. The literature on ethical decision making is loaded with different models for managers to use (Low, Ferrell, & Mansfield, 2000). Some very practical models have been suggested (Cavanaugh, 1984; McDonald, 2001; McNamara, 1999; Trevino, 1986; Zinn, 1993). These models examine a variety of factors and involve multiple steps. For our purposes, we will identify a straightforward model sport managers can apply in the workplace. The model presented below by Hums, Barr, and Guillion (1999, p. 64 [italics added for emphasis]) is an adaptation of Zinn's model:

1. *Identify the correct problem to solve.* When making any type of decision, the decision maker must first identify the *real* problem. Identifying a symptom of the problem and acting on that will not resolve the problem itself.

2. *Gather all pertinent information.* Good decision makers try to be as informed as possible. Is it realistic to think you can gather every piece of information needed? Probably not, but sport managers need to make a good faith effort to find all the information possible to guide them in their decision making.

3. *Explore codes of conduct relevant to one's profession or to this particular dilemma.* More and more sport organizations are developing codes of conduct. Take a look at codes from other sport organizations to see if they provide guidance for your decision.

4. *Examine one's own personal values and beliefs.* We all come to the workplace with our own unique sets of values. Be sure you understand your values and how they could impact your decision.

5. *Consult with peers or other individuals in the industry who may have experience in similar situations.* Sport managers throughout the industry are facing increasing numbers of ethical issues. Perhaps some trusted colleagues have faced a similar dilemma. Talk with them to discuss how they went about solving the issue.

6. *List decision options.* Good decision makers learn to look at as many options as possible so they can make the best choice.

7. *Look for a win–win situation if at all possible.* This is a difficult but critical step. Ethical dilemmas arise when there are questions about the right thing to do. Try to make a decision that maximizes the outcome for the parties involved.

8. *Ask the question,* "How would my family feel if my decision and how and why I arrived at my decision appeared on the Internet

tomorrow?" Remember, as a sport manager, your decisions will be publicly analyzed and criticized. You want to be sure you have done all the right things in making your decision and that there is nothing about your decision you could not be up front about.

9. *Sleep on it.* Do not rush to a decision. In other words, think hard about the situation and the options and consequences facing you. You need to make a well-thought-out decision.

10. *Make the best decision possible, knowing it may not be perfect.* At some point, you will have to make your decision. Knowing you have followed the steps listed above will help you reach the best decision possible. In ethical decision making, reasonable people will often reasonably disagree over decisions.

11. *Evaluate the decision over time.* Often overlooked by managers, it is important to reflect on the decision later to see how it is working, or how changes could be made to improve upon it. This step is especially important if the issue or a similar one arises again.

This model is useful for sport managers because it presents a framework to make ethical decisions. As a sport manager your decision will be publicly scrutinized, so it helps to have a logical approach to such issues.

Another useful decision-making technique for examining ethical decisions is the SLEEPE Principle (presented in Chapter 2). This model helps the sport manager look at the big picture before making a decision. Ethical decisions, by their very nature, are bound to have far-reaching and complex ramifications. The SLEEPE Principle helps a sport manager think in broad terms about the ramifications of ethical decisions. In addition, this model has "Ethical" considerations already built in as the second E in SLEEPE. Regardless of which model a sport manager chooses to use, the models provide structure to help make decisions (Hums, 2006, 2007).

Up to this point, we have concentrated mainly on ethical situations and how individual sport managers will respond to them. Now we must expand that view and look at sport organizations as a whole and their corporate stance on ethical issues. One way to assess the ethical nature of a sport organization is to examine what kind of "citizen" the sport organization represents. This idea of a sport organization as a "citizen" can be looked at through the concept of corporate social responsibility.

Corporate Social Responsibility

Corporate social responsibility (CSR) is a term that often appears in the business ethics literature. What does it mean to be a responsible corporate citizen? A general definition of CSR is

> a concept whereby companies integrate social and environmental concerns in their business operations and in their interaction with their stakeholders on a voluntary basis. Being socially responsible means not only fulfilling legal expectations, but also going beyond compliance and investing "more" into human capital, the environment and the relations with stakeholders. (European Commission, 2001, p. 8)

How is corporate social responsibility measured? There is no singular measure of good citizenship because by its very nature it can be ascertained only from the perspectives of multiple stakeholders. One of the earliest and still often cited measurements of CSR comes from Carroll (1991), who explained how corporations can operate at four different CSR levels:

1. economic
2. legal
3. ethical
4. philanthropic

He examined corporations and the levels where they existed relative to various organizational stakeholders, including owners, customers, employees, the community, and the public at large (Carroll, 1991). The economic level represents the lowest level of CSR, and the philanthropic represents the highest level of CSR. The concept of CSR is usually applied in business settings; rarely has Carroll's model been applied in a sport industry setting.

Applying CSR in a Sport Setting

For our purposes, let's examine a college athletic department and its compliance with Title IX. By law, a college athletic department can comply with Title IX by meeting any one prong of the so-called three-prong approach (Carpenter & Acosta, 2004, pp. 14–15):

1. proportionality—having the same percentage of female athletes and female undergraduates
2. a continuing history of expanding athletic opportunities for women
3. demonstrating success in meeting the interests and abilities of female students

Given this information about Title IX compliance, let's apply the four levels of the CSR model to an intercollegiate athletic department.

1. Economic level. If the department is operating at the economic level, this means it is most interested in achieving purely financial goals. Here the Athletic Department would basically ignore Title IX, doing nothing to comply until forced to do so by outside influences. Using the logic that complying with Title IX is too costly, the Athletic Department would not take any steps to comply with the law unless it became costlier not to comply.

2. Legal level. If the Athletic Department operates at the legal level, it will attempt to meet the minimum legal criterion for compliance. At this stage, organizations strive to meet legal minimums and basically follow the letter of the law. Most certainly it would only attempt to fulfill one of the three prongs currently used to determine compliance. Since Title IX is not a quota system, this Athletic Department may rely on the so-called proportionality rule. It may make the case for continuing progress in developing opportunities for female athletes, or it could show it is meeting the needs and interests of the female student population. Athletic departments at this level are likely to drop men's sports to be in compliance, a quick and efficient way to come into minimum compliance with the proportionality prong of the three-prong approach to compliance. These same departments may often state the reason for dropping the sports was needing more resources for women's sport when in fact the reason was the football "arms race," a football program's increased need for expenditures to keep up with competing teams.

3. Ethical level. The Athletic Department operating at the ethical level would follow not just the letter of the law, but the spirit of the law as well. The department would not just meet but may exceed the legal minimums because it believes that is the proper thing to do. The department would add emerging sports that attract female participants, such as rowing or water polo. Rather than dropping men's sports, the department would find alternative sources of funding or ways to redirect the budget so that female opportunities are increased without adversely affecting opportunities for males.

4. Philanthropic level. Athletic departments operating at the philanthropic level would become active advocates for Title IX. They would develop model programs for compliance and may strive to fulfill all three prongs of the law, instead of the minimal one prong for compliance. These departments would actively offer help to athletic departments at other universities as those departments work to comply with Title IX. By presenting their programs as models and perhaps acting in a consultative mode to help other institutions comply with the law, athletic departments can operate at this level.

Sport Organizations and Corporate Social Responsibility in Practice

More and more sport organizations are beginning to integrate elements of CSR into their everyday business operations. For example, Nike (much maligned for its labor practices, including unsafe working conditions and low wages) has on its website a section called Responsibility that links to sites dealing with community affairs, diversity, environment, manufacturing processes, and reporting. In Nike's 2005–2006 Global Corporate Responsibility report, the company's three main goals are to (1) bring about systemic change for workers in the footwear, apparel, and equipment industries, (2) create sustainable products and business models, and (3) unleash potential through sport via the "Let Me Play" initiative (Nike, 2007, p. 13). In addition, Nike is leading the way with the "Stand Up Speak Up" campaign against racism in soccer and is a sponsoring partner with the Ashoka initiative Changemakers Sport for a Better World Competition. This competition is a "search for innovative ways for sports to promote social change" (Changemakers, 2007, para. 1). Given its past history of controversy with labor practices, Nike is making a concerted effort to present publicly an image of CSR.

The IOC includes several examples of CSR in its required documents for cities bidding to host the Olympic and Paralympic Games. The bid document is divided into a series of themes. In Theme 4, Environmental Protection and Meteorology, the prospective host city must indicate the Games will not adversely affect fragile environments (International Olympic Committee, n.d.). In Theme 9, Paralympic Games, a potential host city must indicate how the needs of people with disabilities will be met by hosting the Games and what legacy the Paralympic Games will leave for people with disabilities after the Games (IOC, n.d.). Capputo and Pennazi (2006) looked at CSR aspects for the 2006 Turino Winter Olympic Games. These authors categorized important Games CSR considerations as economic aspects, environmental sustainability, and the social impact of the Games.

Major professional sports organizations also act in a socially responsible manner through various charitable activities. For example, the NFL has partnered for many years with the United Way. The LPGA and the Women's National Basketball Association (WNBA) both work with the Susan G. Komen Breast Cancer Foundation. MLB's Reviving Baseball in the Inner Cities (RBI) program has grown over the last few years. Many universities support local community activities through programs such as CardsCare at the University of Louisville, where athletes work in community service projects, including reading to school children, visiting hospitals, and participating in charity fundraising events.

Finally, numerous sport organizations are beginning to see the importance of crafting codes of ethics (Jordan, Greenwell, Geist, Pastore, & Mahony, 2004). The content of these codes have been studied to examine what types of behaviors the codes should cover. For example, Greenwell, Geist, Mahony, Jordan, and Pastore (2001) examined the content of codes of ethics for various NCAA conferences. As a follow-up, Jordan and others (2004) asked college coaches their opinions on the contents of NCAA

Nike Corporate Responsibility Report
www.nike.com/nikebiz/nikeresponsibility/pdfs/bw/2_Nike_CRR_CR_Strategy_BW.pdf

conference codes of ethics. The two studies presented similar findings, namely, that the values (including sportsmanship, healthy environment, professional conduct, compliance with rules, welfare of student-athletes, and equitable treatment) contained in the codes were also the same ideals coaches felt should be included.

Codes of ethics vary in content, length, and complexity. Figure 4.3 offers a sample code of ethics from NIRSA that is relatively short (one-and-a-half pages) and concise (NIRSA, n.d.). Figure 4.4 shows the Table of Contents of the IOC Code of Ethics (IOC, 2007). Finally, Figure 4.5 contains a sport template code of behavior created by the ASC (n.d.b). This template provides a sample for almost any sport organization to adapt in constructing its own codes of conduct. Whether the code is long or short, concise or complex, what is most important is that sport organizations are beginning to develop codes of ethics appropriate for use in their segment of the industry.

Ethics and Sport Governance Organizations

Why is it important to include a chapter in this book about ethics? Individual sport managers and sport organizations look to their governing bodies for guidance on a wide range of topics, including legal issues, safety issues, and personnel issues—and ethical issues such as good business practices. Sport governing bodies can set the tone from the top down regarding ethical issues. The stance taken by a governing body will influence decisions made by you as a sport manager in any organization under that governing body's umbrella. An example of this relationship is the effect on International Federations and National Sports Organizations when the IOC makes a ruling on banned substances. State and provincial high school athletic associations are taking stronger stances on tobacco use by children, so individual schools are also instituting such programs. Governing bodies' rulings on ethical issues will hopefully result in behavioral changes and choices by their constituencies as well.

A sport organization's success can be linked directly to the actions of the individuals who make up the organization (Crosset & Hums, 2008), and individual sport managers are these people. Knowing you will face ethical dilemmas, you will need to employ an ethical decision-making model to make decisions about those dilemmas. You will have the opportunity to consider ethical questions in some case studies in this textbook. You will shape the culture of your organization, impacting the sport organization's ethical climate and the organization's stance related to being a good corporate citizen. In other words, the driving force for a sport organization's level of CSR rests with its employees and, most certainly, with its managers. That means you!

Preamble. An outstanding characteristic of a profession is that its members are continually striving to improve the quality of life for the population they serve. In making the choice to affiliate with a professional association, individuals assume the responsibility to conduct themselves in accordance with the ideals and standards set by the organization. For NIRSA members, this means they will strive to uphold the Bylaws in a manner illustrated in the Code of Ethics.

ARTICLE I

The NIRSA member in fulfilling professional obligations, shall:

1. Seek to extend public awareness of the profession and its achievements.
2. Be true in writing, reporting and duplicating information and give proper credit to the contributions of the others.
3. Encourage integrity by avoiding involvement or condoning activities that may degrade the Association, its members or any affiliate agency.
4. Perform dutifully the responsibilities of professional membership and of any offices or assignments to which appointed or elected.
5. Encourage cooperation with other professional associations, educational institutions and agencies.
6. Practice nondiscrimination on the basis of diversity related to age, disability, ethnicity, gender, national origin, race, religion, and sexual orientation.

ARTICLE II

The NIRSA member in relations with employers and employees staff (sic), shall:

1. Promote and implement the concept of equal opportunity and fairness in employment practices and program administration.
2. Refrain from exploiting individuals, institutions or agencies for personal or professional gain.
3. Secure the trust of employees by maintaining, in confidence, privileged information until properly released.
4. Support the contributions of fellow employees by properly crediting their achievements.
5. Assist and encourage the education of employees in the area of professional development.

ARTICLE III

The NIRSA member in providing programs and services, shall:

1. Endeavor to offer the safest and highest quality program achievable with available resources.
2. Take responsibility for employing qualified individuals in positions that require special credentials and/or experience.
3. Strive to keep abreast of current skills and knowledge and encourage innovation in programming and administration.
4. Promote integrity by accepting gratuities for service of no more than nominal value.
5. Encourage promotion of the ideals of Recreational Sports by incorporating such values as sportsmanship, fair play, participation and an atmosphere which promotes equitable opportunity for all.

Source: National Intramural-Recreational Sports Association (n.d.). Reprinted with permission.

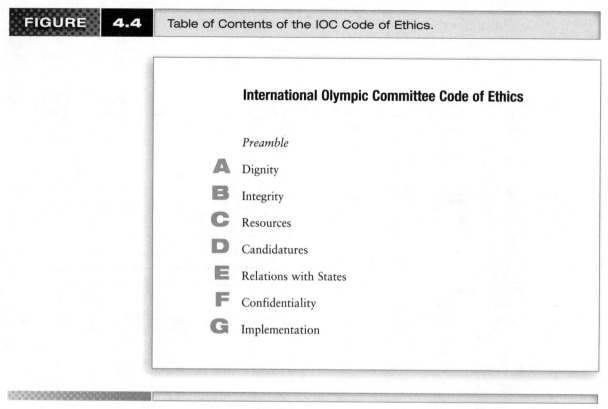

FIGURE 4.4 Table of Contents of the IOC Code of Ethics.

International Olympic Committee Code of Ethics

Preamble

A Dignity

B Integrity

C Resources

D Candidatures

E Relations with States

F Confidentiality

G Implementation

Source: IOC (2007).

SUMMARY

We see numerous examples of ethical dilemmas in society today. The sport industry is part of that greater society; therefore, we encounter ethical issues and dilemmas in the sport industry as well. When sport managers are faced with ethical dilemmas, they have to make decisions about those dilemmas. To make sound decisions, sport managers must follow a systematic ethical decision-making process.

When examining ethics, it is useful to examine ethical activity on the organizational as well as on the individual level. One measure of ethics in a sport organization is CSR, whether it is reflected in a sport organization's stance on a particular issue, its involvement in charitable community events, or its adoption of a code of ethics.

Finally, it is important to examine ethics in the context of governance because of the influence governing bodies have over individual sport organizations. By exhibiting ethical behaviors at the top levels, governing bodies set the ethical tone for their membership.

The Essence of Australian Sport Template Code of Behaviour

This Template Code of Behaviour is intended to be the minimum standard for anyone involved in sport.

- Operate within the rules and spirit of your sport, promoting fair play over winning at any cost.
- Encourage and support opportunities for people to learn appropriate behaviours and skills.
- Support opportunities for participation in all aspects of the sport.
- Treat each person as an individual.
- Display control and courtesy to all involved with the sport.
- Respect the rights and worth of every person regardless of their gender, ability, cultural background or religion.
- Respect the decisions of officials, coaches and administrators in the conduct of the sport.
- Wherever practical, avoid unaccompanied and unobserved one-on-one activity (when in a supervisory capacity or where a power imbalance will exist) with people under the age of 18 years.
- Adopt appropriate and responsible behaviour in all interactions.
- Adopt responsible behaviour in relation to alcohol and other drugs.
- Act with integrity and objectivity, and accept responsibility for your decisions and actions.
- Ensure your decisions and actions contribute to a safe environment.
- Ensure your decisions and actions contribute to a harassment free environment.
- Do not tolerate harmful or abusive behaviours.

ATHLETES

- Give your best at all times.
- Participate for your own enjoyment and benefit.

COACHES

- Place the safety and welfare of the athletes above all else.

- Help each person (athlete, official, etc.) reach their potential—respect the talent, developmental stage and goals of each person and compliment and encourage with positive and supportive feedback.
- Any physical contact with a person should be appropriate to the situation and necessary for the person's skill development.
- Be honest and do not allow your qualifications to be misrepresented.

OFFICIALS

- Place the safety and welfare of the athletes above all else.
- Be consistent and impartial when making decisions.
- Address unsporting behaviour and promote respect for all people.

ADMINISTRATORS

- Act honestly, in good faith and in the best interests of the sport as a whole.
- Ensure that any information acquired or advantage gained from the position is not used improperly.
- Conduct your responsibilities with due care, competence and diligence.
- Do not allow prejudice, conflict of interest or bias to affect your objectivity.

PARENTS

- Encourage children to participate and have fun.
- Focus on the child's effort and performance rather than winning or losing.
- Never ridicule or yell at a child for making a mistake or losing a competition.

SPECTATORS

- Respect the performances and efforts of all people.
- Reject the use of violence in any form, whether it is by spectators, coaches, officials or athletes.

Source: ASC (n.d.b). Reprinted with permission of the Australian Sports Commission.

CASE STUDY *Ethics*

You are the Athletic Director at the local high school. A big baseball fan, you often go to the games and are known and respected by the players on the team. One day one of the players, Matt, comes to your office and asks to speak with you privately. Matt is a very skilled player, one who is predicted to be chosen in the early rounds of the draft. Breaking into tears, he tells you, "I recently went to the doctor and found out that I am HIV+ and I don't know what to do. But please, please, don't tell Coach . . . don't tell Coach. . . ."

1. Using the ethical decision-making model from this chapter, how do you respond to him, and what course or courses of action can you take after he leaves your office?

CHAPTER QUESTIONS

1. Using the model presented in Figure 4.1, choose three additional societal issues and illustrate how they are seen in sport.
2. Apply Carroll's model of CSR to the following sport organizations:
   a. Your choice of a professional sport franchise
   b. Your college or university Athletic Department
   c. Your nation's National Olympic Committee
   d. Can organizations exist at different levels in Carroll's model at the same time?
3. Find codes of conduct or codes of ethics from three different sport organizations, each from a different industry segment. Compare the three for similarities and differences.

REFERENCES

ASC. (n.d.a). Ethics in sport unit. Retrieved October 3, 2007, from www.ausport.gov.au/ethics/issues.asp.

ASC. (n.d.b). The essence of Australian Sports Template Code of Behaviour. Retrieved September 10, 2007, from www.ausport.gov.au/ethics/TemplateCodeof Behaviour.asp.

Asser, M. (2000, June 19). Analysis: Soccer violence an international problem. Retrieved November 17, 2002, from http://news.bbc.co.uk/1/hi/world/europe/797601.stm.

Capputo, A., & Pennazi, V. (2006). Corporate social responsibility in sport: Turino 2006 Winter Olympic Games. Retrieved October 3, 2007, from www.crrconference.org/downloads/2006 cappatopennaziopaperfinal.pdf.

Carpenter, L. J., & Acosta, R. V. (2004). *Title IX*. Champaign, IL: Human Kinetics.

Carroll, A. B. (1991). The pyramid of corporate social responsibility: Toward the moral management of organizational stakeholders. *Business Horizons,* July–August, 39–48.

Cavanaugh, G. (1984). *American values* (2d ed.). Englewood Cliffs, NJ: Prentice Hall.

CCES. (2007). About CCES: CCES position. Retrieved September 25, 2007, from www.cces.ca/forms/index.cfm?dsp=template&act=view3&template_id=62&lang=.

Changemakers. (2007). Sport for a better world. Retrieved October 3, 2007, from www.change makers.net/en-us/competition/sports.

Coakley, J. J. (2006). *Sport in society: Issues and controversies* (9th ed.). Boston: Irwin/McGraw-Hill.

Corporate Social Responsibility Forum. (n.d.). CSR by theme. Retrieved November 14, 2002, from www.csrforum.com/csr/csrwebassist.nsf/web printview/a1a2.html.

Council of Europe Committee of Ministers. (2001). Code of sport ethics. Retrieved October 2, 2007, from https://wcd.coe.int/ViewDoc.jsp?Ref=Rec (92)14&Sector=secCM&Language=lanEnglish&Ver=rev&BackColorInternet=9999CC&BackColor Intranet=FFBB55&BackColorLogged=FFAC75.

Crosset, T., & Hums, M. A. (2008). Ethical principles applied to sport management. In L. P. Masteralexis, C. A. Barr, & M. A. Hums (Eds.), *Principles and practice of sport management* (3d ed., pp. 109–124). Sudbury, MA: Jones and Bartlett.

Etheik Instituut. (2005). Sport ethics. Retrieved October 1, 2007, from www.ethics.uu.nl/sport ethics.html.

European Commission. (2001). Promoting a European framework for corporate social responsibility. Retrieved October 4, 2007, from http://ec.europa.eu/employment_social/soc-dial/csr/greenpaper_en.pdf.

Greenwell, T. C., Geist, A. L., Mahony, D. F., Jordan, J. S., & Pastore, D. L. (2001). Characteristics of NCAA conference codes of ethics. *International Journal of Sport Management, 2*(2), 108–124.

Hums, M. A. (2006, May). Analyzing the impact of changes in classification systems: A sport management analysis model. Paper presented at the VISTA 2006 International Paralympic Committee Congress, Bonn, Germany.

Hums, M. A. (2007, June). The business of the Paralympic Games: Economics and ethics. Paper presented at 7th International Conference on Sports: Economic, Management and Marketing Aspects, Athens, Greece.

Hums, M. A., Barr, C. A., & Guillion, L. (1999). The ethical issues confronting managers in the sport industry. *Journal of Business Ethics, 20,* 51–66.

IOC. (n.d.). Manual for candidate cities for the games of the XXI Winter Games 2010. Retrieved October 3, 2007, from http://multimedia.olympic.org/pdf/en_report_523.pdf.

IOC. (2007). IOC Code of Ethics (Text adopted by the IOC Executive Board April 26, 2007, in Beijing). Retrieved October 2, 2007, from http://multi media.olympic.org/pdf/en_report_17.pdf.

Jordan, J. S., Greenwell, T. C., Geist, A. L., Pastore, D. L., & Mahony, D. F. (2004). Coaches' perceptions of conference codes of ethics. *The Physical Educator, 61,* 131–145.

Lapchick, R. (2005). *2004 Racial and gender report card.* Orlando, FL: Institute for Diversity and Ethics in Sport, University of Central Florida.

Low, T. W., Ferrell, L., & Mansfield, P. A. (2000). Review of empirical studies assessing ethical decision making in business. *Journal of Business Ethics, 25*(3), 185–204.

Maguire, J. A., & Nakayama, M. (2006). *Japan, sport and society: Tradition and change in a globalizing world.* London: Routledge.

McDonald, M. (2001, January). A framework for ethical decision-making: Version 6.0 Ethics shareware. Retrieved November 5, 2002, from www.ethics.ubc.ca/mcdonald/decision.html.

McNamara, C. (2007). Complete guide to ethics management: An ethics toolkit for managers. Retrieved September 20, 2007, from www.management help.org/ethics/ethxgde.htm#anchor53723.

Nike. (2007). Global corporate social responsibility strategy. Retrieved October 2, 2007, from www.nike.com/nikebiz/nikeresponsibility/pdfs/bw/2_Nike_CRR_CR_Strategy_BW.pdf.

NIRSA. (n.d.). NIRSA member code of ethics. Retrieved November 7, 2002, from www.nirsa.org/about/mission.htm.

Oprisan, V. (1999) Aspects and tendencies of voluntary work in Romanian sport. In *Papers of the symposium: Volunteers, global society and the*

Olympic Movement, Lausaunne, Switzerland. Retrieved November 21, 2002, from www.blues. uab.es/olympic.studies/volunteers/oprisan.html.

Ridinger, L., & Greenwell, T. C. (2005). Ethics in the sport industry. In A. Gillentine & R. B. Crow (Eds.), *Foundations of sport management* (pp. 155–168). Morgantown, WV: Fitness Information Technology.

Robinson, M., Hums, M. A., Crow, B., & Phillips, D. (2001). *Profiles of sport management professionals: The people who make the games happen.* Gaithersburg, MD: Aspen.

Trevino, L. (1986). Ethical decision making in organizations: A personal-situation interactionist model. *Academy of Management Review, 11,* 601–617.

University of Nebraska Medical Center. (2007). Every nine seconds a woman is beaten. Retrieved October 3, 2007, from www.unmc.edu/olson/education /dv.htm.

Zinn, L. M. (1993). Do the right thing: Ethical decision making in professional and business practice. *Adult Learning, 5,* 7–8, 27.

5

SCHOLASTIC SPORT

INTRODUCTION

On any given Friday night in the fall, the air is filled with the sounds of fans screaming, helmets pounding, and bands playing. On Saturdays in winter, the ball bounces off the court, and skates glide over the ice. In the spring, the starter's gun marks the beginning of the 100-meter dash, and we hear the familiar sound of softballs and baseballs being caught and hit. On fields, courts, and rinks everywhere, it is time for the weekend ritual—high school sports. All across the land, young athletes compete for their schools, their communities, and themselves. Many of you remember those days, no doubt. This chapter will focus on high school sport, a large area of the sport industry involving thousands of schools and participants.

Although it may surprise you, this is a primarily North American model. In most nations of the world, young people compete for their local municipality's club teams, not for their high school teams. For example, a young athlete living in the town of Megara, outside of Athens, Greece, will play for the local sports club, not for Megara High School. The high school may not even field any teams, since the schools do not compete against each other in sports like schools in North America. In Amsterdam, a talented young football (soccer) player might compete on a developmental team of the Amsterdam Ajax professional football club. While most of this chapter focuses on the North American model, we must remember that this model is not the only competitive model for youth sport. "The opportunity for boys and girls to represent their school and community as they participate in interscholastic activities is a privilege unique to young people in American education" (PIAA, para. 1, 2001). How, then, did it happen that North American high school sport developed into the product we see today? To understand this evolution, it is important to take a look at the history and evolution of sport in high schools.

History of High School Sport

The history of high school sport is long and storied. It began with simple roots, to develop healthy habits in youngsters, and grew to today's widespread spectator popularity, with important steps along the way. For purposes of this textbook, we will examine mainly how the governance of high school sport evolved.

Early Development

In the late 1800s, sport was seen as a vehicle to help solve societal ills such as delinquency and poor health, and so schools began to promote sport (Seymour, 1990). In the early days, high school sport began as a student-initiated, -organized, and -operated activity, similar to the way intercollegiate sport started. However, again similar to intercollegiate sport, the need for adult supervision and direction soon became apparent. To uphold a certain moral image, administrators felt it necessary to extend their authority over interscholastic sport. In the 1890s, the popularity of high school football soared, and its abuses mirrored those of college sport at the time—overemphasis on winning, using ineligible players, and financial mismanagement (Rader, 1999). By the time the 15th Conference on Academies and High Schools met in 1902, faculty control was in place in several states, and the conference issued basic recommendations on faculty control of interscholastic sport. Around the same time, state high school associations were beginning to form, with early associations being organized in Illinois and Wisconsin (Covell, 2008). In the early 1900s, rules began to be put in place for high school athletes that defined minimum course loads and satisfactory progress in school, as well as participation eligibility certification. These rules were a progression from those outlined by the Michigan State Teachers' Association's Committee on High School Athletics in 1896 (Forsythe, 1950). As athletics became more integral in a student's academic experience, government-funded educational institutions assumed increased control over the governance of high school athletics (Vincent, 1994).

Development of the National Federation of State High School Associations (NFHS)

In 1920, representatives of five midwestern states—Illinois, Indiana, Iowa, Michigan, and Wisconsin—met in Chicago to discuss concerns about collegiate and nonschool sponsorship of high school events. As a result of this meeting, a plan was developed to ensure the well-being of high school student-athletes in competitive situations. These five state associations banded together to form the Midwest Federation of State High School Athletic Associations. Eventually, more state associations affiliated with this group, and in 1923, the name "National Federation of State High School Athletic Associations" was officially adopted (NFHS, 2006b). By the 1930s, the group assumed responsibility as the rules-writing and rules-publishing body for high school sports. The organization grew throughout the 20th century, adding members until 1969, when all 50 states and the District of Columbia belonged. In the 1970s, the fine arts were added under the organization's umbrella, and the term *Athletic* was removed from the organization's name. The official name then became the "National Federation of State High School Associations," the name it retains today, and since 1997, the organization has gone by the abbreviation "NFHS" (NFHS, 2007).

Organizational development continued from the 1980s to the present, with increased educational programming, incorporation of debate and spirit programs, and ongoing rules interpretations and publications. In 2000, the NFHS moved its headquarters to Indianapolis, Indiana (NFHS, 2006b).

Value of High School Sport Today

At present, the values and benefits of high school sport have been well defined by its advocates. For example, according to the mission statement of the Alberta Schools' Athletic Association (ASAA), "The mission of ASAA is to promote and regulate sanctioned interscholastic activities, contests and programs as an integral part of quality education of its member schools" (2007a).

www

Alberta Schools' Athletic Association
www.asaa.ca

In addition, the ASAA's Strategic Plan is based on the following beliefs:

Interscholastic activities:

- exist for the intrinsic values they provide for students of member schools;
- are an integral part of the overall educational program;
- provide an opportunity to learn and apply skills beyond the classroom;
- promote character, citizenship, leadership and personal responsibility;
- provide for fair and equitable opportunities for students of member schools;
- provide unique opportunities for students to benefit from cross-cultural contact;
- encourage and enhance the connections between communities and schools, adults and students, and among students; and
- promote positive academic growth and develop sportsmanship. (ASAA, 2007a)

Massachusetts
Interscholastic Athletic
Association

www.miaa.net

As another example, the Massachusetts Interscholastic Athletic Association (MIAA) states on its website (MIAA, n.d.b):

Within high school programs, young people learn the values associated with discipline, performing under stress, teamwork, sacrifice, commitment, effort, accountability, citizenship, sportsmanship, confidence, leadership and organizational skills, participating within rules, physical well-being and chemical health, striving towards excellence, and many other characteristics that come quickly to the mind of any educator to justify sponsoring interscholastic athletics.

For all these reasons, high school sport has become an important component of many students' total educational experience. To make sure all these worthwhile activities happen in a well-planned and organized environment, governance structures must be in place to facilitate proper delivery of the interscholastic sport product.

Governance

Scholastic sport governance occurs on a number of different levels. As mentioned previously, at the national level there is the NFHS, which includes members from the United States and Canada. But unlike some national-level sport governing bodies, this is not where the real power lies. In high school sport the real power and authority rest at the state and provincial levels, where the regulatory power lies. According to

Wong (1994, p. 22), "the power and authority in high school athletics are in the individual state organizations, which determine the rules and regulations for the sport programs and schools within that state." There is also governance on the local level, meaning the school or school district. Let's look at the organizational structures at these different levels and the scope of their authority.

National Federation of State High School Associations (NFHS)

The NFHS (2006a) is the national service and administrative organization of high school athletics and fine arts programs in speech, debate, and music. From its offices in Indianapolis, Indiana, the NFHS serves its 50-member state high school athletic and activity associations, plus those of the District of Columbia. "The NFHS is a member-governed, not-for-profit corporation" (NFHS, 2006b, p. 16). The NFHS publishes playing rules for 16 sports for boys' and girls' competition and provides programs and services that its member state associations can use in working with the 18,500 member high schools and approximately 11 million young people involved in high school activity programs.

From this information, it is important to note two main points. First, the NFHS is considered a service organization. In contrast to the NCAA, which has strong sanctioning power over members, the purpose of the NFHS is to provide service to its members. Second, the NFHS is not involved solely in athletic competition. Subgroups within the NFHS include not only the National Federation Coaches Association, the National Federation Officials Association, and the National Interscholastic Athletic Administrators Association (NIAAA) but also the National Federation Interscholastic Speech and Debate Association, the National Federation Interscholastic Music Association, and the National Federation Interscholastic Spirit Association. Thus, this organization has a broad base across many high school extracurricular activities. This textbook, however, focuses on those aspects of the NFHS dealing directly with interscholastic athletics.

Mission. The mission statement of the NFHS (presented in Figure 5.1) states that the purpose of the NFHS is to promote activities that contribute positively to a student's educational experience. It is also apparent that the organization seeks to develop students into people who are going to be contributing members of society because of the good lessons they learn from their sport experience. From this mission statement it is clear that high school sport is meant to help students achieve educational goals.

Financials. How does the NFHS finance itself? More than half of its income, approximately 52 percent, comes from sales revenue (NFHS,

National Federation of State High School Associations

www.nfhs.org

NFHS Coaches' Association

www.nfhs.org/web/2006/08/coaches_association.aspx

NFHS Officials' Association

www.nfhs.org/web/2006/08/officials_association.aspx

National Interscholastic Athletic Administrators Association

www2.niaaa.org

FIGURE 5.1 Mission statement of the NFHS.

The National Federation of State High School Associations serves its members, related professional organizations and students by providing leadership for the administration of education-based interscholastic activities, which support academic achievement, good citizenship and equitable opportunities.

We believe:

- the NFHS is the recognized national authority on interscholastic activity programs.
- interscholastic activity programs enrich each student's educational experience.
- participation in education-based activity programs promotes student academic achievement.
- student participation in interscholastic activity programs is a privilege.
- interscholastic participation develops good citizenship and healthy lifestyles.
- interscholastic activity programs foster involvement of a diverse population.
- interscholastic activity programs promote positive school/community relations.
- the NFHS is the pre-eminent authority on competition rules for interscholastic activity programs.
- national competition rules promote fair play and minimize risks for student participants.
- cooperation among state associations advances their individual and collective well-being.
- properly trained administrators/coaches/directors promote the educational mission of the interscholastic experience.
- properly trained officials/judges enhance interscholastic competition.

Source: NFHS (2006), p. 1.

2007) from its official publications. These publications include rules publications, miscellaneous sports items, sports guides and handbooks, debate item publications, and speech and debate booklets. In addition, the organization earns funds from membership dues and professional organizations; contributions, royalties, and sponsors; meetings and conferences; and a few lesser sources. How is the money spent? The major expense categories for the NFHS are salaries and benefits, professional organizations, rules making and publications, educational and professional development, and management and general (NFHS, 2007).

Membership. Who belongs to the NFHS? NFHS membership is made up of state associations, not individual people. "The active members of the National Federation of State High School Associations are the 50 state high school athletic/activity associations, plus the District of Columbia. There are also affiliate members, including associations in the U. S. territories, Canada, and other neighboring nations" (NFHS, 2006c). The affiliated members from outside the United States include Canadian School Sport Federations from Alberta, British Columbia, Manitoba, New Brunswick, Nova Scotia, Ontario, Prince Edward Island, Quebec, and Saskatchewan. Other affiliates are from Guam and the U. S. Virgin Islands (NFHS, 2006c).

Organizational structure. The organizational structure of the NFHS indicates that the membership drives the governance of the organization. As illustrated in Figure 5.2, the member state associations are at the top of the chart. The organization is divided into eight sections to ensure fair geographic representation. The National Council is the legislative body of the NFHS and is responsible for enacting amendments to the constitution and bylaws in addition to other duties. The National Council consists of one representative from each voting member, that is, from each member state association. The National Council meets two times a year. The Board of Directors of the NFHS is made up of 12 members, one from each geographic section and four additional at-large members. The board is empowered to conduct the business of the NFHS (NFHS, 2006b), including activities such as approving the annual budget, overseeing the investment and management of all funds, and establishing the standing rules and special committees (NFHS, 2006b). The next group involved in the governance of the NFHS is the Executive Staff, the organization's paid employees, including an Executive Director and Directors of Marketing, Information Services, Financial Services, Publications and Communications, and Educational Services. Several Assistant Directors are also employed, as well as a General Counsel to handle legal questions and issues. Finally, as with most organizations, a series of committees work in designated areas, such as Rules and Sports Committees, general committees, and special committees (NFHS, 2006b).

State and Provincial High School Athletic Associations

Each state and province has its own high school athletic association. As you will see, they have different names. In the United States, for example, we see the Alabama High School Athletic Association, the Colorado High School Activities Association, the Georgia High School Association, the Texas University Interscholastic League, the District of Columbia Interscholastic

www
Canadian School Sport Federations
www.schoolsport.ca/pages/news.php

www
State High School Athletic Associations
www.ahsaa.com
www.chsaa.org
www.ghsa.net
www.uil.utexas.edu

84 CHAPTER 5

FIGURE 5.2 Organizational chart for the National Federation of State High School Associations (NFHS).

```
MEMBER STATE ASSOCIATIONS
        |
NATIONAL COUNCIL ———————— GENERAL COMMITTEE
        |                    Appeal
BOARD OF DIRECTORS ———————— ALL RELATED SUBCOMMITTEES
        |
EXECUTIVE DIRECTOR
        |                    NIAAA
EXECUTIVE STAFF (Support Staff) ——— Certified Athletic
                                     Administrators Program
                                     Leadership Training Program
                                     Professional Publications
```

17 SPORTS RULES AND ACTIVITY COMMITTEES
- Baseball*
- Basketball*
- Field Hockey
- Football*
- Gymnastics Boys/Girls*
- Ice Hockey
- Lacrosse, Boys
- Lacrosse, Girls
- Music
- Soccer*
- Softball*
- Speech
- Spirit*
- Swimming and Diving*/Water Polo
- Track and Field/Cross Country*
- Volleyball*
- Wrestling*

*Interpreters Meetings (11)
- Advertising
- NFHS Website
- Rules Interpretations

GENERAL COMMITTEES
- Annual Meeting Advisory
- Athletic Directors Advisory
- Citizenship
- Equity
- Hall of Fame Screening
- National Records
- NFHS Coaches Education
- Sports Medicine Advisory

SPECIAL COMMITTEES
- Hall of Fame Selection

STAFF COMMITTEE
- Sports Rules Review

- Athletic Sanctions
- Participation Survey
- Rules Interpreters Meetings

SPECIAL MEETINGS/EVENTS
- Debate Topic Selection Meeting
- Hall of Fame Induction
- Legal Meeting
- National High School Activities Week
- Conference for Athletic Directors
- NFHS Summer Meeting
- NFHS Winter Meeting
- NFHS Summit on Current Issues
- Professional Development
  Conferences
- State Music Conference
- Student Leadership Conference

VIDEOS
- Miscellaneous Videos
- Music Videos
- Speech and Debate Videos
- Sports Videos

OTHER SERVICES
- Officials Equipment Center
- Corporate Partnership Program
- Teleconferences on Critical Issues
- Authenticating Mark Program

MEMBER STATE ASSOCIATIONS

PUBLICATIONS
- Court and Field Diagram Guide
- Forensic Quarterly
- High School Sports Record Book
- IAA Magazine
- Lincoln-Douglas Debate Annual
- NFHS Annual Report
- NFHS Brochure
- NFHS Coaches' Quarterly
- NFHS Handbook
- NFHS News
- NFHS Officials' Quarterly
- NFHS Statisticians' Manual
- NFHS Catalog
- Rules Publications 17 Sports
- Speech and Debate Books
- Sports Medicine Handbook

- Rules Exams
- Resource Center
- Rules Questionnaires

EDUCATIONAL SERVICES
- NFHS Coaches Education Program
- Citizenship Curriculum
- Rules Exams and Interpretations
- Rules Posters
- Sports Transparencies/PowerPoint
- Sportsmanship Materials

PROFESSIONAL ORGANIZATIONS
- NFCA (Coaches)
- NFMA (Music)
- NFOA (Officials)
- NFSA (Spirit)
- NFSDA (Speech and Debate)

Legal
- Resource for National Issues
- Citizenship Programs

Source: NFHS (2006b). Reprinted with permission.

Athletic Association, and the Vermont Principals' Association; and in Canada, the Ontario Federation of School Athletic Associations and the Nova Scotia School Athletic Federation. While these organizations have different names, they share common missions and authorities.

State and provincial high school associations serve several important functions. First, they are the regulatory bodies for high school sport in a particular state or province. As stated earlier, the power in high school athletics resides on this level. Second, they are responsible for organizing state or provincial championships, always the highlight of the year for any sport. Finally, they maintain the educational philosophy for high school athletics in their respective state or province. According to Sharp, Moorman, and Claussen (2007, p. 127), "Authority to govern interscholastic athletics within a state is granted to the state association by the state legislature or by judicial decision. Each state's high school athletic association is responsible for implementing and enforcing regulations governing interscholastic athletics participation of the member high schools." This statement clearly establishes that the power in high school sport governance lies at the state level.

The regulatory power in scholastic sport lies mainly at the state level. This level is often vested with this power from the state legislature. State or provincial associations have the authority to revoke eligibility for individual students and to disqualify schools from participating in events if the schools break state or provincial association rules. When there are disputes about eligibility cases and other questions about rules interpretations, the state high school associations are named in these lawsuits. The reason is that in most cases the state association has been found to be a state actor (Altman, 2007), that is, an organization working as if it were empowered by the government to act. You may remember from your Legal Aspects of Sport class that this makes state associations subject to the requirements of the United States Constitution. Whenever a high school athlete feels her or his constitutional rights have been violated because of an association's rule, that athlete names the high school association in the suit. Thus when state associations craft policies, they must be mindful not to enact policies or procedures that could be construed as infringing on a student's fundamental rights, such as the right to due process if a student is denied eligibility for some reason.

Mission. As mentioned earlier, while the associations may differ from state to state, there are still common ideals reflected in each association's mission statement. Sample mission statements from the Oregon School Activities Association (OSAA) and the Ontario Federation of School Athletic Associations (OFSAA) are presented in Figures 5.3 and 5.4, respectively. While these mission statements are somewhat different, one can see similarities between them. Shared themes include the place of ath-

www

Vermont Principals' Association
www.vpaonline.org

Ontario Federation of School Athletic Associations
www.ofsaa.on.ca

Nova Scotia School Athletic Federation
http://nssaf.ednet.ns.ca

www

Oregon School Activities Association
www.osaa.org

FIGURE	5.3	Mission statement of the Oregon School Activities Association.

The mission of the OSAA is to serve member schools by providing leadership and state coordination for the conduct of interscholastic activities, which will enrich the educational experiences of high school students. The OSAA will work to promote interschool activities that provide equitable participation opportunities, positive recognition and learning experiences to students, while enhancing the achievement of educational goals.

Source: OSAA (2001). Reprinted with permission.

FIGURE	5.4	Mission statement of the Ontario Federation of School Athletic Associations.

The Ontario Federation of School Athletic Associations (OFSAA) is a provincial federation of Associations encompassing volunteer coaches, students, and administrators. OFSAA is dedicated to the promotion and enhancement of the educational value of school sport. As an advocate for school sport, OFSAA provides leadership in advancing the educational benefits of participation through its services, resources and the conduct of secondary school sport Championships.

Source: OFSAA (2005). Reprinted with permission.

letics in an educational setting, the values and benefits students derive from high school sport, and provision of service to their members.

Membership. High school associations generally are voluntary, nonprofit organizations whose members are the public and private secondary schools in that particular state or province. In some cases, junior high schools and middle schools may also belong to the association. The size of each association varies, depending on the number of high schools in the state or province. The membership of high school associations is similar to that of the NCAA, where institutions, not individual people, are the members of the organization.

Financials. The sources of funding for athletic associations vary by state. The Arizona Interscholastic Association (AIA) is primarily financed by membership dues, varsity sport participation fees, officials' registration fees, and sales of items including rule books (AIA, n.d.).The MIAA receives no tax money. Rather, the majority of its income comes from sponsorships and ticket sales at regional and state tournaments (MIAA, n.d.). The Nebraska School Activities Association (NSAA) has entered into a corporate partnership with U S Bank, allowing the association to maintain and strengthen its programs without shouldering the additional costs (NSAA, 2007). Dues from member schools, officials, and a share from the tournament series support the $1.2 million annual budget of the Tennessee Secondary School Athletic Association (TSSAA, 1999). The KHSAA includes financial issues in its Operational Strategic Plan. The specific strategies in this document include the following (KHSAA, 2003):

> *Strategy 1.1* Pursue an aggressive fund raising and promotional strategy seeking additional ancillary revenue for the Association while protecting existing programs.
>
> *Strategy 1.2* Continue the practice of fiscal restraint and management controls over the current business operations of the Association.
>
> *Strategy 1.3* Exercise control and optimize usage of Association funds.
>
> *Strategy 1.4* Analyze event structures and financial management practices.

The main sources of funds for the ASAA include the Alberta Sport, Recreation, Parks and Wildlife Foundation (Lottery Funds) through the Ministry of Alberta Community Development, membership fees, fundraising (casinos), and corporate assistance. The money is spent on the following categories: transportation and officiating costs for provincial competitions, delegate expenses to meetings, publications and rule books, medals and trophies, office administration, and staff salaries and benefits (ASAA, 2007b). As budgets become tighter, associations have to come up with more creative means of financing their programs. This topic will be discussed in more detail later in the chapter.

Organizational Structure

State and provincial associations. During the year, an Executive Committee or Board of Directors meets to deal with any ongoing issues. The Executive Committee is made up of Superintendents, Principals, and

Ⓦww

Arizona Interscholastic Association

www.aiaonline.org

Nebraska School Activities Association

www.nsaahome.org

Tennessee Secondary School Athletic Association

www.tssaa.org

Athletic Directors from various high schools around the state or province. In addition, paid Executive Staff members work in the association year round. While the titles may vary, often the highest-ranking paid staff member is called the Commissioner or the Executive Director. There will also be several Associate or Assistant Commissioners or Associate or Assistant Executive Directors, each of whom has distinct responsibilities for certain sports and other areas, such as eligibility, rules interpretation, officials, coaches' clinics, sportsmanship and ethics programs, and trophies and awards. The organizational chart for the Pennsylvania Interscholastic Athletic Association (PIAA) is presented in Figure 5.5.

Pennsylvania Interscholastic Athletic Association

www.piaa.org

School districts. School districts have various responsibilities, including dealing with high school athletic programs in a limited fashion. For example, local school boards approve all employee contracts, including approving coaches' and athletic directors' contracts. It is important again to note that school district responsibilities will differ from state to state. For example, in Indiana, coaches' salaries come from the same general fund as teachers' salaries for that district. Therefore, the school district decides on salaries for coaches from that pool of money. This is not true in all states. In terms of facility construction, decisions on funding sport-related facilities may also be approved by the school district. For example, if a school district decides to fund a gymnasium, the gymnasium would not be built just for athletics. It would be part of a project benefiting the physical education program, and athletics would share the facility. Finally, school districts may also organize capital campaigns to fund individual projects. Sometimes, depending on the success of the campaign and the immediate needs of the school district, the money raised may or may not go to improving athletic facilities, such as renovating a track or developing an exercise room at a particular school (D. Sullivan, personal communication, June 29, 2002).

Individual schools. Each high school has someone who serves as the Athletic Director. Sometimes this person also works as a coach, although that is not the ideal situation. According to Covell (2004, pp. 129–130), the responsibilities and tasks of the Athletic Director include

- hiring, supervising and evaluating coaches;
- coordinating nearly all facets of contest management, including the hiring and paying of officials and event staff; setting . . . training and disciplinary policies; determining . . . budgets; and associated fund-raising;
- determining and verifying game scheduling and athlete eligibility;
- transmitting relevant publicity; and
- handling public relations.

FIGURE 5.5

Organizational chart for the Pennsylvania Interscholastic Athletic Association.

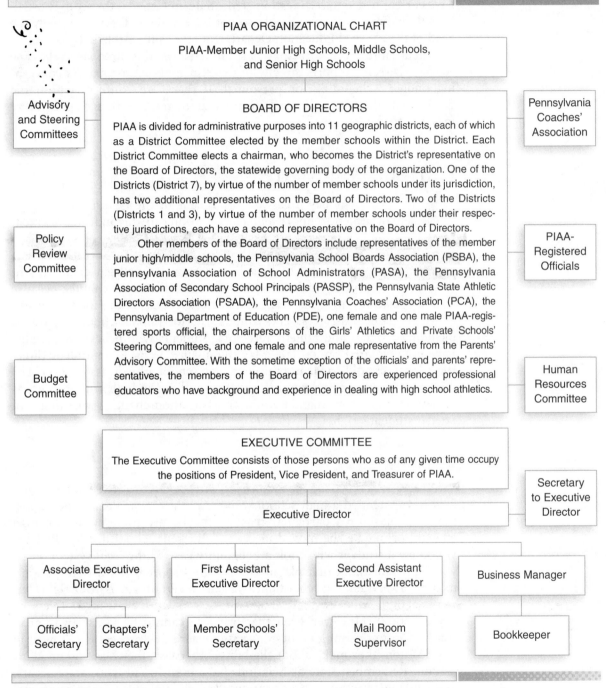

PIAA ORGANIZATIONAL CHART

PIAA-Member Junior High Schools, Middle Schools, and Senior High Schools

Advisory and Steering Committees

Pennsylvania Coaches' Association

BOARD OF DIRECTORS

PIAA is divided for administrative purposes into 11 geographic districts, each of which as a District Committee elected by the member schools within the District. Each District Committee elects a chairman, who becomes the District's representative on the Board of Directors, the statewide governing body of the organization. One of the Districts (District 7), by virtue of the number of member schools under its jurisdiction, has two additional representatives on the Board of Directors. Two of the Districts (Districts 1 and 3), by virtue of the number of member schools under their respective jurisdictions, each have a second representative on the Board of Directors.

Other members of the Board of Directors include representatives of the member junior high/middle schools, the Pennsylvania School Boards Association (PSBA), the Pennsylvania Association of School Administrators (PASA), the Pennsylvania Association of Secondary School Principals (PASSP), the Pennsylvania State Athletic Directors Association (PSADA), the Pennsylvania Coaches' Association (PCA), the Pennsylvania Department of Education (PDE), one female and one male PIAA-registered sports official, the chairpersons of the Girls' Athletics and Private Schools' Steering Committees, and one female and one male representative from the Parents' Advisory Committee. With the sometime exception of the officials' and parents' representatives, the members of the Board of Directors are experienced professional educators who have background and experience in dealing with high school athletics.

Policy Review Committee

PIAA-Registered Officials

Budget Committee

Human Resources Committee

EXECUTIVE COMMITTEE

The Executive Committee consists of those persons who as of any given time occupy the positions of President, Vice President, and Treasurer of PIAA.

Secretary to Executive Director

Executive Director

Associate Executive Director

First Assistant Executive Director

Second Assistant Executive Director

Business Manager

Officials' Secretary

Chapters' Secretary

Member Schools' Secretary

Mail Room Supervisor

Bookkeeper

Source: PIAA (2002). Reprinted with permission.

The Athletic Director is the person who puts forward coaching candidates for the school board's approval. In some states the Athletic Director must also have current teaching certification credentials. In Canada, the setup is usually slightly different. High schools do not have athletic directors; usually the head of the Physical Education Department acts as the Athletic Director.

In addition, the Principal has influence is this area as well. The Athletic Director reports directly to the Principal on any matters concerning budget, scheduling, or personnel. If there are conflicts within the department that the Athletic Director cannot resolve, that responsibility may fall to the Principal.

Current Policy Areas

A number of policy areas are prominent in the governance of high school athletics. Sport managers working in this industry segment must be aware of the constantly changing tides of public opinion about issues surrounding school-age children as these will impact their policy-making decisions. Several of these issues result from legal challenges to existing or proposed policies. As pointed out earlier in the chapter, because state associations are considered state actors, they cannot violate any students' fundamental rights. The same is true for public school employees, including coaches and athletic directors. Students who believe their rights have been violated can initiate a lawsuit against a coach, an athletic director, a local school board, and the state high school athletic association. The outcomes of these cases can directly affect policies in high school sport, as sometimes the courts mandate that an association change a rule that violated a student's rights.

Eligibility

The policy area receiving the majority of attention is eligibility. Some of you may have attended a high school where an athlete was denied the opportunity to play for a particular reason—maybe his grades were not high enough, or maybe she moved in from a different school district. Perhaps you knew a student who took an eligibility case to the legal system. First, you must remember that playing high school sport is *not* a right guaranteed by law. Attending school until you are a certain age *is* your right, but participating in interscholastic sport is *a privilege, not a right* (Ness & Colles, 2007). However, even that privilege cannot be taken away arbitrarily. Sport governing bodies must still ensure due process is followed in any decisions they make about eligibility; otherwise, they may end up in litigation. Remember, state associations have been found to be state actors, and while their actions are not supposed to violate anyone's constitutional rights, there are times when their actions do so, thus resulting in litigation. Eligibility discussions most often relate to questions of academic eligibility, transfer rules covering eligibility, and age limits for participation.

Ethics and eligibility rules. Eligibility rules in general generate some interesting ethical questions. For example, a high school athletic association may have certain rules about "No pass, no play." While this seems acceptable on the surface, what is the effect on academically struggling students for whom sport is the primary motivation to stay in school? If that chance is taken away, are they more likely to drop out? Although transfer rules are based on the educational premise that a student learns best by staying in the same school for an academic career, should students be "punished" for family problems that may result in relocation to another school district? It is important to make sure the outcome of such rules is, in fact, as fair as possible to the student.

Academic eligibility. All high school associations have policies governing academic eligibility. The reason for this is clear. Although high school sports are meant to be an extension of a student's educational experience, they are exactly that—an extension. The purposes of attending high school are to receive an education and earn a diploma so a person can contribute to society in a positive manner. "Overall, academic standards promote educational standards, underscore the educational values of participating in activities, encourage appropriate academic performance and allow the use of interscholastic participation as a motivator for improved classroom performance" (NFHS, 2006b, p. 19).

A focus of discussion in this area is the "No pass, no play" rule. While the specifics differ from state to state, basically this type of rule makes players ineligible to participate for a certain number of weeks if they do not meet certain academic standards. For example, students who fail a class in a given term may be ineligible to participate to play sports the following term. Proponents indicate such rules keep students focused on academics rather than athletics. For athletes seeking college scholarships, these rules also help them to stay on a course to meet the NCAA Clearinghouse standards. Opponents to such rules mention that for some students, being able to play sports is what motivates them to stay in school, and without the opportunity to participate, those students may just drop out of school. Opponents also point out that this rule may lead students to choose a less-challenging curriculum so they do not put themselves in academic jeopardy.

Public Versus Private High Schools

Another issue is the public–private school debate. The discussion often centers around private schools' ability to recruit young athletes to play for them. This point raises ethical issues because of the pressures of recruiting young athletes and the possibility of creating a discrepancy between schools with ample resources and those with limited resources and the unlevel playing fields that may result. In some states, private schools dominate state championships, as with volleyball in Kentucky. The Kentucky High School Athletic Association (KHSAA) has formed a Public–Private Task Force to study this debate (KHSAA, 2006). Other state associations, such as Missouri, have taken votes to determine whether public school and private school playoff systems should be separate (Wheatley, 2007).

KHSAA Taskforce
www.khsaa.org/news/
20052006/nr011006.pdf

Transfer rules. High school associations have transfer rules for various reasons. These rules keep students from moving from school to school for nonfamily reasons. In other words, these rules are in place to keep students from simply enrolling in whichever school has a successful sports program or a well-known coach. School district boundaries are drawn to ensure fair distribution of students across districts. These distributions are tied to the amount of funding the districts receive from the state or province. Students "jumping" out of district to play sports interrupt this balance. Additionally, transferring schools is generally not easy on high-school-age students educationally or socially. If you have ever transferred schools, you may remember the difficulties of making new friends, having new teachers, and learning new rules. In this way, transfer rules work to maintain the ideal of students starting and ending their academic careers in the same school. Another reason for transfer rules is to deter coaches from recruiting students away from other schools. High school athletes, especially the particularly talented ones, have enough pressure on them already. People are wondering where they will go to college, shoe companies may already be approaching them, and they still have to maintain their grades for eligibility. Attempting to recruit these students to rival high schools only adds another layer of pressure to their lives. Transfer rules reduce the opportunity for people to exert undue influence and benefit from a student-athlete's prowess (NFHS, 2006b).

Age limits. Traditionally, a student who reached 18 years of age was no longer eligible to participate in high school sport. In Canada, this age limit is usually 19 years of age. According to the NFHS (2006b), the rationale for age eligibility includes the following:

- inhibiting "red shirting" (allowing an extra year of eligibility)
- allowing younger and less-experienced players opportunities to participate
- allowing more students to participate, thus promoting equality
- avoiding overemphasis on athletics
- maintaining safety

Teenagers grow and mature at different rates. Have you ever looked at a room full of high school freshmen boys? They are all shapes and sizes. Now look at a room of seniors. They are much more physically developed. Athletes in their 20s would be even more well developed. To keep the size differential under control as much as possible and maintain fair competitive levels, state and provincial athletic associations established age limits to keep more physically developed athletes from injuring the smaller athletes. In recent years there have been some modifications in these rules, particularly as they pertain to athletes with cognitive developmental disabilities. The Americans with Disabilities Act comes into play here. As you may have learned in your Legal Aspects of Sport class, the two pieces of federal legislation that most directly impact the sport industry in the United States are Title IX and the Americans with Disabilities Act, commonly referred to as the ADA. Some students with cognitive developmental disabilities such as Down syndrome have successfully challenged existing age-limit rules and have been allowed to play past the age of 18 or the prevailing age limit set by their state athletic association. As evidenced by this section, ongoing debate will continue regarding policy formulation about age limits.

Amateurism

By definition, high school sport means amateur sport. Having limitations on the awards an athlete receives for athletic performance "stimulates participation for the sake of the game itself, prevents exploitation of students, and encourages students to engage in athletic competition for physical, mental and social benefits" (NFHS, 2006b, p. 20). In other words, for high school athletes, sport should be for participation and enjoyment, not a job. Sport should be an extension of the educational mission of the school. To this end, for example, the NFHS has an agreement with professional baseball that professional baseball teams will not sign a high school student to a major or a minor league contract while the student still has high school eligibility (NFHS, 2006b).

Basically, is it in the best interest of the student to leave high school to go directly into the professional ranks? According to NCAA (2007), only .03 percent of boys playing high school basketball make it to the NBA and only .02 percent of girls playing high school basketball make it to the WNBA. For the favored few who actually have the talent and the maturity, professional sport can be an option. But what about those who accept the impractical notion that sport is their "way out"? Coaches and athletic directors need to think about providing realistic information and advice to youngsters who harbor unrealistic hopes and expectations.

Another issue is extreme sports. A large number of extreme sport athletes are teenagers who are performing in national and international competitions and often have lucrative sponsorship deals with skateboard or snowboard companies. For example, Olympic Gold Medalist Shawn White "reportedly pulled in a $6 million income while winning all 11 snowboard contests he entered last season. He signed another million-dollar endorsement deal with Red Bull energy drink" (Willoughby, 2007, p. D12). While White is a world-renowned athlete and earns this income, others are agreeing to endorse products and become spokespeople for products like Mountain Dew or Sobe. These talented athletes are certainly not competing for their high school teams and would be considered professionals in their respective events. While athletes in other sports such as basketball must wait to become professional athletes, extreme sport competitors are already professionals, even in their teen years.

Gender Equity

Whenever we hear the term *gender equity,* one phrase should come to mind immediately—Title IX. Although most of the publicity generated around Title IX has involved college athletics, this piece of legislation also applies to high school sport. The full title of this historic legislation in the United States is Title IX of the Educational Amendments of 1972. Title IX reads as follows: "No person in the United States shall, on the basis of sex, be excluded from participation in, be denied the benefits of, or be subjected to discrimination under any education program or activity receiving Federal financial assistance" (Carpenter, 2007, p. 532). Within high school sport, numerous issues related to Title IX have resulted in court cases, including (1) facility use and (2) girls wanting to play on boys' teams or boys wanting to play on girls' teams.

Facilities. While many gender-equity lawsuits have involved colleges and universities, there have also been a number of cases involving high schools, especially including inequities between girls' softball and boys' baseball. One Florida case, *Daniels v. Brevard County,* focused on inequities between the girls' softball and the boys' baseball programs at Merritt Island High School. Examples of facilities the boys had that the girls lacked included scoreboards, batting cages, restrooms, lights, and a combination concession stand–press box–announcer's booth (Gaskin, 2002). The court ordered the school board to submit a plan to remedy the situation, but the board took the stance "Take it away from the boys" rather than "Improve the girls' facilities." In February 2000, the school board refused to make improvements at two other high schools in the district. Finally, in December 2000, the U. S. District Court found the school board in violation of Title IX because of inadequate facilities for the girls. The school claimed the difference between the boys' and girls' facilities stemmed from the fact that the Baseball Booster Club had raised more money than the Softball Booster Club. However, the court ruled the school district was responsible for equalizing the dollar amount (Schoonmaker, 2001). The judge, knowing the school district had insufficient funds to correct the inequalities, still ordered that Title IX regulations be followed, indicating the inequities should have been rectified long ago (Gaskin, 2002). This case illustrates the interaction between the court system and governance issues occurring at the district, as opposed to the state, level.

Girls on boys' teams, and boys on girls' teams. Consider girls wanting to play on boys' teams and boys wanting to play on girls' teams. If there were no girls' team in a particular sport such as tennis, golf, football, baseball, or wrestling, could a girl play on the existing boys' team? Conversely, if there were no boys' team in a particular sport such as volleyball, softball, or field hockey, could a boy play on the existing girls' team?

This was an early issue with Title IX, and it remains an issue. Early cases involved mostly girls wanting to play on boys' golf or tennis teams. In recent years there has been a shift to cases involving more contact sports, specifically football and wrestling. Most high school associations have rules prohibiting girls playing on boys' teams. The main reasons for these rules were, first, the safety of the girls, and second, the fear that if girls could play on boys' teams then boys could play on girls' teams and would take the girls' roster spots, thus diminishing girls' opportunities. However, girls often prevailed in these cases by using their Fourteenth Amendment right of Equal Protection. The rules were seen as overly broad since not all girls were physically incapable of playing with the boys. In an overview of 29 cases from 1972–2000, the girls prevailed 21 times (Schoonmaker, 2001).

On the other hand, when boys wanted to play on girls' teams, the courts generally denied them that opportunity. State high school associations had rules keeping boys from playing on girls' teams because they thought the boys would dominate on the girls' teams. The majority of court cases have held that this type of rule is valid and does not violate the boys' Equal Protection rights. A review of 13 cases from 1979–1992 indicated the girls prevailed in 11 cases (Schoonmaker, 2001).

Title IX has been the law for over 35 years. The courts have repeatedly been asked to rule on different aspects of the legislation, and in 2002, the Bush administration formed a special committee to examine Title IX, its enforcement, guidelines, and interpretation. Sport managers working in scholastic sport must be aware of any policy interpretations of Title IX issued by the U. S. Department of Education so they can ensure their schools are in compliance with the law.

Gender equity is not a phenomenon limited to the United States. Canada is also dealing with the issue. On the high school level, several provincial associations have policy statements related to gender equity.

FIGURE   5.6   Gender-equity policy of the OFSAA.

Gender equity in school sport is the belief and practice which ensure fair access for female student–athletes, coaches, officials and administrators to participate, compete and lead.

Equity does not necessarily mean that all persons must be treated exactly the same. People may need to be treated differently in order to be treated fairly.

VISION

Women and girls will enjoy a full and equitable range of opportunities for participation, officiating, competition and leadership in school sport activities.

GOAL

Through the implementation of this policy, it is our intent to raise awareness, educate, and change attitudes and behaviours which increase and improve the opportunities for girls and women in school sport.

Policy Statements

OFSAA is committed to gender equity as highlighted in the guiding principles of the Federation's Strategic Plan.

OFSAA is committed to educating and providing support to its members through the development and distribution of a gender equity policy.

OFSAA believes that the elimination of barriers to participation will contribute to the achievement of gender equity.

OFSAA believes that gender equity should serve as a guiding principle for all decisions and operations of the Federation and is a key consideration when developing, updating or delivering Federation programs, policies and projects.

Source: OFSAA (2005). Reprinted with permission.

The OFSAA policy on gender equity (OFSAA, 2005) is included in Figure 5.6. Discussions about gender equity and fairness in participation opportunities will continue, even as the courts and legislative agencies interpret and reinterpret the laws. As outlined in Chapter 4, Ethics in Sport Organizations, athletic administrators should consider how they respond to Title IX in terms of corporate social responsibility and whether they are providing opportunities because the law mandates it or because it is the right thing to do.

Alcohol, Drug, and Tobacco Use

For high school students (usually minors), possessing and consuming alcohol are prohibited by law. Possession and use of recreational and some performance-enhancing drugs are also illegal, no matter what the person's age. There are age restrictions on the purchase of tobacco products. The NFHS takes the following stand:

> The National Federation of State High School Associations (NFHS), the national service organization to all 50 state high school athletic and activity associations as well as the District of Columbia, strongly opposes the abuse of anabolic steroids and other performance-enhancing substances by high school student-athletes. Such use violates legal, ethical and competitive equity standards, and imposes unreasonable long-term health risks. (NFHS, 2005, para. 8)

In terms of legal action in this area, without a doubt the landmark case is *Vernonia School District 47J v. Acton* (1995). The school Acton attended was having difficulties with student drug use. As administrators looked into the problems, they determined that school athletes appeared to be the leaders of the local drug culture. Because of this, the District proposed a Student Athlete Drug Policy that included drug testing. In the fall of 1997, Acton was denied the opportunity to try out for football because he and his parents refused to sign the drug test consent form. They filed suit against the school district on the basis that the drug-testing policy violated the Fourth and Fourteenth Amendments to the U. S. Constitution, as well as Article 1, Section 9, of the Oregon Constitution. However, the Court ruled that the school district had the right to drug test the athletes: based on "the decreased expectation of privacy, the relative unobtrusiveness of the search, and the severity of the need met by the search—we conclude Vernonia's policy is reasonable and hence constitutional" (*Vernonia School District 47J v. Acton*, 1995). This court decision cleared the way for drug testing of high school athletes.

The NFHS has started its own steroid education program, producing a set of materials called "Make the Right Choice." These materials include DVDs, brochures, and posters (NFHS, 2006d). Today some states have

www

NFHS "Make the Right Choice"
www.nfhs.org/web/2006/09/
nfhs_steroids_awareness.aspx

Colin Hood

Executive Director,
Ontario Federation of School Athletic
Associations (OFSAA), Toronto, Canada

F SAA plays a primary role in conducting over 40 provincial high school sport championships each year. As Executive Director, I have three main areas of involvement. My primary task is managing the staff who work with the volunteer championship committees that plan and organize the events. My goal is to ensure that the championships provide quality sporting and educational opportunities for student-athletes. My second function is to assist and guide the OFSAA Board of Directors, which develops the guidelines, policies, and direction for school sport. The Board and its committees deal with a wide range of issues, including sport regulations, equity, eligibility guidelines, and teacher supervision of athletes. I am responsible for helping the Board develop, implement, and manage the policies related to these issues. Finally, I provide leadership to OFSAA with regard to school sport issues affecting the broad spectrum of student-athletes in Ontario, across Canada, and internationally. OFSAA involves itself with such issues as coaching development and keeping school sport safe from violence. I play a key role in promoting the value and importance of school sport within our educational system.

I believe we are struggling with three major issues related to policy development in high school sport. One is ensuring the educational integrity of high school sport programs. We want participants in high school sport activities to be students first. The OFSAA's motto is "Education Through School Sport." In an age when sport dominates much of our attention, students are subject to media and parental pressure to succeed in sport for financial reasons. Some members of the public place demands on the school sport system that are unreasonable and have no place in an education delivery system. All our policies and guidelines are geared to educating students through school sport programs. A second critical area is ensuring that all students have equal access to school competitions. An important task is figuring out how to provide equal access and opportunities within disparate social situations. We must consider gender issues, geography, the size of school, the quality of the program, and transfer and eligibility guidelines, as well as other factors. The third major issue is finding the resources to fund our programs. We've seen significant reductions in government grants to schools, and the competition for available resources is fierce. Providing schools with teacher supervision to cover classes when teachers and coaches travel with teams to tournaments and championships is one of the many fiscal challenges that schools face. Because we know that participants in school sport stay in school longer, get higher grades, and succeed in life after school, we feel that we have a responsibility to do what we can to provide the necessary resources. Finding those resources is a constant battle, but it is important because school sport helps develop better citizens and the lack of these programs comes at significant cost to society.

Our current governance structure is under review. We sense that our old way of managing is no longer working effectively and efficiently. The structure was set up over 50 years ago and does not reflect current legislation or funding support. OFSAA has an Annual General Meeting with over 90 people and a Board of Directors of 55 representatives from 17 member associations. Many feel that the size of the Board is unworkable. OFSSA is in the process of developing a new model that addresses these concerns while maintaining our educational integrity and providing a consistent forum for stakeholder input. We propose combining our executive committee, which has seven people, with the Board of Directors, thus creating an Executive Management Committee of thirteen people who will meet four times a year. We've kept our committees for boys and girls activities, each of which has two representatives from each of our member associations. They will deal with events and rules governing the OFSAA sport regulations. The Executive Management Committee will set policy, establish guidelines, and deal with constitutional issues. Once a year we will invite all stakeholders and others interested in high school sport to our annual meeting. We will conduct a business meeting to elect officers and deal with financial matters. The meeting will be structured to encourage stakeholders to provide input and direction to the Federation. Provincial sport organizations and the Principals Council will meet, and we will select a professional development theme to celebrate school sport. We believe these groups will be able to establish a clear direction for school sport in the province and the new Executive Management Committee will govern from a truly provincial perspective.

As we look toward future challenges, we cannot ignore the need for additional partnerships to provide more opportunities for the student-athlete. We must work with the sport community and other stakeholders to improve the educational opportunities for students.

established their own drug prevention and education programs. For example, the New York State Public High School Athletic Association (NYSPHSAA) has a program called Life of an Athlete (NYSPHSAA, n.d.).

This issue certainly affects the health and safety of young athletes. It also gives coaches and athletic administrators the opportunity to make a statement about the importance of young people making wise behavioral choices in their lives.

New York State Public High School Athletic Association
www.nysphsaa.org

Funding

As with all other aspects of education, high school athletics face enormous budgetary pressure. Only a handful of sports generate any income, mostly from ticket sales and concessions. Some athletic programs have booster clubs, made up mostly of parents and alumni, who donate their time and money to help sustain the program. As mentioned earlier in the chapter, revenue flows into high school associations from various sources, including membership dues, gate receipts, corporate sponsorships, and private donations. Some high school associations are creating new and unique ways to generate funds to ensure their sport programs are financially secure. One source of funding high school programs that is becoming more popular is corporate donations.

A good example is the Virginia High School League (VHSL), which has established the Virginia High School League Foundation, an endowment fund that relies on tax-free contributions from individuals, businesses, and foundations (VHSL, 2006). In addition to operating the Foundation, its strategic plan includes this section on Finances and Foundation (VHSL, 2007, Finances and Foundation section):

Strategy

The VHSL will increase revenue for support, maintenance and expansion of VHSL services and programs.

Action Plans

1. Identify funding needs in terms of name recognition, student services, reserve fund, recognition program, tournament support, non-revenue activities and team reimbursement.

2. Organize an annual fund drive to build constituency support from individuals and a foundation for a capital campaign.

3. Construct a professionally designed case statement to use as a fundraising tool, as well as a modified version for use in League publications.

4. Increase sponsorships by identifying new sources of revenue and seek additional funds by promoting increased attendance at state events and conducting special events.

5. Build the VHSL Foundation through large annual fund donations and League support, as well as grants from other Virginia foundations.

Somewhat similar to the VHSL plan, the North Carolina High School Athletic Association (NCHSAA) established an endowment fund in 1991. Recently, the association announced a new capital campaign (NCHSAA, n.d.).

Other associations are directly targeting corporate sponsorships. Often the corporate sponsors' logos appear on the association's website. For example, the Hawaii High School Athletic Association (HHSAA) lists major corporations such as Chevron, Sports Authority, and Spalding, as well as numerous Hawaii-based corporations such as Hawaiian Airlines and Local Motion. The New Mexico Activities Association (NMAA) lists TLC, Rudy's and Honig's, among its sponsors; the Iowa High School Athletic Association (IHSAA) has the Iowa Farm Bureau; and the NSAA has U S Bank and Windstream Communications. The NSAA lists the following as benefits for sponsors in Nebraska:

- Consistently reaching a dominant percentage of the Nebraska student population, coaches, faculty, administrators, friends and family with your corporate identity and message.

- Enhancing your company's community relations program by demonstrating your commitment to educational benefits realized through school activity participation, and ultimately our state communities' youth.

- Increasing and maximizing your products and/or services awareness at significant times during Nebraska championship events alongside the top performing student interscholastic programs each year. (NSAA, n.d., para. 3)

These examples illustrate some tactics high school associations are taking to generate sufficient funds to cover costs and hopefully expand programs when the need arises.

Certainly the pressure of finding new alternative funding sources is increasing daily. When seeking corporate sponsors, athletic administrators should research the reputation and products of a potential corporate sponsor. The school's and the corporation's images will be intertwined, so associating with ethical business partners is of the utmost importance.

Home Schoolers

An interesting ongoing debate continues around the issue of whether or not home-schooled students should be eligible to compete in high school athletics. In the United States, close to two million children are home schooled annually. What happens when home schoolers decide they want to play organized high school sports? With the occasional exception, most home school settings cannot offer competitive high-school-level athletic opportunities, particularly for team sport athletes, so home schoolers who wish to play must make their request to the local public high school they would have attended or, sometimes, to a local private school. What policies come into play in this situation?

This is a very complex policy area, involving the state legislatures, state high school activities associations, occasionally local school districts, and sometimes even the court system. First, there is no one piece of federal legislation in the United States or Canada relative to home schooling. In other words, decisions on all matters involving home schoolers are left up to the individual states and provinces to decide. No wonder there is so much confusion in this area.

As of 2006, home schoolers from 27 states were barred from playing high school sport, while 8 other states allow them to play if they meet certain academic criteria (Home-Schoolers Want to Play, Too, 2006). The issue of home schoolers' eligibility highlights the complex interaction between high school sport-governing bodies, state legislations, and the court system (Hums, 1996). Home schooling is a policy area that cuts across several governance levels—local, district, and state. At each level, sport managers need to understand the ethical considerations of letting or not letting home schoolers participate. Is it fair to deny home schoolers the chance to play when their families pay taxes that fund public education? Is it fair for home schoolers to take regularly enrolled students' positions on teams? And what educational message is sent when it is acceptable for home schoolers to play sports with, but not go to school with, other students? Questions continue to emerge and policy continues to evolve in this area as home-schooled students in different states seek the opportunity to participate (Killeen, 2002).

SUMMARY

Sport governance takes place at a variety of levels, from international to national to state to local. Remember that the real power in scholastic sport lies with the state or provincial associations, although at times the courts will mandate their activities if any policies violate students' fundamental rights. The rules-setting and regulatory powers truly reside in these associations. The NFHS acts as a service organization for its state or provincial members. School districts, principals, and athletic directors can set rules on their levels, but they must be in accord with the state or provincial rules. In the United States, high school associations have repeatedly been identified as state actors and therefore subject to the U. S. Constitution for their actions.

The types of governance and policy issues scholastic sport administrators must deal with are vast and complex. The governance decisions they make when setting policy will interact with state as well as federal legislative bodies and laws such as Title IX. They will often come in contact with the judicial system as well, and so they must be prepared for their decisions to be questioned in courts of law. Despite these considerations, scholastic sport administrators have the opportunity to provide programming that has a positive impact on the lives of thousands of young athletes. It is an exciting and personally fulfilling segment of the sport industry.

CASE STUDY   *Scholastic Sport*

You are the Boys' Basketball Coach at Cheyenne High School. The night you have your preseason organizational meeting for parents and prospective players, you notice a family you have never seen before. After the meeting, the boy and his parents approach you. "We're Mr. and Mrs. Becker and this is our son David. We home school David, but we'd like him to play basketball here at Cheyenne High. We've heard from other parents who home school their children that many states allow it and that others have challenged for that right in court. We want David have a chance to play and will pursue whatever avenue is necessary."

1. What do you say to the Beckers this evening?
2. You obviously need to talk to your Athletic Director. What information does the Athletic Director need to gather? What governing bodies should the Athletic Director contact?
3. Should home-schooled students be allowed to participate? Use the SLEEPE Principle to examine all aspects of your decision.
4. How can we fairly balance the rights of home schoolers with the rights of students attending the public school daily?

CHAPTER QUESTIONS

1. How does the North American model of adolescent sport participation differ from that in other countries? What do you consider the advantages and disadvantages of this model compared to others?

2. Where does the main power lie in high school sport? Why?

3. High school sport has a number of goals, including education and participation. Should one of these goals be the preparation of college athletes?

4. One emerging source of funds for high school sport is corporate sponsorship. What are the pros and cons of high school athletic departments pursuing corporate sponsors?

REFERENCES

AIA. (n.d.). About AIA. Retrieved August 8, 2007, from www.aiaonline.org/about/index.php.

Altman, S. (2007). State action. In D. J. Cotton, J. T. Wolohan, & T. J. Wilde (Eds.), *Law for recreation and sport managers* (4th ed., pp. 429–438). Dubuque, IA: Kendall-Hunt.

ASAA. (2007a). Mission. Retrieved August 9, 2007, from www.asaa.org/about/mission_statement.html.

ASAA. (2007b). About the Alberta Schools' Athletic Association. Retrieved October 3, 2007, from www.asaa.ca/new/aboutasaa.php.

Biskupic, J., & Henry, T. (2002, June 28). High court OKs vouchers, drug testing for students. *USA Today*, p. 1A.

Carpenter, L. (2007). Gender equity: Opportunities to participate. In D. J. Cotton, J. T. Wolohan, & T. J. Wilde (Eds.), *Law for recreation and sport managers* (4th ed., pp. 530–538). Dubuque, IA: Kendall-Hunt.

Covell, D. (2008). High school and youth sport. In L. P. Masteralexis, C. A. Barr, & M. A. Hums (Eds.), *Principles and practice of sport management* (3d ed., pp. 127–144). Sudbury, MA: Jones and Bartlett.

Forsythe, L. L. (1950). *Athletics in Michigan schools: The first hundred years.* Englewood Cliffs, NJ: Prentice Hall.

Gaskin, L. P. (2002). Title IX and facility adequacy: Daniels v. Brevard County. *2001 Proceedings and directory of the Southern Academy of Women in Physical Activity, Sport, and Health* (Vol. 66). Berea, KY: Berea College.

Home-schoolers want to play, too. (2006, October 8). *The Times Union*, p. C1.

Hums, M. A. (1996). Home schooled students' opportunities to participate in interscholastic sport: Legal issues and policy implications for secondary education. *Journal of Legal Aspects of Sport*, 6(3), 169–177.

KHSAA. (2003). 2003–2007 Kentucky High School Athletic Association operational strategic plan. Retrieved October 8, 2007, from www.khsaa.org/strategicplan/20032007/20032007strategicplangoal1.pdf.

KHSAA. (2006, January 10). KHSAA Public/Private update. Retrieved October 8, 2007, from www.khsaa.org/news/20052006/nr011006.pdf.

Killeen, W. (2002, April 7). Home schooling fight persists. *Boston Globe*, p. 13.

MIAA. (n.d.a). Funding. Retrieved October 4, 2007, from www.miaa.net/miaa-funding.html.

MIAA. (n.d.b). MIAA philosophy. Retrieved October 3, 2007, from www.miaa.net/miaa-philosophy.html.

NCAA. (2007). Estimated probability of competing in athletics beyond the interscholastic level. Retrieved October 4, 2007, from www.ncaa.org/research/prob_of_competing/probability_of_competing2.html.

NCHSAA. (n.d.). The North Carolina High School Athletic Association endowment. Retrieved October 9, 2007, from www.nchsaa.org/gen Page/index.pl?pgid=52.

Ness, G., & Colles, C. (2007). Voluntary associations and eligibility issues. In D. J. Cotton, & J. T. Wolohan (Eds.), *Law for recreation and sport managers* (4th ed., pp. 467–477). Dubuque, IA: Kendall Hunt.

NFHS. (2005). NFHS encourages support of steroid education. Retrieved October 9, 2007, from www.nfhs.org/web/2005/07/nfhs_encourages_support_of_steroid_education.aspx.

NFHS. (2006a). About us. Retrieved August 9, 2007, from www.nfhs.org/web/2006/08/about_us.aspx.

NFHS. (2006b). *Handbook 2006–2007*. Indianapolis, IN: Author.

NFHS. (2006c). Member associations. Retrieved from www.nfshsa.org/members.htm.

NFHS. (2006d). NFHA steroids awareness. Retrieved October 8, 2007, from www.nfhs.org/web/2006/09/nfhs_steroids_awareness.aspx.

NFHS. (2007). *National Federation of State High School Associations 2005–2006 annual report*. Indianapolis, IN: Author.

NMAA. (2001). NMAA philosophy. Retrieved October 22, 2001, from www.nmact.org/phil.htm.

NSAA. (n.d.). NSAA sponsorship programs. Retrieved October 8, 2007, from www.nsaahome.org/nsaa sponsor08.htm.

NYSPHSAA. (n.d.). Life of an athlete. Retrieved October 8, 2007, from www.nysphsaa.org.

OFSAA. (2005). Gender equity policy. Retrieved October 8, 2007, from www.ofsaa.on.ca/site/content/File/ByLaws_July_07.pdf.

OSAA. (2001). About. Retrieved from www.ihigh.com/OSAAgov/about.htm.

PIAA. (2001). Basic philosophy. Retrieved October 23, 2001, from www.piaa.org/overview/PIAA%20Basic%20Philosophy.htm.

PIAA. (2002). PIAA organizational charts. Retrieved September 19, 2003, from www.piaa.org/about//overview/hdbh/Introduction.pdf.

Rader, B. C. (1999). *American sports: From the age of folk games to the age of televised sports* (4th ed.). Upper Saddle River, NJ: Prentice Hall.

Schoonmaker, L. L. (2001, March). Status report: Gender equity and interscholastic athletics. Paper presented at the Annual Conference of the Society for the Study of Legal Aspects of Sport, Branson, MO.

Seymour, H. (1990). *Baseball: The people's game*. New York: Oxford University Press.

Sharp, L. A., Moorman, A. M., & Claussen, C. L. (2007). *Sport law: A managerial approach*. Scottsdale, AZ: Holcomb Hathaway.

TSSAA. (1999). TSSAA: History, facts, and figures. Retrieved October 23, 2001, from www.tssaa.org/History/tssaah.htm#HOW%20IS%20TSSAA%20FINANCED?.

Vernonia School District 47J v. Acton. (1995). 515 U. S. 646.

VHSL. (2001). Virginia High School League Foundation. Retrieved October 23, 2001, from www.vhsl.org/fndtn.htm.

VHSL. (2006). VHSL Foundation. Retrieved October 8, 2007, from http://vhsl.org/fndtn.htm.

VHSL. (2007). Virginia High School League strategic plan. Retrieved October 8, 2007, from www.vhsl.org/MoreAboutVHSL/strategic.htm.

Vincent, T. (1994). *The rise of American sport: Mudville's revenge*. Lincoln: University of Nebraska Press.

Wheatley, T. (2007, May 4). Schools vote against split. *St. Louis Post-Dispatch*, p. D1.

Willoughby, S. (2007, February 13). The crazy world of Senor Blanco. *Denver Post*, p. D12.

Wong, G. M. (1994). *Essentials of sport law*. Westport, CT: Praeger.

6

AMATEUR SPORT IN THE COMMUNITY

INTRODUCTION

The term *amateur sport* describes a diverse set of individual and group sporting activities engaged in by millions of people worldwide. Different people play for different reasons. Enjoyment, group affiliation, fitness, healthy living, and the joy of competition are among the most prominent motivations. Amateur athletes do not get paid for their efforts. Rather, a great many amateur sporting activities involve participants who volunteer to play. The participants range from young children to senior citizens to people with disabilities, and their activity is usually in addition to their primary responsibilities with jobs or schools. Amateur sports include highly competitive events like NCAA Play-Offs and World Little League Baseball Championships, and they also include less-competitive activities such as organized beach volleyball jamborees and father–daughter golf events. Often lots of media coverage attend the glitz and glitter of highly competitive amateur sporting activities such as high school and college championship games, but a local weekend beach volleyball tournament with thousands of participants may go unnoticed. Sport study students need an understanding of how community amateur sport entities are organized and governed because many of you will, at some point in your career, be in a leadership position in such organizations. You may be responsible for setting policy and ensuring the effective pursuit of organization goals in this extensive segment of the sport industry.

Organizations delivering amateur sport in the community for youth and adult populations are both extensive in number and in their variety of activities. In fact, amateur sport in the community has a rich history and an abundance of community structures delivering opportunities for participation. The organizations governing and helping to establish policy for amateur sport are normally categorized as public or nonprofit. To begin this chapter we will discuss how amateur sport for members of the community first developed and became organized.

History of Community and Youth Sport

The roots of modern day amateur sport in North America might be traced to the villages and towns of rural Britain during the industrialization of the 18th and 19th centuries (Kidd, 1999). Mechanization in farming and other industries resulted in the migration of workers from the countryside to cities, and later to North America. Traditionally, farmworkers competed in folk games and other precursors to today's athletic events. Although such activities were repressed in overcrowded cities where an expectation of longer work weeks was the norm, games and active forms of recreation continued to be played in elite, all-male schools (Kidd, 1999). As sport for the elite became more popular and better organized, an interest in participating quickly spread to upper-class girls and women and to working-class boys and men. In this way participating in amateur sport emerged and gained momentum in many parts of the world.

In the United States and Canada, adaptation of British sports and development of new games began in the early 1800s. American Indians were accomplished runners, climbers, swimmers, and canoeists, and they participated in many tests of skill and strength. Settlers from England and other parts of Europe brought their own games and tried the indigenous games as well. While working-class men and women had little leisure time to devote to athletic contests, they still participated and spectated during holidays and other special events. By the mid-19th century, North Americans were engaging in a wide variety of athletic contests. Upper-class women had the time for such activities, but instead they remained on the sidelines rather than run the risk of censure for being too physically active. Boys and men of the upper class were certainly active participants in riding, cricket, tennis, and golf, but they remained active "behind the trimmed hedges of their exclusive clubs" (Kidd, 1999, p. 15). Eventually urban middle-class males succeeded in controlling the emergence of community amateur sport.

The early organizers of community sport were often businessmen. They used business contacts and skills from their managerial backgrounds to create clubs, constitutions, leagues, and schedules (Kidd, 1999). Pre-agreed-to rules and regulations, uniforms, officials—all quickly became normal expectations for competition. As amateur sport became more organized with consistent rules, its popularity spread quickly, and women and children were encouraged to participate. By the 1880s, as steady immigration increased the population in urban centers, the need and the opportunity for sports increased (Kidd, 1999). This increase in population, the changing nature of work in an increasingly mechanized industrial world, and decreased working hours began to provide increased leisure time and paved the way for the development of public and nonprofit sport organizations.

Public Sport Organizations

As the urban population increased at an alarming rate during the mid- to late-19th century, housing density amplified in urban centers. Concerns about municipal activities and the emergence of private sporting clubs led to further scrutiny by local governments. Originally, the interest was in regulating leisure practices. Governments declared public holidays, dedicated land for parks and sporting activities, and enacted laws prohibiting what was considered immoral or improper, such as racing and gambling on Sundays. Municipalities subsidized sport competitions such as rifle shooting and banned the rowdiness and immorality thought to be associated with highly publicized prizefights. With increased activities and publicity, along with a greater number of eager participants, came the development of public sport organizations. Minor sport leagues were formed. Such leagues were managed by groups of individuals who helped set schedules, enforce and adapt rules and regulations, and promote and publicize events such as baseball, football, rugby, and track and field. The leagues frequently led to the development of municipal groups, where teams were assembled from the top local talent to represent the entire community. Such a team would then enter into competition by challenging another team from a nearby town. While travel was difficult and kept to a minimum in the early days, teams often endured substantial travel distances in an effort to reap the glory of victory for their hometowns. Competitions between teams from different communities led to the development of sport festivals and jamborees, the precursors to today's state games in the United States and provincial games in Canada. As sport gained interest and became organized by community groups, soon the need for more opportunities and diversity in sport offerings resulted in the development of nonprofit sport organizations.

Nonprofit Sport Organizations

London Polo Club
www.polonews.com/polo/
london

North Texas Youth Football Association
http://ntyfa.org/index.html

A *nonprofit sport organization* delivers programs and services for a particular sport or group with no intent to gain profit. These types of organizations range from very small (the London Polo Club) to large professional associations (the North Texas Youth Football Association). Nonprofit sport organizations emerged as an alternative to programs such as recreational sport leagues run by city recreation departments, and in addition to those programs developed with the express intent of making money. In the beginning nonprofit organizations filled the gap in programming between the two and provided opportunities for participation in sporting events regardless of class or financial background. For-profit organizations offered programming based on business strategies, inevitably providing only the most popular activities. It was impossible for public recreation departments to offer all possible types of sports. Therefore, interested individuals formed their own organizations according to their own interests. Nonprofit sport organizations emerged all over North America for sporting interests as diverse as waterskiing and bicycling, walking and badminton.

Public and nonprofit sport organizations began developing organizational structures, constitutions, positions of leadership with duties and responsibilities, and programs. What are the governance structures for these types of organizations, and how do they develop policy?

Governance

Climbing Gym Example: Boise Peak Fitness
www.boisepeakfitness.com

Gymnastic Center Example: Gold Medal Gymnastics Centre
www.gmgc.com

Figure Skating Club Example: Scarboro Figure Skating Club
www.sfsc.on.ca

As illustrated by the history of community sport, amateur athletic organizations are structured in a manner consistent with their purpose and mission. While private for-profit ventures exist (such as climbing gyms, gymnastic centers, and figure-skating clubs), most amateur sport in the community is publicly run with funding from some level of government or delivered by nonprofit service organizations. What types of groups fall within these categories, and how are they organized to deliver amateur sport within the community? The following sections will identify the mission, funding, membership, and organizational structure of community amateur sport organizations.

The Governance of Public Sport Organizations

The three main types of public sport organizations delivering amateur sport in our communities are the following:

1. city parks and recreation departments
2. recreational sport leagues
3. state games and provincial games

City Parks and Recreation Departments

City parks and recreation departments have traditionally housed community sport, recreation, and physical activity programs. Cities provide a wide array of services to their citizens, including utilities such as sewers, water, and gas and electric. Cities also provide public transportation and care for infrastructures such as roads and bridges. In addition to these basic services, many cities also take it upon themselves to offer a wide array of sport and recreation facilities.

Mission. City parks and recreation department mission statements are as varied as the activities they offer. They usually include themes such as opportunities for leisure-time activities, learning and playing in a safe environment, provision of a wide variety of facilities, and statements of inclusivity and support for diversity. Two sample mission statements, one of the Parks and Recreation Department of the City of Houston and one of the City of Toronto, are presented in Figures 6.1 and 6.2.

Financials. Because these facilities and staff are provided by the city, city residents' tax money underwrites a good portion of the costs. As a result, some facility use and programming may be offered free of charge, for example, swimming at the neighborhood public pool. Other services may require a fee. For example, a city-sponsored softball league may require teams to pay an entrance fee to cover the costs of umpires, field maintenance, and softballs for each game.

The size of a city parks and recreation budget will vary from city to city. For example, the City of Kissimmee, Florida, had a 2007 budget of $6,231,945, which came from ad valorem taxes, impact fees, sales tax, grants, and a utility surcharge (Kissimmee Parks and Recreation, 2007). A

Houston Parks and Recreation Department
www.houstontx.gov/parks/aboutus.html

City of Toronto Parks and Recreation Department
www.city.toronto.ca/parks/about_us.htm

Mission statement of the City of Houston Parks and Recreation Department.   **FIGURE   6.1**

To enhance the quality of urban life by providing safe, well maintained parks and offering affordable programs for the community.

Source: City of Houston (2007).

| FIGURE | 6.2 | Mission statement of the City of Toronto Parks and Recreation Department. |

> The Parks and Recreation Division's mission is to ensure that people in the diverse communities of Toronto have full and equitable access to high-caliber locally responsive recreational programs, efficiently operated facilities, and safe, clean and beautiful parks, open spaces, ravines and forests.

Source: City of Toronto (2007).

Kissimmee Parks and Recreation

http://kissimmee.org/ch_dept_parks.aspx

City of Snellville Parks and Recreation

www.snellville.org/parks/parksrec.aspx

much smaller city, Snellville, Georgia, budgeted for $1,102,338 in expenses in 2007 (City of Snellville, 2007).

Membership. Generally these programs are open to any and all residents of a particular city. Established policies deal with participation by nonresidents and guests. The people who take part in physical activities offered by city parks and recreation programs have a wide variety of activities to choose from, including offerings such as swimming, soccer, softball, fitness programs, martial arts, tennis, hiking and biking trails, and many others. Activities are not limited to the traditional team sport offerings, as departments try to keep up with trends by offering popular activities. For example, the City of Seattle Parks and Recreation Department offers the following:

> The Department of Parks and Recreation manages a 6,200-acre park system. This includes 224 parks, 185 athletic fields, 112 neighborhood play areas, nine swimming beaches, 18 fishing piers, four golf courses, and 22 miles of boulevards. Other facilities include 151 outdoor tennis courts, 26 community centers, eight indoor and two outdoor swimming pools, 27 wading pools, a nationally recognized Rose Garden, the Seattle Aquarium, and more. The Woodland Park Zoological Society operates the Zoo with City financial support. Hundreds of thousands of residents and visitors use parks and recreation facilities to pursue their passions, from soccer to pottery, kite flying to golf, swimming to community celebrations, to just sitting in quiet reflection. (City of Seattle, 2007)

Seattle Parks and Recreation Department

www.seattle.gov/html/citizen/departments.htm#parks

San Diego Park and Recreation Department

www.sandiego.gov/park-and-recreation

Organizational structure. A city parks and recreation department is one of numerous departments within the organizational structure of a city. Figure 6.3 shows how parks and recreation fits into the overall organizational chart for a large city, San Diego, California. Figure 6.4 illustrates how the organizational chart for the City Parks and Recreation Department can become very complex in larger cities.

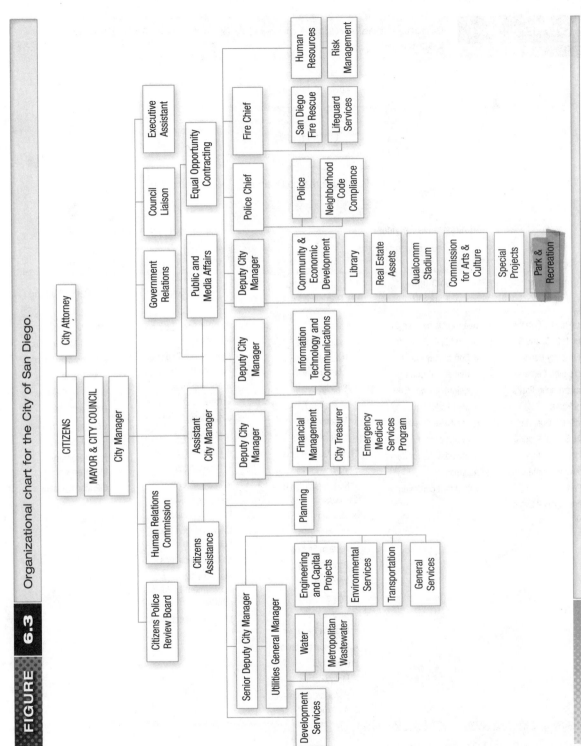

FIGURE 6.3 Organizational chart for the City of San Diego.

Source: City of San Diego (2007). Reprinted with permission.

| FIGURE | 6.4 | Organizational structure of the City of San Diego Park & Recreation Department. |

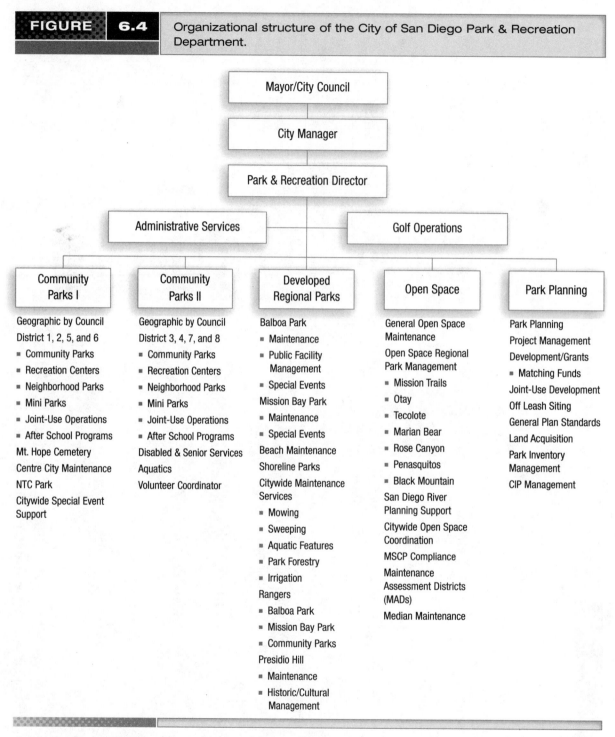

Mayor/City Council

City Manager

Park & Recreation Director

Administrative Services | Golf Operations

Community Parks I

Geographic by Council District 1, 2, 5, and 6
- Community Parks
- Recreation Centers
- Neighborhood Parks
- Mini Parks
- Joint-Use Operations
- After School Programs

Mt. Hope Cemetery
Centre City Maintenance
NTC Park
Citywide Special Event Support

Community Parks II

Geographic by Council District 3, 4, 7, and 8
- Community Parks
- Recreation Centers
- Neighborhood Parks
- Mini Parks
- Joint-Use Operations
- After School Programs

Disabled & Senior Services
Aquatics
Volunteer Coordinator

Developed Regional Parks

Balboa Park
- Maintenance
- Public Facility Management
- Special Events

Mission Bay Park
- Maintenance
- Special Events

Beach Maintenance
Shoreline Parks
Citywide Maintenance Services
- Mowing
- Sweeping
- Aquatic Features
- Park Forestry
- Irrigation

Rangers
- Balboa Park
- Mission Bay Park
- Community Parks

Presidio Hill
- Maintenance
- Historic/Cultural Management

Open Space

General Open Space Maintenance
Open Space Regional Park Management
- Mission Trails
- Otay
- Tecolote
- Marian Bear
- Rose Canyon
- Penasquitos
- Black Mountain

San Diego River Planning Support
Citywide Open Space Coordination
MSCP Compliance
Maintenance Assessment Districts (MADs)
Median Maintenance

Park Planning

Park Planning
Project Management
Development/Grants
- Matching Funds

Joint-Use Development
Off Leash Siting
General Plan Standards
Land Acquisition
Park Inventory Management
CIP Management

Source: City of San Diego (2007). Reprinted with permission.

Recreational Sport Leagues

Recreational sport leagues provide opportunities for regular participation in sport for both children and adults. Leagues might be established by an interested group of individuals who wish to play basketball on a regular basis, or they may be run by community recreation staffs in city parks and recreation facilities. Leagues are commonly available in a wide variety of sports, like football, baseball, hockey, curling, volleyball, soccer, and bowling. Most recreational sport leagues are considered a public service. They are organized to provide individuals the opportunity to participate in their sport of choice.

Mission. A recreational sport league's mission statement will likely include some comment about what sport the league is delivering and to which level of participant. The league may be highly competitive or designed with more of a recreational, fun focus. The inclusion of the concepts of fair play, respect, and ethical conduct are common components of recreational sport league mission statements. See Figures 6.5 and 6.6 for the mission statements of the Cabot Youth Baseball Association in Cabot, Arkansas, and of the Pickering Hockey Association in Pickering, Ontario.

Financials. Funding for recreational sport leagues is often provided through municipal sources and supplemented by league fees charged to each participant. The salaries of administrators designing and delivering the league may be paid through municipal departments. The costs of facilities are also borne by the community. Often, participants will pay a small fee to generate some revenue toward paying for administrative costs, officials, and equipment. Of course, the "pay for play" fee could be more substantial if the particular sport has expensive requirements such as ice

www

Cabot Youth Baseball Association
http://cabotbaseball.com

Pickering Hockey Association
http://pickeringhockey.com

Mission statement of the Cabot Youth Baseball Association.   **FIGURE 6.5**

The mission and purpose of Cabot Youth Baseball Association is to provide a safe place where children can enjoy being part of a team, learn and improve their physical skills, learn life lessons that victory and defeat can provide, and revel in the occasional attention that comes with being the hero with that great play or timely hit.

Source: Cabot Youth Baseball Association (2007).

Doug Voss

Administrator, Park Aquatic Programs
Louisville Parks and Recreation, Louisville, KY

Currently, I serve as the Administrator of Metro Louisville Parks Aquatic Programs. I am responsible for the administration and management of the staff and aquatic programs for 12 aquatic facilities operated by the Parks and Recreation Department. My major job responsibilities include directing the day-to-day operation of aquatic facilities; developing and enforcing policies and procedures related to aquatic operations; coordinating the maintenance and repair of all equipment used at aquatic facilities; developing, recommending, and administering the aquatic budget; determining the maintenance and equipment needs at all aquatic facilities; guiding, training, and directing the activities of subordinate personnel; preparing annual reports on operations; developing and conducting programs, training, and special events; determining personnel needs for the division; ensuring safety standards are met at aquatic facilities; and interviewing, selecting, and recommending staff.

Several major policy issues confront our Parks and Recreation Department. One of the most critical issues concerns the number of aging facilities, including community centers, athletic fields, and aquatic facilities. Lack of funds make even basic improvements to many of these facilities unattainable. Because a great many of the parks' operations are funded by general fund tax dollars, funding for upkeep is often tenuous at best. This is particularly true when the renovations or improvements (such as plumbing, roofing, and other basic but necessary repairs) are not glamorous and do not have visible benefits for the public. As vibrant communities continue to grow in population and expand locations, more funds are needed to provide services.

Policy decisions regarding the use of funds to create new recreational areas must be balanced by decisions on how to improve and maintain existing resources.

The most recent governance issue I have been involved with concerns the way in which employees within the department are classified. As government employees we are all held to high degrees of accountability and are expected to maintain efficiencies. We are expected to provide more with less, especially during an economic downturn. For example, we must determine the minimum number of employees required to perform certain functions while maintaining quality services. This process involves reexamining the way in which we normally operate to create job classifications that meet the public need while staying within budget constraints.

The current governance structure of the Metro Parks Department follows a well-established chain of command. The Mayor is the leader of the department. The Mayor receives information regarding parks issues from his Deputy Mayor, who in turn receives information from a Cabinet Secretary who oversees the parks and other quality of life departments such as the Louisville Zoo. The Parks Director reports to the Cabinet Secretary. Metro Parks has four Assistant Directors reporting to the Parks Director. Each of these Assistant Directors has a clearly defined role within the department. Currently there are Assistant Directors for Recreation, Finance, Operations, and Planning and Design/Olmstead Conservancy. One major drawback of this structure is that communication between the four divisions is often not as good as it could be. The structure is beneficial, however, in that areas of responsibility are well defined and a structured chain of command exists within each department. A newly merged city and county government structure adopted by the community in January 2003 has also highlighted the need for interdepartmental communication and the pooling of all available resources. This merger might lead to collaborations between, for example, Louisville Public Works and Metro Parks, the Louisville Zoo and the Office of Youth Development, and so on.

The biggest policy development challenge is creating revenue streams with less reliance on general fund tax dollars. To do this we must create methods that increase fee generation for programs and services and develop new methods of attaining grants and public donations. By increasing the amount of revenue gener-ated through non–tax dollar sources, funding for programs and services will be made more secure and less reliant on legislative appropriations. Policy decisions must also ensure that citizens who cannot pay are not left out. Another challenge we face is to work well with the other agencies within Metro government and with private agencies to ensure that additional land is acquired to meet the needs of Louisville's future population. The acquisition of park land, athletic space, and athletic fields must go hand in hand with future residential and commercial development in the metro area.

Ms. Barbara Kalkhof, Metro Parks Assistant Director for Finance, contributed to this portrait.

rental for hockey leagues. The major expense categories for minor sport leagues include facility rental, officials, purchase of equipment, and promotion and publicity.

Membership. Recreational sport leagues are organized for a vast array of participants. Some activities target children and youth groups, other leagues are run specifically for teens and young adults, and still others include adults, both young and old. Leagues might be gender specific or coed.

Organizational structure. A group of officers is usually elected to help organize and govern the activities of the league. These voluntary positions might include a president, vice president, and chairs of a few committees specific to the particular sport. For example, one might expect a Beach

---

Mission statement of the Pickering Hockey Association, Ontario.   **FIGURE   6.6**

To provide hockey for all persons, regardless of race, creed, ability or financial circumstances who abide by the rules and regulations of the Association; to provide for the affiliation of other hockey organizations in the City of Pickering; and to promote a harmonious relationship with the City of Pickering Recreation Department and their employees.

Source: Pickering Hockey Association (2007).

Volleyball League to be governed by a League Executive Committee that comprises the President, Vice President, Chair of Scheduling, and Chair of Facilities. The President runs meetings and provides overall direction and leadership, while the Vice President might be responsible for league promotion, complaints, and discipline. The Scheduling Chair develops and communicates all league scheduling, and the Facilities Chair schedules event locations and coordinates with facility staff for equipment. The elected members of the Executive Committee develop policy, and these administrators debate issues and ideas regarding league operation at the Annual Meeting. Policy might be required to guide the league activities in each of the major areas of responsibility and to incorporate where, when, and how the games are played.

Iowa Games
http://iowagames.org

State Games and Provincial Games

State games (U. S.) and provincial games (Canada) are amateur sport festivals held every year or two. Individuals and teams may have to qualify to attend the games by successfully advancing through regional competition(s) or by gaining entry through a lottery or a first-come, first-served basis. These games are usually multisport events, held in both summer and winter. For example, the Iowa Games Annual Sport Festival is held in winter and summer locations each year. Over 50 summer and 15 winter sports are organized for both adult and youth performers. The Iowa Games are a multisport festival of Olympic-style competition for Iowa's amateur athletes, and in this case age, ability, and gender are not considered criteria of participation.

Mission. The mission of state and provincial games focuses on delivering a well-organized amateur sport competition for athletes of a variety of ages within the region. The idea of the games is to offer the opportunity to compete, to gain experience, and to bring together citizens of a region in a festival atmosphere. The games are usually multisport and designed for participants, coaches, officials, spectators, volunteers, and sport managers—an experience for everyone. See Figure 6.7 for the mission statement of the Iowa State Games.

Iowa Sports Foundation
www.iowasportsfoundation.org

Financials. State and provincial games are funded through both public and private sources, entry fees, and money raised through sponsors and marketing initiatives. The Iowa Games, for example, is a project of the Iowa Sports Foundation "made possible because of the financial support from corporate sponsors, in-kind and cash donations" (Iowa Sports Foundation, 2007).

The members of summer or winter games hosted by an American state or Canadian province include mostly participants and volunteers. The

FIGURE 6.7

Mission statement of the Iowa State Games.

The mission of the Iowa Games is to provide Iowa citizens with a wholesome avenue for positive personal development through sports and physical activity, to recognize their dedication and achievement, to enable all citizens the opportunity to utilize quality sport facilities and to create an amateur sports network of administrators, officials and volunteers throughout Iowa to further the development of amateur athletic programs. In addition, the Iowa Games encourages all Iowans to practice sportsmanship, trustworthiness, respect, responsibility, fairness, caring and citizenship, while striving to be a champion on and off the field of play.

Source: Iowa Games (2007). Reprinted with permission.

organization does not have a group of individual members outside the event but is composed of a paid professional staff and a volunteer group that functions as a Board of Directors to organize the events.

Organizational structure. The paid staff usually comprises an Executive Director, one or more Directors of Sports, Event Operations, and Finance, and a number of assistant positions that help to organize specific components of the games. The Board of Directors, all volunteers, includes a Chair or President, Vice President, Treasurer, Secretary, and a number of board members who may be responsible for specific aspects of the events. The organizational structure of the Iowa Games is presented in Figure 6.8.

The Governance of Nonprofit Sport Organizations

The term *nonprofit* aptly describes sport organizations. They are organizations developed to deliver sporting activities and services with no intent of making a profit. This type of organization may be large or small and may have a simple or an intricate organizational structure. Two of the most prominent examples of nonprofit amateur sport organizations are the Young Men's Christian Association (YMCA) and the Boys & Girls Clubs. Other less-prominent local nonprofit community groups provide opportunities for amateur sport.

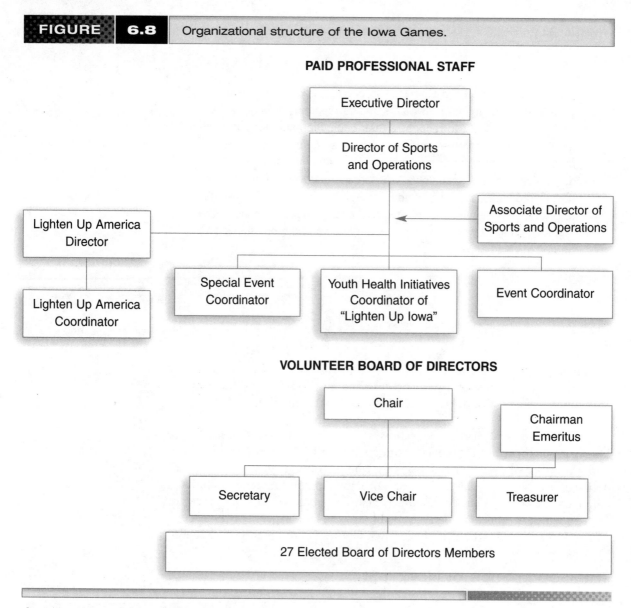

FIGURE | **6.8** | Organizational structure of the Iowa Games.

PAID PROFESSIONAL STAFF

Executive Director

Director of Sports
and Operations

Associate Director of
Sports and Operations

Lighten Up America
Director

Special Event
Coordinator

Youth Health Initiatives
Coordinator of
"Lighten Up Iowa"

Event Coordinator

Lighten Up America
Coordinator

VOLUNTEER BOARD OF DIRECTORS

Chair

Chairman
Emeritus

Secretary

Vice Chair

Treasurer

27 Elected Board of Directors Members

Source: Iowa Games (2007). Reprinted with permission.

YMCA

YMCAs are service organizations, collectively the largest not-for-profit community organizations in America (YMCA, 2007). Ys provide programming for children and adults, for males and females of all races, abilities, ages, and incomes. They have a significant history in basketball, volleyball, and racquetball and were the original leaders in camping and fitness, as well as in providing children with swimming lessons (YMCA, 2007). The Ys serve more than 45 million people in more than 120 countries around the world; 2,617 Ys are located in the United States. There are 50 YMCAs and 10 Young Women's Christian Associations (YWCAs) located in Canada (YMCA Canada, 2007).

YMCA
http://ymca.net

YMCA Canada
www.ymca.ca

Mission. A large component of the YMCA mandate is delivered via amateur sports programs, including leagues, instructional classes, family nights, youth sports programming, mentoring, and exchange programs. Each YMCA strives to nurture the healthy development of children and teens, strengthen families, and make the community a better place. The mission involves the development of the "whole body" through programs that often incorporate physical activity. See Figure 6.9 for the mission statement of the YMCA.

Financials. Each local YMCA is an independent, charitable, nonprofit organization required to pay dues to a National Association. Of the total revenue the National Association collects per year, approximately 31 percent comes from program fees, 32 percent from memberships, 19 percent from charitable contributions, 6 percent from resident camping and living quarters, 12 percent from government contracts and grants, and 1 percent from miscellaneous sources (YMCA, 2007). No one is turned away for inability to pay.

Membership. YMCAs are a part of community life in neighborhoods and towns across North America. In the United States over 18 million individuals enjoy their services each year. Several types of memberships are available, along with the ability to join only specific programs or groups.

Organizational structure. YMCAs have volunteers and professional, full-time, paid staff who help to set policy that is then implemented by

---

Mission statement of the YMCA.   **FIGURE 6.9**

The YMCA mission is "to put Christian principles into practice through programs that build healthy spirit, mind and body for all" through the motto "we build strong kids, strong families and strong communities."

Source: YMCA (2007).

both employees and volunteers. Most operate with a volunteer Board of Directors, steered by an Executive Committee elected from board members. Other committees work on specific types of programs or initiatives, like youth sports, clubs and camps, and family nights. The local board has jurisdiction over the development of policy for the independent YMCA, as long as the independent YMCA meets the following requirements as outlined in the national constitution (YMCA, 2007):

1. Annual dues are paid by the local Y to the national office, the YMCA of the U. S. A.

2. The Y refrains from any practices that discriminate against any individual or group.

3. The national mission is supported.

Accordingly, "all other decisions are local choices, including programs offered, staffing, and style of operation" (YMCA, 2007).

The organizational structure of a typical YMCA is shown in Figure 6.10.

YWCA

www Ⓦ
YWCA
http://ywca.org

The YWCA is the oldest and largest multinational women's organization in the world (YWCA, 2007). It aims to provide safe places for girls and women no matter what their situation. According to YWCA USA (2007, n. p.), "Women come to us in times of crisis, as survivors of rape or domestic violence. They come for job training and career counseling. They come for childcare. They come for health and fitness. They come for a variety of reasons. But they come. And they leave with a renewed spirit, new skills, and stronger lives."

Mission. YWCA's intent is to eliminate racism and empower women. Their formal mission statement is

> The YWCA USA is a women's membership movement nourished by its roots in the Christian faith and sustained by the richness of many beliefs and values. Strengthened by diversity, the YWCA draws together members who strive to create opportunities for women's growth, leadership, and power in order to attain a common vision: peace, justice, freedom, and dignity for all people. The YWCA will thrust its collective power toward the elimination of racism, wherever it exists, and by any means necessary. (YWCA, 2007)

Financials. The total revenues of YWCA USA per year are almost $550 million. Of this amount, 44 percent is from government grants, 28 percent comes from public support (individuals, foundations, and corporations) and membership fees, and 18 percent comes from program service fees (YWCA, 2007).

Organization chart for the Harlem YMCA.   **FIGURE**   **6.10**

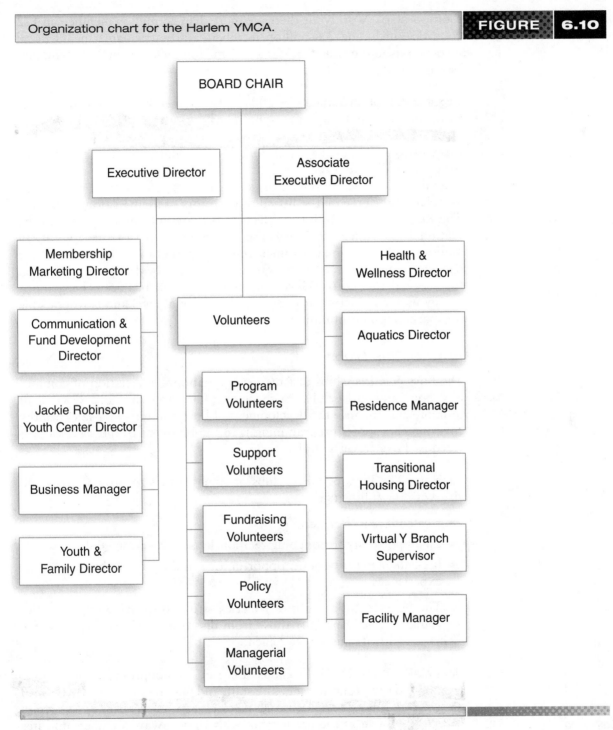

Source: YMCA of Greater New York (2008).

Membership. Worldwide there are more than 25 million members in 122 countries, including 2.6 million members and participants in 300 local associations in the United States and 1 million members in 200 communities in Canada.

Organizational structure. In 2001, YWCA members voted to restructure the national organization. The grassroots Change Initiative changed the top-down structure to a bottom-up structure grounded in the work of the local associations. Nine separate Regional Councils were created, and each local association affiliated with a Regional Council. Each local association sends two representatives from their association to serve on the Board of Directors of their Regional Council. The Regional Council in turn elects two representatives to serve on the National Coordinating Board, the governing board of the YWCA. In addition, each Regional Council sends representatives to serve on the national committees, thereby giving extensive local representation on the regional and national level. The national office has been charged primarily with conducting advocacy at the national level and is responsible for marketing and branding.

Boys & Girls Clubs

www**W**

Boys & Girls Clubs of America
www.bgca.org

The Boys & Girls Clubs of America is a national association of community boys and girls clubs. Such clubs offer programs and services to promote and enhance the development of boys and girls in a safe, healthy environment. Sports programming is one component of the services provided by Boys & Girls Clubs.

Mission. The Boys & Girls Clubs of America acts to provide boys and girls with the following:

- a safe place to learn and grow
- the opportunity for ongoing relationships with caring adults
- life-enhancing programs, opportunities, and character-building experiences

The Boys & Girls Clubs of America strives to provide opportunities for young people, especially those from disadvantaged backgrounds. See Figure 6.11 for its mission statement.

Financials. Boys & Girls Clubs are run as nonprofit organizations. Revenues to run programming, hire staff, and maintain facilities come from membership dues, private donations, corporate funding, and community partnerships such as the partnership with United Way. Membership rates are kept to a minimum ($10 to $35 per year), and no one is turned away

| Mission statement of the Boys & Girls Clubs of America. | FIGURE | 6.11 |

> The mission of the Boys & Girls Clubs of America is "to enable all young people especially those who need us the most, to reach their full potential as productive, caring responsible citizens."

Source: Boys & Girls Clubs of America (2007). Reprinted with permission.

from programming because of an inability to pay. On average about $250 is spent per youth in a given year.

Membership. Over 4.6 million boys and girls participated in programming at over 4,000 clubs in the United States, with approximately 55 percent male and 45 percent female participants (Boys & Girls Clubs of America, 2007). A variety of unique sport programming is provided through clubs, tournaments, and the JrNBA and JrWNBA programs. Other specialized learning programs such as the Athletic Director University program teach youngsters leadership and skills to organize and administer their own leagues, clubs, and teams.

Organizational structure. The City of Atlanta operates an organization that helps clubs within its region to effectively deliver programs to boys and girls. There may be as many as 20 clubs in a region, each operating with a small professional staff and many volunteers. The Boys & Girls Clubs of Metro Atlanta are organized with a volunteer Board of Directors, to which members from each club belong (Boys & Girls Clubs of Metro Atlanta, 2007). The board is elected and is composed of 14 unit board presidents from regions within the geographical area and 57 board members (Boys & Girls Clubs of Metro Atlanta, 2007). The Board of Directors and the association members are responsible for developing policy, for example, the policy regarding the division of revenues between each of the metro clubs. Policy may determine that the use of revenues collected by individual clubs be defined without restriction by the club, but that revenues distributed to individual clubs by the overarching Atlanta parent group be used in specific areas such as programming, professional staff, and facilities.

www

Boys & Girls Clubs of Metro Atlanta www.bgcma.org

The organizational structure of a typical Boys & Girls Club that can be found in communities across the United States is shown in Figure 6.12.

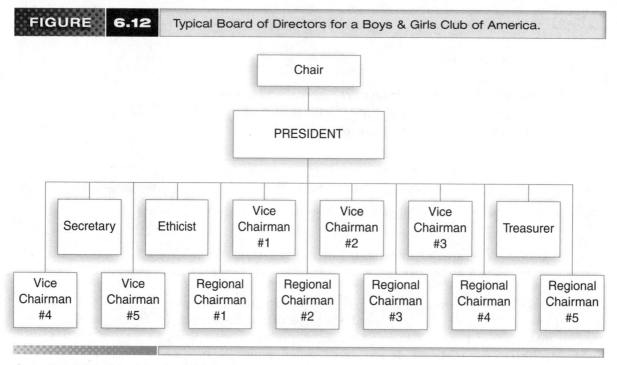

FIGURE **6.12**   Typical Board of Directors for a Boys & Girls Club of America.

Source: Boys & Girls Clubs of America (2007). Reprinted with permission.

Jewish Community Centers

**Jewish Community
Center Association
of North America**

www.jcca.org

Jewish Community Centers (JCC) are nonprofit organizations under the authority of the Jewish Community Center Association of North America, an umbrella organization including more than 350 JCCs, Young Men's Hebrew Associations/Young Women's Hebrew Associations (YMHAs/YWHAs), and campsites in the United States and Canada (JCC, 2007). The Jewish Community Center Association offers a wide range of services and resources to help its affiliates provide educational, cultural, social, Jewish identity-building, and recreational programs for people of all ages and backgrounds.

Each year the JCC Association puts together a sporting festival for Jewish teens known as the JCC Maccabi Games. These games are an Olympic-style sporting competition held each summer on multiple sites in North America and is the largest organized sports program for Jewish teenagers in the world (Orange County Maccabi Games, 2007). In addition, the JCC Association helps sponsor the Maccabiah Games, the quadrennial Jewish Olympics, held in Israel the year following the Olympic Games.

Mission. The mission of the JCC Association of North America is "to encourage and help everyone at the JCC to continue learning, growing, and thriving. It's all about teaching and learning for a lifetime" (JCC,

2005a). As an example of the mission of a local JCC, the mission statement of the Jewish Community Center of Greater Baltimore, the inaugural JCC, is: "The Jewish Community Center of Greater Baltimore is dedicated to promoting and strengthening Jewish life and values through its programs and services to individuals, groups, and families" (Jewish Community Center of Greater Baltimore, 2000).

JCC Maccabi Games
www.jccmaccabigames.org

Financials. In 2005, the JCC Association of America operated with a budget just below $10 million. Revenues came from the following sources: JCC dues (38%), program revenue (24%), NFC and federation support (21%), foundation grants (10%), corporate sponsorship (5%), and earnings from investments (2%). Association expenses included: program enrichment services (40%), community consultation services (15%), professional development (10%), management and finance (10%), marketing and communications (9%), Jewish education (7%), financial resource development (6%), and services to the military (4%) (JCC, 2005b).

In 2006, the JCC of San Francisco had operating revenues of $23.5 million that were derived from the following sources: activity income (40%), center membership (33%), gifts and grants (13%), Jewish Community Federation annual grant (4%), investments (3%), and other income (7%). Expenses included programs (68%), management (15%), building repairs and improvements (14%), and fundraising (3%) (JCC of San Francisco, 2007).

Membership. The JCC Association serves more than 350 JCC, YM/YWHA, and campsites in North America. Each of these members pays annual dues to the association. The association offers its members a wide range of services and resources in educational, cultural, social, Jewish identity-building, and recreational programs for people of all ages and backgrounds (JCC, 2007).

Individual JCCs offer memberships in various categories. There are individual memberships, family memberships, senior memberships, and some local JCCs even offer full community memberships. Membership dues depend on the individual JCC as well as the category of membership.

Organizational structure. The JCC Association of North America is organized with an Executive Committee and a Board of Directors. The Executive Committee, formed by elected officers, consists of a President, a Chair, nine Vice-Chairs, a Secretary, three Associate Secretaries, a Treasurer, three Associate Treasurers, five Honorary Chairs, and a President Emeritus. The Board of Directors is very large, consisting of 78 members (JCC, 2005b). The JCC Association has three North American offices, as well as one in Jerusalem, Israel. The North American offices are located in New York City; Austin, Texas; and New Orleans, Louisiana.

JCC of San Francisco

www.jccsf.org

Pacers and Racers Running and Walking Group

www.pacersandracers.com

Saskatchewan Road Runners Association

www.saskatchewanroad runners.ca

San Juan Sledders Snowmobile Club

www.sanjuansledders.org

Muskegon County Amateur Hockey Association

www.muskegonchiefs.org

The JCC of San Francisco is directed by an Executive Director, a group of elected officers, and a volunteer Board of Directors. Along with the Executive Director, the elected officers include a President, the First Vice-President, the Vice-President, a Treasurer, a Secretary, and a Chief Financial Officer. The volunteer Board of Directors is also large, consisting of 19 members (JCC of San Francisco, 2007).

Community Groups

There are many individuals and groups running nonprofit organizations for sport and physical activity. They are community based but not run by community government agencies such as city parks and recreation departments. Community groups such as the Pacers and Racers Running and Walking Group located in New Albany, Indiana, and the Saskatchewan Road Runners Association have organized themselves to deliver events in particular activities. The San Juan Sledders Snowmobile Club of Bayfield, Colorado, is another example of a nonprofit amateur sport organization. This group acts to mark and groom winter trails in the area, encouraging use for multiple outdoor winter sports such as dogsledding, cross-country skiing, snowshoeing, and snowmobiling. The Muskegon (Michigan) County Amateur Hockey Association (MCAHA), another example of a nonprofit organization for amateur sport, provides opportunities for youth to participate in amateur hockey in the city of Muskegon.

Mission. The mission of a nonprofit community-based amateur sport organization involves delivering a particular activity by providing facilities and related services, such as arranging for individual participation or competition. Many community groups involve leagues or clubs through which regular activities are scheduled. Encouraging safe, ethical conduct for all participants is a common theme. The mission statement of the MCAHA is presented in Figure 6.13.

Financials. Nonprofit community groups are typically funded through participant membership fees, sponsorship, and other methods of fundraising. They may also be eligible for grants extended by municipal government agencies or private foundations. For example, a "Fun Run" organized by a city running club might involve municipal support (facilities and race-day logistics), sponsorships (printing costs, post-race refreshments, and awards), and a small entry fee to cover the costs of race T-shirts.

Membership. Volunteers run community nonprofit amateur sport organizations. Members of the organization are solicited to help organize; in turn, they gain the benefit of services such as events, tournaments, and championships. Membership dues are usually collected on a yearly basis.

| Mission statement of the Muskegon Chiefs Amateur Hockey Association. | FIGURE | 6.13 |

The Muskegon Chiefs Amateur Hockey Association (MCAHA) is a non-profit organization governed by a volunteer Board of Directors. For over twenty (20) years, our organization's main goal has been providing the youth of the greater Muskegon area the opportunity to grow and develop as individuals in the great sport of hockey. Through participation in this team sport, our programs will provide:

- The development and encouragement of sportsmanship between all players for the betterment of physical and social well-being
- Encouragement and improvement in the quality of ice hockey in Western Michigan
- Both instructional and competitive ice hockey opportunities to its members
- Association with the Michigan Amateur Hockey Association (MAHA), USA Hockey, and other hockey associations
- Help to defray the expense associated with ice hockey and team events through fundraisers
- Any and all acts desirable in the furtherance of the forgoing purposes

Our USA Hockey certified coaches, governed by a review board, are taught to stress that putting forth an individual's best effort is of primary importance. If an individual can increase his or her self-esteem, physical ability and have fun while doing so, we have accomplished our goals.

Source: MCAHA (2007). Reprinted with permission.

Organizational structure. Depending on its size, a community sport organization might be loosely configured or highly structured. A smaller organization such as the San Juan Sledders Snowmobile Club might have a small Executive Committee consisting of a few members in positions such as the President, Vice-President, and Treasurer. Other members of the group are then given tasks, but often they hold no specific titles. More often, the President will provide overall leadership, and the members of the group will complete tasks for each sporting event. An expectation exists for a fair division of labor among all group members. Once initial policy is established for managing the events, the group focuses on service as opposed to being a rules-making or sanctioning body. Conversely, in a larger organization such as the MCAHA, a structured managerial group may provide leadership, with a President, several Vice Presidents, and a number of Committee Chairs.

Current Policy Areas

A number of policy areas are prominent for managers of amateur sport organizations in the community. It is important that policy be defined for each of the areas described in this section because the issues are critical to the effective delivery of amateur sport, especially as related to children and children's programming. Effective policy enables effective decision making.

Fundraising

Policy enabling decision making for fundraising is a prominent issue for amateur sport organizations in the community. Community-based amateur sport organizations rely on raising capital for both programming and infrastructure. Public sport organizations compete with every other level of social programming for funding, and government grants often fall short of their needs. As important as fundraising is to public sport organizations, policy that enables effective financial management is even more important with nonprofit sport organizations. Managers in the nonprofit sector are continually concerned with policy setting and maintaining strict measures for raising money, along with ensuring that budgets are balanced and that spending is effective and shared among as many programs as possible. For instance, the Boys & Girls Clubs of America rely heavily on donations from both the private and the public sectors. While club administrators acknowledge that it takes money to run a Boys & Girls Club (about $250 per youth per year), they point out that the alternative costs of keeping a young adult in jail for a year ($50,000 to $100,000) makes their programming "one of the best bargains in America" (Boys & Girls Clubs of America, 2002). Understandably, they take great pride in the national recognition they received from *The Chronicle of Philanthropy*, a publication that ranked them number one among nonprofit youth organizations for efficient use of financial resources for the twelfth consecutive year in 2005.

The fundraising policy areas receiving most of the attention are the following:

1. identifying funding sources
2. soliciting donations and sponsorships
3. servicing and maintaining donor relationships

1. *Identifying funding sources.* Most organizations set specific policy that identifies sources of funds worth pursuing. Virtually all solicit private donations, government grants, and corporate sponsorships. Specific policy might list donors in order of priority based on which are most likely to enter a partnership and in specific categories of new contacts to pursue. In addition, such policy will certainly outline categories of unacceptable sources of funding. For instance, no Boys & Girls Club would solicit funds from a tobacco company. On the contrary, the club will work hard to disassociate unhealthy practices such as smoking from the club's programming for children and teenagers. The policy might also define special-event types of fundraising (charity dinners, silent auctions, golf tournaments, etc.), and set some parameters on exactly what events will be hosted and what goals will define success.

2. *Soliciting donations and sponsorships.* Other policy will define exactly how donations and sponsorships are solicited and by whom. Will potential donors be called, contacted by mail or e-mail? Will the club website be used to initiate fundraising? How will money be received, and how will records be kept? Such questions can be answered by developing effective policy.

3. *Servicing and maintaining donor relationships.* Ensuring donors and sponsors are "serviced" is very important as well. Servicing involves "giving back" to the donor or sponsor. Once support is found for programming, every effort must be made to inform, involve, and thank the sponsors for their involvement. Courtesy and reciprocity are critical to building relationships and are the best ways to maintain donor or sponsor involvement from year to year. Newsletters, invitations to see programs in action, thank-you letters from participants, and summarized information outlining the positives resulting from the donation are all effective means of servicing. The Boys & Girls Clubs of America use an extremely prominent National Board of Governors and Officers in their fundraising efforts, as illustrated by Honorary Co-Chairs President George W. Bush and First Lady Laura Bush and Officers Ken Griffey Jr. and Denzel Washington.

Inactivity of Girls and Women

Currently, the inactivity of girls and women generally and the declining numbers of females engaging in amateur sport have been targeted as problems that amateur sport programs at the community level can help to reverse. Policy is often set to deal with recurring issues and to enable decision making to effect change regarding such issues. All too often, a girl's role in sport is peripheral to the action, watching the boys play. Research shows that girls' participation in sport and physical activity declines

Canadian Association
for the Advancement
of Women in Sport
and Physical Activity

www.caaws.ca/e/

between ages five and twelve (Kernaghan, 2002). Another large drop in girls' participation occurs at high school age (Pate, Long, & Heath, 1994). The Canadian Association for the Advancement of Women in Sport and Physical Activity (CAAWS, 2002) has identified three key issues associated with increasing the inactivity of girls and women in sport:

- lack of media coverage of female sporting heroes
- a need for quality programming for school-age girls
- decreased levels of corporate funding for female athletes

It has also been demonstrated that institutional inequities exist where girls and women lack access to local municipal recreation programs (American Civil Liberties Union [ACLU], 1999). The ACLU of Southern California successfully asserted that girls and women lacked opportunities for participation because programming, services, and facilities were not provided equitably in the City of Los Angeles (ACLU, 1999).

As a result of such lawsuits, and also because it is the fair thing to do, community-based amateur sport organizations have set policy to ensure programming exists for girls and women. The goal is to provide fun-filled, supportive, female-only sport and physical activity experiences for nonactive girls and women in the 9–18 age group. Such policy has helped to promote the development of sport and physical activity skills, along with healthy lifestyles and improved self-esteem, for females. For example, the settlement of the lawsuit against Los Angeles referred to above resulted in "Raise the Bar," a gender-equity policy that specifically addresses programming and access to facilities for girls and women (City of Los Angeles, Department of Parks and Recreation, 2003). Today the purpose of the program focuses more on youth: encouraging girls to get involved in sports and recreation, increasing the number of girls in traditionally male activities, and distributing resources equitably across all youth activities (City of Los Angeles, Department of Recreation and Parks, 2007).

Los Angeles Department
of Parks and Recreation

www.laparks.org

Women's Sports Foundation

www.womenssports
foundation.org

Gender-equity policies also already exist in many community amateur athletic organizations such as the City of Vancouver Recreation Department, which now offers T-ball programs and Little League Baseball for little girls as well as little boys. Such policy is also promoted by groups such as the Women's Sports Foundation (WSF), a charitable organization dedicated to ensuring equal access to participation and leadership opportunities for girls and women in sport (WSF, 2007). The foundation announced the awarding of $675,000 to 85 separate organizations and 10,462 individuals in 2006 as part of the grant program "GoGirlGo." The funding is intended to "provide girls and women with educational materials and scholarships, research on leadership development and opportunities to participate in sports and physical activity" (WSF, 2007).

Parental Involvement

Parental involvement has been the topic of youth sport over the past several years (Center for Sports Parenting, 2007). Stories of parents being "muzzled" or banned from events are too frequently presented in the media. Adult misbehaviors have become more commonplace: splashing hot coffee in the face of an official; verbal abuse of officials, coaches, and kids; and overt fighting, threats, and other forms of confrontations. According to Dan Bylsma, former NHL player and Assistant Captain of the Mighty Ducks of Anaheim, two questions must be addressed: Why have parents become so invested in the progress of their children in youth sports to the exclusion of other arguably more important endeavors, such as academic pursuits? And why is parental involvement usually unrelated to a focus on the benefit for the child (Institute for International Sport [IIS], 2002)? Amateur sport in the community is about fun, about learning teamwork and dedication, and about respect for authority. Excessive parental involvement in amateur sport, especially involvement that overshadows other important aspects of growing up, such as doing homework and chores and gaining experience in a number of activities, serves to teach children the wrong lessons. Consider the values being taught a child when *thousands* of dollars are spent on hockey travel when a parent would not consider spending tens of dollars on a math tutor (IIS, 2002).

If the purpose of youth sports is to have fun, increase athleticism, and learn the value of teamwork and discipline, then some adults are helping to teach the wrong lessons. Sport managers and program administrators are working to reverse such involvement by setting policy to curtail "parental overinvolvement." Examples of such policy include spectator codes of conduct, parental contracts agreeing to acceptable types of conduct and involvement, and conferences and seminars for parents of children in youth sport. The City of Henderson and the Nevada Parks and Recreation Department are encouraging parents to get involved and stay involved in amateur sports. They have been proactive by setting policy to educate all participants' parents, and that policy is enacted through YouthFirst, a youth sports orientation program for parents (YouthFirst, 2007). The orientation has been developed by the University of Nevada, Las Vegas, and is designed to encourage parental involvement, emphasize fun, and boost participant retention. The intent is to curb violence in youth sports by orienting all parents to their role, the coach's role, and to what parents can do to foster continued participation by kids. The program requires parents to complete a certification quiz and to sign a code of conduct (YouthFirst, 2007).

Amateur sport groups in the community are well advised to have policy governing parental involvement. As Dan Bylsma states, "It's long past the time some adults in youth sports clean up their act [and] focus on the wholesome purposes of youth sports and improve the lessons they're teaching their children. Or I fear the next trial for manslaughter will be

www

Center for Sports Parenting
www.sportsparenting.org

Institute for International Sport
www.internationalsport.com

www

YouthFirst
www.youthfirst.info

held in Juvenile Court" (IIS, 2002). Dan Doyle (2007) suggests "parents must help young athletes understand the meaning of gamesmanship as it applies to their sport(s), and that maintaining one's integrity begins with adhering not only to the rules of the sports, but to the spirit of the rules.

Violence in Sport

Violent behaviors associated with amateur sport are not restricted to parents. Overly aggressive and violent acts by participants and spectators are regularly reported in the media. Violence is associated with physical acts of aggression, both verbal and nonverbal. Reducing sport violence involves curtailing athlete and spectator aggression. Policies dealing with reducing athlete violence seek to achieve the following:

- provide proper, nonaggressive role models for young athletes
- develop rules that allow low tolerance for acts of violence
- apply severe and swift penalties for violence involving the actions of athletes, referees, and coaches
- apply severe and swift penalties for coaches who support and promote violent or aggressive play
- remove stimuli that provoke aggression
- organize referee, coach, parent, and athlete workshops
- provide ample positive reinforcement for appropriate displays of behavior in sport
- teach and practice emotional control (Kids First Soccer, 2007)

Amateur athletic organizations can curtail spectator violence through policies that deal with the following items:

- banning alcoholic beverages
- making it a family affair
- ensuring that the media are not contributing to the buildup of tension
- focusing on achieving excellence rather than fighting the enemy
- fining unruly spectators (Kids First Soccer, 2007)

Kids First Soccer
www.kidsfirstsoccer.com

Rediscovering Youth Sportsmanship
www.discoversportsmanship.com

For example, administrators of the Saint Barnabas Health Care System (SBHCS) in New Jersey set policy to curb violence in sport by developing the Rediscovering Youth Sportsmanship program. The key elements of the program include training and education sessions for parents, coaches, officials, facility managers, and sport administrators that provide a system of boundaries, positive reinforcement, and sanctions for certain behaviors, delivered through videos, pledges, surveys, and rewards (SBHCS, 2007). Another example is SportSafe, a program developed by the government of British

Columbia, Canada, that seeks to create a safer environment in sport and recreation. The Anti-Violence Policy for Recreation Facilities enacted as part of SportSafe seeks to raise awareness among spectators and parents of their role in creating a positive environment and gives volunteers and staff the mandate and power to deal with violent and antisocial behavior (Government of British Columbia, 2007). The policy defines *violent behavior* as the following:

- loud verbal assaults
- intimidation and threats
- aggressive actions such as approaching another individual or throwing articles
- striking another individual
- attempting to incite violence

Individuals engaging in any of the above activities are immediately ejected from the facility by program- or facility-designated leaders and banned from all local recreation facilities for a period of time defined by the recreation facility staff (Government of British Columbia, 2007).

Selecting Youth Sport Coaches

Programming for kids depends on having supervision and instruction, the normal role of the coach. About 4 million volunteer coaches work with more than 40 million young athletes in the United States alone (Positive Coaching Alliance, 2003). Unfortunately, the large number of volunteer coaches required sometimes results in the hiring of untrained, unprepared coaches. Far more deadly and devastating is the potential for placing a pedophile or some other criminal in contact with children and youth. To ensure this error does not happen, all sport organizations need to use specific criteria for hiring youth coaches and to utilize reference and criminal-background checks before hiring coaches. All sport organizations must have a personnel policy that contains procedures and requirements for youth sport coaches and volunteers and that includes items such as the following:

- required coach training and background
- background information disclosure
- police record check
- coaching expectations and code of conduct
- coaching your own child
- understanding the goals and objectives of the association
- feedback on coaching performance
- dismissing a coach
- an individual's right to appeal

SportSafe Program
www.tsa.gov.bc.ca/sport/
programs/sportsafe.htm

Positive Coaching Alliance
www.positivecoach.org

SUMMARY

Hundreds of amateur sport organizations are community based. Their mandate is to provide opportunities for sport participation, and such organizations provide for a broad spectrum of sports for a range of age groups. Such organizations can be categorized as public or non-profit, depending on their purpose and type of funding. Amateur sport at the community level has a rich history and is considered to be one of the foundations of a society in which happiness, health, and well-being are central. Such organizations include leagues, groups, clubs, special-interest groups, and organizations such as the YMCA.

The managers of community-based amateur sport organizations deal with a wide variety of governance and policy issues. Funding is a key area, because fundraising is at the core of the operation of the organization. Programming dependent on both funding and interest and the inactivity of girls and women are areas of concern and policy development. Inappropriate conduct or interference by parents and violence are other current policy issues concerning amateur sport. Despite these issues, community-based sport managers provide programming that positively impacts the lives of hundreds of thousands of participants. It is an exceptionally important component of the sport industry.

CASE STUDY | *Unbecoming Conduct in Youth Sport*

As the Director of Children's Sport Programming for the town of Clarington, you are organizing a Soccer League for girls and boys from 6 to 10 years old. Experience tells you that the parents and kids of Clarington are a competitive group. At the winter hockey leagues several groups of parents were banned, and suspensions for violent behavior were common among the participants. In an effort to be proactive and eliminate such behaviors in the Soccer League, you have developed a Code of Conduct for both participants and spectators.

1. Describe your Code of Conduct for directing the behavior of (a) participants, (b) parents, and (c) general spectators.
2. How do you plan to communicate the Code of Conduct?
3. How do you plan to enforce the Code of Conduct?
4. How might you go about getting both participants and spectators to buy in to the Code?
5. What ethical dilemmas might you face implementing the policy, and how will you solve them?

CHAPTER QUESTIONS

1. What is the difference between a public and a nonprofit sport organization? How do the governance structures of the two categories differ? Why do different types of recreational sport organizations exist?

2. Using the Internet, locate a community sport organization. With which category of those mentioned in this chapter does it most closely align? Summarize its governance structure by describing the following: mission, financials, membership, and organizational structure.

3. You have just been voted President of the Marysville Minor Soccer Association. Your organization provides opportunities for competition for boys and girls in five age groups, with nearly 700 participants on 35 teams. You are dismayed by the recent conduct of both athletes and parents on and off the field, and no policy exists to establish expected behaviors. Address these concerns by doing the following: (a) develop a policy of expected behaviors for players, parents, and coaches; (b) define an overall program of education to ensure that the policy and reasons behind the program are well understood; (c) define a list of sanctions for violating the policy; and (d) decide on a course of action to help you to convince your Executive Committee that the policy is important and that it needs to be implemented next season.

REFERENCES

ACLU. (1999). Settlement of CA lawsuit brings equality, victory for girls' and women's sports, ACLU says. Retrieved June 19, 2003, from www.aclu.org/WomensRights/WomensRights.

Boys & Girls Clubs of America. (2002). The board—who we are. Retrieved September 30, 2002, from www.bgca.org/whoweare/board.asp.

Boys & Girls Clubs of America. (2007). Our mission. Retrieved May 5, 2007, from www.bgca.org/whoweare/mission.asp.

Boys & Girls Clubs of Metro Atlanta. (2007). Boys & Girls Clubs of Metro Atlanta—A positive place for kids. Retrieved October 6, 2002, from www.bgcma.org.

CAAWS. (2002). Girls @ play—Getting more girls in the game. Retrieved October 7, 2002, from www.caaws.ca/girlsatplay/index.htm.

Cabot Youth Baseball Association. (2007). About CYBA. Retrieved May 3, 2007, from www.cabotbaseball.com.

Center for Sports Parenting. (2007). Institute for International Sports, Center for sports Parenting. Retrieved June 6, 2007, from www.sportsparenting.org/csp.

City of Houston (2007). Overview of the Parks Department. Retrieved May 3, 2007, from www.houstontx.gov/parks/AboutUs.html.

City of Los Angeles, Department of Parks and Recreation. (2003). Raise the bar. Retrieved June 19, 2003, from www.laparks.org/dos/sports/raisethebar/introduction.html.

City of Los Angeles, Department of Parks and Recreation. (2007). Raise the bar: Achieve gender equity in youth sports. Retrieved August 22, 2007, from www.laparks.org/dos/sports/raisethebar/raisethebar.htm.

City of San Diego. (2007). Neighbourhood and Customer Services Department. Retrieved August 21, 2007, from www.sandiego.gov/orgchart/pdf/ncs.pdf.

City of Seattle. (2007). 2007 Adopted & 2008 endorsed budget. Retrieved May 3, 2007, from www.seattle.gov/financedepartment.

City of Snellville. (2007). General Fund—Budget for fiscal year 2007. Retrieved August 20, 2007, from www.snellville.org/administration/budget.aspx.

City of Toronto. (2007). About us. Retrieved August 22, 2007, from www.city.toronto.ca/parks/about_us.htm#mission.

Doyle, D. (2007). The practical value of good sportsmanship. Retrieved August 22, 2007, from www.internationalsport.com/nsd/nsd_letter.cfm.

Government of British Columbia. (2007). Ministry of Tourism, Sports, and the Arts: The SportSafe program. Retrieved August 22, 2007, from www.tsa.gov.bc.ca/sport/programs/sportsafe.htm.

IIS. (2002). Untitled article. Retrieved October 7, 2002, from www.internationalsport.com/nsd/nsd_opeds.cfm?n=bylsma.

Iowa Games. (2007). Iowa Games mission statement. Retrieved May 3, 2007, from www.iowagames.org/history.aspx.

Iowa Sports Foundation. (2007). Becoming a sponsor. Retrieved August 21, 2007, from http://IowaGames.org/becomingasponsor.aspx.

JCC. (2005a). JCC association annual report 2005 (p. 2). Retrieved May 17, 2007, from www.jcca.org/about_us.html.

JCC. (2005b). Annual report 2005. Retrieved May 22, 2007, from www.jcca.org/about_us.html.

JCC. (2007). About JCC association. Retrieved May 17, 2007, from www.jcca.org/about_us.html.

JCC of Greater Baltimore. (2000). JCC mission statement. Retrieved May 17, 2007, from www.jcc.org/template.php?section=AM.

JCC of San Francisco. (2007). 2006 Annual report. Retrieved May 22, 2007, from www.jccsf.org/content_main.aspx?catid=374.

Kernaghan, J. (2002). What stops the girls from playing? *The Hamilton Spectator.* Retrieved April 6, 2003, from www.caaws.ca/Whats_New/2002/nov/Hamilton_article.htm.

Kidd, B. (1999). *The struggle for Canadian sport.* Toronto: University of Toronto Press.

Kids First Soccer. (2007). Aggression and violence in sport. Retrieved August 22, 2007, from www.kidsfirstsoccer.com/violence.htm.

Kissimmee Parks and Recreation. (2007). Florida Parks and Recreation. Retrieved May 3, 2007, from www.kissimmee.org/ch_dept_parks.aspx?id+323.

MCAHA. (2007). Muskegon Chiefs Hockey mission statement. Retrieved August 22, 2007, from www.muskegonchiefs.org/mission.htm.

Orange County Maccabi Games. (2007). About the games. Retrieved May 17, 2007, from http://ocmaccabi.org/index.php?page=AboutTheGames.

Pate, R. R., Long, B. J., & Heath, G. W. (1994). Descriptive epidemiology of physical activity in adolescents. *Pediatric Exercise Science, 6,* 302–314.

Pickering Hockey Association. (2007). PHAinfo. Retrieved May 3, 2007, from www.pickeringhockey.com/about/about.html.

Positive Coaching Alliance. (2003). The problem and the opportunity. Retrieved June 23, 2003, from www.positivecoach.org.

The San Juan Sledders Snowmobile Club. (2007). The San Juan Sledders Snowmobile Club. Retrieved August 22, 2007, from www.sanjuansledders.org.

SBHCS. (2007). Rediscovering youth sportsmanship program. Retrieved August 22, 2007, from www.discoveringsportsmanship.com.

WSF. (2007). Grants and scholarships. Retrieved August 22, 2007, from www.womenssportsfoundation.org/cgi-bin/iowa/index.html.

YouthFirst. (2007). YouthFirst: Parents Learning About Youth Sports. Retrieved August 22, 2007, from www.youthfirst.info.

YMCA. (2007). Welcome to YMCA.net. Retrieved October 6, 2007, from www.ymca.net/index.jsp.

YMCA Canada. (2007). YMCA Canada. Retrieved May 15, 2007, from www.ymca.ca/eng_ycda.htm.

YMCA of Greater New York. (2008). About us. Retrieved March 31, 2008, from www.ymcanyc.org.

YWCA. (2007). YWCA USA. Retrieved May 15, 2007, from www.ywca.org.

CAMPUS RECREATION

INTRODUCTION

Campus recreation is the umbrella term used to describe a myriad of recreation and leisure activity programming on university and college campuses throughout North America. Recreation departments exist on virtually every college and university campus in North America. This segment of the industry has extensive facilities and numbers of personnel, and many of you may include campus recreation departments in your career plans. Understanding the organization, governance, and policy issues pertinent to this extensive segment of the sport industry will help you prepare for such management positions located on college campuses or within umbrella organizations helping to lead the campus recreation industry.

Historically, college and university administrators have accepted responsibility not only for the education but also for the general welfare of their students. Since the promotion of health and well-being was identified as critical for student welfare, campus recreation departments became essential components of institutions of higher learning. In general, the mandate of the Campus Recreation Department was to offer opportunities to participate in recreational activities, both programmed activities and activities open to definition by the participants. The importance of this mandate gained momentum because college campuses were often community oriented and could accommodate and serve large populations of students, faculty, and staff members. Today, campus recreation departments aim to enrich student life and are often considered tools for recruiting and retaining college students.

The size of campus recreation departments varies depending upon the campus setting; however, their purpose is often strikingly similar. Campus recreation provides opportunities to engage in sport and leisure activities. The prime target audience of such programming is the student body. However, programming is usually also accessible to faculty and staff members, and sometimes their families. In addition, many activities are made available to the community at large (Van Mierlo, 1996). The basic premises underlying campus recreation programming are enjoyment and promotion of a healthy lifestyle through physical activity. The missions and visions of such programs are represented by slogans such as "Something for Everyone," "Fit for Life," "Intramurals, Where It's Done for Fun," and "Active Living for Health and Happiness."

Let's have a look at a few mission statements used by campus recreation departments in colleges and universities around North America. Ohio State University (OSU) is one of the largest single-campus institutions with an enrollment of approximately 59,000 students. The mission of the OSU Department of Recreational Sports follows (OSU, 2007):

www
Ohio State University Recreational Sports
http://recsports.osu.edu

We are committed to providing the finest programs, services, facilities, and equipment to enrich the university learning experience. We also want to foster a lifetime appreciation of wellness and recreational sports and activities among our students, faculty and staff.

Founded in 1842, Queen's University (QU) is one of the oldest and finest institutions of higher learning in Canada. Located in the smaller City of Kingston, Ontario, the campus is known for being residential; many of the 14,000 students live on or near the campus. The university offers a large campus recreation program and has a similar mission to that of Ohio State (QU, 2007):

www
Queen's University Athletics and Recreation
www.goldengaels.com/recreation

The Recreation program at Queen's provides opportunities for all students, staff, faculty and their families to participate in an extensive and varied program. The philosophy of the program is to ensure that all members of the Queen's community have access to the many facilities available in order to pursue their personal health, fitness and recreational interests.

Drew University (DU) is much smaller than OSU or QU. Located in Madison, New Jersey, the college has an enrollment of about 1,600 liberal arts students. Even so, it offers a large intramural, recreational, and instructional program for its students. The purpose of Drew's Department of Campus Recreation Services is as follows (DU Campus Recreation Services, 2007):

> Campus Recreation Services' programs are designed to meet the athletic and recreational needs of the whole community—all students, staff, and faculty. Programs provide opportunities for the worthwhile use of leisure time and maintenance of high-level health and wellness.

Ⓦww
Drew University Campus Recreation Services
http://depts.drew.edu/crs

Each of these mission statements implicitly links the importance of campus facilities to the operation of recreational programming. In addition, the vision of the Campus Recreation Department involves inclusivity, since it operates as a vital part of the university community at large. The mission and vision of campus recreation departments often include a set of values as summarized in Table 7.1.

With this basic understanding of campus recreation, let's look at the roots of campus recreation departments, why they were developed, and how they are organized and governed nationally.

A summary of the typical values of a campus recreation department.   **TABLE 7.1**

Access for All	Provide opportunities for a wide diversity of interests, age groups, and abilities, including individuals with disabilities.
Customer Satisfaction	Develop a friendly, knowledgeable staff and clean, safe, accessible, and attractive facilities.
Awareness	Employ promotional strategies to ensure programs and services are well communicated to new and current participants.
Mutual Respect	Ensure a welcoming environment, and promote opportunities for activity in an environment of respect.
Diversity	Create an environment embracing individual differences and reflecting campus diversity.
Variety	Provide opportunities reflecting the diverse interests of the campus community.
Fun	Ensure enjoyment is the mainstay of each programming area.
Development	Provide opportunities for students to guide the programming and gain valuable leadership and management skills.
Evaluation	Maintain a cutting-edge set of programs and facilities reflecting current trends and interests.

The History of Campus Recreation

R ecreation and leisure activities undoubtedly contributed to the early growth of competitive athletics (Langley & Hawkins, 1999). The interest in playing, learning to engage in new activities, or simply getting active is well documented in the history of sport and the pursuit of good health. Early on, goals were likely pure enjoyment, opportunities to socialize with friends, and relief from the boredom of work, study, or everyday life. If physical activity is viewed as a continuum from informal play and recreation that is not necessarily competitive to formal and institutionalized competitive sport (Kane, 2007), it is easy to understand that the early history of recreation on campus is certainly interwoven with campus sport as we know it today.

The First Campus Recreation Programs

Early sport and leisure activities originated in English sport clubs and German gymnastics. As long ago as 1743, "Benjamin Franklin recommended that schools have a healthful situation and provide gardens and fields for students to engage in running, leaping, wrestling and swimming" (Colgate, 1978, p. 3). Around the midpoint of the 19th century, North Americans were looking for opportunities to be physically active other than in highly competitive sports or in the rigid routine of gymnastics. This interest resulted in the founding of the YMCA in 1851 and the YWCA in 1866 (Langley & Hawkins, 1999). Part of the emergence of these organizations involved the development of facilities. More important, the range of programming offered physical activity for a wide variety of interests.

This interest in pursuing physical and recreational activities and sport was naturally present on college campuses. The campus was an ideal setting for spontaneous games, with divisions already defined by academic class, major, or residence housing. As well, the energy level of the college age group resulted in regular involvement in physical activities. Thus the first football game was played at Yale University on the public greens as an intramural activity in 1807 (Colgate, 1978). Students at Princeton University organized intramural sports in 1857 when the freshman class challenged the sophomore group to a baseball game (Presbrey, 1901). By 1859, intramural boating clubs were established with organized crew competitions between classes (Mueller & Reznik, 1979). The term *intramural*, used to describe these first programs of campus recreation, comes from the Latin words for "within" (*intra*) and "wall" (*murus*), that is, within the walls of an organization (Brown, 1998).

Competition between different classes soon became commonplace. Colleges and universities embraced the notion that programming for leisure and recreational pursuits, along with competitive athletics, was an important component in the overall education and well-being of their students. In 1904, Cornell University (CU) developed a system of what is known today as instructional sport for students not participating at the varsity level. During the next decade the surge of student interest in recreational sports resulted in the development of a department to manage such student programming. OSU and the University of Michigan (UM) each defined organized intramural departments in 1913 (Mueller & Reznik, 1979). CU quickly followed, along with other colleges and universities in the United States and Canada.

A Rationale for Campus Recreation

When considering the history of higher education, intramural sport is perhaps one of the oldest organized campus activities (Smith, 1991). Campus recreation emerged as a formal department on campus and recreational programming subsequently experienced extensive growth and popularity for several reasons. A significant factor in legitimizing campus recreation occurred in the early part of the 20th century. In 1918, the National Education Association (NEA) in the United States coined the phrase "worthy use of leisure time" as one of the Seven Principles of Education (Colgate, 1978). In essence, the idea of capitalizing on one's leisure time became a tenet of an effective education. Greater meaning was attached to educating the whole person and to the importance of out-of-classroom educational experiences (Smith, 1991). Over time, the notion that healthy individuals are active, involved, and accomplished in activities of both mind and body became another cornerstone supporting the need for open recreation and intramural programming on campus. As the world became more technologically sophisticated, the amount of leisure time increased and the demand for recreational activities on campus continued to grow. Recreational activities were social in nature and offered opportunities both for affiliation with one's classmates or roommates and for friendly competition for bragging rights associated with pride in that group's accomplishment.

Each of these reasons for the establishment and growth of the Campus Recreation Department remains today. In addition, the extensive facilities developed to house recreational programming and the breadth of such programming in today's university are drawing cards for potential students. Students and their parents are naturally drawn to those institutions with excellent facilities and programs, providing a natural link between the Campus Recreation Department and the overall mission of the university. Research indicates that student retention is favorably influenced by getting students involved in extracurricular activities such as those housed within campus recreation (Leppel, 2006; Melendez, 2006; Zhang, DeMichele, & Connaughton, 2004). Finally and perhaps most important, campus recreation programs began and continue to flourish because of student interest. Enormous popularity and interest by the general student body grew over the years, leading to a proliferation of facilities and program offerings. In 1928, UM was the first institution to devote a building primarily to intramurals (Mueller & Reznik, 1979). Today, many campuses have complete facilities solely dedicated to recreational use.

The Formation and Evolution of National Intramural-Recreation Associations

Following World War II, while athletic and physical education groups were holding Annual Meetings and looking to associate with one another for a variety of purposes, recreation programmers were without such opportunities. To fill this void in the United States, Dr. William N. Wasson of Dillard University in New Orleans formed the National Intramural Association (NIA) in 1950. The mandate of the NIA was to provide an association for professionals working in college and university intramural sports programs in the United States to share ideas, develop policy, and encourage professional development. In 1975, the NIA membership voted to change its name to the current National Intramural-Recreational Sport Association (NIRSA). The membership felt NIRSA more aptly described the expanded and diversified role of recreation departments on college campuses. Such units organize and deliver programming far beyond the boundaries of intramural sports, and the scope and mission of NIRSA has expanded phenomenally to what is currently an extensive national association. The governance structure of NIRSA will be described later in this chapter.

The Canadian Intramural Recreation Association (CIRA) was founded in 1977 in response to a void in Canada similar to the one in the United States. The mission of CIRA was somewhat broader than NIRSA's, extending its reach to school as well as college and university intramural and recreation programming. The ultimate goal of CIRA was to promote active living and healthy lifestyles through intramural and recreation programming within the Canadian educational community. It was a membership-based, not-for-profit national association located in Ottawa, the nation's capital. CIRA membership primarily comprised practitioners (teachers), administrators, and students involved with intramurals and recreation from all provinces and territories within Canada. CIRA was the only national organization promoting and supporting intramurals in Canada until April 1, 2003, when CIRA transferred its activities and resources to the Canadian Association for Health, Physical Education, Recreation, and Dance (CAHPERD). The change was prompted by a reduction in federal funding to CIRA and the goal of effectively delivering one system of physical activity programming for all schools in Canada. CAHPERD now places a greater emphasis on intramurals through the development of the Intramural

Recreation Program Advisory Committee and programs such as the Quality School Intramural Recreation initiative (CAHPERD, 2007).

The next section describes the governance structures of NIRSA and CAHPERD in further detail and defines how campus recreation departments are organized on college and university campuses.

Governance

Municipal and state or provincial organizations exist as umbrella organizations with which campus recreation departments may affiliate on a local level. This section examines the two national associations to which most campus recreation professionals in the United States and Canada belong. We will attempt to answer the following questions about NIRSA and CIRA: What are the missions of these organizations? How do they obtain funding? Who are their members? How are these organizations structured?

National Intramural-Recreational Sport Association (NIRSA)

Mission. The purpose of NIRSA, the original organization promoting intramural sport, has expanded greatly since it was founded in 1950. Beyond intramurals, areas of interest include aquatics, extramurals, wellness and fitness, informal recreation, instructional programs, outdoor recreation, programs for people with disabilities, special events, sport clubs, and student leadership and development. NIRSA strives to provide its members with research, teaching, presenting, and publishing opportunities as well. NIRSA is a nonprofit professional association dedicated to promoting quality recreational sports programs. The association is equally committed to providing continuing education and development for recreational sport professionals and students. NIRSA's mission statement is presented in Figure 7.1.

Financials. NIRSA is a nonprofit organization. However, recent material and financial growth led the organization members to reorganize into three independent legal entities, each of which has a significant role in managing NIRSA finances. In addition to the parent NIRSA organization, the NIRSA Foundation and the NIRSA Services Corporation were formed (NIRSA, 2007).

NIRSA is a membership organization with approximately 4,000 individual and organization members. Membership fees constitute a major source of funding. The NIRSA Foundation is also a not-for-profit organization mandated to support the NIRSA mission; it receives donations to

www

National Intramural-Recreational Sport Association
www.nirsa.org

FIGURE   7.1   Mission statement of NIRSA.

The mission of the National Intramural-Recreational Sports Association is to provide for the education and development of professional and student members and to foster quality recreational programs, facilities and services for diverse populations. NIRSA demonstrates its commitment to excellence by utilizing resources which promote ethical and healthy lifestyle choices.

Source: NIRSA (2007). Reprinted with permission.

- **NIRSA.** The NIRSA Services Corporation is the taxable, business-oriented component of NIRSA. It was established to receive revenues from advertising, sponsorship, sales of licensed goods, and sport club championships (NIRSA, 2007).

Membership. Today, NIRSA has an extensive reach and membership across North America, but this has not always been the case. Whereas the first organizational meeting in 1950 included 13 individuals, the association now boasts a membership of thousands of professionals and students from colleges, universities, correctional facilities, military installations, and parks and recreation departments. NIRSA initiatives and programming reach millions of recreational sport enthusiasts, including an estimated 5.5 million college students. NIRSA also extends north of the border to professionals and students in Canadian schools, colleges, and universities.

Membership is offered at the institutional, professional, and student levels, as well as the associate level for commercial organizations who provide products or services to the NIRSA membership. Within each category NIRSA offers many opportunities to get involved. With its sole focus on the advancement of intramural-recreational sport programs and their professionals and students, NIRSA provides access to program standards, a code of ethics, an extensive resource library, career opportunity services, and the Sports Officials' Development Center. In addition, NIRSA's message is delivered to professionals through state and regional conferences, symposia and workshops, and the Annual National Conference and Exhibit Show. NIRSA Institutional Members represent large and small, public and private, two- and four-year colleges, and universities. For those with an institutional-level membership, access is provided to nationally sponsored programs and events ranging from individual and team sport events to fitness and wellness exhibitions and special publications. An example of an event touching each area within the association's mandate is the NIRSA Natural High program, an alcohol and other-drug awareness program.

Organizational structure. NIRSA is governed by a General Assembly and managed by a 12-member Board of Directors that conducts the association's business throughout the year. The Board of Directors (see Figure 7.2) comprises the following elected positions: President, Past-President, President-Elect, Past Presidents' Representative, National Student Representative, Executive Director, and six Regional Vice Presidents (Regions I–VI). The individuals elected to these positions hold one- to three-year terms, staggered to ensure continuity on the Board of Directors from year to year. The board is assisted by a nonvoting position of Secretary.

Organizational chart of the NIRSA Board of Directors. **FIGURE 7.2**

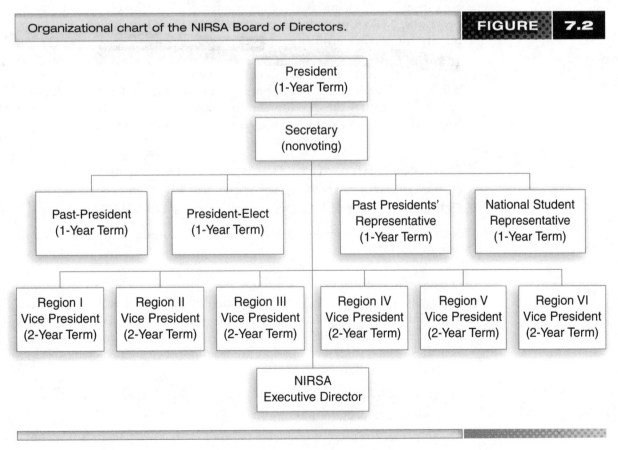

Source: NIRSA (2007). Reprinted with permission.

The Executive Director (ED) of NIRSA answers to the Board of Directors and is responsible for the daily activities of the organization. The NIRSA National Center, located in Corvallis, Oregon, is further divided into six main areas of focus, with each area leader reporting either to the ED or to the Chief Operating Officer (COO), who in turn reports to the ED. The five activity areas within the organization are (1) Education, (2) Finance, (3) Publications & Educational Resources, (4) Marketing, and (5) National Sport Programs. Approximately 20 individuals are employed as National Center staff. The NIRSA National Center, organizational chart is shown in Figure 7.3.

Also included in the governance structure are State Directors and a variety of committees. NIRSA State Directors are elected by and from their state of origin and are subdivided into six regionally defined affiliations. In total, over 40 professional meetings are conducted at the various levels throughout the year.

NIRSA is primarily a service organization, dedicated to continuing education for its members and the promotion of quality recreational sport programs. NIRSA provides its members with knowledge, ideas, and community for solving problems. Its prime policy role is the development of program standards for events and activities within recreation programs. Ensuring the safety of participants and quality of programming has been one focus of such policy development. Another focus of policy initiatives at NIRSA includes the development of codes of ethical practices for professionals and participants within recreational sport settings.

Canadian Intramural Recreation Association (CIRA)/Canadian Association for Health, Physical Education, Recreation, and Dance (CAHPERD)

As mentioned previously, in 2003, CAHPERD assumed the activities and resources of CIRA.

Mission. CAHPERD now promotes the mission (see Figure 7.4), vision, and goals statements originally articulated by CIRA. The vision is to have active intramural programs in all schools and post-secondary institutions and to ensure that children and youth are participating in daily physical activities. This vision and mission are accomplished by achieving the following goals (CIRA, 2002):

I. To decrease physical inactivity among children and youth through community programming;

II. To provide resources and leadership to enable teachers and students to lead intramural and campus recreation programs;

FIGURE 7.3   Organizational chart of the NIRSA National Center.

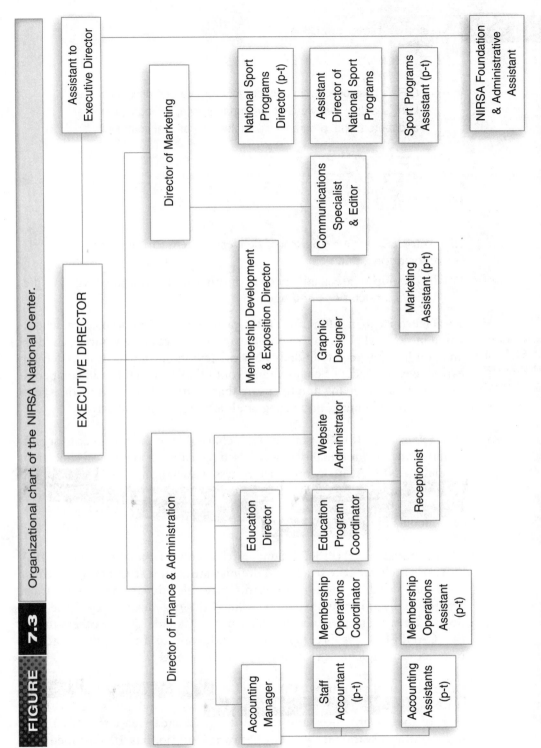

Source: NIRSA (2007). Reprinted with permission.

FIGURE | **7.4** | Mission statement of CIRA.

> CIRA's mission was "to encourage, promote and develop active living, healthy lifestyles and personal growth, through intramural and recreational programs within the educational community."

Source: CIRA (2002).

III. To foster a strong grassroots-delivery system through the provincial associations; and

IV. To develop strategic alliances with other national and provincial like-minded associations and agencies.

Canadian Association for Health, Physical Education, Recreation, and Dance

www.cahperd.ca

To achieve its mandate, CAHPERD promotes the importance of school-based intramural programs to provide opportunities and encourage children and youth to participate in daily physical activities. The intent is to develop early life experiences of children and youth that will enable a lifelong commitment to active living and to ensure that youth are involved in all aspects of recruiting, planning, organizing, and delivering physical activity.

Financials. CAHPERD is a national, charitable, voluntary-sector organization advocating for quality school-based recreation and physical education. Similar to NIRSA, it operates a business association called Physical and Health Education Canada to manage advertising, sponsorship, and program revenues and to manage its growing customer base. Other sources of revenue include membership fees.

Membership. CAHPERD members that came from the former CIRA structure are primarily teachers, administrators, and students who deliver intramural and recreation programs through educational institutions. Several thousand individuals have joined the organization over the past decade from every province and territory in Canada. Many others utilize the CAHPERD resource catalogue and website to acquire practical resources to implement recreational programming.

Organizational structure. CAHPERD is led by a President and governed by an Executive Council of 12 individuals, one of whom is elected from each of the 10 provinces and territories in Canada (see Figure 7.5). The organization's National Office in Ottawa, Ontario, has 10 staff members

Organizational chart of the CAHPERD Executive Council.	FIGURE	7.5

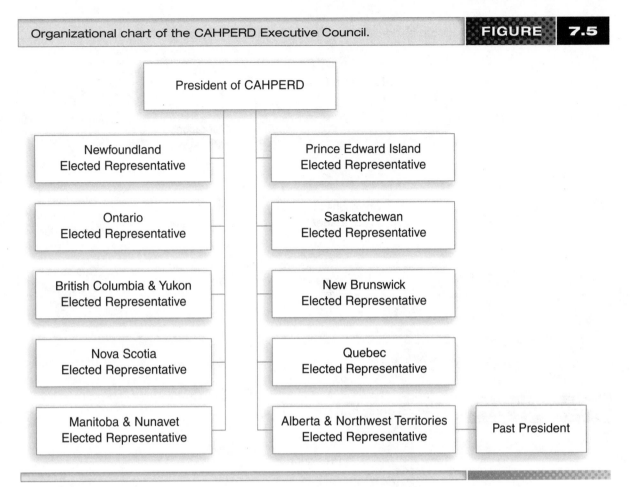

Source: CAHPERD (2007).

(see Figure 7.6) and is organized into two major Councils, the Council of Provinces and the Council of University Presidents. The Councils divide into five main areas of activity: (1) Executive Office, (2) Communications, (3) Programs, (4) Business Development, and (5) Finance. Each Council is represented by an elected expert to help CAHPERD set policy and direction within its respective jurisdiction of schools and professional preparation. The Intramural Recreation Program Advisory Committee comprises a number of key former CIRA members, continuing to play an advocacy and programmatic role for the promotion of intramural sport. The organizational structure of CAHPERD is presented in Figure 7.7.

CAHPERD does not play a large role in intramural-recreation policy development. Its main purpose is to promote and encourage active living and healthy lifestyles through intramural and recreational programming.

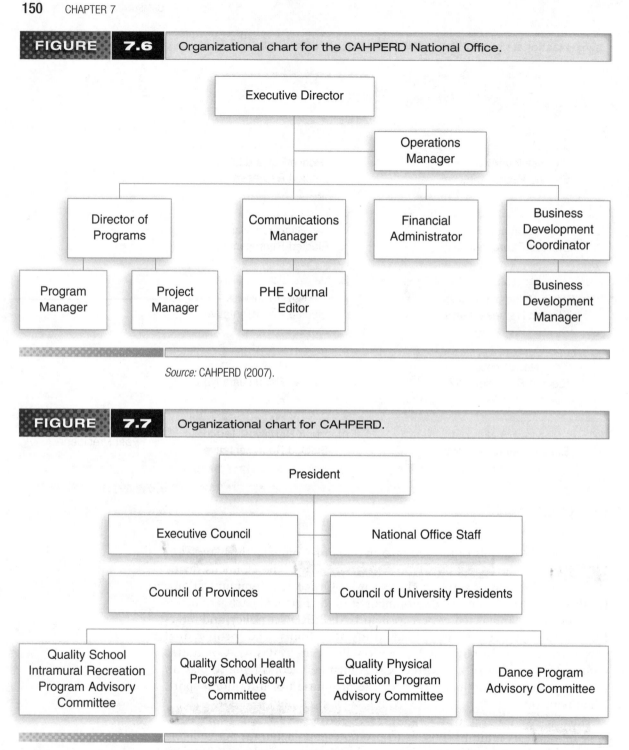

FIGURE 7.6   Organizational chart for the CAHPERD National Office.

Source: CAHPERD (2007).

FIGURE 7.7   Organizational chart for CAHPERD.

Source: CAHPERD (2007).

It achieves its mandate by providing resources and programming ideas to the educational community. CAHPERD often works in partnership with Canada's federal and provincial levels of government to decrease the inactivity of children. It plays a role in advocating for healthy, active lifestyles and works to advise the appropriate levels of government in the health and education sectors regarding policy development.

Campus Recreation Department Structure

Virtually every college and university in North America has a Campus Recreation Department. The campus is viewed as a community, and the pursuit of fitness and play through sport is an important part of any community operation.

Mission. The structure and function of the campus recreation department is directly linked to the unit's mission and goal statements, which are based upon participants' and clients' goals. A typical mission statement for a campus recreation department might read: "We are committed to providing the finest programs and services in order to enrich the University learning experience and to foster a lifetime appreciation of and involvement in recreational sport and wellness activities for our students, faculty, and staff." For sample mission statements, see Figure 7.8.

Financials. The financial operations of the small versus the large Campus Recreation Department will vary. Some institutions support programming and facilities through central budgets housed in Student Affairs. Revenue might be generated through varsity athletic budgets or through academic Physical Education or Kinesiology budgets. Budgetary support ranges from full to partial funding by the institution; more commonly, university budgets provide one of several sources of the overall recreation budget. Another common source of revenue for recreation is a compulsory recreation fee charged to every university student to help support student programs and facilities. Such fees are collected in addition to tuition and other compulsory academic and nonacademic fees at the beginning of each semester or quarter. Another revenue source includes "pay for play" fees collected from the participants in a league, class, or special event. Other budget components include rentals, facility membership or daily-use fees, advertising, and other marketing initiatives. In this case, the operation is run on a break-even basis, equating operational and program spending to the revenues generated through some combination of the sources defined above.

Other campus recreation programs are run as *profit centers*. Many institutions, regardless of size, have built multimillion-dollar facilities to service the needs of their current constituents. This proactive stance recognizes the role campus facilities can play in attracting and retaining future stu-

University of Idaho Campus Recreation

www.campusrec.uidaho.edu

Southern Polytechnic State University Recreational Sports and Athletics

www.spsu.edu/home/sports/index.html

University of California Los Angeles Recreation

www.recreation.ucla.edu/recreate/float.aspx?id=4112

| FIGURE | 7.8 | Sample mission statements of campus recreation programs. |

University of Idaho (Moscow, Idaho)

> Campus Recreation provides the finest programs, services, facilities, and equipment to enrich the University of Idaho learning experience. The department fosters a lifetime appreciation and involvement in recreation and wellness activities for our students, faculty, staff, and community. Campus Recreation contributes to the physical, social, intellectual, and cultural development of those we serve.

Southern Polytechnic State University (Marietta, Georgia):

> The Recreational Sports program shares in the educational mission of the university by offering opportunities to experience interpersonal growth, social development, improve physical and mental health, and to develop lifetime leisure skills for a healthier lifestyle. The department organizes, administers, and promotes a broad program of competitive, recreational, and educational activities for students, faculty, and staff.

University of California Los Angeles (UCLA)

> UCLA Recreation is committed to high quality recreational experiences that benefit the campus community.

Sources: University of Idaho (2007); Southern Polytechnic State University (2007); UCLA (2007).

dents, faculty, and staff. Profit centers generate revenue to offset the costs beyond those related to operations, for example, to pay a facility mortgage. Often, using the facility involves a membership fee. Students may pay through the recreation fee charged within the tuition package, and faculty and staff may be required to pay monthly membership fees. Opportunity for memberships may also be extended to alumni, family members, and community users on separate fee schedules. The proposal for building such a facility sometimes involves a student referendum for an additional building fee that might extend from as few as 5 years to as many as 20 years. In this case, an additional facility or building fee is charged to all students.

Some institutions look beyond their students to additional sources of revenue for building recreation facilities. An alternative model for financing the construction or renovation of facilities involves developing partnerships. In such cases, the university partners with the community, with local governments, or with the private sector to raise capital.

Agreements for use and profit allocation are developed in return for building capital. The facility is run as a business with market rates charged for use. The Director of Recreation must ensure certain profit levels are maintained through memberships and sources of program revenue. Significant sources of revenues in the millions of dollars can accrue from rental payments, instructional programs, and sport camps, to name a few.

Membership. As mentioned previously, the constituents of a modern campus recreation program include the students, faculty, and staff. However, this consumer group may well be broadened to include alumni, families of faculty and staff, and community members interested in acquiring recreation opportunities (O'Dell & Ross, 1996).

Organizational structure. The structure of the Recreation Department is also partially determined by its size. A small college may have a fairly simple organizational structure due to fewer constituents, limited facilities, smaller levels of programming, and less need for full-time staff. On the other hand, a large college will have a complex organizational structure that provides extensive levels of programming for multiple constituents through state-of-the-art facilities. Let's have a look at the administration and operation of two examples.

Small Recreation Programs

Consider a small, private college with 900 students and 75 faculty and staff members situated in a rural community of 5,000 people. It is possible the only constituents of the campus recreation program are students and a few faculty or staff. In this case recreation may be housed within a larger unit of Athletics and Recreation, so that the continuum of competitive and noncompetitive activity, along with the management of facilities, is combined within one department led by an individual with the title of Manager, Coordinator, or Assistant Director. Campus recreation thus coexists within a larger administrative unit responsible for varsity athletics and facilities; this alignment encourages an equitable distribution of resources (financial, physical, and human); good communication between multiple users of the same facilities; and effective, seamless delivery of the many physical activity options available to the participants. The head administrator of the overall operation, usually called the Director, is charged with maintaining some balance between the competitive and noncompetitive programming units.

In such cases, the Campus Recreation Manager may be the only full-time employee with direct responsibilities for recreational programming. She may have an assistant but often manages the area alone, with support from the Director and from employees who manage the facilities. In small programs it is easy to comprehend the large role students play in organizing and delivering the campus recreation program. Of necessity, in the beginning such programming was student run, and recreational programming today is still largely student run (Brown, 1998). Full-time university employees are hired to direct the overall program, set policy, and manage finances, but the actual development and delivery of programming is led by students. This fact is certainly celebrated by colleges and universities, where administrators wholly applaud the concept of "for the students, by the students." These programs allow students to gain valuable management and leadership skills. Clearly these students have their finger on the pulse of their classmates' interests when it comes to assessing programming. It is not uncommon to have 50 student leaders in both paid and volunteer positions as supervisors, officials, and event managers even within a small campus recreation program. Student leaders help govern the program as well, often by way of management teams and advisory councils that feed information through to the full-time university employees. For example, student-led committees dealing with areas such as intramurals, participant conduct, special events, clubs, and officials may report through the Student Supervisors' Council to the Campus Recreation Manager. Student input and leadership is the foundation of the program. In this case, student employees and supervisors, along with the Manager of Recreation, are likely to be heavily involved in the development and implementation of policy. The Director of Athletics and Recreation and any departmental coordinating council or management team will also play a role in confirming policy. An example of the administrative structure for a small college is presented in Figure 7.9.

Large Recreation Programs

The scope of a large campus recreation program can differ significantly from that of the small college presented above (Little & Guse, 1988). Many colleges and universities have a significant number of student, faculty and staff, and alumni populations. Some are housed in large urban centers. In such cases, the administration and operation of the Campus Recreation Department is generally large and complex, with many full-time professional staff and several programming divisions. Consider, for example, a large public university with an enrollment of 50,000 students. The Department of Recreation may be led by a Director who is the administrative head reporting to a Vice President or Provost responsible for Student Life (see Figure 7.10), or it may be led by an Associate Athletic Director responsible for recreation, in which case campus recreation is once again linked to the Department of Athletics (see Figure 7.11).

In either case, the structure of the Campus Recreation Department will be extensive and will be compartmentalized into several operational and management areas based on the defined programming. Students will

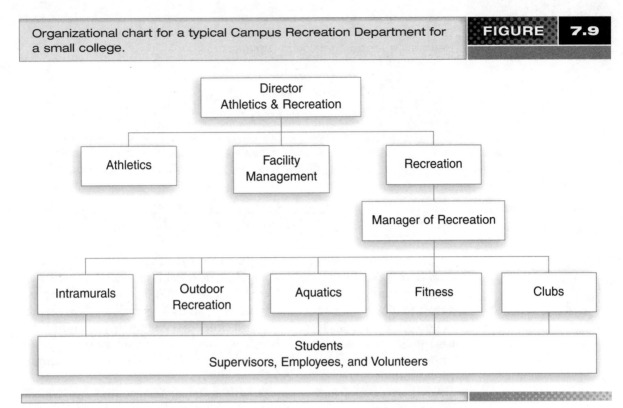

Organizational chart for a typical Campus Recreation Department for a small college.   **FIGURE 7.9**

help run the respective areas through advisory boards and committees, but a large professional staff will manage the department. Associate Directors responsible for different types of programming are common, each reporting directly to the head administrator. The different programming areas depend on the campus constituents and their needs and environment. The following major areas are most common: Intramural Sport, Extramural

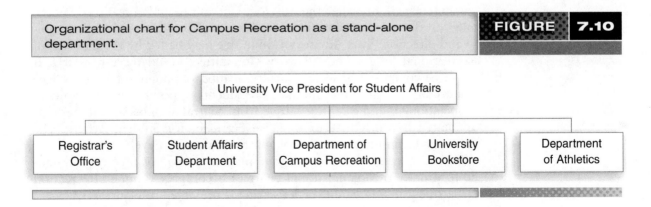

Organizational chart for Campus Recreation as a stand-alone department.   **FIGURE 7.10**

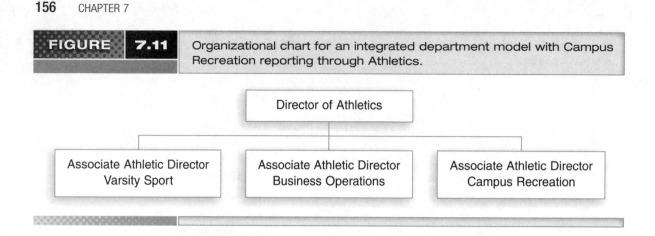

FIGURE 7.11 Organizational chart for an integrated department model with Campus Recreation reporting through Athletics.

Sport, Sport Camps, Outdoor Adventure, Sport Clubs, Fitness Activities, Special Events, Wellness Programming, Instructional Programming, Aquatics, Dance, Martial Arts, Family Recreation, Informal Recreation, Adapted Recreational Sports, Equipment Rentals, Facility Operations, Marketing, Technology, Business Operations, and Student Personnel. Depending on the scope of programming, it is not uncommon for each major area to operate as a separate department, with its own central office and administrative staff.

Advisory committees composed of students, faculty and staff members, and designated area (intramural sports, residence halls, fraternities and sororities) representatives provide input to a wide spectrum of programming and management issues. The deliberations of these committees contribute to policy development that might ultimately funnel to the Director of Recreational Sports, for example, policy regarding penalties imposed on teams that are late for or fail to show up for an intramural event. To erase such practices, policy is developed to fine the offending team and impose a ban on competition for teams with further offenses. Such policy is common in intramurals today. Another level of advisory committee, perhaps called the Advisory Committee on Recreational Sports, takes on the responsibility for overall issues of program and facility equity and direction. This Advisory Committee may be led by the Director of Recreational Sport. The Advisory Committee would meet regularly. It might be composed of several faculty members appointed by the College Faculty Senate, an equal number of students appointed by the Student Association(s), and a representative from central administration, perhaps appointed by the Office of the Vice President for Student Affairs. The Advisory Committee will also play a role in policy development, usually considering issues of overall program magnitude, equity, finance, and public relations. An organizational chart of a complex Campus Recreation Department in a large university setting is presented in Figure 7.12.

Organizational chart for a typical Campus Recreation Department for a large university.

FIGURE 7.12

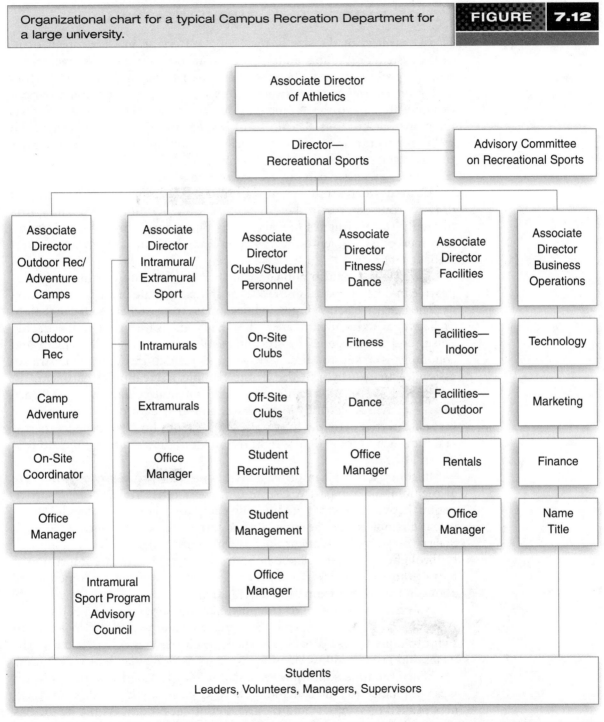

Programming in Campus Recreation

Regardless of the size of the Campus Recreation Department or its system of funding, an important issue on every campus involves the scope of programming. When the question of scope arises, almost without exception, the one-word answer is *extensive*. Campus recreation programs certainly live up to the "something for everyone" theme, with offerings ranging from intramural team sport leagues to instructional activities to wellness programs to events for special populations. Even small programs run by a single professional staff member with limited access to facilities can deliver extensive campus recreation programs.

Campus recreation began as intramural sport, and this area still draws strong interest today. Intramurals include not only team sports normally run in leagues but also individual sports. Intramurals encompass men-only, women-only, and coed leagues in virtually every sport of student interest.

Club sports are also popular. Clubs are student-run organizations that provide in-depth opportunities to learn and participate in a particular activity. The extensive array of possibilities ranges from archery to broomball to cycling to kayaking to ultimate frisbee. Each club is formed, developed, governed, and administered by student membership. Student leadership and continuity is a key to success. Rules and regulations and administrative assistance are usually provided by the Campus Recreation Department.

Instructional activities include classes in fitness, dance, yoga, "learn to . . ." activities, certification courses, and unstructured facility-use time for self-directed activities. Self-directed activities involve sport for fitness and fun, such as individual weight training or lane swimming, pickup basketball, or tennis.

In contrast to such informal activities are extramural sports, which are also gaining in popularity. *Extramural sport* refers to structured participation between groups on different campuses. For example, the intramural champion may be invited to a state or national event, or the Law Society may enroll a team at the Law Student Games Festival run annually throughout Canada. The emphasis is still on fun, but competition is part of the event. Participants may engage in each of the areas mentioned above in traditional team and individual sports.

Another popular area of campus recreation programming is the pool. Aquatic activities range from self-directed lane swimming to learn-to-swim to aqua-fitness programming. Aqua-fitness classes are taken in the water and usually follow the same formats as in regular fitness activities.

When the fitness industry exploded in North America in the 1970s, it was not long before the demand for aerobic classes, yoga, and personal fitness peaked on campus, and the trend continues today. As the public has become better informed of the health benefits and personal satisfaction associated with recreation and leisure activities, campus recreation has expanded its wellness offerings with such classes as aromatherapy, reflexology, tai chi, pilates, and power yoga.

Events for special populations have been developed to provide opportunities for students other than the traditional 18- to 24-year-old, able-bodied students. Events of interest to individuals with disabilities (for example, wheelchair basketball) or to populations of international students (for example, a cricket festival) are commonly offered.

Most of the activities and events described above take place indoors. The final area of programming in campus recreation involves outdoor recreation and adventure activities. Outdoor recreation involves activities in and sometimes trips to the great outdoors to take advantage of the lakes, mountains, and forest terrain. Cycling, kayaking, canoeing, hiking, mountain biking, and scuba diving are popular pursuits, with classes for beginners to advanced participants. Adventure activities usually step up the element of risk and include such activities as outdoor rock climbing, extreme triathlon, or open-water kayaking.

It is easy to understand why campus recreation programmers have coined the slogans "Something for everyone" and "We do more than just play games." They clearly live up to these mottoes, providing an extensive and diverse array of recreation and leisure-time-activity opportunities. The sheer breadth of programming can be a "pressure point" for the Campus Recreation Director. Policy issues also require the attention of campus recreation providers, and some key policy areas are discussed next.

Current Policy Areas

Policy is defined as those guidelines or procedures an organization follows in an effort to achieve the overall goals of the organization. Like any other department in an institution of higher education, the recreation unit must develop and update policy. The Campus Recreation Director will lead the debate on issues of policy, gathering input from both full- and part-time recreation employees and participants. Some issues will be impacted by policy enacted by the institution or the Athletic Department. Some of the current policy areas that undoubtedly impact campus recreation leaders today are discussed in this section.

Funding

The Sport Manager, and perhaps any kind of manager, is always concerned with finances. What are our sources of funding? Are we maximizing our avenues of funding, and are we spending efficiently? Is the cost–benefit ratio of our programming effective? Can we justify our choices? Certainly the campus recreation administrator must set effective financial management policy and is required to do so by the institution.

One regularly discussed issue involves financing a broad program. How do we define what activities or events should be offered, and how do we ensure the financial support exists in the form of human and physical resources to deliver an effective program? Remember, colleges and universities are about excellence, and the delivery of excellent service and programming is a cornerstone of the Campus Recreation Department's mandate. Campus recreation leaders deal with this issue by setting policy around the viability of program offerings. Program managers conduct research to gather participants' views on the effectiveness of their programs. The Director on a yearly basis then charts hard data on participant numbers in specific activities and longitudinal participant trends. This information feeds the decision-making process by providing the leaders with quantitative information about what is of interest to participants and how they view the quality of the current offerings. Then administrators consider other relevant parameters, such as availability of funds and facilities, in their decision-making formula. The Campus Recreation Director needs to research questions such as the following:

- Do we have the facilities to support a particular endeavor?
- Are we willing to enter into a "pay for play" schema in order to collect supplementary dollars to rent extra facilities?
- How much interest must support a decision to add programming on a "pay for play" basis?
- Which activities are core support activities, that is, activities covered entirely by the campus recreation budget?
- Which events are run on a break-even basis only, requiring registration dollars and other mechanisms of funding in order to support the program?

These types of questions, plus others specific to a particular institution, will help the Campus Recreation Department deal with and set financial management policy.

Competition for Limited Facilities

Campus recreation is often in competition with other programming. The departments of Physical Education, Athletics, and Summer Camps often vie for the same facility and equipment use. These competing units may even exist within the same department or faculty. When facilities are shared, it is important that leaders develop policy to ensure that rules exist to balance the needs of all areas. The Campus Recreation Director needs to take a proactive leadership role, advocating for the implementation of such boundaries. Otherwise, those interested in getting active will have no opportunity and will, instead, be forced to watch others perform. The recreation administrator needs to be armed with good information when policy is negotiated. Participant numbers, student numbers, activity interests and levels, and knowledge of user preferences are important. Setting procedures for priority status and for bumping programs is necessary to divert interruptions to planned activities and prevent major user conflicts.

Activity Trends

Defining which activities to offer, mentioned above as an issue in funding campus recreation programs, is an important area for policy development. Interest in specific leisure and recreation activities tends to blow with the wind. Fads and popular trends are normal in recreation, and they shift quickly. Campus recreation leaders need to have their fingers on the pulse of shifting interests, and they can gather the information they need through three important mechanisms. First, they can administer participant and non-participant questionnaires to collect interests, likes, and dislikes. Second, recreation department student employees can gather informal data about interests and patterns of behavior. Finally, sport leaders can observe behaviors to learn where people are recreating, what events are popular, what events fail to draw, what the competition is up to, and who is the competition. Through program evaluation managers can gather information needed to make appropriate change. This is critically important to meet the interests and needs of constituent groups, which are ever evolving and sometimes change radically. After all, the campus recreation program is nothing without participants.

Access

While having a large base of participants is fundamentally important to the mission of the campus recreation program, participation, normally referred to as *participant eligibility,* is restricted. The Campus Recreation Director and his advisors are required to set eligibility policy based upon their unique environment and departmental goals. Normally, intramural and extramural sports are accessible only to the institution's currently registered students (both full- and part-time). Instructional and special-event programming may be open to faculty and staff members and their families, alumni, and community members. Other programming may have a priority listing for first-come, first-served entrance into leagues or events. To manage access, administrators of the department set policy stipulating who is eligible for a particular program. They may go so far as to create a priority listing for some activities. They may close other activities to only a certain set of the possible participant constituents. Some participants

Mike Dunn

Director, The Ohio State University
Campus Recreation Program, Columbus, Ohio

I am the Director of one of the more comprehensive university recreational sports departments in the country. We operate facilities and programming for about 50,000 students on campus and about 25,000 faculty and staff members and their families. We currently manage four indoor facilities totaling about 47,000 square feet and 100 acres of outdoor space, including two parks. We have built a $140 million structure that is about 16,000 square feet. Another facility of about 80,000 square feet houses our outdoor adventure programs and includes two indoor multipurpose turf surfaces for indoor soccer and lacrosse.

Several policy issues confront campus recreation today. One of the most important department-wide policy issues we confront is the need to have a clear understanding of our mission, vision, and values. We have invested a significant amount of time developing each of these, and we've shared them widely across campus. In terms of establishing policies, we do a lot of benchmarking as well as visiting other campuses—particularly those in the Big Ten—to discover what is cutting edge around the country and around the state. In addition, we certainly keep in touch with our history. Some policies at Ohio State might not work at Michigan or Penn State, but they work at Ohio State because they've been around so long.

We're very conscious of our user group. Our University Recreational Sports Committee is made up of 13 voting members, including 6 undergraduate students, 2 graduate students, 2 faculty members selected by the faculty senate, and 2 staff members selected by the University Staff Advisory Council. None of these individuals are on our payroll. Each position on the committee is appointed for two years, with the terms staggered so that we lose half the people every year, which is problematic. It's a challenge to keep the new people informed about their responsibilities. The committee, which is student led, reviews all policies, old and new, that may need to be changed. Because we focus on customer service, we believe policies must be easy to understand. I think one of the greatest changes in the campus recreation setting over the past 10 to 15 years has been raising the bar of what customer service means.

One of the real challenges we're facing right now involves facility use. Students, faculty, and staff don't want to pay fees for facility use. However, we require students, faculty, and staff to pay significant fees to use our facilities. Through our market research we have been able to get that information out, but now we must change the culture of usership. We have facilities with state-of-the-art equipment, technology, and security, but users will have to be willing to pay for these improvements. A second challenge we face is helping students become empowered customers. We need to hear user voices to effectively deliver the programs they want in the facilities they need. We intend our facilities to set a standard for customer service.

Another major challenge we face is our increasingly diverse campus population. It's sometimes difficult to put policies in place that capably serve each of our populations: men and women; students, faculty and staff; younger students; older students; ethnically diverse students. We have 130 different cultures from around the world represented on this campus, so it's a challenge to serve everyone. For example, one difficult area has been the issue of same-sex partners. We were able to put in place a policy to ensure inclusivity for all members of our campus, regardless of gender, ethnicity, sexual orientation, or other grouping factors. We're very proud of this.

may enroll for free, while others pay differential fees depending on the mission of the Campus Recreation Department and of the university at large. It is important, however, that such policy exists and is clearly communicated to participant groups and staff.

In addition to establishing participant eligibility, the Campus Recreation Department must also establish and enforce rules limiting access to facilities and events. For example, employees must consistently check identification (ID) cards so only eligible participants enter a facility. Disagreement and confrontations often develop when participants forget their ID cards. Establishing clear policies for handling such situations helps maintain program safety and integrity.

Event Management

Recreation on today's university campus is often a huge enterprise, and consumers' expectations for excellence have kept pace with the diverse approach to programming and multimillion-dollar facilities. Students, their parents, and members of the community expect the highest quality in service and environment. To satisfy the expectations of all consumers, campus recreation administrators must ensure that policy regarding event management exists.

Recognizing the need to develop policy may seem like common sense. However, consider the roots of the campus recreation program: "for the students, by the students." Even today, mostly student employees and student volunteers deliver recreation programs. Therefore, it is important that full-time managers of the Campus Recreation Department establish policy to define standards of event management. These may involve time lines and standards of physical setup, expectations of student managers and officials, rules for the use of logos and department letterhead, requirements concerning marketing and sponsorship, guidelines for decision making and problem solving, emergency-response plans and other items related to managing risk, and media liaison and reporting of results. Of course, other issues connected to event management and requiring policy development will arise. Thus risk management becomes particularly important to an effective and efficient Campus Recreation Department.

Risk Management

Campus Recreation Directors must be concerned with risk management (Barcelona, 2004). Of course, some risk is associated with crossing the street or playing a game of baseball. One may be run over by a speeding car or hit in the head by the baseball. Society attempts to minimize the possibility of being run over by a car by posting speed limits, building sidewalks, and setting up traffic lights and stop signs. Similarly, recreation administrators attempt to minimize risk in physical activity by requiring participants to wear protective equipment, ensuring that participants are taught proper techniques, and strictly enforcing safety rules. If the baseball player is hit in the head with a ball, it is hoped that the helmet she wears will protect her. It is impossible to eliminate risk; the challenge is managing the risk. In other words, the recreation professional has the responsibility to set up and deliver programs reducing overt risks and communicating other levels of risks to participants. According to Miller (1998), to achieve this, policy is required to

- develop a written risk-management plan to show evidence of proactive prevention
- keep accurate and detailed records on participants and injuries that occur
- ensure that the rules of play are properly enforced and communicated
- train and certify leaders in the areas they teach and supervise
- ensure proper supervision of areas needing supervision and restrict access to some unsupervised areas
- check equipment regularly to ensure it is in good working order
- require paperwork that provides for lists of participants, identification information, and possibly health information
- develop and communicate emergency-response procedures
- train event leaders in first aid and cardiopulmonary resuscitation (CPR)
- develop and implement informed-consent forms and health-related questionnaires for all but the very minimal risk activities

For example, an aerobics class should be led by a trained, certified instructor. He should have a class list, and participants should be required to complete a medical screening questionnaire such as the Physical Activity Readiness Questionnaire (PAR-Q) to identify any potential risk factors. In another activity, such as an outdoor adventure trip in white-water kayaking, medical clearance may be required, and program leaders will use waiver forms to have participants acknowledge the risks involved and to take responsibility for such risk. Waivers and informed-consent forms are commonly employed and should be a required component of the policy surrounding risk management for the Campus Recreation Department, especially where off-site travel or high-risk activities are involved.

PAR-Q
www.phac-aspc.gc.ca/sth-evs/english/parq.htm

Sport Management Resources
www.sportsmanagementresources.com/library/participant-waivers

Medical Issues

Pre-activity screening is important when dealing with medical conditions. However, it will not prepare employees in a recreation department for the acute medical emergencies that may result during sporting events and other physical activities. Inevitably, one player will step on another's foot while playing intramural basketball and sprain or break an ankle. The Campus Recreation Department must have set policy on procedures to help the injured participant. Having emergency supplies on-site is important. Having an emergency action plan and trained supervisors who know what to do is even more important. Some activities require collecting and keeping information on-site in the event of an emergency. The group leaders on a daylong cycling tour should have information on a participant who is allergic to insect stings, including medical insurance information and contact numbers and names. Medical information needs to be collected and collated into a manageable, perhaps laminated form that can be tucked into a sidesaddle or a fanny pack. Having on-site information and knowing what to do in the event of an emergency are critical areas for policy development and a clear responsibility of the Recreation Department in terms of employee training.

Access for People with Disabilities

The most critical issue with respect to recreational opportunities for students with disabilities is gaining an accurate demographic picture of who has needs and defining those needs (Frost, 1987). To achieve this end, campus recreation professionals must set policy enabling the collection of important information regarding maximizing opportunity for students with disabilities. This is readily achieved through a Disabled Student Advisory Council, which sets a schedule for defining appropriate activities, defines a mechanism for publicizing activities and facility schedules, creates opportunities for training with respect to facilities and equipment, and provides ongoing leadership in the assessment of the effectiveness of the overall effort. Colleges and universities across North America must work harder to provide recreational programming designed specifically for individuals with disabilities (Anonymous, 2006).

SUMMARY

The delivery of recreational programming is thriving on college campuses. Universities have embraced the notion that higher education involves much more than lectures and examinations and that the quality of student life is an important concern. The Campus Recreation Department helps to further the overall goals of the institution by offering student activities that promote health, happiness, and affiliation. The diversity of programming is often extensive and usually student led. As a result of the considerable recreational scheduling on the college campus, several organizations have been established at the community, state or provincial, and national levels to promote recreation and offer recreation leaders sources of both professional development and practical resources. Two of the largest national-level associations are NIRSA in the United States and the Intramural Recreation Program Advisory Committee of CAHPERD, formerly known as CIRA. Both comprise elected recreation officials from state or provincial associations, many of whom are campus recreation professionals.

The Campus Recreation Department can be organized as a unit with a small number of professional staff, housed within the university Athletics Department, or it can function as a stand-alone unit within the Student Affairs operation of the university, with many departments led by recreation professionals employed on a full-time basis. In either case, the organizational structure will rely on an extensive group of student employees and student volunteers who help to deliver a vast array of programming. Recreation professionals manage the affairs of the department by defining mission, vision, and goals; by managing facility operation and finances; and by setting and enforcing policy. Many policy areas will draw the attention of the Campus Recreation Department leaders, from defining how the unit is funded and maximizing funding sources to program offerings and participant eligibility to access for people with disabilities. The Campus Recreation Department plays an extensive role in the delivery of recreational opportunities for the constituents on the modern university campus.

CASE STUDY — *Facility Development*

As the newly hired Assistant Director of Campus Recreation at Big State University, your first assignment is to upgrade program offerings in your new facility. You have the following facilities:

- 1 gym—big enough for eight basketball courts
- 1 pool measuring 25 meters
- 1 cardiovascular room with treadmills and stationary bikes
- 1 weight room with free weights and a weight-machine system
- 2 activity rooms with 10-foot ceilings
- 4 multipurpose grass fields

Your student body enrollment of 18,000 includes many nontraditional students, and residence halls coexist with fraternities and sororities on campus.

1. What programs would you set up? Times? Leagues versus tournaments? How would you decide which activities to drop and which to add?

2. How would you go about getting funding for your programs? Whom would you ask?

3. Where would you get building and program staff? What would you include in their training program?

4. How would you ensure that your programs and facilities fairly and effectively provide for all your users?

5. You wish to ensure that your programs meet local and national standards. Which organizations would you join, and how would you go about ensuring that your programming reflected the best practices around the country?

CHAPTER QUESTIONS

1. Using the Internet, search for the committee structure of NIRSA or the recreational component of CAHPERD. Build an organizational chart of the committees showing how they link together and where they report. How are the ideas generated and the problems solved at the committee level turned into policy? Trace and describe one example of such policy development by reading the committee meeting minutes as posted on the Web.

2. Investigate the campus recreation program at your institution. How is it structured, and how is policy developed? Who has the authority to make decisions? How is the program financed? How would you go about creating a new program activity?

3. Varsity athletics and campus recreation often compete for facilities and resources on campus. Develop an organizational structure with the best chance of downplaying this internal rivalry.

REFERENCES

Anonymous. (2006). Accessibility in campus recreation programs. *Palaestra, 22,* 6.

Barcelona, B. (2004). Looking beyond the jockocracy. *Parks & Recreation, 39*(1), 22–29.

Brown, S. C. (1998). Campus recreation. In J. B. Parks, B. Zanger, & J. Quarterman (Eds.), *Contemporary sport management* (pp. 139–154). Champaign, IL: Human Kinetics.

CAHPERD. (2007). Physical and health education. Retrieved August 21, 2007, from www.cahperd.ca.

CIRA. (2002). Canada's physical activity guides for children and youth. Retrieved January 3, 2002, from www.intramurals.ca/cira/overview.htm.

Colgate, J. A. (1978). *Administration of intramural and recreational activities: Everyone can participate.* New York: John Wiley.

DU. (2007). Campus recreation services. Retrieved August 23, 2007, from http://depts.drew.edu/crs.

Frost, R. L. (1987). Campus recreation and the handicapped students: Attitude and opportunity. *NIRSA Journal, 11*(3), 35–36, 50.

Kane, M. J. (2007). Sociological aspects of sport. In J. B. Parks, J. Quarterman, & L. Thibault (Eds.), *Contemporary sport management* (pp. 389–413). Champaign, IL: Human Kinetics.

Langley, T. D., & Hawkins, J. D. (1999). *Administration for exercise-related professions.* Englewood, CO: Morton.

Leppel, K. (2006). The impact of sport and non-sport activities on college persistence of freshmen. *College Student Retention, 7*(3-4), 165–188.

Little, S. L., & Guse, D. (1988). Campus recreation services: An enterprise in higher education. *Journal of Physical Education, Recreation & Dance, 59*(8), 62–63.

Melendez, M. C. (2006). The influence of athletic participation on the college adjustment of freshmen and sophomore student athletes. *College Student Retention, 8*(1), 39–55.

Miller, R. D. (1998). Campus recreation risk management. *NIRSA Journal, 22*(3), 23–25.

Mueller, P., & Reznik, W. (1979). *Intramural-recreational sports programming and administration* (5th ed.). New York: John Wiley.

NIRSA. (2007). Mission and more. Retrieved May 7, 2007, from www.nirsa.org/about/mission.

O'Dell, I., & Ross, C. (1996). Campus recreation for families. *NIRSA Journal, 20*(3), 10.

OSU. (2007). Retrieved May 7, 2007, from http://rec sports.osu.edu/contactus_mission.asp.

Presbrey, F. (1901). *Athletics at Princeton.* New York: Author.

QU. (2007). Campus recreation. Retrieved May 7, 2007, from www.goldengaels.com/recreation/index.html.

Smith, P. (1991). Positioning recreational sport in higher education. In R. L. Boucher & W. J. Weese (Eds.), *Management of recreational sports in higher education* (pp. 5–12). Madison, WI: WCB Brown & Benchmark.

Southern Polytechnic State University. (2007). Recreation mission statement. Retrieved May 17, 2007, from www.spsu.edu/home/sports/index.html.

UCLA. (2007). Recreation department mission statement. Retrieved May 17, 2007, from www.recreation.ucla.edu/recreate/index.aspx.

University of Idaho. (2007). Campus recreation mission statement. Retrieved May 17, 2007, from www.campusrec.uidaho.edu/Mission.

Van Mierlo, P. (1996). Wellness: Bridging the gap between departments, community and campus recreation. *NIRSA Journal, 20*(2), 16, 18–19.

Zhang, J. J., DeMichele, D. J., & Connaughton, D. P. (2004). Job satisfaction among mid-level collegiate campus recreation program administrators. *Journal of Sport Behavior, 27*(2), 184–212.

8

INTERCOLLEGIATE ATHLETICS

INTRODUCTION

Click on a college website, open a newspaper, or turn on the television and you will immediately see the interest in North American college athletics. National championship event titles such as "The Final Four" are known worldwide. The spectacle of college sport will likely continue to grow and endure the test of time, due in part to the mass media's role in strengthening its appeal by bringing events and personalities directly into our homes. The appeal is strongest in the United

States, but colleges and universities in many countries around the world also sponsor competitive athletic opportunities for their students. In the United States and Canada, colleges and universities support extensive competitive athletic programs. This type of competition is commonly known as *intercollegiate athletics.*

The appeal of intercollegiate athletics is unquestionable and at the same time paradoxical. On one hand, the loyalty of cheering college students, with painted faces, fully caught up in the excitement of events, with intense rivalries, sometimes with national distinction at stake, is all completely understandable. But viewed from another perspective, intercollegiate athletics is woven with problems. From the consumer viewpoint, the quality of play might not compare with professional leagues. In addition, a long history of abuses, excesses, and cheating has plagued intercollegiate athletics, challenging the very core concepts of sport in general and amateurism specifically. Ideals such as fairness, honesty, character development, competitive balance, and the dual role of the student-athlete have been questioned. In some cases the very existence of such an enterprise in connection with an educational institution has been called into question. Some of these issues, along with the huge costs of programming, have resulted in some schools dropping programs. *The Chronicle of Higher Education* reported that 60 Division I sports teams have been dropped between 2000 and 2002. For example, Iowa State dropped baseball and men's swimming in 2001, and Massachusetts eliminated seven sports in March 2002 (*Waterloo-Cedar Falls Courier,* 2003). Recently James Madison University dropped 10 (7 men's and 3 women's) of its 28 varsity teams for Title IX compliance (Brainard, 2006). Despite these issues, consumer attraction for intercollegiate athletics continues to grow as evidenced by levels of ticket sales and television revenues (Kahn, 2006).

"Growth" might serve as the perfect one-word descriptor of 20th-century intercollegiate athletics in the United States. Interest in supporting the local team seemed to build on its own momentum to a point where now more than a thousand colleges and universities offer intercollegiate sport in the United States alone. Fueled by this momentum, the sheer magnitude of intercollegiate athletics may be one reason for its enduring and expanding appeal.

Different perspectives provide different insights into this phenomenal growth. A historian might suggest that the leadership of President Theodore Roosevelt and a group of college presidents provided the original momentum for the growth of college athletics when they intervened in college football to promote more extensive rules and safety requirements in 1905. A sociologist might point to the place of sport in American society and the feelings of personal success and hometown pride when the local team wins (Ingham & Loy, 1993). A psychologist might point to improved psychological health with individuals identifying strongly with a local sport team (Wann, 2006). The economist might suggest that colleges and universities need the revenue generated by athletics, whether from television, recruiting students, or developing and managing the image of the institution. Other viewpoints exist, but one thing is sure: intercollegiate athletics is a huge component of the sport industry of North America.

This chapter focuses on the many differences between the governance of organizations delivering collegiate sport in the United States (the NCAA and the National Association of Intercollegiate Athletics [NAIA]) and Canada (the CIS and the Canadian Collegiate Athletic Association [CCAA]) such as size, financial capacity, committee structures, scope of operations, sports supported, rules and philosophical underpinnings, among others. Distinctions also exist in the governance and policy development between collegiate sport organizations in other countries around the world. Although collegiate sport exists in hundreds of countries worldwide, and athletes from these organizations represent their countries at the World University Games (Federation Internationale du Sport Universitaire [FISU] Games; see Chapter 9), their college sport programs may differ substantially from those in the United States and Canada. For instance, the British Universities Sporting Association (BUSA) has over 150 members while University Sport New Zealand (USNZ) has 10 universities in its membership. Some countries within Africa and South America may have very limited sport offerings, with heavier emphasis on sports considered unknown or less popular in North America such as footvolley (mix of football and volleyball), jujitsu, football (soccer), biribol (volleyball in a swimming pool), and running events. The big business nature of American collegiate sport fueled by considerable fan interest and television reach (and revenue) is not necessarily mirrored in other collegiate sport settings around the world. The organizations that manage sport, creating the governance structures and policy for operations are similarly unique to the settings, political environment, and historical events of the location. Therefore, the umbrella organizations delivering collegiate sport in countries around the world vary significantly in their size, capacity, sport programs, rules and regulations, and structures.

Let's turn our attention now to the governance of collegiate athletics in North America. Exactly how is it organized? How are rules made, and who decides the issues of the day? A brief look at the history and evolution of intercollegiate sport will answer those questions.

History of North American Intercollegiate Athletics

Often the largest and most popular events are borne of the humblest beginnings, and this is exactly the case with intercollegiate athletics. The idea for athletic competition did not come from educators, nor was it a part of the curriculum. Rather, it originated with the student body.

The Beginning

College athletics began as recreational activities organized by students to meet their needs for both physical and social activities (Davenport, 1985). Although faculty members were not involved, they accepted the idea that students needed some diversions from classroom activity. It is easy to understand how college athletics developed. Two groups of students got together to play a game in the late afternoon sun; later, over dinner, the victors boasted of their success. Perhaps their classmates listened in and decided to show up for the next game to cheer on their friends. Next, for even more bragging rights, the victorious group then challenged the college in the next town. This, basically, is the story of the first intercollegiate competition, when a crew (rowing) race was organized between Harvard and Yale in 1852 (Scott, 1951). Interestingly, this first intercollegiate contest had a corporate sponsor. The Boston, Concord & Montreal Railroad Company sponsored the competition as a means to publicize their business (Dealy, 1990). Of course, the railroad provided the only means of transportation to the Harvard versus Yale rowing contest: The inaugural college athletic event in the United States had exclusive sponsorship (Barr, 2005)! From this original event came other ideas about sport competitions, and challenges between colleges soon became commonplace.

Original Events

The next organized intercollegiate activity was baseball. The first baseball game was between Amherst College and Williams College in 1859 (Davenport, 1985). Such student-led activities gained significant interest among spectators and some notice from college faculty and administration. Administration noticed that winning athletic contests helped recruit students to campus and provide some positive attention for the college. Only 10 years later, on November 6, 1869, the first intercollegiate football game was played between Rutgers and Princeton (Davenport, 1985). Challenges for competition became more and more common. This growth was not always viewed positively, however. Concerns by administrators about the unproductive nature of athletic contests were also common, and more than a little resistance was voiced against the emerging popularity of intercollegiate football. This opposition may have grown out of the deeply religious roots of American higher education, or the concern that students would become soft from more play than work (Gerdy, 1997). In 1873, Cornell University President Andrew White, citing his disdain for traveling 400 miles, turned down an invitation from University of Michigan students asking the Cornell team to attend a football competition in Cleveland (Rudolph, 1990).

Despite the attitude of some university administrators, tremendous interest in collegiate football was evident by the 1890s. A win-at-any-cost mentality developed, and to please the members of the overflowing college grandstands, players and coaches without affiliation to the college were inserted in the lineup. Street brawls became common after games. "In 1893 New York was thrown into a virtual frenzy by the annual Thanksgiving game between Yale and Princeton. Hotels were jammed. . . .

Clergymen cut short their Thanksgiving Day services in order to get off to the game in time. Clearly, football had arrived" (Rudolph, 1990, p. 375). Sports were becoming so popular on college campuses as to be likened to small business enterprises (Davenport, 1985).

Need to Control

Up to this point, college athletic activities were organized and operated by students, and merely tolerated by the university administration. But it was becoming evident that athletic teams served as a unifying function among members of the college. Heroes emerged; public interest grew, as did the public relations opportunities. All of these factors, along with the potential for revenue generation, resulted in university administrations changing their position. College presidents and their inner circles realized successful sports teams could generate additional resources for their cash-strapped institutions, as well as draw both political favor and alumni support. As Gerdy (1997, p. 29) comments, "college presidents believed that a successful football program legitimized their institution as a major, big-time university." These factors changed the administration's outlook on formerly student-run activities. College administrators, especially college faculty members, moved to take over management and control. Athletic personnel as we know them today did not exist.

On January 11, 1895, a historic meeting of faculty representatives was held in Chicago to develop eligibility and participation rules. This was the inaugural meeting of the Intercollegiate Conference of Faculty Representatives, forerunner to the Big Ten (Davenport, 1985). Soon thereafter, personnel in other regions of the United States also met and copied many of the rules developed at the initial meeting. Faculty exercised control over schedule development and equipment purchase. Playing rules and regulations were enforced, and some eligibility and financial restrictions were put in place.

At about this same time, an alarming number of serious football injuries were reported as a result of popular practices such as gang tackling and mass formations. In 1905, 18 athletes were reported killed and 143 seriously injured while playing collegiate football (Gerdy, 1997), prompting President Theodore Roosevelt to intervene. He called representatives from Harvard, Yale, and Princeton to two White House conferences to discuss the problems. At the request of Chancellor Henry M. Mac-Cracken of New York University, representatives of 13 institutions met in New York City in December 1905 (NCAA, 2007a). The original intent of this meeting and a follow-up meeting later that month was to resolve issues related to football. However, a much larger result occurred. More university administrators shared concerns, and as a result, 62 members founded the Intercollegiate Athletic Association of the United States

(IAAUS) to oversee and regulate all college sports. The association was officially constituted on March 31, 1906.

At the same time, north of the U. S. border, Canadian colleges were experiencing growth and interest in intercollegiate activities. In response to this growing need, in the very same year the IAAUS was constituted, the Canadian Interuniversity Athletic Union–Central (CIAU–Central) was formed. This association comprised faculty representatives from universities in Ontario and Quebec. Rapid growth, facility development, and the need for rules and regulations dominated CIAU–Central's initial agenda.

Evolution of College Sport Organizations

The development of the IAAUS and the CIAU–Central represented pivotal moments in the history of North American intercollegiate athletics and marked the beginning of an era in which collegiate sport was understood to require rules, regulations, supervision, and philosophical direction. In the beginning, rules compliance was expected but not actively enforced by either organization. The intent was to ensure that all collegiate athletic activities were managed ethically, with a balanced playing field, in keeping with the dignity and high purpose of colleges and universities (Applin, 1979). Faculty members in physical education departments were hired to coach teams and administer programs.

In 1910, the IAAUS renamed itself the National Collegiate Athletic Association (NCAA). During its initial years, the NCAA was composed only of faculty members from its affiliate institutions. It was a discussion group and rules-making body. Collegiate sports continued to grow, and more rules committees were formed. The evolution of the NCAA continued, and in 1921, the first national championship was held in track and field (NCAA, 2007a). Other sports and more championships were gradually added over the years. The growth in championships and members, along with reported abuses in recruiting and financial aid, resulted in a crisis after World War II. Television became a concern, along with attendance and the enticement of student-athletes. It became apparent that collegiate athletics was becoming a business. Full-time professional leadership was needed, and the NCAA hired Walter Byers as its first Executive Director in 1951. A national headquarters was then established in Kansas City, and work proceeded rapidly to set policy to regulate the most pressing issues of the association. By 1973, the membership was divided into three legislative and competitive divisions (Divisions I, II, and III) based on institutional size. Subsequently, Division I members voted to subdivide football into Divisions I-A and I-AA. Today, the NCAA is staffed by more than 320 full-time employees and runs 38 national championships (19 for men and 19 for women) in 22 sports; its National Office is located in Indianapolis (NCAA, 2007a).

In Canada, the same period (1906–1919) saw major growth for athletics on university campuses; after World War II, conditions became relatively stable (CIS, 2007a). The CIAU–Central existed until 1955. Its main purpose was to develop common intercollegiate athletics rules and regulations. At that time regional organizations in one to four provincial areas emerged. For instance, the Atlantic Intercollegiate Athletic Association (AIAA) governed intercollegiate competition for the four Atlantic Provinces (New Brunswick, Prince Edward Island, Nova Scotia, and Newfoundland). Other organizations governed sport in Ontario and Quebec (Ontario–Quebec University Athletic Association and Ottawa–St. Lawrence Athletic Association) and in Western Canada (Western Intercollegiate Athletic Association), including British Columbia, Alberta, Saskatchewan, and Manitoba. Eventually the need for a truly national association became apparent, and the Canadian Interuniversity Athletic Union (CIAU) was reconstituted in 1961. The CIAU sustained gradual growth, moved to a central office at the National Sport Centre in Ottawa, and gained membership from all Canadian universities, a modest group of 49 institutions. In June 2001, the CIAU changed its name to Canadian Interuniversity Sport (CIS). The organization is still housed in Canada's capital city of Ottawa, and a small staff of eleven employees manages 19 National Championships and special events (CIS, 2007b).

Growth of Women's Sport

As women's intercollegiate sport in Canada grew and expanded, it needed organization. In 1923, the Women's Intercollegiate Athletic Union (WIAU) was established to oversee and provide programming for women's competition in Ontario, and the Ontario–Quebec Women's Intercollegiate Athletics (OQWIA) coordinated programming for female students in these regions. These two associations joined in 1971 to form the Ontario Women's Intercollegiate Athletic Association (OWIAA). Other regions gradually added women's programming as well. Much later, in 1997, the OWIAA merged with the men's association Ontario University Athletics Association (OUAA) to form one association, Ontario University Athletics (OUA), to provide better services for delivering college athletics to both female and male athletes (OUA, 2007).

www

Ontario University Athletics
http://oua.ca/about

In the United States, unfortunately, female participation in intercollegiate sport was conspicuously missing in the beginning. Until the mid-20th century, little in the way of formal competition existed for women until 1971, when women physical educators established the Association for Intercollegiate Athletics for Women (AIAW). Several national championships were sponsored, and women's intercollegiate athletics gained momentum, quickly becoming an important component of college athletics. This interest prompted the NCAA to expand its structure to include programming for women, only 10 years after the AIAW had been established. The first NCAA programming for women occurred in 1980 when Divisions II and III took a leadership role by adding 10 national championships for women. This historic action prompted an extensive governance plan to be passed in 1981–1982, including 19 additional women's championships, along with services and representation in decision making for administrators of women's athletics.

The circumstances surrounding the original programming for women in the NCAA were unfortunate, to say the least. The AIAW–NCAA merger was essentially a hostile takeover. The NCAA enticed women's athletic departments to join by subsidizing team expenses to national championships and increasing television coverage for women's events (Hult, 1994). Such enticements resulted in an immediate 20 percent drop in AIAW memberships and even higher decreases in championship participation (Barr, 2005). With the absence of a television contract (a substantial component of AIAW revenues) and a failed lawsuit against the NCAA, the AIAW had no ability to compete and therefore dissolved in 1982.

Historically Black Colleges and Universities (HBCUs)

In the United States, Historically Black Colleges and Universities (HBCUs) are liberal arts institutions that were established before 1964 with the intention of serving the African American community. Those institutions with large African American student populations but founded after the *Brown v. Board of Education* ruling that outlawed racial segregation are known as "predominantly black," but not "historically black."

According to the White House Initiative on Historically Black Colleges and Universities,

> HBCUs are a source of accomplishment and great pride for the African American community as well as the entire nation. The Higher Education Act of 1965, as amended, defines an HBCU as: "any historically black college or university that was established prior to 1964, whose principal mission was, and is, the education of black Americans, and that is accredited by a nationally recognized accrediting agency or association determined by the Secretary [of Education] to be a reliable authority as to the quality of training offered or is, according to such an agency or association, making reasonable progress toward accreditation." HBCUs offer all students, regardless of race, an opportunity to develop their skills and talents. These institutions train young people who go on to serve domestically and internationally in the professions as entrepreneurs and in the public and private sectors. (U.S. Department of Education, 2007)

Today, 103 HBCUs in 23 states are divided into four categories: 40 four-year public institutions, 49 four-year private institutions, 11 two-year public institutions, and 3 two-year private institutions. Over the years, HBCU graduates have gone on to make names for themselves in all spectrums of society including athletics, where some notable graduates include NFL MVP Steve McNair (Alcorn State University) and Eddie Robinson (Grambling State University), the winningest coach in college football history. HBCUs are affiliated with both the NCAA and the NAIA.

Although the name Historically Black Colleges and Universities might lead one to believe that only black student-athletes attend HBCUs, today their student populations, while predominantly black, do contain a more representative picture of society. As such, most HBCU athletic mission statements emphasize this diverse aspect to their population. For example, Alcorn State University's athletic mission statement is the following:

> Alcorn State University is committed to providing a broad-based program that prepares student-athletes to succeed in their chosen field of study and to excel in their chosen sport. The mission of the Athletics Department is to provide equal opportunity for a diverse student population through competitive programs that encourage integrity, personal development, leadership, and teamwork at the highest level of academic and athletic excellence. This quest for academic excellence undergirds the University's mission of teaching, research and service through strong academics support programs for student–athletes and through the participation of all student–athletes in community service activities which lead to the development of competent, civic-minded graduates. (Alcorn State University, 2007)

However, in comparison to more "traditional" colleges and universities, HBCU athletic budgets are much lower. In 2006, Delaware State was the only black school that ranked among the top 200 (out of 331) athletic budgets in Division I (Jones, 2007). Some small schools, such as Division I-AA Southern University, rely heavily on one or two games to bring the majority of the revenue for their athletic departments, usually an annual game between two schools, or what is termed "a guarantee game," where small schools travel to face national powerhouses. While this game usually guarantees a substantial payday for the small school, it is hard to compete against more resource-rich institutions.

Alcorn State Sports
http://alcornsports.com/home.php

Governance

The growth, popularity, and subsequent reform in college sport dictated a more-formal approach to managing and governing intercollegiate athletics. The NCAA is the largest and oldest organization formed for this purpose, and its history is closely intertwined with the growth of intercolle-

National Junior College Athletic Association

www.njcaa.org

National Christian College Athletic Association

www.thenccaa.org/news.html

giate athletics. However, other organizations also govern intercollegiate athletics. In the United States, the NAIA is another umbrella organization of like-minded institutions, often compared in philosophical orientation to NCAA Division II schools. The National Junior College Athletic Association (NJCAA) and the National Small College Athletic Association (NSCAA) each exist to oversee the athletic programs of junior and small colleges, respectively. Finally, the National Christian College Athletic Association (NCCAA) administers intercollegiate competition for Christian schools.

Canada, with approximately one-tenth the population and a fraction of the number of universities and colleges found in the United States, has two divisions of institutions of higher education: degree-granting *universities* that offer three- and four-year undergraduate and graduate programs, and diploma-granting *colleges* that offer two- and three-year programs. (Colleges in Canada are comparable to technical schools in the United States.) Intercollegiate athletics is organized and governed by these two classifications: CIS is the organization that manages intercollegiate athletics for degree-granting universities, and the CCAA oversees intercollegiate competition for diploma-granting colleges across the nation. Following is an in-depth look at the actual structures of some of these organizations and the governance of intercollegiate athletics throughout North America.

National Collegiate Athletic Association

National Collegiate Athletic Association

www.ncaa.org

The NCAA has some global recognition, thanks to television and marketing efforts. It is a voluntary association of colleges and universities, run by a President and staffed by several hundred employees. Members of the NCAA consider issues and policies affecting more than one region, thus making them national issues.

Mission. The NCAA is devoted to the expert administration of intercollegiate athletics for its membership. The purpose of the NCAA is to provide programming and deliver national championships for intercollegiate athletes. According to the NCAA (2007a), the goals of the organization are very specific to the student-athlete: to promote college athletics, to protect the interest of the athlete by ensuring fairness and integrity, to prepare the athlete for a lifetime of leadership, and to provide funding to help accomplish these goals. The association supplies a governance structure to provide rules and establish consistent policy through which all NCAA member institutions operate. NCAA literature states eight specific purposes, as presented in Figure 8.1.

Financials. The NCAA is a nonprofit organization, yet it is also a multi-million-dollar enterprise. Given the breadth of focus described above, it requires substantial revenue to fund an incredibly wide-ranging agenda.

Purposes of the NCAA.	FIGURE	8.1

- To initiate, stimulate and improve intercollegiate athletics programs for student-athletes and to promote and develop educational leadership, physical fitness, athletics excellence and athletics participation as a recreational pursuit.

- To uphold the principle of institutional control of, and responsibility for, all intercollegiate sports in conformity with the constitution and bylaws of the Association.

- To encourage its members to adopt eligibility rules to comply with satisfactory standards of scholarship, sportsmanship and amateurism.

- To formulate, copyright and publish rules of play governing intercollegiate athletics.

- To preserve intercollegiate athletics records.

- To supervise the conduct of, and to establish eligibility standards for, regional and national athletics events under the auspices of the Association.

- To legislate, through bylaws or by resolutions of a Convention, upon any subject of general concern to the members related to the administration of intercollegiate athletics.

- To study in general all phases of competitive intercollegiate athletics and establish standards whereby the colleges and universities of the United States can maintain their athletics programs on a high level.

Source: NCAA (2007b). Reprinted with permission.

It is in a healthy financial situation, reporting revenues over expenses of $13.6 million in 2007. Revenues are generated from television rights, championships, royalties, investments, sales and services, and philanthropic contributions. The association's expenses include championships, special events, revenue sharing, association-wide programs, management, and the NCAA Foundation (NCAA, 2007b). At the end of 2006, the NCAA held net assets in excess of $280 million.

Membership. The NCAA comprises member institutions whose representatives retain voting privileges on setting policy and directing the future of intercollegiate athletics. In 2006 the organization reported that 1,287 institutions, conferences, and organizations were members of the NCAA (NCAA, 2007c).

It is important to note that NCAA members are institutions, not individuals. Institutions are afforded membership by virtue of their mission in higher education, along with other membership criteria. All sizes and types of institutions are eligible for membership, as long as they are accredited by the recognized agency within their academic region, offer at least one sport for both men and women in each of the three traditional sport seasons, abide by the rules and regulations set forth by the NCAA (as certified by the Chief Executive Officer [CEO]), and agree to cooperate fully with NCAA enforcement programs (NCAA, 2007c).

NCAA member institutions belong to one of three divisions labeled Division I, II, or III. The main criteria used for establishing an institution's divisional classification are size, number of sports offered, financial base and sport-sponsorship minimums, focus of programming, football and basketball scheduling requirements, and availability of athletic grants-in-aid (Staurowsky & Abney, 2007; NCAA, 2007c). Division I (DI) football institutions are further subdivided into I–FBS (Football Bowl Subdivision) and I–FCS (Football Championship Subdivision): Division I–FBS programs must meet minimum paid-football attendance criteria. Institutions competing in Division I in sports other than football are categorized simply as Division I. Just over 1,025 institutional members are divided fairly evenly among each division: DI has 326, DII has 281, and DIII has 420 (NCAA, 2007d). The composition of the NCAA in each of its membership categories is presented in Table 8.1.

Association-Wide and Division-Specific Structure

As with most other self-governing organizations, the NCAA began and existed for many years with a governance structure allotting one vote to each member institution. An annual national convention debated issues

TABLE 8.1   Member composition of the NCAA.

	I-FBS	I-FCS	Division I	Total	Division II	Division III	Total
Active	119	116	91	326	281	420	1027
Provisional	0	0	1	1	15	21	37
Voting Conference	11	10	10	31	22	43	96
Nonvoting Conference	0	3	18	21	1	13	35
Corresponding							15
Affiliated							72
TOTAL							1282

Source: NCAA (2003e). Reprinted with permission.

and voted on matters of policy. This organizational structure was reformed on August 1, 1997. In general, the reform provided each division greater autonomy for managing division-specific matters and gave university presidents more involvement in and control of developing legislation. For instance, in Division I the one-vote-per-institution principle was replaced with a system based on conference representation. Rather than every member voting on each issue at an annual convention, an 18-member Board of Directors is charged with managing all legislation, and one elected member from each conference votes on behalf of the conference. Members of the Board of Directors are institutional CEOs or college presidents, a move made, as mentioned above, to ensure more presidential involvement in intercollegiate athletics. Of course, the Board of Directors is not able to complete all of the Division's business.

Divisional governance structure. Reporting to the Board of Directors is the Division I Management Council. It comprises both athletic administrators and faculty athletic representatives, academics from the college faculty appointed to provide an academic perspective to athletic policy making. The Division I Management Council has two main functions. First, it receives the reports of the Division I cabinets (groups responsible for specific areas of Division I activities). Second, it serves in an advisory capacity for the Board of Directors, funneling information from the cabinets and committees up to the board. Cabinets, which report to the Management Council, comprise either 49 or 34 members and are responsible for one specific area, such as academic affairs, eligibility and compliance, and championships and competition. Each cabinet then has a series of committees (such as Rules and Sports Committees) reporting to it, each committee focusing on specific tasks and areas within the purview of the cabinet. In effect, NCAA Division I is organized with four layers within its decision-making structure (see Figure 8.2).

Divisions II and III are structured similarly to Division I but have several important distinctions for conducting division-specific business. Each has a Board of Directors made up of institutional CEOs, but the body is called the Division Presidents Council, not a Board. The Division II Presidents Council includes 14 presidents, while the Division III Presidents Council comprises 18 presidents of institutions belonging to Division III. Both Divisions II and III also have Management Councils (with 25 and 19 members, respectively), but Division III has broadened the representation on this group by adding both institutional CEOs and student-athlete representatives to the athletic administrators and faculty athletic representatives comprising the Division I and II councils. Although Division II and III are structured in a similar way to Division I, one very important distinction remains: Legislation in both divisions is considered by the traditional one-school, one-vote method, as opposed to the conference representation used

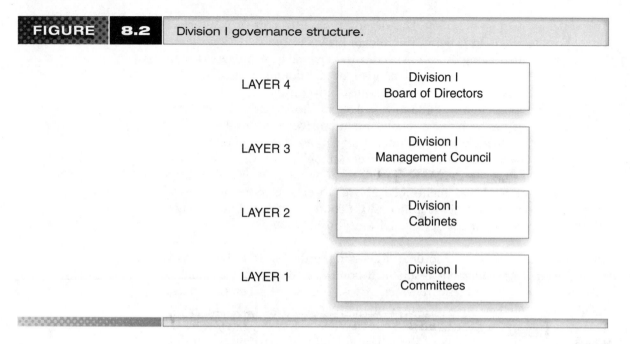

FIGURE   8.2   Division I governance structure.

LAYER 4 — Division I Board of Directors

LAYER 3 — Division I Management Council

LAYER 2 — Division I Cabinets

LAYER 1 — Division I Committees

by Division I. Both Divisions II and III have a committee structure to deal with issues specific to their business and sports.

Association-wide governance structure. As you can see, the NCAA is a huge enterprise. Each division has extensive numbers of members and layers of committee structures for managing the business of intercollegiate sport. As with any large conglomerate, however, there is always the need to oversee association-wide issues. This coordinating function falls to the NCAA Executive Committee, comprising the 16 voting members of the Board of Directors and the Presidents Councils of the three divisions (eight from Division I–FBS, two from Division I–FCS, two from Division I, two from Division II, and two from Division III). The NCAA President and Chairs of the Division Management Councils also belong to the Executive Committee as ex officio (nonvoting) members. The Executive Committee is commissioned to ensure each division operates consistently with the overall principles, policies, and values of the NCAA.

In addition, about a dozen association-wide committees exist to ensure that the principles, policies, and values of the NCAA on common issues like medical and safety concerns are articulated and communicated. They include Olympic Sports Liaison, Research, Women's Athletics, Sportsmanship and Ethical Conduct, and Minority Opportunities and Interests.

See Figure 8.3 for a summary of the governance structure of the NCAA.

The NCAA has undergone much change during the last couple of decades. Major initiatives in enforcement and governance have occurred

Governance structure of the NCAA. **FIGURE 8.3**

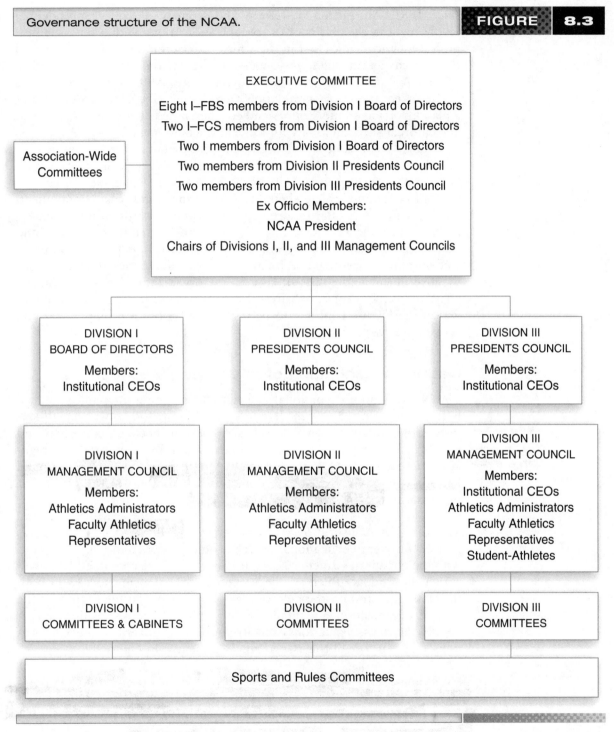

Source: NCAA (2007). Reprinted with permission.

since 1981. An agenda of reform and strategy of college presidential involvement in the affairs of the organization, along with a philosophical push to put academics first in the athlete–education dyad was emphasized through changes to rules, governance structures, and institutional change. The NCAA's focus on Academic Progress Rate (APR) is indicative of the action taken to improve graduation rates. Essentially, APR is conceived as a plan involving administrators and coaches aimed at tracking, managing, and enforcing accountability for academic achievement by NCAA athletes.

Many would continue to argue that the changes have not worked or do not go far enough. Evidence of the change, however, is irrefutably public given the size and complexity of the *NCAA Rule Book*. New rules have evolved governing athlete eligibility and financial aid, cost containment, recruitment, coach salaries, drug testing, championships, women's issues, and student-athlete welfare. Television has contributed to the growth, and publicized such issues as academics and amateurism, expectations put on student-athletes, growth and finance, diversity, and external interventions by government and courts of law. As the organization and its members' goals and values evolve, one area of change has not faded away: problems within the NCAA continue to be visible and critics are more vocal and active than ever before.

National Association of Intercollegiate Athletics

National Association of Intercollegiate Athletics

www.naia.cstv.org

The NAIA is another national association governing intercollegiate athletics in the United States. It comprises about 300 mostly small-size institutions, many of which emphasize the link between education and athletics more strongly than revenue generation. Initially formed to regulate intercollegiate basketball, the association was called the National Association of Intercollegiate Basketball (NAIB) until 1952, when the organization changed its name to the NAIA.

Mission. NAIA institutions view athletics as "co-curricular," that is, as part of the overall educational process, something that goes hand in hand with the pursuit of academic goals. It believes involvement in athletics will enrich the student-athlete's college experience, balancing success in both the classroom and on the field of play. The NAIA National Office is the hub of organization and planning for national championships, and it defines the rules, regulations, and structures that govern member institutions. The purpose of the association is presented in Figure 8.4.

Financials. The NAIA is a not-for-profit association funded through membership fees, sponsorship, championship revenues, and merchandise sales. It collects fees for running national championships and other special programs and shares net revenues with its membership.

FIGURE 8.4

Purpose of the NAIA.

The purpose of the NAIA is to "promote the education and development of students through intercollegiate athletic participation. Member institutions, although varied and diverse, share a common commitment to high standards and the principle that participation in athletics serves as an integral part of the total educational process."

Source: NAIA (2007a). Reprinted with permission.

Membership. Like the NCAA, NAIA members are institutions. NAIA membership is rather diverse, with an assorted group of institutions around the United States and a few members from Canada. The NAIA has just over 280 members and is divided into 14 regions and 25 conferences across the United States (NAIA, 2007a). It has two categories of membership: active and associate members (NAIA, 2007b). Active members consist of four-year colleges and universities and upper-level two-year institutions in the United States or Canada that award undergraduate degrees. These institutions must be fully accredited by one of six institutional accrediting bodies from regions across the United States (such as the Southern Association of Colleges and Schools–Commission on Colleges and the New England Association of Schools and Colleges–Commission on Institutions of Higher Education), must abide by the constitution and bylaws of the NAIA, must be accepted for membership by the Council of Presidents, and must pay the appropriate membership fees. Associate members are required to meet the same standards as active members except for full accreditation by one of the six accrediting bodies. These institutions must, however, be committed to the development of a fully accredited baccalaureate (undergraduate) program. Associate members are not eligible for postseason competition, nor do their institutional representatives vote on issues, serve on committees, or participate in national awards programs.

Individual institutions become members of one of the NAIA's organized regions and conferences. Conference issues having overall association impact or dealing with national championships are deliberated at national meetings or in committee forums.

Organizational structure. The NAIA is organized to govern its business through a series of councils and committees. The association deliberately places the membership at the top of the organizational chart to emphasize the importance of each member institution and the student-athletes for whom programming is organized. Responsive to the membership is the Council of Presidents. Similar to the NCAA, the NAIA relegates control and responsibility for the intercollegiate athletic program to the President or Chief Executive Officer of the institution. Each of the 14 regions within the NAIA elects one to three institutional CEOs to represent the conference membership on the Council of Presidents. The Council is composed of 40 representatives, of whom 15 are independent, at-large, or ex officio (nonvoting) members. An elected Administrative Committee, made up of a chair, three other members, and the NAIA administrative head, manages the Council. Each member of the Council holds one vote. Figure 8.5 illustrates the governance structure of the NAIA.

The NAIA is further subdivided into three major councils: the Council of Athletics Administrators, the Council of Faculty Athletics Representatives, and the Council of Affiliated Conferences and Independents.

1. *Council of Athletics Administrators.* The Council of Athletics Administrators is responsible for all sport-related business. It is composed of 19 members, the Chair of each of the 14 regions of the NAIA, along with two elected at-large members. An elected President and Vice President, chosen from among the regional chairs, and a Vice Chair govern it. The purpose of the Council of Athletics Administrators is to develop policy and enact procedure consistent with the values of NAIA institutions through four main groups: (1) Athletics Directors Association, (2) Athletics Trainers Association, (3) Conduct and Ethics Committee, and (4) NAIA Coaches Associations (which are sport specific). Each group brings its own specific focus to the issues under discussion, and each helps form the philosophy and the delivery of NAIA events.

2. *Council of Faculty Athletics Representatives.* The Council of Faculty Athletics Representatives promotes the student and academic priorities clearly endorsed by the NAIA. This Council is slightly larger in number than the Athletics Administrators groups, with a Chair and Vice Chair, 14 regional representatives, three at-large members, the Faculty Athletics Representatives Association (FARA) Chair and Chair-Elect, and a staff liaison person. FARA is responsible for promoting the continued prominent role of education in NAIA athletics.

3. *Council of Affiliated Conferences and Independents.* This Council oversees operational policies and supervises regional events and plays a primary role in competitive alignments and divisions, along with sports information and awards. A Regional Management Committee comprises representatives from the various members and independents governs each region. A Chair and Chair-Elect, along with a Vice Chair and Secretary, serve as officers of the association and govern the Council. In addition to these four

Organizational chart for the NAIA. FIGURE 8.5

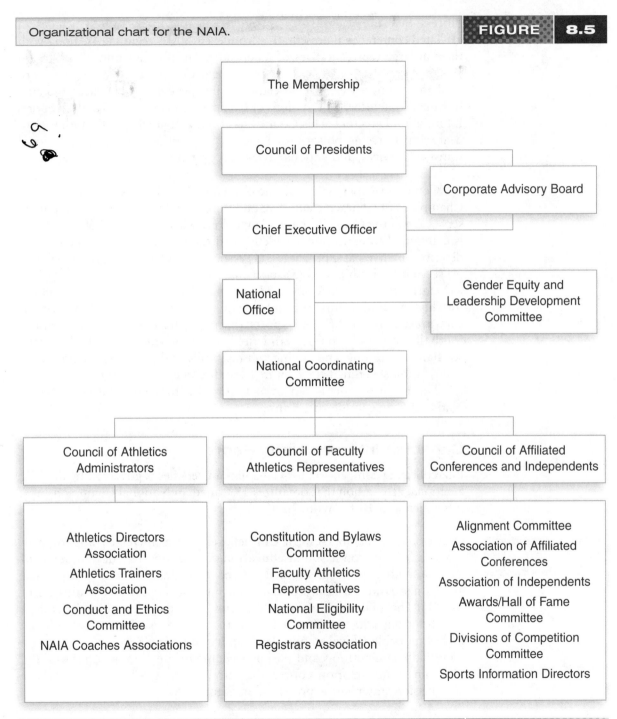

Source: NAIA. Reprinted with permission.

officers, the Council of Affiliated Conferences and Independents includes an affiliated conference representative from each NAIA region (14), along with three at-large representatives of independent member institutions. Six main groups comprise this Council: (1) Alignment Committee, (2) Association of Affiliated Conferences, (3) Association of Independents, (4) Awards and Hall of Fame Committee, (5) Divisions of Competition Committee, and (6) Sports Information Directors. This Council has been delegated specific authority to deal with operating policies for regional competitions and events, national statistical services, and national award programs.

Committees managing specific elements of NAIA business, such as the Champions of Character initiative and the NAIA Hall of Fame Committee, serve each of the Councils. Each group, along with the Council of Presidents, is committed to educational athletics and the true spirit of competition as described by five basic principles: (1) respect, (2) integrity, (3) responsibility, (4) servant leadership, and (5) sportsmanship (NAIA, 2007c).

Currently, the NAIA offers 23 national championships. Teams qualify for their championships through regional conferences. The NAIA sponsors a slate of 13 different sports (baseball, basketball, cross-country, football, golf, indoor track and field, outdoor track and field, soccer, softball, swimming and diving, tennis, volleyball, and wrestling), with competition scheduled for men in 12 and women in 11 sports.

The organization is led by a CEO who manages the large NAIA National Office in Olathe, Kansas.

Canadian Interuniversity Sport

Intercollegiate competition for Canadian universities is governed by the CIS, a national association that organizes 19 Canadian National Championships, 9 for men and 10 for women.

www

Canadian Interuniversity
Sport
www.universitysport.ca

Mission. The membership of CIS believes that a university athletic program is founded on a sound educational program. The development of such individual programs, aided by and through a national forum that allows discussion of issues of common interest, is part of the mission of the CIS. The goals of the CIS are very similar to those espoused by college athletic groups in the United States: to achieve excellence through the highest possible ethical standards of equity and fair play, to encourage and coordinate competition and national championships, and to publish and disseminate information concerning interuniversity athletic activity. The CIS mission statement is presented in Figure 8.6.

Financials. The CIS is a small, modest enterprise with a 2007 annual budget of $2.2 million (CIS, 2007c). Much of its focus is on delivering

Mission statement of CIS.	**FIGURE**	**8.6**

It is the mission of Canadian Interuniversity Sport to enrich the educational experience of the athlete through a national sport program that fosters excellence through quality educational and athletic experience; unity of purpose, respect for autonomy; integrity and fair play; trust and mutual respect; equity and equity experience.

Source: CIS (2007a). Reprinted with permission.

national championships and other special events in conjunction with its members. Finances are always tight, and fiscal responsibility is a major focus. The organization manages to balance its spending with revenues each year. Revenues are generated from championship guarantees, sponsorship and events, government support through Sport Canada, membership fees, publications, and investments; expenses are for championships, special events, association-wide programs, office and meeting management, and sport development (CIS, 2007c).

Membership. Members are institutions of higher education in Canada that grant undergraduate degrees. These institutions are divided into four Regional Associations (Atlantic University Sport, Quebec Student Sports Federation, Ontario University Athletics, and Canada West), each with a minimum of eight members. With a total of 51 members, the CIS has a much smaller membership than either the NCAA or the NAIA. This number includes virtually all of the degree-granting universities in Canada. Each CIS member agrees to abide by the organization's constitution, bylaws, and rules and regulations; to pay yearly dues; to be a member in good standing of a CIS regional association; and to offer at least one intercollegiate sport for both men and women. Each institution names two delegates (one must be male, one female) to attend the organization's General Assembly meetings, an event normally held once a year.

Organizational structure. Between General Assembly meetings, the Board of Directors governs the CIS and has "the jurisdiction to do all things necessary for carrying out the Constitutional Objectives and fulfilling the Mission Statement of Canadian Interuniversity Sport" (CIS, 2007d, p. BL6). This includes the power to manage policies and procedures, direct disputes, discipline members, and direct personnel. The Board of Directors consists of the President and President-Elect, along with the Chair of the Finance Committee; three Vice Presidents elected by the General Assembly responsible for portfolios in Sport, Research and Development, and Marketing; Chair of the Equity and Equality Committee; and one person from each of the four Regional Associations. Each Regional Association names one male and one female nominee, and board members are selected for a two-year term from among the regional association members and are balanced in number of women and men. The CEO is an ex officio (nonvoting) member of the board. The Board of Directors meets at least twice a year.

The elected officers of the board comprise the Executive Committee, which is charged to act on behalf of the board between meetings. The Executive Committee is also responsible for dealing with strategic planning, budgeting, public relations, and other important items impacting the organizational effectiveness of the CIS. Its members include the President, President-Elect, Past President, Vice Presidents (Programs, Marketing, and Research and Development), Finance Committee Chair, and Chief Executive Officer (ex officio). Committees include Eligibility, Equity and Equality, Marketing, International, Discipline, Sport, Finance, and Research and Development. The committees have regional association membership and responsibility for managing specific CIS business.

The CEO and other paid employees of the organization are located in Ottawa, Ontario. Figure 8.7 summarizes the governance structure of the CIS.

Canadian Colleges Athletic Association

The CCAA was founded in 1974 to coordinate college sport in Canada (CCAA, 2007a). Remember, Canadian colleges are similar to technical schools in the United States.

www

Canadian Colleges Athletic
Association (CCAA)

www.ccaa.ca

Mission. Like the CIS, the primary objectives of the CCAA are to conduct and to promote athletic competitions for their member institutions, Canadian colleges that offer mostly two- and three-year programs. The organization is a coordinating body and thus seeks to bring together a group of administrators from a diverse set of colleges to make decisions concerning the development of college athletics in Canada. The mission statement of the CCAA is presented in Figure 8.8.

Financials. The CCAA is even smaller in scope and finances than the CIS. Revenues are generated largely from championships, sponsorship and events, and membership fees; expenses are for championships, special events, association-wide programs, and office management.

Membership. With 104 members, the CCAA comprises a wide variety of post-secondary institutions, including community colleges, university-col-

FIGURE   8.7

Organizational structure of CIS.

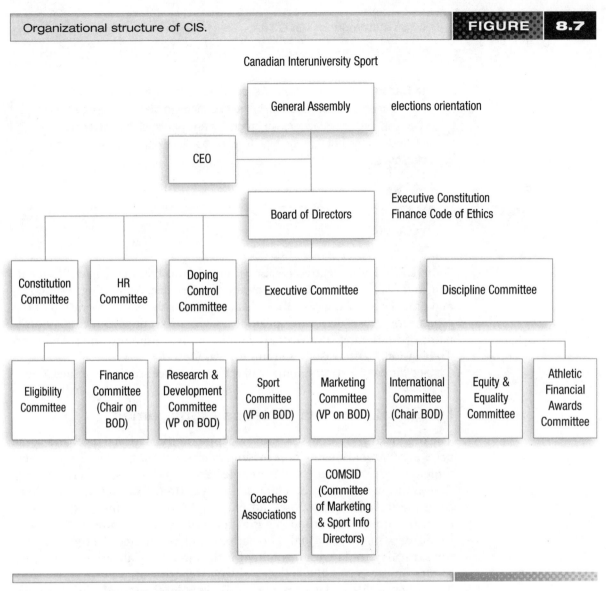

Canadian Interuniversity Sport

General Assembly — elections orientation

CEO

Board of Directors — Executive Constitution Finance Code of Ethics

Constitution Committee

HR Committee

Doping Control Committee

Executive Committee

Discipline Committee

Eligibility Committee

Finance Committee (Chair on BOD)

Research & Development Committee (VP on BOD)

Sport Committee (VP on BOD)

Marketing Committee (VP on BOD)

International Committee (Chair BOD)

Equity & Equality Committee

Athletic Financial Awards Committee

Coaches Associations

COMSID (Committee of Marketing & Sport Info Directors)

Source: CIS (2003). Reprinted with permission.

leges, and technical institutes. It is composed of five regional athletic conferences from coast to coast in Canada. College student-athletes compete for national championships in eight sports (three men's, three women's, two coed).

Organizational structure. The CCAA is governed by a Board of Directors comprising six elected executive positions and a representative from each

FIGURE	8.8	Mission statement of the CCAA.

> The Canadian College Athletic Association, as an active partner in the integrated Canadian Sport System, is the coordinating body for college sport in Canada, providing leadership, programs and services that foster student-athlete development through high level competitive opportunities in intercollegiate sport.

Source: CCAA (2007a).

conference. The executive positions include the President, Past President, and four Vice Presidents, one each for Governance, Marketing, Programs, and Finance and Administration. Leadership for the entire operation of the organization rests with three positions: CCAA Executive Director, Coordinator of Marketing and Media Relations, and an Administrative Assistant. The National Office is housed in Ottawa, Ontario.

See Figure 8.9 for a summary of the governance structure of the CCAA.

Individual Campus Athletics Management

The organizations discussed above operate on the national level and comprise institutional members providing competitive opportunities for their athletes and coaches. A series of rules and regulations, policies, procedures, and bylaws help regulate the competition, focusing on everything from the underlying purpose and philosophy of the competition to how events are operated. Although a great deal of regulatory power exists with the leaders of the national associations and coalitions of larger institutions, the day-to-day responsibility for the intercollegiate athletic program resides on campus in the college Athletic Department.

College athletic departments can be very large or very small, as illustrated in Figures 8.10 and 8.11. Larger colleges and universities employ a wide variety of sport professionals to manage, deliver, and supervise intercollegiate athletics: administrators, coaches, trainers, facility and event managers, and faculty representatives all play important roles in the intercollegiate program. Of course, all campus initiatives fall under the auspices of the President's Office. Over the years, the college or university president has had varying degrees of involvement in the athletic program. Today, direct involvement by the college president is more the rule than the exception. For example, university presidents in Ontario pushed for gender

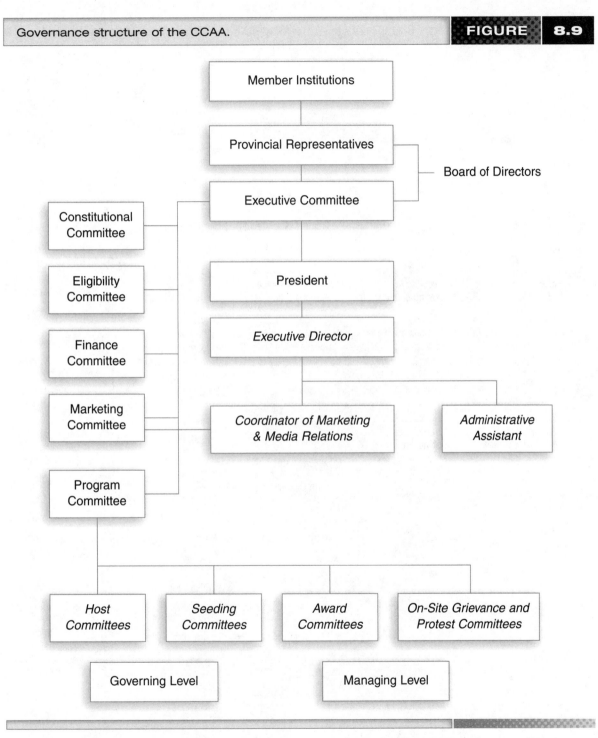

Governance structure of the CCAA.   **FIGURE   8.9**

Source: CCAA (2007c).

FIGURE 8.10   Organizational structure for OSU's Department of Athletics.

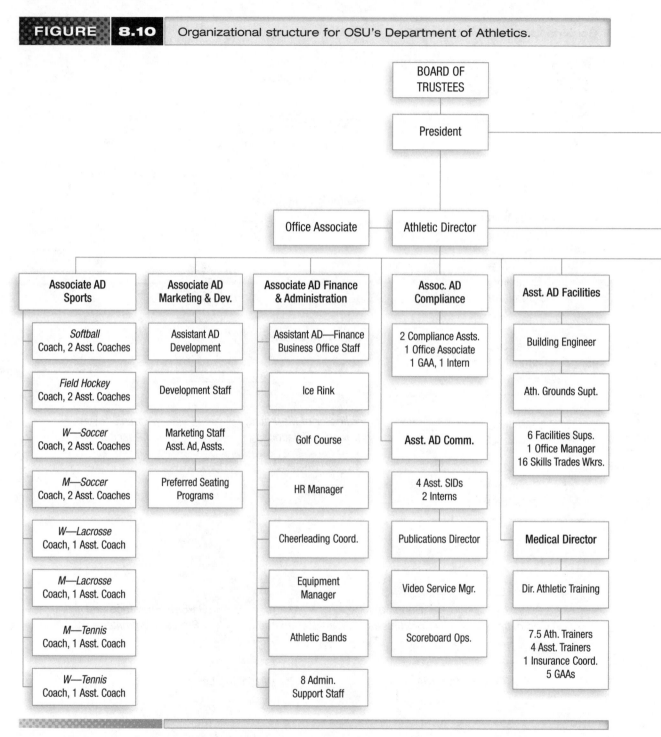

Source: The OSU Department of Athletics (2008). Reprinted with permission.

Continued.

FIGURE 8.10

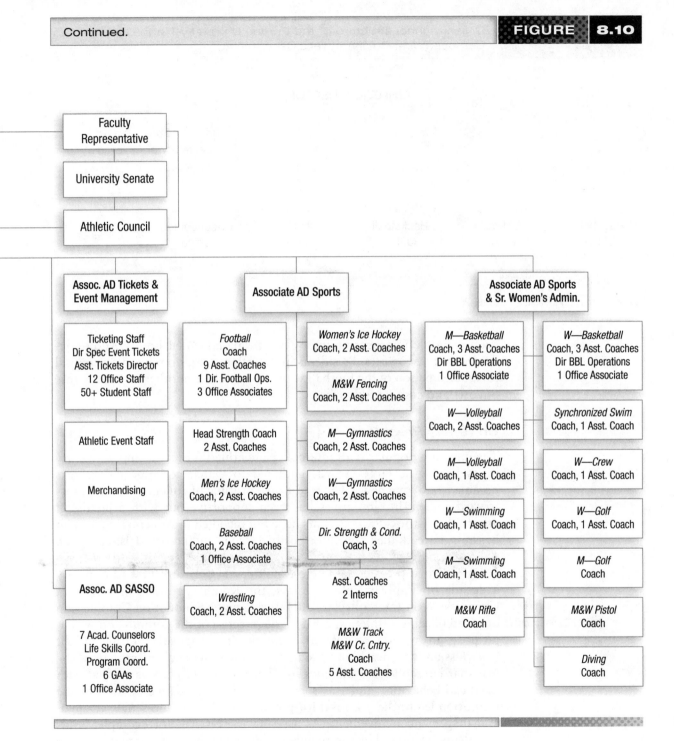

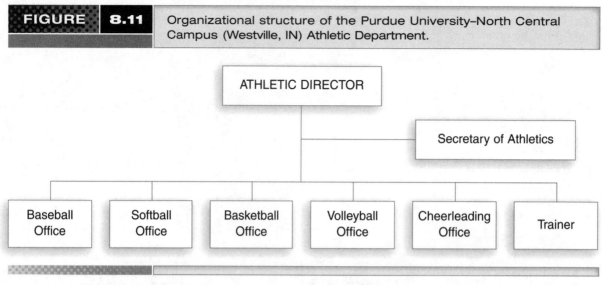

FIGURE 8.11 Organizational structure of the Purdue University–North Central Campus (Westville, IN) Athletic Department.

Source: Purdue North–Central Athletics (2008).

equity in athletic programming by instituting a Gender-Equity Audit conducted every two years. Presidents in the Atlantic region refused a proposal for amalgamation of the football schedule to include another region because of costs and competitive issues.

University President

The immense popularity of intercollegiate athletics became apparent early in its history as large crowds gathered to watch contests and reports became front-page news. The traditional attitude of college administrators toward student-life initiatives has been supportive but with a hands-off approach. Historically, presidents have not meddled in Athletic Department business; instead, they hoped for positive results and no scandals. However, the proliferation of highly publicized violations and reported abuses garnered increased presidential interest in intercollegiate athletics. After nearly a decade of highly visible scandals, the Knight Foundation created a Commission on Intercollegiate Athletics (Knight Foundation Commission on Intercollegiate Athletics, 2001). The purpose of the commission was to propose an agenda of reform. One of the proposals of the Knight Commission was increased presidential control over college athletics. The fear that intercollegiate athletics had become too large, was riddled with unethical behaviors, and was separate from the academic mission of the institution led to the proposal for greater presidential and senior academic management involvement. As a result, the NCAA, for example, holds presidents accountable for member conduct and requires that they be

Knight Commission
www.knightcommission.org

involved in developing and managing policy through the Board of Directors and the Council of Presidents. In essence, presidential involvement has resulted from negativity, corruption, and deceit. On the other hand, increased presidential involvement has also resulted from the potential institutional benefits of athletics participation, not the least of which is money. Developing an institutional image of excellence, increasing alumni involvement, and recruiting new students have always been positive goals for university presidents, but the potential for revenue generation has led to a more serious focus.

Gerdy (1997) summarizes the enhanced role of the university president in college athletics:

> This explosion of media attention, coupled with the growing need to market higher education to an increasingly skeptical public, suggests that presidents, and the academic community they represent, take a more active role in managing that exposure. Thus, the heretofore hands-off, keep-me-off-the-front-page approach to managing this powerful university resource no longer serves greater institutional purposes. In short, athletics' visibility and public influence must be looked upon as something not simply to be tolerated but rather harnessed and exploited for larger university gain. (p. 9)

The level of presidential involvement varies from institution to institution. Many presidents have supported the formation of an Athletic Board and a Faculty Athletics Representative to help scrutinize policy, direction, and operations of the Athletic Department and advise the president on athletic activities and issues.

In January 2006 the Summit on the Collegiate Athlete Experience was held, bringing together coaches, journalists, and athletes, among others, to discuss the collegiate athlete experience, substance abuse, and recruiting ethics. The results of the summit, along with recent NCAA statistics regarding rules violations, has prompted the Knight Commission to strongly urge college presidents to support academic reform in college athletics (Knight Foundation Commission on Intercollegiate Athletics, 2007).

The Athletic Board

The Athletic Board is a committee normally placed at the top of the Athletic Department hierarchy between the Director and the college President. Its purpose is to advise the Athletic Director and possibly the president and to oversee Athletic Department operations. The Athletic Board is generally composed of a large number of constituents, including faculty, students, alumni, community businesspersons, and university administrators. The group meets regularly each semester to oversee policy development and implementation and to scrutinize budgets. Since the Athletic Director is *responsible* to the university President, the Athletic Board in effect serves as part of the checks and balances on Athletic Department operations, a sounding board for the development of new initiatives, and a mechanism for control of operations. The Athletic Director is *responsive* to the Athletic Board and works closely with and in consultation with it, but usually reports directly to the university President (or indirectly via a Dean or Vice President).

In theory the Athletic Board wields considerable power; however, in reality it is often relatively powerless, receiving general information and rubber-stamping reports that are peripheral to the major issues facing the unit and its personnel. Even so, perhaps the least powerful position associated with this group, which is sometimes actually marginalized by the Athletic Department, is the Faculty Athletics Representative (FAR).

Faculty Athletics Representative

The FAR is normally appointed by the President and is responsible for ensuring that the operation of the Athletic Department remains within the educational context of the institution. The FAR addresses a variety of topics but most likely oversees policy regarding educational priorities of athletes, scheduling and time commitments, graduation rates, academic support programs, and policy enforcement. The FAR undoubtedly reports to the President and works in concert with the Athletic Board and the Athletic Director. The reporting structure described above can have a marginalizing effect for the FAR because members of the Athletic Department can construe her presence and her mandate as intrusive. Since she reports directly to the President, struggles over jurisdiction and perspective between the role and value of athletics versus the importance of education can occasionally result. This conflict can reduce the effectiveness of the FAR's role, an unfortunate and unproductive result for the Athletic Director and the Athletic Department.

Athletic Director

The Athletic Director (AD) is the head of the Athletic Department. As the top manager, the AD is responsible for the unit and must understand the policies, activities, and actions of those working within each department area. Recently, in many large athletic departments, the AD's activities have become more externally driven, adding fundraising responsibilities, community and alumni relations, and capital building to his portfolio. Ultimately, this individual is responsible for planning, organizing, leading, and evaluating both programs and personnel. Depending on the scope of these external initiatives, an Associate AD (sometimes referred to as an Athletic Coordinator) may manage the day-to-day operations of the unit. In any event, the specific responsibilities for the AD include finance, facilities, medical services, travel, event management, compliance, media, scheduling, marketing, ticket sales, public relations, personnel, communication, risk management, television, and student-athlete services. Effective ADs possess a great deal of business sense, critical-thinking and problem-solving ability, and strong communication skills. They must ensure the Athletic Department's mission coexists effectively with the mandate of higher education. Striving for excellence in two domains means conflicts will certainly arise between athletics and academics. For example, how should the AD respond when a coach develops a schedule requiring a student-athlete to be away from campus 10 days in the middle of the semester? The games may be highly beneficial from a competitive standpoint, but taking a student out of class for this length of time might prove disastrous. The AD must balance academic and athletic goals, in this case by decreasing the length of the trip. Educational concerns must supersede athletic goals because colleges and universities are first and foremost institutions of higher learning. Without a doubt there are ADs who lose sight of this founding principle in their quest for athletic excellence. Having the management skills to plan and organize is important, but it is perhaps more important that the leader of the Athletic Department effectively promotes the educational priorities of the institution and the personal achievement and welfare of student-athletes. The most important role for the AD is the role of educator. This is also true for coaches, the other main constituent of the Athletic Department.

Coaches

Coaches truly are managers in that they plan, organize, lead, and evaluate their teams like small, independent organizations. You might think of the coach as the CEO of the most important component of the Athletic Department, the athletic team. A coach wears many hats in addition to being an educator. In managing and building the athletic program, she establishes liaisons with constituent groups such as student-athletes, students in general, high school recruits, the media, parents, alumni, Athletic Department administrators and colleagues, sponsors, members of the college community, and professional colleagues. Today's college coaches are skilled in a particular sport and knowledgeable generally about teaching, developing tactics and strategies, communicating, motivating athletes, and building support for their program. They represent an integral component of the structure of the college Athletic Department because they drive the main business of the organization. Coaches hold a major position of influence and authority. In their highly visible positions, they greatly affect the welfare of their student-athletes and the images of their institutions. Coaches also can have an important voice in the critical policy areas currently under review within intercollegiate athletics.

Current Policy Areas

Many areas within intercollegiate athletics require the development of policy to ensure fairness results from common practices. Many policy areas are debated in college athletics regardless of the country of origin, division, or affiliation. The sheer numbers involved with these organizations and the issues evolving from the unique sport environment require a problem-solving, action-oriented culture. The focus on developing new and amending old policy helps administrators effectively manage the evolving, dynamic environment of intercollegiate athletics. Let's investigate some recurring and some new governance policy areas facing collegiate athletics.

Eligibility

Eligibility defines who is allowed to play. In the early days of college sport, concerns arose when an individual not affiliated in any way with the college emerged as the star of the team. If collegiate athletics is about representing one's particular institution, it follows that the members of the team must also be students at the college. *Eligibility,* then, is the global term used to define the rules for entering, in-progress, and transferring student-athletes.

Initial eligibility. To be eligible to compete in intercollegiate athletics, a high school graduate must possess the required grades on a set of core courses acceptable to the college or university for entrance. Normally, meeting the entrance requirements to a college or university as a full-time student in Canada will enable the student to be an athlete. In the United States, however, the NCAA uses an external body called the NCAA Initial Eligibility Clearinghouse to process student-athlete eligibility in order to ensure common standards are enforced (NCAA, 2007e). Students register with the Clearinghouse (normally after their junior year) by filling out forms and submitting high school transcripts and standardized test scores (such as the Scholastic Aptitude Test [SAT] or American College Test [ACT]) for approval. The Clearinghouse then approves an application when an institution requests information about a particular student's status. Currently, the NCAA requires 14 core courses to be completed satisfactorily along with a minimum standardized test score defined in conjunction with grade-point average (GPA). For example, a student with a 2.3 GPA must score at least a 900 on the SAT or 75 on the ACT to compete on an athletic team. However, a core GPA of 2.5 or higher requires 820 on the SAT or 68 on the ACT (NCAA, 2007e).

The NAIA (2005) requires two of the following three items for eligibility: (1) a minimum 2.0 GPA (on a 4.0 scale), (2) graduation in the upper half of the high school graduating class, (3) a minimum score of 18 on the

NCAA Initial Eligibility Clearinghouse
www1.ncaaclearinghouse.net

enhanced ACT or 860 on the SAT. Students who gain admission to a college but have scores below these NCAA or NAIA standards are ineligible to compete for their first full year of attendance (two semesters, three quarters, or the equivalent).

Academic progress. To maintain eligibility, student-athletes must take and achieve passing grades for a specific number of courses (or maintain a specific GPA).

In Canada the CIS (2007e) requires that a student pass 3 full courses, 6 half courses, or 18 credit hours in order to be eligible for competition the following year. In the NAIA a freshman student must successfully complete 9 institutional credit hours in his first term of competition to be eligible for his second term of play. Thereafter, he must accumulate a minimum of 24 credit hours a year to be eligible for competition the next year. No more than half of the 24 credit hours can be earned during the summer or noncompetition terms.

As stated earlier, the NCAA has initiated an academic reform package. In the NCAA, student-athletes must demonstrate steady progress toward graduation: They must be pursuing full-time study, be in good standing, and be making satisfactory progress toward a degree. In addition, the NCAA Division I member institutions must be accountable for the academic success of their student-athletes, and each Division I sports team receives an APR score. An APR of 925 (out of 1,000) approximates a 60 percent Graduation Success Rate. While teams with high APRs receive public recognition from the NCAA, teams that score below 925 can be sanctioned (NCAA, 2008a).

Transfer students. Rules regarding transfer students are an important aspect of intercollegiate athletics eligibility policy. Transfers to institutions for the sole purpose of playing intercollegiate athletics are discouraged because such moves contradict the philosophy of student first, athlete second. The purpose of attending a college or a university is to get an education, earn a degree, and become a contributing member of society. To promote this philosophy, intercollegiate athletics commonly enforces a transfer rule requiring the transferring student-athlete to refrain from competition for some period of time. The NCAA transfer rule requires a student-athlete to complete one full academic year of residence (two semesters or three quarters) at a certified institution before being declared eligible to compete. The NAIA requires a 16-week residency period prior to competition after transfer from a four-year institution; it allows a transfer from a two-year institution after filing the appropriate disclosure forms. In Canada the CIS requires a student to forgo competition for one year following transfer to another institution, while the CCAA allows open transfer from one institution to another.

www

NCAA Academic Reform Package

www2.ncaa.org/portal/
academics_and_athletes/
education_and_research/
academic_reform/index.html

Eligibility is a common policy issue in intercollegiate athletics because competing institutions have always valued fairness and a balanced starting point in competition. These are achieved when the respective league-eligibility committees define benchmark standards to guide the agreed-upon concept that collegiate athletics is for full-time college students progressing toward a bona fide diploma or degree. Such eligibility requirements differentiate collegiate athletics from other avenues of amateur and professional sport.

Amateurism

Over the years, intercollegiate athletic administrators have worked hard to ensure college competition is identified as amateur as opposed to professional sport. Many will debate their success, given the requirements placed on student-athletes and the big business nature of college athletics, especially at the NCAA Division I level. According to NCAA (2007f) bylaws, the principle of *amateurism* is that

> student-athletes shall be amateurs in an intercollegiate sport, and their participation should be motivated primarily by education and by the physical, mental and social benefits to be derived. Student participation in intercollegiate athletics is an avocation, and student-athletes should be protected from exploitation by professional and commercial enterprises.

In any event, college student-athletes are not paid salaries for their services. Their involvement is noncontractual, and their primary purpose for attending the institution is educational. Does this ring true? Perhaps not always, and this is the specific reason amateurism is hotly debated by administrators at the institutional, regional, and national levels.

Are college athletes employees? The answer, of course, is "no" in theory and "no" in operation, at least most of the time. College athletics should reflect the tenets of amateurism without any difficulty: competition for the glory of achievement, in a voluntary environment in which no salary is paid for competing. In most cases amateur competition is consistently portrayed in college athletics. However, the competitive nature of NCAA Division I athletics, in which both coaches and athletic administrators push to win games and balance budgets, certainly tests (if not crosses) the line between amateur and professional sport. In this case many critics have complained of a "say . . . do" gap. College athletics is said to be amateur athletics in the context of education, but the demands and the stakes suggest a more-professional sport environment to some critics who maintain that colleges should pay athletes for their performance, just as professionals are compensated for the entertainment they bring.

Regardless of the debate, collegiate athletic administrators continue to embrace amateurism and have invoked rules to prohibit professionals from competition. Student-athletes are not paid to compete, but most receive athletic scholarships or grants-in-aid to help offset the costs of a college education. An "athlete turned pro" is prohibited by league policy from returning to college competition in her sport. The amateur policy of the NCAA describes many activities that result in an athlete's losing amateur status (NCAA, 2007g):

- playing for pay
- accepting a promise for pay
- signing a contract to play professionally
- receiving financial reimbursement
- competing for a professional team
- entering into a draft prior to collegiate enrollment
- entering into an agreement with an agent

Without a doubt, college administrators still believe it is important for college athletes to be students first, competing in amateur athletics as law-abiding, drug-free role models reflective of the entire student body. Policies play a role in fulfilling this mission.

Substance Abuse and Performance Enhancement

Collegiate athletic administrators are united in their opposition to performance-enhancing drugs and other forms of substance abuse by anyone involved in college athletics. Evidence of unequivocal opposition is reflected in policy statements. National and regional associations governing collegiate sport throughout North America respect the list of banned substances and methods as reported by Olympic and National and International Sport Federations, along with the FISU, which governs the World University Games held every two years. Policies oppose the use of any banned or restricted substances or methods and the encouragement of such practices by anyone associated with college sport (coaches, administrators, athletic staff, medical practitioners, sport scientists, alumni, boosters, athletes, etc.). The opposition to doping strongly discourages participants from seeking an artificially induced advantage in competition. Student-athletes sign consent forms demonstrating their understanding of drug-testing programs and their willingness to abide by the rules. In Canada such consent forms are a component of eligibility.

To establish doping control, policy has been invoked on two levels: education and enforcement. Educational programs have been established by the NCAA (2007h) and the CIS (2007g) and are mandatory for athletes in order to ensure awareness of the rules and the lists of banned substances and methods. In addition, programs of unannounced testing www W

**Canadian Centre for
Ethics in Sports**

www.cces.ca

have been established by the leagues mentioned above, which give no notice or short notice and target drug testing in college athletics. In Canada the doping-control program for intercollegiate athletics falls under the auspices of the CCES, in conjunction with the CIS and the CCAA. Testing is done randomly and, in certain sports such as swimming and track and field, on the basis of finish. In the NCAA, random drug testing is used, and a positive test for any banned substance results in loss of eligibility for one calendar year. A second positive test results in permanent loss of eligibility in all sports.

Policies, procedures, and rules regarding performance enhancement in intercollegiate sport help guide all participants (coaches, athletes, trainers, etc.) in understanding the broader issue of fairness and healthy practices. Other policy areas such as financial aid and gender equity are defined to help guide university personnel to ensure that equitable practices are maintained from one campus to the next.

Financial Aid

Providing athletes with financial aid, commonly known as an athletic scholarship, has been a source of debate within college athletics for decades. Within the NCAA, Divisions I and II have set policy providing for awarding a certain number of athletic scholarships, whereas Division III, the NAIA, and the CIS have been more restrictive in their rules. For example, NCAA Division I and II schools sponsor a certain number of athletic scholarships per sport, whereas Division III schools do not offer such awards. Canadian schools have recently begun to offer athletic scholarships but have more stringent restrictions on the value of the award and when it can be given to the athlete. In the United States the source of funding for these awards has not been the most important issue. Rather, intercollegiate leagues such as the NCAA have developed policy to ensure fair practices among institutions regarding how much financial aid can be given a particular athlete (to ensure a distinction from paid professional athletes), to balance awards given to males and females, and to regulate when such an award can be withdrawn. Some questionable practices, such as overpaying or unjustly withdrawing an athletic scholarship, prompted a focus on these issues.

Financial aid continues to be an area of policy debate. Specifically, the NCAA has debated the issue of whether student-athletes should be permitted to hold part-time jobs. A large proportion of the student population works part-time to offset the high costs of university tuition and living expenses. Yet, in the past, athlete eligibility rules forbade athletes to hold part-time jobs. Although the rule against part-time employment was in the students' best interests, the NCAA felt that, considering the demands of the classroom combined with the demands of athletic commitment, a change in policy was necessary. In 2003 the work rule was changed to allow employment on campus to a maximum of $2,000 (NCAA, 2003a). More currently a student-athlete is permitted to hold on- or off-campus employment for which monies do not count toward maximum financial aid allowances, provided that compensation is based solely on work performed and does not exceed the going rate for similar service (NCAA, 2007f). In addition, NCAA athletes are now permitted "pay for teaching to play," that is, using their skills as athletes to teach as music majors and fitness majors often do. Members of the NCAA believe this change is fair, given today's high costs of living and a philosophy that athletes should be treated more like the rest of the student body. The emergence and evolution of policy regarding gender equity is another good example.

Gender Equity

Virtually every administrative body governing intercollegiate athletics has policy pertaining to gender equity. In the United States, Title IX provides the impetus for committee and task force discussions and implementation for change in order to achieve equitable intercollegiate athletic programs for both men and women. The NCAA Gender-Equity Task Force delivered the following policy statement: "An athletics program can be considered gender equitable when the participants in both the men's and women's sports programs would accept as fair and equitable the overall program of the other gender. No individual should be discriminated against on the basis of gender, institutionally or nationally, in intercollegiate athletics" (NCAA, 2007i, p. 1). University Presidents and Athletic Directors determine specific compliance with Title IX on individual campuses. However, numerous lawsuits have been initiated by athletes and parents that challenge actual Title IX compliance. The specific duty to comply with equitable practices rests on individual campuses and must be the joint responsibility of the President, Athletic Director, and Athletic Board.

In Canada, the CIS defined its Policy for Equity and Equality in the following statement: "Canadian Interuniversity Sport accepts the principles of equity and equality and will ensure that these principles are adhered to in all its activities. . . . Equity refers to treatment that is fair and just. . . . Equality means that all persons enjoy the same status regardless of gender . . . [and] . . . have equal conditions for realizing their full rights and potential and to benefit from the results" (CIS, 2004, p. OM/50). The CIS also defined 13 operational goals for enacting the Equity and Equality Policy. The difficulty, of course, is that the national policy might have little impact for change on individual campuses.

Gender equity has been a long-standing contentious issue in college athletics. The inequities are played out in many different, often systemic,

Dr. Robertha Abney

Associate Athletic Director,
Slippery Rock University,
Slippery Rock, Pennsylvania

Currently I am the Associate Athletic Director at Slippery Rock University, an NCAA Division II institution. I also am the Senior Women's Administrator and the Director of Equal Opportunity in Sport. Those are my three official duties with the university, in addition to being a faculty member in the Sport Management program. We have over 20 sports, and as the Associate AD I have about 10 sports that report directly to me for day-to-day operations. I do all of the scheduling for both men's and women's sports, and both men's and women's sports report to me. I'm also in charge of promoting some of our events. In addition, equity and Title IX compliance are included in my portfolio as the Director of Equal Opportunity in Sport.

On our campus we seem to be in constant governance mode because of the need to review our own internal Athletic Department structure and its effectiveness and fit within the university environment. We've had an outside consultant assess our hierarchy and structure as well as the complete unit to ensure that we are in compliance with gender equity and Title IX. Title IX has forced us to reevaluate specific programs and resource allocations such as scholarships, but it has also forced us to study more systemic, embedded inequities. We're very committed to equity and to making sure that we are being fair and flexible as the same time.

The President of the NCAA, Miles Brand, had made it his charge to create a more responsive and less bureaucratic NCAA. So, under his guidance and leadership, each of the Divisions is reviewing the regulatory culture of its system with reference to the entire organization. Many think that the by-laws, policies, and procedures of the NCAA are designed to ensure competitive or recruiting equity, but our policies need to be viewed not only as effective, fair, and appropriate, but also as flexible. The NCAA has multiple, unique relationships to manage with student-athletes and institutions. To manage these unique relationships, we are reviewing our current policies to make sure they are responsive to the needs of the student-athlete.

I think it will be a major challenge for the NCAA to review its by-laws, because those by-laws, policies, and procedures are a big part of the organization's identity. The move away from strict rules, policies, and procedures will be a major challenge. Ultimately I think it is going to be very beneficial, not only to the association as a whole and its image, but also to the membership and all the NCAA constituents. The major policy challenges currently facing the NCAA are academic reform and advocacy. Of course, it is imperative that we be as inclusive as possible and hear the voices of the entire membership, as diverse as it is.

ways. Participation opportunities for men have historically exceeded those for women; many sports, such as football and hockey, existed for men only. The budgets allocated to men's teams and salaries paid to coaches of men's teams are significantly higher than for women's teams. The decision makers in athletic program administration, university central administration, and coaching have dominantly been males. Many more males than females coach women's teams. These and other imbalances in gender that elevate men's sport over women's continue to create issues of inequity that must remain a focus of the reform required in collegiate athletics.

Gambling

Gambling has experienced extensive growth in society; sports gambling is a multibillion-dollar business. This growth, coupled with the expansion and media hype surrounding college sports, has resulted in a noticeable increase in gambling associated with collegiate sport. The NCAA reports a significant increase in the number of cases it processed related to sports wagering. Particular concern is currently focused on the prevalence of Internet wagering, which is increasingly appealing to college-age, computer-savvy students. Administrators and members of the NCAA are very concerned about the potential for sports wagering and believe that it threatens the very existence of college sports (NCAA, 2002). For example:

> A study by the University of Cincinnati of 648 Division I intercollegiate men's basketball and football respondents indicated that 25.5% had gambled money on other college sporting events, 3.7% had gambled money on a game in which they had played, and that 0.5% received money from a gambler for not playing well in a game. (NCAA, 2002, n.p.)

The NCAA opposes sports gambling in all its forms, legal and illegal. The zero-tolerance policy adopted by the NCAA prohibits Athletic Department staff and student-athletes from engaging in any form of gambling activities. The policy prohibits gambling on both intercollegiate and professional sports and stipulates that an individual involved in collegiate sport must not knowingly provide information to individuals involved in organized gambling, solicit a bet, accept a bet, or participate in any gambling activity through any method (NCAA, 2002).

In 2003, the NCAA published a study on collegiate sports wagering that found

> males consistently reported engaging in gambling or sports wagering activities in much higher proportions than their female counterparts. . . . Approximately 69 percent of male student-athletes reported participating in *any gambling behavior* in the past year. . . . About 35 percent of males and 10 percent of females reported wagering on *any sporting events* in the past year, in direct violation of NCAA bylaws regarding sports wagering. . . . Approximately one percent of football players reported accepting money for playing poorly in a game. One half of one percent of men's basketball players reported the same." (NCAA, 2003b)

The harshness of the policy results from the NCAA's belief that illegal sports wagering is big business, and big business attracts organized crime. The involvement of impressionable college-age students is a concern. Not only is the welfare of student-athletes jeopardized, the very integrity of sports contests can be undermined. According to the NCAA (2002), "Sports wagering demeans the competition and competitors alike by a message that is contrary to the purposes and meaning of 'sport.' Sports competition should be appreciated for the inherent benefits related to participation of student-athletes, coaches and institutions in fair contests, not the amount of money wagered on the outcome of the competition" (p. 2). The NCAA has responded aggressively to combat the problem and communicate its stance on sports wagering. A media campaign, educational meetings with Final Four participants, Web postings, liaison activities with the FBI and other law enforcement units, background checks on game officials, signatures by athletes on affidavit forms prior to some championships, public service announcements, and education programs on campuses—all are active components of the NCAA's sports-wagering education activities (NCAA, 2002).

The issue of gambling in college sport is not unique to the NCAA. Members of the NAIA, who believe gambling undermines the very values of NAIA athletics, have also discussed the issue. A zero-tolerance policy exists for any form of sports wagering. In Canada the issue has drawn notice by researchers including those at the University of Toronto who are conducting studies to assess the incidence of sports gambling and its impact on Canadian student-athletes.

Administrators and governing bodies such as the NCAA have moved quickly to set policy prohibiting the association between gambling and college athletics. Enforcing the rules emerging from such policy becomes the next hurdle.

Enforcement

Since intercollegiate athletic organizations are collectives of member institutions, legislation is created *by* the members of the organization *for* the members of the organization. Enforcement Services, also called *Compliance,* refers to a department within the organization with employees who ensure that all institutions are abiding by the rules, thus maintaining the integrity of the rules and fair play among all participants. The intent of enforcement programs is to reduce violations by education, discovery, and the disbursement of appropriate penalties.

College athletic departments in both the United States and Canada are expected to monitor their rules compliance and self-report any violation. In addition, the NCAA has a Vice President for Enforcement Services assisted by 6 Directors and 19 enforcement representatives who have significant volumes of work as field investigators. The importance of the enforcement policy is underscored by the fact that a senior NCAA executive, a Vice President, is responsible for enforcement policy. Unfortunately, however, this arrangement is frequently perceived as inadequate by members of the NCAA because of the huge investigation workload assumed by only 20 people. The inquiry process involves field investigations, formal correspondence of inquiry, the development of a case summary, hearings before a Committee on Infractions, and, if necessary, a ruling regarding the violation and penalty (NCAA, 2003b). An appeal process is also provided, and attempts are made to ensure due process is followed in any investigation.

Enforcement is not accorded as much focus in the NAIA, CIS, and CCAA, where self-reporting is virtually the sole means of policing infractions. Each organization has a committee to deal with allegations of impropriety but no full-time enforcement officers. This is primarily a financial issue; these organizations do not have the resources available for full-time enforcement officers. For many sport organizations, funding is problematic, and intercollegiate athletics is no different.

Funding

It seems that every conceivable level of sport has funding woes. Children's sport programs are being dropped, professional sport is losing franchises, and recreational sport is becoming more an option only for those who are financially well off. Funding, or lack of funding, has also become a major issue for college athletic administrators. Many are surprised that funding is included in the policy issues of intercollegiate athletics. But consider the following myths: College sports make money; competitive sports fund recreational sports; no other sports would exist without football. These statements, in fact, are not accurate most of the time, but they are convenient arguments sometimes used to drive certain status quo decisions (Sperber, 2000). More accurate is the statement that funding is a major concern in intercollegiate athletics on every level (Fizel, Gustafson, & Hadley, 1999; Zimbalist, 1999). The cost of a Division IA football program is astronomical; the revenues derived, even through television contracts, quickly vanish in the expense column. In addition, problems of the national economies in both Canada and the United States can lead to reductions in university funding in general.

Lenskyj (2004) identified two changes that seem to reflect athletic funding pressures: "increasing corporatization of both Canadian and American university campuses, and the attempts by university administrators to build stadium facilities by imposing higher student fees." Likewise, Keels (2004) discussed the cancellation of the football program at the historically black Central State University in Ohio due to funding shortages.

To ensure the continuance of intercollegiate athletics, the Finance Committees of the NCAA and CIS are defining policies to help curb spending and reduce excess. Rules defining a maximum roster size, the allowable number of games, starting dates, and scheduling efficiencies have resulted and will continue to be an important focus for intercollegiate athletic administrators.

SUMMARY

The fall season is here! More than likely, fall conjures up thoughts of cooler weather, bright red and yellow leaves, apple picking, and college football games. For many people, the beginning of the college sports season is synonymous with the new year, as a new school year begins for all levels and vacations associated with the summer months are over. This association indicates the appeal of college athletics, not just for the participants and student body but also for the wider public who attend games and tune in to the mass media. Widespread interest in intercollegiate athletics has resulted in colleges offering a wide array of teams and developing excellent facilities for participants and spectators on campuses. It has also resulted in the need for college administrators to actively supervise the intercollegiate sport enterprise, its governance, operations, and policy development. From the humble beginning of a crew race between Harvard and Yale in 1852, thousands of competitions among institutions all over the United States and Canada are played today.

To compete with other colleges and universities with similar philosophies and values about competition, institutions become members of governing associations such as the NCAA, the NAIA, and the NJCAA in the United States, and the CIS and the CCAA in Canada. Members of these organizations meet to set policy, procedures, rules and regulations, and legislation regulating competitions, and to deal with the current climate.

The policies regulating competition debated from year to year depend on the current climate and financial environment. Eligibility seems to be a concern surfacing every year. The preservation of amateurism is also a timeless issue. The use of performance-enhancing drugs and the implementation of fair practices in providing gender equity have surfaced as issues in more recent decades. Setting policy regarding gambling and enforcement are even newer issues in intercollegiate athletics, whereas financial aid and overall program funding have ignited debate from the beginning.

Intercollegiate athletics and its governance will continue as hot topics on university campuses, and the governing structures will play an ever-increasing and important role in ensuring a safe and fair environment for competitions between colleges for participants and spectators alike.

Agents

You are the Athletic Director at Big State University. It has been reported in the nearest large newspaper, *The Elkhart Truth,* that your standout player, Billy Dover, a native of Elkhart, has been receiving cash and gifts from at least one agent during the past season, and maybe even during his sophomore year. He has been seen driving around campus in a brand-new Navigator and wearing expensive-looking gold jewelry, and you know for a fact that neither he nor his family could ever have purchased these items. Your high-profile coach, John Becher, has visions of making his mark so he can coach in the NBA someday soon, and he guided the Dover-led team to the Final Four, where they lost in the semifinal game.

This afternoon, a press conference is scheduled where you will have to face members of the press and comment on the allegations.

1. If in fact Dover received these items (in obvious violation of NCAA rules), who shares responsibility here? Dover? The agent? Coach Becher? The NCAA? Who needs to be held accountable?

2. If you were a college Athletic Director at a Division I school with athletes who potentially could go pro, what sort of agent-screening system could you put in place? Who would be involved? What would be the process to help protect and educate athletes about the dangers of dealing with agents?

3. Put yourself in the shoes of the President of Big State University. Using one of the ethical decision-making models described in Chapter 4, list the steps you would take to assess the employment status and situation of Coach Becher.

CHAPTER QUESTIONS

1. Compare and contrast the organizational structures of the NCAA, the NAIA, and the CIS. What is different in these three organizations, and why?

2. How might a policy help an athlete deal with the struggle of balancing requirements and expectations of academics versus athletics? Write a policy encouraging balance between both components of the term *student-athlete.*

3. Suppose you are the Athletic Director of a large Division I university with teams competing in the NCAA. It has come to your attention that the men's basketball coach has broken a series of recruiting rules in order to attract a 7-foot center to the team. In the end the

coach was unsuccessful in recruiting the athlete, but self-disclosure rules still exist in the NCAA. Using the SLEEPE Principle presented in Chapter 2, analyze the situation to help understand each of the ramifications of your decision. In the end, what will you do?

REFERENCES

Alcorn State University. (2007). Athletic mission. Retrieved May 16, 2007, from http://alcorn sports.com/tradition.php.

Applin, A. C. (1979, May). The recent historical development of the NCAA. Paper presented at the Annual Meeting of the North American Society for Sport History, Austin, TX.

Barr, C. A. (2005). Collegiate sport. In L. Pike Masteralexis, C. A. Barr, & M. A. Hums (Eds.), *Principles and practice of sport management* (2d ed., pp. 141–165). Sudbury, MA: Jones and Bartlett.

Brainard, J. (2006, October 20). James Madison U. will drop 10 sports teams, including 7 for men, to achieve gender balance. *Chronicle of Higher Education, 53*(9), 43.

CCAA. (2007a). CCAA profile. Retrieved May 8, 2007, from www.ccaa.ca/profile.htm.

CCAA. (2007b). Operating code. Retrieved May 8, 2007, from www.ccaa.ca/pdf/CCAAOperating Code2006-07.pdf.

CCAA. (2007c). Organizational chart. Retrieved May 8, 2007, from www.ccaa.ca/orgchart.html.

CIS. (2004). Equity and equality policy. Retrieved August 27, 2007, from http://universitysport.ca/ e/student/equity.cfm.

CIS. (2007a). History. Retrieved May 8, 2007, from www.universitysport.ca/e/bout/history.htm.

CIS. (2007b). Programs and services. Retrieved May 8, 2007, from http://universitysport.ca/e/about/ index.cfm.

CIS. (2007c). Board of directors. Retrieved May 8, 2007, from http://universitysport.ca/e/meetings/ documents/Nov.06BODMeetingMinutes.pdf.

CIS. (2007d). By-laws. P..BL9. Retrieved May 8, 2007, from http://universitysport.ca/e/pol_proc/ index.cfm.

CIS. (2007e). Athletes guide. Retrieved August 27, 2007, from http://universitysport.ca/e/student/ index.cfm#eligibility.

CIS. (2007f). Organizational chart. Retrieved May 8, 2007, from http://universitysport.ca/e/about/ org_chart.html.

CIS. (2007g). Doping and substance use. Retrieved August 27, 2007, from http://universitysport.ca/ e/student/index.cfm#doping.

Davenport, J. (1985). From crew to commercialism— The paradox of sport in higher education. In D. Chu, J. O. Segrave, & B. J. Becker (Eds.), *Sport and higher education* (pp. 5–16). Champaign, IL: Human Kinetics.

Dealy, F. X. (1990). *Win at any cost*. New York: Carol.

Fizel, J., Gustafson, E., & Hadley, L. (1999). *Sports economics: Current research*. London: Praeger.

Gerdy, J. R. (1997). *The successful college athletic program—The new standard*. Phoenix, AZ: Oryx Press.

Hult, J. S. (1994). The story of women's athletics: Manipulating a dream 1890–1985. In D. M. Costa & S. R. Guthrie (Eds.), *Women and sport: Interdisciplinary perspectives* (pp. 83–106). Champaign, IL: Human Kinetics.

Ingham, A. G., & Loy, J. W. (1993). *Sport in social development: Traditions, transitions, and transformations*. Champaign, IL: Human Kinetics.

Jones, B. (2007). *Progress, yes; but HBCUs paid a price for it*. Retrieved May 17, 2007, from http://sports.espn.go.com/espn/blackhistory2007/ news/story?id=2780876.

Kahn, L. M. (2006). The economics of college sports: Cartel behavior vs. amateurism. Institute for the Study of Labor Discussion Series (IZA DP No. 2186). Retrieved August 27, 2007, from ftp://repec. iza.org/RePEc/Discussionpaper/dp2186.pdf.

Keels, C. L. (2004). Funding shortages push back central state football program. *Black Issues in Higher Education, 21*(6), 12.

Knight Foundation Commission on Intercollegiate Athletics. (2001). A call to action: Reconnecting college sports and higher education. Retrieved June 12, 2003, from www.ncaa.org/databases/knight_commission/2001_report.

Knight Foundation Commission on Intercollegiate Athletics. (2007). Students and athletes. Retrieved August 27, 2007, from www./knightcommission.org.

Lenskyj, H. (2004). Funding Canadian university sport facilities: The University of Toronto stadium referendum. *Journal of Sport & Social Issues, 28*(4), 379–396.

NAIA. (2005). A guide for the college bound student athlete. Retrieved May 9, 2007, from http://naia.cstv.com/member-services/attend.html.

NAIA. (2007a). About the NAIA. Retrieved May 8, 2007, from http://naia.cstv.com/member-services/about.

NAIA. (2007b). Member institutions. Retrieved May 8, 2007, from http://naia.cstv.com/member-services/about/members.html.

NAIA. (2007c). Councils. Retrieved May 8, 2007, from http://naia.cstv.com/member-services/legislative/Councils.html.

NCAA. (2002). Gambling—Sports wagering. Retrieved April 20, 2002, from www.ncca.org/membership/enforcement/gambling/index.html.

NCAA. (2003a). Pay for (teaching to) play: Fee for lesson rules afford Division I student-athletes new benefits. Retrieved June 12, 2003, from www.ncca.org/news/2003/20030609/awide/4012n04.html.

NCAA. (2003b). NCAA study on sports wagering. Retrieved May 10, 2007, from www1.ncaa.org/membership/enforcement/gambling/study_on_sw/index.html.

NCAA. (2007a). History. Retrieved May 8, 2007, from www.ncaa.org/about/history.html.

NCAA. (2007b). About the NCAA: Purposes and goals. Retrieved May 8, 2007, from www.ncaa.org/about/purposes.html.

NCAA. (2007c). NCAA budget. Retrieved May 8, 2007, from www1.ncaa.org/finance/2006-07_budget.html.

NCAA. (2007d). NCAA membership report. Retrieved May 8, 2007, from www.ncaa.org/library/membership/membership_report/2006/2006_ncaa_membership_report.pdf.

NCAA. (2007e). Composition of the NCAA. Retrieved May 8, 2007, from www1.ncaa.org/membership/membership_svcs/membership_breakdown.html.

NCAA. (2007f). 2006–07 Guide for the college-bound student-athlete. Retrieved May 9, 2007, from www1.ncaaclearinghouse.net/NCAA/student/index_student.html.

NCAA. (2007g). Division I manual. Retrieved May 9, 2007, from www2.ncaa.org/portal/media_and_events/ncaa/publications/membership/index.html.

NCAA. (2007h).Useful resources. Retrieved May 10, 2007, from www2.ncaa.org/portal/legislation_and_governance/eligibility_and_recruiting/eligibility.html.

NCAA. (2007i). 2006–07 NCAA drug testing program book. Retrieved May 10, 2007, from www2.ncaa.org/portal/legislation_and_governance/eligibility_and_recruiting/drug_testing.html.

NCAA. (2007j). Gender equity in intercollegiate athletics. Retrieved May 10, 2007, from www1.ncaa.org/library/gereral/gender_equity/gender_equity_manual.pdf.

NCAA. (2008a). NCAA backgrounder on academic reform. Retrieved February 12, 2008, from www2.ncaa.org/portal/academics_and_athletes/education_and_research/academic_reform/backgrounder_academic_reform.html.

NCAA. (2008b). Playing rules. Retrieved March 31, 2008, from www.ncaa.org/wps/portal/legacysiteviewer?CONTENT_URL=http://www2.ncaa.org/portal/media_and_events/ncaa_publications/playing_rules.

OUA. (2007). The history of Ontario University Athletics. Retrieved May 8, 2007, from http://oua.ca/about.

OSU. (2008). Athletic Department Directory. Retrieved April 1, 2008, from www.ohiostatebuckeyes.com/ViewArticle.dbml?DB_OEM_ID=17300&KEY=&ATCLID=925292.

Purdue North Central. (2008). Our staff. Retrieved April 1, 2008, from www.pnc.edu/athletics/staff.html.

Rudolph, F. (1990). *The American college and university: A history.* Athens: University of Georgia Press.

Scott, H. A. (1951). *Competitive sports in schools and colleges.* New York: Harper and Brothers.

Sperber, M. (2000). *Beer and circus: How big-time college sports is crippling undergraduate education.* New York: Holt.

Staurowsky, E. J., & Abney, R. (2007). Intercollegiate athletics. In J. B. Parks, B. R. K. Zanger, & J. Quarterman (Eds.), *Contemporary sport management* (3d ed., pp. 67–96). Champaign, IL: Human Kinetics.

U. S. Department of Education. (2007). White House initiative on historically black colleges and universities. Retrieved May 16, 2007, from www.ed.gov/about/inits/list/whhbcu/edlite-index.html.

Wann, D. L. (2006). Examining the potential causal relationship between sport team identification and psychological well-being. *Journal of Sport Behavior, 29*(1), 79–95.

Waterloo-Cedar Falls Courier. (2003). Bowlsby: Sports safe at Iowa. Retrieved June 20, 2003, from www.wcfcourier.com/articles/2003/06/17/sports/local/0645d9f497c2565086256d48005401df.txt.

Zimbalist, A. S. (1999). *Unpaid professionals: Commercialism and conflict in big-time college sports.* Princeton, NJ: Princeton University Press.

9

THE MAJOR GAMES IN AMATEUR SPORT

Think of amateur sport as a highway. The highway is a stretch of road spanning informal, recreational opportunities (such as pickup basketball and Sunday afternoon touch football) to elite, multi-event competitions (such as World Championships and the Olympic Games). Lanes are open for participants, coaches, officials, and spectators. Participants can easily enter and exit the highway as their interests and abilities dictate. Events are organized all along the highway, filling specific needs for competition for the age group and competitive level of the athletes. Along the road amateur sport evolves from recreation into competitions for elite athletes. Such events exist for a variety of age groups at the local, national, and international levels. For example, teams compete for National Championships. Athletes are selected to represent their country on national teams competing in the World Championships, World University Games (also called the FISU Games), and Pan American Games. Such competitions normally lead to the pinnacle event staged every four years—the Olympic and the Paralympic Games. The purpose of this chapter is to investigate the governance structures of the organizations delivering the major games of elite amateur athletics. Given the scope and the importance of the Olympic and Paralympic Games, the organization and governance of the Olympics and the Paralympics will be discussed in separate chapters.

How did other major games come to exist, and how are they organized and governed? This chapter will approach this question in two ways. First, the governance of different organizations that provide athletes for major games will be discussed. Second, several major games will be presented to illustrate the governance structures of the actual events. Let's look briefly at the evolution and history of the major games of amateur sport.

History of the Major Games

Major advances in technology and urbanization led historians to describe the 19th century as "the age of progress" (Riess, 1995). Sport progressed at a phenomenal rate as well: "[T]he international foundation was truly laid for the gigantic proportions of sport today" (Glassford & Redmond, 1988, p. 140). Inventions such as the railroad (1830), the motorcar (1885), the camera (1826), the electric lamp (1881), and the radio (1901) were among the profound technological changes contributing to the evolution of sport (Glassford & Redmond, 1988).

Urbanization was also a major factor in the growth of the sport industry. Although cities have existed for thousands of years, a greater proportion of the population became centered in larger metropolitan areas during this period. The city became the site of huge stadiums and other facilities and the focal point for natural masses of participants and spectators. Tournaments, festivals, and special events became more commonplace as both leisure time and general affluence increased (Kidd, 1999). Technology, especially related to easing long-distance transportation, provided the opportunity for both national and international competition. Before long, governments focused on the idea of sport as an alternative to war, in which political ideologies and national strength could be displayed by winning international sporting competitions (Riordan & Kruger, 1999).

The advancement of political ideology through sport likely occurred around the time Baron Pierre de Coubertin revived the ancient Olympic

Games in the late 19th century. Baron de Coubertin's dream was that sport could be used to increase goodwill among nations of the world. He reinstated Olympic competition when, in 1894, officials from 12 countries endorsed a modern cycle of Olympic Games (Glassford & Redmond, 1988).

Baron de Coubertin's Olympic Games were not entirely original. Games in England in the Cotswolds and the Highland Games of Scotland were staged in the 19th century. The concept of major games and festivals spread quickly. The Far Eastern Championship Games were organized in 1913 as regional games after the rebirth of the modern Olympics. Teams from China, Japan, the Philippines, Thailand, and Malaysia participated (Glassford & Redmond, 1988). Similar games were established in Central America, and teams from Puerto Rico, Cuba, Mexico, and other Latin American countries participated. The first British Empire Games (later renamed the Commonwealth Games) took place in Hamilton, Canada, in 1930. Other countries organized regional games such as State Games and National Championships. In addition, international competitions such as the Asian Games, the Pan American Games, the Goodwill Games, and other special group events were developed. For instance, the International Student Games were first held in 1924 (renamed the Universiade in 1959). In 1960 the first Paralympic Games were held for individuals with disabilities. Today games exist for every age group in virtually every sport. The World Little League Baseball Championships, the America's Cup yachting competition, World Championships for speed skating, and the World Deaf Games are examples of major amateur sporting events that dominate today's world sporting calendar. Who organizes these events, and how are they operated? Next, we investigate the organizations and governance structures of several major games in amateur sport.

Governance

The governance of amateur sport differs in countries around the world. The extent of government focus on policy involving the delivery of amateur sport became more prominent in the latter half of the 20th century (Chalip, Johnson, & Stachura, 1996). Even so, the degree to which government is involved in sport policy differs depending on social, cultural, and political national perspectives. In the United States, sport is intensely popular and a cause for national unity. However, American public policy has historically claimed (some say rhetorically) that sport is independent of government (Chalip & Johnson, 1996). In Canada the promotion of national unity and identity are central themes in government involvement in sport-policy development. In both nations, some level of government involvement helps to shape the policies governing the athletes representing their nations at the major games of amateur athletics.

Governing Structures for Amateur Sport in North America

Three branches of government exist in the United States: The legislative branch is responsible for policy making; the executive branch implements laws and public policies; and the judicial branch interprets the law. Each branch plays an important role in policy development, along with state and local governments. In fact, many state and local governments are influenced by national policies. The policy developed at each level of government has implications for amateur sport. At the national level, laws specific to sport have been enacted; for example, the Amateur Sports Act of 1978 promotes, coordinates, and sets national goals for amateur sport in the United States through the development of national governing bodies (United States Amateur Sports Act, 1978). Another example is the Stevens Amendment of 1998, which changed the Amateur Sports Act so that it became known as the Ted Stevens Olympic and Amateur Sports Act; the new law strengthened athletes' rights, provided procedures for dispute resolution, and incorporated the Paralympics into the Act by updating provisions for disabled athletes (U.S. Senate Committee on Commerce, Science, and Transportation, 1998). Policies affecting sport might also result from the application of laws not written specifically for sport, such as the Americans with Disabilities Act of 1990, established to prevent discrimination on the basis of disability, or through federal government agencies such as the President's Council on Physical Fitness and Sport, which sets policy dealing with issues related to physical fitness and sport (Chalip & Johnson, 1996; Americans with Disabilities Act, 1990).

State and national organizations exist in order to provide rules, regulations, promotion, and competition for specific sports. In the next sections three examples of state and national organizations are presented. First, the Amateur Athletic Union (AAU) is described. It is one of the largest multisport organizations in the United States, incorporating both state and national offices with the mandate to promote and develop amateur sport opportunities in a variety of sports. Second, Sport Canada is discussed. In Canada, the federal government oversees the development of amateur sport through Sport Canada, a department helping to set policy and provide leadership for Canadian national teams. Finally, USA Basketball is presented. It's an example of a national sport organization that serves to organize basketball in the United States by operating in conjunction with 15 affiliate associations. How are these groups organized and how is policy developed?

The Amateur Athletic Union

The AAU is a multisport organization dedicated to promoting and developing amateur sport and physical fitness programs. It was founded in 1888 to establish standards for amateur sport participation (AAU, 2007). In the early days, the AAU represented all amateur sports at International Federation meetings and was the association responsible for organizing national teams to represent the United States at international competitions, including the Olympic Games. As mentioned earlier, in 1978 the U.S. Senate and the U.S. House of Representatives enacted the Amateur Sports Act, the purpose of which was to coordinate amateur sport throughout the United States. This was done, in part, by establishing individual organizations for the purpose of developing specific sports. The Amateur Sports Act had a profound effect on the mandate of the AAU and caused the organization to refocus its purpose away from representing U. S. teams internationally and toward the development and provision of sports programs for a wider spectrum of participants (AAU, 2007). At this point the AAU introduced the "sports for all, forever" philosophy. Today, the AAU offers a broad spectrum of activities, from baton twirling to flag football and pretty much everything in between.

Ⓦww

Amateur Athletic Union
www.aausports.org

Mission. The AAU seeks to promote and deliver amateur sport widely within the United States. It exists as a network of local chapters that provides programs for children, men, and women, in a large number of activities. The breadth of its mandate is illustrated by the inclusiveness of its programming. The mission statement of the AAU is presented in Figure 9.1.

Financials. The AAU is a nonprofit organization funded through membership dues and donations. Yearly member dues are modest: Any youth can belong for only $12, and the Added Benefits Membership option (which allows participation in nonsanctioned events) is only an additional $14. Dues for coaches and adults are only slightly higher. Sponsorships and partnerships are solicited, such as the alliance made between the AAU and Walt Disney World in 1996, which precipitated the relocation of the AAU National Office to Orlando, Florida. Each year more than 40 AAU national events are held at Disney's Wide World® of Sports Complex.

Ⓦww

Disney's Wide World of Sports® Complex

http://disneyworldsports.disney.go.com/dwws/en_US/home/home?name=HomePage&bhcp=1

Mission statement of the AAU.   **FIGURE 9.1**

To offer amateur sports programs through a volunteer base for all people to have the physical, mental, and moral development of amateur athletes and to promote good sportsmanship and good citizenship.

Source: AAU (2007).

Membership. Athletes, coaches, volunteers, and officials make up the membership of the AAU. The organization has thousands of members (500,000 participants and 50,000 volunteers) and offers programming for both youth and adult participants.

Organizational structure. Fifty-seven associations make up the AAU, each representing either a state (for example, Oklahoma) or a region (for example, New England) of the United States. The Board of Directors comprises association officers, sport committee chairs, and national committee members (similar to a national assembly or council in other organizations). The AAU is managed by a smaller Executive Committee, which comprises an elected group of officers: the President, First and Second Vice President, Secretary, Treasurer, plus one representative from each of the four national regions. The entire operation is managed by a group of full-time staff members led by the Executive Director. In addition, a host of committees deal with AAU activities such as Finance, Insurance, Youth Sport, Adult Sport, and Law and Legislation. Policy is developed through committees, analyzed and voted on by the Executive Committee, and then voted upon by the Board of Directors at annual national meetings. Much of the policy discussion involves the development of rules, regulations, and hosting guidelines for events. Figure 9.2 depicts the organizational structure of the AAU.

FIGURE	9.2	Organizational structure of the AAU.

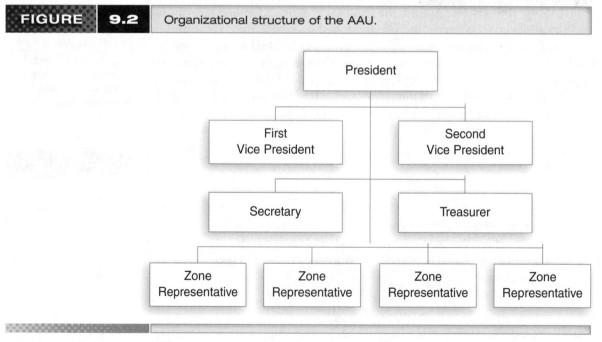

Source: AAU (2007).

Sport Canada

Sport Canada is a branch within the Department of Canadian Heritage of the Canadian federal government. It is responsible for elite sport programming and sport policy development, and is dedicated to valuing and strengthening the Canadian sport experience. Sport Canada has 10 strategic directions (Sport Canada, 2007a):

1. strengthening sport leadership
2. providing strategic support for high performance programming
3. promoting technically sound sport development
4. enhancing opportunities for sport participation
5. maximizing the benefits of hosting
6. promoting linguistic duality in the Canadian sport system
7. strengthening the ethical foundation of sport
8. expanding the body of knowledge about sport
9. strengthen sport Canada program and policy evaluation
10. harmonizing the Canadian sport system

Mission. The mission of Sport Canada is to promote sport. The organization seeks to coordinate and encourage the achievement of excellence by Canadian athletes on the world stage, as well as to work with a variety of partners such as national sport organizations, coaches, and other levels of government to provide the necessary environment for high-performance athletes to achieve. Sport Canada's mission also extends to promoting sport as a source of pleasure, personal satisfaction, and a means of achieving good health. Each of these pursuits is captured in the Canadian Sport Policy, a document defining the goals for sport in Canada by 2012 (Canadian Sport Policy, 2002). These goals include enhancing participation, excellence, capacity, and interaction of members of the sport community. The mission statement of Sport Canada is presented in Figure 9.3.

Financials. Sport Canada derives its funding from the Canadian federal government. It then establishes funding priorities and guidelines for the Canadian sport system. Sport Canada finances the following programs (Sport Canada, 2007c):

1. Athlete Assistance Program—living and training allowances for athletes
2. National Sport Organization Support Program—national team funding; development of coaches and officials
3. Sport Hosting Program—financial assistance for the hosting of international single-sport events (World Championships, World Cups, Qualification Tournaments) in Canada

WWW

Sport Canada
www.pch.gc.ca/progs/sc

| FIGURE | 9.3 | Mission statement of Sport Canada. |

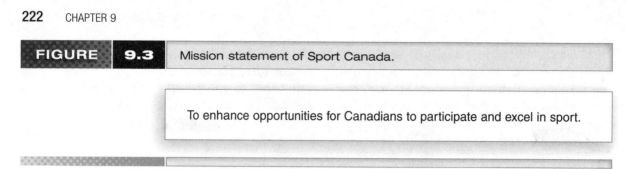

To enhance opportunities for Canadians to participate and excel in sport.

Source: Sport Canada (2007b).

Membership. Sport Canada is an umbrella organization seeking to support the mandate of high-performance sport. As such, it does not have a membership as national or state sport organizations have. It comprises civil servants of the Canadian federal government. It is important to note that Sport Canada is separate and distinct from Canadian National Sport Organizations (NSOs) as well as from the Canadian Olympic Committee (COC). The former is linked to Sport Canada because it provides some degree of funding in return for compliance with policy and directives as set by Sport Canada. The COC, however, is completely separate from Sport Canada. While consultation and an open chain of communication is encouraged by both organizations, no formal relationship or reporting structure exists.

Organizational structure. Sport Canada is led by a Director General who reports through a Deputy Minister to the Secretary of Sport. The organization is subdivided into five areas: Policy and Planning, Sport Support, Sport Excellence, Major Games and Hosting, and Business Operations. The areas of sport policy and sport programs are further subdivided to deal with specific areas of focus, for instance, national sport policy. Within this unit, policy is set regarding eligible forms of funding for athletes, NSO requirements regarding gender and language equity, and intergovernmental strategy and communication. A variety of program managers and sport consultants handle the duties within each subunit of Sport Canada. The organizational structure of Sport Canada is presented in Figure 9.4.

USA Baseball
http://mlb.mlb.com/usa_baseball/index.jsp

Judo Canada
www.judocanada.org

Hellenic Beach Volleyball Federation
www.sport.gov.gr/3/30k/e30k1.html

National Sport-Governing Bodies

Within each country, one national-level sport organization generally is recognized as the regulatory body for a particular sport. Sometimes these are governmental units, and other times they are freestanding sport organizations. These organizations have names like USA Baseball, Judo Canada, or Hellenic Beach Volleyball Federation. Depending on the nation, these organizations are called national governing bodies (NGBs) or national sport organizations (NSOs). To illustrate the governance structure, USA Basketball is an excellent example.

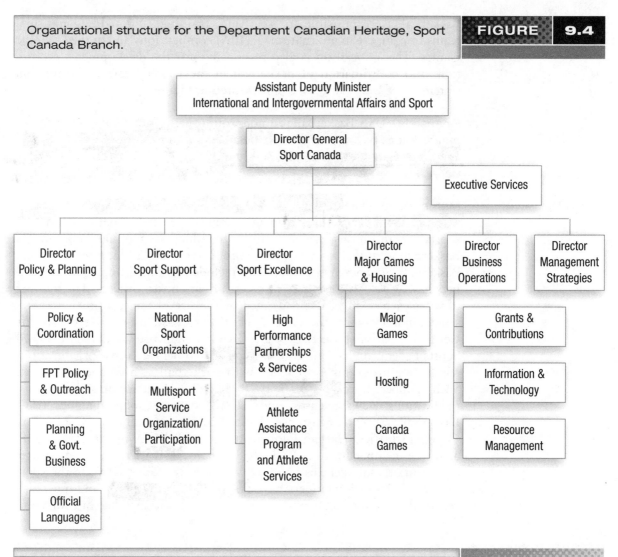

Organizational structure for the Department Canadian Heritage, Sport Canada Branch.

FIGURE 9.4

Source: Sport Canada (2007d).

USA Basketball

USA Basketball is the NGB for basketball in the United States. As such, its employees oversee the development of the game of basketball from the grass roots through the elite levels.

USA Basketball
www.usabasketball.com

Mission. USA Basketball is the international U. S. representative to the USOC, and acts as the FIBA member in the United States (USA Basketball, 2007). FIBA is the international governing body for basketball. USA

Basketball is responsible for selecting, training, and fielding national teams to compete in international (FIBA) competitions and in the Olympic Games. The association is also responsible for the development, promotion, and coordination of basketball in the United States. The mission statement of USA Basketball is presented in Figure 9.5.

Financials. USA Basketball is a nonprofit organization. Although member organizations pay annual dues, the majority of funding is derived from revenues associated with corporate partnerships and sponsorships, television, sales of apparel and souvenirs, hosting rights, and Olympic revenue sharing.

Membership. The three types of USA Basketball memberships are active, associate, and affiliate. Active membership is open to "all national amateur sports organizations which actively conduct a national program in Basketball as a competitive sport" (USA Basketball, 2002, n.p.). National Basketball Coaches Associations are included in this group. Active members have voting representation through their chosen officers. The number of votes each member has is defined by the size of the constituency represented. For instance, the AAU is entitled to cast three votes before the Congress (National Meeting), the NCAA has eight votes, and the USA Deaf Sports Federation has one vote. Associate members are those organizations conducting programs in or allied with basketball as a competitive sport. Such members have "neither voice nor vote" in the association but receive publications, news releases, and selected organizational mailings (USA Basketball, 2007). For instance, Athletes in Action, California Community College Athletics, Harlem Globetrotters, and YMCA of the USA are all associate members of USA Basketball. Finally, affiliate members are travel and promotional agencies or other commercial groups active in the sport of basketball. Such members have "neither voice nor vote" and must also certify their willingness to abstain from using the membership for com-

FIGURE 9.5   Mission statement of USA Basketball.

> The purpose of this Association is to act as the national governing body for the sport of basketball in the United States, and in such connection, to be recognized as such by the USOC and to act as the FIBA member in the U.S.

Source: USA Basketball (2007).

mercial purposes. Affiliate members receive regular publications and other mailings from the association. USA Basketball affiliate members include Basketball Travelers, Inc., and Sport Tours International, Inc.

Organizational structure. USA Basketball members meet yearly at a Congress of the association. In addition to the memberships defined above, active athletes are eligible for 20 percent of the total Congress voting power and are elected to the Congress. The Congress is required to receive reports from the President on past and future activities, receive a Nominating Committee Report, hold elections, and act on business before the association.

The affairs of USA Basketball are governed and conducted by a Board of Directors. The board consists of 25 members, of which 5 are active athletes and 1 is the immediate Past President. Constituents of USA Basketball are permitted to name members to the board as follows: one representative each to the AAU, NAIA, NFHS, NJCAA, and U. S. Armed Forces; four representatives each to the NBA and NCAA. Five other members of the Board of Directors who are not active members are elected at-large members. The board meets at least annually and has primary responsibility for developing policy and approving actions regarding the competitive basketball programs of the association (USA Basketball, 2007). A slate of elected officers makes up the Executive Committee, which is empowered to deal with day-to-day operations on behalf of the Board of Directors, in conjunction with the organization's Executive Director and professional staff. The officers consist of the President, Vice President, Vice President (Senior Men), Vice President (Senior Women), Vice President (Men), Vice President (Women), Secretary, Treasurer, and two Athlete Representatives. The President is elected from among the members of the board, but no other officer can simultaneously serve as an officer and board member (USA Basketball, 2007). Policy is defined by the board and the Executive Committee and via committee work. Standing committees of the association include Constitution and Bylaws, Disabled, Finance, Membership, Officials, and committees defined by the board for specific basketball programs and events. The organizational structure of USA Basketball is presented in Figure 9.6.

The organizations discussed above are all involved in organizing athletic competitions for elite-level athletes or sending elite athletes to major competitions. State and provincial organizations feed into NGBs and NSOs, respectively. NSOs are aided by other organizations such as the AAU, Sport Canada, the National Coaches Associations, and the NCAA via their roles in training elite athletes, coaches, and officials. One component of their collective missions is to enhance the ability of athletes to perform on the world stage at international competitions and major games. Next, we investigate the governance structures of some of the major games of amateur athletics.

FIGURE   9.6   Organizational structure of the Executive Committee of USA Basketball.

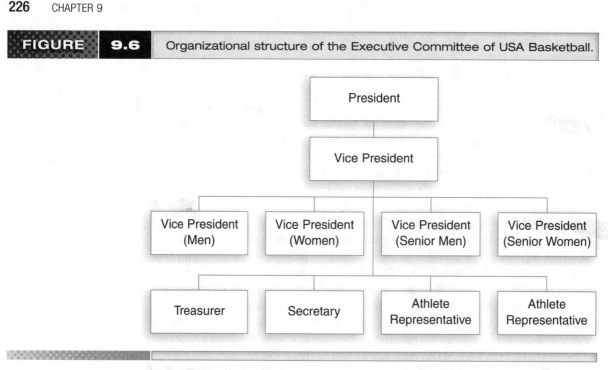

Source: USA Basketball (2007).

Organizations That Manage Major Games in Amateur Sport

Fédération Internationale de Basketball Amateur

www.fiba.com

Fédération Internationale Football Association

www.fifa.com

Major games are national or international events run as single-sport or multisport championships. International world championships that are sport specific are common to many sports, for example, the FIBA World Basketball Championships and the FIFA Soccer World Cup. Also common are major international multisport games for which participation is restricted by eligibility criteria (such as country of origin, age group, or disability), such as the Pan American Games, Commonwealth Games, World University Games, World Deaf Games, and Special Olympics International Games. How are these major games organized? The next sections will address these multisport competitions.

Pan American Games

The Pan American Games are a celebration of sport, competition, and international friendship for nations of the Americas in the Western Hemisphere (Rio 2007 Pan American Games, 2007). The Games have run on a strict quadrennial cycle since the first competition in 1951, typically scheduled for the summer in the year directly preceding the Olympic Games (Pan American Games Summer, 2002).

Pan American Games
www.rio2007.org.br

Mission. The Pan American Games are first and foremost an international multisport competition. However, since the event's inception the organizers have sought a broader purpose. Along with sporting competition, the Pan American Games are about friendship, life, culture, and the strength of human spirit (Pan American Games '99, 2002). They are also a celebration of the Americas' community and of each country's dedication to the nations making up the Americas. The motto of the Pan American Sports Organization (PASO) incorporates Spanish, Portuguese, English, and French: "America, Espirito, Sport, Fraternite," which translates loosely as "The American spirit of friendship through sports" (Pan American Games Summer, 2002). The mission statement of the Pan Am Games is presented in Figure 9.7.

Financials. The Pan American Games are a huge undertaking, third in scope after the Olympic Games and World University Games (Pan American Games '99, 2002). Depending upon the extent of facility development required, the budget for the games can top $200 million. The majority of the expenses include building or upgrading facilities, organizing the games and festivals, housing the competitors, and hosting dignitaries. While competing nations are responsible for their own travel costs, the host committee covers on-site expenses. A fee is guaranteed to PASO for the hosting rights, and additional revenues are generated from television ($10 million in 2003), sales, sponsorships and advertising, and entry fees.

Membership. Athletes from countries in the Americas are eligible to compete in the Pan American Games. The Americas include North, Central, and South America, as well as Caribbean nations. More than 2,500 athletes from 22 nations competed at the first Pan Am Games in 1951 (Pan American Games Summer, 2002). Currently, 42 nations belong to PASO.

Mission statement of the Pan American Games.	**FIGURE**	**9.7**

The Pan American Games bring together athletes from the countries of the Americas in a festival of sport and international friendship. The games are held every four years in the year preceding the Olympic Games.

Source: XIV Pan American Games (2002).

Organizational structure. PASO governs the games, awarding the hosting rights and setting policy and direction for the competition. PASO headquarters is located in Mexico City and is presided over by a President and an Executive Council. Each host country then establishes its own organizing committee. Normally the organizing committee comprises the President, Executive Vice President, Secretary, Treasurer, Second Vice President, Sports Commissioner, and an extensive number of Organizing Committee members who are assigned portfolios and committees (XIV Pan American Games, 2002). An example of the host organizing committee structure for the XV Pan American Games in Rio de Janeiro, Brazil is presented in Figure 9.8.

Commonwealth Games

Commonwealth Games
www.thecgf.com

The Commonwealth Games are a multisport competition bringing together countries from around the world that are united by history, as opposed to geography (as in the Pan American Games). The Commonwealth Games involve competition for those once belonging to the British Empire (see Figure 9.9) and for nations and territories that subsequently joined the British Commonwealth after the empire (Dheensaw, 1994). The countries comprising the Commonwealth share a history and acceptance of a common past. The Commonwealth Games continue to bring athletes and spectators of these nations together every four years for a significant festival of sport.

FIGURE 9.8 Organizational structure of the 2003 Pan Am Games.

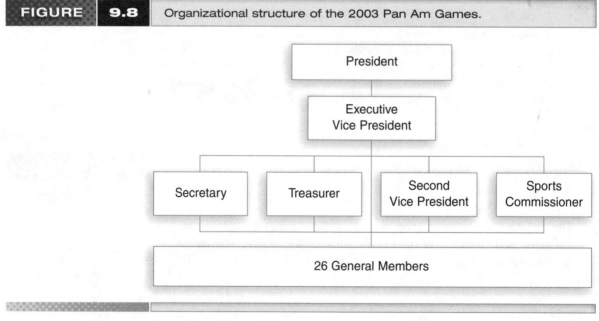

Source: Pan Am Games (2002).

THE MAJOR GAMES IN AMATEUR SPORT

Competing countries of the 2006 Commonwealth Games.   **FIGURE   9.9**

AFRICA

Botswana	Lesotho	Nigeria	Tanzania
The Gambia	Malawi	Seychelles	Uganda
Cameroon	Mauritius	Sierra Leone	Zambia
Ghana	Mozambique	South Africa	
Kenya	Namibia	Swaziland	

AMERICAS

Belize	Canada	Guyana	St. Helena
Bermuda	Falkland Islands		

OCEANIA

Australia	Nauru	Papua New Guinea	Tuvalu
Cook Islands	New Zealand	Samoa	Vanuatu
Fiji	Niue	Solomon Islands	
Kiribati	Norfolk Islands	Tongo	

CARIBBEAN

Anguilla	Barbados	Jamaica	St. Vincent
Antigua	Cayman Islands	Montserrat	Trinidad and Tobago
Bahamas	Dominica	St. Kitts	Turks and Caicos
Virgin Islands	Grenada	St. Lucia	Isles

EUROPE

Cyprus	Guernsey	Malta	Wales
England	Isle of Man	Northern Ireland	
Gibraltar	Jersey	Scotland	

ASIA

Bangladesh	India	Maldives	Singapore
Brunei	Malaysia	Pakistan	Sri Lanka

Source: Commonwealth Games (2006).

Mission. The mission of the Commonwealth Games follows a vision of hosting a world-class multisport event for peoples of Commonwealth nations. The idea of a friendly festival of competition, held on a four-year cycle, is common to their mission statement, presented in Figure 9.10.

Financials. The economics of the Commonwealth Games are very similar to the Pan American Games. Revenues are generated through television, sponsorship and advertising, and sales. Perhaps more importantly, the games are seen as playing an economic role and creating a legacy for the hosting community. The games were hosted by Manchester, England, in 2002, and part of Manchester's platform for hosting was based on the economic impact to be gained for the region, as the organizing committee stated: "The games will play a crucial role in the continued physical, economic and social regeneration of Manchester, but will also bring regional economic benefits and provide a boost to national claims to host future international sporting events" (Manchester Commonwealth Games, 2002, n.p.). The 2006 Commonwealth Games were also successful in creating a financial legacy for the City of Melbourne, Australia (Tucker, 2006).

Membership. Athletes from 71 nations worldwide compete in a variety of individual and team sports at the Commonwealth Games. These nations and territories belong to the Commonwealth and are located in parts of Africa, the Americas, Asia, Caribbean, Europe, and Oceania.

Organizational structure. The Commonwealth Games Federation (CGF) is the umbrella organization responsible for regulating the competition. It is led by a President and two Vice Presidents, along with an Executive Board composed of Vice Patron (nonvoting); six elected Regional Vice Presidents (representing Africa, America, Asia, Caribbean, Europe, Oceania,

FIGURE 9.10 Mission statement of the Commonwealth Games.

> Our vision is to promote a unique, friendly, world class Games and to develop sport for the benefit of the people, the nations, and the territories of the Commonwealth, and thereby strengthen the Commonwealth. Every four years the Games celebrate the shared values, traditions, and language of the Commonwealth.

Source: Commonwealth Games Federation (2002). Reprinted with permission.

and Australia, but not the host region); honorary positions of Secretary, Treasurer, Legal Advisor, and Medical Advisor; an Athlete's Representative; a member representing the host region; and a group of Officers (CGF, 2006). The Executive Board and Officers help to set policy enacted by a CGF professional staff led by the CEO.

Similar to the Pan American Games, the local hosting community develops an organizing committee to deliver the competition. This group forms to bid for the event and, if successful, operates for several years prior to staging the Commonwealth Games. The committee then dissolves in the year after the games, when final financial and operational reports are completed. The next Commonwealth Games will be staged in Delhi, India, in October 2010.

World University Games

The World University Games (also called the Universiade) is a sporting and cultural festival held every two years for university-level athletes, a large multisport games governed by FISU (FISU, 2007a).

Mission. Founded in 1949, FISU is responsible for supervising the summer and the winter Universiades, as well as World University Championships in select sports. Universiades are held to bring university-level student-athletes from around the world to different countries to compete in 12 compulsory and up to 5 optional sports as chosen by the host country (FISU, 2007b). For example, the 2007 FISU Summer Games were held in Bangkok, Thailand. The theme for the Universiade was "All Become One" (24th Universiade, 2007). The Bangkok FISU Games included competition in the 12 compulsory sports of athletics (track and field), basketball, fencing, football (soccer), gymnastics (rhythmic and artistic), judo, swimming, diving, water polo, table tennis, tennis, and volleyball, and the 5 optional sports of badminton, golf, shooting, softball, and tae kwon do (24th Universiade, 2007). The mission statement of FISU is presented in Figure 9.11.

Financials. FISU is funded through marketing activities, television incomes, organizing fees, and subscriptions (FISU, 2002). The Universiade is run as a multisport festival, bid for by a host country, and run as a business. Revenues are generated in a similar manner to the Pan American and the Commonwealth Games, with government funding, corporate sponsorship, television-rights fees, entry fees, and sales making up the largest components of the budget. Summer World University Games are second in size to the Olympic Games, involving as many as 174 nations (in Daegu, Korea, in 2003) and 7,805 participants (in Izmir, Turkey, in 2005) (FISU, 2007b). Size alone often dictates the need to develop new facilities to stage the FISU Games.

World University Games
www.fisu.net

| FIGURE | 9.11 | Mission statement of the FISU. |

> FISU (International University Sports Federation) was formed within university institutions in order to promote sporting values and encourage sporting practice in harmony with, and complementary to, the university spirit. To promote sporting values means encouraging friendship, fraternity, fair play, perseverance, integrity, co-operation, and application amongst students who will one day hold responsible and key positions in politics, the economy, culture and industry.

Source: FISU (2007b).

Membership. FISU comprises 142 National University Sports Federations (FISU, 2007b). The United States Collegiate Sports Council is composed of representatives of the various administrators and support staff of the NCAA, NAIA, and their member institutions. This Council and CIS are the federations representing the United States and Canada, respectively, at FISU. National university sports federations gain membership by paying fees and providing proof of eligibility. The Universiades are open to all student-athletes between the ages of 17 and 28 who are eligible to compete in university sport at home and who have not been out of school for more than a year (FISU, 2007b).

Organizational structure. FISU is composed of a General Assembly where each of the 141 member nations have representation. The General Assembly elects an Executive Committee to act on its behalf between meetings of the Assembly. The Executive Committee of FISU is elected on the basis of a four-year term and is composed of 23 positions. It is led by the President and comprises a First Vice President, four Vice Presidents, Secretary-General, Treasurer, First Assessor, 14 Assessors, and a Senior Auditor. This committee is the main policy-making group within FISU. In addition, the host city for the Universiade will name an Organizing Committee to plan and manage the staging of the World University Games.

World Games for the Deaf

The first International Games for the Deaf (renamed World Games for the Deaf in 1969) were held in 1924 in Paris, France (Carbin, 1996). Just prior to the inaugural games, a group of Deaf European men organized the International Committee of Silent Sports, abbreviated CISS. Today, CISS refers to the International Committee of Sports of the Deaf (CISS, 2007a). This organization oversees the World Games for the Deaf (recently termed the *Deaflympics*) and the Deaf World Championships.

Mission. The motto of the CISS is "Equal Through Sports." The organization aims to bring deaf athletes together to compete in a range of athletic events, offering them the opportunity to compete and celebrate their achievements, uniqueness as deaf athletes, and accomplishments. The CISS mission statement is presented in Figure 9.12. It is operationalized by "creating more and better athletes with higher standards of excellence; a significant level of international recognition; an increased and sound budget; and an efficient and effective organization" (CISS, 2007b).

Financials. The CISS is funded through annual membership fees and levies, along with contributions, donations, sponsorships, and government grants (CISS, 2007a). Local communities bid for the hosting rights of the World Games or sport-specific world championships and raise dollars in support of the event through government funding, corporate sponsorship, sales, and other marketing initiatives.

Membership. The CISS has four membership categories: full and associate members, regional confederations, and honorary life members. Full members, national associations, have voting privileges and participate at the Congress, the governing body of the CISS. National associations are admitted to the Congress upon review of the report of the Legal Committee of CISS, which investigates each applicant's constitution, documents of incorporation, financial reports, and qualifications for membership. Only one national association per country may be admitted as a full member of the CISS. Currently the organization has 83 full members from around the

www

World Games for the Deaf
www.fisu.net

Mission statement of the CISS.   **FIGURE 9.12**

The mission of CISS is to celebrate the spirit of Deaf Sports where deaf athletes come together as members of a cultural and linguistic minority to strive to reach the pinnacle of competition.

Source: CISS (2007b). Reprinted with permission.

world and 1 associate member. Associate memberships are at the discretion of the Executive Committee; currently the International Martial Arts Federation for the Deaf is the only associate member. Honorary membership may be conferred for meritorious services. Members pay annual fees.

Organizational structure. Each member has a vote at the Congress. Between congresses, an Executive Committee has the power to deal with the business of the association. The Executive Committee is composed of the President, Vice President, three at-large members, a Sports Director, and the President of each regional confederation (nonvoting). In a similar fashion to other World Games, the World Games for the Deaf are awarded to a city on the basis of a bid to host the championships. An organizing committee, structured to meet the needs of the event, includes the President, Vice President, Secretary, Treasurer, and Chairs for Facilities, Marketing, Sport Operations, Transportation, Special Events, and Media Relations.

Special Olympics World Games

www@

Special Olympics World
Games
www.specialolympics.org

Most people are familiar with Special Olympics. Perhaps you have volunteered at local- or state-level events. But did you know that Special Olympics also holds a major international-level event? Special Olympics World Games is a multisport world festival held every four years for individuals with cognitive and developmental disabilities at all levels. Special Olympics and Paralympics are two separate organizations recognized by the IOC. Special Olympics provides sports opportunities for individuals with cognitive and developmental disabilities, while the Paralympics provides sports opportunities for elite athletes with physical disabilities. The Special Olympics World Games take place the year before the Olympic Games, while the Paralympic Games are conducted immediately following the Olympics (2007 Special Olympics World Games, 2007a).

Mission. The mission of the Special Olympics World Games includes providing an exceptional sporting experience for participants with disabilities from around the world. The vision of the Special Olympics World Games (2007a) in Shanghai, China, was to do the following:

> Embrace the diversity of all individuals' abilities worldwide and celebrate all differences. Through these World Games, Special Olympics athletes transcend the boundaries of geography, nationality, political philosophy, gender, age, culture and religion. It is the common pursuit of achievement, the shared moment of victory, which brings even the most diverse people together. This spirit of unity on the playing fields, in families and communities throughout the world makes for a better way of life for all. Special Olympics celebrates the fundamental com-

monality of all people. Together, we can learn to accept each other, and this will allow us all to contribute to society and to the world we all share.

The mission statement of the organizers of the 2007 Special Olympics World Games is presented in Figure 9.13.

Financials. The host committee of the 2003 Games in Ireland estimated the Special Olympics World Games would cost €34 million (US $32 million at that time) cash and a further €23 million (US $21 million) for in-kind products and services. To deliver the event, sponsorship and corporate partnerships were needed, along with revenue from sales and municipal support. For 2003 the Bank of Ireland was the premier partner for the Games and over €15.23 million (US $14 million) had been raised in sponsorship one year out from the games (2003 Special Olympics World Games, 2002). Beyond corporate sponsorship, fundraising was initiated through programs such as Support an Athlete, Golf Challenge, Race Day, and a Gala Ball.

Membership. The Special Olympics World Games have participants rather than members. The 2007 Games showcased the athletic skills, courage, and dignity of thousands of athletes with cognitive and developmental disabilities from around the world. Approximately 7,500 athletes, 40,000 volunteers, 3,500 event officials, and thousands of families, journalists, and spectators attended the games (2007 Special Olympics World Games, 2007c). The athletes' oath for the Games is "Let me win, but if I cannot win, let me be brave in the attempt."

Mission statement of the Special Olympics World Games Organizing Committee. **FIGURE 9.13**

The mission statement of the Special Olympics is to provide year-round sports training and athletic competition in a variety of Olympic-type sports for children and adults with intellectual disabilities, giving them continuing opportunities to develop physical fitness, demonstrate courage, experience joy and participate in a sharing of gifts, skills and friendship with their families, other Special Olympics athletes and the community.

Source: 2007 Special Olympics World Games (2007b).

Organizational structure. The Special Olympics World Games are managed by a Games Organizing Committee (GOC). The GOC is led by a Chair and is composed of a fairly large number of high-profile community members who act as Directors. The 2003 Ireland GOC had 23 Directors and 2007 Games in Shanghai maintain a large organizational structure and over 20 Directors. The GOCs are incorporated as a company under the name of the Games being organized. The GOC's Board of Directors included highly experienced individuals from a variety of public and private sector backgrounds. These volunteers, led by a CEO, oversaw the activities of paid staff. For the 2007 Shanghai Games, committees such as Security, Quality Management, Transportation, Information Technology, Competitions, Volunteers, among many others, were employed.

Current Policy Areas

Hosting major games as described above is a significant undertaking. Each event requires considerable organizational efforts, large financial support, and thousands of workers, both paid and volunteer. The organizing committee may plan for three or four years to ensure a safe and effective competition. Along the way, organizers will surely deal with many issues and problems. Some are internal to the particular event, such as fundraising and security. Many others are externally imposed, often by the governing international federation and include issues such as doping control and the influences of mass media. Other concerns stem from our global society and involve the world's perspective on global conflict, political involvement in sport, and the very definition of *amateurism*. Each of these issues involves current policy areas considered by the organizers of major games in amateur sport.

Sport and International Politics

The association between sport and politics, and the subsequent political maneuvering that might occur through major games, is another current policy area of interest to event participants and organizers. Recent issues of the international politics of sport include the advance of political ideologies such as democracy versus communism versus fascism, nazism, and Francoism; religion, women, the rise of the black athlete, and disability sport; sport and terrorism; and sport in South Africa (Riordan & Kruger, 1999). Sport has traditionally been used for nation building. It symbolizes the values of success, "of our ways compared to your ways," "of our people over your people." Sport illustrates power, wealth, business might, and general superiority. It has even been used as a show of moral authority and political legitimization (Houlihan, 1994).

Political factors have influenced the location of game sites. For instance, international federations have chosen host sites on the basis of generating economic support and facilitating legacy to an underdeveloped part of the world. Boycotting tactics—a nation refusing to send athletes and teams to an event in protest over another country's action regarding domestic or foreign policy—have been used as a form of political maneuvering. In this case national policy might directly influence sport policy, and a nation may decide the extent to which sport will be used on the world stage to further other national objectives. The degree to which sport is used to enhance a national political agenda directly affects the political maneuvering associated with major games. Another factor might include the involvement of business and the commercialization of sporting events. Houlihan (1994) suggests the long-term involvement of business in sport might actually weaken the ability of government to manipulate and exploit sport as a means for promoting a diplomatic agenda.

Marketing and Fundraising

The concepts of fundraising and marketing have become increasingly important to hosting major games in amateur athletics (Howard & Crompton, 1995). While several levels of government might commit to contributing some financial support, such an offering is seen as a component of a larger financial landscape. Therefore, since hosting requires significant resources, particularly when new facilities are required, developing the financial backing to deliver the event is critical for success.

The importance of marketing for the major amateur athletic event is a given (Slack, 1998). While significant positive results can accrue from attracting donor funds and marketing the event (even to the extent that one without the other may well be impossible), other issues arise from marketing and fundraising practices. Members of organizing committees are debating methods of increasing the value of television and sponsorship packages. Increased commercialization of amateur sport results in a shift of power and control toward sponsors. Struggles develop as a result of exclusive sponsorship categories. For example, water and isotonic drinks are obviously an important sponsorship category associated with major games. When exclusive sponsorship rights are awarded to one soft drink company for these categories, the extent of the sponsorship agreement might well become a source of problems. Does the sponsorship agreement extend to all other products associated with the company? This becomes an issue because today's multinational conglomerates produce a vast array of products. A balance for coexistence between the sponsor's needs and the major games is required. Without fundraising, sponsorship, and marketing, the very existence of major games could be jeopardized, given the significant requirement for operating revenues.

Today's global economy drives both cost and value. On the one hand the hosting of most major games runs in the millions of dollars or euros. The value of selling certain properties associated with major games, such as title sponsorship or television rights, slides on a scale depending on the location and economic factors. Organizers are constantly concerned with keeping costs down and value up. While costs can remain fairly neutral once established, the values of the properties of major games are more difficult to pinpoint. These values depend on many factors, and they change as a result of economic and political factors. For instance, how does the value of television rights for hosting the Pan American Games differ between a host site in North America versus South America? Many factors, such as the number of potential television carriers, the size of target markets, the time of year, competition with other established events, and the ability of the host to attract other corporate partners affect the value of the television package. Of course, the organizing committee enacts policies to drive the value of the contract as high as possible. These policies might suggest the importance of publicity to increase the television audience, scheduling games and events at the best time of day to ensure the highest possible television numbers, and so on.

Broadcasting and sponsorship revenues come with an associated cost. When outside groups buy services or properties, conflict may arise over how the event is run. Policies to define rights and privileges associated with each partnership are critical to successfully hosting major games. For instance, the organizing committee must define a specific television policy that establishes explicit guidelines for how the event will be scheduled, with game-day time lines determined in advance. The policy will also suggest how changes to the time lines can be made, naming the groups or individuals who must be consulted.

Exclusivity is a term used for selling sponsorships that involves dividing the event into sponsorship categories and allowing for each category to be sold only one time, thereby providing one sponsor with "exclusive rights" without competition for its product. For instance, selling soft drink sponsorship exclusively to Pepsi would preclude any sponsorship with Coca-Cola or any other soft drink company. It may be difficult to decide which categories of sponsorship should be sold exclusively. Often, the sponsorship policy defines exactly which sales categories will be sold with exclusivity. Preferably, the marketing and sales personnel of the organizing committee will carefully define and communicate this practice to sponsors in advance, thereby lessening the potential for conflict between sponsors and enhancing the sponsors' interest in being associated with the event.

Amateur athletic organizers rely heavily on marketing and sponsorship to deliver an event of the magnitude of FISU or Commonwealth Games. As Slack (1998) points out, "in no previous time period have we seen the type of growth in the commercialization of sport that we have seen in the last two decades. Today, sport is big business and big businesses are heavily involved in sport" (p. 1). Such reliance, however, is of concern to event organizers. In a best-case scenario, a major games could run as an entity by itself. Given this is not the case, international federations and major games organizing committees set policy to encourage revenue generation beyond corporate sponsorship and advertising. For example, the Finance Committee of a major games would define sources of funding in order to manage the event. Those sources will be as diverse as possible in order to decrease the threat of reliance on any one funding category. Government funding, television rights, categories of exclusive and nonexclusive sponsors and corporate partners, pure advertising, ticket sales, merchandising, entry fees—all are sought by organizing committees to diversify revenue sources, decrease the threat of running an overall deficit, and deflect undue influence and/or control of the games by outside groups.

Global Conflict, Terrorism, and Security

Global conflict and the war on terrorism seem to be a constant issue on the world agenda. War, conflict, terrorism, political maneuvering, and alliance building are at the forefront of issues for virtually every government. The increased acts of terrorism in recent decades have the particular attention of world leaders; specifically, the September 11, 2001, attack on the United States has the world on alert. Terrorism is defined as a politically motivated form of violence, usually employed to overthrow governments (Wedemeyer, 1999).

The changes to daily life associated with a world on alert are manifested in many ways. Citizenship, travel, security, privacy, and global politics each take on heightened meaning. The impact on gatherings and event management is particularly important. Imagine being the Director of Security for a large international event in this environment. Your task is to ensure the safety of 5,000 competitors from 145 countries and the 400,000 people who will gather to enjoy the competition and related cultural events. Given recent world events, this is a monumental task and the focus of extensive debate and policy development. Unfortunately, the issue is not brand new. The tragic hostage crisis in the Olympic Village during the Munich Olympic Games of 1972 resulted in the killing of 11 Israeli athletes and coaches, 5 Palestinian terrorists, and 1 German police officer. Major games bring global representatives and world media attention. The potential for terrorist action at major games is of real concern.

Policy to deal with issues of safety, conflict, terrorism, and political maneuvering at major athletic games involves the collaboration of several levels of administration. Security and law enforcement personnel from local and governmental offices provide the foundation. Sport federations might provide background and past experience that proves valuable for future actions. The organizing committee ensures the coordination of all agencies and the implementation of the policy. Other levels within the government of the host country help with coordination. The governments of competing countries may offer assistance and will undoubtedly require assurances of readiness. In the end the policy will define parameters for safe and secure travel, admittance, contact, and conduct of participants, spectators, and affiliates of the major games.

Glasgow Bid for the 2014 Commonwealth Games

www.glasgow2014.com

The successful bid by Glasgow, Scotland, to host the 2014 Commonwealth Games identifies security as a main planning theme. Historical evidence of managing security, having the capacity and systems in place to coordinate huge numbers of visitors and venues, and experience in command and control are a consistent requirement of major games hosting. At this event, as with Pan American Games, World University Games, and other events and championships, security is of paramount concern and significant resources, planning, and collaboration with local and national law enforcement is required.

Performance Enhancement

The use of drugs to enhance performance and direct the outcomes of athletic contests is termed *doping*. Worldwide, sport agencies and federations view doping as cheating and prohibit the use of performance-enhancing drugs. Athletic competition is about pitting the athleticism and skills of an individual or group against another. Inherent in sport is a baseline common to all from which competition begins. In fairness, each individual or group works within a common set of parameters for competition. Performance-enhancing drugs are considered detours around the rigors of training and preparation. As such, doping is considered artificial and is thus banned as a means of achieving an edge in athletics. In addition, many doping practices are dangerous, in direct opposition to the concept of "healthy mind, healthy body," one of the inherent benefits of sport and physical activity. To combat the issue of doping in sports, national associations such as the United States Anti-Doping Association (USADA) and the Canadian Centre for Ethics in Sport (CCES) have been organized to work in conjunction with the World Anti-Doping Agency (WADA). Policy on doping in sport has been defined in order to

United States Anti-Doping Association

www.usantidoping.org

Canadian Centre for Ethics in Sport

www.cces.ca

World Anti-Doping Agency

www.wada-ama.org

- protect those who play fair
- deter those who might cheat
- apply common sanctions for doping infractions
- provide detailed procedures for establishing a breach in the rules (CCES, 2007)

All major games, international sport federations, and the Olympic Movement have provided a unified approach to setting policy that outlines banned substances and practices and outlaws anyone contributing to doping in sport. WADA provides for this required unified approach to developing doping-control policy. Testing procedures, penalties, laboratory analyses, results management, protests and appeals, and reinstatement procedures are basic elements of doping-control policy. The issue is defined as a current policy area because it remains a dynamic issue. The use of banned substances and subsequent reports of positive tests remains to be a common occurrence at major games such as the Commonwealth Games and Pan American Games. Testing and strict anti-doping procedures are enacted at all major games by organizing committees. However, the will to win and the stakes for winning on the world stage help promulgate a win-at-any-cost attitude, which results in the development of new performance-enhancing techniques and substances. Thus policy makers at virtually all national and international levels continue to focus on this issue to curb such behaviors.

SUMMARY

The major games of amateur sport have a rich and diverse history. The Olympic Games are still the world's largest and most prestigious sport festival, but between Olympics many other events are organized and attended by nations worldwide. Major games are organized mostly for amateur competitors, and NGBs and NSOs help initiate and manage the competitors selected to represent their nation at major games. In the United States, the AAU has played a major role in developing and organizing competitive athletics. State and national governing bodies then govern national-level competition and representatives to international games. In Canada, provincial and national sport organizations have the same governance role, and Sport Canada helps to set policy and provide funding for teams to compete at world championships.

Major international games include events such as the Pan American Games, Commonwealth Games, FISU Games, and World Games for the Deaf. Such events require extensive planning and organizing and are major financial undertakings. Organizing committees spend years preparing and managing many policy areas in an effort to ensure a safe, effective sporting competition. Current policy issues include the very definition of *amateurism*, political maneuvering, funding, security and issues of global conflict, mass media influences, and doping control. The stakes are high for participants and organizers, given the enormity of the overall profile, size, and financial commitment involved in major games.

CASE STUDY   *Major Games in Amateur Sport*

You are working for your local area sports commission. You are putting together your strategic plans for the next 10 years and have decided to put in a bid for the Commonwealth Games. You are located in a major metropolitan area with a population of approximately two million residents. Your city has a large university with excellent sport facilities and a college with good outdoor facilities. You also have one AAA minor league baseball team; considerable other sports facilities, both private and public; and extensive park areas that could serve as potential venues.

Using the bid created by the City of Glasgow for the 2014 Commonwealth Games for assistance, answer the following questions:

Glasgow Bid for the 2014 Commonwealth Games

www.glasgow2014.com

1. Make a list identifying each area of information that will be required, forming an outline of the sections of the bid document.

2. With which governing bodies (local, national, international) will you need to communicate?

3. Exactly which sports will be on the games program, and what is your plan for selecting the venues you would like to use for each sport?

4. Whom will you work with to ensure the security of athletes, coaches, and fans?

5. What local community groups will you actively pursue to assist with your bid, and what will their specific roles be?

CHAPTER QUESTIONS

1. Choose any two of the major games presented in this chapter. Using the Internet, compare the content of their constitution and bylaws. How are they different or similar?

2. How do major games market their product and entice sponsors? Using the websites of any three major games, review the fundraising practices of the organizing committee. Given the four strategic management practices (presented in Chapter 3, pp. 47–48) used by sport managers to maximize their potential, assess the degree to which the organizing committees maximize their revenue-generating potential.

3. What is WADA, and why does it exist? Explain WADA's goal. What role do major games organizers play in helping WADA achieve its mission?

AAU. (2007). About AAU. Retrieved August 14, 2007, from http://aausports.org/default.asp?a=pg_about_aau.html.

Canadian Sport Policy. (2002). The Canadian sport policy. Retrieved June 20, 2003, from www.sport.mb.ca/Canadian_Sport_Policy.pdf.

Carbin, C. F. (1996). *Deaf heritage in Canada: A distinctive, diverse and enduring culture*. Toronto: McGraw-Hill Ryerson.

CCES. (2007). About CCES. Retrieved August 30, 2007, from www.cces.ca/forms/index.cfm?dsp=template&act=view3&template_id=62&lang=e.

CGF. (2006). Constitution. Retrieved May 11, 2007, from www.thecgf.com/about/constitution.pdf.

Chalip, L., & Johnson, A. (1996). Sport policy in the United States. In L. Chalip, A. Johnson, & L. Stachura (Eds.), *National sport policies: An international handbook* (pp. 404–430). Westport, CT: Greenwood Press.

Chalip, L., Johnson, A., & Stachura, L. (1996). *National sport policies: An international handbook*. Westport, CT: Greenwood Press.

CISS. (2007a). International Committee of Sports for the Deaf. Retrieved August 21, 2007, from www.deaflympics.com.

CISS. (2007b). Mission statement. Retrieved August 21, 2007, from www.deaflympics.com/about/index.asp?ID=1107.

Dheensaw, C. (1994). *The Commonwealth Games*. Victoria, BC: Orca.

FISU. (2002). What's FISU? Retrieved October 26, 2002, from www.fisu.net/html.

FISU. (2007a). FISU history. Retrieved May 11, 2007, from www.fisu.net.

FISU. (2007b). FISU today. Retrieved May 11, 2007, from www.fisu.net/site/page_517.php.

XIV Pan American Games. (2002). XIV Pan American games. Retrieved October 26, 2002, from www.santodomingo2003.org.do/ingles/paginas/comite/Ecomiteorganizador.html.

Glassford, R. G., & Redmond, G. (1988). Physical education and sport in modern times. In E. F. Zeigler (Ed.), *History of physical education and sport* (pp. 103–171). Champaign, IL: Stipes.

Houlihan, B. (1994). *Sport and international politics*. London: Harvester Wheatsheaf.

Howard, D. R., & Crompton, J. L. (1995). *Financing sport*. Morgantown, WV: Fitness Information Technology.

Kidd, B. (1999). *The struggle for Canadian sport*. Toronto: University of Toronto Press.

Manchester Commonwealth Games. (2002). Background to the Manchester 2002 Games. Retrieved October 26, 2002, from www.commonwealthgames.com/The_Games.

Pan American Games '99. (2002). Pan American Games '99—Winnipeg, Manitoba, Canada. Retrieved October 26, 2002, from www.americascanada.org/eventpanam/menu-e.asp.

Pan American Games Summer. (2002). A history of the Pan American Games. Retrieved October 26, 2002, from www.aafla.org/8saa/PanAm/pan_am_history.html.

Riess, S. A. (1995). *Sport in industrial America 1850–1920*. Wheeling, IL: Harlan Davidson.

Rio 2007 Pan American Games. (2007). XV Pan American Games Rio 2007. Retrieved May 11, 2007, from www.rio2007.org.br/pan2007/ingles/indexing.asp.

Riordan, J., & Kruger, A. (1999). *The international politics of sport in the 20th century*. New York: Routledge.

Slack, T. (1998). Studying the commercialisation of sport: The need for critical analysis. *Sociology of Sport Online, 1*(1). Retrieved October 30, 2002, from www.physed.otago.ac.nz/sosol/v1i1/v1i1a6.htm.

Sport Canada. (2007a). Sport Canada strategic directions. Retrieved May 10, 2007, from www.pch.gc.ca/progs/sc/mission/index_e.cfm.

Sport Canada. (2007b). Sport Canada mission. Retrieved May 10, 2007, from www.pch.gc.ca/progs/sc/mission/index_e.cfm.

Sport Canada. (2007c). Sport Canada funding programs. Retrieved May 10, 2007, from www.pch.gc.ca/progs/sc/prog/index_e.cfm.

Sport Canada. (2007d). Sport Canada organization chart. Retrieved May 10, 2007, from www.pch.gc.ca/progs/sc/mission/org_chart_e.cfm.

Ted Stevens Olympic and Amateur Sports Act. (1998). 36 U.S.C. sec. 220501 et seq. of the United States Code.

Tucker, S. (2006, April 8). Rewards for a city that lifted its game. *Financial Times,* p. 16.

24th Universiade. (2007). Bangkok 2007. Retrieved May 11, 2007, from www.bangkok2007.com/en/main/index2.php#.

2001 X Games—Philadelphia. (2002). Retrieved January 16, 2002, from http://philadelphia.about.com.

2003 Special Olympics World Games. (2002). Games organizing committee board members. Retrieved December 12, 2002, from www.2003special olympics.com/en/?page=goc_boa_01.

2007 Special Olympics World Games. (2007a). World Summer Games Shanghai 2007. Retrieved May 11, 2007, from www.2007specialolympics.org.

2007 Special Olympics World Games. (2007b). World Summer Games Shanghai 2007. Retrieved May 11, 2007, from www.2007specialolympics.org/about_us/mission_vision/default.html.

2007 Special Olympics World Games. (2007c). 2007 Special Olympics World Summer Games.

Retrieved May 11, 2007, from www.2007 specialolympics.org/world_games/2007_world_summer_games/default.html.

United States Amateur Sports Act. (1978). United States Amateur Sports Act. Retrieved June 16, 2003, from www.whitewaterslalom.org/rules/asa-1978.html.

USA Basketball. (2002). *USAB today.* Retrieved October 26, 2002, from www.usabasketball.com/general/index.html.

USA Basketball. (2007). USA basketball today. Retrieved August 20, 2007, from www.usa basketball.com/general/index.html.

U. S. Senate Committee on Commerce, Science, and Transportation. (1998). Committee clears legislation, nominations. Retrieved June 16, 2003, from www.senate.gov/~commerce/press/105-278.htm.

Wedemeyer, B. (1999). Sport and terrorism. In J. Riordan & A. Kruger (Eds.), *The international politics of sport in the 20th century* (pp. 217–233). London: Taylor & Francis.

10

OLYMPIC SPORT

INTRODUCTION

Imagine what it must be like to strive to be the best in the world in your chosen sport: the years and years of preparation, the excitement of the competitions, the media attention, the applause of fans, the travel, the agony of defeat, and the thrill of victory. Now imagine the feelings of competing at the Olympic Games, often described by athletes as the adventure of a lifetime. Without doubt, the Olympics are the most significant sporting competition in the world,

245

scheduled every four years for both summer and winter events. Athletes at virtually every level dream of one day competing for their nation on the world stage in the Olympic Games. Winning an Olympic Gold Medal holds tremendous meaning worldwide. Not only does it signify world supremacy for the athlete(s) involved, Olympic Gold means instant recognition, notoriety, financial success, nation building, and legitimization of political ideologies. Olympic Gold Medals are symbolic of success throughout the society the winner represents. No wonder the Olympic Games are held in such high regard and taken so seriously by nations around the world.

Citius, Altius, Fortius ("Faster, Higher, Stronger") is the motto of the modern Olympic Games. The Summer and Winter Olympics alternate every two years so that four years (a *quadrennial*) passes in a full cycle. More than 3.9 billion people watched the 2004 Athens Games worldwide, making them more than just a sporting event (IOC, 2004; Senn, 1999; Schaffer & Smith, 2000). The Olympic Games are a media extravaganza, a cultural festival, an international political stage, an economic colossus, and a location for meeting and developing friendships. Everyone strives for excellence, from the athletes in competition to the host city. The Olympic Games are a showcase and "Faster, Higher, Stronger" is the very essence of everything associated with the Olympic Games. This chapter looks at the history of the Games, their current organization and governance, and the policy issues currently confronting organizers.

History of the Olympic Games

A history of the Olympic Games can be divided into two distinct time frames. The games originated in Ancient Greece, were discontinued for several hundred years, and then were reinstituted in the late 19th century. In the Early Olympic Games, the ancient Greeks competed for the glory of their gods. Much later in history, in the so-called modern era of the games, the ancient festival was reintroduced and evolved into the event we know today.

The Ancient Olympic Games

Early Greek civilizations loved athletics and assimilated strength and vigor with a love of rhythm, beauty, and music in their style of games and pursuits (Howell & Howell, 1988). The Greeks participated in contests and athletic events like chariot racing, boxing, wrestling, footraces, discus throwing, and archery. The first Olympic Games were held in 776 BC and were celebrated again every four years until their abolition by the Roman Emperor Theodosius in AD 393 (Howell & Howell, 1988).

The four years between games were called an *Olympiad*, a system upon which time was calculated in ancient Greek history (The Ancient

Olympics, 2004). The specific events changed over the centuries, but footraces, pentathlon, boxing, and various types of chariot races were common. The Olympic Games originated with primitive religious festivals held at the shrine of Olympia, and sports were played to honor the gods. Any violation of the rules was considered an affront to the gods, helping enforce the rules and preserving the purity of the contests. However, this did not stop the practice of bribing officials and trying to find that illusive edge for victory. These games were considered so important that wars were stopped to allow for the staging of the events. The ancient Olympic Games were restricted to Greek men. It was not until the modern Olympic era that women were included (either as competitors or as spectators) and that people of different nations were allowed to compete.

The Modern Era of the Olympic Games

From 1859 until the actual revival of the Olympic Games in 1896, the idea of reinstituting the festival of the Olympiad was discussed by both Greek nationalist Evagelis Zappas and Englishman William Brooks (1896 Athens, Greece, 2007). Baron Pierre de Coubertin of Paris visited with Brooks and is the individual now credited with successfully launching the modern Olympic Games we know today. Baron de Coubertin believed strongly in the healthy mind–healthy body connection (de Coubertin, 2000). He envisioned amateur athletes from all around the world competing in a festival of sports similar to those of ancient Greece. In 1894, the Baron presided over a congress held at the Sorbonne in Paris. Representatives from 13 countries attended the meeting, and another 21 wrote to support the concept of reviving the Olympic Games (Tyler & Soar, 1980). The assembled nations unanimously supported the revival of the Greek Olympic festival, to be held every four years, and to which every nation would be invited to send representatives. Baron de Coubertin envisioned the inaugural event to be held in Paris in 1900. However, the Greek delegates made an impassioned plea that Greece host the first modern games, given the history and the tradition of the ancient festivals. The modern Olympic Games were reborn in 1896 and were held in Athens, Greece. Two hundred and forty-one athletes (all men) from 13 nations participated in nine sports in the First Modern Olympiad (IOC, 2007a).

Many traditions taken for granted in the Olympic Games today were born during the early modern Olympics. For instance, the opening ceremony and the parade of nations into a stadium were instituted early on; the medal ceremonies in which the flag raising of the Gold Medal–winning athlete occurred became symbolic of world excellence; the housing of participants in an Olympic Village at the site of the games; and beginning and ending the Games with the lighting and the extinguishing of the Olympic flame, brought to the site from the ancient site in Olympia, Greece.

Quickly the Olympic Games became a world focus, and today young men and women come from all over the world to compete in various sports for the glory of representing their nation (Tyler & Soar, 1980). The Games were not always a brilliant success (Wallechinsky, 1984). The 1896 Games in Athens had only two years to prepare and experienced significant financial duress. The Paris Olympics of 1900 were badly overshadowed by the Paris International Expedition, an irony for organizers, since the two events had been scheduled together on purpose. The 1904 Olympics were scheduled to take place in Chicago, but infighting between Chicago and St. Louis resulted in moving the Games to St. Louis. As a result of the utter disorganization, very few athletes participated.

Since the revitalization of the modern Games, the Olympics have grown in size and complexity, requiring an increasingly sophisticated international governance structure. Exactly how are the Olympics governed, and how is an Olympic Games planned, organized, and managed?

Governance

Mention "the Olympic Games" and immediate images of competition, ceremony, and colors of the world come to mind, along with memories of the spectacle and stories of unimaginable achievements. But from a sport management perspective, what makes these Games happen? In fact, an enormous amount of planning and coordination is required, in addition to volumes of policy that set standards for what and how things are done. Three main levels of organizational influence direct the Olympic Games as we know them. First, the Olympics are organized through the jurisdiction of the International Olympic Committee (IOC), led by its President, the Session (an annual General Assembly or Annual Meeting), and the Executive Board (similar to an Executive Committee). Bids to host the Olympic Games are made by National Olympic Committees (NOC) from interested countries. Finally, once a bid has been awarded to a particular country, the responsibility for organizing an Olympics falls upon the Organizing Committee for the Olympic Games (OCOG). Each, in turn, contributes significantly to the staging of the Olympic Games.

International Olympic Committee (IOC)

The IOC, founded on June 23, 1894, is a group of officials governing Olympic organization and policy. The members are elected from the worldwide sport community. The headquarters of the IOC is located in Lausanne, Switzerland, and the committee is a nonprofit organization independent of any government or nationality. Having an NOC organizing Olympic teams does not guarantee that a country will be eligible to have an IOC representative. However, an effort is made to ensure that IOC membership represents geographical regions of the world. In addition, while countries that have hosted Olympic competitions are eligible to have two IOC members, some other countries choose not to fill their IOC seat, and they are not required to do so. Some countries have more than two IOC members because their additional members are citizens of those countries but are selected as IOC members because they head an International Sports Federation (IFC) for one of the sports on the program of the Olympic Games.

www

International Olympic Committee
www.olympic.org

Mission. The roles of IOC members are rather specific: First, they are expected to serve the Olympic Movement (that is, to promote the tenets of Olympism) by helping to organize and govern policy relative to the staging of the Olympic Games. They are also expected to further the cause and understanding of all things associated with the Olympic Movement in their respective countries. IOC members are not representatives of their nation to the IOC. Rather, they are representatives of the IOC to their nations. They are expected to care first and foremost about what's best for the Olympics and work only on furthering the Olympic Movement. Overall, the IOC's "fundamental task is to supervise the regular celebrations of the Olympic Games, and toward that end, it promotes the 'development of those physical and moral qualities which are the basis of sport' and of propagating the 'Olympic ideal' so as to create 'international goodwill'" (Senn, 1999, p. 7). The IOC (2007b) defines its mission as follows:

> The International Olympic Committee is the supreme authority of the Olympic Movement. Its role is to promote top-level sport as well as sport for all in accordance with the Olympic Charter. It ensures the regular celebration of the Olympic Games and strongly encourages, by appropriate means, the promotion of women in sport, that of sports ethics and the protection of athletes.

The goals of the IOC are presented in Figure 10.1.

Financials. The IOC generates extensive revenues through its ownership of the rights to the Olympic Games and associated marks and terminology. These marks and terminology include the Olympic symbol consisting of the five interlocking Olympic rings and the Olympic motto, anthem, and flag, along with the Olympic flame and torch. Permission to use these symbols is granted to the host organizing committee, and NOCs are permitted to use the rings in developing their own national Olympic symbol. (In the United States, a special statute requires the USOC's consent to all commercial uses of Olympic-related marks and terminology in the United States.) Countries hoping to host the Olympics guarantee a percentage of the money they will raise to the IOC in return for the rights to host. The size of the IOC's share became an issue after the 1984 Summer Olympics in Los Angeles. These

| FIGURE | 10.1 | Goals of the IOC. |

The goal of the Olympic Movement is to contribute to building a peaceful and better world by educating youth through sport practiced without discrimination of any kind and in the Olympic spirit, which requires mutual understanding with a spirit of friendship, solidarity, and fair play.

- Choice of the host city
- Organization of the Olympic Games
- Equality in sport
- Promotion of women in sport
- Protection of athletes
- Human development assistance
- Protection of the environment
- The Olympic Truce

Source: IOC (2007b). Reprinted with permission.

IOC Marketing Fact File
http://multimedia.olympic.org
/pdf/en_report_344.pdf

games generated a surplus of $225 million. The IOC was unsuccessful in getting a share of the revenue, but it intensified its resolve to get a fair share of Olympic revenues in the future. The committee accepted the decree of then-President Samaranch, who said, "Sport without money is impossible today" (*Korea Herald*, 1986). The IOC resolved to increase its revenue share from hosting rights and acted to establish its own sources of income through marketing the Olympic symbols with amazing success (Senn, 1999). According to the IOC Marketing Fact File (2006, n.p.):

> The Olympic Movement generates revenue through five major programmes. The IOC manages broadcast partnerships and the TOP worldwide sponsorship programme. The OCOGs manage domestic sponsorship, ticketing and licensing programmes within the host country, under the direction of the IOC.

The total revenue for the 2001–2004 quadrennium was just under $4.2 billion (IOC Marketing Fact File, 2006).

Membership. Historically, IOC members were elected by the other members of the committee, a practice contributing to criticism that labeled the committee as being elitist, incestuous, and existing for the gratification of its members. In the beginning, the committee was an extended group of friends and business associates of original members, mostly from the upper class of society. Following the corruption allegations associated with the

2002 Salt Lake City Winter Olympic Games bid, the IOC changed some of its procedures. For instance, the IOC is now composed of a maximum of 115 members (IOC, 2007b). Members of the IOC are allowed to serve until age 70 (lowered from 75), although some choose to retire prior to that age. Positions are still elected by the members of the General Assembly, but a breakdown of the 115 positions was changed as follows: 70 are reserved for individual members, 15 are active Olympic athletes elected by their peers at the Olympic Games, 15 members come from ISFs, and 15 from NOCs.

Organizational structure. Three components are central to IOC governance and the development of policy:

1. The Session
2. The Executive Board
3. The Office of the President

   1. *The Session.* The Session, comparable to a General Assembly, is a general meeting of all IOC members. The purpose of the Session is to adopt or modify policy relating to the Olympic Charter. The Olympic Charter includes the purpose and description of the ideals of Olympic participation, along with the rules and regulations for Olympic events, membership in and recognition by the IOC (IOC, 2007c; USOC, 2007a). The Olympic Charter provides the framework for governing the organization and operation of the Olympic Movement, and stipulates conditions for hosting the Olympic Games. Elections for accepting new IOC members are also held during the Session. Meetings are held annually unless unusual circumstances dictate the calling of a special meeting.

   2. *The Executive Board.* The Executive Board is a smaller subset of the Session and is responsible for the management and overall direction of the IOC between meetings of the Session. It was first conceived by Baron de Coubertin in order to share the responsibility for directing the IOC and to prepare for an orderly succession of leadership (Senn, 1999). Executive Board membership (Figure 10.2) includes 15 positions: the President, 4 Vice Presidents, and 10 additional members elected by the Session. Each Executive Board member's term of office is a minimum of four years, with the exception of the President, who is elected to an eight-year term. The board meets regularly, at the call of the President or at the request of a majority of its members. The Executive Board of the IOC has the following specific responsibilities (Schaffer & Smith, 2000; Senn, 1999; Thoma & Chalip, 1996):

- ensures that the Olympic Charter is observed and promoted
- administers the IOC and appoint the Director General, who oversees the daily business affairs of the IOC
- manages IOC finances and financial reporting

FIGURE 10.2   Executive Board of the IOC.

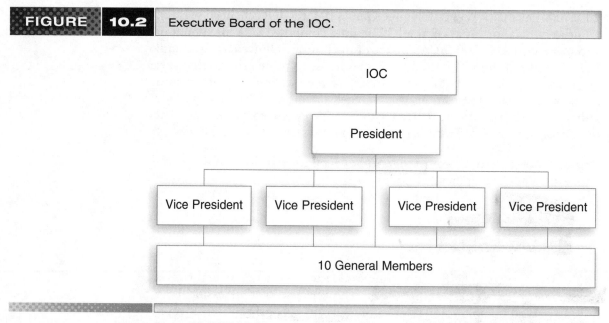

Source: IOC (2007b). Reprinted with permission.

- formulates bylaw or rule changes for implementation by the General Assembly
- approves the organizational chart of the IOC
- makes recommendations for elections
- establishes the agenda for all IOC meetings
- enacts all regulations for the proper organization of the Olympic Games
- maintains the records of the IOC

3. *The Office of the President.* The President of the IOC is elected from members of the Session. It is a critical position with power and responsibility for directing the general course of the IOC. The President is the official spokesperson of the IOC and presides over the Executive Board. It is the President's role to convene the Executive Board and lead the business of the IOC. The term of office is initially eight years, and the incumbent President may be reelected for one subsequent four-year term. The modern era of the Olympic Games has known only eight different Presidents (see Table 10.1).

The officers of the IOC do not actually organize the Olympic Games. Rather, the IOC works with the groups responsible for Olympic sport and hosting activities within individual nations, NOCs, and OCOGs.

| Presidents of the IOC. | | **TABLE** | **10.1** |

President	Country of Origin	Years of Service
Dimitrius Vikelas	Greece	1894–1896
Pierre de Coubertin	France	1896–1925
Henri Baillet-Latour	Belgium	1925–1942
J. Sigfrid Edstrom	Sweden	1942–1946 (acting) 1946–1952
Avery Brundage	United States	1952–1972
Lord Killanin	Ireland	1972–1980
Juan Antonio Samaranch	Spain	1980–2001
Jacques Rogge	Belgium	2001–

Source: USOC (2002). Reprinted with permission.

National Olympic Committees (NOCs)

NOCs control operations and policy relative to the Olympics for a particular country, as well as the delegation sent to represent a nation at the Olympic Games. With rare exceptions, only athletes certified by an NOC are permitted to compete at the Olympics. The NOC is required to check participant eligibility rules, defined by Olympic, ISF, and NOC policies. NOCs have been described as "the basic building blocks in the structure of the Olympic Games" (Senn, 1999, p. 11).

If a nation is interested in hosting an Olympic Games, the NOC is responsible for choosing one city to go forward to the IOC for consideration. The NOC selects that city no later than nine years in advance of the Games. For example, in 2002 the USOC chose New York City as a potential host for the 2012 Summer Olympic Games. The NOC makes this choice nine years in advance because the IOC makes its final selection seven years in advance of the Games.

The USOC (founded in 1894) and the COC (founded in 1907) represent Olympic interests within their respective countries.

United States Olympic Committee (USOC)

The USOC governs, manages, promotes, and liaises within and outside the United States for all activities of the Olympic, Paralympic, and Pan American Games. As mentioned in Chapter 9, in 1978 the U. S. Congress

United States Olympic
Committee

www.usoc.org

passed the Amateur Sports Act, which was amended in 1998 and is now called the Ted Stevens Olympic and Amateur Sports Act. The amended law included activities associated with the Paralympic Games and addressed athletes' rights and other matters. The law specifically mandates the USOC to govern all American activities for the three major Games. The USOC is the self-professed "premier sports organization" in the United States. It is composed of a group of individuals and organizations whose common goals are athletic excellence and achievement on the world stage and promoting nation building through the achievement of athletes.

The year 2003 represented a historic time for the USOC. In 2002, the USOC's President was forced to resign because of misstatements on her resume. In 2003, the organization was confronted with allegations of violations of its Code of Ethics by its CEO, and infighting between the CEO and the President of the organization. The good name of the USOC was tarnished, and the image of the association was at an all-time low. Concern was even voiced in the U. S. Congress: Three Senators requested an independent commission be appointed to investigate the practices of the organization and recommend change. In addition, the USOC appointed a Governance and Ethics Task Force to recommend a course of action for changing the practices, mandate, and expectations of the USOC. The sizes of the Board of Directors and Executive Committee were particularly criticized, along with the breadth of the USOC's all-encompassing mandate, which extends very broadly beyond training athletes, building facilities, and designing equipment.

The independent commission and the USOC Governance and Ethics Task Force focused their recommendations on these three major issues (USOC, 2003):

1. narrowing the USOC mandate to focus on training athletes for national and international competition related to the Olympic and Paralympic Games

2. ensuring ethical, responsible, and transparent business and financial practices

3. creating a workable governance structure that better defines the responsibility of volunteers and professional staff and that reduces and changes the numbers and constituents involved in decision making

They recommended that (1) the mission, goals, and objectives of the organization be focused to ensure that the ideals of the Olympics be preserved and reflected in practice and conduct; (2) the governance structure of the USOC be clearly redefined concerning responsibilities, authority, and accountability; (3) the overall governance structure of the USOC be streamlined and downsized; and (4) that ethical policy and compliance with ethical policy be instituted (USOC, 2003).

Mission. The USOC mission connects to the themes and the meanings of the Olympics as outlined by the IOC. The mission statement speaks to the ideals of Olympism, the promotion of ethical conduct and peace between nations achieved through sport competitions. The USOC hopes to drive national unity and pride within the United States through the accomplishments of U. S. athletes in competition with their peers from other countries. The USOC mission statement is presented in Figure 10.3.

Financials. In the past 20 years the USOC's budget for the four-year span between Olympic Games has grown from $13 million to $491.5 million (USOC, 2002). The organization is continually ranked among the top 100 nonprofit organizations in the United States. Funding comes from several sources. The USOC owns the rights to all Olympic symbols within the United States and generates considerable revenue from sales of Olympic products. It also has extensive reach in the corporate world, with a corporate partnership and advertising program contributing large yearly revenues. In addition, the USOC developed a trust fund after the successful Los Angeles Olympics in 1984. Established as an endowment for Olympic sports, the trust fund is called the United States Olympic Foundation and operates as a separate not-for-profit corporation. Although the initial endowment of $111 million must remain intact according to the terms of the trust, it generates an annual grant that has varied by year between 5 percent and 10 percent (or just under $9 million) to the USOC for the promotion of Olympic-related sports in the United States (IOC, 2007a).

Membership. The USOC has an extensive membership. There are 78 member organizations divided among seven categories. The membership categories include Olympic sport organizations, Pan American sport organizations, community-based multisport organizations, affiliated sport organizations, education-based multisport organizations, and the armed forces (USOC, 2004). The entire membership of the USOC is presented in Table 10.2.

Mission statement of the USOC. **FIGURE 10.3**

To support United States Olympic and Paralympic athletes in achieving sustained competitive excellence and preserve the Olympic ideals, and thereby inspire all Americans.

Source: United States Olympic Committee (2005). Reprinted with permission.

TABLE	10.2	Member organizations of the USOC.

Olympic Sport Organizations (48)

U.S. Archery	U.S. Equestrian	U.S. Rowing	USA Synchronized Swimming
USA Badminton	U.S. Fencing	U.S. Sailing	USA Table Tennis
USA Baseball	U.S. Field Hockey	USA Shooting	USA Taekwondo
USA Basketball	U.S. Figure Skating	U.S. Short Track	USA Team Handball
U.S. Biathlon	USA Gymnastics	U.S. Skeleton	U.S. Tennis
U.S. Bobsled	USA Hockey	U.S. Skiing	USA Track & Field
USA Bowling	USA Judo	U.S. Snowboarding	USA Triathlon
USA Boxing	USA Karate	U.S. Soccer	USA Volleyball
USA Canoe/Kayak	U.S. Luge	USA Softball	USA Water Polo
USA Curling	USA Pentathlon	U.S. Speedskating	USA Water Skiing
USA Cycling	USA Racquetball	U.S. Squash	USA Weightlifting
U.S. Diving	USA Roller Sports	USA Swimming	USA Wrestling

Affiliated Organizations (6)

Sports Acrobatics	U.S. Armed Forces	Underwater Society of America
U.S. Orienteering	USA Rugby	USA Dance Sport

Community-Based Organizations (13)

Amateur Athletic Union	Boys and Girls Clubs of America	National Congress of State Games
American Alliance for Health, Physical Education, Recreation, and Dance	Catholic Youth Organization	National Senior Games Association
	Jewish Community Centers Association	Native American Sports Alliance
American Legion		YMCA of the USA
Boy Scouts of America	National Association of Police Athletics/Activities League, Inc.	YWCA of the USA

Community-Based Multisport Organizations (7)

Disabled Sports USA	National Disability Sports Alliance	USA Deaf Sports Foundation
Dwarf Athletic Association of America	Special Olympics, Inc.	Wheelchair Sports USA
	U.S. Association for Blind Athletes	

Education-Based Multisport Organizations (4)

National Association of Intercollegiate Athletics (NAIA)

National Collegiate Athletic Association (NCAA)

National Federation of State High School Associations (NFSHSA)

National Junior College Athletic Associations (NJCAA)

Source: U.S. Olympic Committee Directory (2007). Reprinted with permission.

Organizational structure. The USOC employs almost 500 staff members and relies heavily on the expertise of its volunteer leadership (USOC, 2005). Volunteers involved with the USOC include some of the most influential leaders in both sport and business from around the United States. The organization is structured such that elected officers, a Board of Directors, Executive Committee, and various other committees help provide direction the staff implements (see Figure 10.4).

Officers. The most important leaders of the USOC are the President (an elected volunteer) and the CEO (a paid employee). Both fulfill leadership

Organizational structure of the USOC. **FIGURE 10.4**

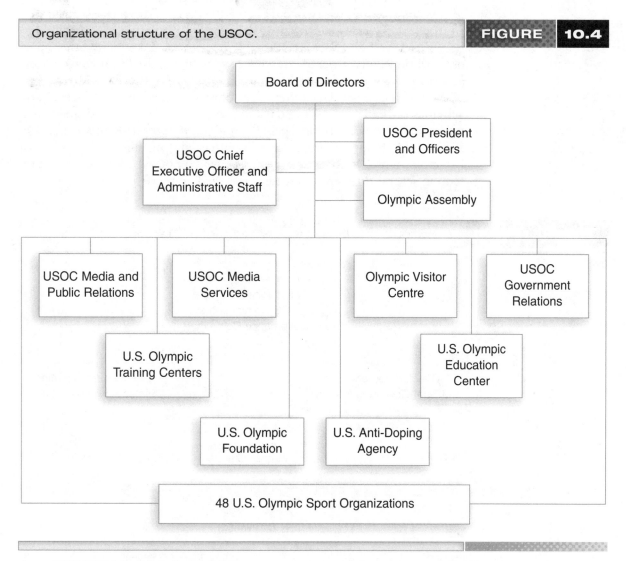

Source: USOC (2007a). Reprinted with permission.

roles in establishing USOC policy and are the principal spokespersons for the organization. The CEO is also responsible for day-to-day operations, strategic policy initiatives and directions, and management of the professional staff (USOC, 2006). In addition to the President, the elected officers of the organization include three Vice Presidents, Secretary, and Treasurer.

Board of Directors. The task force investigating USOC reform began working on a new leadership structure for the organization in February 2003. The organization was viewed as being too large and overly bureaucratic. To overcome these issues, the Task Force recommended that the Board of Directors be reduced in size (125 members to 11), the numbers of standing committees be reduced, the Executive Committee be eliminated from the governance structure, delineation of roles and responsibilities be enacted, and an Olympic Assembly be created. Like many other sport organizations, a two-tiered governance structure is used to manage USOC affairs. The Board of Directors has the ultimate authority and responsibility for the business, policy development, election of officers, and activities of the USOC. The Board has the authority to amend the constitution and bylaws of the USOC, admit and terminate members, and receive and review reports from committees and members. The Board of Directors, which meets twice each year, is composed of members representing several different constituencies (see Figure 10.5).

FIGURE	10.5	Constituent members of the USOC Board of Directors.

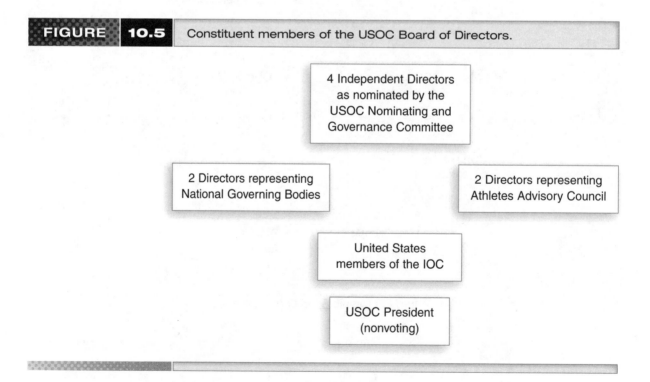

Olympic Assembly. The Olympic Assembly is held once per year, and is an event for which all constituent groups of the USOC gather to discuss the achievements of the organization and communicate to the Board of Directors. According to the USOC (2006) Bylaws, the Olympic Assembly has the following purpose:

> The Board, in conjunction with the CEO, shall provide information to the members of the Olympic Assembly on the affairs of the corporation, which shall include information on the performance of the organization, the financial performance and well being of the corporation, preparations for the Olympic, Pan American, and Paralympic Games, achievement of the corporation's mission, and actions taken, results achieved, and programs being implemented by the corporation. At the Olympic Assembly the members of the Olympic Assembly will have an opportunity to provide information and to communicate with the Board and the CEO concerning the performance, policies and other matters related to the corporation. Such input shall be advisory in nature and shall not be deemed to direct the Board or the CEO to take or not take any particular action. The Olympic Assembly shall not conduct or perform any governance functions. (pp. 19–20)

Other committees. Additionally, four other committees deal with specific USOC areas of importance, interest, and concern. There are named the (1) Audit, (2) Compensation, (3) Ethics, and (4) Nominating and Governance committees. The Athletes' Advisory Council and the NGB Council are also important USOC committees.

Canadian Olympic Committee (COC)

The COC is responsible for Canada's involvement in the Olympic movement. It is a private, not-for-profit corporation managing Canada's participation in the Olympic, Paralympic, and Pan American Games, promoting Olympic values within Canada, and selecting and supporting Canadian cities bidding to host Olympic or Pan American Games.

Mission. The COC's mission statement (see Figure 10.6) proclaims developing and advancing sport and the Olympic Movement for all Canadians (COC, 2007a). This mission to promote, organize, develop, and manage the ideals of Olympic participation within Canada is extended to include a vision for sport in Canada. The stated vision is intended as an impetus for the COC and the rest of the Canadian sport community to improve the high-performance system of sport for the country. The plan provides steps designed to make Canada one of the top 10 sporting countries in the world by 2010. The plan involves grassroots sport development, identification of and training for athletes and coaches, coordination between constituents of the sport system, funding for and monitoring of success,

USOC Bylaws
www.usolympicteam.com/ NGBCouncilBylawswonline numbers.pdf.pdf

Canadian Olympic Committee
www.usoc.org

FIGURE	10.6	Mission statement of the COC.

> The Canadian Olympic Committee is dedicated to developing and advancing sport and the Olympic Movement for all Canadians from coast-to-coast-to-coast.

Source: COC (2007a). Reprinted with permission.

development and application of sport research, facility development, and hosting world events. For further information regarding the COC's performance indicators and vision, see www.olympic.ca.

Financials. In the year 2005, the COC's consolidated revenues were C$15.155 million. These moneys, all stated in Canadian dollars, were derived from the following sources (COC, 2006):

- marketing initiatives in sponsorship, licensing of goods, and special event programs (C$7.765 million)
- investment income (C$6.073 million)
- grants and donations (C$1.317 million)

In contrast, COC expenses involve grants and scholarships to athletes and coaches, National Sport Federation (NSF) and Games Mission costs (60%); marketing and business operation outlay (31%); athlete and community relations (5%); governance (2%); advocacy and partner relations (2%); and communications (1%) (COC, 2006). The COC also operates a legacy trust from the 1988 Calgary Winter Olympic Games that provided original capital of C$53,152,000. The fund, called the Canadian Olympic Family Fund, was worth C$100 million on December 31, 2005, of which C$71 million is protected as investment capital under the direction of the fund managers. Revenues over investments are available to help finance COC programs.

Membership and organizational structure. The COC is organized using a two-tiered system of governance. A large Board of Directors manages and develops policy and direction for the COC, and this policy is implemented through an array of full-time paid staff positions. The board is led by a President and Executive Committee elected by Board members. The Board of Directors consists of the following members (COC, 2007b):

- 60 Olympic and Pan American Canadian Sport Federation representatives

- 12 COC members at large
- 1 Olympic or Pan American Games Coaches representative
- 2 individuals affiliated with sport
- all IOC members in Canada

The Executive Committee is composed of 16 members, including elected officers and at least 2 athlete members of the board. The organizational structure of the COC is presented in Figure 10.7.

Organizational structure of the COC. **FIGURE 10.7**

Source: COC (2007b). Reprinted with permission.

Mark Lowry

Executive Director, Sport;
Canadian Olympic Committee, Ottawa, Canada

My position involves a variety of responsibilities dealing with all aspects of the Canadian team's participation in the Olympic Games and Pan American Games, in addition to the development and support of the National Sport System in Canada. We support Canadian athletes participating in the Olympics, and we are ultimately responsible for pre-planning, travel support, on-site operations, and team management. Coordinating the logistics of taking a team to the Olympic Games is one of my responsibilities, but probably my greatest responsibility is developing the Canadian sport system and focusing on performance excellence. This involves long-term planning, working collaboratively with major funding partners, working for a better model for sport in Canada, and helping athletes optimize their performance.

With regard to governance, one of the most interesting challenges is finding support for and reaching agreement on organizational priorities and direction. The COC has a Board of Directors of about 90 people, all Olympic and Pan American Sport Federations and Directors. It is a challenge for members to rise above individual self-interest to look at the good of the overall sport system and decide on how the COC can have the greatest positive impact. The COC has addressed the size and efficiency of its board structure through a policy governance review. The review sought to determine if other governance models would allow for better development of future policy. The review also expanded efficiency issues and potential conflicts of interest. There are two ways of looking at our current structure. On one hand, we have the ultimate democracy where everyone affected by a decision is part of the decision-making process. That's a clear positive. On the other hand, special interest groups can block a policy direction of the organization, even if it is consistent with the COC's stated objectives. In such situations, compromise, flexibility, and balance are essential for accomplishing anything. There are always challenges to face when moving beyond the status quo. For example, our previous grants policy provided all member NSFs with similar levels of support. However, the new COC direction provides greater support to those Federations with better performance results. This significant change has resulted in winners and losers in the area of financial support and will likely be a key issue as we create a new governance model, as we will have to address concerns about NSFs losing influence on financial or policy decisions if they are not able to participate.

The IOC has a unique governance model: Its 123 members are mostly appointed, with a minority elected. The IOC went through a difficult time as a result of the 1998 scandals, but I think they've come through much stronger. Because of their independence, and because they are able to generate such huge sums of money, they have the ability to move quickly, make changes, and be prescriptive with their decisions. For example, consider the anti-doping issue. At the 2003 World Conference on Anti-Doping, the IOC President made the statement that any government not supporting the World Anti-Doping code will never be able to host an Olympic Games in their country, and any International Sport Federation that doesn't support the Anti-Doping code will not be granted participation privileges in future Olympic Games. You rarely see an organization with the authority to make such sweeping international demands. With regard to governance, the IOC has tremendous freedom and power to make positive changes. Needless to say, critics of the IOC will say that the organization has no accountability to the sporting participants around the world and that this lack of accountability can result in abuse of power. An organization without some accountability always has the potential for problems. The key to successful sport governance is maintaining accountability without losing the capacity for proactive change.

NOCs, like the USOC and COC, are the rights-holders to the Olympics within their respective countries. They play a role in endorsing an individual city that may wish to bid for the Olympic Games, and they certainly help to liaise with and assist the bidding city, but they do not actually act to host the Olympic Games. Rather, they turn over the duties of planning and managing the hosting of the Olympic Games to an organizing committee specifically created for that purpose.

Organizing Committees for the Olympic Games (OCOGs)

OCOGs are another vital component of the Olympic structure. An OCOG is formed within a community after it has successfully won the bid for the Olympic Games hosting rights. The work for the OCOG begins many years (perhaps 10 to 14 years) in advance of the actual Olympic event. The predecessor to this committee prepares the bid and plans for all aspects of hosting. With the support of the host country's NOC, the bid is submitted to the IOC and judged on a host of criteria. If the bid is unsuccessful, the bid committee finalizes its affairs and dissolves. The bid committee that is awarded the hosting rights becomes an OCOG and continues and intensifies planning. Some examples of successful OCOG bids were the Vancouver–Whistler (Canada) Organizing Committee (VANOC), which is organizing the 2010 Winter Games, and the London Organizing Committee for the Olympic Games (LOCOG), which is organizing the 2012 Summer Games.

Vancouver–Whistler Organizing Committee
www.vancouver2010.com

London Organizing Committee for the Olympic Games
www.london2012.org

Given that the Olympic Games occur in a different location each four years, OCOGs are developed to manage one event at a time. As mentioned in the discussion on NOCs, bids for hosting the Olympic Games are made well in advance of the event to allow for facility development and proper event planning. Developing a bid is a process that takes years from idea to plan to concept. The IOC awards the Games to a host city seven years in advance of the Games (Senn, 1999). Although the bid is presented to the IOC by a city interested in hosting, the OCOG must demonstrate the support of various levels of government and the NOC. The process is so competitive that few cities receive the IOC's support after their first application. Once the application to bid is supported, the OCOG will move into action to prepare for the Games and will stay active for about a year after the event to finalize all financial accounting and final reports. In total, members of the OCOG are likely to be involved in some stage of bidding, planning, executing, or reporting for 10 to 12 years. At any given time, four OCOGs (two for Winter and two for Summer Games) are in some stage of this process. Many OCOG employees come from the host city, while some sport and event managers travel the world with the Olympic Games, moving from position to position as specialists in some capacity with the organizing committees.

Mission. The mission of an OCOG clearly reflects the ideals of the Olympic movement: to be the best, to host the best, to show the world the best Olympic Games ever. When the President of the IOC speaks at the Olympic closing ceremonies, the local organizers listen carefully to his comments about the job done of hosting. They want to hear something to the effect of "This was the best Olympic Games ever"—clearly the goal of the OCOG. An example mission statement of the Torino, Italy, OCOG is presented in Figure 10.8.

Financials. The Olympic Games are run like a business. The goal is to have surplus funds available after the Games in order to leave an Olympic

FIGURE 10.8 Mission statement of an Olympic Games Organizing Committee—Torino, Italy, 2006.

TOROC, which is the official acronym used to identify the Organising Committee of the XX Olympic Winter Games in Torino, is a no-profit private foundation established to organize the sports events and the opening and closing ceremonies, to manage the Olympic villages, which will provide hospitality to athletes and technical staff, and to deal with matters related to the Media Villages, the Main Press Centre and the International Broadcasting Centre for television and radio services. The Committee will co-ordinate transportation and medical services, set up the temporary structures needed for athletes and spectators, plan and promote the cultural program, organize accommodation and transportation for athletes, sports staff, the media and all other personnel involved in the event. Finally, the Committee will be responsible for drawing up a marketing programme with the co-operation of the IOC and CONI.

Source: Torino 2006 (2003).

legacy for the next hosting city and country. An inordinate amount of money goes into hosting, and it is raised through government grants and funding, television rights, corporate sponsorship and advertising, licensing and sale of merchandise, ticket sales, and other marketing and special event functions. For example, VANOC's budget for the 2010 Winter Olympic Games is just over C$2 billion (VANOC, 2006).

Membership and organizational structure. OCOG members include both paid professional staff and volunteers. The OCOG is usually led by a volunteer President and Board of Directors, and a staff CEO. The OCOG is then subdivided into areas of responsibility such as finance, facility development, sports, technical liaison, marketing and sponsorship, volunteers, security, ticket sales, merchandising, television, doping control, and so forth.

Each of the governing structures presented above plays a role in setting or enforcing policy for the Olympic Games. The IOC is charged with this mandate, and NOCs and OCOGs help to enact it. Policy is often under revision and scrutiny, depending upon the prevailing issues of the day. For example, the 1999 scandal associated with IOC members accepting bribes from the Salt Lake City Organizing Committee resulted in a focus on procedures for choosing the host city. The continued presence of doping, as illustrated by positive drug tests at virtually every recent Olympic Games, continues to focus attention on testing procedures. World terrorism has resulted in heightened security measures and scrutiny of security procedures. These and other current policy issues of concern for Olympic organizers are discussed next.

Current Policy Areas

Baron Pierre de Coubertin envisioned the modern Olympics as the focus of the world spotlight, and he purposely kept the four-year time span between games so the spotlight would continue to burn bright long into the future. Given the continued interest and prestige of the Games today, de Coubertin and his collaborators would be well pleased. Every so often during the interlude between Olympics the media focuses on an issue related to international sport and ultimately the Olympic Games. These areas of intense interest and speculation are a good starting point for discussing current Olympic policy issues.

Doping Control Through Drug Testing

The Mexico City Summer Games in 1968 marked the beginning of drug testing for Olympic athletes. Rumors of athletes using performance-enhancing drugs to gain the slight edge required to win were becoming more and more frequent. The subject of drug use by athletes had "long constituted a hazy subject in the shadow of the Games, brought into the open only occasionally as after the death of the Danish cyclist in 1960" (Senn, 1999, pp. 142–143). The IOC responded by establishing the Medical Commission in 1967, which defined a list of banned substances and instituted testing at the Games. In the early days very few episodes of drug use were uncovered. Some members of the IOC encouraged the idea that athlete drug use at the Olympics was not a problem. In reality the science and technology required to detect many of the banned substances simply did not exist.

The use of drugs to boost performance is a major concern today. As Mitchell and Yates (2000) put it, "What trust can or should the public place in the 'heroic' achievements of sports stars if their success is gained illegally or because of a double standard in the rules regarding drug taking and testing?" (p. 199). Using artificial means for enhancing performance, through taking drugs, is considered cheating. Although only sometimes illegal, drug use to create a physical or mental edge over another individual competing without chemical aids is considered immoral and shameful.

Why would an athlete engage in such activity, considered wrong, possibly harmful to one's health, and clearly outside the rules of athletic engagement? Athletes justify their actions in several ways. Everyone wants to win, and the margin for success on the world stage is often so small that any slight advantage could produce an Olympic medal. It's easy for athletes and coaches to rationalize that everyone else is using, and therefore to keep up, I must too. The stakes are very high, with Gold Medal–winning athletes getting significant sponsorship and endorsement contracts. Finally, the will to win on behalf of one's nation, to bring glory home to one's fellow citizens, to gain the fame of being the best in the world—each is an incredible pull. So why *not* use drugs to enhance performance? There are many reasons, far more compelling than those just suggested. Doping is the very antithesis of fair competition, in which the beginning of the game or race or event is equal for all competitors. Otherwise, how about giving some competitors a head start, or provide one team a point cushion over the other? Such a concept is absurd in the athletic context and would never be supported. Doping, in effect, is the same as a head start or a point cushion, except that it usually cannot be detected overtly. Thus we see the implementation of drug testing and doping-control practices.

The policy developed and enacted by the IOC and NSFs is designed to eradicate doping practices by educating athletes and coaches and by catching and punishing those who cheat. The development of the World Anti-Doping Agency (WADA) by the IOC in November 1999 was a major step toward maintaining an edge over illicit drug use in sport. The organization has equal representation by members involved in the Olympic

Movement and by public authorities so that individual governments will play a role in anti-doping affairs (WADA, 2007). WADA established its headquarters in Montreal, Canada, in 2001. Having reached agreements with 56 International Sport Federations (ISFs) to conduct unannounced, out-of-competition testing, its mandate is to enact a harmonized, universal anti-doping policy that defines banned substances and practices, testing procedures, and penalties. The policy, enacted by the IOC, WADA, and ISFs, prescribes doping-control action in the following four areas:

1. communicating—ensuring that coaches, athletes, officials, and administrators understand the rules and the reasons for doping control
2. defining—identifying exactly what substances and practices are illegal
3. testing—detecting doping practices
4. sanctioning—imposing swift and severe penalties

World Anti-Doping Agency
www.wada-ama.org

Doping control and drug testing is a current policy issue because it continually evolves. As new substances and methods of illegally boosting performance are invented, new methods of detecting them are subsequently invoked. The result is an ongoing need to update the banned list and to communicate to participants. There are also problems in coordinating exactly which products or practices should be tested for which sports. In addition, the IOC and ISFs deal with the increasing possibility of legal wrangling over testing procedures, false positive tests, and sanctions. Without doubt, doping control will remain a concern and issue for policy refinement well into the future.

Defining Amateurism

Amateurism can be defined as doing things for the love of them, without reward or material gain. In its earliest context, the word *amateur* described a belief in action arising from taste rather than instrumental self-interest (Allison, 2001). Amateurism in sport has been defined and redefined over the years, arousing considerable social and political emotions. The issue is the product of a society that aspires to the conflicting models of commercialism and professionalism (Allison, 2001). Through the 19th century commercialism rose, and legitimacy was no longer guaranteed through religious or ethical behaviors. Instead, the power of money became emphasized, and the importance of honor and aristocratic values faded. Sport became a vehicle for professionals as well as amateurs, and debate regarding the importance of amateurism in competition raged. In the new millennium most competitors at Olympic Games are amateurs. However, historians describe the time between 1961 and 1995 as the Decline of Amateurism (Allison, 2001). The Olympic Games was historically the leader in furthering the support for amateurism in sport. Many of the IOC members and leaders remained committed to the concept until late in the 20th century, at which time some international federations such as FIBA (basketball) modified their rules to allow professional athletes to compete.

As long ago as 1971 the IOC eliminated the term *amateur* from the Olympic Charter. After the Moscow Olympics in 1980, Juan Antonio Samaranch was elected President of the IOC. "He aspired to make the games a world championship in all sports and had little interest in strict interpretations of the amateur principle" (Allison, 2001, p. 169). Samaranch sought to allow individual sports to implement their own definitions of *amateurism*. Thus the IOC accepted a proposal from Track and Field in 1983 to allow athletes who earn money through competition the opportunity to keep it in trust until the end of their careers. In 1984, the IOC permitted professional hockey players (other than NHL players) access to the Winter Olympics. The door was opened, and the Olympic Games embraced professional athletes as competitors in the 1990s. These events in turn fueled the debate among leaders of other events, sparking a change in eligibility rules at some major games.

The debate about establishing policy regarding amateurism has faded somewhat but has not been resolved all together. Professional athletes are now common place at Olympic Games, but not without reservation by many Olympic enthusiasts. Around the world countries make distinctions between amateur and professional athletes, with spectator interest helping to define the competition status. Rowing is a sport that continues to retain amateur status in its purest form but professional leagues now exist in sports from curling to volleyball. Defining the place of the amateur versus professional athlete will undoubtedly continue well into the 21st century.

Choosing a Host City

Imagine this setting: the President of the IOC moving toward the microphone, paper in hand, to announce the successful bid for hosting the next Summer Olympic Games. You and other members of the Organizing Committee sit in the audience of the capacity-crowd press conference, thinking back over the last seven years of work spent on the bid: hundreds of meetings; millions of dollars or euros raised and a good sum spent; victory upon victory in convincing citizens, city workers, and government officials of the value of bringing the Olympics home; visits by Olympic and IOC members; a massive enterprise coordinated. Yet, you still have not won the bid to host the Olympic Games. The President of the IOC announces, "And the winner is . . . ."

At the press conference to award the bid to host the Olympic Games, the stakes are huge because of the time and money invested as well as the potential for gain in achieving the bid. It is a city's chance to host the world, to gain the world spotlight. The stakes are indeed monumental.

Given this situation, it's easy to understand why the IOC procedures for awarding the bid to host are considered an important area for policy development. The policy must stipulate exactly how the decision will be made, based on what criteria, and within what time line. In this case, a policy will provide a framework for the bidding committee. What is important to the IOC in terms of staging the Olympics? Who will make the decision, and when will the decision be made? How can we position our bid to be held in the best possible regard by members of the IOC? The IOC has established a set of themes to guide this process. Consider the example of the U. S. bid for the 2012 Summer Olympic Games presented in Figure 10.9. The selection criteria themes upon which Olympic bids are judged have a dual purpose. They define the content of the bid and also provide a framework for members of the IOC who will vote for the successful bidding city. Policy to guide IOC voting members in deciding the successful bid has long been a topic of discussion. The process has come under increased and intense criticism recently. Rumors of IOC members accepting bribes of money, trips, gifts, and promises had been debated for years, but the December 1998 scandal that erupted as a result of alleged bribes associated with the 2002 Salt Lake City Olympic bid resulted in a thorough scrutiny and revision of the policy that mandates the conduct of IOC members. In the past, the IOC did not condone IOC Bid Selection Committee members accepting gifts, but it also did little to monitor the actions of its members. In effect, it produced a scenario where it appeared, and perhaps more than just appeared, that in order to win the bid the votes of IOC members had to be secured through bribes. Organizing committees spent considerable time, money, and strategic thought on planning how to best influence members of the IOC. However, the public outcry resulting from the Salt Lake City corruption allegations resulted in the IOC sanctioning those involved, a rather historic Olympic moment. Investigators discovered that the Salt Lake City Bid Committee paid hundreds of thousands of dollars in cash, gifts, travel, and medical aid to IOC members. In the end, 4 IOC violators resigned, 6 were expelled, and 10 received official warnings by the IOC President (IOC, 2002). The IOC Vice President at the time, Canadian Richard Pound, was tasked with investigating the bribery scandal and developing policies to "modernize" IOC procedures. The following changes were implemented in 1999 as a result of his investigation (IOC, 2002):

- Specific procedures for electing the candidate cities for 2006 onwards were amended.
- Visits by IOC members to candidate cities were abolished.
- An IOC Ethics Commission was created.
- IOC General Assembly (Sessions) were opened to the media for the first time.

FIGURE | 10.9 | Example of time lines and selection criteria in the U.S.A. bid to host the 2012 Summer Olympic Games.

Time Lines	
December 15, 2000	Deadline to submit bid to USOC by interested cities
December 15, 2000– February 28, 2001	USOC staff reviews bids
March 1, 2001	Bids sent back to cities for clarification/ changes
June 1, 2001	Deadline for resubmission of bids to USOC
June 1, 2001– September 30, 2001	USOC site visits
October 26, 2001	USOC Executive Committee selects finalist cities
April 8, 2002	Bid additions due to USOC
June 28–29, 2002	Washington, DC, site visit
June 30–July 1, 2002	New York City site visit
July 12–13, 2002	Houston site visit
July 14–15, 2002	San Francisco site visit
August 27, 2002	USOC to short-list to two candidate cities
October 1, 2002	Bid cities executive summary due to USOC
November 2, 2002	USOC Board of Directors selects U.S. candidate city (New York City)
July 2003	USOC nominates U.S. candidate city to IOC
May 2004	9 Bids reduced to 5 for 2nd stage of selection process. NYC is still in consideration
July 2005	IOC selects host (London) for the 2012 Olympic Games

Continued.

FIGURE | **10.9**

Selection Criteria Themes

18 Required Themes from the IOC: National, Regional and Bid City Characteristics, Legal Aspects, Customs and Immigration Formalities, Environmental Protection, Meteorological and Environmental Conditions, Security, Medical and Health Services, Official Program of the XXX Olympiad, General Sports Organization, Sports, Olympism and Culture, Olympic Village, Accommodations, Transportation, Technology, Media, Finance, Marketing, Guarantees

Additional Themes from the USOC: Sport Event Experience, Sports Infrastructure, Olympic Village, Finance, Paralympic Games, OCOG Governance/Ethics, International Strategies

Fifty-four percent of the scoring is according to International Olympic Committee guidelines for host city candidates, 15 percent will relate to financial and budget stability, and 31 percent judges USOC partnership opportunities, Paralympics planning, and the ability to win a vote before the IOC.

Highlights of Nominated Bid

New York City, U.S.A.

Proposed Budget: $3.2 billion

Dates: July 27–August 12, 2012

Highlights: Melting pot of America welcomes the world; business/media center; tourist area

Challenges: traffic congestion; security issues; massive construction projects

Source: New York City 2012 Summer Olympic Games Bid (2003). Reprinted with permission.

- Financial transparency was mandated through publication of sources of revenue and expenditures.

In addition to the changes implemented in 1999, the election procedure has been revised to consist of two phases: (1) the Applicant City phase, which includes applicant cities completing a comprehensive questionnaire about their bid intentions; and (2) the Candidature phase, in which cities provide information responding to a set of instructions by the IOC in creating bid planning documents (IOC, 2007d).

Corporate Sponsorship

Financing an Olympic Games may be the biggest issue facing an OCOG (Sleeman, 1992). "With the sheer size and complexity of today's Olympic Games, it is evident that if there were no sponsors, there would be no Games according to the IOC" (VISA, 2007). Some countries rely on their government for funding, others get funding from public sources such as lottery returns, and many will raise money privately through corporate sponsorship. The United States and Australia relied heavily on revenues raised from corporate partnerships for hosting the 2002 Salt Lake City Winter Games and the 2000 Sydney Summer Games, respectively.

Sponsorship is a complicated area. The stakes are high because of the potential for revenue generation. The area is complicated because of the need to define exactly who owns the rights to Olympic symbols and marks. Given the different levels of governance for Olympic sport (defined earlier in this chapter), it should be easy to understand why this area is so complicated. Three layers of organizations have an interest or a right to sponsorship associated with the Olympics: the IOC, the NOC, and the OCOG.

The IOC has therefore written policy to define who has the right to market and sell which sponsorships. Beyond outlining who has the right to which properties, Olympic sponsorship policy is intended to set guidelines for the practices of the different levels of governance. For example, are Title Sponsorships allowed? Could the Olympic Games be called the Coke Olympics? Obviously, neither practice is allowed by the IOC. However, defining the limits of acceptance regarding sponsors is a hot topic for debate and definition.

The IOC regularly debates the issue of commercialization of the Olympics. From the beginning, organizers have worked to keep the Games from becoming overly commercial, to ensure that the advertising at and around Olympic venues is tasteful and discreet. The issue, of course, is power. What happens if a sponsor contributing millions of dollars requests an action or accommodation? As former IOC President Samaranch told the press in Atlanta, "This commercialization must not run the games; the games must be run by the IOC" (Senn, 1999, p. 258). Concern over commercialization and a carnival atmosphere with too many sponsors and spectators was discussed after the Atlanta Olympics because of the extensive number of sponsors involved. In taking action to combat this problem, the IOC updated its sponsorship policies by adding a clause giving them veto power over sponsors' marketing plans. The IOC also required a financial guarantee from the government of the host city in order to balance funding and eliminate Olympic reliance on commercial sponsorship (Senn, 1999). But according to then IOC Vice President Richard Pound, the increasing commercialism of the Olympics was inevitable: "You can't have organized sports without corporate involvement" (Palmer, 2001).

Television Rights

Of all the sponsorship, advertising, and marketing opportunities available at the Olympics, no property for potential revenue generation is larger than television. In the aftermath of the 1984 Los Angeles Olympics, when huge profits were realized from hosting, the IOC began intense scrutiny of its own funding portfolio. It focused first on hosting guarantees and revenue-sharing methods and second on the revenues to be generated from selling television broadcast rights. The IOC decided to retain the right to negotiate television contracts and to share the revenues among the IOC, NOCs, OGOCs, and ISFs. For example, in December 1996 the IOC sold the American television rights to the Summer Games of 2004 and 2008 and the Winter Games of 2006 for $2.3 billion (Senn, 1999), an unprecedented action, given that host sites for some of those games had not yet been awarded. The policy issue regarding television rights involves ownership and value. The IOC has acted to retain the rights of negotiation and dispersal of television revenues. Its purpose included control, consistency, and ensuring value. By setting policy ensuring central control of this important negotiation, the IOC has ensured the potential for developing consistent, long-term contracts of the highest possible value. Of course, OGOCs would prefer to hold the rights themselves, and they can be expected to push for further debate on this issue. In addition, in the United States, the USOC takes the position, and the IOC recognizes, that the Ted Stevens Olympic and Amateur Sports Act grants it certain rights to participate in and to share in the proceeds of the U. S. television-rights broadcast negotiations.

New Olympic Sports

The size of the Olympic festival has been a topic of recent debate. The masses of visitors and spectators at the Sydney Olympics resulted in further scrutiny and policy development by the IOC, and the concern is revisited with each Olympic hosting. The issue of the number of competitors and sports has been added to the debate. Of course, many ISFs intensely lobby to be included in the Olympics. How many sports should the Olympics include? How many competitors are too many? How can the IOC balance the wonderful interest in Olympic competition and its mandate to provide opportunities for nations all around the world (203 NOCs), with the management issues that arise from competitions that are simply too large? Should every nation be permitted to send Olympic participants in all sports, even though the individuals may not meet world standards?

The IOC has developed policy to define exactly which sports will compete in the Olympics and how to add new sports. Currently there are 35 Summer and Winter Games sports with nearly 400 events (The Olympic

Movement, 2007). Within the Olympic Charter, policy is written to define the following:

- Olympic sports (for example, only sports practiced by men in 75 countries and on four continents, and by women in 40 countries and three continents may be included in the Olympic program)
- disciplines (different events within sports)
- events (competitions resulting in medals)
- criteria for admitting each sport

Often, the IOC will name an addition to the sport program at a particular Olympics in accordance with the wishes of the Organizing Committee. As you might imagine, a significant amount of lobbying occurs in an attempt to have a sport recognized for Olympic competition. Policy is required to define the criteria, procedure, and timing of decisions relative to the sports program of an Olympic Games. A recent debate involved whether to drop baseball and softball from the Olympic program and to add rugby and golf. The discussions revolved around spectator interest, worldwide participation in these sports, and the number of competitors in the Games. In another example, snowboarding was added to the Winter Olympic Games program to attract young viewers and thereby boost television ratings and sponsorship revenues.

Defining which sports will be offered at Olympic Games is the responsibility of the Olympic Programme Commission. This committee is charged with reviewing and analyzing the program of sports and defining the permissible number of athletes in each Olympic sport. It is also responsible for developing recommendations on the principles and structure of the Olympic program. Members of the commission vote upon adding or removing sports from the program, and traditionally it took a simple majority of votes (50% plus 1) to add a sport and two-thirds of the votes (67%) to remove one. In July 2007 this voting procedure was changed so that a simple majority of votes is now required to add or remove sports from the Olympic program. The maximum number of sports to be offered is set at 28, with 25 being the purview of the IOC and up to 3 others that may be added by the host organizing committee. The Olympic Programme Commission makes recommendations to the IOC Executive Board and presents reports to the IOC Session.

www

Olympic Programme Commission

www.olympic.org/uk/ organisation/commissions/ programme/index_uk.asp

Image

For more than a century, members of the Olympic Movement have been concerned with image. Significant effort has been put forth to ensure that the Olympic Games are perceived to be outside the realms of government interference, beyond partisanship and corruption, and grand contributors to improving conditions in the world. Caring for the image of the Olympic Movement is in concert with other tenets of Olympism. The Olympics involve excellence; being and doing your best; demonstrating strong ethical and moral behavior; building up, never breaking down; and giving, as opposed to just taking away. The Olympics are proposed as a festival of nations, with sporting competition as its mainstay, but also including cultural events and other ways of promoting world peace.

The IOC has taken great pains to maintain its image of excellence. Policy exists within the Olympic Charter illustrating an Olympic mandate far beyond a sporting competition. The IOC has positioned the Olympics and the Olympic Movement as contributing positively to world conditions. In building this Olympic image, the IOC has spoken out in favor of world peace; improved living conditions in poorer parts of the world; environmental renewal and care; cultural, ethnic, religious, and racial tolerance; economic growth and legacy for underdeveloped areas; and overall social responsibility for balancing resources between the haves and the have-nots in the world. The IOC wants the public to associate the Olympics with the image of a caring, contributing, concerned partner working toward a better world.

Some might argue the degree to which the IOC has succeeded in achieving these goals. Regardless, striving to create such an image has motivated the IOC to act in recent years. The corruption allegations and subsequent findings of the commission against members of the IOC Bid Selection Committee resulted in expelling members from the IOC. Increasing the number of active Olympic athletes elected to the IOC and changing policy relative to IOC vacancies and terms of office are also results of outside criticisms. In fact, the IOC had gained the reputation of being a closed shop, void of women and out-of-touch with the real world. Then IOC President Samaranch acted to increase the number of women on the committee (somewhat successfully) and to open the activities of the IOC by promoting financial transparency through public reports and by opening meetings to the press. Each of these actions, revisions to IOC policy, reflect practices to promote the image of all things Olympic.

Security

Security is a major issue for any large event that attracts world attention and the presence of world leaders, and the Olympic Games are no exception. Perhaps more to the point, it is an excellent example of the importance of providing for the security of participants and spectators at any large gathering. The Olympic Games attract many groups of individuals with their own agendas. Some come to participate, coach, or watch. Other groups come to further their cause, relying on the publicity gained in the high-profile-media presence of the Olympics. Examples of groups demonstrating to further world awareness of environmental or social or political concerns have been cited at many previous Olympic Games (Schaffer & Smith, 2000; Senn, 1999). For example, Australian aboriginal groups used the 2000 Sydney Olympics to publicize their protests against government land policies. Amnesty International protested the State of Georgia's position on the death penalty at the 1996 Atlanta Games. People for the Ethical Treatment of Animals protested the inclusion of rodeo in the cultural Olympiad that preceded the 2002 Salt Lake City Games. A group identified as "No Games 2010 Coalition" staged anti-Olympic protests during the IOC pre-election visits to Vancouver, and a group of American tourists demonstrated for a free Tibet and protested the 2008 Olympics leading to their deportation from China. The combination of world gathering, groups promoting their own interests, masses of people, and intense media scrutiny and availability has made organizers aware of the distinct need for security.

The bomb detonation in the Olympic park area at the Atlanta Olympics sent a clear message to organizers of the need for security. And of course, the darkest moment in Olympic history undoubtedly occurred in Munich in 1972 when a number of Israelis and Palestinians were killed in a hostage incident.

The IOC, NOC, and OCOG—each has a role in defining security policy such as emergency action plans and access areas for the Olympic Games. The IOC role involves scrutiny of the overall plan and insistence on base levels of acceptable practice. The NOC and OCOG define the exact practices related to access of fans, participants, and dignitaries; security of the Olympic Village; and practices such as managing cash at venues. Partners in the security details are the local and federal levels of police, intelligence, and armed forces. For example, the 2008 Beijing OCOG worked closely with the Beijing Municipal Public Security Bureau to plan for the safety of the Olympic participants, spectators, and volunteers. They identified nine major categories of risk including fire, illegal intrusion to facilities, urban harassment, crimes, technological risk to key service systems, traffic safety, natural calamities, other calamities, and terrorist activities as points of emphasis in Beijing.

A delicate balance is sought between allowing spectators to watch events and participate in cultural activities, and an effort to protect the participants and national delegations from outside attack or interference. In the final analysis, access to all official Olympic venues (competition and select noncompetition) is highly controlled. The Olympic Village is a closed, high-security area housing the delegations of each country. Access is controlled through accreditation badges worn by participants. Each accreditation contains photo identification and areas for which access is allowed. Only Olympic participants, officials, organizers, IOC members, and other official delegation members are accredited for the Olympic Games.

Politics at the Olympic Games

The originators of the Olympic Games sought to avert governmental interference by forming the IOC as a group in isolation from the funding requirements, politics, and power of a particular nation's administration. In reality, however, it has been impossible to keep politics out of the Olympics. The IOC is a very political organization in which alliances are regularly formed to enact some vision or goal. Even more so, political involvement in the Olympic Games occurs as a result of the gains possible for a national government and its ruling ideology. The Olympic Games have a huge following of people around the world, and governments naturally try to exploit the Games for their own purpose. In this way, the Olympics provide an avenue to unite people, to develop a national consciousness, and to provide ammunition to suggest that "our ways" are better than "your ways." Governments have used sport to send political messages to another country by sending a team to compete prior to an Olympics; for example, when the U. S. table tennis team went to China, it signaled a renewed interest in discussing foreign policy between the two nations. There are many other examples of political motives driving decisions associated with athletic competitions. However, none is more profound than a nation boycotting an Olympic Games.

The term *boycott* refers to shutting off access to something in order to punish or coerce for political motives. In the context of the Olympics, *boycott* refers to a nation's (or nations') refusing to attend a particular Games to protest some action or policy that can be profiled through such a refusal to participate. Several boycotts have taken place over the years: the U. S.-led boycott of the 1980 Moscow Olympics over the Soviet invasion of Afghanistan, and the subsequent retaliatory boycott of the Los Angeles Games by the Soviet Union and other Eastern Bloc nations in 1984; the African nations' boycott of the 1976 Montreal Olympics after the New Zealand rugby team toured apartheid South Africa; and the boycott of the 1956 Melbourne Olympics over the Soviet Union's invasion of Hungary and the United States' involvement in the Suez crisis (Schaffer & Smith, 2000). During these and other boycotts the Games went on without the athletes of the boycotting nations. Without a doubt, political statements were made, fewer athletes competed, and some individuals won medals they may not otherwise have won.

Extensive debate rages on regarding the usefulness of boycotting events. Today, protesting at Olympic-related events offers great visibility and impact, given the speed and global nature of media coverage. For example, the whole world witnessed protests during the Olympic torch global relay prior to the 2008 Beijing Summer Olympic Games. Rights groups and citizens in countries within Europe and around the world (United States, Australia, and Canada) used rallys to publicize and protest China's policies and actions in Tibet, viewed as repressive and in violation of basic human rights. The protests caused political leaders such as the President of the European Union to reconsider their nations' involvement in the Games, and the notion of boycotting was discussed, particularly in regard to political leaders attending the Opening Ceremonies. As of this writing, the final impact of these protests had not been determined.

Political ramifications of the Olympic Games are definitely an issue for policy definition, whether the political issues are related to the internal workings of the IOC or external to the governments of the participating nations. Each group will set policies to manage their own interests and perspectives. Perhaps organizing committees and their sponsors engage in political maneuvering. Or perhaps all parties are worried about the dangers of terrorist violence, the embarrassment of positive tests for performance-enhancing drugs, legal injunctions over team membership, or the authority of ISFs. One thing is for sure: Policies to deal with issues of power and politics in the Olympics will be necessary into the foreseeable future. As Senn (1999) put it, "Those who refuse to recognize the politics of the Games put themselves at the mercy of the people and organizations who actively participate in the political competition" (p. 296).

SUMMARY

The Olympic Games are at the pinnacle of sporting events in the world. Even professional athletes dream of winning an Olympic Gold Medal. Participating at an Olympics is described as an experience of a lifetime, and athletic careers are routinely described in terms of Olympic Medals won and number of Games attended. Such is the prestige of the Olympic Games.

All things Olympic are governed by the IOC, an elected group of Olympic enthusiasts charged with overseeing Olympic events and promoting the Olympic Charter. Policies of the Olympic Charter are developed by IOC committees and approved by the Session of the IOC, which meets at least once per year.

CASE STUDY   *Olympic Sports*

You have been lucky enough to land an opportunity to be involved with putting together the Olympic bid for the Summer Olympic Games in 2016. You have a choice of the following cities: Boston, Central Florida, Dallas, Edmonton, Los Angeles, Seattle, St. Louis, Windsor, and Winnipeg.

For your choice of cities, you have been asked to help assemble the bid documents for 6 of the 18 required IOC bid themes.

1. Choose a city.

2. Choose any 6 of the 18 themes presented in Figure 10.9 that are required components of the Olympic bid.

3. For your choice of city, explain as thoroughly as possible what information would go into the sections you are writing. You may need to do some Internet research to learn more about the specific city.

4. What procedures might you implement to ensure that all procedures and actions detailed in the bid document meet the highest legal and ethical standards?

CHAPTER QUESTIONS

1. Build a chart that depicts the levels of all organizations involved in delivering Olympic sport. Since the IOC has supreme authority, put it at the top of the chart and work down to state or provincial sport organizations.

2. Does television have a positive or negative effect on the Olympic Games? Make a list of both positive and negative effects before making your final decision.

3. How do sports become Olympic sports? Review the list of current Olympic sports. Are they popular and interesting? Are there any sports that might be replaced? If so, which ones, and what would replace them? What rationale would you provide the IOC for adding or dropping a sport?

4. Consider the costs of hosting an Olympic Games. Using a search engine such as Google Research, compare the predicted costs of hosting identified in London's 2012 bid to actual costs involved in hosting. If there is a change in predicted versus actual costs, where does it come from?

REFERENCES

Allison, L. (2001). *Amateurism in sport: An analysis and defense*. London: Frank Cass.

The Ancient Olympics. (2004). Frequently asked questions about the ancient Olympic Games. Retrieved May 12, 2007, from www.perseus.tufts.edu/edu/Olympics/faq11.html.

COC. (2006). Annual Report 2005. Retrieved September 26, 2007, from www.olympic.ca/EN/organization/publications/publications/.shtml.

COC. (2007a). Role of COC. Retrieved September 26, 2007, from www.olympic.ca/EN/organization/aboutus/.shtml.

COC. (2007b). Canadian Olympic Committee governance structure. Retrieved September 26, 2007, from www.olympic.ca/EN/organization/governance/index.shtml.

de Coubertin, P. (2000). Olympism: Selected writings. (Norbert Muller, Ed.). Lausanne: IOC.

1896 Athens, Greece. (2007). The Olympic Games. Retrieved September 28, 2007, from www.cartage.org.lb/en/themes/Sports/olympicgames/1896/athens.htm.

Howell, M. L., & Howell, R. (1988). Physical activities and sport in early societies. In E. F. Zeigler (Ed.), *History of physical education and sport* (pp. 1–56). Champaign, IL: Stipes.

IOC. (2002). Evolution of its structure. Retrieved October 30, 2002, from www.olympic.org/uk/organisation/ioc/organisation/index_uk.asp.

IOC. (2004). Global TV viewing of Athens 2004 Olympic Games breaks records. Retrieved May 12, 2007, from http://en.beijing2008.com/16/87/article211928716.shtml.

IOC. (2007a). Athens 1896. Retrieved May 12, 2007, from www.olympic.org/uk/games/past/index_uk.asp?OLGT=1&OLGY=1896.

IOC. (2007b). Organization. Retrieved May 12, 2007, from www.olympic.org/uk/organization/index_uk.asp.

IOC. (2007c). Organization. Retrieved May 12, 2007, from www.olympic.org/uk/organization/missions/charter_uk.asp.

IOC. (2007d). Choice of the host city. Retrieved May 14, 2007, from www.olympic.org/uk/organization/missions/cities_uk.asp.

IOC Marketing Fact File. (2006). Olympic marketing revenue generation. Retrieved May 12, 2007, from http://multimedia.olympic.org/pdf/en_report_344.pdf.

Korea Herald. (1986, May 24). In A. E. Senn (1999). *Power, politics, and the Olympic Games.* Champaign, IL: Human Kinetics.

Mitchell, A., & Yates, H. (2000). Who's sorry now? Drugs, sports, and the media toward 2000. In K. Schaffer & S. Smith (Eds.), *The Olympics at the millennium* (pp. 197–212). London: Rutgers Press.

New York City 2012 Summer Olympic Games Bid. (2003). Bid city profile and games sheet—New York, U. S. A. Retrieved June 17, 2003, from www.gamesbids.com/english/bids/usa.shtml.

The Olympic Movement. (2007). Sports. Retrieved September 24, 2007, from www.olympic.org/uk/sports/index_uk.asp.

Palmer, S. (2001). Executive says thrill of games trumps scandal. *The Eugene Register-Guard.*

Retrieved June 17, 2003, from www.warsawcenter.com/news_2001_0322.html.

Schaffer, K., & Smith, S. (2000). *The Olympics at the millennium.* London: Rutgers Press.

Senn, A. E. (1999). *Power, politics, and the Olympic Games.* Champaign, IL: Human Kinetics.

Sleeman, R. (1992). What price Sydney 2000? *Inside Sport, 1*(10), 14–16, 19–20, 115.

Thoma, J. E., & Chalip, L. (1996). *Sport governance in the global community.* Morgantown, WV: Fitness Information Technology.

Torino 2006. (2003). XX Olympic Winter Games, 10–26 February, 2006: Mission. Retrieved June 23, 2003, from www.Torino2006.it/eng/toroc_1.html.

Tyler, M., & Soar, P. (1980). *The history of the Olympics.* London: Marshall Cavendish.

USOC. (2002). United States Olympic Committee. Retrieved November 8, 2002, from www.usoc.org.

USOC. (2003). Board of directors meeting. April 12–13, 2003. Retrieved July 14, 2003, from www.olympic-usa.org/about_us/document.htm.

USOC. (2004). Olympic link directory. Retrieved September 24, 2007, from www.usoc.org/12181_36427.htm.

USOC. (2005). 2005 Annual report. Retrieved May 12, 2007, from www.usoc.org/12699.htm.

USOC. (2006). USOC bylaws. Retrieved May 3, 2007, from www.usolympicteam.com/12699.htm.

USOC. (2007a). United States Olympic Committee. Retrieved September 27, 2007, from www.usoc.org.

USOC. (2007b). Olympic link directory. Retrieved September 24, 2007, from www.usoc.org/12181_36427.htm.

VANOC. (2006). VANOC business plan and games budget. Retrieved May 14, 2007, from www.vancouver2010.com/en/OrganizingCommittee/AboutOrganizingCommittee/BusinessPlanGamesBudget.

VISA. (2007). VISA Olympic partnership. Retrieved September 28, 2007, from http://sponsorships.visa.com/olympic/corporate_sponsorship.jsp.

Wallechinsky, D. (1984). *The complete book of the Olympics.* New York: Penguin.

WADA. (2007). WADA history. Retrieved May 14, 2007, from www.wada-ama.org/en.

11

PARALYMPIC SPORT

INTRODUCTION

When we hear the word *athlete,* certain images come to mind. We envision people who are strong and fast, can throw or run great distances, shoot three pointers, or ski downhill at incredible speed. When we read about athletes running the 100 meters in just under 12 seconds, high jumping more than 6 feet (1.97 meters), or lifting 550 pounds (250 kilograms), we know they most certainly are elite athletes. All these *are* accomplishments of elite athletes, elite athletes with disabilities who competed in the Paralympic Games, an event that draws thousands of elite athletes with disabilities from over 130 nations every four years and that enjoys millions of corporate sponsorship dollars and worldwide media coverage. Who are these athletes, and what are the Paralympic Games?

Defining Disability Sport

When hearing the term *disability sport,* the image that often comes to mind first is that of the Special Olympian. However, that is not the only form of sport for people with disabilities. DePauw and Gavron (2005, p. 8) define *disability sport* as "sport designed for or specifically practiced by athletes with disabilities." For the purposes of this chapter, the focus will be on highly competitive, international, elite-level disability sport, specifically, the Paralympic Games.

Participants

The Paralympic Games showcase elite-level athletes with disabilities. Incorporating the same ideology as the Olympic Games in celebrating the accomplishments of elite international athletes, the Paralympic Games are scheduled approximately two weeks later than the Olympic Games in the same cities and venues, and are staged by the same organizing committee. When a host city is awarded the Olympic Games, the Paralympic Games are an obligatory part of the package, as one of the themes in the host city bid process.

The motto of the Paralympic Games is "Spirit in Motion." The International Paralympic Committee (IPC) considers this motto to represent its vision, "to enable Paralympic athletes to achieve sporting excellence and excite the world." The sports on the official Paralympic Games Programme are presented in Table 11.1. Not all disability types are eligible to participate in the Paralympic Games. The athletes who compete in the Paralympic Games have a range of disabilities, including visual impairment, cerebral palsy, amputations, spinal cord injuries, and on a very limited basis, athletes with intellectual disabilities. Please note that athletes with hearing impairments do not participate; they compete in separate World Games and other competitions for the deaf, including the Deaflympics. Athletes with cognitive disabilities such as Down syndrome do not participate in the Paralympics. The Special Olympics were established to provide opportunities for people with cognitive and developmental disabilities. The mission of Special Olympics includes skill development and social interaction, not the development of international elite-level athletes, which is the mission of the Paralympics.

Current sports on the official Paralympic Programme.		TABLE 11.1

Paralympic Games Programme for Beijing 2008 Summer Games		
Archery	Goalball	Table Tennis
Athletics	Judo	Volleyball (Sitting)
Boccia	Powerlifting	Wheelchair Basketball
Cycling	Rowing	Wheelchair Fencing
Equestrian	Sailing	Wheelchair Rugby
Football 5-a-Side	Shooting	Wheelchair Tennis
Football 7-a-Side	Swimming	

Paralympic Games Programme for Torino 2006 Winter Games		
Alpine Skiing	Cross-Country Skiing	Wheelchair Curling
Biathlon	Ice Sledge Hockey	

History of the Paralympic Games

Sport for people with disabilities existed for many years before the founding of the Paralympic Games and began to grow after World War II, when sport was used to rehabilitate the many injured military and civilian persons. In 1944, Sir Ludwig Guttmann opened the Spinal Injuries Center at Stoke Mandeville Hospital in England and incorporated sport as an integral part of the rehabilitation process for people there. On July 28, 1948, the first Stoke Mandeville Wheelchair Games were held. The date was significant because it corresponded to the Opening Ceremonies for the Summer Olympic Games in London that same day. As disability sport continued to expand beyond athletes who used wheelchairs, the International Sport Organization for the Disabled (ISOD) was formed in 1964. ISOD brought together athletes with disabilities such as visual impairments, cerebral palsy, and amputees. Additional sport organizations for people with disabilities formed as well, such as the Cerebral Palsy International Sport and Recreation Association (CP-ISRA) and the International Blind Sports Association (IBSA), organized in 1978 and 1980, respectively. To help these and other sport organizations for athletes with disabilities to coordinate their activities, the IPC was founded in 1989 in Düsseldorf, Germany. The IPC remains today the only multidisability international sport organization in the world recognized by the IOC (IPC, 2007a).

When the IPC lists statistics for the Summer Paralympic Games, it begins with the 1952 Summer Games at Stoke Mandeville, the first international games for athletes with disabilities. The first Winter Paralympic Games were held in 1976 in Sweden. The first Paralympic Games under the direct management of the IPC were the Winter Paralympic Games in Lillehammer in 1994. Table 11.2 lists the dates of the Paralympic Summer and Winter Games, the numbers of athletes and nations participating, and additional information. As the statistics show, the Paralympic Games are showing steady growth in the number of both athletes and nation members participating. The 2004 Paralympic Summer Games in Athens, Greece, had more than 3,800 athletes from 136 nations—just four fewer nations than participated in the 1984 Summer Olympic Games in Los Angeles.

TABLE 11.2 Overview of Paralympic Games.

Summer Games Overview

Year	Location	Disabilities Included	Number of Countries	Number of Athletes	Shared Venue with Olympics	Highlights
2012	London, UK	Spinal injury Amputee Visual impairment Cerebral palsy Les Autres Intellectual disability	150*	4200*	Yes	
2008	Beijing, China	Spinal injury Amputee Visual impairment Cerebral palsy Les Autres	150*	4000*	Yes	Rowing to be added
2004	Athens, Greece	Spinal injury Amputee Visual impairment Cerebral palsy Les Autres	136	3806	Yes	Football 5-a-side added Record media attendance
2000	Sydney, Australia	Spinal injury Amputee Visual impairment Cerebral palsy Les Autres Intellectual disability	122	3843	Yes	Sailing and wheelchair rugby added Record ticket sales

* Expected number

Overview of Paralympic Games, *continued.*   **TABLE   11.2**

Year	Location	Disabilities Included	Number of Countries	Number of Athletes	Shared Venue with Olympics	Highlights
1996	Atlanta, USA	Spinal injury Amputee Visual impairment Cerebral palsy Les Autres Intellectual disability	103	3195	Yes	Equestrian added Track cycling added First worldwide corporate sponsorship
1992	Barcelona, Spain	Spinal injury Amputee Visual impairment Cerebral palsy Les Autres	82	3021	Yes	Event benchmark in organizational excellence
1988	Seoul, Korea	Spinal injury Amputee Visual impairment Cerebral palsy Les Autres	61	3013	Yes	Judo, wheelchair tennis added Cooperation between Olympic and Paralympic Organizing Committees
1984	Stoke Mandeville, UK, & New York, USA	Spinal injury Amputee Visual impairment Cerebral palsy Les Autres	41 (UK) 45 (USA)	1100 (UK) 1800 (USA)	No	Football 7-a-side and Boccia added Road cycling added Demonstration event at Olympic Games in L.A.: Wheelchair racing
1980	Arnhem, Netherlands	Spinal injury Amputee Visual impairment Cerebral palsy Les Autres	42	1973	No	Sitting volleyball added Events for athletes with cerebral palsy included
1976	Toronto, Canada	Spinal injury Amputee Visual impairment Les Autres	38	1657	No	First use of specialized racing wheelchairs Volleyball (standing), goalball, and shooting added

(continued)

| TABLE | 11.2 | Overview of Paralympic Games, *continued*. |

Year	Location	Disabilities Included	Number of Countries	Number of Athletes	Shared Venue with Olympics	Highlights
1972	Heidelberg, Germany	Spinal injury	43	984	No	First quadriplegic competition added Demonstration events for athletes with a visual impairment
1968	Tel Aviv, Israel	Spinal injury	29	750	No	Lawn bowling added
1964	Tokyo, Japan	Spinal injury	21	357	Yes	Weightlifting added
1960	Rome, Italy	Spinal injury	23	400	Yes	First games for athletes with a disability held in same venue as Olympic games
1952	Stoke Mandeville, UK	Spinal injury	2	130	No	First international games for athletes with a disability

Winter Games Overview

Year	Location	Disabilities Included	Number of Countries	Number of Athletes	Shared Venue with Olympics	Highlights
2010	Vancouver, Canada	Spinal injury Amputee Visual impairment Cerebral palsy Les Autres	45*	650*	Yes	
2006	Torino, Italy	Spinal injury Amputee Visual impairment Cerebral palsy Les Autres	39	477	Yes	Wheelchair curling added
2002	Salt Lake City, USA	Spinal injury Amputee Visual impairment Cerebral palsy Les Autres	36	416	Yes	Number of tickets on sale had to be augmented due to high demand

* Expected number

Overview of Paralympic Games, *continued.*   **TABLE   11.2**

Year	Location	Disabilities Included	Number of Countries	Number of Athletes	Shared Venue with Olympics	Highlights
1998	Nagano, Japan	Spinal injury Amputee Visual impairment Cerebral palsy Les Autres	32	571	Yes	Demonstrated rising media and public interest in Paralympic winter sport
1994	Lillehammer, Norway	Spinal injury Amputee Visual impairment Cerebral palsy Les Autres	31	492	Yes	Ice sledge hockey added
1992	Tignes-Albertville, France	Spinal injury Amputee Visual impairment Cerebral palsy Les Autres	24	475	Yes	Biathlon added Demonstration events: Alpine and cross-country skiing for athletes with an intellectual disability
1988	Innsbruck, Austria	Spinal injury Amputee Visual impairment Cerebral palsy Les Autres	22	397	No	Sit-ski events introduced in the sports of Alpine and Nordic skiing
1984	Innsbruck, Austria	Spinal injury Amputee Visual impairment Cerebral palsy Les Autres	21	457	No	Demonstration event at Olympics in Sarajevo: Giant slalom
1980	Geilo, Norway	Spinal injury Amputee Visual impairment Cerebral palsy Les Autres	18	350	No	Demonstration event: Downhill sledge racing
1976	Örnsköldsvik, Sweden	Visual impairment Amputee	17	250+	No	Demonstration event: Sledge racing

Source: IPC (2007g).

Governance

Just as with the Olympic Movement, the Paralympic Movement and specifically the Paralympic Games fit into a complex set of governance structures. A number of governing bodies are involved with Paralympic Sport, including the IPC, National Paralympic Committees (NPCs), and International Paralympic Sport Federations (IPSFs).

International Paralympic Committee (IPC)

www@

International Paralympic
Committee
www.paralympic.org

The IPC, the supreme authority of the Paralympic Movement, is the international representative organization of elite sports for athletes with disabilities. IPC organizes, supervises, and coordinates the Paralympic Games and other multidisability competitions on the elite sports level, of which the most important are world and regional championships.

Vision/Mission. The IPC has a vision statement and a mission statement. (See Figures 11.1 and 11.2.) The vision statement for the IPC contains an overall picture of IPC philosophy. Its mission statement is more detailed, including statements that could also be seen as goals for the organization. This mission statement is a bit longer than mission statements for some sport organizations, but does provide a detailed picture of what the IPC does and strives for.

FIGURE   11.1   Vision statement of the IPC.

PARALYMPIC VISION

To Enable Paralympic Athletes to Achieve Sporting Excellence and Inspire and Excite the World

- To enable—This is the primary role of the IPC as an organization: To create the conditions for athlete empowerment through self-determination

- Paralympic athletes—The primary focus of the IPC's activities, in the context of Paralympic athletes, is the development of all athletes from initiation to elite level

- To achieve sporting excellence—The goal of a sports-centered organization

- To inspire and excite the world—The external result is our contribution to a better world for all people with a disability. To achieve this, relations with external organizations and the promotion of the Paralympic Movement as a whole are of prime importance.

Source: IPC (2003).

Mission statement of the IPC.	FIGURE 11.2

PARALYMPIC VISION

- To guarantee and supervise the organization of successful Paralympic Games
- To ensure the growth and strength of the Paralympic Movement through the development of National Paralympic Committees in all countries and the support to the activities of all IPC member organizations
- To promote and contribute to the development of sport opportunities and competitions, from initiation to elite level, for Paralympic athletes as the foundation of elite Paralympic sport
- To develop opportunities for female athletes and athletes with a severe disability in sport at all levels and in all structures
- To support and encourage educational, cultural, research and scientific activities that contribute to the development and promotion of the Paralympic Movement
- To seek the continuous global promotion and media coverage of the Paralympic Movement, its vision of inspiration and excitement through sport, its ideals and activities
- To promote the self-governance of each Paralympic sport either as an integral part of the international sport movement for able-bodied athletes, or as an independent sport organization, whilst at all times safeguarding and preserving its own identity
- To ensure that in sport practiced within the Paralympic Movement the spirit of fair play prevails, violence is banned, the health risk of the athletes is managed and fundamental ethical principles are upheld
- To contribute to the creation of a drug-free sport environment for all Paralympic athletes in conjunction with the World Anti-Doping Agency (WADA)
- To promote Paralympic sport without discrimination for political, religious, economic, disability, gender, sexual orientation, or race reasons
- To ensure the means necessary to support the future growth of the Paralympic Movement

Source: IPC (2003).

Financials. One source of funding for the IPC comes from annual membership dues. However, most funding comes from the IPC's partnerships with private and public bodies, including revenues received from the rights given to organizing committees for hosting the Paralympic Games. Income used by organizing committees to operate the Games themselves is derived from a combination of government support, Olympic support, and sponsorship deals. Currently, the IPC has four Worldwide partners: VISA, Otto Bock, Atos Origin, and Samsung. In addition, Deutsche Telekom and Allianz are Gold Patrons. Other companies sign on to be sponsors of a specific Games, for example, Alpha Bank during the 2004 Summer Games in Athens.

Membership. The members of the IPC include the International Organizations of Sport for the Disabled (IOSDs), NPCs, IPSFs, and Regional/Continental Paralympic Organizations.

The IOSD organizations are as follows:

CP-ISRA	Cerebral Palsy International Sport and Recreation Association
IBSA	International Blind Sport Federation
INAS-FID	International Association of Sport for People with an Intellectual Disability
IWAS	International Wheelchair and Amputee Sports Federation

In addition to these international sports organizations, NPCs or National Contact Agencies from different nations are also full members of the IPC. Currently 162 NPCs are members of the IPC. Three regional organizations—African Sports Confederation for the Disabled (ASCOD), European Paralympic Committee (EPC), and Oceania Paralympic Committee—as well as two regional committees—Americas Paralympic Committee and Asian Paralympic Committee—are also members. These full members have voting rights at the IPC's General Assembly. In addition to the above-mentioned full members, the IPSFs have voting and speaking rights at the IPC's General Assembly. Besides being the supreme authority for the supervision and organization of the Paralympic Games, the IPC also fulfills an important role as the international federation for several sports.

Organizational structure. The structure of the IPC consists of the General Assembly, the Governing Board, Management Team, and a number of Standing Committees. Figure 11.3 illustrates the general structure of the IPC.

The General Assembly is the governance body for the IPC and its highest authority. The General Assembly decides on any matters relevant to the IPC and is the biannual assembly of the IPC members (IPC, 2007c). Members of the General Assembly meet at least once every two years to discuss and vote on policy matters of concern to the Paralympic Games. At the General Assembly, each full member has one vote. The Governing Board members include a President, Vice President, 10 Members-at-Large, one Athlete Representative and one CEO ex-officio member.

The Governing Board

is primarily responsible for the implementation of policies and directions set by the General Assembly. Additionally, the Governing Board provides

www

CP-ISRA

www.cpisra.org

IBSA

www.ibsa.es/eng

www

African Sports Confederation for the Disabled

www.ascod.org

European Paralympic Committee

www.europaralympic.org

Asian Paralympic Committee

www.asianparalympic.org

General structure of the IPC.   **FIGURE   11.3**

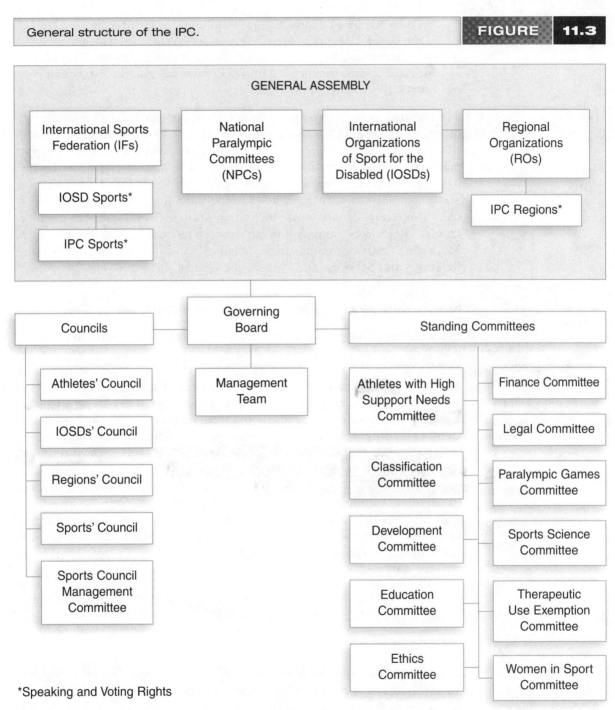

GENERAL ASSEMBLY

International Sports Federation (IFs)

National Paralympic Committees (NPCs)

International Organizations of Sport for the Disabled (IOSDs)

Regional Organizations (ROs)

IOSD Sports*

IPC Regions*

IPC Sports*

Governing Board

Councils

Standing Committees

Management Team

Athletes' Council

IOSDs' Council

Regions' Council

Sports' Council

Sports Council Management Committee

Athletes with High Suppport Needs Committee

Classification Committee

Development Committee

Education Committee

Ethics Committee

Finance Committee

Legal Committee

Paralympic Games Committee

Sports Science Committee

Therapeutic Use Exemption Committee

Women in Sport Committee

*Speaking and Voting Rights

Source: IPC (2007c, d).

recommendations on membership (conditions for membership and fees) to the General Assembly, including motions received from members. It is also responsible for approving budgets and auditing accounts, IPC Rules and Regulations, membership of IPC Committees and the Paralympic Games. (IPC, 2007c, ¶3)

The IPC Team "consists of the professional staff working under the direction of the CEO (special representative, §30 German Civil Code)" (IPC, 2004, IPC Management Team section). These are the paid sport managers who work at IPC Headquarters. The headquarters for the IPC has been located in Bonn, Germany, since 1999. Several paid Executive Staff members work at the headquarters, including the COO, who oversees numerous departments including Sports; Development; Finance, Human Resources, and Administration; Fundraising and Sponsorship; Marketing and Communication; Medical and Scientific; Membership Relations and Services; and Paralympic Games (IPC, 2007e).

National Paralympic Committees (NPCs)

Every nation participating in the Paralympic Games must have an NPC or, if an NPC has not yet been established, a National Contact Agency. What is an NPC's role in Paralympic sport governance? NPCs have the following functions: "NPCs undertake the co-ordination and support of IPC activities and Paralympic Sport within their respective territory. They are also responsible for the entrance, management and team preparation for the Paralympic Games and other IPC sanctioned competitions" (IPC, 2007f, ¶3).

In the United States, the USOC acts as the NPC and is constitutionally obligated to do so by the Amateur Sports Act. This is very unusual, as most nations have a separate NPC. For example, in Canada the Canadian Paralympic Committee is responsible for the Paralympic Movement, Australia has the Australian Paralympic Committee, and Greece has the Hellenic Paralympic Committee. In 2002, the USOC established U. S. Paralympics, a division of the USOC, to manage Paralympic sport. The mission statement of U. S. Paralympics reads as follows:

> U. S. Paralympics, a division of the U. S. Olympic Committee, is dedicated to becoming the world leader in the Paralympic sports movement, and promoting excellence in the lives of persons with physical disabilities. (USOC, 2005)

U. S. Paralympics and the appropriate NGB help prepare and select the athletes who represent the United States at the Paralympic Games. It also works with local organizations to promote sport programs for children and developing athletes who have disabilities. U. S. Paralympics helps spread the Olympic ideals to people with disabilities in the United States (USOC, 2005).

www.Ⓦ

Canadian Paralympic Committee

www.paralympic.ca

Australian Paralympic Committee

www.paralympic.org.au

Hellenic Paralympic Committee

www.paralympic.gr/index.php?lang=en

U. S. Paralympics

www.usparalympics.com

David Grevemberg

Sport Director, International Paralympic Committee, Bonn, Germany

As Sports Director for the IPC, I am responsible for the supervision and management of the established sport organizational standards and requirements necessary for the successful hosting of the Paralympic Games. Relative to the Paralympic Games, some of my specific tasks include (1) the evaluation of the sports, disciplines, and events on the Paralympic Programme, (2) the development of qualification standards, (3) the determination of standard levels of service provided to technical officials, and (4) the evaluation and determination of appropriate competition and training venues and equipment requirements. Because all Paralympic Games issues are subject to the final authority of the IPC Executive Committee, I develop proposals, reports, and policies for consideration by this governing body and other IPC Standing Committees to ensure the successful hosting of the Paralympic Games by organizing committees.

Currently, the most pressing policy issues confronting the Paralympic Movement concern the identification, development, and retention of athletes with disabilities in both developing and advantaged nations. With the disability demographic profiles worldwide changing due to vaccinations, research, war, and technology, the IPC faces the unique challenge of creating, updating, and balancing policies that establish competitive sport standards at the elite level while encouraging physical activity and general participation in sport at the local level.

A notable governance issue that I have been involved in solving is related to the development of formal cooperative agreements between Paralympic sport governing bodies governed by the IPC and their equivalent Olympic ISF. By identifying existing synergies and assessing value-added areas, I have developed strategies and initiated exploratory meetings to facilitate a joint understanding of existing and potential opportunities. The focus has been not only on developing relationships that emphasize the inclusive or social values of Olympic ISFs, but on laying the foundation for greater self-sustainable sport property development.

Currently, the IPC has a very broad mandate and therefore has created many standing committees and commissions to achieve its vision and mission. A positive aspect of such a broad structure is that it encourages specialization and the potential for vast recruitment of expertise in select areas. However, from a purely operational perspective, the management and administration of these bodies require significant human and financial resources. For sports organizations like the IPC, it is therefore essential that a strong emphasis be placed on the effective prioritization of issues, streamlining operations to maximize work efficiency, and eliminating work redundancy.

International Paralympic Sport Federations (IPSFs)

These organizations, similar to the international federations discussed in the chapter on Olympic sport, act as governing bodies for a particular sport on the international level. They have voting and speaking rights at the IPC General Assembly. In addition, the IPC itself acts as the international federation for a number of sports.

Current Policy Areas

Like any major international sport entity, the Paralympic Movement faces a wide variety of issues about which it must formulate policies. Because of its global nature, many of these policy issues take on increased complexity, and many of these complex issues have strong ethical components (Hums, 2006). Some of the specific challenges facing managers in Paralympic sport are as follows: changing technology (Hums, 2006, 2007), sport in developing nations (Hums, 2006, 2007), performance-enhancing substances and methods, differing global concepts of gender (Cody, 2002), sport and human rights (Hums, 2007), and integration and inclusion of athletes with disabilities into able-bodied sport (Grevemberg, Wolff, & Hums, 2001).

Changing Technologies

Advances in technology have an impact on sport every day, whether through introduction of a new golf club, lighter football shoes, or improved athletic turf. The impact of technology is felt deeply in the Paralympic Games, as prosthetics and wheelchairs for competition become lighter and stronger and as athletes become faster. Oscar Pistorius, a double-amputee runner from South Africa, rose to international recognition in his pursuit of qualifying for the Olympic Games as a sprinter. His quest was not without controversy, however, as some people in sport questioned whether his prosthetic devices gave him an unfair advantage.

How technology affects sport presents larger questions for sport managers. Just because new equipment can be manufactured that allows for increased performance, does that mean the equipment should be allowed in competition? For example, just because a company can manufacture a golf ball that can fly 500 meters does not necessarily mean golf governing bodies must sanction the ball for competition. In deciding which equipment to sanction for competition, sport governing bodies need to assess three things: (1) safety, (2) ability of people to access or acquire the equipment, and (3) fairness. First and foremost, sport equipment must be safe for the athletes using the equipment and for the other athletes competing in the same game or event. Second, governing bodies must assess whether the cost of the new equipment is excessive, thereby eliminating the possibility for athletes, particularly those from developing countries, to acquire the equipment. Finally is the basic question of fairness. Does using certain equipment provide one athlete an unfair advantage over the competition?

Developing Nations

As a result of poverty, natural disaster, or conflict, people in many developing nations struggle mightily with daily life. People with disabilities in these nations face even greater barriers. The Paralympic Movement is committed to encouraging the development of sport for people with disabilities in all nations and recognizes the special challenges prospective athletes in developing nations face. One factor that cannot be overlooked in this discussion as well is the cost of these before-mentioned technologies. Cost can affect the ability of people in developing nations to access advanced technology. People in these nations have enough difficulty accessing what they need to maintain their own lives. Thus, due to financial restrictions, they are not going to have access to the newest technology in prosthetics, sport chairs, or training practices for sport. Aspiring athletes may therefore be shut out of opportunities because of financial barriers (Hums, 2006, 2007).

Performance-Enhancing Activities

It has been shown repeatedly that some athletes will do "whatever it takes" to win. This rationale for illegal drug use also applies to some athletes in disability sport. The use of performance-enhancement techniques including banned substances is an area of great concern for the Paralympic Movement. Therefore, the IPC established the IPC Anti-Doping Code in January 2004. The rationale behind the code is that

> Anti-doping programmes seek to preserve what is intrinsically valuable about sport, "The spirit of sport." Thus, the rationale for doping control in sport is twofold: first, to protect athletes from the potential harmful side effects that some drugs can produce; and second, to ensure fair and ethical competition by preventing athletes from taking prohibited substances or using prohibited methods in an attempt to increase performance or violating the spirit of sport. (IPC, 2007b, ¶5)

The IPC Anti-Doping Code is congruent with the World Anti-Doping Code put forth by the WADA. Despite the establishment of the code, three athletes tested positive in Powerlifting at the Athens 2004 Summer Games and were sanctioned with lifetime ineligibility. Unfortunately, as in the Olympic Games, instances of doping still occur.

Paralympic sport has one special issue concerning drug testing: Some athletes have a disability due to an accident or adult-onset illness that requires medications for everyday life, and these medications may be considered banned substances (e.g., steroids). Therefore, decisions must be made about what is appropriate use, as opposed to excessive use, of certain substances.

Women in Paralympic Sport

Just as with the Olympic Movement, the Paralympic Movement is also attempting to create more participation opportunities for female athletes. In the 2004 Summer Games in Athens, Greece, only 31 percent of the total

IPC Anti-Doping Code

www.paralympic.org/release/ Main_Sections_Menu/Anti_ Doping/2006_06_IPC_Anti-Doping_Code_-_January_ 2004_-_Revised.pdf

World Anti-Doping Code

www.wada-ama.org/ rtecontent/document/ code_v3.pdf

athletes were women because of the difficulty for women with disabilities to compete. They face a "double barrier" of gender and disability (Hums, 2007). What are some of the barriers women wishing to participate face? According to Cody (2002):

> The duality of discrimination based on disability and gender presents significant barriers to achieving independence and self-determination. These barriers influence a woman's ability to seek employment, education, and economic self-sufficiency, relegating them to poverty and dependency on others. It is difficult to participate in sport without financial resources. Women also must make difficult choices about their commitment to sport versus careers, family, children, etc. The majority of people with disabilities are introduced to disabled sports later in life (16–25). For women, this leaves a much smaller window of opportunity in which to engage in competitive sport and reach the elite level. Women face additional societal and familial pressures to start families and run households earlier than men.

In an attempt to increase female participation, the Sport Technical Department of the IPC (2001) introduced a number of initiatives for the Sydney 2000 Paralympic Games, including the following:

- equity in allocation of country wildcards (extra athlete participation slots)
- emphasis on at-risk events for women and athletes with severe disabilities in allocation of sport wildcards
- addition of viable events and disciplines for women
- equitable allocation of slots by sports and nation
- emphasis on increasing awareness of Sport and NPC leadership of issues related to women and sports

Women and Sport Commission

www.olympic.org/uk/ organisation/missions/ women/index_uk.asp

For the 2008 Beijing Games, the IPC has set desired levels of participation by women. The target gender representation for Beijing is 65 percent male and 35 percent female athletes (IPC, 2005). The IPC also established the Women and Sport Commission in 2003 to address the low numbers of women in the Paralympic Movement at all levels. In addition, Cody (2007, p. 263) offers two suggestions. "One strategy is to work toward inclusion of women with disabilities into the women and sport movement generally . . . Working within international organizations responsible for sport for people with disabilities to remove barriers and bring about policies and practices that encourage participation by girls and women in every aspect of sport will also be an important place to focus efforts as well."

It is hoped that over time initiatives such as these will increase opportunities for female athletes with disabilities to compete to their potential. Women with disabilities face a two-tiered barrier in sport—they are female athletes, and they are athletes with disabilities. Making every effort to improve opportunities for these elite athletes provides opportunities on two fronts.

Sport and Human Rights

The United Nations General Assembly recently adopted the Treaty on the Rights of Persons with Disabilities. Article 30.5 of this Treaty pertains directly to access to sport and physical activity. In addition, in 2004 the International Paralympic Committee Governing Board approved a position statement on sport and human rights. The notion of sport and human rights extends beyond the days of competition of the Paralympic Games:

> Not everyone can qualify for the Paralympic Games, but people with disabilities can still be part of the Paralympic Movement at the grass roots level. We need to inform people the Movement is broader than the 10-day competition we call the Paralympic Games. Any person with a disability should be able to be a part of the Paralympic Movement. The overall Paralympic Movement is more about sport for all, similar to the notion of Olympism. (Hums, 2007)

Increasingly, scholars, activists, and sport management professionals are including the notion of sport and human rights into their programs of action.

Integration and Inclusion of Athletes with Disabilities into Able-Bodied Sport

This extremely complex policy area is one in which the solutions are evolving differently in different parts of the world. How can integration of athletes with disabilities be measured? The extent to which athletes with disabilities have been integrated can be measured by the following organizational components: (1) governance, (2) media and information distribution, (3) management, (4) funding and sponsorship, (5) awareness and education, (6) events and programs, (7) awards and recognition, (8) philosophy, and (9) advocacy (Hums, Legg, & Wolff, 2003; Wolff, 2000). Each of these components can be examined as follows:

1. Governance can be evaluated by looking at organizational policies and procedures dealing with athletes with disabilities.

2. Media and information distribution can be examined by looking for representation of athletes with disabilities in organizational publications or media guides.

3. Management can be assessed by examining the number of persons with disabilities working in management positions or sitting on governing boards.

www

Position Statement of the IPC on Human Rights

www.paralympic.org/release/
Main_Sections_Menu/News/
Paralympic_News/Days/IPC_
Position_Statement_HR.pdf

4. Funding and sponsorship can be ascertained from budgets. How much money being raised by the organization is going to support athletes with disabilities?

5. Awareness and education refer to how informed and how knowledgeable people within the organization are about disability sport.

6. The number of events and programs the organization delivers for athletes with disabilities indicates the number of competitive opportunities the organization is providing.

7. Awards and recognitions deal with how the organization publicly recognizes the accomplishments of its athletes with disabilities.

8. The organization's philosophy is reflected in its mission statement. Are athletes with disabilities mentioned in that mission statement?

9. Advocacy can be examined by seeing whether a sport organization is actively promoting sport for people with disabilities via special programming.

How can these components relate to policy development within a sport organization? For media and information distribution, sport organizations could make sure athletes with disabilities are presented on a consistent basis in printed materials or press releases. Under management, sport organizations could establish hiring procedures creating opportunities for people with disabilities to be represented in the pool of candidates for open management positions. Under events and programs, sport organizations could establish participation categories for athletes with disabilities, just as there are categories of participation for men and women. For funding, sport organizations could establish funding opportunities designated for athletes with disabilities so that when organizational representatives meet with potential donors, disability sport is always in the conversation. These selected examples show how these criteria for inclusion can result in organizational policy making, and they also provide a solid framework for assessing the status of athletes and people with disabilities within sport organizations.

Organizations that embrace diversity are acting as socially responsible partners with society. Including athletes with disabilities into the management structure of sport organizations increases the size of the networks involved and allows for more voices at the table.

SUMMARY

The Paralympic Games motto is "Spirit in Motion." The Games are an ever-growing, international, multidisability, multisport competition. Attracting thousands of athletes from numerous nations, the Games showcase the best of the best of elite athletes with disabilities. As a sport property, the Games are gaining the interest of corporations eager to connect with millions of consumers around the world. The governing structure of the Paralympics parallels that of the Olympic Games in many ways; both are large multisport international events. Just as women and racial and ethnic minorities have contributed by diversifying the sport industry, so too are people with disabilities beginning to make an impact. This large part of the sport industry is often overlooked in spite of its size and importance, and students are well advised to keep an eye on the growth and development in this area.

The Paralympic Games, as a growing competition, must deal with evolving policy issues. As with the Olympic Games, use of performance-enhancing substances by athletes is a major concern. The question of inclusion of athletes with disabilities into able-bodied sport will continue to be an ongoing debate. As the Games grow, pressure will increase to maximize corporate sponsorship opportunities. It is an exciting time for the Paralympic Games, given their future growth potential.

Sport for People with Disabilities
CASE STUDY

You are working with USA Hockey, the NGB for ice hockey in the United States. Recently, the USOC has asked you to examine the status of the inclusion of the Paralympic men's ice sledge hockey team into USA Hockey. At the 2002 Salt Lake City Paralympic Games, the U. S. men's team brought home the Gold Medal, capping a four-year rebuilding process for the team, which had finished in last place in the Winter Games in Nagano, Japan, in 1998. Playing before sold-out audiences in the E Center in Salt Lake City, the team's performance was far and away the biggest story to come out of the 2002 Salt Lake City Paralympic Games.

The ultimate goal after making the assessment is to integrate the activities of the Paralympic sledge hockey team within USA Hockey, the NSF for hockey in the United States. What types of events or activities of the Paralympic sledge hockey team could USA Hockey sponsor? What types of publicity could it provide? In other words, what are some concrete strategies USA Hockey could use to help sledge hockey grow and prosper? How should you go about starting your task?

1. The best place to start is to use the nine-component model designed by Wolff (2000) and presented in this chapter (see pp. 297–298). Using each component, show how USA Hockey could incorporate the ice sledge hockey team into its organization.

2. Think of other sports organizations that could assist you in your tasks, such as the NHL, Hockey Canada, or any other sport organization that could potentially be working with hockey players with disabilities.

3. Some people would argue that athletes with disabilities should retain a separate identity from able-bodied sport and compete only with other athletes with disabilities. Do you agree or disagree, and why? What benefits do disability sport, and athletes with disabilities, offer to able-bodied sport organizations?

CHAPTER QUESTIONS

1. The IPC is considering expanding the Summer and Winter Games by one sport each. Which sports would you choose to add, and why?

2. The U. S. Paralympic men's soccer team is playing a series of exhibition matches against the Brazilian Paralympic men's soccer team. Your college or university has been awarded one of the matches. Develop a series of marketing strategies to promote the event. What community groups and sponsors will you want to involve?

3. What are some specific strategies the IPC could use to attempt to increase sport participation by athletes with disabilities who live in developing nations?

REFERENCES

Cody, A. (2002). Women in the Paralympic Movement. *ICSSPE Bulletin.*

Cody, A. (2007). Sport for people with disabilities. In M. A. Hums, G. G. Bower, and H. Grappendorf (Eds.), *Women as leaders in sport: Impact and influence* (pp. 261–268). Reston, VA: National Association for Girls and Women in Sport.

DePauw, K., & Gavron, S. (2005). *Disability and sport* (2d ed.). Champaign, IL: Human Kinetics.

Grevemberg, D., Wolff, E. A., & Hums, M. A. (2001, May). Integration of Paralympic sport in international sport federations: Comparative international models. Paper presented at the Annual Conference of the North American Society for Sport Management, Virginia Beach, VA.

Hums, M. A. (2002, March 11–17). Another bid for gold, but TV fades to black. *Street & Smith's SportsBusiness Journal, 4,* 40–41.

Hums, M. A. (2006, July). Ethical issues facing the Paralympic Movement. Paper presented at the International Olympic Academy Educator's Session, Olympia, Greece.

Hums, M. A. (2007). Ethical issues of changing classification systems. *Proceedings of the II Conferencia Internacional sobre Deporte Adaptado,* Malaga, Spain.

Hums, M. A., Legg, D., & Wolff, E. A. (2003, June). Examining opportunities for athletes with disabilities within the International Olympic Committee. Paper presented at the Annual Conference of the North American Society for Sport Management, Ithaca, NY.

IPC. (2001). Women and Sport—Progress report. *The Paralympics Online Newsletter.* Retrieved September 20, 2003, from www.paralympic.org.

IPC. (2003). Handbook: Chapter 1.1 Vision and mission. Retrieved October 7, 2007, from www.paralympic.org/release/Main_Sections_Menu/ IPC/IPC_Handbook/Section_1/Sec_i_chapter_ 1.1_Paralympic_Vision_and_Mission.pdf.

IPC. (2004). Handbook: Constitution. Retrieved October 7, 2007, from www.paralympic.org/release/ Main_Sections_Menu/IPC/IPC_Handbook/Section _1/IPC_Constitution.pdf.

IPC. (2005, April 20). Beijing Paralympic programme. Bonn, Germany: Author.

IPC. (2007a). About the IPC. Retrieved October 7, 2007, from www.paralympic.org/release/Main_Sections_Menu/IPC/About_the_IPC.

IPC. (2007b). Anti-Doping. Retrieved October 9, 2007, from www.paralympic.org/release/Main_Sections_Menu/Anti_Doping.

IPC. (2007c). General assembly. Retrieved October 8, 2007, from www.paralympic.org/release/Main_Sections_Menu/IPC/Organization/General_Assembly.

IPC. (2007d). Governing board. Retrieved October 8, 2007, from www.paralympic.org/release/Main_Sections_Menu/IPC/Organization/Governing_Board.

IPC. (2007e). Management team. Retrieved October 6, 2007, from www.paralympic.org/release/Main_Sections_Menu/IPC/Organization/IPC_Head quarters/index.html.

IPC. (2007f). National Paralympic Committees (NPCs). Retrieved October 8, 2007, from www.paralympic.org/release/Main_Sections_Menu/IPC/Organization/General_Assembly/NPCs/index.html.

IPC. (2007g). Summer Games overview. Retrieved October 8, 2007, from www.paralympic.org/release/Main_Sections_Menu/Paralympic_Games/Past_Games/Summer_Games_Overview.html.

USOC. (2005). Mission statement. Retrieved October 8, 2007, from www.usolympicteam.com/para lympics/about_33722.htm.

Wolff, E. A. (2000). Inclusion and integration of soccer opportunities for players with disabilities within the United States Soccer Federation: Strategies and recommendations. Senior Honors Thesis. Brown University.

12

NORTH AMERICAN PROFESSIONAL SPORT

Many people dream of hitting a home run in the bottom of the ninth inning to win the World Series, making the game-winning shot at the buzzer in the NBA Finals, throwing a touchdown pass to a wide-open receiver in the Super Bowl, or scoring the game-winning goal in the final game of the Stanley Cup. In North America we have grown up watching these exciting moments live on TV or seeing the highlights on ESPN or TSN. All these spectacular plays belong to the most visible of all our sport industry segments—professional sport. Yet most of us have warning track power at best, shoot the occasional air ball, are unable to throw a true spiral, and cannot even skate backward. The odds against making it as a professional athlete in the Big Four—MLB, the NBA, the NFL, and the NHL—are astronomical, but these athletes' games would not happen and their exploits would remain relatively unknown if not for the sport managers, "The People Who Make the Games Happen" (Robinson, Hums, Crow, & Phillips, 2001). Without these people, the games and the athletes would not be nearly as popular. No season tickets would be for sale, no sponsorships available, no games broadcast on TV, no T-shirts with our favorite team's logo, and no new high-tech stadiums and arenas to visit.

Professional sport in North America takes many forms. We think first of the Big Four. Professional sport also takes place in other forms: tours or organized series, such as we see in professional golf with the PGA, LPGA, and the Champion's Tour; or in motor sports with the Nextel Cup Series and the Craftsman Truck Series, both from the National Association of Stock Car Auto Racing (NASCAR). Other professional leagues exist as well, including the WNBA, and MLS, and we should not overlook the current popularity of MMA—Mixed Martial Arts! There are also minor league sports, particularly baseball, hockey, and basketball. Other sports also have professional competition, such as the Professional Bull Riders Association (PBRA), Professional Bowlers Association (PBA), and Bass Anglers Sportsman Society (B.A.S.S.) Masters Fishing. (Now some of you will want to ask about professional wrestling, like World Wrestling Entertainment [WWE]—well, let's save that topic for another day and another class.)

How are these professional sports organized? Who are the people delivering the product to the public? Who are the power players and groups governing these sports? This chapter focuses on the governance structures of professional sport in North America. The main focus of the chapter is on the traditional Big Four. The following chapter will explain the governance structures of professional sport in other nations.

History and Development of Professional Sport

The history of the development of professional sport in North America is beyond the scope of this particular book. However, it is important to note key dates for certain events in the histories of each of the Big Four, for example, when the leagues took the form they have today. It is also important to note governance issues, for example, when rival leagues formed to compete with existing leagues.

Major League Baseball (MLB)

MLB has the longest history of any professional sport in North America. The first professional club, the Cincinnati Red Stockings, was founded in

1869. The first professional sports league was baseball's National League, established in 1876, followed by the American League in 1901. The signing of the National Agreement between the National League and the American League established much of the basic governance structure for MLB (Scully, 1989). Early on, the players formed a number of rival leagues such as the Players' League and the Federal League. Players objected to management's strict rules, such as the reserve system that "reserved" a player to his club and prohibited other clubs from negotiating with him, thus controlling players' salaries. While these leagues presented brief challenges to professional baseball's structure, all eventually failed (Abrams, 1998). MLB has not had a serious competitor since 1914–1915 (Wise & Meyer, 1997). As you will discover, this long-standing unchallenged status is quite different from the history of the other Big Four leagues.

Currently, MLB has 30 teams. The American League has 14 (5 in the East, 5 in the Central, and 4 in the West Divisions). The National League has 16 (5 in the East, 6 in the Central, and 5 in the West Divisions).

National Football League (NFL)

The first professional football league, the American Professional Football Association, was established in 1920. It changed its name to the National Football League in 1922 (NFL Enterprises, 2007). The NFL has experienced a long history of rival leagues, dating all the way back to its first inter-league battle in 1926 with the American Football League (AFL) (Quirk & Fort, 1992). Different forms of the AFL would emerge and challenge the NFL, and finally in 1966 the leagues signed an agreement establishing an inter-league championship, and full amalgamation began in 1970. This event marked the first time that TV income played a critical role in survival of a rival league, since the AFL had an existing TV contract that by 1969 would give each team approximately $900,000 (Quirk & Fort, 1992). Since then, the NFL was challenged by the World Football League (WFL) in 1974–1975, the United States Football League (USFL) in 1983–1985, and very recently the Xtreme Football League (XFL) in 2001.

Currently the NFL has 32 teams with two conferences, the American Football Conference (AFC) and the National Football Conference (NFC). The AFC North, AFC South, AFC East, and AFC West each have 4 teams, as do the NFC North, NFC South, NFC East, and NFC West.

National Basketball Association (NBA)

The very first professional basketball league was established in 1924 as the American Basketball League. It eventually went out of business in 1947, and another league emerged, the Basketball Association of America

www

Major League Baseball
www.mlb.com

www

National Football League
www.nfl.com

National Basketball Association
www.nba.com

(BAA) (Quirk & Fort, 1992). At the same time a league called the National Basketball League (NBL) was also in existence. By 1949 the BAA absorbed the remaining NBL teams, and the organization renamed itself the National Basketball Association (NBA Media Ventures, 2007). In 1967, a rival league named the American Basketball Association formed, one which had sufficient financial backing and talent to pose a threat to the NBA. In 1976, an agreement was reached between the two leagues in that four franchises from the ABA—Denver, Indiana, New York, and San Antonio—moved to the NBA (Quirk & Fort, 1992). No rival leagues have attempted to compete with the NBA since then.

Currently the NBA has 30 teams in two conferences. The Eastern Conference has 5 teams in the Atlantic Division, 5 teams in the Central Division, and 5 teams in the Southeast Division. The Western Conference has 5 teams in the Northwest Division, 5 teams in the Pacific Division, and 5 teams in the Southwest Division.

National Hockey League (NHL)

National Hockey League
www.nhl.com

The NHL started in 1917 with four teams located in Canada—Toronto, Ottawa, and two teams in Montreal. The league expanded to the United States in 1924 (Quirk & Fort, 1992). The NHL faced its biggest challenge from rival leagues from the World Hockey Association (WHA), a league that began in 1972. The WHA attempted to establish itself in medium-size Canadian markets without NHL franchises as well as in major United States cities in direct competition with existing NHL teams. After a seven-year war with the NHL, four remaining franchises—Winnipeg, Quebec, Edmonton, and Hartford—moved to the NHL in 1979 (Quirk & Fort, 1992).

Currently the NHL has 30 teams in two conferences. The Eastern Conference has 5 teams each in the Northeast, Southeast, and Atlantic Divisions. The Western Conference has 5 teams each in the Central, Northwest, and Pacific Divisions.

Governance

Each professional sport league has various levels of governance structures. The governance structures exist at the league level and the front-office level. The league level includes the league offices and the Office of the Commissioner, which constitute the governance structures on the management side of professional sport. The players' side is governed by Players Associations. Although the governance structures of the various leagues are not identical, they share common governance components. According to Sutton and Gladden (2007, p. 102), these components are the following:

1. a league Commissioner
2. a Board of Governors or a committee composed of team owners
3. a central administrative unit that negotiates contracts and agreements on behalf of the league

In addition to these components, governance issues are also dealt with at the individual team level. We will briefly examine each of these components.

Commissioner's Office

Major professional sports leagues are led by a Commissioner. The first Commissioner in professional sport was Kennesaw Mountain Landis, who became Major League Baseball Commissioner in 1921 (Abrams, 1998). As Commissioner, he ruled with an iron fist, basing his decisions on his interpretation of what was in the game's best interest. Although the original concept of a Commissioner's role was modeled on Landis, commissioners in different sports did not follow his lead completely (Masteralexis, 2008).

The Office of the Commissioner is typically created and defined within a league's constitution and bylaws. According to Wise and Meyer (1997, p. 150), the Commissioner's

> jurisdiction, authority, and duties are principally derived from the league constitution and/or by-laws adopted by the league members, or a special contract among them, although some powers flow from and/or are limited by collective bargaining agreements. . . . Under these documents they are granted a broad and often extensive array of powers over players, management, teams, owners, and others connected with their league or organization.

The Commissioner is in some ways an employee of the owners, as the owners have the power to hire and terminate the Commissioner. However, in other ways the Commissioner is the owners' boss, having disciplinary power over the owners (Wong, 2002).

The role of the Commissioner in professional sport has evolved over time, but some of the basic powers of the office have remained throughout the years in different sports. In general, the discretionary powers of the Commissioner include (Yasser, McGurdy, Goplerud, & Weston, 2000, p. 411):

- approval of player contracts
- resolution of disputes between players and clubs
- resolution of disputes between clubs
- resolution of disputes between players or clubs and the league
- disciplinary matters involving players, clubs, front-office personnel, owners, etc.
- rule-making authority

Wise and Meyer (1997, p. 150) further explain these powers by stating, "In addition to specific authority in particular situations, the constitution, by-laws or some other agreement generally contain a 'best interest in the league and/or sport' clause, the wording varying by sport, under which the Commissioner . . . has wide authority to act."

The Professional Baseball Agreement (MLB, n.d., p. 1) contains the following language:

> (B) Conduct Not in the Best Interest of Baseball. The Commissioner shall have jurisdiction:

> (1) To investigate, either upon complaint or upon the Commissioner's own initiative, any act, transaction, or practice charged, alleged, or suspected not to be in the best interests of the national game of Baseball, and with authority to summon persons and to order the production of documents, and in the case of refusal to appear or produce, to impose and enforce penalties as are hereinafter provided . . .

> (C) Penalties. Punitive action that the Commissioner may take against any offender for conduct not to be in the best interest of Baseball shall include any one or more of the following: a public reprimand, a fine not exceeding one hundred thousand dollars ($100,000) for any one offense, suspension, removal from office, or a declaration of temporary or permanent ineligibility.

Commissioners' actions often go unnoticed by the public, as they are handled internal to the league. However, some notable exceptions include MLB Commissioner Bart Giamatti's banning Pete Rose from baseball for life for gambling, NFL Commissioner Roger Goodell's suspension of Michael Vick for involvement with dog-fighting, and NBA Commissioner David Stern's imposition of a severe penalty on Latrell Sprewell for choking his coach, P. J. Carlissimo. The Commissioner's Office exercises it regulatory power in professional sports leagues through decisions concerning fines, suspensions, and disciplinary actions. Some regulatory power also rests on the league level and with the Players Associations.

Board of Governors or Owners Committee

Despite a wide range of powers, the Commissioner is not necessarily the final decision maker in issues involving governance of professional sport leagues. Although the Commissioner is very influential, the owners still have the ultimate say in policy development (Robinson, Lizandra, & Vail, 2001). We read about the annual league owners' meetings, where policies, rules, and business decisions concerning league operations are addressed. Each league has a committee structure made up of owners who ultimately make decisions on matters concerning franchise relocation, league expansion or contraction, playing facility issues, collective bargaining rules and rule changes, and revenue sharing (Sharp, Moorman, & Claussen, 2007). This committee also represents management in labor negotiations with players (Robinson et al., 2001b). At this level policy making often takes place, within the frameworks of each league's constitution and bylaws. In professional sport this level is where the power lies on the management side. As we will see shortly, the players' side has a governance structure as well. Although policy making occurs at this level, daily league operations occur at another league-wide governance level. Each league has a league office employing paid sport managers to handle these tasks.

Central Administrative Unit—League Office

As mentioned earlier, this governance level deals with league-wide issues. A unique aspect of professional sport, as opposed to other businesses, is that the teams must simultaneously compete and cooperate (Mullin, Hardy, & Sutton, 2007). League offices schedule games, hire and train officials, discipline players, market and license logoed merchandise, and negotiate broadcast contracts (Sharp et al., 2007). League offices are usually organized by function, with a range of different departments. For example, in addition to the Commissioner and President or CEO, the MLB League Office includes the following departments: Baseball Operations, Security and Facilities, Public Relations, Licensing, Publishing and Photographs, Special Events, Broadcasting, Corporate Sales, Advertising, Community Affairs and Educational Programming, General Administration, International, MLB Western Operations, and Umpires (Baseball America, 2007). The NBA League Office includes the following departments: Commissioner's Office, Administration, Basketball Operations, Broadcast Operations, Communications Group, Community and Player Programs, Creative Services, Events and Attractions, Facility Operations, Finance, Global Merchandising, Human Resource Information System and Benefits, Human Resources, Information Technology, Interactive Services, International, International Television, Legal, Marketing, Marketing and Media, NBA Development League, NBA Store, NBA TV, Security, Team Marketing and Operations, and WNBA (NBA Media Ventures, 2005).

Individual Team Level

The day-to-day operations of a professional sports franchise take place on the individual team level. The two major groups—the owners and the front-office staff—that are responsible for daily operations are discussed in the following sections.

Owners

Who are the people who own major professional sport franchises? According to Schaaf (2003, p. 348), "The best future owner is a lot like the old owner: very wealthy, egotistical, and interested in building a winner." Gone are the days when teams were owned by relatively ordinary people who made their living from operating a ballclub (Quirk & Fort, 1999). Today's owners are multibillionaires, many of whom are members of the Forbes 400 richest individuals in the nation. Some of the more recognizable team owners are Microsoft's Paul Allen (Portland Trailblazers), Black Entertainment Television's Robert L. Johnson (Charlotte Bobcats), not to mention the New York Yankees' George Steinbrenner and the Dallas Mavericks' Mark Cuban. What motivates a person with so much money to purchase a professional sports franchise? Several reasons exist, including the excitement of being involved in professional sport and certainly the publicity and spotlight that accompany owning a team, especially a winning team. But do not be fooled—these individuals did not get to be wealthy without a sharp eye on the bottom line. According to Quirk and Fort (1999, p. 97), "As important as winning is to them, it might well be a matter of ego and personal pride that they manage to do this while pocketing a good profit at the same time." Owners also know that in the long run, very few franchises have ever been sold for less than their purchase price, basically ensuring future long-term capital gains.

While some owners, such as George Steinbrenner, want to be closely involved with the daily operations of their franchises, for the most part the owners leave those daily chores to the people who work in the front offices. The owners' place in the policy-making process lies mainly on the league level, as discussed earlier. Some owners may impose policies on their front-office staff, but that is not necessarily the norm.

Front-Office Staff

The front office is the place where the day-to-day operational and business decisions are made for the individual professional sports franchise. Similar to league offices, the front office staff is usually departmentalized by function. In Major League Baseball, a typical front office is divided into two main areas: Business Operations and Baseball Operations. For example, on the Business Operations side the front-office staff of the Atlanta Braves includes an Executive VP, Business Operations; Senior VP, Sales and Marketing; VP and Team Counsel; Finance; Marketing and Sales; Public Relations and Communications; Stadium Operations; Ticketing; and Travel and Clubhouse. The Baseball Operations side includes the Major League Staff (manager and coaches), Medical and Training, Player Development, and Scouting (Baseball America, 2007).

A typical NBA front office has departments such as Basketball Operations, Sports Media Relations, Marketing, Operations, Finance, Corporate Partnerships, Ticket Operations and Services, Human Resources, Player Personnel, and General Counsel (Miami Heat, 2007). As you can see, front-office staffs across the Big Four are similar in composition.

The entities and governance levels described so far in this chapter all deal with the management side of professional sport. However, governance structures also exist on the players' side of professional sport. These organizations, the players' unions, are commonly referred to as *Players Associations*.

Players Associations

Each of the Big Four professional leagues has what is known as a Players Association. These Players Associations, or PAs as they are sometimes called, are the players' unions. Professional baseball has the longest history of labor organization of all the professional sports. A player named John Montgomery Ward led the earliest unionization efforts. Ward founded the first players' union in 1885 and the Players League of 1890 (Abrams, 1998). Baseball players saw themselves as skilled tradespeople, just as those workers who filled the factories of that era. Professional baseball witnessed several failed attempts at unionization until the Major League Baseball Players Association (MLBPA) was established with former United Steelworkers employee Marvin Miller as its first Executive Director. Miller negotiated the players' first collective bargaining agreement in 1968 (MLBPA, 2005b). The National Hockey League Players Association (NHLPA) began in 1967 when player representatives from the original six clubs met, adopted a constitution, and elected a president (NHLPA, 2007). For the NBA, in 1954 NBA All Star Bob Cousy began organizing the players, ultimately forming the National Basketball Players Association (NBPA) (NBPA, n.d.d). The NFL players' efforts were first organized in 1956, when a group of NFL players authorized a man named Creighton Miller and the newly formed National Football League Players Association (NFLPA) to represent them (NFLPA, 2002c).

Mission statements. Each PA has its own mission statement. The mission statement of the NBPA is presented in Figure 12.1. This mission statement clarifies that the number-one priority of any PA is its members—the players—and protecting their rights.

PAs share the common goals of representing players in matters related to wages, hours, working conditions, and protecting players' rights. They help players with any type of dispute or problem they may have with management. They also deal with insurance benefits, retirement, and charitable opportunities, similar to nonsport labor unions. The NFLPA, for

www

Major League Baseball Players Association
www.mlbplayers.com

National Hockey League Players Association
www.nhlpa.com

National Basketball Players Association
www.nbpa.com

National Football League Players Association
www.nflpa.org

| FIGURE | 12.1 | Mission statement of the NBPA. |

> To ensure that the rights of NBA players are protected, and that everything possible is being done to help players maximize their opportunities and achieve their goals on and off the court.

Source: NBPA. (n.d.a).

example, is a member of the American Federation of Labor-Congress of Industrial Organizations (AFL-CIO), a major nonsport union representing workers from a variety of industries.

Financials. PAs rely on two primary sources of revenues. The first is individual membership dues. For example, in the MLBPA in 2005, the players' dues were set at $45 per day during the season (MLBPA, 2005b). The second revenue source is each association's licensing division. For example, National Football League Players Incorporated, which is known as PLAYERS INC, is the for-profit licensing, marketing, sponsorship, and content development subsidiary of the NFL Players Association (PLAYERS INC, 2007). Created in 1994, its mission is "taking the helmets off" the players and marketing them as personalities as well as professional athletes.

PLAYERS INC
www.nflplayers.com/
about_us/main.aspx

Membership. The membership of any PA may include more than just active players. MLBPA membership includes all players, managers, coaches, and trainers holding a signed contract with MLB (MLBPA, 2005a).

Organizational structure. PAs share relatively common governance structures, with Player Representatives, an Executive Board, and an Executive Committee. However, ultimate power rests with the players themselves. Every year each team elects, by secret ballot, a Player Representative (called a "Player Rep") and an Alternate Player Representative to serve on a Board of Player Representatives (for the NFL) or on an Executive Board (for MLB and the NHL). Player Reps generally serve one-year terms and act as liaisons between the union and the team members. According to the NFLPA, the Player Reps serve the following roles (NFLPA, 2007b , p. 9)

- assist in the implementation of the Collective Bargaining Agreement;
- exercise direct responsibility for new memberships and for the execution of check-off authorizations by members and nonmembers;

- receive and provide information concerning the processing of grievances;
- cooperate with the officers and staff of the NFLPA in the promotion and operation of the NFLPA programs;
- attend, unless physically incapacitated, all meetings of the Board of Representatives, and all NFLPA conventions;
- appoint and coordinate the operation of the Team Council which will assist him in performing his duties;
- advance the policies and interests of the NFLPA;
- perform such duties as may be from time to time directed by the Board; and
- facilitate communication between members and the NFLPA.

The Player Reps come together to form the governance structure on the Board level. In the NFL the Board of Player Reps is responsible for the following tasks (NFLPA, 2002b, 2007b, p. 15):

- enactment of policies governing the affairs of the NFLPA;
- provision for the location and maintenance of a principal and any regional offices;
- election of an Executive Director who shall be an ex officio member of all committees;
- appointment of the representatives of the NFLPA to boards, commissions and other organizations;
- the general conduct of collective bargaining and the ratification of the Collective Bargaining Agreement;
- the establishment and specification of the duties of standing and temporary committees;
- approval of the annual budget of the NFLPA;
- establishment of the annual membership dues;
- establishment of trusts for disabled, needy or deceased players or former players; and
- adoption and administration of a system of regulation of player agents.

These Boards of Player Reps select the members of an Executive Committee. For the NBPA the Executive Committee consists of nine players, and for the NHLPA the Executive Committee consists of seven players, one of whom holds the title of President. PAs also employ full-time sport managers to staff their offices. The staff members of the MLBPA have titles such as Executive Director, Chief Operating Officer, General Counsel, Manager of Financial Operations, Contract Administrator, Director, Business Affairs and Licensing, Category Director of Interactive Games,

Category Director of Apparel and Novelties, Category Director of Trading Cards and collectibles (Baseball America, 2007). The NBPA is divided into departments including the Executive Director's Office, Agent Regulations and Security, Communications, Finance, Legal, Special Events and Sponsorships, Player Programs, Career Development, and WNBPA Operations (NBPA, n.d.c) Currently, the offices for the MLBPA, NBPA, and NFLPA are located in New York City, while the offices for the NHLPA are housed in Toronto.

Current Policy Areas

As with any sport industry segment, professional sport has a myriad of policy areas to discuss. Among these are labor issues (particularly salary caps), drug use, criminal activity by players, gambling, and increased hiring of racial and ethnic minorities into management positions.

Labor Issues

As long as labor and management continue to coexist in professional sport, labor issues will remain. Players have a deep-seated distrust of management, dating back to the days when management first established the reserve system in professional baseball and kept the system secret among themselves (Abrams, 2000). Strikes and lockouts are common disruptions to sports fans. Who can ever forget the 1994 MLB strike when then-Acting Commissioner Bud Selig went so far as to cancel the World Series? Players and owners are in constant struggles over revenue sharing, salary caps, salaries, pensions, and benefits.

www.W

NBPA Collective Bargaining Agreement
www.nbpa.com/cba.php

NFLPA Collective Bargaining Agreement
www.nflpa.org/CBA/
CBA_Complete.aspx

One particular policy issue affecting all of the Big Four is the salary cap. According to the NBPA Collective Bargaining Agreement (NBPA, n.d.b), a *salary cap* is defined as "the maximum allowable Team Salary for each Team for a Salary Cap year, subject to the rules and exceptions set forth in this Agreement." A salary cap or luxury tax is established as part of the collective bargaining process and undergoes many iterations through the process (Zimbalist, 2003). In the NFLPA Collective Bargaining Agreement (NFLPA, 1998), a *salary cap* is defined as "the absolute maximum amount of Salary that each Club may pay or be obligated to pay or provide to Players or Player Affiliates, or may pay or be obligated to pay to third parties at the request of and for the benefit of Players or Player Affiliates, at any time during a particular League Year, in accordance with the rules set forth." In other words, a salary cap sets a limit on the amount a team can designate for its total team payroll.

For example, the NFL salary cap has grown from $34.6 million in its initial year of 1994 to $52.4 million in 1998, to $71.1 million in 2002, to

$102.5 million in 2006 (Duberstein, 2002b; Weisman, 2006). Although teams may slightly exceed the cap, it is still considered a "hard cap." For example, in 2000 the salary cap limit was $62.2 million, but average club salary expenditures were $68.3 million (Duberstein, 2002a); in 2006 the cap was $85.5 million, but the average team was approximately $1.3 million over that (Horrow, 2006). The NBA cap was set at $53.135 million for the 2006–2007 season, an increase of $3.6 million from the previous year (Ford, 2006). The NBA salary cap has specified built-in exceptions, including exceptions for veteran free agents, disabled players, rookies, and assigned players (NBPA, n.d.). This acts as a "soft cap."

After the latest round of talks between labor and management, the NHL now has a salary cap. The cap was set for $44 million in the 2006–2007 season (Burnside, 2006). MLB does not have a salary cap, but instead imposes a luxury tax on owners whose payroll exceeds a certain amount. In the latest collective bargaining agreement, the luxury tax levels were set as follows: "Thresholds for luxury tax on team payrolls set at $148 million for 2007, $155 million for 2008, $162 million in 2009, $170 million in 2010 and $178 million in 2011. Tax rates on amount over threshold remain at 22.5 percent for first time over threshold, 30 percent for second time over threshold, 40 percent for third or subsequent time over threshold" (Associated Press, 2006). A luxury tax, while not a hard cap, can act as a disincentive to clubs to spend on player salaries (Erdes, 2002).

With spending reaching astronomical proportions in professional sport, discussions of salaries and salary caps will continue. Owners favor the caps, and players vehemently oppose them, as they serve as a method to limit player salaries. Salary caps are not as simple as they may appear; many interpretations and options are available. For example, the section in the NBPA Collective Bargaining Agreement related to the salary cap is 83 pages long. This topic will continue to be an ongoing battlefield.

Because of the monetary amounts involved in this industry, sometimes it is difficult to see issues of fairness. When fans see billionaire owners battling millionaire athletes, it can be difficult to realize that labor-management disputes still come down to issues of fairness in the workplace. Just because the workplace is a professional sports arena, fundamental rights in the workplace cannot be ignored.

Drug Policies

Reports of professional athletes using performance-enhancing substances, including illegal drugs, are everyday occurrences. To help ensure that athletic competitions are as fair as possible, sport organizations have constructed drug policies. Each of the Big Four has developed extensive drug policies. The policies enacted at this level are notably different from the ones at, say, the high school level. In professional sport, everyone is an adult. Also, one could argue these professional athletes are role models to others, especially children and young athletes.

Major League Baseball was set solidly at the forefront of this debate when its current and former stars took the stand in congressional hearings about use of steroids. Player icons such as Mark Maguire, Sammy Sosa, Rafael Palmiero, Curt Schilling, and Jose Canseco, as well as MLB executives, faced public scrutiny in these televised hearings. Neither the players, nor the league, emerged from the hearings unscathed. Major League Baseball again became the focus in 2007 with the release of the Mitchell Report, an 18-month, independent investigation headed by Senator George Mitchell into use of performance-enhancing substances in Major League Baseball. The 409-page report included 86 names, ranging from utility players to superstars, and painted a picture of a game stained by what is sure to be known as "the steroid era" (ESPN, 2007). To further improve the joint drug prevention and treatment program, the report recommended that the program should

Mitchell Report
http://mlb.mlb.com/mlb/
news/mitchell/index.jsp

1. be independent
2. be transparent
3. perform adequate year-round unannounced drug testing
4. be flexible enough to employ best practices as they develop
5. continue to respect the legitimate rights of players
6. have adequate funding (Mitchell, 2007)

When developing these policies, professional sport organizations must be mindful of numerous legal considerations. Because professional athletes are employees and specifically are members of unions (PAs), leagues must be aware of the fact that drug testing is a condition of employment, and therefore any alterations to a drug-testing policy is a mandatory subject of bargaining between the players and the league (Wong, 2002). The NFLPA Collective Bargaining Agreement section titled Substance Abuse contains the following statement (NFLPA, 1998):

> The parties agree that substance abuse and the use of anabolic steroids are unacceptable within the NFL and that it is the responsibilities of the parties to deter and detect substance abuse and steroid use and to offer programs of intervention, rehabilitation, and support to the players who have substance abuse problems.

Some main points of difference among the four leagues' testing policies are as follows: NHL players can be tested only with probable cause. In the NBA, all players are tested when training camp begins. Rookies are tested on a random basis four times during the season. All other players can be tested during the season if an arbitrator decides there is reasonable cause (Drug Test Provision in New Baseball Contract Seen as Wanting, 2002).

The NFL tests all players at the start of training camp for drugs like marijuana and cocaine. Players undergo random testing for steroids during the season and the off-season. The NFL Drug Policy states (NFLPA, 2002b):

> The illegal use of drugs and the abuse of prescription drugs, over the counter drugs, and alcohol (hereinafter referred to as "substances of abuse") is prohibited for players in the National Football League (NFL). . . . Substance abuse can lead to on-the-field injuries, to alienation of the fans, to diminished performance, and to personal hardship. The deaths of several NFL players have demonstrated the potentially tragic consequences of substance abuse. NFL players should not by their conduct suggest that substance abuse is either acceptable or safe. . . . The primary purpose of this policy is to assist players who misuse substances of abuse, but players who do not comply with the requirements of this Policy will be subject to discipline. An important principle of this Policy is that a player will be held responsible for whatever goes into his body. (NFLPA, 2007a, p. 1)

Professional sport leagues' drug policies typically contain information about the administration of the program, testing procedures, discipline, and lists of prohibited substances. The NFL Drug Policy also includes the following sections (NFLPA, 2007a):

- administration
- confidentiality
- testing for substances of abuse
- entrance into the intervention stages
- intervention stages
- notice
- discipline for violations of law related to substances of abuse other than alcohol
- discipline for alcohol-related violations of the law or abuse of alcohol
- imposition of fines and penalties
- appeal rights

For comparison, the NBA Anti-Drug Program, as contained in the NBPA Collective Bargaining Agreement, consists of the following sections (NBPA, n.d.):

- definitions
- administration
- confidentiality
- testing
- reasonable cause testing or hearing

- drugs of abuse program
- marijuana program
- use or possession of steroids
- noncompliance with treatment
- dismissal and disqualification
- reinstatement
- exclusivity of the program
- additional bases for testing additional prohibited substances

In 2005, MLB instituted a new drug-testing policy. The increased number of home runs coupled with allegations of rampant steroid use by players prompted this policy. The policy includes the following:

> The first positive test will result in a suspension of up to ten days. The second positive test will result in a suspension of thirty days. The third positive test will result in a suspension of sixty days. The fourth positive test will result in a suspension of one full year. Finally, the fifth positive test will result in a penalty at the discretion of the Commissioner of Major League Baseball. Players will be tested at least once per year, with a chance that several players can be tested numerous times per year. (Baseball Almanac, 2007, ¶3).

In the 2005 season, 12 MLB players were suspended for violating the policy, 3 players were suspended in 2006, and 2 in 2007 (Baseball Almanac, 2007). These suspensions were all related to steroid use. Questions still remain as to whether MLB has done enough to rid itself of the shadow cast over it, particularly during the 2007 home-run record chase by Barry Bonds, which was surrounded by controversy and allegations about Bonds' use of steroids. Certainly other sport organizations use much stricter codes, such as the Anti-Doping Code of the World Anti-Doping Agency. The use of performance enhancers can create an uneven playing field. Use of banned performance enhancers taints the essence of sport and fair play for fans and athletes alike.

Criminal Activity by Players

Unfortunately, professional athletes' names are linked to run-ins with the law almost daily. The stories of current and former NFL players Michael Vick, Pacman Jones, Jamal Lewis, and Rae Carruth and former NBA player Jayson Williams are all too familiar to sports fans in North America. Benedict and Yaeger (1998) reported the number of incidents in which NFL players were involved with assaults, domestic violence, and other off-the-field incidents, citing statistics that approximately 21 percent of NFL players have been charged with a serious crime. Dealing with off-the-field incidents is difficult from the league perspective. First, the incidents are widely covered in the media. Second, taking punitive action may give the appearance of guilt even if the legal system has not yet passed judgment on an accused athlete. Third, if a team or league controls information about an incident, it is often accused of covering up information. Finally, the issue of how the PA will react to punishing players for off-the-field incidents remains. In 1997, the NFL introduced a new violent-crime policy to deter criminal behavior by its players (Wong, 2002). The Conduct Policy for NFL Players includes this statement (NFLPA, 2002b):

> Engaging in violent and/or criminal activity is unacceptable and constitutes conduct detrimental to the integrity of and public confidence in the National Football League. Such conduct alienates the fans on whom the success of the League depends and has negative and sometimes tragic consequences for both the victim and the perpetrator. The League is committed to promoting and encouraging lawful conduct and to providing a safe and professional workplace for its employees.

The policy further defines *prohibited conduct* as including, but not limited to, violent or criminal activity such as crimes involving use or threat of physical violence, use of a deadly weapon in committing a crime, domestic violence, and sex offenses, as well as involvement in hate crimes. Players charged with criminal activity must undergo immediate clinical evaluation and counseling, if necessary. Players convicted of criminal activity are subject to discipline as determined by the Commissioner, including possible fines and suspensions (NFLPA, 2002b). Players always have the right to appeal any sanctions.

In 2007, Roger Goodell faced serious issues in his early time as NFL Commissioner. He responded quickly and forcefully when dealing with both Michael Vick and Pacman Jones, whose brushes with the law placed the NFL in a poor light for the public. The message was clear—the good name and brand value of the NFL are essential for league success—and players acting inappropriately will be punished.

Responding to allegations of player misconduct is a delicate area for sport managers, and one where the SLEEPE Principle is very important in deciding on a course of action, because the decisions have social, legal, ethical, economic, and political ramifications. Athletes are role models, and criminal activities, like issues involving drugs, are not positive reflections on the players or the leagues. Thus codes of conduct are necessary.

Gambling

"What's the line on tonight's game?" How often have you heard this question on the day of an important game? The amount of money wagered on professional sport events is astronomical. *Street & Smith's SportsBusiness*

Conduct Policy for NFL Players
www.nflpa.org/RulesAnd Regs/ConductPolicy.aspx

Journal (2002) estimated that approximately $18.9 million was wagered on sporting events in 2001. Policies on gambling for the Big Four are relatively straightforward. Leagues do not want the public to question the integrity of the players' performances. Therefore, Uniform Players' Contracts contain specific language about involvement with any gambling-related activities. For example, the Integrity of the Game section from the NFL Player Contract is as follows:

> Player recognizes the detriment to the League and professional football that would result from impairment of public confidence in the honest and orderly conduct of NFL games or the integrity and good character of NFL players. Player therefore acknowledges his awareness that if he accepts a bribe or agrees to throw or fix an NFL game; fails to promptly report a bribe offer or an attempt to throw or fix an NFL game; bets on an NFL game; knowingly associates with gamblers or gambling activity; uses or provides other players with stimulants or other drugs for the purpose of attempting to enhance on-field performance; or is guilty of any form of conduct reasonably judged by the League Commissioner to be detrimental to the League or professional football, the Commissioner will have the right, but only after giving the Player the opportunity for a hearing at which he may be represented by counsel of his choice, to fine Player in a reasonable amount, to suspend Player for a period certain or indefinitely, and/or to terminate this contract.

Other leagues' contracts contain similar language and similar potential punishment for engaging in any activities related to gambling. In this area, policies among the leagues are relatively consistent (NFLPA, 2006, p. 166).

Gambling problems do not only apply to players. The issue with officials came to the forefront in 2007 with the incidents involving NBA referee Tim Donaghy's gambling activities. Donaghy became the target of an FBI investigation for allegedly betting on NBA games, including some of which he had officiated. Commissioner David Stern described the case involving Donaghy's discretions as the worst situation he ever experienced regarding the NBA and its image.

Fans want to think that games contested on the field are fair and that the outcomes are not fixed (Crosset & Hums, 2008). The appearance of activities associated with gambling does not shed a positive light on the games. Athletes need to act in a manner that maintains the integrity of the outcomes of the games played on the field.

Policies on Increasing Diversity in Front Offices

Over the years, the faces of professional athletes have changed. Sports previously played by predominantly white athletes are now diversified, and we see players from different racial and ethnic groups and numerous international players. We have seen these changes on the field, but off the field in positions with power over the governance of professional sport, we have not, unfortunately, seen nearly enough progress.

The Racial and Gender Report Card, published by the Institute for Diversity and Ethics in Sport in the DeVos Sport Business Management Program at the University of Central Florida, serves as a barometer to measure representation of women and racial and ethnic minorities in management positions in sport. The institute assigns "grades" to each sport organization as a way to evaluate how that organization is doing in terms of diversity. For race, because 24 percent of the U. S. population is made up of people of color, organizations with people of color holding 24 percent of managerial positions received an A grade. Organizations received a B if the percentage was 12 percent, a C for 9 percent, D for 6 percent, and an F for 5 percent or less. For gender, an organization received an A if 45 percent of employees were women, a B for 40 percent, a C for 35 percent, a D for 30 percent, and an F for less than 30 percent (Lapchick, 2005). As shown in Table 12.1, front offices do not have much diversity. By looking at the grades given to the organizations, the WNBA leads in the Race and Gender Report Card, followed by the NBA (Lapchick, 2005). Check the website in the margin for updates to the 2005 Racial and Gender Report Card. In April 2008, for example, the institute released an updated report card for Major League Baseball. The league was award an A– for race and a C+ for gender for a combined score of a solid B.

How have professional leagues responded to this issue, and what is being done to attempt to achieve diversity in front-office personnel and others in management positions? MLB Commissioner Bud Selig issued a memo in 1999 ordering teams to consider minority candidates in five positions: General Manager, Assistant General Manager, Field Manager, Directors of

Institute for Diversity and Ethics in Sport
www.bus.ucf.edu/sport/cgi-bin/site/sitew.cgi?page=/ides/index.htx

TABLE 12.1 2005 Racial and Gender Report Card grades.

	Combined Grade	Race Grade	Gender Grade
NBA	B+	A	B–
NFL	N/A	B+	N/A
MLB	C+	B+	D+
MLS	N/A	N/A	N/A
WNBA	A	A	A
College Sport	B	B–	B

Source: Lapchick (2005). Reprinted with permission.

www

Diverse Business Partners Program

http://mlb.mlb.com/mlb/
official_info/dbp/about.jsp

RBI

http://mlb.mlb.com/mlb/
official_info/community/
rbi.jsp

Youth Baseball Academy

http://mlb.mlb.com/mlb/
official_info/community/
urban_youth.jsp

Breaking Barriers Program

http://mlb.mlb.com/mlb/
official_info/community/
bb.jsp

Baseball Tomorrow Fund

http://mlbplayers.mlb.com/
mlb/official_info/community/
btf.jsp

Player Development, and Directors of Scouting. In the memo Selig wrote, "If a club has an opening in any of these positions, the club must notify me personally. In addition, your list of candidates must be provided to me. I expect the list to include minority candidates whom you and your staff have identified. I will provide assistance to you if you cannot identify candidates on your own" (Bodley, 2002, p. 11C). This initiative occurred in 1999, but the numbers still do not reflect increased representation.

MLB, however, does have a number of other diversity initiatives. First is MLB's Diverse Business Partners Program. This program has resulted in millions of dollars being spent with minority- and women-owned businesses who are suppliers for MLB and for the individual teams. MLB also has established a number of urban youth initiatives, including Reviving Baseball in the Inner Cities (RBI); MLB's Youth Baseball Academy; Breaking Barriers in Sports, in Life; and the Baseball Tomorrow Fund (Lapchick, 2006).

The NFL developed a policy addressing the issue of diversity. In the NFL's policy, announced in December 2002, owners agreed to "seriously" interview at least one minority candidate for each coaching vacancy. The policy was developed by a committee appointed in October and headed by Pittsburgh Steelers' owner Dan Rooney, following a report on minority hiring issued by a group headed by attorney Cyrus Mehri (Cochran: NFL Can Do Better, 2003). Time will tell whether these initiatives are taken seriously and result in any significant changes in the makeup of front-office staffs.

Research is also under way examining opportunities for people with disabilities in sport management positions. Race and gender are already being examined, and now researchers at the Disability in Sport Program at Northeastern University's Center for Sport in Society are extending the definition of diversity in front offices to include people with disabilities as well (Wolff & Hums, in progress).

As stated in the previous chapter, increasingly diversified sport organizations allow for more voices to be heard and for continued growth. As mentioned in the chapter on ethics, sport reflects society. With society as a whole becoming more diverse, so must the sport industry embrace this diversity, not just on the player level but on the management level as well.

SUMMARY

Professional sport in North America takes many forms. Most prominent are the Big Four—MLB, NBA, NFL, and NHL. These major sport organizations have different governance levels, including Commissioners, league offices, and individual franchise levels on the management side, and PAs on the players' side. The policy issues facing managers in the professional sport industry segment are numerous and include areas such as drug policies, player misconduct, gambling, and labor-related issues such as salary caps and luxury taxes. These areas become more complex when players belong to the players' union, so both sides must be cognizant of their respective Collective Bargaining Agreement when developing policy and deciding on governance issues.

North American Professional Sport

CASE STUDY

You have probably heard or read about the Mitchell Report, which exposed the use of performance-enhancing substances in Major League Baseball. It is obvious that some highly successful professional athletes will choose to use these substances as a way to gain an advantage over their competition. The use of performance-enhancing substances presents a number of governance-related questions and issues. Assume the role of an MLB team owner and consider the following questions:

1. Should professional sports leagues adopt the more stringent rules and regulations set forth by WADA? What are the pros and cons to doing so?
2. What should happen to the records set by players during the so-called "steroid era"? Should they be nullified, somehow marked with an asterisk, or left as they are?
3. As the recommendations of the Mitchell Report are discussed, how will the relationship between management and labor (MLBPA) play out?
4. Most people agree that athletes are role models and many young athletes look up to the players named in this report. Should athletes be role models? Do athletes have an ethical obligation to be role models?

CHAPTER QUESTIONS

1. Which of the Big Four do you consider to be the model example of a professional sport league? Why?
2. You have been hired to work in the Marketing Department of an NHL franchise. In your position, how will you interact with the various governance levels in the NHL, both directly and indirectly?
3. Who are the Commissioners of each of the Big Four, and what are their employment backgrounds? Which do you consider to be the most powerful, and why? You have the opportunity in answering this question to write a letter to one Commissioner and give that Commissioner five suggestions to improve that league's operation. Which league would you choose, and what suggestions would you offer?

REFERENCES

Abrams, R. I. (1998). *Legal bases: Baseball and the law.* Philadelphia: Temple University Press.

Abrams, R. I. (2000). *The money pitch: Baseball free agency and salary arbitration.* Philadelphia: Temple University Press.

Associated Press. (2006, October 25). MLB players, owners announce five-year labor deal. Retrieved October 5, 2007, from http://sports.espn.go.com/mlb/news/story?id=2637615.

Baseball Almanac. (2007). Steroid suspensions. Retrieved October 5, 2007, from www.baseball-almanac.com/legendary/steroids_baseball.shtml.

Baseball America. (2007). *Baseball America directory 2007.* Durham, NC: Author.

Benedict, J., & Yaeger, D. (1998). *Pros and cons: The criminals who play in the NFL.* New York: Warner.

Bodley, H. (2002, November 15). Major leagues take big step forward then step back in minority manager hires. *USA Today,* p. 11C.

Burnside, S. (2006, December 5). With happy cap news, board set to settle schedule. Retrieved October 9, 2007, from http://sports.espn.go.com/nhl/columns/story?columnist=burnside_scott&id=2686411.

Cochran: NFL can do better in hiring minorities. (2003, January 23). Associated Press. Retrieved on January 23, 2003, from http://web.lexis-nexis.com/universe/document?_m=d930e1bd9e1e166da95555c6c9bce077&_docnum=1&wchp=dGLbVtb-lSlAl&_md5=06abffded79316f0a488e7786caa5c30.

Crosset, T., & Hums, M. A. (2008). Ethical principles applied to sport management. In L. P. Masteralexis, C. A. Barr, & M. A. Hums, (Eds.), *Principles and practice of sport management* (4th ed.), pp. 109–124). Sudbury, MA: Jones & Bartlett.

Drug test provision in new baseball contract seen as wanting. (2002, October 18). *Workplace Substance Abuse Advisor, 16*(22). Retrieved January 23, 2003, from http://web.lexisnexis.com/universe/document?_m=3dab03c18b9f16df7eacbc97f46acc01&_docnum=4&wchp=dGLbVzzlSlzV&_md5=30f6d1f67e489bf3326fff7da69c10ab.

Duberstein, M. J. (2002a). It happens every February: Media misperceptions of the current NFL system. New York: NFLPA Research Department.

Duberstein, M. J. (2002b). NFL economics primer. New York: NFLPA Research Department.

Erdes, G. (2002, August 31). Baseball strike averted. *Boston Globe,* p. E1.

ESPN. (2007). Mitchell report: Baseball slow to react to players steroid use. Retrieved January 2, 2008, from http://sports.espn.go.com/mlb/news/story?id=3153509.

Ford, C. (2006). Salary cap for 2006–2007 set at $53.135 million. Retrieved October 5, 2007, from http://sports.espn.go.com/nba/news/story?id=2516704.

Horrow, R. (2006, January 20). Heading to Super Bowl XL: NFL business issues. Retrieved October 9, 2007, from http://cbs.sportsline.com/general/story/9177560.

Lapchick, R. (2005). *2005 Racial and gender report card.* Orlando, FL: Institute for Diversity and Ethics in Sport, University of Central Florida.

Lapchick, R. (2006). *The 2005 racial and gender report card: Major League Baseball.* Orlando, FL: Institute for Diversity and Ethics in Sport, University of Central Florida.

Masteralexis, L. P. (2008). Professional sport. In L. P. Masteralexis, C. A. Barr, & M. A. Hums (Eds.), *Principles and practice of sport management* (3d ed., pp. 205–232). Sudbury, MA: Jones and Bartlett.

Miami Heat. (2007). Contact directory list. Retrieved October 5, 2007, from www.nba.com/heat/contact/directory_list.html.

Mitchell, G. J. (2007, December 13). Report to the Commissioner of Baseball of an independent investigation into the illegal use of steroids and other performance enhancing substances by players in Major League Baseball. Retrieved December 31, 2007, from http://mlb.mlb.com/mlb/news/mitchell/index.jsp.

MLB. (n.d.). *Professional Baseball Agreement.* New York: Author.

MLBPA. (2002a). Contact us. Retrieved November 3, 2002, from http://bigleaguers.yahoo.com/mlbpa/contact.html.

MLBPA. (2002b). Frequently asked questions. Retrieved November 3, 2002, from http://bigleaguers.yahoo.com/mlbpa/faq.html.

MLBPA. (2005a). Frequently asked questions. Retrieved October 5, 2007, from http://mlbplayers.mlb.com/pa/info/faq.jsp#membership.

MLBPA. (2005b). History of the Major League Baseball Players Association. Retrieved October 5, 2007, from http://mlbplayers.mlb.com/pa/info/history.jsp.

Mullin, B. J., Hardy, S., & Sutton, W. A. (2007). *Sport marketing* (3d ed.). Champaign, IL: Human Kinetics.

NBA Media Ventures. (2005). League office career opportunities. Retrieved October 1, 2007, from http://careers.peopleclick.com/careerscp/client_nba/external/search.do.

NBA Media Ventures. (2007). History: 1949–50 Season. Retrieved October 3, 2007, from www.nba.com/history/season/19491950.html.

NBPA. (n.d.a). About the NBPA. Retrieved October 5, 2007, from www.nbpa.com/about_nbpa.php.

NBPA. (n.d.b). *NBPA Collective bargaining agreement*. New York: Author.

NBPA. (n.d.c). NBPA departments. Retrieved October 5, 2007, from www.nbpa.com/departments.php.

NBPA. (n.d.d). NBPA history. Retrieved October 5, 2007, from www.nbpa.com/history.php.

NFL Enterprises. (2007). NFL history: Chronology. Retrieved October 2, 2007, from www.nfl.com/history/chronology/1921-1930.

NFLPA. (1998). Collective bargaining agreement. Retrieved October 22, 2002, from http://nflpa.org/shared/CBAPrinter.asp.

NFLPA. (2002a). Conduct policy. Retrieved October 5, 2007, from www.nflpa.org/RulesAndRegs/ConductPolicy.aspx.

NFLPA. (2002b). Drug policy. Retrieved October 18, 2002, from www.nflpa.org/agents/main.asp?subPage=Drug+Policy.

NFLPA. (2002c). History. Retrieved October 22, 2002, from www.nflpa.org/agents/main.asp?subPage=History.

NFLPA. (2006). *Collective bargaining agreement between the NFL Management Council and the NFL Players Association.* New York: Author.

NFLPA. (2007a). *National Football League policy and program for substances of abuse.* New York: Author.

NFLPA. (2007b). NFL Players Association constitution. Retrieved October 5, 2007, from www.nflpa.org/pdfs/Shared/NFLPA_Constitution.pdf.

NHLPA. (2007). Origins of the NHLPA. Retrieved October 5, 2007, from www.nhlpa.com/AboutTheNHLPA/WhatIs.asp.

PLAYERS INC. (2007). About us. Retrieved October 6, 2007, from www.nflplayers.com/about_us/main.aspx.

Quirk, J., & Fort, R. (1992). *Pay dirt: The business of professional team sports.* Princeton, NJ: Princeton University Press.

Quirk, J., & Fort, R. (1999). *Hard ball: The abuse of power in pro team sports.* Princeton, NJ: Princeton University Press.

Robinson, M. J., Hums, M. A., Crow, B., & Phillips, D. (2001a). *Profiles of sport management professionals: The people who make the games happen.* Gaithersburg, MD: Aspen.

Robinson, M. J., Lizandra, M., & Vail, S. (2001b). Sport governance. In B. L. Parkhouse (Ed.), *The management of sport: Its foundation and application* (3d ed., pp. 237–269). Boston: McGraw-Hill.

Schaaf, P. (2003). *Sports, Inc. 100 years of sports business.* Amherst, NY: Prometheus.

Scully, G. W. (1989). *The business of Major League Baseball.* Chicago, IL: University of Chicago Press.

Sharp, L. A., Moorman, A. M., & Claussen, C. L. (2007). *Sport law: A managerial approach.* Scottsdale, AZ: Holcomb Hathaway.

Street & Smith's SportsBusiness Journal. (2002). By the numbers. Charlotte, NC: Author.

Sutton, W. A., & Gladden, J. (2007). Professional sport. In J. B. Parks, J. Quarterman, & L. Thibault (Eds.), *Contemporary sport management* (3d ed., pp. 97–123). Champaign, IL: Human Kinetics.

Weisman, L. (2006, July 7). Expect NFL salary cap to keep going through the roof. Retrieved October 5, 2007, from www.usatoday.com/sports/football/nfl/2006-07-07-salary-report_x.htm.

Wise, A. N., & Meyer, B. S. (1997). *International sports law and business* (Vol. 1). The Hague, The Netherlands: Kluwer Law International.

Wolff, E. A., & Hums, M. A. (in progress). Disability report card. Boston: Northeastern University Center for Sport and Society.

Wong, G. M. (2002). *Essentials of sport law* (3d ed.). Westport, CT: Praeger.

Yasser, R., McCurdy, J., Goplerud, P., & Weston, M. A. (2000). *Sports law: Cases and materials*. Cincinnati, OH: Anderson.

Zimbalist, A. (2003). *May the best team win: Baseball economics and public policy*. Washington, DC: Brookings Institute.

13

INTERNATIONAL PROFESSIONAL SPORT

When you think of professional sport, the first leagues that come to mind are often the NBA, the NFL, the NHL, and MLB. However, in many parts of the world, these leagues do not come to mind, and the topics of discussion at the office the day after a game are also different. Perhaps a debate rages over the upcoming soccer match involving Manchester United and Amsterdam Ajax, the ongoing rivalry between Olympiakos and Panathanaikos, or whether

327

anyone can catch Michael Schumacher in the next Formula One Grand Prix. If you are wondering what these examples refer to, then welcome to the exciting world of professional sport beyond North America, where football means "soccer," basketball has a few different rules, motor sports does not mean NASCAR, and baseball is often completely unknown!

The sport industry has a truly global nature. Similar to other global products such as Coca-Cola or McDonald's, sport transcends borders. The North American way of organizing and managing sport is not the only, and certainly not always the best, way to organize sport. Sport managers working in an international environment must learn to be respectful of local cultures, norms, and expertise. According to Apostolopoulou and Papadimitriou (2005, p. 170), "it is imperative for sport managers to understand the international environment in which they operate. Sport professionals must be aware of the opportunities that are available on a global scale, as well as the challenges that arise from conducting business in this new, global market."

This chapter introduces the basics of selected international sport leagues and events. For the most part, people in North America have a relatively narrow view of professional sport—the Big Four, NASCAR, golf, and tennis. Hopefully, this chapter will help expand your horizons to professional sport around the world. The chapter will focus on two particular examples—soccer and motor sports—that are extremely popular around the world, as witnessed by the enormous numbers of fans who follow the World Cup and the Formula One World Championship.

The governance of professional sport internationally is very different from that of North America. Interrelationships among several levels of sport governing bodies are involved. Specifically, leagues are tied to the NGB for the sport in each nation, the international federation (IF) for each particular sport, and sometimes to a regional governing body. For example, the Premier League in England has ties to the Football Association of England (FA), the Union of European Football Associations (UEFA), and FIFA (Premier League, 2007a).

Another striking difference between professional leagues in North America and Europe is the system of promotion and relegation used in European leagues (Szymanski & Valetti, 2003). Briefly, this system operates as follows: "While there are several ways in which this scheme can operate, the most commonly used format is one where the worst performing teams in a league during the season, measured by the number of points won (a measure that is close to win percentage) are demoted to an immediately junior league to be replaced by the best performing teams in that league" (Szymanski, 2006, p. 685). As a useful comparison, what might this system look like if applied to Major League Baseball? Let's say that in a given year the team with the worst record in the National League was the Pittsburgh Pirates, and the team with the worst record in the America League was the Kansas City Royals. Next let's say the team with the best record in the AAA level International League was the Louisville Bats, and the team with the best record in the AAA level Pacific Coast League was the Memphis Redbirds. Applying the European scheme, the Bats may be promoted to the National League, while the Redbirds would be promoted to the American League. Consequently, the Pirates would be relegated to the Pacific Coast League, and the Royals would be relegated to the International League. Perhaps you are thinking "That sounds pretty crazy! What about stadiums and season tickets and corporate sponsorships?" Although you may wonder how it could possibly work, promotion and relegation is a common practice in professional sports leagues outside of North America and has worked successfully for many years.

Governance

The first sport we will analyze is soccer. In this section we will concentrate on two professional leagues—the Premier League in England and the J. League in Japan.

Soccer

As an organized sport, soccer has been around for an extremely long time. Professional soccer has a shorter past. In this section, we will briefly trace the history of the Premier League and the J. League, and then we will focus more directly on league operations and governance.

Before discussing any specific soccer league, we must take a quick look at the overall governance of international soccer. The IF for soccer, FIFA, is the international governing body for the game. FIFA consists of six regional organizations, including the Asian Football Confederation (AFC), the Confédération Africaine de Fútball (CAF), the Confederation of North, Central American and Caribbean Association Football (CONCACAF), the Confederacion Sudamericana de Footbol (CONMEBOL), the Oceania Football Confederation (OFC), and UEFA. Within these regions, every nation has its own FIFA-recognized national soccer governing body, such as U.S. Soccer Federation, Canadian Soccer Association, and the Hellenic Football Federation. Professional soccer leagues within specific nations must belong to their FIFA-recognized national soccer governing body to be eligible to advance in international play. For example, in the United States, MLS belongs to the U.S. Soccer Federation. The U.S. Soccer Federation, in turn, is a member of CONCACAF, which is the regional division of FIFA that includes North America. Because of this arrangement, MLS, or any FIFA-recognized professional soccer league in any nation, must follow the rules and regulations set forth by FIFA. Although the leagues have their own individual league governance systems for daily operation, they must follow many basic policies handed down from FIFA on issues such as drug use, match scheduling, and player transfers.

History

In the late 1980s, English soccer was in need of restructuring. A fire at a match cost many lives, as did a number of violent incidents involving fans. The game's image was in tatters, and it also suffered from a lack of financial

www

Premier League
www.premierleague.com

J. League
www.j-league.or.jp/eng

www **W**

Fédération Internationale
de Football Association

www.fifa.com

Asian Football Confederation

www.the-afc.com/eng/
index.jsp.html

Confédération Africaine
de Football

www.cafonline.com

Confederation of North,
Central American and
Caribbean Association
Football

www.concacaf.com

Confederación
Sudamericana de Fútbol

www.conmebol.com/index,
E.html

Oceania Football
Confederation

www.oceaniafootball.com

Union of European Football
Associations

www.uefa.com

U.S. Soccer Federation

http://ussoccer.com

Canadian Soccer Association

www.canadasoccer.com

Hellenic Football Federation

www.epo.gr/default_uk.asp

Major League Soccer

http://web.mlsnet.com/
index.jsp

investment. Establishing itself as a business entity separate from the nation's FA allowed the FA Premier League to negotiate its own television and sponsorship contracts, sources of income that have helped the league transition to its success today. The FA Premier League was formed in 1992 and took over as the top professional league in 1992–1993 (Premier League, 2007b). The league attracts players and fans from all over the world and is a successful business entity. In 2007, it changed its name to simply Premier League.

In Japan soccer became more popular after the 1964 Tokyo Olympics and the nation's Bronze Medal finish in the 1968 Mexico City Olympics. The game was played on a national league level as the Japan Soccer League (JSL), but this was an amateur league until professional athletes were officially admitted to the Olympic Games in 1984 and the JSL officially recognized professional players in 1986. The JSL established an action committee that discussed ways to grow the game and suggested formation of a professional league. The Japan Football Association (JFA) accepted the committee's recommendation. Thus, the J. League officially began in 1993, in a game in Tokyo before 59,626 spectators. By 2004, the league's aggregate attendance reached 7.4 million fans (J. League, 2005).

Numerous professional soccer leagues exist throughout the world, in addition to the Premier League in England and the J. League in Japan, including the Bundesliga in Germany, the Super League in Greece, and MLS in the United States. In addition multination leagues, such as the UEFA Champions League, exist. To illustrate governance structures, this section will focus on the Premier League and the J. League. Both are the top-level leagues in their nations, with lower leagues below them. These lower leagues are not technically minor leagues as we know them; they are separate clubs, not affiliates of the top division clubs. For example, the J. League technically consists of two leagues—J1 and J2. J1 is the top league, the one we refer to as J. League in this section.

Mission. The Premier League mission statement is in Figure 13.1, and the J. League's mission statement is presented in Figure 13.2. While both mention the development of the game, the Premier League presents more information concerning the business aspects of the league.

Membership. The members of these two professional leagues are the teams themselves. The Premier League is owned by 20 shareholders—the member clubs (e.g., Blackburn Rovers, Newcastle United, Liverpool, and 17 others), whose membership in the league is dependent upon the performance of their football team (Premier League, 2007a). The J. League's 16 member teams/shareholders include Gamba Osaka, Kyoto Purple Sanga, and Urawa Red Diamonds. The J. League has very specific conditions of membership. These conditions fall into these categories (J. League, 2005):

Mission statement of the Premier League.   **FIGURE** **13.1**

The Premier League must:

- Manage, continually improve and be regarded as the world's best league football competition—on and off the field
- Increase interest in our competitions, promote accessibility to live games and ensure that media exposure is used to optimum effect
- Generate increased commercial value, using the resulting revenues to further enhance our competition and strengthen the long-term future of the Premier League and its clubs
- Use our power and influence responsibly to improve the game in this country and abroad through partnership with the FA, UEFA and other bodies
- Create a quality of competition that provides a platform from which our member clubs can achieve unparalleled success in European or World competitions
- Use our resources to develop playing talent that will provide for international success with the England team at all levels—with the status of World Champions being the realistic goal

Source: Premier League (2007a).

Mission statement of the J. League.   **FIGURE** **13.2**

- To raise the level of Japanese football and promote the diffusion of the game through the medium of professional football
- To foster the development of Japan's sporting culture, to assist in the healthy mental and physical growth of Japanese people
- To contribute to international friendship and exchange

Source: J. League (2005).

1. *Incorporation.* Each club must be a registered corporation specializing in football, thus ensuring a secure management base.

2. *Hometowns.* Each club must designate a particular locality as its hometown and then must be active in its local community, promoting sports in the region.

3. *Player contracts.* Players (minimum of 15) must have signed the standard league-approved professional contract.

4. *Coaching licenses.* The coaches must also have attained the appropriate coaching license approved by the JFA.

5. *Team structure.* Each J1 team must have a top satellite club in the J2 League, a U-18 team, a U-15 team, and a U-12 team.

6. *Stadium facilities.* Each J. League team must have a stadium of a minimum size, meeting minimum lighting standards, and seating at least 15,000 spectators.

7. *Promotion to Division 1.* A Division 2 club can only be promoted if it satisfies the requirements for entry into Division 1.

To maintain membership, these leagues use a "ladder system" to determine ongoing membership. This system, common in international sport leagues, works as follows: The teams that finish last and next to last in the J. League (or J1) one season are relegated to J2 the next season. Simultaneously, the two top finishers in the J2 are elevated to J1 status the next year, assuming they meet the criteria for J1 membership. This system, referred to as "promotion and relegation," is different from the system used by leagues in North America. An analogy would be sending down the two teams in MLB with the worst records to AAA while sending up the two AAA teams with the best records to MLB, either to the American or the National League.

Financials. The sources of revenues for these leagues are similar to those in North America; they include merchandising programs, broadcast revenues, and corporate sponsorships, in addition to ticket sales. The Premier League is also known as the Barclay's Premier League, because Barclay's is the official title sponsor for the league. Other official partners of the Premier League are Budweiser, Lucozade, Nike, and Wrigley's Extra. In fiscal year 2005, the J. League projected revenues of over ¥11 billion (yen) or approximately US$105 million or €66 million (J. League, 2005). Some of J. League's official sponsors include Calbee Foods, Canon, Suntory Limited, JOMO, NicoS, Konami, AIDEM, HEIWA, and GE Money (J. League, 2007).

Organizational structure. The Premier League, as mentioned earlier, is owned by 20 shareholders—the member clubs. According to the league (Premier League, 2007a, Our Relationship with the Clubs section):

The shareholders meet quarterly. Any shareholder can table a motion to be discussed at the meeting. Each shareholder is entitled to one vote and all rule changes and major commercial contracts require the support of two-thirds of the clubs voting at a general meeting.

The [English] Football Association is also a special shareholder. They have the right of veto in certain crucial areas, such as the appointment of a Chairman and Chief Executive and promotion and relegation, but have no say on other areas of Premier League work.

The day-to-day business and statutory company responsibilities are handled by the Board of Directors, comprising the Chairman and Chief Executive, and the full-time members of the staff at the Premier League.

Shareholder meetings are held every other month during the season and the AGM [Annual General Meeting] is a two-day meeting held during the closed season.

The organizational structure for the J. League is illustrated in Figure 13.3. The J. League has a Board of Directors, with directors and auditors elected at the regularly scheduled General Meeting. The Board of Directors, the J. League's ultimate governing body, oversees two Executive Committees, one for J1 (the J. League), and the other for J2 (the second-division league). According to the J. League (2005, p. 21)), "The Executive Committees put the league's aims and policies into effect and deliberate and decide on matters entrusted to them by the Board of Directors. Each Executive Committee is made up of the chairman, directors with specific responsibilities, and one representative selected from each club." The Board of Directors also determines the authority and responsibilities of the Disciplinary Committee, Referees' Committee, Technical Committee, Legal Affairs Committee, Match Commissioners' Committee, and Doping Control Committee (J. League, 2005).

The Premier League and the J. League offer us interesting information about the operation of international team sport leagues. Another well-publicized and highly regarded international professional sport is motor sports. Let's take a look at the most prominent of these—Formula One racing.

Motor Sports

Motor sports take on many forms, including stock car racing, as in NASCAR; open-wheel racing, as in the Indy Racing League (IRL); and drag racing sponsored by the National Hot Rod Association (NHRA). However, the form of motor sports reaching the largest number of fans around the world is none of the above. The most widely watched motor sport is Formula One racing. But what exactly is Formula One and how is it governed?

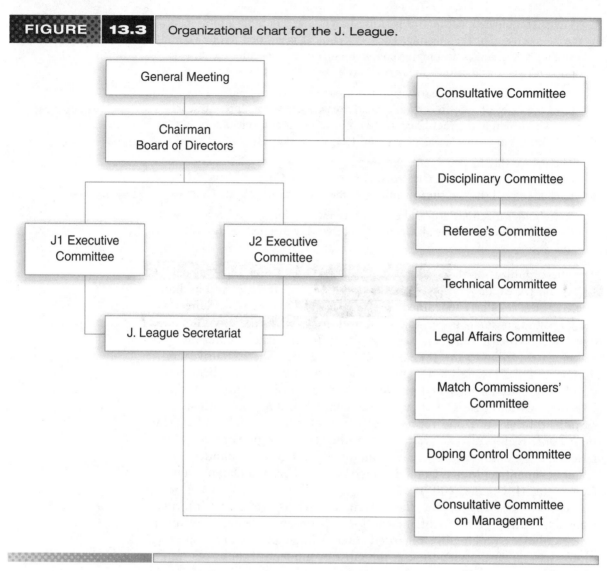

FIGURE 13.3 Organizational chart for the J. League.

Source: J. League (2005).

History

The IF governing motor sports is Fédération Internationale de l'Automobile (FIA), which organizes Formula One World Championships as well as all other international motor sports (FIA, 2004a). FIA not only governs motor sports but also oversees issues concerning traffic safety and automobile safety in general. Created in 1904, FIA today is "a non-profit making association which brings together 213 national motoring organizations from 125 countries on five continents" (FIA, 2004a, ¶ 3).

Formula refers to a certain combination of car specifications, including minimum and maximum weights, fuel consumption, and cylinder capacity. In the early days of racing, no *formula* designation existed. The first basic formula, introduced in 1904, simply restricted maximum car weight. The term *Formula One* did not appear until after World War II. Created in 1950, the Formula One World Championship is the oldest of the FIA championships. According to FIA, *Formula One* is defined as

> a set of technical regulations for single seater racing cars which is published annually by the FIA. The regulations specify maximum and minimum dimensions, engine capacity, what is permitted technically and what is not prohibited, and perhaps most important of all, a large number of safety measures to be incorporated into the car with a view of protecting the driver. (F1 Racing, n.d., question 1)

Currently the Formula One World Championship consists of 17 events in 17 nations. The 2007 FIA Formula One World Championship consisted of 17 Grand Prix events in the following locations: Australia, Malaysia, Bahrain, Spain, Monaco, Canada, the United States, France, Great Britain, Germany, Hungary, Turkey, Italy, Belgium, Japan, China, and Brazil. Two World Champion titles are awarded—one for drivers and one for constructors. Points are awarded for order of finish, and the driver and the constructor with the most points after the season series are awarded their respective titles.

Mission. FIA is the governing body for Formula One. Its mission statement, according to the statutes adopted by the FIA General Assembly in 2002 and modified in 2006, is presented in Figure 13.4. In contrast to the mission statement for the Premier League, FIA's mission statement describes its organization as a nonprofit, serving as an umbrella IF for activities in addition to racing.

FIA also lists a number of objectives, one of which is "promoting the development of motor sport, enacting, interpreting and enforcing common rules applicable to the organization and running of motor sports events" (FIA, 2006b, Article 2). Formula One racing falls under this particular objective.

Membership. The voting members of the FIA include (FIA, 2006c) the following:

- national automobile clubs and national automobile associations (for example, American Automobile Association and Canadian Automobile Association)
- clubs, associations, or federations covering road traffic, touring, or camping

NASCAR
www.nascar.com

Indy Racing League
www.indycar.com

National Hot Rod Association
www.nhra.com

Fédération Internationale de l'Automobile
www.fia.com/index_1024.html

| FIGURE | 13.4 | Mission statement of the FIA. |

The Fédération Internationale de l'Automobile (FIA), a non-profit-making world organization and an international association of national Automobile Clubs, Automobile Associations, Touring Clubs, and National Federations for motoring and motor sport, was founded in 1904 and enjoys consultative status with the U.N. It has its headquarters in Paris, or in such place as the General Assembly may determine.

The FIA shall refrain from manifesting racial, political, or religious discrimination in the course of its activities and from taking any action in this respect.

Source: FIA (2006a).

ASN Canada FIA
www.asncanada.com

Deustche Motor Sport Bund e.V.
www.dmsb.de

■ clubs, associations, or federations whose activity concerns motor sports (for example, ASN Canada FIA, Deustche Motor Sport Bund e.V. [Germany]). Once admitted as members, these clubs, associations, or federations exercise Sporting Power.

Clearly, the governance and operation of Formula One racing falls under "Sporting Power" in the third category above.

Financials. Formula One Grand Prix events are multimillion-dollar or -euro events. For example, according to the Motorsports Industry Association (MIA),

Motorsports Industry Association
www.the-mia.com

> the 2002 British round of the FIA Formula One World Championship attracted nearly £35 million [US$68 million or €44 million] of expenditure and maintained the equivalent of approximately 1,150 full-time jobs. . . . As well as the substantial direct economic benefit of staging the event, the British Grand Prix brings additional intangible benefits for the UK motorsport industry in Motorsport Valley by providing a platform to showcase high performance engineering expertise and resources. In addition, the event has significant, yet unquantifiable, benefits for the wider economy by presenting the UK and the region in a positive light to a worldwide TV audience of over 300 million viewers. (MIA, 2003, p. 1)

According to Lilley and DeFranco (1999), the Grand Prix Formula One race held in the European Union drew more than 2 million spectators to 11 events, and these spectators spent approximately $500 million (€325 million). In addition, these spectators spent money in 127,000 local businesses with almost 740,000 employees over an area of 81,000 square kilometers. The average spectator spent approximately US$230 (€150) per day on tickets, parking, gasoline, hotels, food, drink, entertainment, transportation, and tourist retail (Lilley & DeFranco, 1999). These statistics apply to events in Austria, Belgium, the UK, France, Germany, Italy, Monaco, Portugal, San Marino, and Spain. Fans turn out in large numbers for the Grand Prix events. In 2007, fans numbering 105,000 watched the Australian Formula One Grand Prix, 140,300 attended the Spanish Grand Prix, and 120,000 attended the Canadian Formula One Grand Prix (Grand Prix Cities, n.d.). In addition, Formula One attracts 850 million television viewers per year (Bool, 2006). Formula One racing is heavily driven by corporate sponsorship. Formula One racing receives the second highest amount of euros spent by corporate sponsors on sporting events in Europe, second only to soccer. Major corporate sponsors include companies such as Bridgestone, ING, Petronas, Gulf Air, Petrol Ofisi, Fuji Television, and Sinopec.

Canadian Formula One Grand Prix
www.grandprix.ca/home.html

Organizational structure. Because Formula One is governed by FIA, we must first look at the governance structure of that organization to see where Formula One fits in. FIA's highest level of authority is the General Assembly, composed of delegations from the FIA member clubs, associations, or federations (FIA, 2006d). The General Assembly elects two World Councils—the World Council for Mobility and the Automobile (for all nonsporting activities) and the World Motor Sport Council, which governs all international motor sport (FIA, 2004b). Each World Council, in turn, is governed by its respective General Assembly and the FIA Articles describe the membership of these Councils. Figure 13.5 illustrates the governance structure of the FIA.

The World Motor Sport Council has numerous Sporting Commissions that assist in its tasks. Some of these Commissions include the Medical Commission, Technical Commission, Rally Commission, Off-Road Commission, Safety Commission, Sporting Manufacturers' Commission, and of course, a Formula One Commission (FIA, 2006e).

In Formula One racing, a Formula One technical group consists of the technical directors of each team who "make recommendations to the FIA Formula One Commission on which the teams, race promoters, engine manufacturers, sponsors, tire manufacturers, and of course, FIA, are represented. Decisions of the Formula One Commission then go to the FIA World Sport Council and ultimately the FIA General Assembly for approval" (F1 Racing, n.d., question 2).

FIGURE   13.5   Governance structure of the FIA.

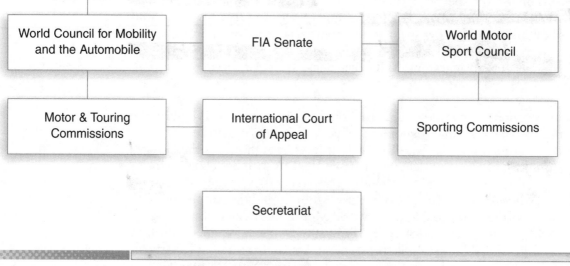

Source: FIA (2004b).

Current Policy Areas

Just as with professional sport in North America, international professional sport faces a broad range of policy issues that need to be addressed. Two of these issues are racism in football and the fallout from the Formula One scandal.

Racism in Football

Over the past years, we have seen an increase in the number of incidents involving racist behavior on the part of football fans. Unfortunately, racism is still quite alive in some sectors of European football. "FC Barcelona stars Ronaldinho and Samuel Eto'o are taunted with monkey noises at Spanish matches. AS Roma fans display banners with neo-Nazi and anti-Semitic slogans. Gypsies are targeted by Romanian supporters" (Mackey, 2006, p. 1). Superstar Thierry Henry is insulted by an opposing coach. An Italian footballer gives a fascist salute to spectators.

So what have sport organizations done to try and deal with this? At the 2006 World Cup in Germany, the "Say No to Racism" message was expressed often and visibly. FIFA dedicated all four of the quarter finals to spreading the word against racism. Players and officials held banners on the field reading "Say No to Racism" before these games. In addition, all the stadiums where matches were played were equipped with a racism monitoring system using trained security personnel (FIFA, 2007).

UEFA has joined with Football Against Racism in Europe (FARE) in a campaign called Unite Against Racism, and has produced a booklet describing racism and how to respond to racist fans. UEFA offers the following 10-point program (UEFA, 2006, p. 18):

1. Issue a statement saying that racism or any other kind of discrimination will not be tolerated, spelling out the action that will be taken against those who engage in racist chanting. The statement should be printed in all match programmes and displayed permanently and prominently around the ground.

2. Make public address announcements condemning racist chanting at matches.

3. Make it a condition for season ticket holders that they do not take part in racist abuse.

4. Take action to prevent the sale of racist literature inside and around the ground.

5. Take disciplinary action against players who engage in racial abuse.

6. Contact other associations or clubs to make sure they understand the association's or club's policy on racism.

7. Encourage a common strategy between stewards and police for dealing with racist abuse.

8. Remove all racist graffiti from the ground as a matter of urgency.

9. Adopt an equal opportunities' policy in relation to employment and service provision.

10. Work with all other groups and agencies, such as the players' union, supporters, schools, voluntary organisations, youth clubs, sponsors, local authorities, local businesses and the police, to develop proactive programmes and make progress to raise awareness of campaigning to eliminate racial abuse and discrimination.

www

Football Against Racism in Europe
www.farenet.org

Unite Against Racism
www.uefa.com/Multimedia Files/Download/uefa/ KeyTopics/448328_ DOWNLOAD.pdf

Formula One Scandal

In the summer of 2007, Formula One was rocked by a scandal of epic proportions. In an attempt to gain a competitive advantage, "McLaren chief designer Mike Coughlan was found in possession of a 780-page dossier of Formula-1 rival Ferrari's technical data. The information allegedly had all the data on the Italian team's 2007 car" (Maphosa, 2007, p. 1). With a backdrop of espionage and intrigue, the punishments levied were newsworthy. Ultimately, the McLaren Mercedes team was eliminated from the constructors' standings and fined $100 million (€65 million) in a scandal that cast a shadow over the racing season (Spurgeon, 2007).

FIA issued the following statement regarding the penalties, after a special session of the World Motor Sports Council (WMSC):

> The WMSC has stripped Vodafone McLaren Mercedes of all constructors' points in the 2007 FIA Formula One World Championship and the team can score no points for the remainder of the season. Furthermore, the team will pay a fine equal to 100 million dollars, less the FOM income lost as a result of the points deduction. However, due to the exceptional circumstances in which the FIA gave the team's drivers an immunity in return for providing evidence, there is no penalty in regards to drivers' points. The WMSC will receive a full technical report on the 2008 McLaren car and will take a decision at its December 2007 meeting as to what sanction, if any, will be imposed on the team for the 2008 season. (Formula 1, 2007, ¶ 7–10)

SUMMARY

The world of international professional sport is complex. The interrelationships among professional leagues, IFs, regional federations, and NGBs are unlike any we are used to seeing in North America. Despite those differences, similarities exist, particularly when it comes to player movement and corporate sponsorship concerns. What is important to realize, however, is how global a product sport really is.

CASE STUDY | *International Professional Sport*

The time for you to start planning your internship is quickly approaching. After reading this book (especially this chapter), you realize opportunities exist for you to pursue internships in nations outside of North America. The opportunities include professional sports, national sport organizations, IFs, and major games and events.

1. List a number of nations where you would like to live or visit.

2. List a number of organizations, sports, or events you would consider.

3. How can you find out more detailed information about these sport organizations?

4. Ask if any of your classmates have either visited or lived in other parts of the world. What questions would you like to ask them about their experiences?

5. What are three specific industry experiences an international internship could offer you that a domestic internship could not?

6. How do you see the global face of the sport industry changing in the next 10 years?

CHAPTER QUESTIONS

1. Choose another professional sport league outside of North America and research its history, mission, membership, financials, and governance structure.

2. Choose a nation outside of North America. Research the different professional sport opportunities available in that nation.

3. In addition to the governance structures described in this chapter, some nations also have a governmental agency that oversees all sports, including professional sport, in that nation. Sometimes this agency is named the Ministry of Sport. If such a structure were created in the United States, who would serve on it, and how would it be organized?

REFERENCES

Apostolopoulou, A., & Papadimitriou, D. (2005). Global sport industry. In A. Gillentine & R. B. Crow (Eds.), *Foundations of sport management.* Morgantown, WV: Fitness Information Technology.

Bool, H. (2006, October 17). Sponsorship and sports—The ING example: Running & Formula One. *EzineArticles.* Retrieved October 7, 2007, from http://ezinearticles.com/?Sponsorship-and-Sports—The-ING-Example:-Running-and-Formula-One&id=331165.

FIA. (2004a). Introduction. Retrieved October 6, 2007, from www.fia.com/thefia/Organisation/organisation.html.

FIA. (2004b). Structure. Retrieved October 6, 2007, from www.fia.com/thefia/Structure/index.html.

FIA. (2006a). Article 1. Retrieved October 6, 2007, from www.fia.com/thefia/statutes/Files/article01_fia.html.

FIA. (2006b). Article 2—Object of the FIA. Retrieved October 6, 2007, from www.fia.com/thefia/statutes/Files/index.html.

FIA. (2006c). Article 3—Composition of the FIA. Retrieved October 6, 2007, from www.fia.com/thefia/statutes/Files/index.html.

FIA. (2006d). Article 8—General assembly. Retrieved October 6, 2007, from www.fia.com/thefia/statutes/Files/index.html.

FIA. (2006e). Article 21—Sporting commissions. Retrieved October 7, 2007, from www.fia.com/thefia/statutes/Files/index.html.

FIFA. (2007). Anti-racism at the 2006 WFIFA World Cup. Retrieved October 6, 2007, from www.fifa.com/aboutfifa/worldwideprograms/footballfor hope/news/newsid=518222.html.

F1 Racing. (n.d.). Formula One racing. Retrieved October 6, 2007, from www.f1-racing.org/frames1.html.

Formula 1. (2007, September 13). McLaren fined and stripped of constructors' points. Retrieved October 6, 2007, from www.formula1.com/news/headlines/2007/9/6767.html.

Grand Prix Cities. (n.d.). World motorsport attendances. Retrieved October 6, 2007, from www.grandprixcities.com/raceattendances.html.

J. League. (2005). *2005 J. League Guide.* Tokyo: Author.

J. League. (2007). Official site. Retrieved October 6, 2007, from www.j-league.or.jp/eng.

Lilley, W., & DeFranco, L. J. (1999). *The economic impact of the European Grand Prix.* Brussels, BEL: FIA.

Mackey, S. (2006, January 31). European soccer's anti-racism conference. Retrieved October 6, 2007, from www.lexisnexis.com/us/Inacademic/results/docview/docview.do?risb=21_T22054399 49&format=GNBFI&sort=BOOLEAN&startDoc No=1&resultsUrlKey=29_T2205439955&cisb= 22_T2205439954&treeMax=true&treeWidth= 0&csi=138211&docNo=2.

Maphosa, T. (2007, September 13). McLaren fined in Formula-1 scandal. Retrieved January 2, 2008, from www.voanews.com/english/archive/2007-09/2007-09-13-voa51.cfm?CFID=9354429& CFTOKEN=58519804.

MIA. (2003, September 16). Major survey shows British Grand Prix brought £35 million into the UK in 2002. Retrieved October 6, 2007, from www.the-mia.com/view_press_release.cfm?id=53.

Premier League. (2007a). About us. Retrieved October 6, 2007, from www.premierleague.com/page/Contact/0,,12306,00.html.

Premier League. (2007b). A history of the Premier League. Retrieved October 6, 2007, from www.premierleague.com/page/History/0,,12306,00.html.

Spurgeon, B. (2007, September 30). After spying scandal, embarrassing results. *International Herald Tribune.* Retrieved October 6, 2007, from www.nytimes.com/2007/09/30/sports/othersports/30prix.html?fta=y.

Szymanski, S. (2006). The promotion and relegation system. In W. Andreff and S. Szymanski (Eds.), *Handbook on the economics of sport* (pp. 685–688). London: Edward Elgar.

Szymanski, S., & Valetti, T. (2003). Promotion and relegation in sporting contests. Retrieved January 2, 2008, from www.nhh.no/sam/stabssem/2003/szymanski.pdf.

UEFA. (2006). *Tackling racism in club football: A guide for clubs.* Retrieved October 6, 2007, from www.uefa.com/MultimediaFiles/Download/uefa/KeyTopics/448328_DOWNLOAD.pdf.

14

THE FUTURE OF SPORT GOVERNANCE

A future without change would be pretty bleak. Imagine if everything always stayed the same—the same people, same events, same physical layout, same schedule. Consider a professional baseball franchise: What if the rosters never changed, the competition was always the same, and the stadium or schedules were never upgraded? For fans, this scenario would be boring and lack energy, and over time simply would be no fun. While an unchanging situation can be

343

problematic, the exact opposite—rapid or unplanned change—can be equally difficult. Rapid change can be unsettling, creating confusion and uncertainty. Suppose the roster of the baseball team was shuffled every week, so that no one could follow who played for which team. MLB fans would find it impossible to feel loyalty for a team that changes players so quickly. A world without change is inconceivable, and a world in constant, rapid, and unplanned change can be chaotic.

Change is nonetheless important and inevitable. Change is often a component of progress; viewed hopefully, change provides not just different, but better, ways of doing things. Sport organizations are perfect illustrations of the importance of change, and are good examples of the negative results accruing from overly rapid or poorly planned change.

To grow and thrive, a sport organization must be able to change and adapt to its environment. Factors in the environment include its size, members, competition, strategy, and technology (Chelladurai, 2005; Slack & Parent, 2006). As the size or membership of an organization grows, it changes to best serve its constituents. The organization defines strategy based on its competition and adapts to effectively utilize technology. Consider the NOCs in Chapter 10. The COC is a good illustration of an NOC that changed its operating structure to effectively deliver its mandate. As the Olympic Games evolved from a world festival of sport into a multimillion-dollar extravaganza and a voice for political agendas, the COC changed to accommodate this new environment, while still effectively delivering services to its members. The importance of winning Olympic medals as part of the national political agenda of Canada was one factor providing impetus for organizational change. This organizational change involved a new name, a new internal structure, and new criteria for funding Olympic sports within Canada.

One major concern to sport organizations as they undergo change is the pressure of future economic survival. The world economy fluctuates. During periods of downsliding, government spending on high school and college or university athletic and recreation programs is in jeopardy, as well as funding for city and municipal recreation programs. Professional sport, as well as Olympic and Paralympic sport, which rely on corporate sponsorships, also feel pressure as corporations make decisions about how much to invest in sport properties. Increased financial pressure, coupled with changing environments, present sport managers with a complex future.

This chapter serves to complete our look at the governance of sport organizations. Its purpose is to provide a look at the future of governance in the sport industry segments described in this text. Predicting the future, of course, is risky business. However, the future surely involves the continued evolution of sport organizations to meet their needs and the needs of their various stakeholders. The globalization of business practices, including the business of sport, has resulted in unprecedented change evolving faster than ever before (Moorhead & Griffin, 2007). We hope such change will be planned change, as opposed to forced change.

Change Within Organizations

Structures and governance policies of sport organizations evolve to improve effectiveness. The importance of change for sport organizations is in keeping with business and other organizations worldwide. As Beer and Nohria (2000, p. ix) point out, "The demands of an ever competitive and changing environment are increasing the need for knowledge about how to lead and manage organizational change rapidly, efficiently, and effectively. The management mantra as we enter the 21st century is 'lead change.'" Change should be planned and strategic, not some revolving door, constantly shuffling in new ideas while bouncing out the old.

According to Slack and Parent (2006), planned change can occur in four different areas of a sport organization: (1) the structures and systems of the organization, (2) the conduct of the organization's personnel, (3) the products and services delivered through the organization, or (4) the technology supporting the organization. So where do the pressures for change originate?

Pressures for Change

Pressure for organizational change may originate from three sources (Brill & Worth, 1997):

1. events occurring within the organization
2. factors arising outside the organization
3. an interaction of external and internal factors

For example, the NCAA membership provided the impetus for restructuring the organization into divisions based on the changing philosophical perspectives of its members. In the past, changes in legislation and rules were made at the organization's annual meeting, where members from all divisions met together. When voting on issues, every school had one vote, and all divisions voted on all issues. Today the Division I, II, and III categories are taken for granted in the governance structure of the organization. The changing perspectives of various institutions within the organization provided the impetus for this change.

Sport organizations work within fairly complex environments, both internal to the specific organization and external to its many partners and constituencies. What are the goals of planned organizational change?

Goals of Planned Change

Planned change involves the systematic development and initiation of new modes of operating to gain competitive advantage. It may be prompted by the need for action resulting from events internal or external to the organization. The goal of planned change within a sport organization likely involves either matters of finance or organizational capability (Beer & Nohria, 2000). The impetus for change often results from financial belt-tightening within an organization. Specifically, a goal often involves increasing revenues or decreasing expenditures, or both, in an effort to balance the budget or enhance organizational services. When finances are not at the root of planned change, improving the organization's capability usually is. In this case the purpose of planned change is to enhance the organization's capacity to learn to respond better to its environment. Further, the goal might be to go beyond *responding* to the environment and, instead, proactively *shaping* that environment. Achieving this second goal allows an organization to exercise more control over future directions and be on the cutting edge of the industry. Understanding the goals of planned change within an organization is important in determining strategy for change. How is such change initiated, and what procedures are used to invoke organizational change?

Procedures for Organizational Change

Planned change occurs when several stages of activities result in organizational action (Slack, 1997; Slack & Parent, 2006). According to Greiner (1967), change begins because pressure is exerted either from inside or outside the organization, or from an interaction of these two. First, a request for change is made to senior management. The request carries the most influence when it comes simultaneously from sources both within and outside the organization. Often the request for change is blocked by senior management because this group has a tendency to rationalize organizational problems (Brill & Worth, 1997). A consultant is regularly used to overcome such rationalization or hesitancy. Second, the specific problem causing change is diagnosed and recognized throughout all the levels of the organization. Third, solutions to the problems are invented, and a commitment to a course of action is sought by testing several possible solutions to the identified problems. Finally, change is implemented through a number of small-scale decisions serving to reinforce a course of action and acceptance of larger-scale associated changes. The change process just described is presented diagrammatically in Figure 14.1.

Future Industry Segment Issues

Change within organizations is often slow and difficult. The previous chapters of this book outlined governance structure and policy development for several segments of the sport industry. Let's look briefly at some of the issues that might cause change within those industry segments.

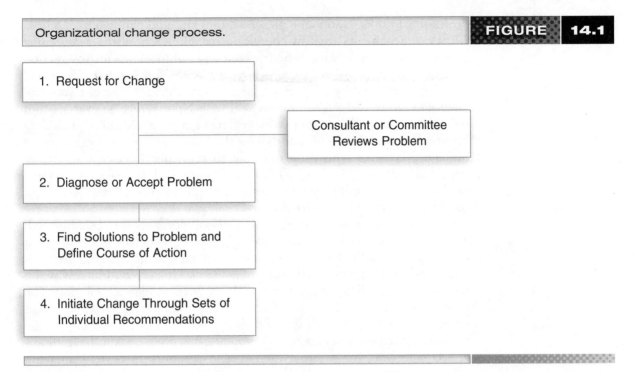

Organizational change process.

FIGURE 14.1

1. Request for Change

Consultant or Committee Reviews Problem

2. Diagnose or Accept Problem

3. Find Solutions to Problem and Define Course of Action

4. Initiate Change Through Sets of Individual Recommendations

Scholastic Sport

Today's youth has more opportunities than ever to participate in organized sport. With year-round traveling soccer teams, sports offered in the European club sport model, Little League Baseball, summer camps, and more, children (and their parents) have more choices than ever. While this is great, it also creates a more competitive climate for scholastic sport. Should a child play on a year-round soccer team or for the local high school team? Should a young athlete play one sport all year and specialize or change sports as the seasons change? Often choices such as these are driven by the thought that the more visible the competition level is to college coaches, the more likely it is that the young athlete may have an opportunity for a college scholarship.

These considerations lead to another key issue—what is the purpose of high school sport? Is it participation, healthy activity, and socialization opportunities, or is it preparation for intercollegiate athletics? A college education is a basic expectation, but these days as tuition costs rise and the economy stumbles, parents are looking for ways to finance their children's education. Although the odds are against it, many parents in the United States see athletic scholarships as a way to cover these costs, and they see high school sport as the platform for their child's future success.

Sometimes high school sport becomes an even higher platform. More and more often, high school athletes consider jumping directly into the professional ranks. National high school rankings and national high school All Star tournaments are now commonplace. High school sport governing bodies must make decisions about which types of tournaments to sanction and must examine more closely their definitions of *amateurism*. This trend is well documented by the LeBron James story, the high school basketball phenom who signed a $90 million deal with Nike before he ever set foot on an NBA court. While some winners emerged from his story—including his family, his high school, and Nike—the losers will be the large number of young athletes who now may try to replicate James's statistically improbable career (Elmore, 2003). In the future, high school sport governing bodies will continually revisit important philosophical questions about the basic nature of high school sports.

Finally, the issue of funding for high school sports needs to be addressed. More and more corporate dollars are being put into interscholastic sport. In addition, some individual high schools are selling naming rights to their stadiums and entering into deals with companies such as Nike. In many ways, the intercollegiate financing model is trickling down to high school sport. The implications of high school sport becoming more commercialized and reliant on outside funding through sponsorship is twofold. First, it will impact the competition for sponsorship dollars as sponsoring organizations have another sector striving for external funding and sponsorship beyond amateur, collegiate, and professional sport. Second, it may result in elevating high school competitions to levels expected of entertainment properties such as professional sport, which involves high costs and may further contribute to potential budget crises for administrators. Some may question this increasing commercialization of high school sport and whether it will influence the basic premise for why high school sport exists—educational purposes. Yet without these alternative funding sources, some students may lose out on the opportunities for these experiences.

Amateur Sport in the Community

Amateur community sport is the grass roots of competitive athletics. However, individuals in administrative positions will very likely be challenged to maintain the current breadth of programming. This challenge comes from competition for resources. Regardless of age group or type of sport, it takes significant human and financial resources to deliver programs. Competition for facilities is fierce. Finding people to coach, officiate, and organize programming is becoming more and more difficult. While public sport organizations will continue to strive to deliver recreational sport leagues, a lack of funding coupled with deteriorating infrastructure will combine to create a major impetus for change. Policy decisions might well be enacted to create much larger sources of funding to offset the need for money to renovate facilities. Current user fees will likely be increased to produce a larger revenue source. Recruiting volunteers such as coaches, officials, and league administrators will become more problematic and be given higher priority, along with volunteer training. Competition among public and private groups will create an environment more prone to accepting change, spurred on by the importance of making use of every opportunity. Programming innovations and offerings will need to adapt to changing demographics, as the populations of North American seniors and of racial and ethnic minorities continue to increase. The future success of the YMCA, the JCC, the Boys & Girls Clubs, and city parks and recreation departments will depend largely on their leadership and the ability of their boards of directors to understand the competition, to harness new forms of financial and human resources, and to enact policy that will take advantage of and accommodate shifting interests and trends for amateur athletes.

Campus Recreation

The leaders of campus recreation programs will oversee unprecedented change in the next decade. The future will be one of balancing service and customer-care issues in state-of-the-art facilities, while managing the balance among user groups. In the past, campus recreation programming and facilities were primarily for constituent groups of the campus, including students, staff, faculty, and perhaps immediate family members. This mandate will continue to broaden as program emphasis broadens to include members from the community. This might well involve parallel changes to organizational structures to include representatives from the community and their program interests in campus recreation governance. It will surely include changes to campus recreation policies aiming to involve and protect the interests of an expanded group of constituents. Service will be the mantra, and unprecedented growth will create opportunities and challenges. Constructing additional facilities, expanding the numbers of professional staff, and increasing programming will be balanced with maintaining a firm understanding of priorities so that the interests of university users, especially students, are not lost. The ongoing struggle among campus recreation, intercollegiate athletics, and physical education over shared facilities will also continue into the future. The governance structure and efficiency of policy-making procedures within future campus recreation programs, especially relating to risk management and access for people with disabilities, will be more important than ever before.

Intercollegiate Athletics

Although the commercial mandate of recreation programs on campus is generally accepted and supported, intercollegiate athletics policy makers will continue to confront negativity associated with commercialization in college football and basketball in the United States. It is unlikely, however, that any real change will occur. The issue, of course, will revolve around the role of college athletic programs in higher education. Are athletes at Division I colleges playing football and basketball really "students"? They more closely resemble professionals, except they are not directly paid to play. Why are they not paid to play? Colleges and universities make significant sums of money from their athletes. How is it that our colleges and universities, supposed collectives of truth and light, have created a system so very incongruous with their mandate and their purpose? The questions could go on and on to include issues of fairness, equity, corruption, and control. The issue is articulated well by Duderstadt (2000, p. 8), Professor Emeritus at the University of Michigan:

> We are obliged to ask the difficult question of whether it makes sense for the 21st Century university to conduct commercial activities at the current level of big-time college football and basketball. Is there any logical reason for an academic institution, with the fundamental mission of teaching and scholarship, to mount and sustain a professional and commercial enterprise simply to satisfy the public desire for entertainment, and the commercial goals of the marketplace? Why should the university squander its resources, distract its leadership, and erode its most fundamental values and integrity with these commercial activities, particularly at a time when it will face so many other challenges in responding to the changing educational needs of our society?

Although the debate will rage on, change is not on the horizon.

The Major Games in Amateur Sport

Managerial activities associated with major games policy development will receive considerable attention and will be the focus of governance activities for hosting events in the future. Two important issues are at stake. First, organizers will focus on the development of policy to ensure the safety and security of participants and spectators. World events such as the Pan American Games, Special Olympics, and World University Games are major events, receiving considerable attention from the media, spectators, and television. Organizers must plan for every contingency to ensure security and safety are not compromised by any group attempting to use the event for political gain. Major games administrators must be prepared to deal with issues of security, given the events confronting the world in the 21st century. Second, the governance structures in place for organizing major games must be able to deliver effective policy to manage the issues of the day in a timely manner. The committee structures are considerably large, requiring massive support to make change and allowing only a few members to effectively block the ability to move on issues quickly. Also, the procedures for developing policy and initiating change are unwieldy; inertia resists change, and thus the old, conservative way of doing things prevails. Organizers of major games will be forced to manage issues such as security, and it will be paramount that they have the governance structure and technology in place to set policy in a timely manner.

The Olympic Games

The IOC will continue to evaluate the future of the Olympic Games. Currently, the IOC suggests the four Olympic Movement cornerstones under future review include (1) assessing the Olympic Programme of sports and events; (2) studying the cost and complexity of the Games; (3) continuing to implement recent reform; and (4) auditing operation and financial administration (IOC, 2007). A major policy area demanding considerable attention of IOC members involves the size of the Games. The current Olympic Games are considered the "overgrown Games," which have too many sports and too many athletes, and cost too much money to deliver. As a comparison, in 1948 the Summer Olympic Games involved 17 sports, 140 events, and 4,099 athletes, whereas the Athens 2004 Games had 28 sports, 301 events, and 11,099 athletes (IOC, 2007).

Given the four issues for reform mentioned above, reviewing the actual sport program will enact policy and create reform that might, at least in part, address the other areas of concern. In 2002 the IOC moved forward and created policy to systematically review the composition of the sports program after every Games to ensure its relevancy for future sporting generations. This work is undertaken by the IOC Olympic Programme Commission and IFs. According to the Olympic Charter, the number of sports on the program can be anywhere between 15 and 28. Sports can be voted on for inclusion on the program at the Sessions. For a sport to become an Olympic sport, and thus be eligible for inclusion on the program, a two-thirds majority vote is needed at an IOC Session. Enacting this policy to manage sports in the Olympic Programme will dominate the agenda of the future. An assessment of the overall governance structure of the IOC should parallel that process. Moving sports off the Olympic competition roster, however, will continue to be very challenging.

The Paralympic Games

The Paralympic Games are gaining international recognition as an elite sport product. Along with this growth, numerous questions will arise regarding the Paralympic Movement. One of the first issues deals with integration of athletes with disabilities into mainstream able-bodied sport. Some IFs and events have already integrated competitions and rules (Grevemberg, Hums, & Wolff, 2001). For example, the Boston Marathon has included wheelchair

Boston Marathon

www.bostonmarathon.org/
BostonMarathon/
Disabilities.asp

**International Tennis
Federation**

www.itftennis.com

athletes as competitors for over 25 years (DePauw, Driscoll, Fay, Hums, & Joukowsky, 2003). The International Tennis Federation website has links to information on tennis for athletes with disabilities. Should athletes with disabilities be fully integrated into mainstream sport organizations, or should they remain separate with their own unique identities?

Another major issue facing the Paralympic Games involves illegal performance enhancement. Just as this is an issue in the Olympics, so too is it an issue in the Paralympic Games: Elite athletes are always looking for an edge over the competition. Cooperation between the IPC and organizations such as the WADA will be critical in this area.

Advances in technology will also impact the Paralympic Games. As the technology of prosthetics for people with disabilities develops, the development will be reflected in the performances of athletes with disabilities. Racing chairs will be made out of lighter-weight materials, and prosthetic limbs will be made stronger and more flexible. As these technologies develop, athletes will begin to achieve performances never seen before, and world records will be broken, establishing new standards of performance for these elite athletes. Technology's impact in this area will be far-reaching. But while examining the impact of technology, one must ask three questions: (1) Is the technology safe? (2) Is the technology fair? and (3) Is the technology accessible to all? These questions pertain not just to the Paralympic Games, but also to the policy making bodies of any sport governing body dealing with advances in technology.

Finally, just as with the Olympics, major games, and professional sport, security will continue to be important for the Paralympic Games. Whenever there are large gatherings of elite athletes from many nations, security and risk management become critical for the athletes, spectators, and workers.

As the Paralympic Games continue to grow, the governing bodies associated with the Games, including the IPC, NPCs, and IFs will need to adjust to an ever-changing environment. They will need to be responsive to governance decisions made by able-bodied sports organizations that may impact events, rules, and eligibility for athletes with disabilities.

**UN Treaty on the Rights of
Persons with Disabilities**

www.un.org/disabilities

Finally, the United Nations' General Assembly's adoption of the Treaty on the Rights of Persons with Disabilities will have long-term effects on the Paralympic Movement. The Treaty contains language specific to sport in Article 30.5 of the document, thus sport and physical activity clearly fall under the umbrella of this Treaty. It may take some time for the document to be put into practice, but the long-term results will provide increased opportunities for athletes with disabilities (Wolff, Hums, & Roy, 2007).

Professional Sport

While financial and security concerns remain important to professional sport, leagues, teams, and the players associations doubtlessly are going to need to step up their stances on misconduct by athletes, coaches, and officials. The summer of 2007 saw scandals involving the NFL player Michael Vick and dogfighting as well as NFL Coach Bill Belichick's taping of the opposing team's defensive signals, NBA official Tim Donaghy and gambling, and the release of the Mitchell Report that discussed steroid and human growth hormone (HGH) use by MLB players, including stars such as Roger Clemons and Andy Pettite. The seeming rampant behavior problems, ranging from boorishness to unlawful activity, beg for leagues to take truly strong stands against misconduct.

Although many people seemed to believe the professional sport industry was relatively impervious to the twists and turns of the economy and world events, those notions were swept away on September 11, 2001. In the wake of that day, professional sport has had to face the reality of unstable international economies and environments. The value of the U. S. dollar continues to plummet in relation to the euro, and the U. S. middle class has not benefited significantly from national economic policies since 2000. For sport managers, this economic environment is significant because the middle class makes up the lion's share of a team's or league's fan base.

In an unstable economy, professional sport sponsorship is surely to be affected. Not only is the struggling economy an issue for sponsors when trying to negotiate long-term deals, the conduct of the players or teams associated with the sponsor is also a major issue in sport today. With more and more athletes getting in trouble with the law and receiving subsequent bad press and a tarnished image, sponsors have to be very careful in choosing players with whom to associate. Following his 2004 trial for suspected rape, Kobe Bryant's image plunged and some of his sponsors, including McDonald's and Nutella, declined to renew their contracts with him (Associated Press, 2004).

Many security measures implemented in stadiums and arenas for professional sport events have remained in place since September 11 (Slezak, 2002). Stadiums continue to ban coolers and backpacks, and armed security personnel remain a visible presence. These are the changes visible to fans. Behind the scenes, the Big Four has increased measures to protect teams and players when they travel, and teams are required to carry special insurance plans as well. Security at sporting events has moved to the top item facing industry executives (Hyman, 2002; Security Info Watch, 2007). Governing bodies, specifically leagues, have had to create and enforce new security policies and procedures in a somewhat uncertain environment.

While security and the economy remain at the top of the list, other issues remain constant in professional sport. Leagues and PAs will continue to debate collective bargaining agreements. Labor issues in sport will always be with us, and leagues and PAs will continually hammer out new policies regarding everything from performance-enhancing substances to athlete misconduct. For example, in 2004–2005, the NHL became the first professional sports league in North America to cancel an entire season due to a work stoppage. This stoppage was the culmination of a year-long standoff between the players and the owners in an attempt to negotiate a new collective bargaining agreement (CBA). The main point of contention was the escalation of player salaries, leading the owners to demand a hard salary cap and the players steadfastly refusing to accept one. After months of on-and-off negotiations between the NHLPA and the owners, an agreement was reached in July 2005. The new CBA would not only include a hard salary cap, but the players also accepted an immediate 24 percent rollback in salaries league-wide and a limit on individual season salaries, whereby no player can earn more than 20 percent of the team cap. Collective bargaining and labor relations will continue to surface within professional sport, for both men's and women's teams.

Mentioning women's sport brings forth another issue—the future of women's professional sport. The WNBA, while beginning to turn small profits, is still receiving "anemic" television ratings, and most of their teams lose money (Heath, 2006). However, while women's team sports seem to continue struggling, individual female athletes are thriving; some of them are even making inroads in male professional sport. Both the LPGA and the Women's Tennis Association (WTA) have prize money approaching the levels of their male counterparts, and both golfer Michelle Wie and race car driver Danica Patrick have competed, and held their own, against men. It will be interesting to see if these or other women will be able to achieve consistent success against men in the future and to observe how sport governing bodies in women's sport continue developing.

Professional sport in North America has begun to take on a more international flavor. The number of athletes from around the world is increasing, with numerous athletes from South America, Central America, and Japan playing MLB and many European players filling the rosters of the NHL and the NBA. In fact, many of today's biggest pro sport stars come from outside North America, including Ichiro Suzuki (Japan) and Albert Pujols (Dominican Republic) in MLB; Dirk Nowitzki (Germany), Yao Ming (China), and Pau Gasol (Spain) in the NBA; and Jaromir Jagr (Czech Republic) and Alexander Ovechkin (Russia) in the NHL.

League and play-off games are being broadcast to different nations and in different languages, as the professional leagues become a more global product. Each of these leagues are taking further advantage of this relatively new global market by scheduling regular season games in international cities, such as the NFL holding a 2007–2008 regular season game between the Miami Dolphins and New York Giants at Wembley Stadium in London, England. In addition, international "best-on-best" tournaments such as the World Cups of Baseball and Hockey showcase their respective games to the world, helping the game to grow even more.

www W

MLB Players from around the World

http://mlb.mlb.com/mlb/official_info/dbp/about_players.jsp

International Professional Sport

It is interesting to speculate on the future of professional sport internationally. Political and economic factors will no doubt impact the sport industry. Sponsors internationally will continue to reexamine their choices for investing in sporting leagues and events. Accordingly, the sport governing bodies for these sports will have to make decisions regarding financial matters in order to maintain and improve operations in the coming years. Because of the interrelationship of IFs such as FIA or FIFA to the operation of professional leagues internationally, these organizations will be considering policies related to garnering sufficient financial resources, just as the professional leagues in North America will. Internationally, professional sport will continue to grow. Soccer will remain the most popular sport globally and a viable investment for corporations. Formula One racing will need to find a way to recover after the McLaren-Ferrari scandal that resulted in a US$100 million (€65 million) fine for stealing trade secrets. In addition, sports such as rugby and cricket are coming onto the scene rapidly, bringing with them new fan bases and new sponsor opportunities to get their products in front of people around the globe.

SUMMARY

Change is inevitable. The future is uncertain. The future of sport will be full of changes! How sport governing bodies respond to these facts will determine their success in the future. Some people resist change, while others welcome it. In each segment of the sport industry, sport governing bodies will face change. Some of these changes will be unique to one industry segment, while others will cut across a number of segments.

And you future sport managers, how will you choose to face this future with all its uncertainties and questions and changes? As they say, "The ball is in your court now!"

CHAPTER QUESTIONS

1. Choose three industry segments from the textbook and identify two additional future issues for each.
2. Using the model presented in this chapter, analyze the steps for change for one of the following:
   a. a professional athlete being accused or convicted of criminal behavior
   b. a state or provincial association creating a wheelchair division for track-and-field competition
   c. a campus recreation program facing declining participation numbers

3. Choose one sport organization you would like to see experience changes in membership, eligibility, or organizational structure. Describe the changes you would like to see take place and how these changes will improve the organization.

REFERENCES

Associated Press. (2004, January 19). McDonald's cuts ties with Kobe Bryant. *USA Today*. Retrieved June 7, 2007, from www.usatoday.com/sports/basketball/nba/2004-01-19-mcdonalds-bryant_x.htm.

Beer, M., & Nohria, N. (2000). *Breaking the code of change*. Boston: Harvard Business School Press.

Brill, P. L., & Worth, R. (1997). *The four levers of corporate change*. New York: American Management Association.

Chelladurai, P. (2005). *Managing organizations for sport and physical activity: A systems perspective* (2d ed.). Scottsdale, AZ: Holcomb Hathaway.

COC. (2002). Home page. Retrieved November 8, 2002, from www.coa.ca.

DePauw, K., Driscoll, J., Fay, T., Hums, M. A., & Joukowsky, A. (2003). The Boston Marathon: Breaking barriers. Paper presented at the Disability Sport Symposium, Boston, MA.

Duderstadt, J. J. (2000, October 18). Some observations on the current state and the future of intercollegiate athletics. Remarks presented to the Knight Commission, Washington, DC. Retrieved January 21, 2003, from http://milproj.ummu.umich.edu/publications/knight_commission/knight_commission.pdf.

Elmore, P. (2003, January 20–26). James' juggernaut a dream—and a nightmare. *Street & Smith's SportsBusiness Journal, 5*(39), 33.

Greiner, L. E. (1967). Patterns of organizational change. *Harvard Business Review, 45*, 119–130.

Grevemberg, D., Hums, M. A., & Wolff, E. A. (2001). Integration of Paralympic Sport into International Sport Federations: Comparative international models. Paper presented at the Annual Meeting of the North American Society for Sport Management, Virginia Beach, VA.

Heath, T. (2006, July 12). A matter of value instead of profit. *Washington Post*. Retrieved June 7, 2007, from www.washingtonpost.com.

Howell, M. L., & Howell, R. (1988). Physical activities and sport in early societies. In E. F. Zeigler (Ed.), *History of physical education and sport* (pp. 1–56). Champaign, IL: Stipes.

Hyman, M. (2002, April 29). Security issues rise to the top of the docket for sport lawyers. *Street & Smith's SportsBusiness Journal*. Retrieved April 26, 2003, from www.sportsbusinessjournal.com/article.cms?articleId=21087&s=1.

IOC. (2007). Athens 2004. Retrieved May 14, 2007, from www.olympic.org/uk/games/past/index_uk.asp?OLGT=1&OLGY=2004.

Moorhead, G., & Griffin, R. W. (2007). *Organizational behavior: Managing people and organizations* (Canadian Ed.). Boston: Houghton Mifflin.

Robbins, S. P. (1990). *Organizational theory: Structure, design, and applications* (3d ed.). Englewood Cliffs, NJ: Prentice Hall.

Security Info Watch. (2007). Venues and arenas. Retrieved June 6, 2007, from www.securityinfowatch.com/article/article.jsp?siteSection=394&id=10790.

Slack, T., & Parent, M. (2006). *Understanding sport organizations: The application of organization theory* (2d ed.). Champaign, IL: Human Kinetics.

Slezak, C. (2002, September 8). Sporting a different look. *Chicago Sun-Times*, p. 123.

Steadward, R. (2001). IPC Strategic Planning Congress. Retrieved April 24, 2003, from www.paralympic.org.

Wolff, E. A., Hums, M. A., & Roy, E. (2007). *Sport in the United Nations Convention on the Rights of Persons with Disabilities*. Boston, MA: International Disability in Sport Working Group/United Nations Office of the Special Advisor of the Secretary-General on Sport for Development and Peace.

INDEX